METRO Street Atlas of
YORK & ADAMS
COUNTIES IN PENNSYLVANIA

Table of Contents

LEGEND

Toll Roads	Beaches	Libraries
Limited Access Roads	Block Numbers ...2036	Lighthouses
US and State Routes	Boardwalk	Mountain Peak
Other Major Roads	Boat Ramps	Municipal Buildings ...With Police
Rt. Markers: Interstates, US & (83) (30)	Bodies of Water	Nuclear Power Station
State (74)	Bridges	Parks
Exits (28) (19)A	Buildings	State Forest Lands
One Way Streets	Campgrounds	State Game Lands &
Streets FULTON RD.	Casinos	Picnic Areas
Railroads	Cemeteries	Physical Features Blue Mountain
Trails	Covered Bridges	Places of Worship
Borough Names Glen Rock	Court Houses	Points of Interest
Township Names HOPEWELL	Fire Houses	Police Stations ...In Municipal Bldg.
Place Names Keeny	Fire Tower / Lookout Tower	Quarries, Sand / Gravel Pits
Municipal Boundaries	Golf Courses & Country Clubs	Schools
Post Offices, Delivery (PO)	Government Facilities	Colleges & Universities
Post Offices, Non-Delivery Railroad 17355	Hiking Trails	Shopping Centers
Zip Codes, Delivery 17363	Hospitals	Ski Areas / Resorts
Airports	Industrial Parks & Business Centers	Wineries

STREET INDEX EXPLANATION

Example:
PLANK RD., Hopewell..........17349 E5 3584

Explanation:
Plank Rd. in Hopewell Township
is found in Grid Key E5 on Map Page 3584.
It is in Zip Code 17349.

The orientation of the map pages
in this atlas is true north.

Copyright 2005 by FRANKLIN MAPS
333 S. Henderson Road
King of Prussia, PA 19406
610·265·6277 / Fax 610·337·1575
1-800-356-8676
FIRST EDITION

Scale 1" = 2100'

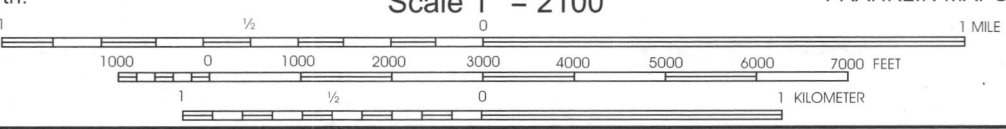

INDEX TO
METRO Street Atlas Of
YORK & ADAMS
COUNTIES IN PENNSYLVANIA

LEGEND

Toll Roads....................	
Limited Access Roads...........	
US and State Routes............	
Rt. Markers: Interstates, US, State....	83 30 462
Exits................................	242
County Names....................	**ADAMS**
Boro & City Names..............	**Dover**
Boro & City.....................	
Bodies of Water................	*Pinchot Lake*

1" = 6.65 MILES

0   3.325   6.65   9.975   13.3

Copyright 2005 by Franklin Maps
333 S. Henderson Road
King of Prussia, PA 19406
1•800•356•8676
Fax 610•337•1575

About the Map Numbering System!

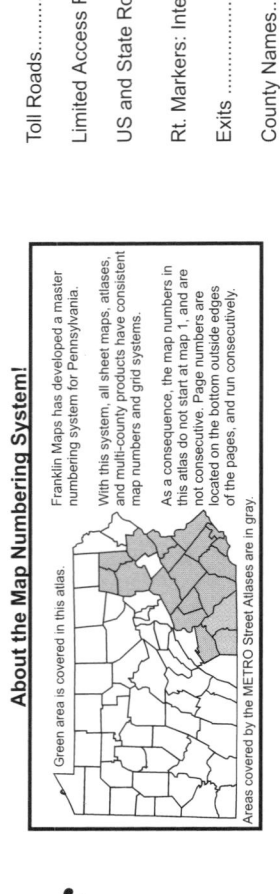

Franklin Maps has developed a master numbering system for Pennsylvania.

With this system, all sheet maps, atlases, and multi-county products have consistent map numbers and grid systems.

As a consequence, the map numbers in this atlas do not start at map 1, and are not consecutive. Page numbers are located on the bottom outside edges of the pages, and run consecutively.

Green area is covered in this atlas.

Areas covered by the METRO Street Atlases are in gray.

Franklin Maps
Custom Mapping Department
will customize maps to suit your needs.

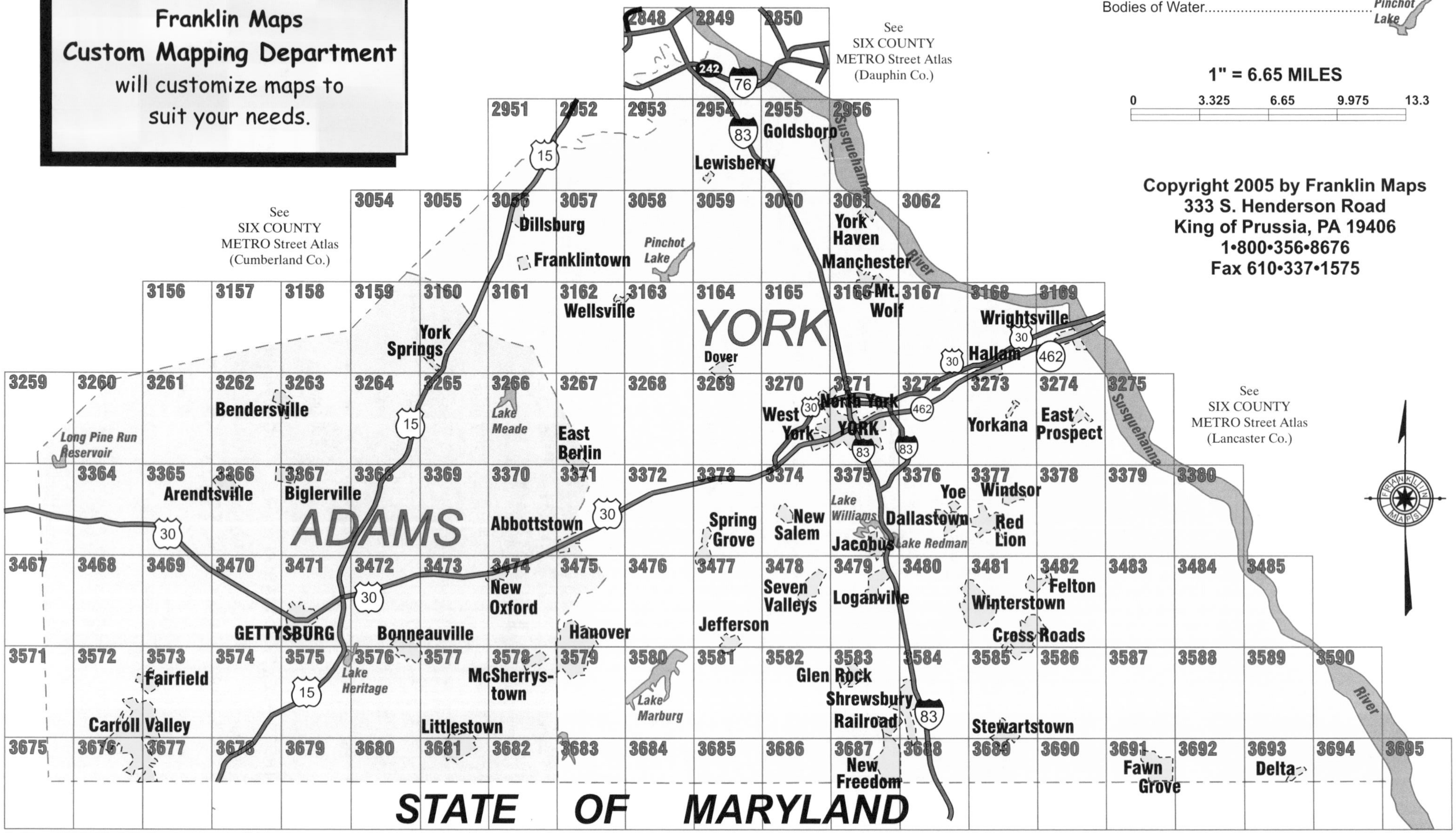

York County map grid:

2951 · 3054 · 3055 · 3056 · 3057 · 3058 · 3059 · 300 · 295 · 2955 · 2956
3156 · 3157 · 3158 · 3159 · 3160 · 3161 · 3162 · 3163 · 3164 · 3165 · 3166 Mt. Wolf · 3167 · 3168 · 3169

Franklintown · Wellsville · Dillsburg · York Springs

YORK · ADAMS

Goldsborg · Lewisberry · York Haven · Manchester

East Berlin · Abbottstown · New Oxford · Bonneauville · GETTYSBURG · Biglerville · Arendtsville · Bendersville

Spring Grove · Jefferson · Seven Valleys · New Salem · West York · York · Dover

Wrightsville · Hallam · Yorkana · East Prospect

York · Windsor · Red Lion · Felton · Winterstown · Cross Roads

Yoe · Dallastown · Loganville · Glen Rock · Shrewsbury · Railroad · New Freedom · Stewartstown

Hanover · Littlestown · McSherrystown · Fairfield · Carroll Valley

ADAMS

STATE OF MARYLAND

See SIX COUNTY METRO Street Atlas (Dauphin Co.)
See SIX COUNTY METRO Street Atlas (Lancaster Co.)
See SIX COUNTY METRO Street Atlas (Cumberland Co.)

Susquehanna River · *Pinchot Lake* · *Lake Marburg* · *Lake Williams* · *Lake Redman* · *Lake Meade* · *Lake Heritage* · *Long Pine Run Reservoir*

Fawn Grove · Delta

15 · 30 · 76 · 83 · 242 · 462

3259 3260 | 3348 3349 3850 3950 2951 2952 2953 3955 2956
3467 3468 · 3571 3572 · 3675 3676 Carroll Valley · 3677 · 3573 Fairfield · 3674

3690 Stewartstown · 3691 Fawn Grove · 3692 · 3693 Delta · 3694 · 3695
3580 3589 3590 3485 3380 3275 River

Index of Map Pages for
METRO *ADAMS* COUNTY, PA

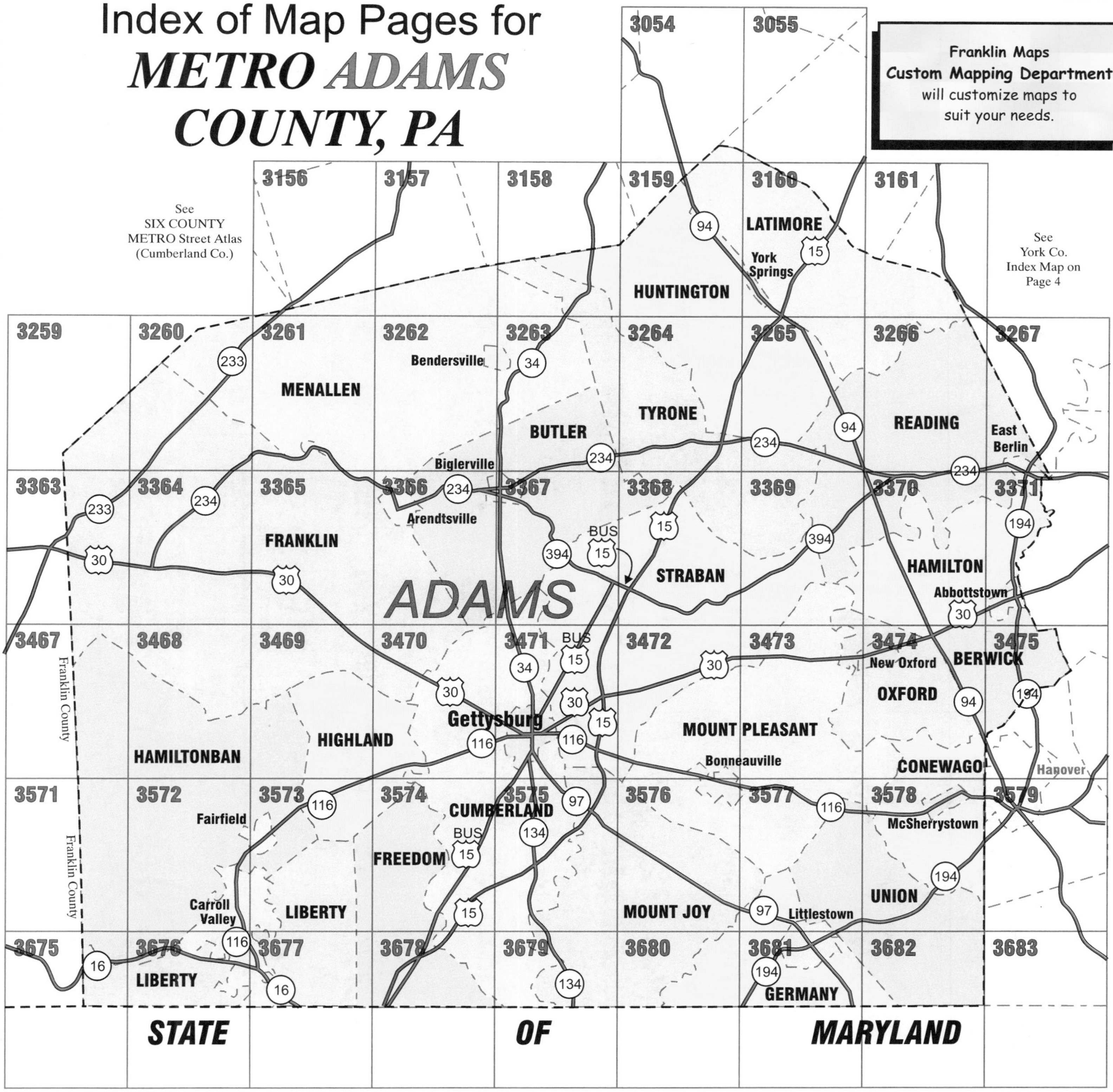

See
SIX COUNTY
METRO Street Atlas
(Cumberland Co.)

Franklin Maps
Custom Mapping Department
will customize maps to
suit your needs.

See
York Co.
Index Map on
Page 4

3054
3055

3156
3157
3158
3159
3160
3161

LATIMORE
York Springs

HUNTINGTON

3259
3260
3261
3262
3263
3264
3265
3266
3267

Bendersville

MENALLEN

TYRONE

READING

East Berlin

BUTLER

Biglerville

3363
3364
3365
3366
3367
3368
3369
3370
3371

Arendtsville

FRANKLIN

HAMILTON

BUS 15

ADAMS

Abbottstown

STRABAN

3467
3468
3469
3470
3471
3472
3473
3474
3475

BUS

New Oxford
BERWICK

Gettysburg

OXFORD

HAMILTONBAN
HIGHLAND

MOUNT PLEASANT

Bonneauville

CONEWAGO

Hanover

3571
3572
3573
3574
3575
3576
3577
3578
3579

Fairfield

CUMBERLAND

McSherrystown

BUS 15

FREEDOM

Carroll Valley

LIBERTY

UNION

MOUNT JOY

Littlestown

Franklin County

3675
3676
3677
3678
3679
3680
3681
3682
3683

LIBERTY

GERMANY

STATE
OF
MARYLAND

LEGEND

Limited Access Roads.................................
US and State Routes...................................
Rt. Markers: US Routes, State Routes.... 30 34
County Names.. *ADAMS*
Township Names...................................... **LIBERTY**
Boro Names.................................. **Gettysburg**

MILES

0   1.663   3.325   6.65

About the Map Numbering System!

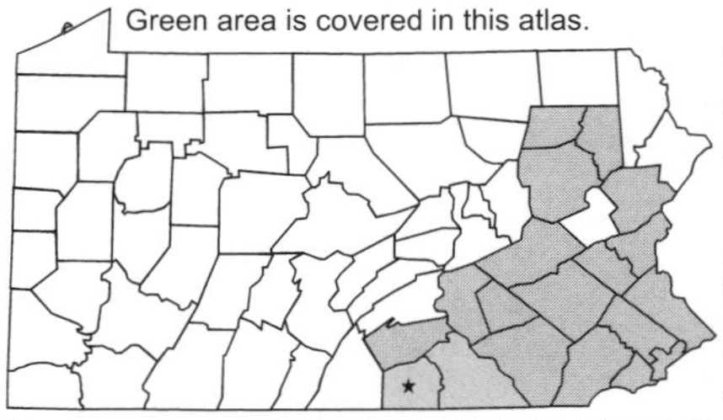

Green area is covered in this atlas.

Franklin Maps has developed a master numbering system for Pennsylvania.

With this system, all sheet maps, atlases, and multi-county products have consistent map numbers and grid systems.

As a consequence, the map numbers in this atlas do not start at map 1, and are not consecutive. Page numbers are located on the bottom outside edges of the pages, and run consecutively.

Other areas covered by the METRO Street Atlas Series are gray.

Index of Map Pages for *METRO YORK COUNTY, PA*

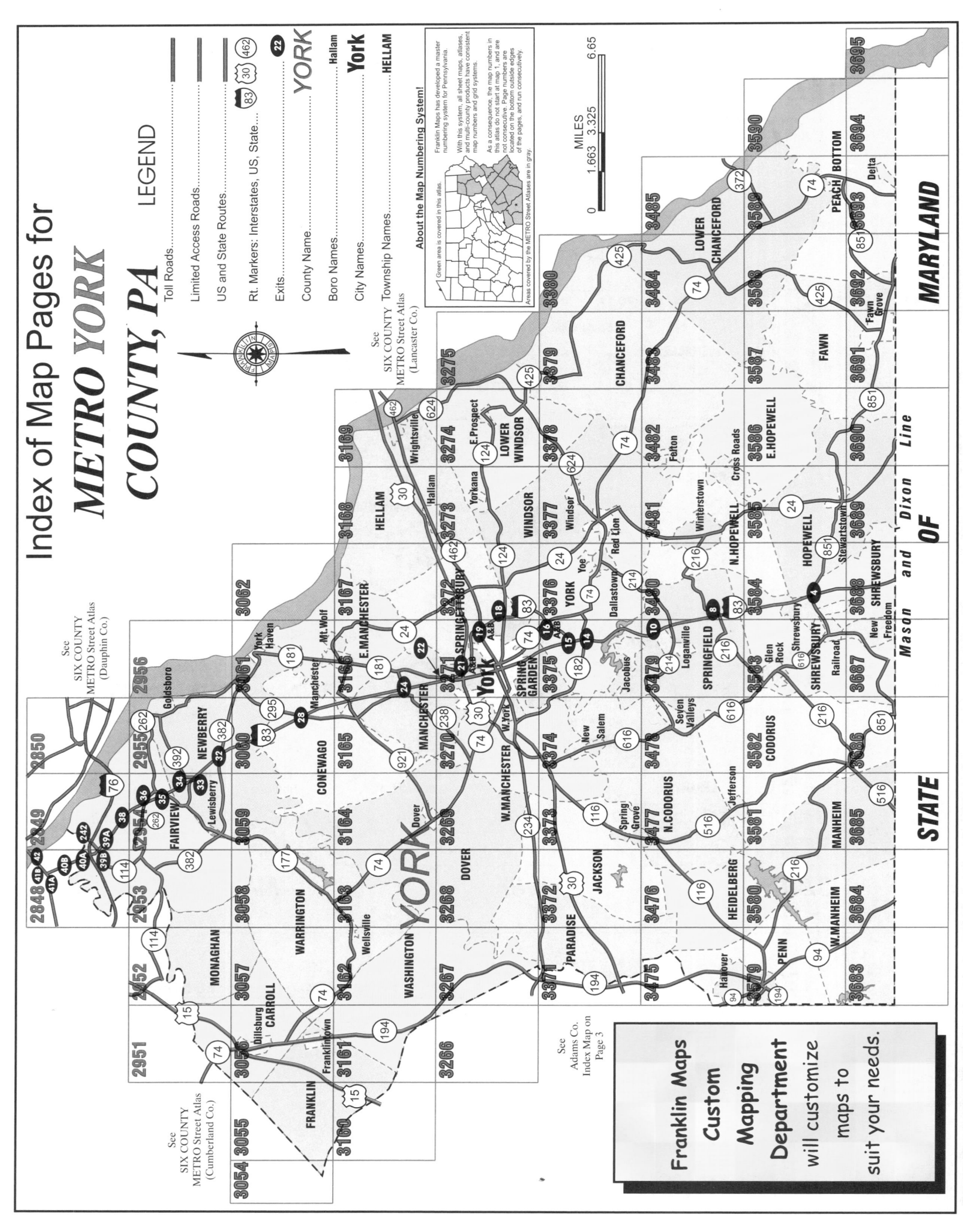

LEGEND

Toll Roads	
Limited Access Roads	
US and State Routes	
Rt. Markers: Interstates, US, State	⟨83⟩ ⟨83⟩ ⟨30⟩ ⟨462⟩
Exits	⬤22
County Name	YORK
Boro Names	Hallam
City Names	**York**
SIX COUNTY METRO Street Atlas Township Names	HELLAM

About the Map Numbering System!

Franklin Maps has developed a master numbering system for Pennsylvania.

With this system, all sheet maps, atlases, and multi-county products have consistent map numbers and grid systems.

As a consequence, the map numbers in this atlas do not start at map 1, and are not consecutive. Page numbers are located on the bottom outside edges of the pages, and run consecutively.

Green area is covered in this atlas.

Areas covered by the METRO Street Atlases are in gray.

MILES
0   1.663   3.325   6.65

See SIX COUNTY METRO Street Atlas (Cumberland Co.)

See SIX COUNTY METRO Street Atlas (Dauphin Co.)

See SIX COUNTY METRO Street Atlas (Lancaster Co.)

See Adams Co. Index Map on Page 3

Franklin Maps Custom Mapping Department will customize maps to suit your needs.

Franklin Maps

Map grid numbers: 2951, 2850, 2849, 2848, 2452, 2453, 2956, 2955, 2954, 3055, 3056, 3057, 3058, 3059, 3060, 3061, 3062, 3054, 3160, 3161, 3162, 3163, 3164, 3165, 3166, 3167, 3168, 3169, 3266, 3267, 3268, 3269, 3270, 3271, 3272, 3273, 3274, 3275, 3371, 3372, 3373, 3374, 3375, 3376, 3377, 3378, 3379, 3380, 3475, 3476, 3477, 3478, 3479, 3480, 3481, 3482, 3483, 3484, 3485, 3579, 3580, 3581, 3582, 3583, 3584, 3585, 3586, 3587, 3588, 3589, 3590, 3683, 3684, 3685, 3686, 3687, 3688, 3689, 3690, 3691, 3692, 3693, 3694, 3695

Townships/places: MONAGHAN, CARROLL, FRANKLIN, WARRINGTON, WASHINGTON, DOVER, PARADISE, JACKSON, HEIDELBERG, PENN, W.MANHEIM, MANHEIM, CODORUS, N.CODORUS, SPRINGFIELD, SHREWSBURY, N.HOPEWELL, HOPEWELL, E.HOPEWELL, FAWN, PEACH BOTTOM, LOWER CHANCEFORD, CHANCEFORD, FAWN GROVE, WINDSOR, LOWER WINDSOR, SPRINGETTSBURY, SPRING GARDEN, YORK, W.YORK, W.MANCHESTER, MANCHESTER, E.MANCHESTER, CONEWAGO, NEWBERRY, FAIRVIEW, HELLAM

Cities/towns: Dillsburg, Franklintown, Wellsville, Goldsboro, Lewisberry, York Haven, Mt. Wolf, Manchester, Dover, Hanover, Spring Grove, New Salem, Seven Valleys, Jacobus, Loganville, Glen Rock, Shrewsbury, Railroad, New Freedom, Stewartstown, Winterstown, Red Lion, Dallastown, Yoe, Windsor, Yorkana, Hallam, Wrightsville, E.Prospect, Delta, Fawn Grove, Cross Roads, Felton, Jefferson

YORK

MARYLAND

STATE OF

Mason and Dixon Line

5

Rossville	Yk	B11	3058	WINDSOR TWP	Yk	F6	3377
Round Top	Ad	C3	3575	WINTERSTOWN	Yk	B6	3481
Roundtown	Yk	H8	3165	Woodbine	Yk	D5	3588
Rye	Yk	D11	3376	Woodland View	Yk	D11	3166
Saginaw	Yk	A11	3062	WRIGHTSVILLE	Yk	B6	3169
Sechrist Mill	Yk	D2	3481	Wyndham Hills	Yk	B1	3375
Seven Stars	Ad	C3	3470	Yocumtown	Yk	A5	2955
SEVEN VALLEYS	Yk	G3	3478	YOE	Yk	G5	3376
Shenks Ferry	Yk	F7	3380	YORK CITY	Yk	A6	3271
Shiloh	Yk	C4	3270	York Furnace	Yk	G1	3484
SHREWSBURY BORO	Yk	B8	3584	YORK HAVEN	Yk	D3	3061
SHREWSBURY TWP	Yk	B2	3584	YORK TWP	Yk	C4	3376
Shrivers Corner	Ad	H8	3367	YORKANA	Yk	F5	3273
Siddonsburg	Yk	E8	2952	Yorkshire	Yk	D5	3272
Sinsheim	Yk	B2	3581	Zeigler	Yk	B11	3585
Slate Hill	Yk	D2	3694	ZION VIEW	Yk	F3	3165
Slate Ridge	Ad	E3	3681	Zora	Ad	B3	3677
Smiths Station	Yk	A11	3476				
Snyder Corner	Yk	D3	3378				
South Side	Yk	F6	3588				
SPRING GARRDEN	Yk	D5	3271				
SPRING GROVE	Yk	B11	3373				
Spring Plains	Yk	F4	3272				
Springdale	Yk	D10	3271				
SPRINGETTSBURY	Yk	C3	3272				
SPRINGFIELD	Yk	B4	3479				
Springvale	Yk	E8	3377				
Spry	Yk	A4	3376				
Square Corner	Ad	B1	3577				
Starview	Yk	H3	3166				
Stevenstown	Yk	B5	3057				
STEWARTSTOWN	Yk	C10	3585				
Sticks	Yk	A1	3686				
Stitlz	Yk	G5	3686				
Stoner	Yk	F11	3168				
Stonybrook	Yk	F3	3272				
Stoverstown	Yk	H10	3373				
STRABAN	Ad	D5	3368				
Stremmels	Ad	F5	3470				
Strickhousers	Yk	A6	3478				
Strickler	Yk	B10	3169				
Strinestown	Yk	G7	3060				
Sunnyburn	Yk	A2	3589				
Table Rock	Ad	D5	3367				
Taxville	Yk	A8	3270				
Texas	Ad	A7	3367				
The Knob	Ad	H4	3467				
Thomasville	Yk	C2	3373				
Tillie	Ad	G4	3469				
Tolna	Yk	E9	3584				
Trust	Ad	F3	3364				
Two Taverns	Ad	D7	3576				
TYRONE	Ad	D9	3158				
UNION	Ad	E4	3682				
Uno	Yk	C4	3057				
Valley Forge	Yk	E4	3271				
Valley Junction	Yk	A1	3581				
Valley View Park	Yk	D3	3273				
Villa Green	Yk	G9	3271				
Violet Hill	Yk	E11	3271				
Virginia Mills	Ad	H2	3572				
Wago Junction	Yk	G7	3061				
Waldheim	Ad	A6	3370				
WARRINGTON	Yk	B6	3058				
WASHINGTON	Yk	C6	3162				
Weigelstown	Yk	G4	3269				
WELLSVILLE	Yk	H3	3162				
Wenksville	Ad	A3	3262				
West Bangor	Yk	H4	3693				
WEST MANCHESTER	Yk	A9	3270				
West Manheim	Yk	C5	3684				
WEST MANHEIM	Yk	C3	3683				
WEST YORK	Yk	G9	3270				
Whitehall	Ad	A4	3577				
Wiley	Yk	C5	3690				
Wilshire Hills	Yk	G5	3272				
WINDSOR BORO	Yk	E4	3377				
Windsor Park	Yk	D4	3271				

FRANKLIN MAPS PENNSYLVANIA COVERAGE
About the Map Numbering System!

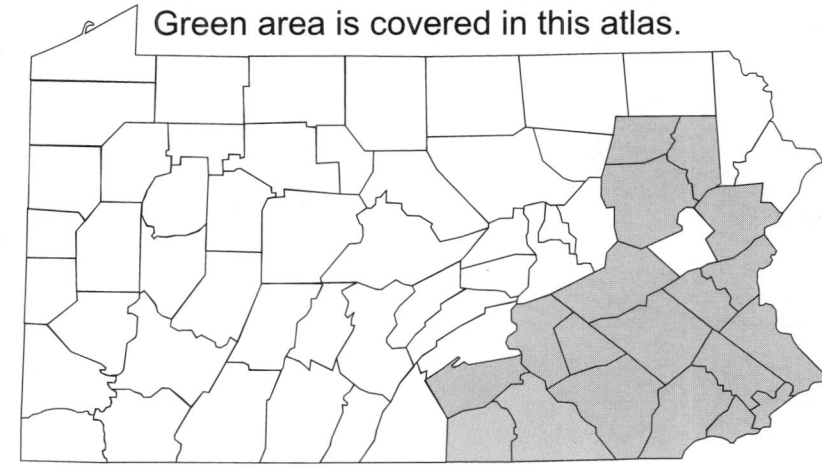

Green area is covered in this atlas.

Areas covered by the METRO Street Atlases are in gray.

Franklin Maps has developed a master numbering system for Pennsylvania.

With this system, all sheet maps, atlases, and multi-county products have consistent map numbers and grid systems.

As a consequence, the map numbers in this atlas do not start at map 1, and are not consecutive. <u>Page numbers</u> are located on the bottom outside edges of the pages, and run consecutively.

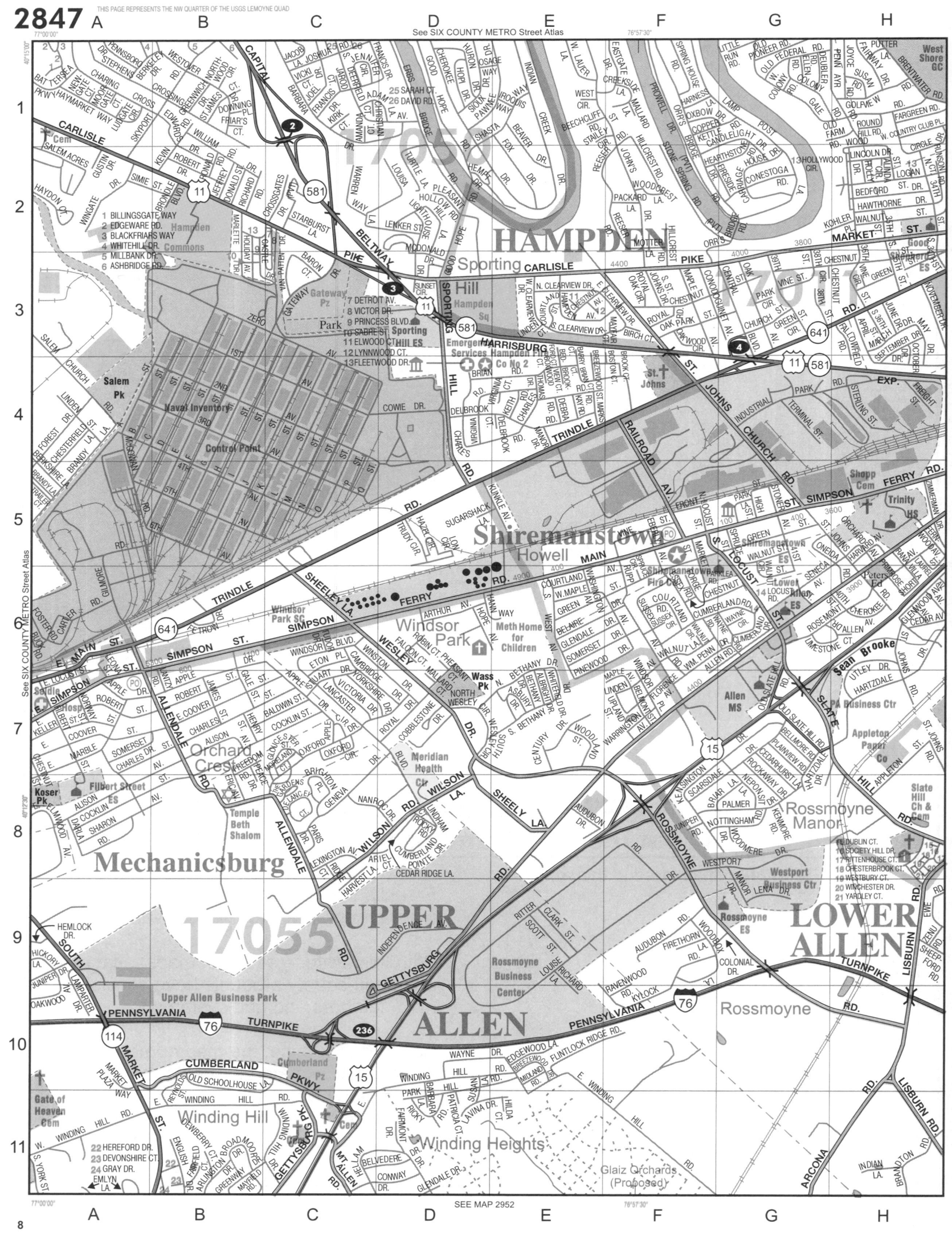

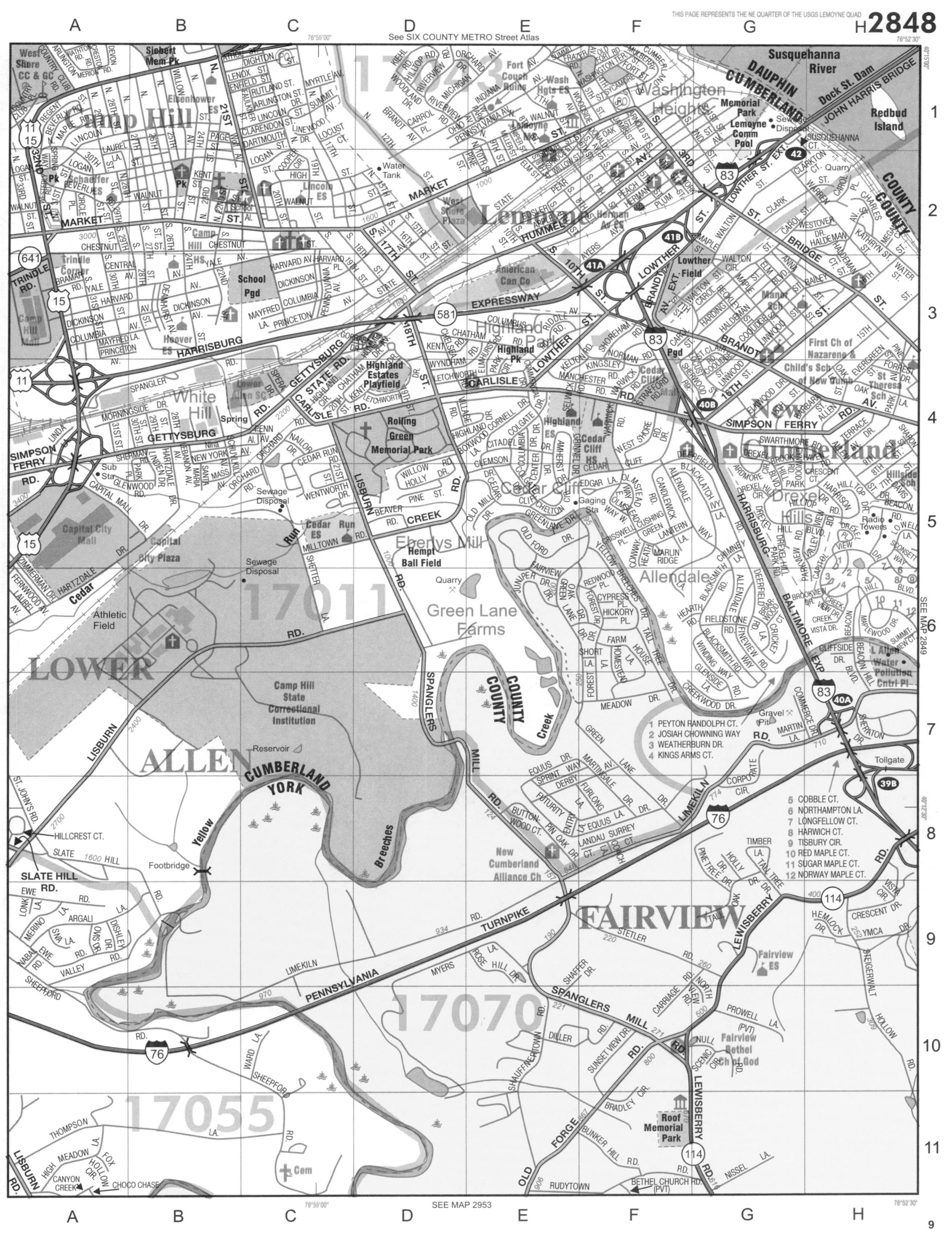

See SIX COUNTY METRO Street Atlas

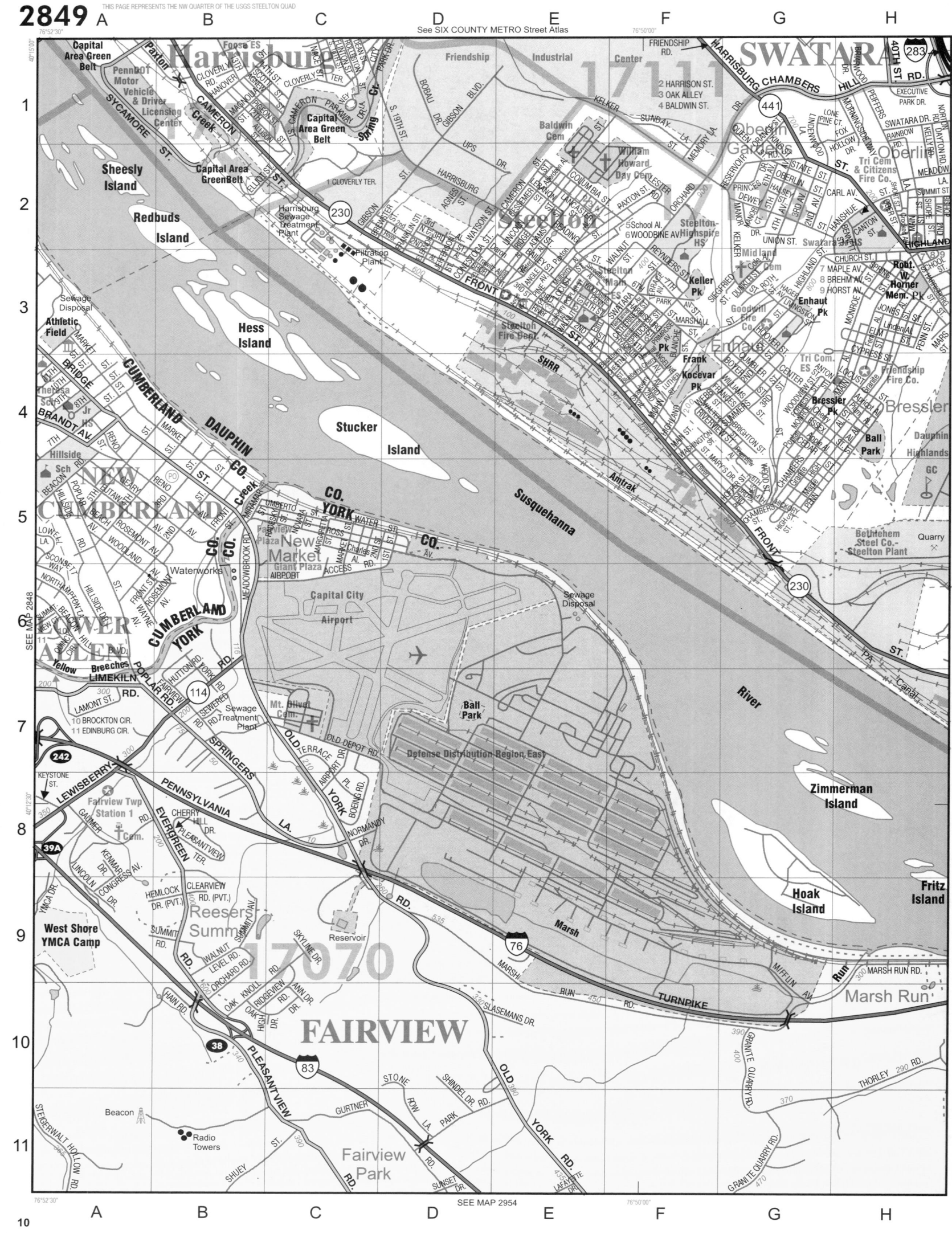

See SIX COUNTY METRO Street Atlas

SWATARA

17111

Harrisburg

Capital Area Green Belt

PennDOT Motor Vehicle & Driver Licensing Center

Sheesly Island

Capital Area GreenBelt

Redbuds Island

Hess Island

Stucker Island

Steelton

Friendship

Industrial

Center

2 HARRISON ST.
3 OAK ALLEY
4 BALDWIN ST.

FRIENDSHIP RD.

HARRISBURG CHAMBERS

Baldwin Cem

William Howard Day Cem

Oberlin Gardens

Oberlin

Tri Cem & Citizens Fire Co.

17809

Steelton-Highspire HS

Robt. W. Horner Mem. Pk

7 MAPLE AV.
8 BREHM AV.
9 HORST AV.

Enhaut Pk

Bressler Pk

Bressler

Dauphin Highlands

Susquehanna

Amtrak

Harrisburg Sewage Treatment Plant

Filtration Plant

NEW CUMBERLAND

Sewage Disposal

Athletic Field

Hillside Sch

CUMBERLAND CO.
DAUPHIN CO.
YORK CO.

LOWER ALLEN

Breeches LIMEKILN RD.

10 BROCKTON CIR.
11 EDINBURG CIR.

NEW MARKET

Giant Plaza
New Market Giant Plaza

Capital City Airport

Sewage Treatment Plant

Mt. Olivet Cem.

Defense Distribution Region, East

Ball Park

Sewage Disposal

River

Zimmerman Island

Hoak Island

Fritz Island

Bethlehem Steel Co.- Steelton Plant

Quarry

Marsh

Marsh Run

Fairview Twp Station 1

West Shore YMCA Camp

Reeser Summit

17070

FAIRVIEW

Radio Towers

Beacon

Fairview Park

TURNPIKE

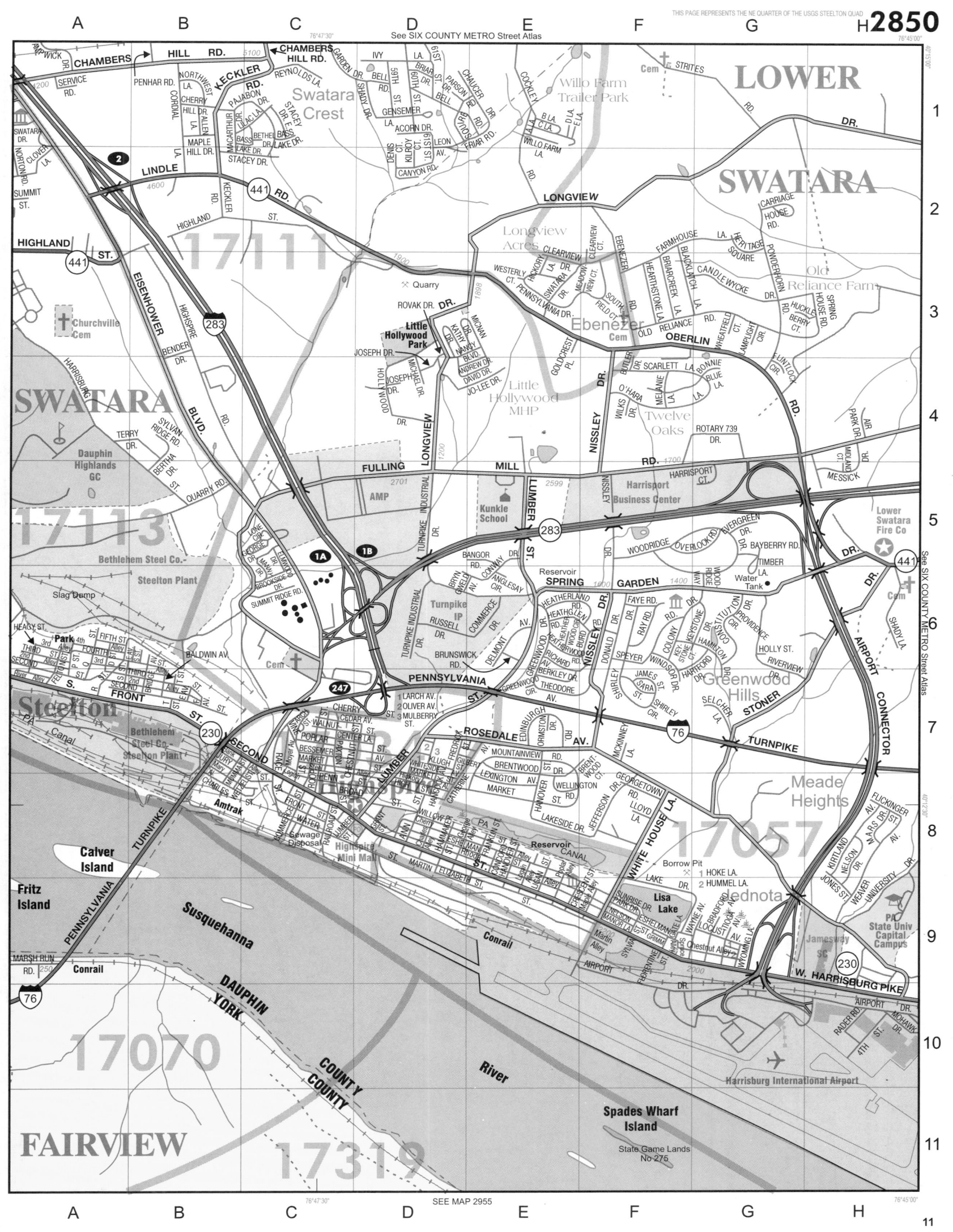

See SIX COUNTY METRO Street Atlas

LOWER

SWATARA

SWATARA

17111

Churchville Cem

Dauphin
Highlands
GC

17113

Bethlehem Steel Co.-
Steelton Plant

Slag Dump

Steelton
PA

Bethlehem
Steel Co.-
Steelton Plant

Calver
Island

Fritz
Island

17070

FAIRVIEW

Susquehanna

DAUPHIN
YORK
COUNTY
COUNTY

River

17319

Swatara
Crest

Quarry

Little
Hollywood
Park

Little
Hollywood
MHP

Longview
Acres

Ebenezer
Cem

Twelve
Oaks

FULLING   MILL

AMP

Kunkle
School

Turnpike
IP
RUSSELL
DR.

Harrisport
Business Center

Reservoir
Spring Garden

Water
Tank

Greenwood
Hills
STONER

Meade
Heights

17057

Reservoir

Lisa
Lake

Jednota

PA
State Univ
Capital
Campus

Jamesway
SC

W. HARRISBURG PIKE

Harrisburg International Airport

Spades Wharf
Island

State Game Lands
No 275

See SIX COUNTY METRO Street Atlas

SEE MAP 2955

Lower
Swatara
Fire Co

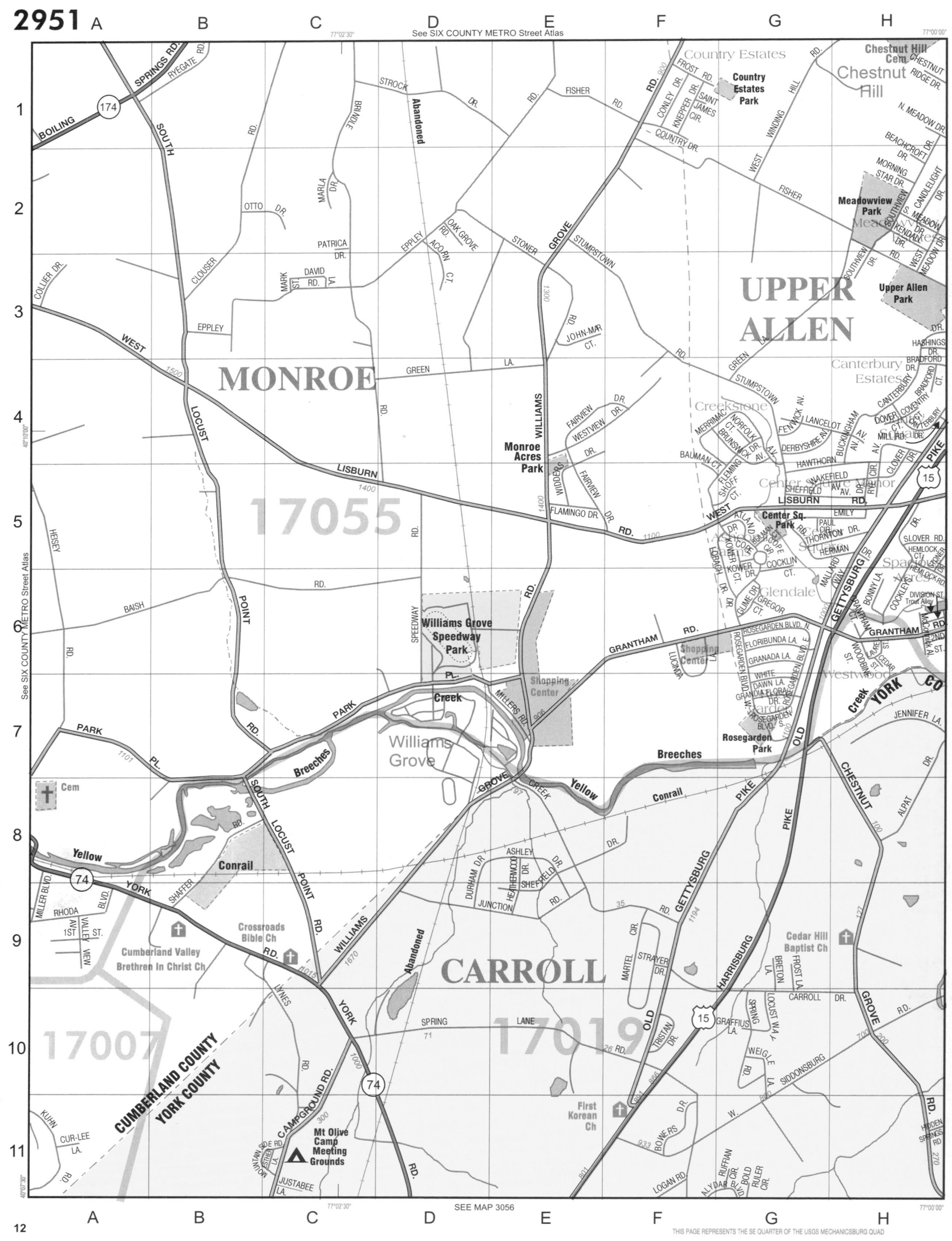

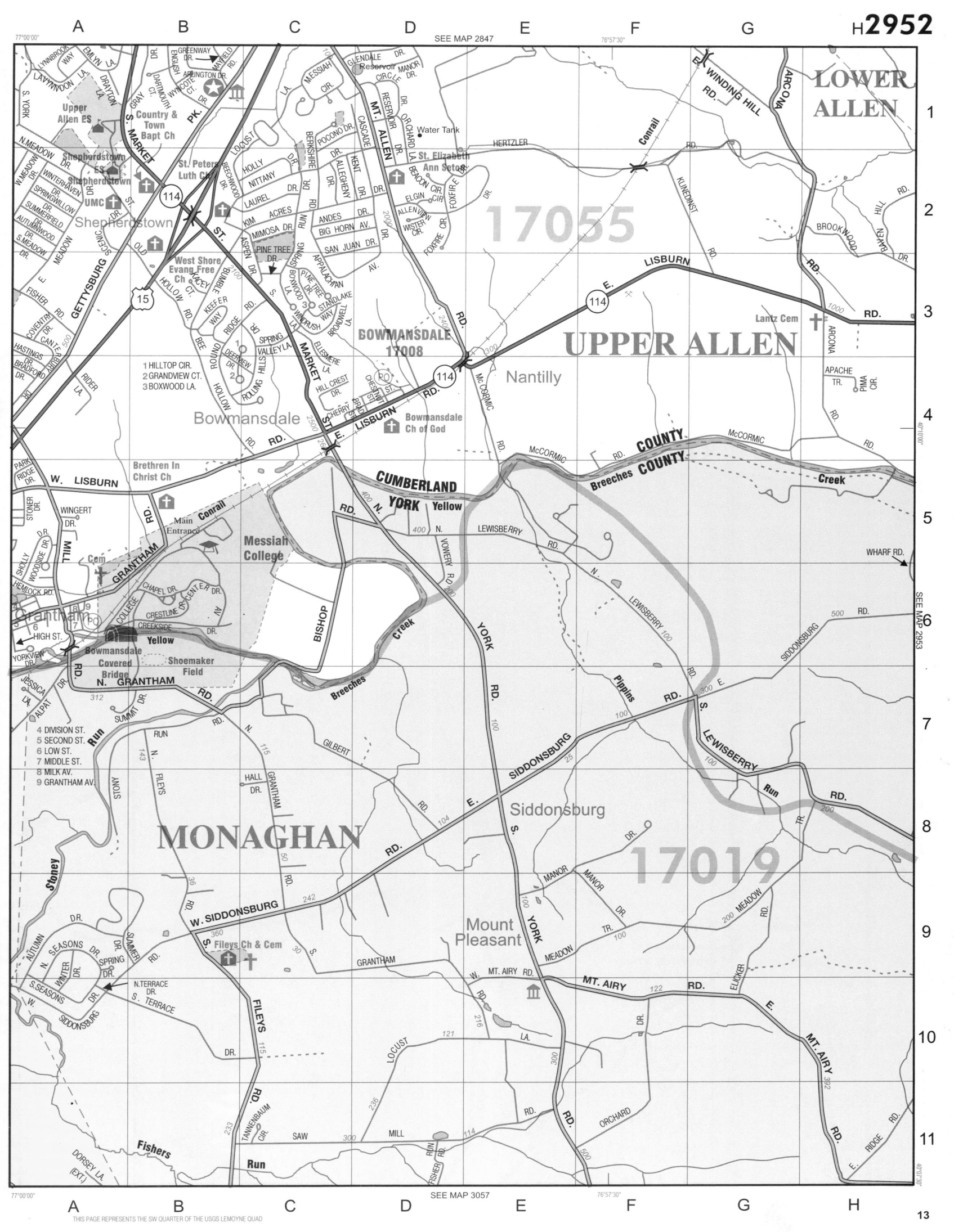

LOWER ALLEN

17055

UPPER ALLEN

Nantilly

BOWMANSDALE
17008

Bowmansdale

Shepherdstown

Grantham

Messiah College

CUMBERLAND
YORK
Yellow

COUNTY
Breeches COUNTY
Creek

WHARF RD.

MONAGHAN

Siddonsburg

17019

Mount
Pleasant

Fishers
Run

1 HILLTOP CIR.
2 GRANDVIEW CT.
3 BOXWOOD LA.

4 DIVISION ST.
5 SECOND ST.
6 LOW ST.
7 MIDDLE ST.
8 MILK AV.
9 GRANTHAM AV.

SEE MAP 2847
SEE MAP 2963
SEE MAP 3057

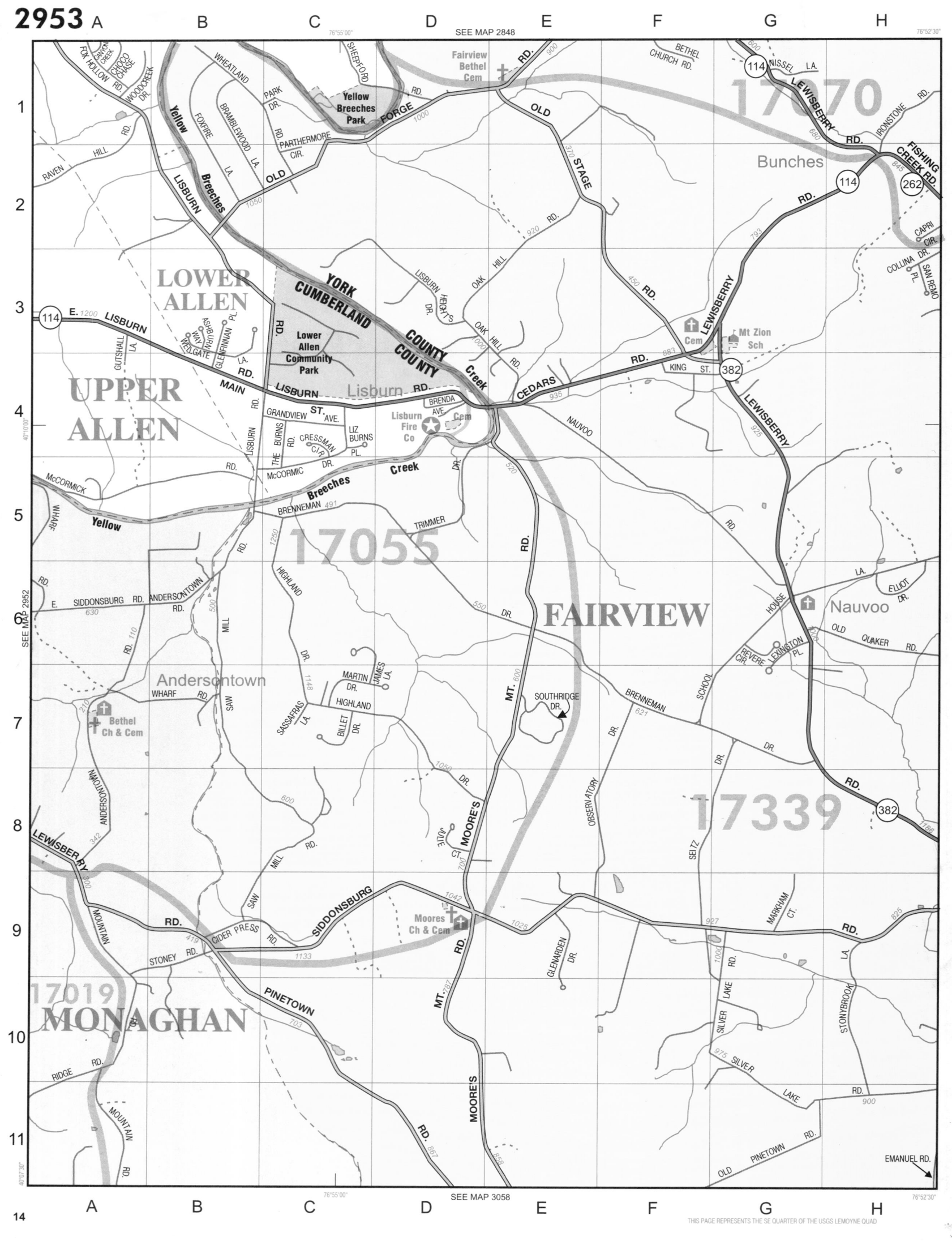

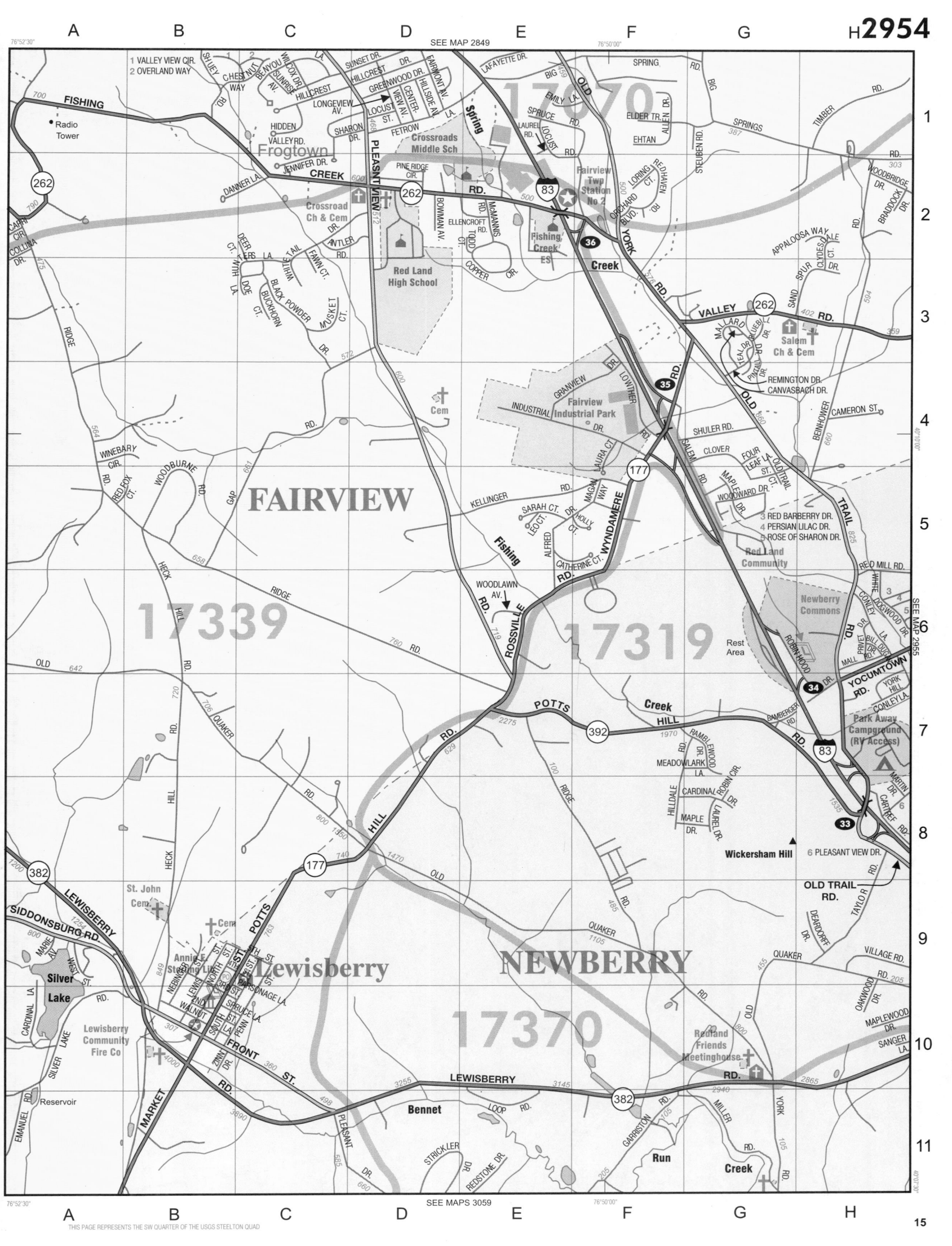

SEE MAP 2849

SEE MAP 2965

SEE MAPS 3059

THIS PAGE REPRESENTS THE SW QUARTER OF THE USGS STEELTON QUAD

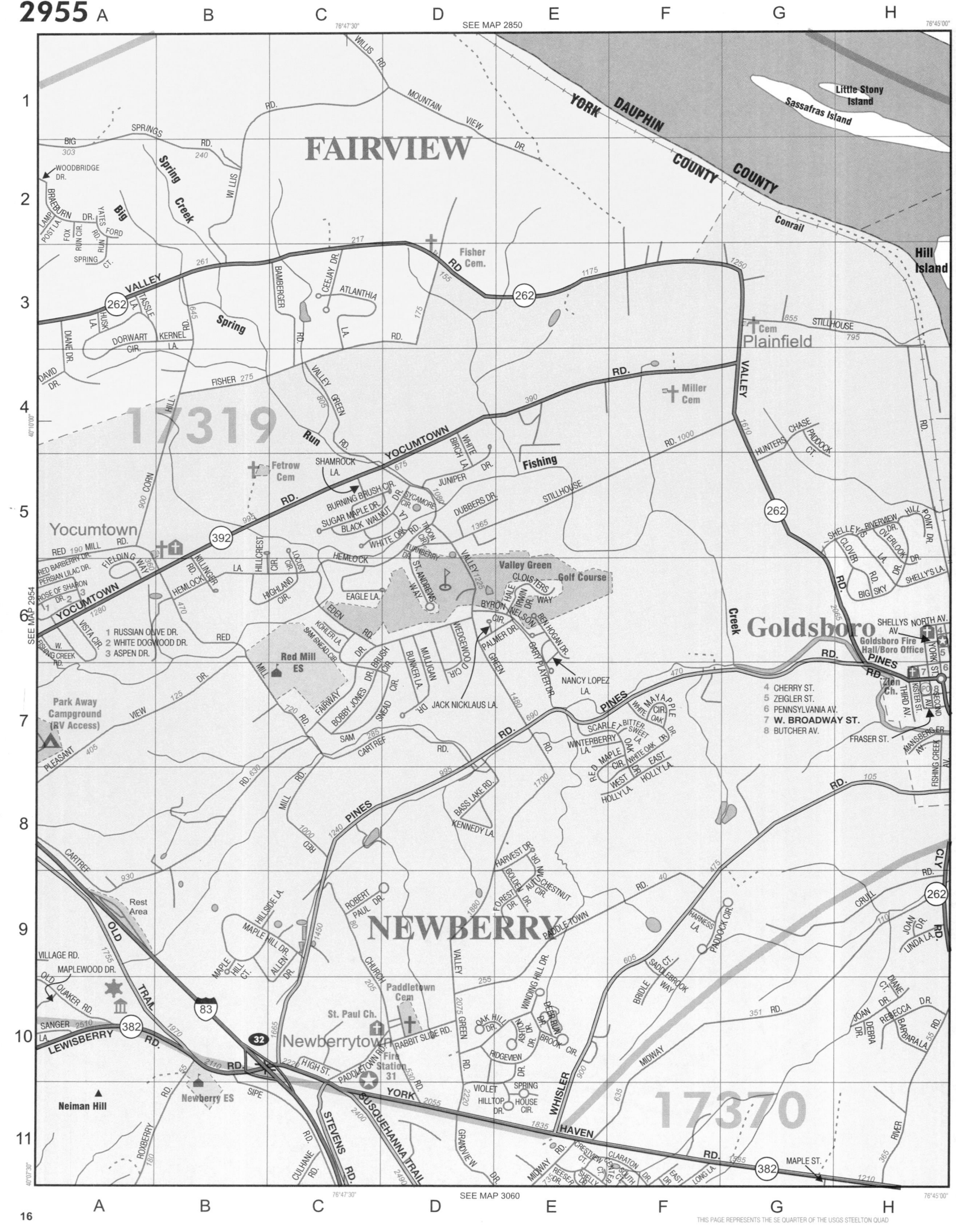

SEE MAP 2850

FAIRVIEW

York DAUPHIN COUNTY

York COUNTY

Little Stony Island

Sassafras Island

Hill Island

Big SPRINGS RD. 240

Spring Creek

WOODBRIDGE DR.

BRAEBURN DR.

LAMP POST LA.

FOX RUN CIR.

YATES FORD

Big FORD

SPRING CT.

VALLEY

262

LASSIE LA.

HUSKY RD.

DIANE DR.

DAVID DR.

DORWART CIR.

KERNEL LA.

645

WILLIS RD.

MOUNTAIN VIEW DR.

217

261

BAMBERGER

CEEJAY DR.

ATLANTHIA LA.

Fisher Cem.

RD. 155

262

1175

1250

Conrail

855

STILLHOUSE 795

Cem Plainfield

Spring

FISHER 275

VALLEY GREEN RD. 805

Run

RD.

YOCUMTOWN

WHITE BIRCH LA.

Fishing

RD. 1000

390

1610

HUNTERS

CHASE

PADDOCK CT.

17319

900 CORN RD.

392

Fetrow Cem

SHAMROCK LA.

BURNING BRUSH CIR.

SUGAR MAPLE DR.

BLACK WALNUT

675

SYCAMORE CIR.

JUNIPER DR.

TROON

DUBBERS DR.

1088

STILLHOUSE

1365

262

SHELLEYS RIVERVIEW DR.

HILL POINT DR.

Yocumtown

RED 190 MILL RD.

FIELDING WAY 360

KILLINGER RD.

HEMLOCK RD.

HILLCREST LA.

CIR. LOCUST LA.

WHITE OAK

RD.

LUMBERRY DR.

HALE

Valley Green Golf Course

CLOVER LA.

OVERLOOK DR.

SHELLY'S LA.

PERSIAN LILAC DR.

RED BARBERRY DR.

ROSE OF SHARON

HEMLOCK

HIGHLAND CIR.

ST. ANDREWS WAY

EAGLE LA.

EDEN

VALLEY 1225

CLOISTERS WAY

BYRON CIR.

IRWIN

NELSON

BEN HOGAN DR.

BIG SKY

VISTA CIR.

1280

YOCUMTOWN

W. SPRING CREEK RD.

1 Russian Olive Dr.
2 White Dogwood Dr.
3 Aspen Dr.

RED

KOHLER LA.

SAM SNEAD CIR.

DR.

BRUSH CIR.

BUNKER LA.

MULLIGAN

WEDGEWOOD CIR.

GREEN

PALMER DR.

GARY PLAYER DR.

Creek

Goldsboro

SHELLYS NORTH AV.

Goldsboro Fire Hall/Boro Office

PINES RD.

Park Away Campground (RV Access)

PLEASANT 405

VIEW

125

Red Mill ES

720 RD.

FAIRWAY

BOBBY JONES

SAM SNEAD CIR.

SNEAD CIR.

JACK NICKLAUS LA.

NANCY LOPEZ LA.

4 CHERRY ST.
5 ZEIGLER ST.
6 PENNSYLVANIA AV.
7 W. BROADWAY ST.
8 BUTCHER AV.

Zion Ch.

THIRD AV.

SECOND AV.

YORK ST.

MANSBERGER

FRASER ST.

FISHING CREEK AV.

RD. 630

MILL RD.

SAM CARTREF RD.

285

PINES

RD.

690

PINES RD.

1490

MAYAPPLE DR.

WHITE OAK CIR.

SCARLET

BITTER SWEET LA.

WINTERBERRY LA.

RED MAPLE CIR.

WHITE OAK DR.

EAST

WEST DR

HOLLY LA.

HOLLY LA.

BASS LAKE RD.

999

1700

RD. 105

CARTREF

930

RED RD. 1000

PINES 1240

KENNEDY LA.

NEWBERRY

HARVEST DR.

FOREST DR.

NW CHESTNUT CIR.

GOLDEN AUT.

RD.

40

475

RD.

CLY RD.

262

Rest Area

HILLSIDE LA.

MAPLE HILL DR.

1450

ROBERT PAUL DR.

1880

PADDLETOWN

HARNESS LA.

PADDOCK CIR.

SADDLEBROOK WAY

JOAN DR.

LINDA LA.

VILLAGE RD.

MAPLEWOOD DR.

1755

MAPLE HILL CT.

ALLEN DR.

MAPLE HILL

VALLEY

255

605

BRIDLE

351 RD.

JOAN DR.

DIANE CT.

REBECCA DR.

OLD QUAKER RD.

OLD

TRAIL

83

CHURCH RD. 205

Paddletown Cem

2075 GREEN

OAK HILL DR.

WINDING HILL DR.

ASHTON DR.

DEERBURN DR.

BROOK CIR.

MIDWAY

DEBRA DR.

BARBARA LA.

SANGER LA.

2510

382

RD.

1970

32

St. Paul Ch.

Newberrytown

RABBIT SLIDE RD.

RIDGEVIEW DR.

WHISLER RD.

900

635

55

LEWISBERRY

RD.

2110

HIGH ST.

2225

PADDLETOWN

530 RD.

Fire Station 31

VIOLET HILLTOP DR.

SPRING HOUSE CIR.

HAVEN

1835

17370

Neiman Hill

Newberry ES

SIPE

YORK

2055

2220

1365

382

MAPLE ST.

1210

ROXBERRY RD. 180

CULHANE RD.

STEVENS RD. 2400

SUSQUEHANNA TRAIL 2490

GRANDVIEW DR.

MIDWAY

CRESTVIEW CT.

CLARATON CT.

REESER

SHELLY

LONG LA.

EAST DR.

365

RIVER

76°47'30"

SEE MAP 3060

76°45'00"

THIS PAGE REPRESENTS THE SE QUARTER OF THE USGS STEELTON QUAD

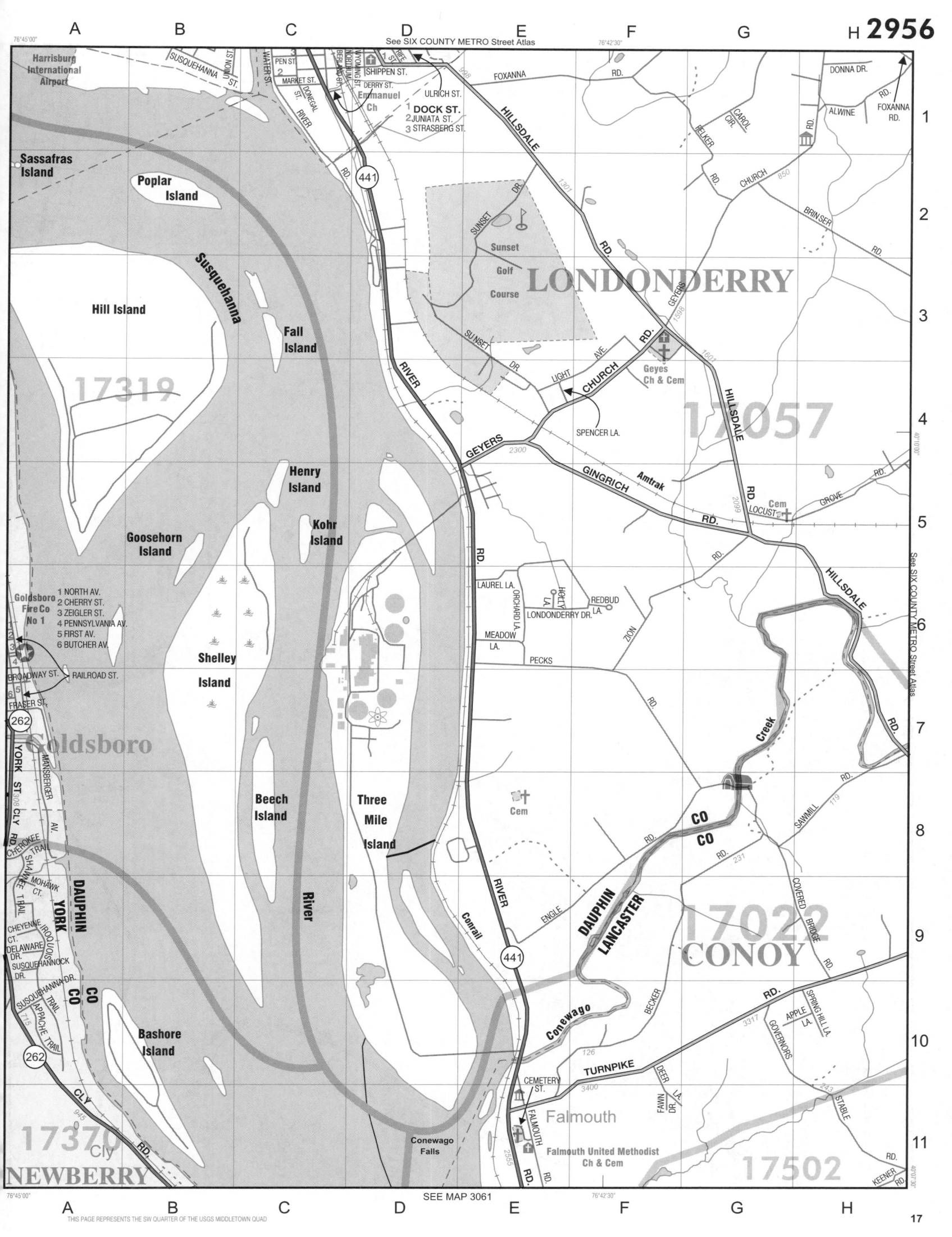

76°45'00"

A B C D See SIX COUNTY METRO Street Atlas E F 76°42'30" G H

Harrisburg
International
Airport

DONNA DR.

FOXANNA   RD.

RD.
FOXANNA
RD.

ALWINE

HELKER

CAROL
CIR.

CHURCH

850

1

Sassafras
Island

Poplar
Island

PEN ST.
WAHER ST.
UNION ST.
SUSQUEHANNA
MARKET ST.
DONEGAL
SHIPPEN ST.
NORTH AV.
BERLAND ST.
WYOMING ST.
DERRY ST.
Emmanuel
Ch
ULRICH ST.
1 DOCK ST.
2 JUNIATA ST.
3 STRASBERG ST.

HILLSDALE

1301

SUNSET
DR.

RD.

BRINSER

RD.

2

441

Susquehanna

Hill Island

Fall
Island

Sunset
Golf
Course

LONDONDERRY

GEYERS

1598

HILLSDALE

17057

3

17319

RIVER

SUNSET DR

LIGHT AVE.

CHURCH

RD.

Geyes
Ch & Cem

1601

RD.

40°10'00"

4

Henry
Island

GEYERS

2300

SPENCER LA.

GINGRICH

Amtrak

2099

Cem
LOCUST

GROVE

RD.

5

Kohr
Island

Goosehorn
Island

RD.

LAUREL LA.

ORCHARD LA.

HOLTY
LA.

REDBUD
LA.

Londonderry Dr.

ZION

HILLSDALE

6

Goldsboro
Fire Co
No 1

1 NORTH AV.
2 CHERRY ST.
3 ZEIGLER ST.
4 PENNSYLVANIA AV.
5 FIRST AV.
6 BUTCHER AV.

Shelley
Island

MEADOW
LA.

PECKS

Creek

RD.

7

BROADWAY ST.
RAILROAD ST.
FRASER ST.
262

Goldsboro

YORK ST
MANSBERGER
CLY
708
RD.

Beech
Island

Three
Mile
Island

Cem

CO
CO

SAWMILL

119

8

CHEROKEE
TRAIL
SHAWNEE AV.
DAUPHIN
YORK
MOHAWK
CT.

River

Contrail

RIVER

DAUPHIN
LANCASTER

ENGLE

RD.

RD.

231

COVERED
BRIDGE
RD.

9

CHEYENNE
CT.
IROQUOIS
DELAWARE
DR.
SUSQUEHANNOCK
DR.
CO
CO

441

17022
CONOY

APPLE
LA.

SPRING HILL LA.

GOVERNORS

3317

2432

STABLE

10

SUSQUEHANNA
TRAIL
715
APPACHE TRAIL

Bashore
Island

Conewago

BECKER
RD.

RD.

FAWN
DR.

DEER
LA.

262

CLY
945
RD.

Conewago
Falls

CEMETERY
ST.

TURNPIKE

126

3400

FALMOUTH

Falmouth
Falmouth United Methodist
Ch & Cem

2555

KEENER
RD.

RD.

11

17370
Cly
NEWBERRY

17502

40°07'30"

76°45'00"

A B C SEE MAP 3061 D E F 76°42'30" G H

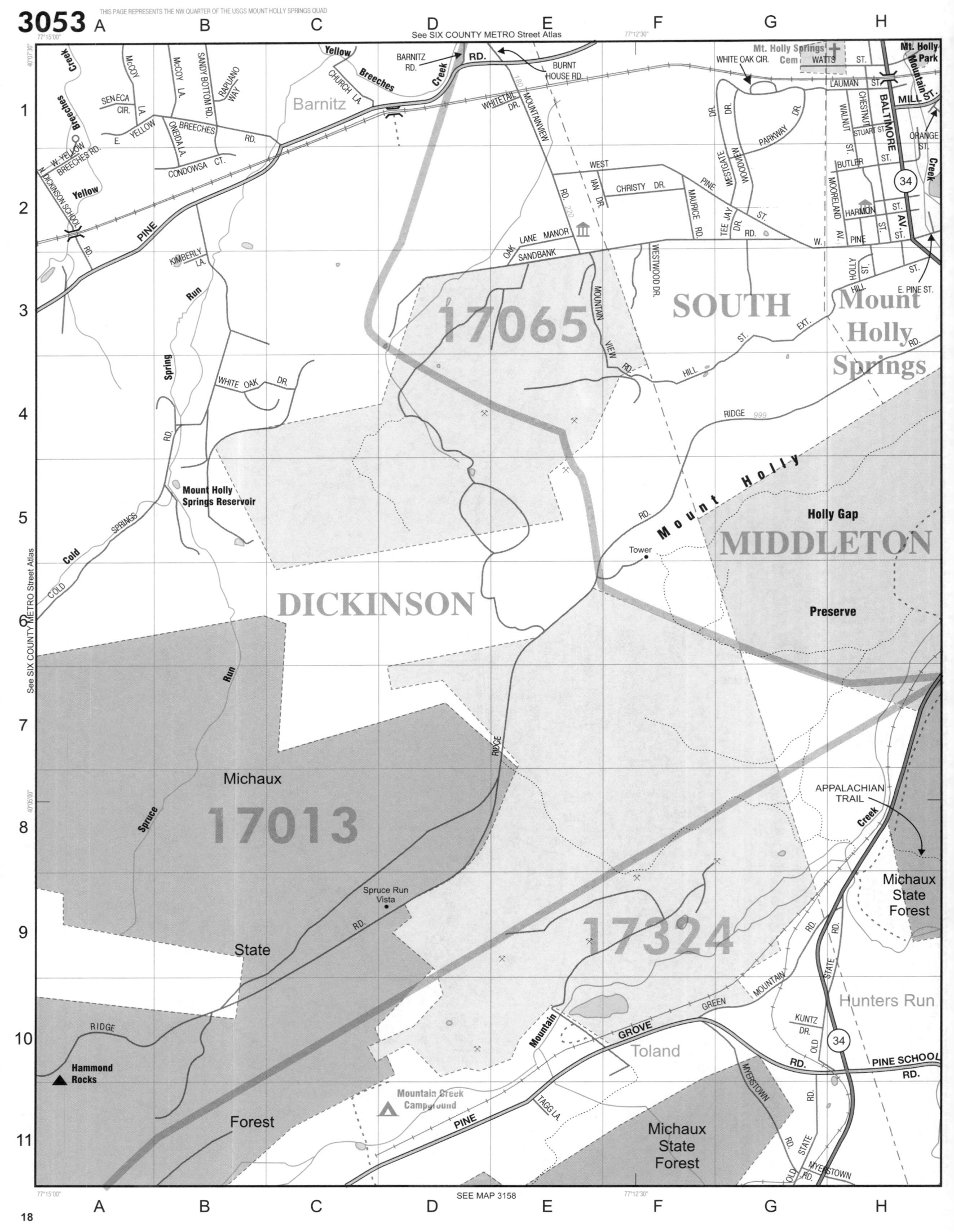

THIS PAGE REPRESENTS THE NW QUARTER OF THE USGS MOUNT HOLLY SPRINGS QUAD

See SIX COUNTY METRO Street Atlas

77°15'00"   77°12'30"

A   B   C   D   E   F   G   H

Creek

W. YELLOW BREECHES RD.
N. DICKINSON SCHOOL RD.
Breeches
McCOY
SENECA CIR.
E. YELLOW
McCOY LA.
SANDY BOTTOM RD.
RAPUANO WAY
ONEIDA LA.
BREECHES
CONDOWSA CT.
CHURCH LA.
Yellow
Yellow
BARNITZ RD.
Breeches
Creek
RD.
BURNT HOUSE RD.
WHITETAIL DR.
MOUNTAINVIEW
Mt. Holly Springs Cem
WHITE OAK CIR.
WATTS ST.
Mt. Holly Mountain ST.
Mt. Holly Park
LAUMAN ST.
CHESTNUT ST.
BALTIMORE
MILL ST.
STUART ST.
WALNUT ST.
ORANGE ST.

Barnitz

1

PINE
Yellow
KIMBERLY LA.
RD.
WEST
IAN DR.
CHRISTY DR.
PINE
MAURICE RD.
TEE JAY
WESTGATE
WOODVIEW
DR.
DR.
PARKWAY
BUTLER ST.
ST.
MOORELAND
HARMON
W.
AV.
PINE
ST.
RD.
220
34

2

Spring
Run
WHITE OAK
DR.
OAK LANE MANOR
SANDBANK
WESTWOOD DR.
MOUNTAIN VIEW RD.
17065
SOUTH
HILL
ST.
ST.
EXT.
Mount Holly Springs
HILL
E. PINE ST.

3

Mount Holly Springs Reservoir
RIDGE 999
Mount Holly
4

Cold
SPRINGS
COLD
Holly Gap
MIDDLETON
RD.
Tower
5

See SIX COUNTY METRO Street Atlas

DICKINSON
Preserve

6

Run
RIDGE
7

Spruce
Michaux
17013
APPALACHIAN TRAIL
Creek

8

Spruce Run Vista
RD.
17324
Michaux State Forest

9

State
GREEN
Hunters Run
MOUNTAIN
RD.
RD.
KUNTZ DR.
STATE
OLD
34

10

RIDGE
Hammond Rocks
Mountain
GROVE
Toland
MYERSTOWN
PINE SCHOOL RD.

11

Forest
Mountain Creek Campground
TAGG LA.
PINE
Michaux State Forest
OLD STATE RD.
MYERSTOWN

77°15'00"   SEE MAP 3158   77°12'30"

A   B   C   D   E   F   G   H

18

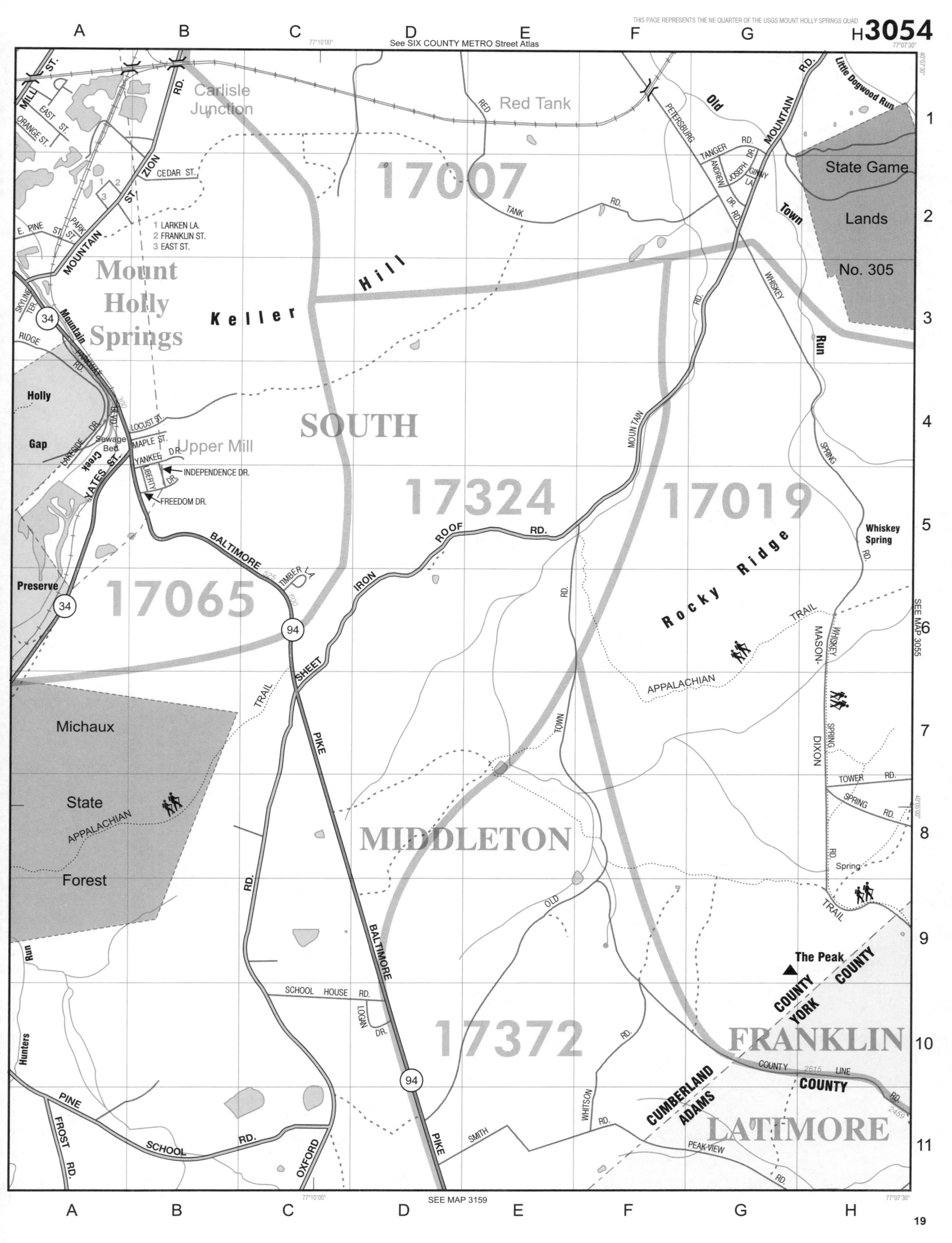

See SIX COUNTY METRO Street Atlas

Carlisle Junction

Red Tank

17007

1 LARKEN LA.
2 FRANKLIN ST.
3 EAST ST.

Mount Holly Springs

State Game

Lands

No. 305

Keller   Hill

Holly

Gap

SOUTH

Upper Mill

INDEPENDENCE DR.

FREEDOM DR.

17324   17019

Whiskey Spring

Preserve

17065

Rocky Ridge

APPALACHIAN

Michaux

State

APPALACHIAN

Forest

MIDDLETON

The Peak

17372

FRANKLIN

CUMBERLAND
ADAMS

YORK
COUNTY

LATIMORE

SEE MAP 3055

SEE MAP 3159

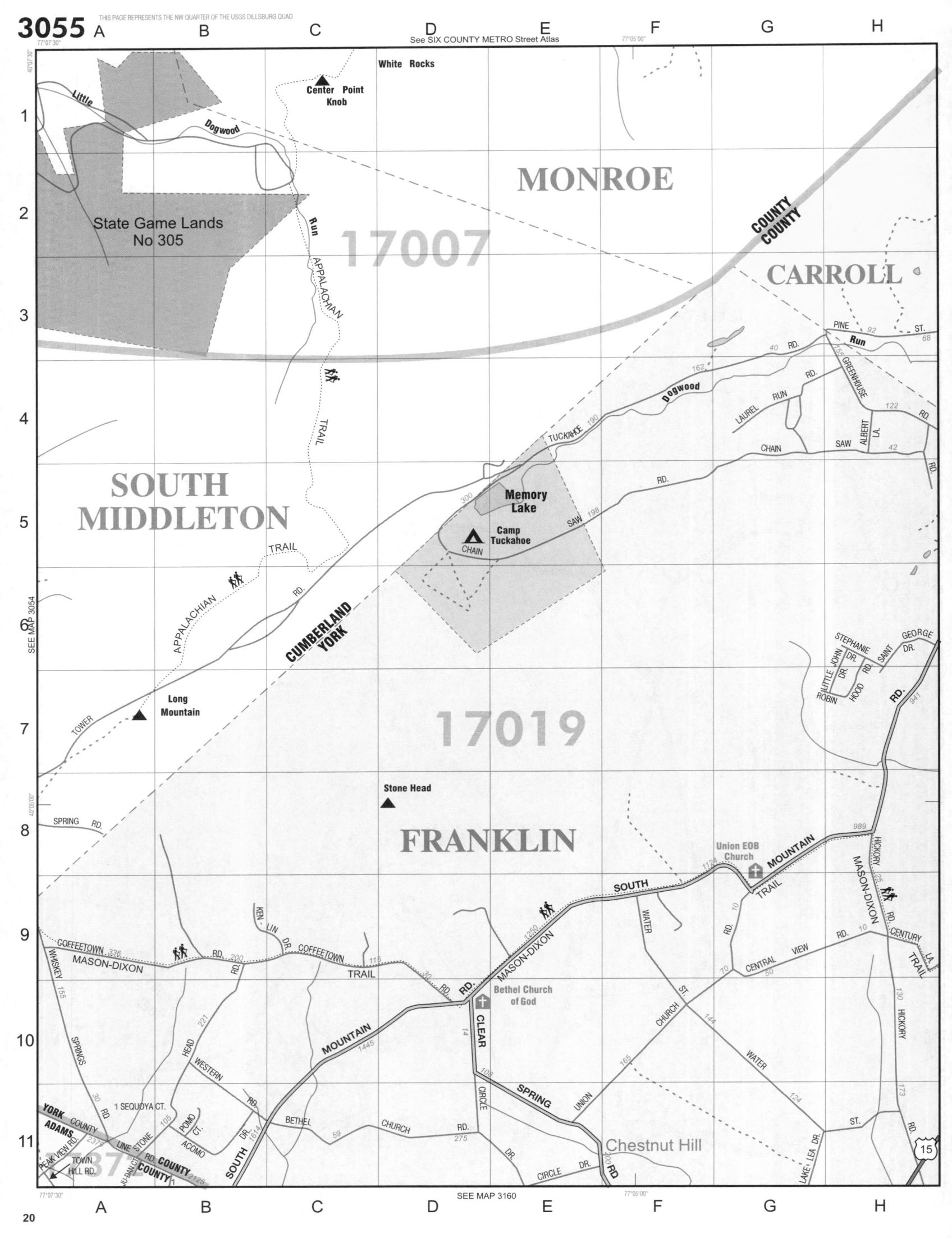

B   C   D   E   F   G   H

White Rocks

Center Point
Knob

MONROE

17007

CARROLL

Little

Dogwood

Run

State Game Lands
No 305

PINE 92 ST. 68
RD.
Run
40 RD.
162 GREENHOUSE
Dogwood
LAUREL RUN RD.
TUCKAHOE 190
CHAIN SAW ALBERT LA. 42
RD.
300
Memory
Lake
Camp
Tuckahoe
SAW 198
CHAIN

**SOUTH
MIDDLETON**

APPALACHIAN

TRAIL

TRAIL

APPALACHIAN RD.

CUMBERLAND
YORK

TOWER

Long
Mountain

STEPHANIE DR.
LITTLE JOHN DR.
GEORGE DR.
HOOD RD. SAINT
ROBIN
RD. 941

17019

Stone Head

FRANKLIN

Union EOB
Church
MOUNTAIN
1124
SOUTH
TRAIL
989
HICKORY 225
MASON-DIXON RD. 10
CENTURY
LA.
130
HICKORY

SPRING RD.

COFFEETOWN 336
MASON-DIXON
WHISKEY 155
KEN- LIN DR.
RD. 200
COFFEETOWN 115
TRAIL
MASON-DIXON
RD.
30 RD.
WATER
RD. 10
CENTRAL 50 VIEW
70
CHURCH ST.
1124

SPRINGS
HEAD 221
WESTERN
RD.
MOUNTAIN 1445
RD. 14
CLEAR
Bethel Church
of God
108 CIRCLE
SPRING
UNION
165
WATER
124
Chestnut Hill
LAKE LEA DR.
173

**YORK
ADAMS**
PEAK VIEW RD. 237B
TOWN HILL RD.
LINE STONE RD.
POMO CT.
ACOMO
SOUTH DR. 1614
SEQUOYA CT.
30 RD.
JU-DALG CT. 21125
105
1
COUNTY
BETHEL
59
CHURCH
RD. 275
DR.
CIRCLE DR.
100 RD.
15

A   B   C   D   E   F   G   H

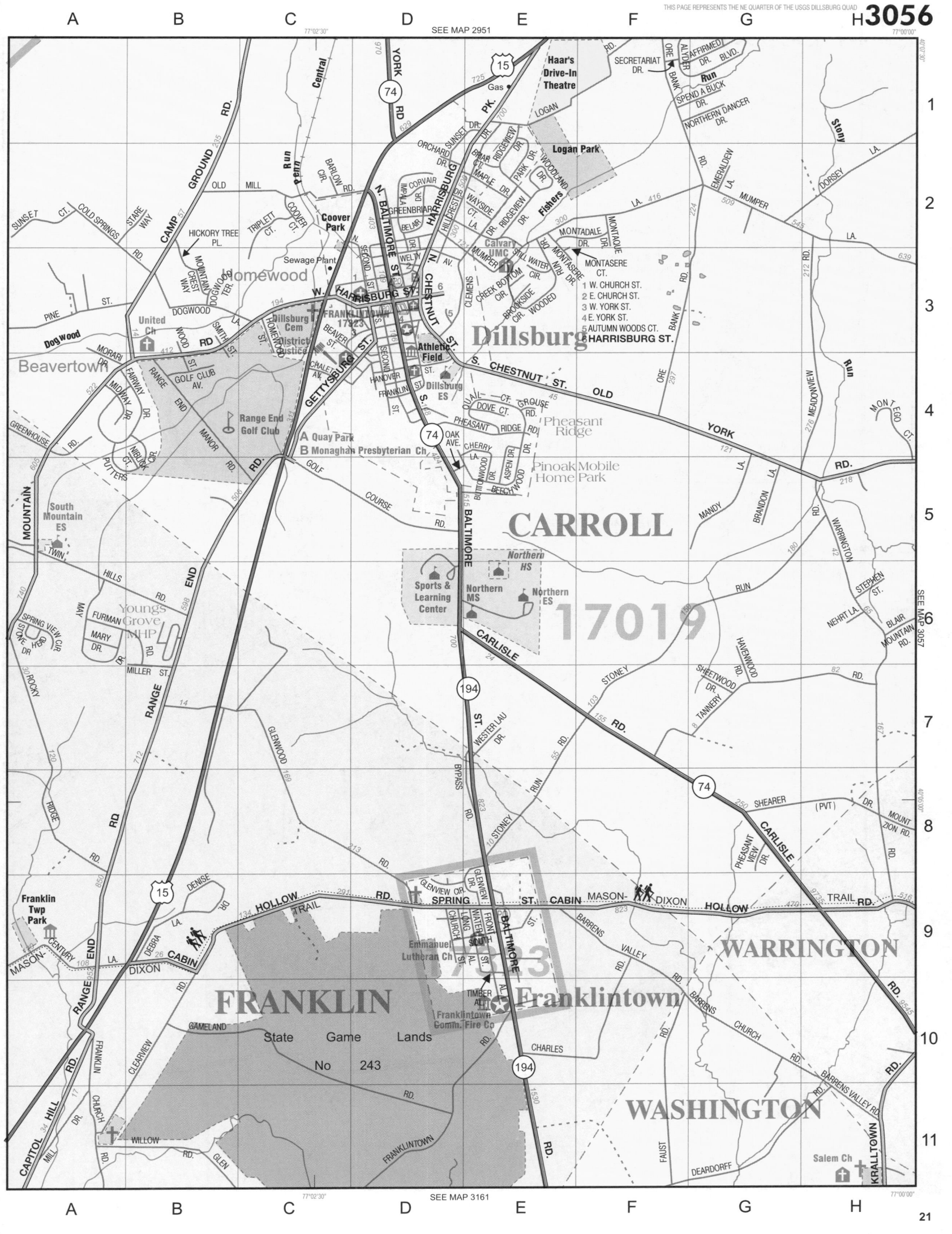

SEE MAP 2951

A B C D E F G

Haar's Drive-In Theatre

Logan Park

SECRETARIAT DR.

AFFIRMED DR. ALYDAR BLVD.

SPEND A BUCK DR.

NORTHERN DANCER DR.

Stony LA.

Gas

15

YORK RD.

74

Central

CAMP GROUND RD.

OLD MILL

Run Penn

Coover Park

HICKORY TREE PL.

United Ch

Homewood

Sewage Plant

Beavertown

Dogwood

Range End Golf Club

A Quay Park
B Monaghan Presbyterian Ch

South Mountain ES

Youngs Grove MHP

RANGE END RD.

GLENWOOD

FRANKLIN

State   Game   Lands

No   243

15

Franklin Twp Park

CAPITOL HILL RD.

MASON-DIXON

HOLLOW TRAIL RD.

Emmanuel Lutheran Ch

Franklintown Comm. Fire Co

Franklintown

FRANKLINTOWN RD.

W. HARRISBURG ST.

Dillsburg

FRANKLINTOWN 17323

Dillsburg Cem

District Justice

Athletic Field

Dillsburg ES

S. CHESTNUT ST.

Calvary UMC

Fishers

1 W. CHURCH ST.
2 E. CHURCH ST.
3 W. YORK ST.
4 E. YORK ST.
5 AUTUMN WOODS CT.
6 HARRISBURG ST.

Pheasant Ridge

Pinoak Mobile Home Park

OLD YORK RD.

CARROLL

17019

Sports & Learning Center

Northern HS

Northern MS

Northern ES

CARLISLE RD.

194

74

SHEARER DR.

CARLISLE RD.

WARRINGTON

WASHINGTON

Salem Ch

KRALLTOWN RD.

BARRENS VALLEY RD.

SEE MAP 3057

SEE MAP 3161

A B C D E F G H

77°00'00"

21

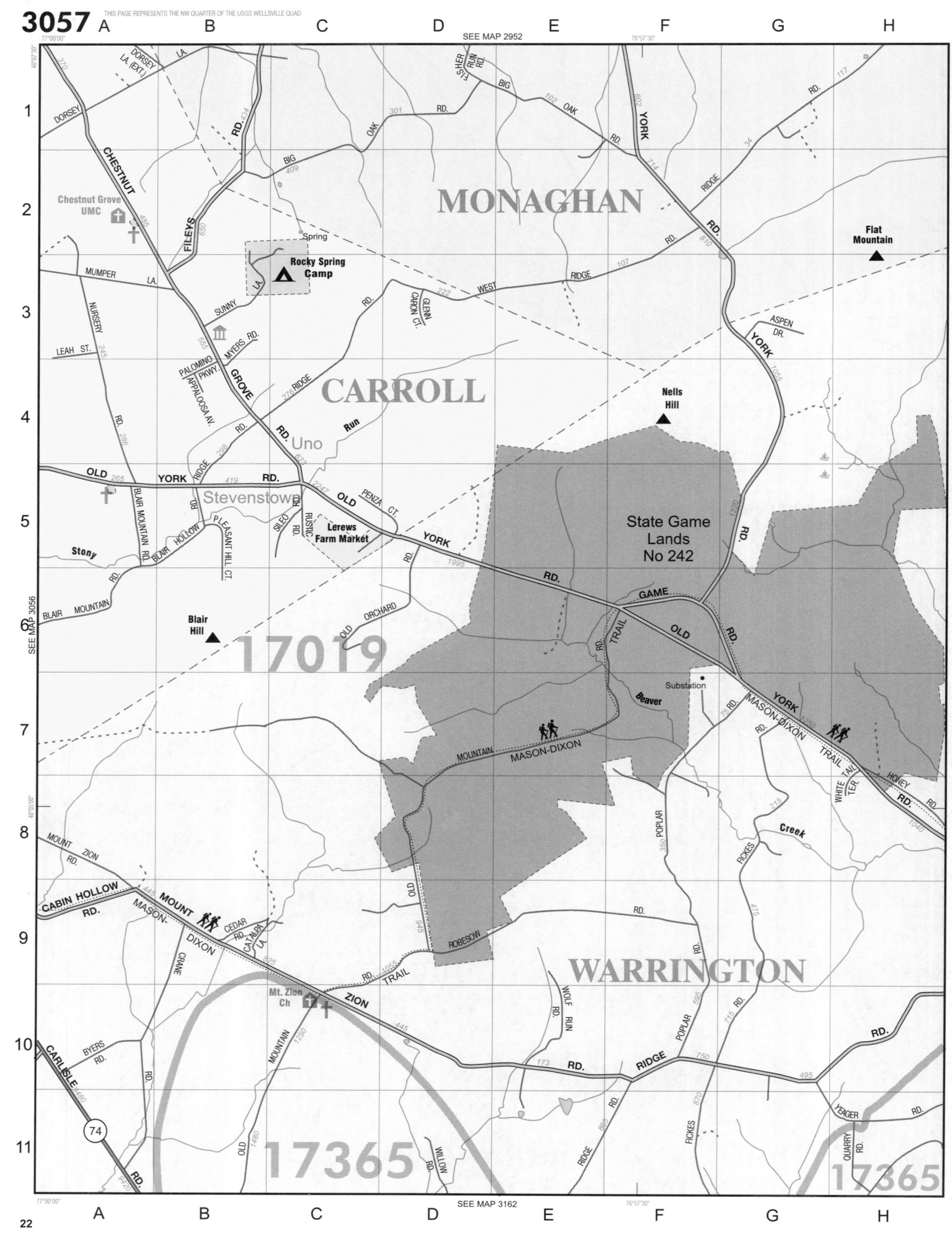

SEE MAP 2952

A   B   C   D   E   F   G   H

MONAGHAN

Flat
Mountain ▲

Chestnut Grove
UMC

Spring

Rocky Spring
Camp ▲

CARROLL

Nells
Hill ▲

Stevenstown

Uno

Run

Lerews
Farm Market

State Game
Lands
No 242

Stony

Blair
Hill ▲

17019

Substation

Beaver

MASON-DIXON

Creek

WARRINGTON

Cabin Hollow

Mt. Zion
Ch

17365

74

17365

SEE MAP 3162

A   B   C   D   E   F   G   H

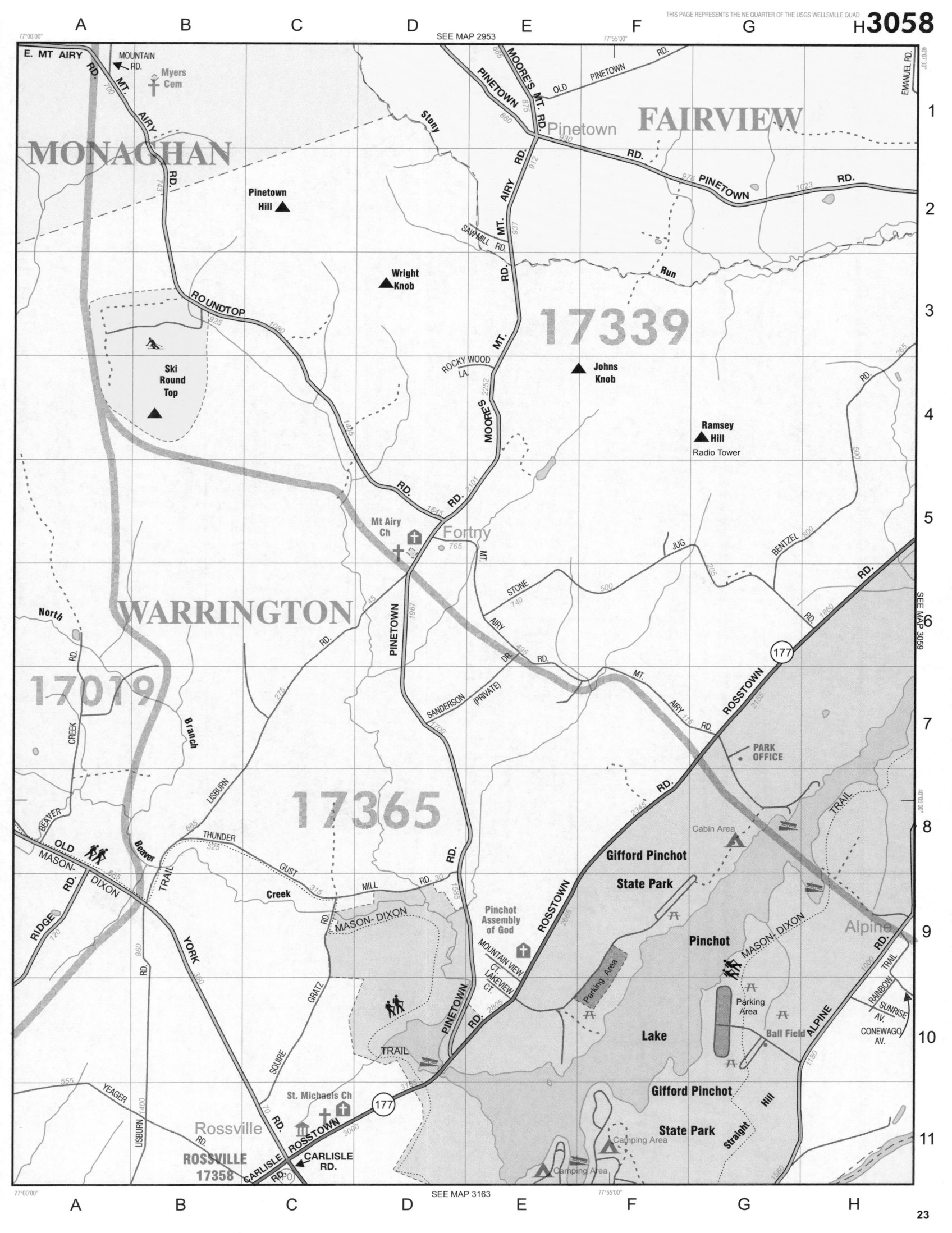

A · B · C · D · E · F · G · H

E. MT AIRY RD.
MOUNTAIN RD.
Myers Cem

MONAGHAN

Pinetown Hill ▲

SEE MAP 2953

Stony

PINETOWN RD.

MOORES MT. RD.

OLD PINETOWN

Pinetown

FAIRVIEW

PINETOWN RD.

EMANUEL RD.

ROUNDTOP

Wright Knob ▲

SAWMILL RD.

MT. AIRY RD.

17339

Run

Ski Round Top ▲

ROCKY WOOD LA.

MOORE'S MT.

Johns Knob ▲

Ramsey Hill ▲
Radio Tower

RD.

RD.

Mt Airy Ch

Fortny
765

JUG

BENTZEL

WARRINGTON

MT. AIRY DR.

STONE 740

17019

North

CREEK

Branch

PINETOWN RD.

Sanderson (PRIVATE)

MT. AIRY RD.

177

ROSSTOWN RD.

PARK OFFICE

LISBURN

THUNDER TRAIL

Creek

GUST

MILL RD.

RD.

MASON-DIXON

17365

Cabin Area

TRAIL

BEAVER

Beaver

OLD MASON-DIXON RD.

RIDGE RD.

YORK RD.

GRATZ

MASON-DIXON

Pinchot Assembly of God

ROSSTOWN RD.

Gifford Pinchot State Park

Pinchot

Alpine

MOUNTAIN VIEW CT.
LAKEVIEW CT.

Parking Area

Parking Area

Ball Field

ALPINE RD.

RAINBOW TRAIL

SQUIRE RD.

YEAGER

LISBURN

St. Michaels Ch

CARLISLE RD.

177

PINETOWN RD.

TRAIL

Lake

SUNRISE AV.

CONEWAGO AV.

Rossville

ROSSTOWN RD.

ROSSVILLE 17358

CARLISLE RD.

SEE MAP 3163

Gifford Pinchot State Park

Straight Hill

Camping Area

Camping Area

A · B · C · D · E · F · G · H

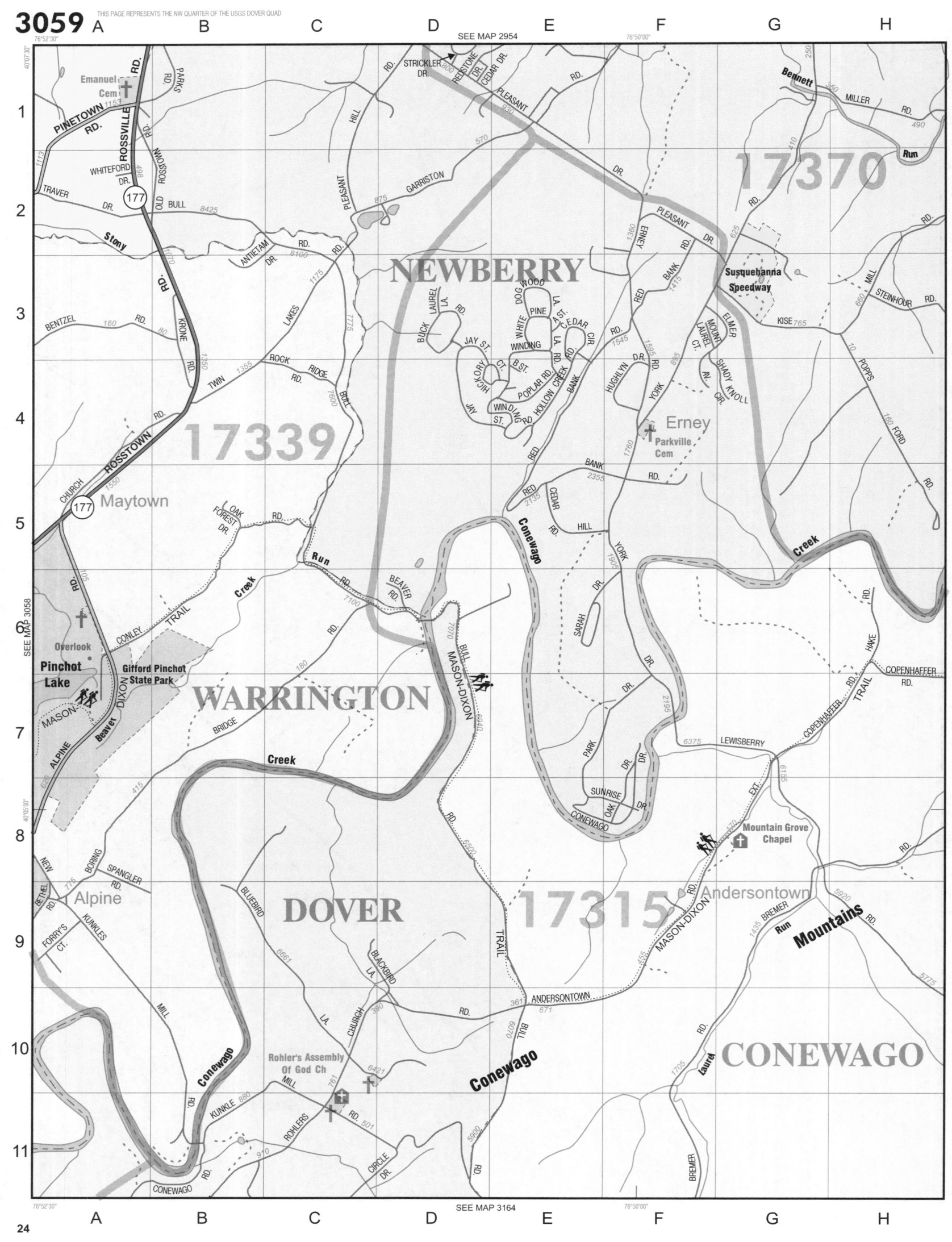

THIS PAGE REPRESENTS THE NW QUARTER OF THE USGS DOVER QUAD

SEE MAP 2954

17370

NEWBERRY

17339

17315

WARRINGTON

DOVER

CONEWAGO

Maytown

Pinchot Lake

Gifford Pinchot State Park

Overlook

Alpine

Andersontown

Mountains

Mountain Grove Chapel

Susquehanna Speedway

Erney

Parkville Cem

Emanuel Cem

Rohler's Assembly Of God Ch

Bennett

SEE MAP 3164

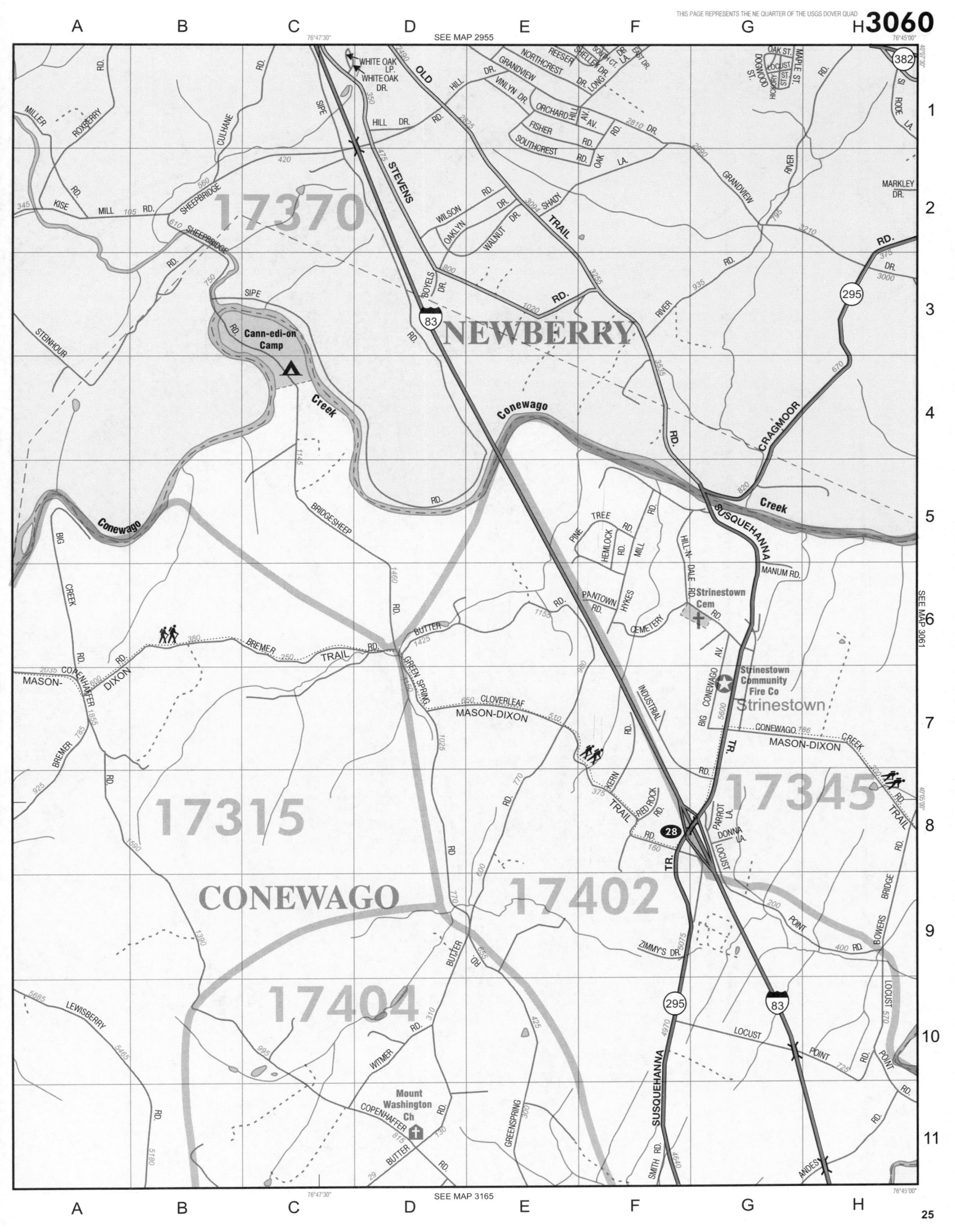

A   B   C   D   E   F   G   H

SEE MAP 2955

WHITE OAK LP.
WHITE OAK DR.

17370

Cann-edi-on Camp

NEWBERRY

Conewago

Creek

Conewago

SEE MAP 3061

17315

17345

CONEWAGO

17402

Strinestown
Community
Fire Co
Strinestown

Strinestown Cem

Susquehanna Creek

MASON-DIXON

17404

Mount
Washington
Ch

SEE MAP 3165

A   B   C   D   E   F   G   H

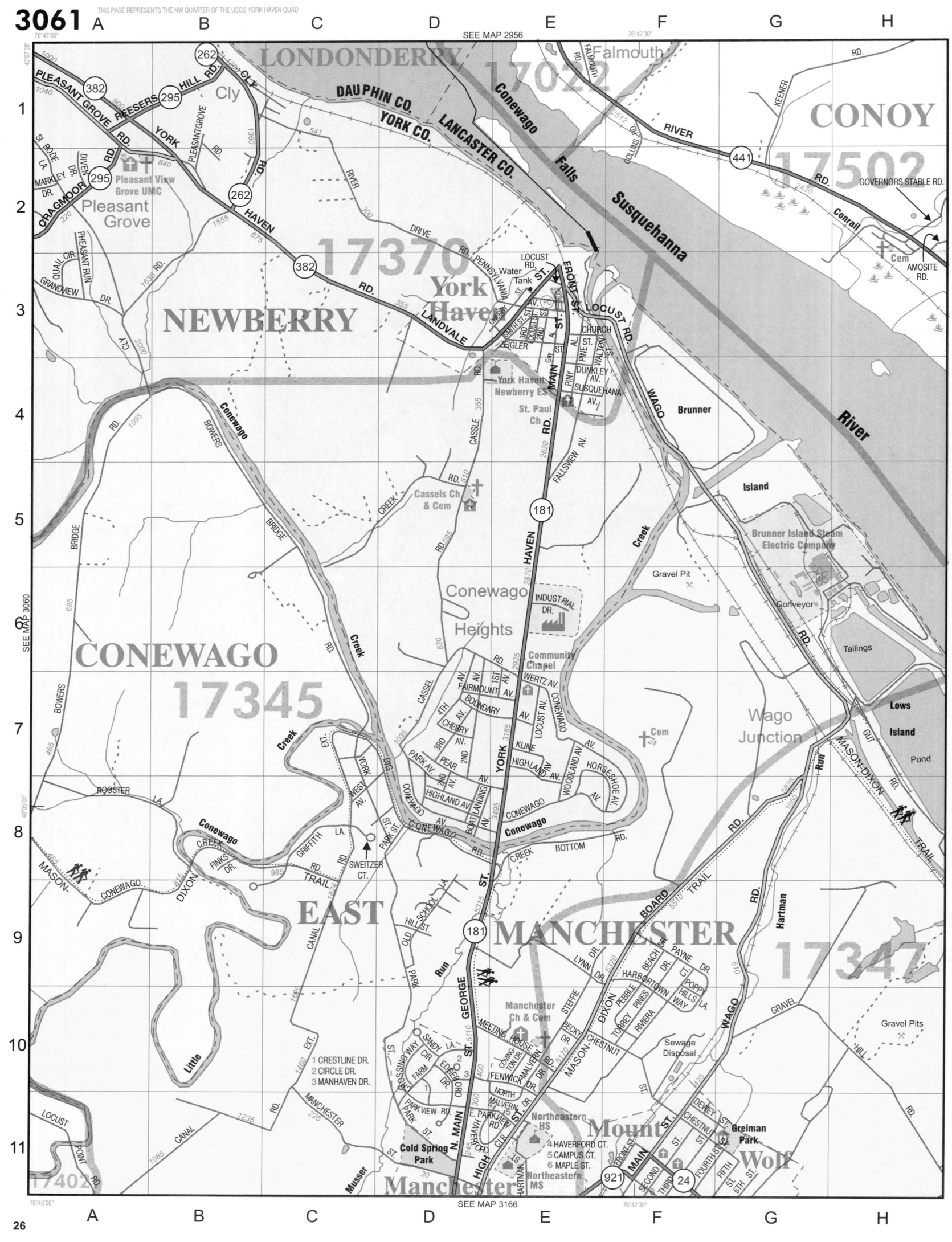

THIS PAGE REPRESENTS THE NW QUARTER OF THE USGS YORK HAVEN QUAD

A B C D E F G H

SEE MAP 2956

CONOY

17502

LONDONDERRY

1702.2

Falmouth

DAUPHIN CO.

YORK CO.

LANCASTER CO.

Conewago

River

Susquehanna

GOVERNORS STABLE RD.

Conrail

Cem

AMOSITE RD.

441

17370

York Haven

NEWBERRY

Water Tank

LOCUST RD.

CHURCH

York Haven
Newberry ES

St. Paul Ch

Brunner

WAGO

River

Island

Brunner Island Steam
Electric Company

Conveyor

Gravel Pit

Cassels Ch
& Cem

181

HAVEN

Conewago
Heights

INDUSTRIAL DR.

Community
Chapel

Tailings

CONEWAGO

17345

Creek

Wago
Junction

Lows
Island
Pond

Cem

Wertz Av.

Fairmount Av.

Boundary

Cherry

Park Av.

Highland Av.

Conewago

Kline

Highland

Woodland Av.

Horseshoe Av.

MASON-DIXON

EAST

MANCHESTER

17347

Conewago

Creek

Sweitzer
Ct.

Conewago

Bottom

Board

TRAIL

Hartman

RD.

181

Manchester
Ch & Cem

Meeting
House

Payne
Dr.

Harbortown
Dr.

Poppy
Hills La.

Sewage
Disposal

Gravel Pits

Little

Crossing Way

Sandy La.

Steffie

Dixon

Becky

Pebble

Torrey

Pines

Riviera

Chestnut

1 CRESTLINE DR.
2 CIRCLE DR.
3 MANHAVEN DR.

Fenwick

North

Malvern

Northeastern
HS

4 HAVERFORD CT.
5 CAMPUS CT.
6 MAPLE ST.

Greiman
Park

Mount

Wolf

Cold Spring
Park

Park View Rd.

Northeastern
MS

Dewey

Chestnut

Fourth

Fifth

6th

Manchester

SEE MAP 3166

921

24

A B C D E F G H

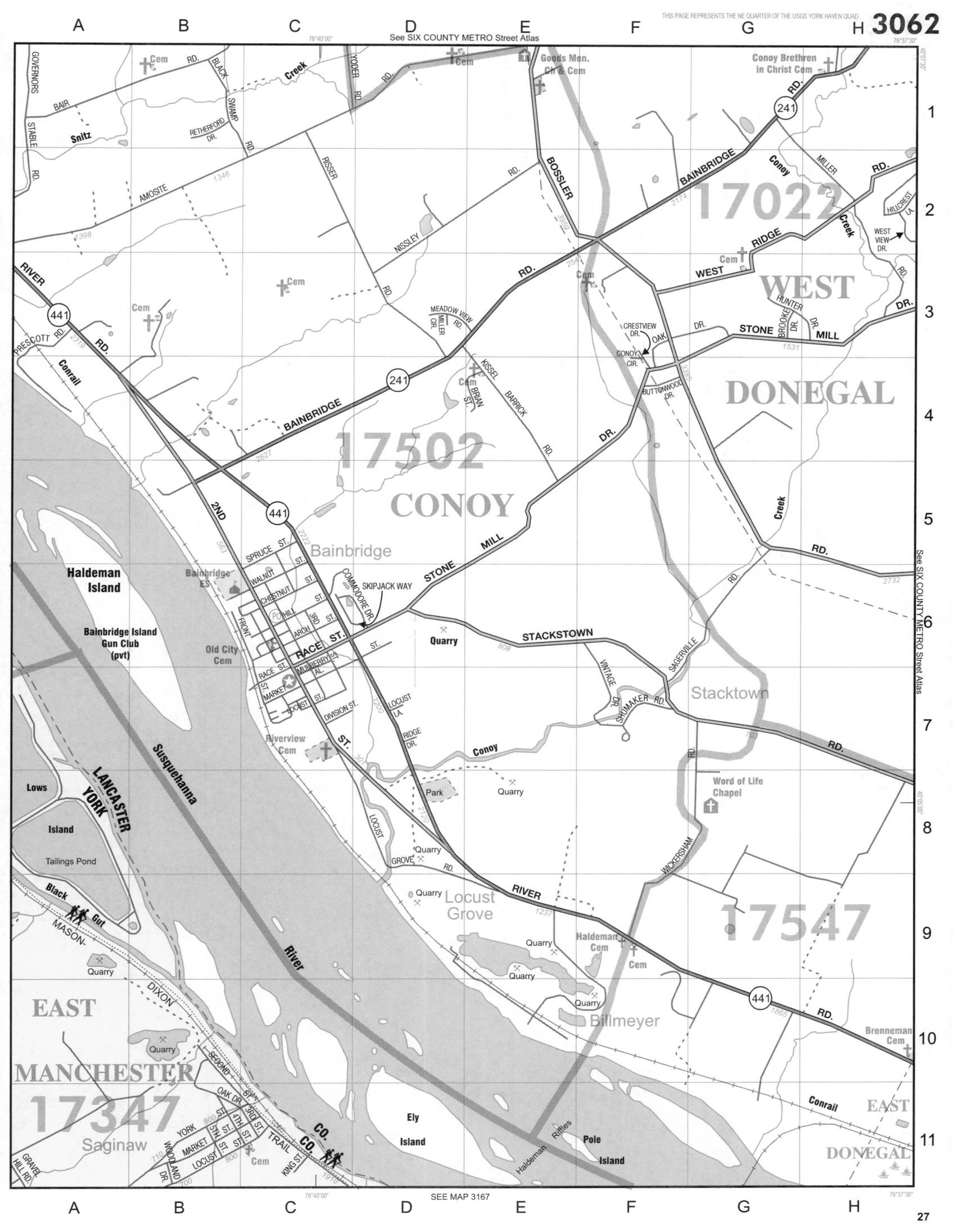

See SIX COUNTY METRO Street Atlas

A   B   C   D   E   F   G   H

76°40'00"

40°07'30"

1

Cem   RD.   BLACK   SWAMP   RD.   Creek   YODER   RD.   Cem   Goods Men. Ch & Cem   Conoy Brethren in Christ Cem

GOVERNORS   BAIR   Snitz   RETHERFORD DR.   RISSER   BOSSLER   BAINBRIDGE   241   Conoy   MILLER RD.

STABLE   RD.   AMOSITE   1346   1398   NISSLEY   RD.   2174   WEST   RIDGE   Cem   HILLCREST LA.

WEST VIEW DR.

2

17022

RIVER   441   Cem   Cem   MEADOW VIEW RD.   MILLER CIR.   RD.   Cem   254   WEST   HUNTER DR.   BROOKE DR.   STONE   MILL   Creek   RD. DR.   WEST

PRESCOTT   RD.   2319   241   Conrail   CRESTVIEW DR.   OAK   CONOY CIR.   DR.   1531   3385   DR.

3

Conrail   BAINBRIDGE   KISSEL   Cem BRIAN ST.   BARRICK   BUTTONWOOD DR.   DONEGAL

17502

4

2627   RD.   DR.

Susquehanna   2ND   441   563   2222   CONOY   STONE   MILL   Creek   2732   RD.

5

Haldeman Island   SPRUCE ST.   ST.   Bainbridge   SKIPJACK WAY   COMMODORE DR.   STONE   MILL   RD.

Bainbridge ES   WALNUT   ST.   CHESTNUT   ST.   3RD   ST.   808   STACKSTOWN   SAGERVILLE   RD.   Stacktown

6

Bainbridge Island Gun Club (pvt)   PO HILL   ARCH   ST.   RACE ST.   ST.   Quarry   VINTAGE DR.   SHUMAKER RD.

FRONT   Old City Cem   RACE ST.   MULBERRY AL.   LOCUST LA.   Conoy   RD.   Word of Life Chapel

7

MARKET   DIVISION ST.   LOCUST   ST.   RIDGE DR.   Quarry   Park   Quarry   RD.

Riverview Cem   ST.   2200   3200   WICKERSHAM

8

Lows   LANCASTER   YORK   Island   Tailings Pond   GROVE   RD.   Quarry   RIVER   Locust Grove   Quarry

17547

9

Black   Gut   MASON   Quarry   River   1237   Quarry   Haldeman Cem   Cem   441

DIXON   Quarry   1865   RD.   Brenneman Cem

10

EAST   Quarry   SECOND   Billmeyer   Conrail   EAST

MANCHESTER   OAK DR   6TH   3RD ST.   TRAIL   Ely Island   Rifles   Pole   DONEGAL

17347   YORK   5TH ST.   4TH ST.   LOCUST   CO.   Haldeman   Pole Island

Saginaw   WOODLAND DR.   MARKET   LOCUST   Cem   KING ST.   CO.   1970

GRAVEL HILL RD.   700   800

11

A   B   C   D   E   F   G   H

76°40'00"   SEE MAP 3167   76°37'30"

See SIX COUNTY METRO Street Atlas

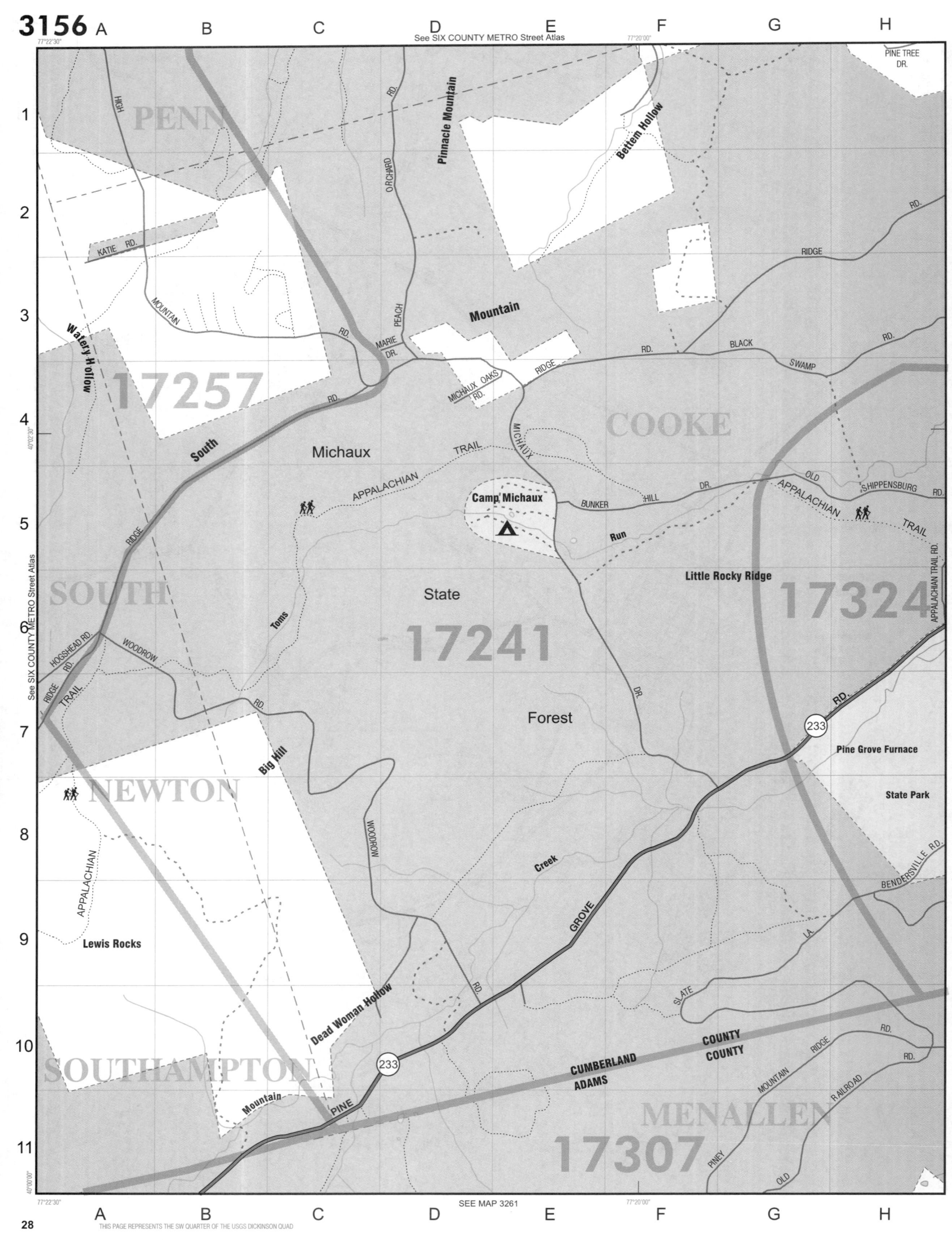

3156 A

77°22'30"
77°20'00"

PINE TREE DR.

PENN

1

Pinnacle Mountain

Bettem Hollow

ORCHARD RD.

2

KATIE RD.

RIDGE RD.

MOUNTAIN

PEACH

3

Watery Hollow

RD.

Mountain

RD.

BLACK

SWAMP

RD.

17257

MARIE DR.

MICHAUX OAKS RD.

RIDGE

COOKE

40°02'30"

4

South

Michaux

TRAIL

MICHAUX

OLD SHIPPENSBURG RD.

APPALACHIAN

Camp Michaux

BUNKER HILL DR.

APPALACHIAN TRAIL

5

RIDGE

Run

Little Rocky Ridge

17324

SOUTH

Toms

State

Run

APPALACHIAN TRAIL RD.

See SIX COUNTY METRO Street Atlas

6

HOGSHEAD RD.

WOODROW

17241

DR.

7

RIDGE TRAIL

RD.

Forest

233 RD.

Pine Grove Furnace

Big Hill

8

NEWTON

WOODROW

Creek

GROVE

State Park

BENDERSVILLE RD.

APPALACHIAN

9

Lewis Rocks

RD.

SLATE LA

RIDGE RD.

10

SOUTHAMPTON

Dead Woman Hollow

233

CUMBERLAND COUNTY

ADAMS COUNTY

MENALLEN

MOUNTAIN RD.

RAILROAD RD.

Mountain

PINE

17307

PINEY

OLD

11

40°00'00"

77°22'30"

SEE MAP 3261

77°20'00"

A B C D E F G H

THIS PAGE REPRESENTS THE SW QUARTER OF THE USGS DICKINSON QUAD

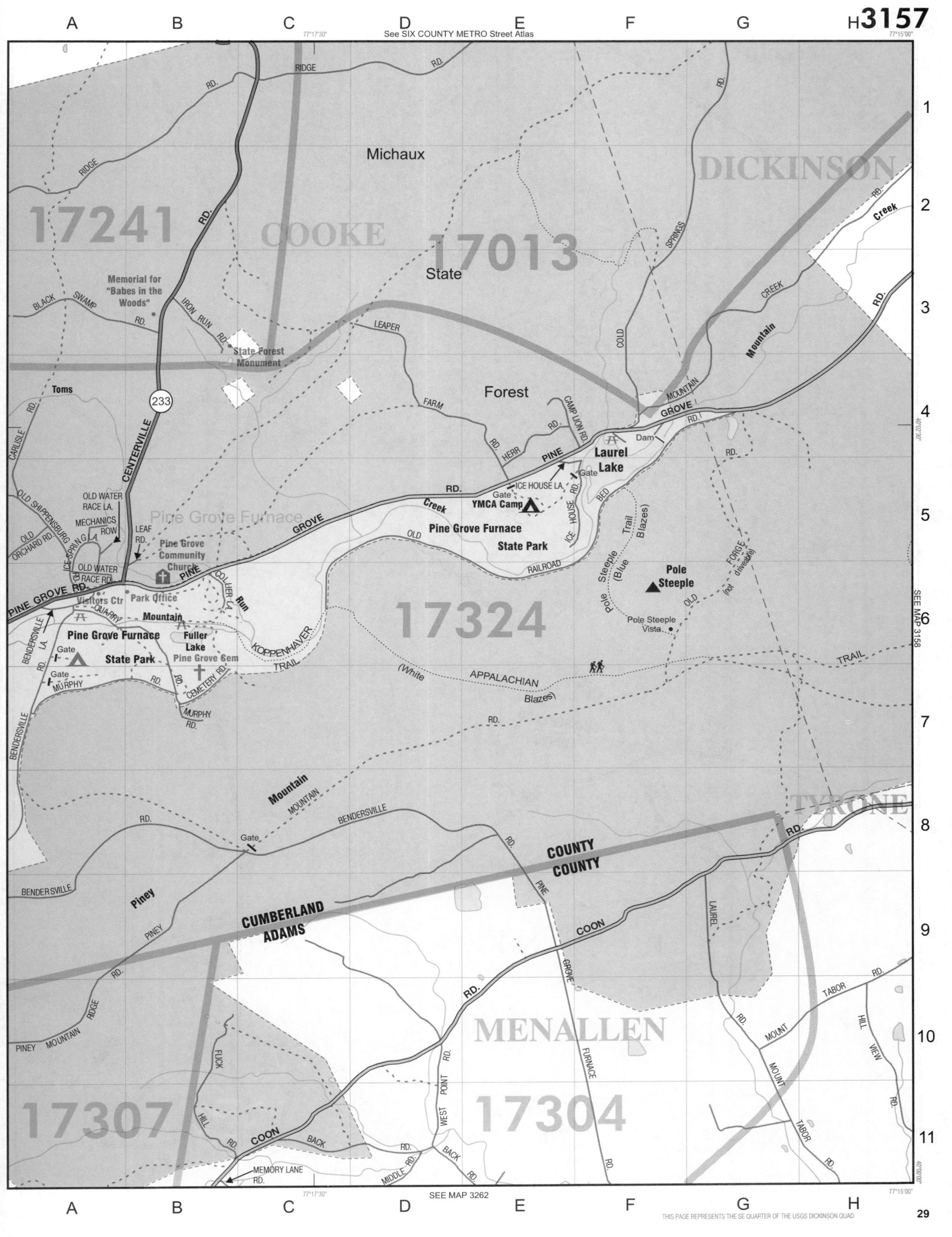

See SIX COUNTY METRO Street Atlas

77°17'30"

77°15'00"

A B C D E F G

1
2
3
4
5
6
7
8
9
10
11

40°02'30"

SEE MAP 3158

Michaux

DICKINSON

17241

COOKE

17013

State

Creek

Memorial for "Babes in the Woods"

State Forest Monument

LEAPER

Forest

COLD SPRINGS

MOUNTAIN CREEK

Mountain

Toms

FARM

Camp Lion Rd.

GROVE

Dam

HERR

PINE

Laurel Lake

Carlisle Rd.

ICE HOUSE LA.

Gate

233

Old Shippensburg Rd.

Old Orchard Rd.

Old Water Race La.

Mechanics Row

LEAF RD.

CENTERVILLE

Pine Grove Furnace

GROVE

Creek

YMCA Camp

Gate

Pine Grove Furnace State Park

RAILROAD

OLD

Pole Steeple (Blue Trail Blazes)

Pole Steeple

FORGE (not driveable)

OLD

Pine Grove Community Church

PINE

COLLIER LA.

Run

17324

Pole Steeple Vista

Pine Grove Rd.

Visitors Ctr

Park Office

QUARRY

Mountain

Fuller Lake

KOPPENHAVER

TRAIL

(White

APPALACHIAN

Blazes)

TRAIL

Bendersville

Pine Grove Furnace

State Park

Pine Grove Cem

CEMETERY RD.

RD.

Gate

MURPHY

MURPHY RD.

RD.

Mountain

Mountain

MOUNTAIN

Bendersville

Gate

TYRONE

PINE

COUNTY

COUNTY

RD.

Piney

LAUREL

PINEY

CUMBERLAND

ADAMS

COON

GROVE

MENALLEN

17307

PINEY MOUNTAIN RIDGE

FLICK

MOUNT

TABOR RD.

HILL VIEW

FURNACE

MOUNT

TABOR RD.

17304

HILL RD.

COON

BACK

RD.

BACK

WEST POINT RD.

MIDDLE RD.

RD.

MEMORY LANE RD.

40°00'00"

77°17'30"

SEE MAP 3262

77°15'00"

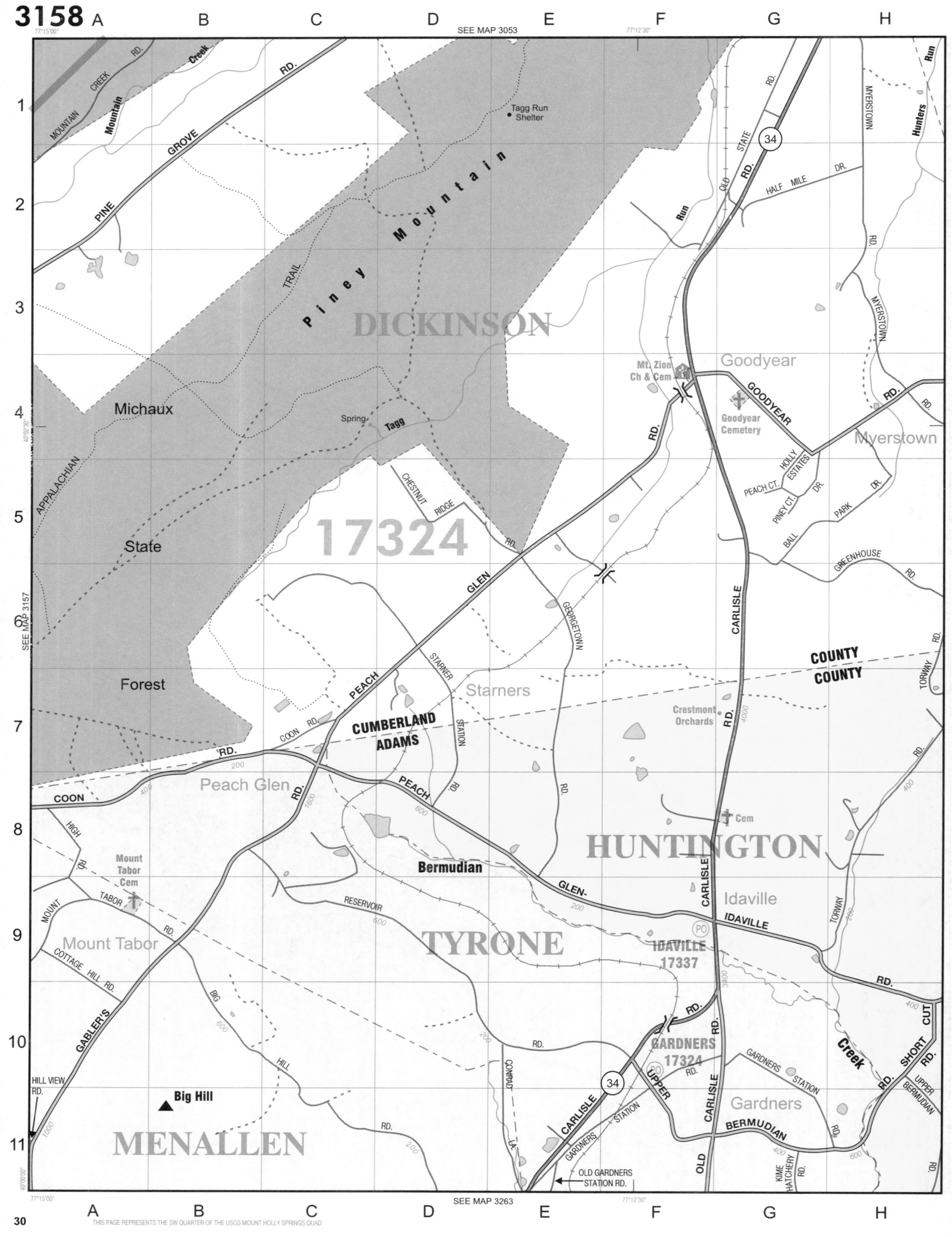

SEE MAP 3053

77°15'00"

77°12'30"

MOUNTAIN

CREEK RD.

Creek

Mountain

GROVE

PINE

RD.

Run

Run

STATE

OLD

RD.

34

HALF MILE

DR.

MYERSTOWN

Hunters Run

Piney Mountain

TRAIL

Piney

DICKINSON

MYERSTOWN

Tagg Run Shelter

RD.

RD.

Goodyear

Michaux

APPALACHIAN

Spring

Tagg

GOODYEAR

Mt. Zion Ch & Cem

Goodyear Cemetery

HOLLY ESTATES

PEACH CT.

PINEY CT.

DR.

BALL

DR.

PARK

DR.

Myerstown

State

CHESTNUT RIDGE

17324

RD.

GLEN

CARLISLE

GREENHOUSE RD.

Forest

PEACH

COON RD.

STARNER

GEORGETOWN RD.

Starners

COUNTY
COUNTY

Crestmont Orchards

RD.

4000

TORWAY RD.

CUMBERLAND
ADAMS

STATION

RD.

RD.

Peach Glen

COON

RD.

400

RD.

200

1600

PEACH

600

RD.

HUNTINGTON

Cem

High

RD.

Mount Tabor Cem

TABOR

RD.

Bermudian

GLEN-

200

CARLISLE

Idaville

TORWAY

RD.

MOUNT

COTTAGE HILL RD.

RESERVOIR

600

TYRONE

IDAVILLE

PO

IDAVILLE
17337

RD.

Mount Tabor

RD.

BIG

600

HILL

200

RD.

RD.

3400

400

CUT

GABLERS RD.

HILL VIEW RD.

▲ Big Hill

CONRAD

LA.

RD.

GARDNERS
17324

PO

UPPER

CARLISLE

RD.

GARDNERS STATION

Creek

SHORT RD.

UPPER BERMUDIAN

MENALLEN

7000

200

34

CARLISLE

GARDNERS STATION RD.

OLD

UPPER

BERMUDIAN

Gardners

KIME

HATCHERY RD.

RD.

400

600

← OLD GARDNERS
STATION RD.

40°00'00"

77°15'00"

SEE MAP 3263

77°12'30"

40°00'00"

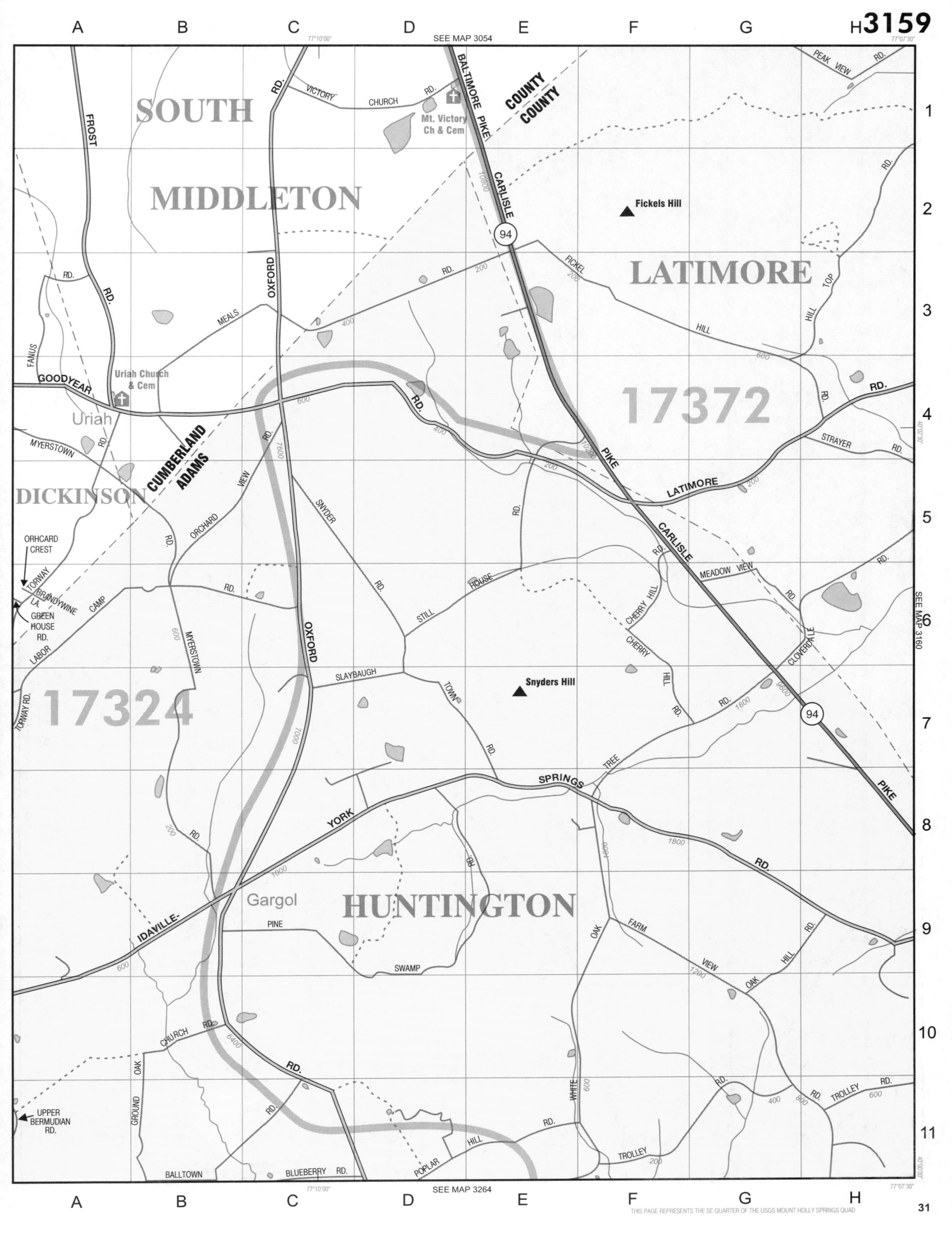

SOUTH

MIDDLETON

LATIMORE

17372

DICKINSON

17324

HUNTINGTON

Fickels Hill

Snyders Hill

Uriah Church & Cem

Mt. Victory Ch & Cem

Uriah

Goodyear

Myerstown

Orhcard Crest

Torway La.

Brandywine

Green House Rd.

Labor

Gargol

Idaville

Upper Bermudian Rd.

Balltown

Blueberry Rd.

SEE MAP 3054

SEE MAP 3264

SEE MAP 3160

COUNTY COUNTY

CUMBERLAND ADAMS

77°10'00"

77°07'30"

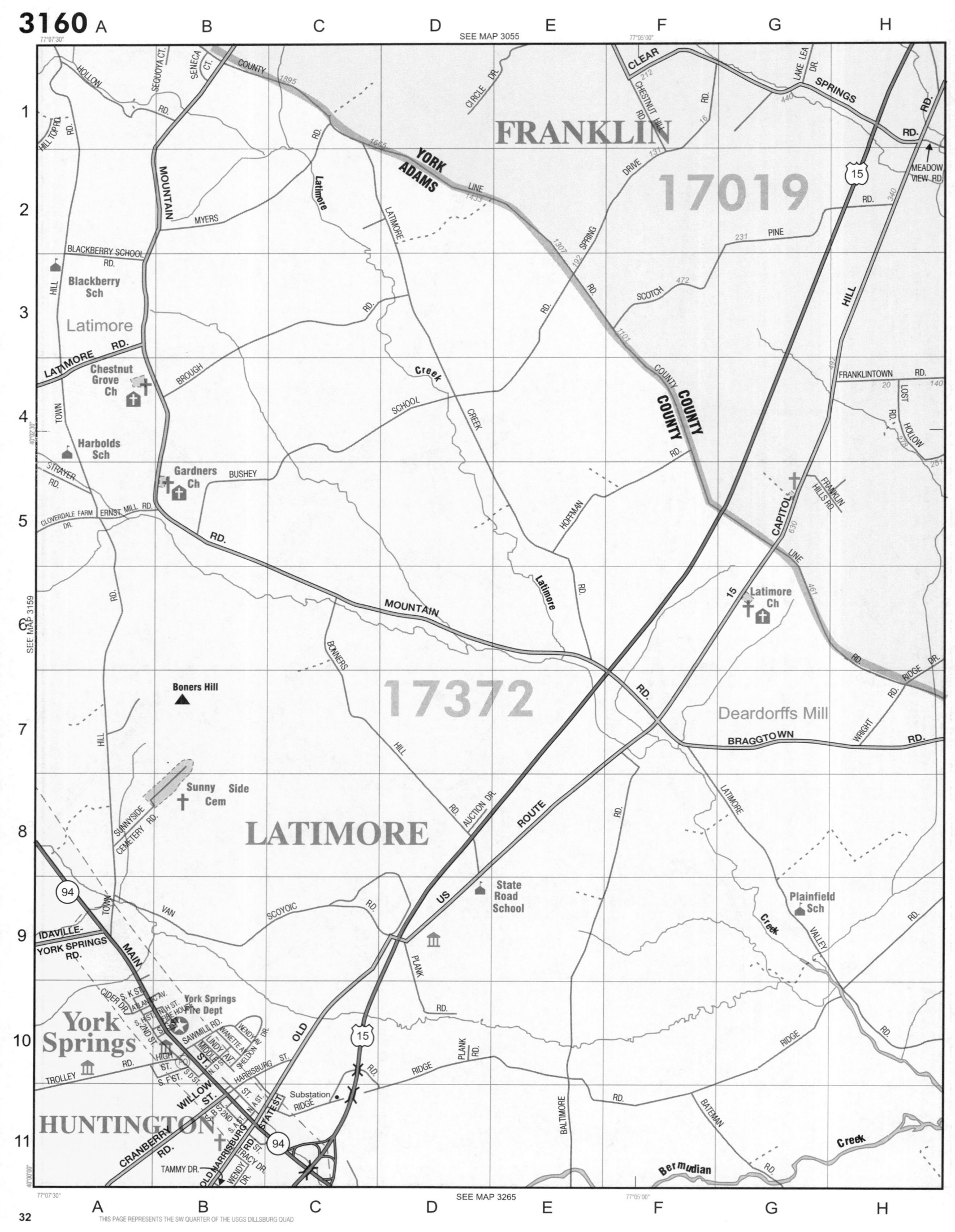

77°07'30"

SEE MAP 3055

77°05'00"

A   B   C   D   E   F   G   H

1

HILL TOP RD.

HOLLOW

SEQUOYA CT.

SENECA

CT.

RD.

COUNTY

1895

CIRCLE DR.

CLEAR

CHESTNUT HILL

212

440

LAKE LEA DR.

SPRINGS

RD.

FRANKLIN

RD.

16

15

MEADOW VIEW RD.

MOUNTAIN

MYERS

Latimore

1685

YORK

ADAMS

LINE

1435

LATIMORE

1307

DRIVE

1371

SPRING

192

17019

231

PINE

340

HILL

2

BLACKBERRY SCHOOL RD.

HILL

Blackberry Sch

Latimore

RD.

RD.

SCOTCH

472

1101

COUNTY

472

FRANKLINTOWN RD.

20

140

3

LATIMORE RD.

TOWN

Chestnut Grove Ch

BROUGH

Creek

SCHOOL

CREEK

RD.

COUNTY

COUNTY

LOST HOLLOW RD.

251

4

STRAYER RD.

Harbolds Sch

Gardners Ch

BUSHEY

CREEK

CAPITOL

FRANKLIN HILLS RD.

5

CLOVERDALE FARM DR.

ERNST MILL RD.

RD.

RD.

HOFFMAN

Latimore

RD.

15

LINE

630

Latimore Ch

461

6

SEE MAP 3159

RD.

MOUNTAIN

BONERS

Latimore

RD.

RD.

RIDGE DR.

7

HILL

Boners Hill

17372

HILL

RD.

Deardorffs Mill

BRAGGTOWN

WRIGHT

RD.

8

SUNNYSIDE CEMETERY RD.

Sunny Side Cem

LATIMORE

RD.

AUCTION DR.

ROUTE

RD.

LATIMORE

9

94

IDAVILLE-YORK SPRINGS RD.

TOWN

VAN

SCOYOIC

RD.

US

State Road School

Creek

Plainfield Sch

RD.

PLANK

VALLEY

10

CIDER DR.

S. K ST.

ATLANTIC AV.

York Springs

MAIN

York Springs Fire Dept

SAWMILL RD.

WENDY AV.

MANETTE AV.

SHELDON

OLD

94

15

RD.

PLANK RD.

RIDGE

RD.

11

TROLLEY

RD.

HIGH ST.

MIDDLE ST.

S. F ST.

LINDY AV.

HARRISBURG ST.

RIDGE

PLANK RD.

RD.

BATEMAN

WILLOW ST.

STATE ST.

Substation

RIDGE

BALTIMORE

RD.

Creek

HUNTINGTON

CRANBERRY RD.

OLD HARRISBURG RD.

TAMMY DR.

TRACY DR.

WENDY DR.

94

Bermudian

RD.

77°07'30"

SEE MAP 3265

77°05'00"

A   B   C   D   E   F   G   H

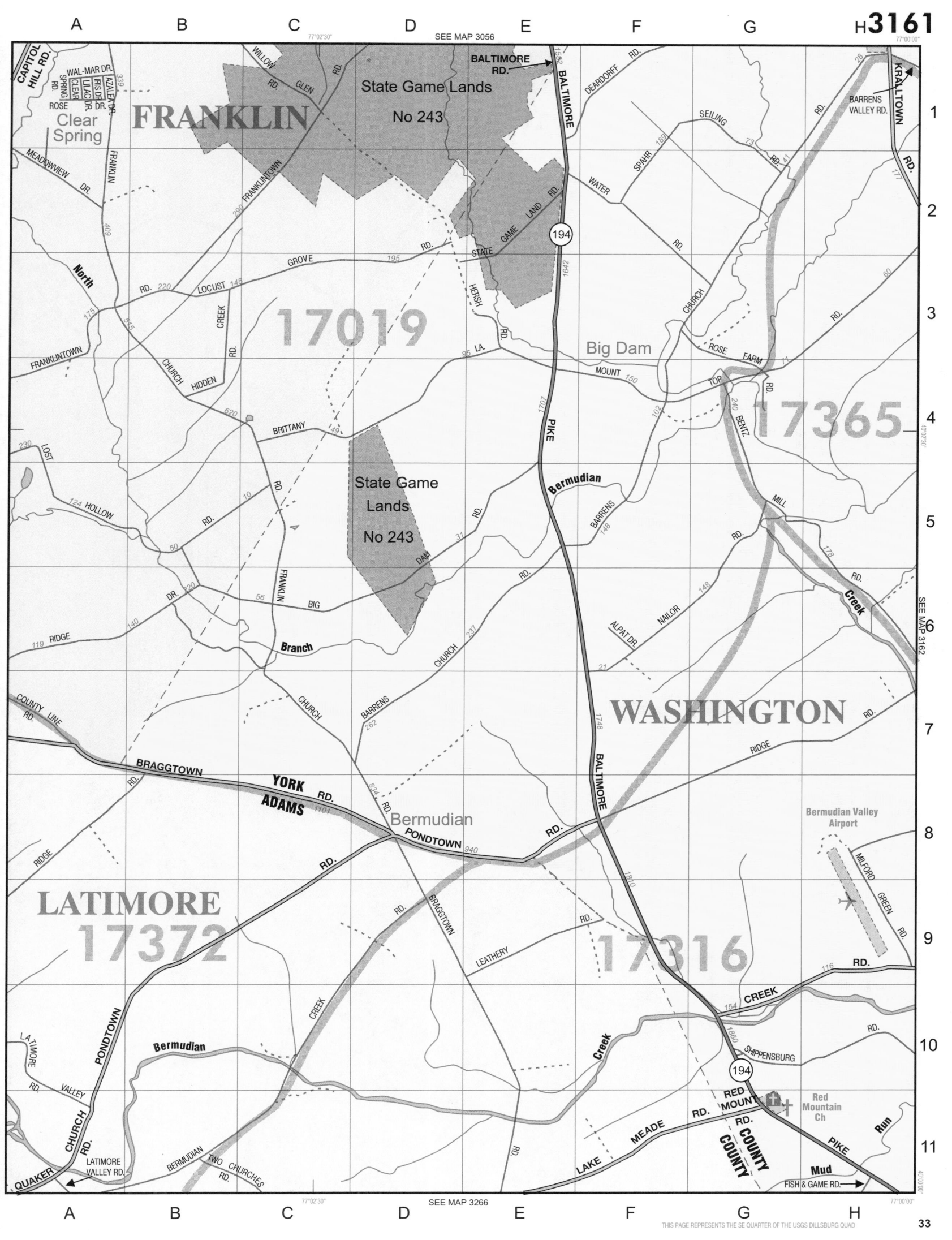

A · B · C · D · E · F · G

CAPITOL HILL RD.
WAL-MAR DR.
SPRING RD.
AZALEA DR.
IRIS DR.
LILAC DR.
CLEAR RD.
ROSE
MEADOWVIEW DR.

Clear Spring

FRANKLIN

North

FRANKLINTOWN

FRANKLIN 409
339
290
175
220 RD.
345
LOCUST 145
CHURCH
HIDDEN 620
CREEK
RD.

FRANKLINTOWN

GROVE
195
WILLOW RD.
GLEN RD.
RD.

SEE MAP 3056

BALTIMORE RD.

State Game Lands

No 243

1642
BALTIMORE 28
KRALLTOWN RD.
BARRENS VALLEY RD.
177

DEARDORFF RD.
SEILING
RD.
SPAHR 189
WATER RD.
73
41
RD.
60

STATE GAME LAND RD.
194
HERSH
RD.
95 LA.

17019

BRITTANY 49

State Game Lands

No 243

230
LOST 124 HOLLOW
RD.
50
DR. 320
140
119 RIDGE
10
RD.
FRANKLIN
56
BIG
Branch
31
DAM
237
CHURCH

PIKE 1707
Bermudian
Big Dam
MOUNT 150
102
BARRENS 148
RD.
NAILOR 148
ALPAT DR.
21
CHURCH
RD.
BARRENS 262

ROSE FARM
74
TOP
MOUNT 240
BENTZ
MILL
178 RD.
Creek
RD.
RD.

17365

40°02'30"

SEE MAP 3162

COUNTY LINE RD.
BRAGGTOWN RD.
YORK
ADAMS RD. 1101
834 RD.
CHURCH
RIDGE

WASHINGTON

RIDGE
BALTIMORE 1748

LATIMORE
17372

RIDGE
PONDTOWN
Bermudian
PONDTOWN 940
RD.
BRAGGTOWN
RD.
CREEK
LEATHERY
RD.
Creek

BALTIMORE 1810

17316

Bermudian Valley Airport
MILFORD
GREEN RD.
116 RD.
154 CREEK RD.
1860
SHIPPENSBURG
RD.

LA TIMORE RD.
PONDTOWN
VALLEY RD.
CHURCH RD.
QUAKER RD.
LATIMORE VALLEY RD.
Bermudian
BERMUDIAN TWO CHURCHES RD.
VALLEY

194
RED MOUNT
RD.
MEADE
LAKE
COUNTY
COUNTY
BALTIMORE RD.
RED MOUNT RD.
Red Mountain Ch
PIKE
Run
Mud
FISH & GAME RD.

40°00'00"

SEE MAP 3266

A · B · C · D · E · F · G · H

1
2
3
4
5
6
7
8
9
10
11

A B C D E F G H

SEE MAP 3057

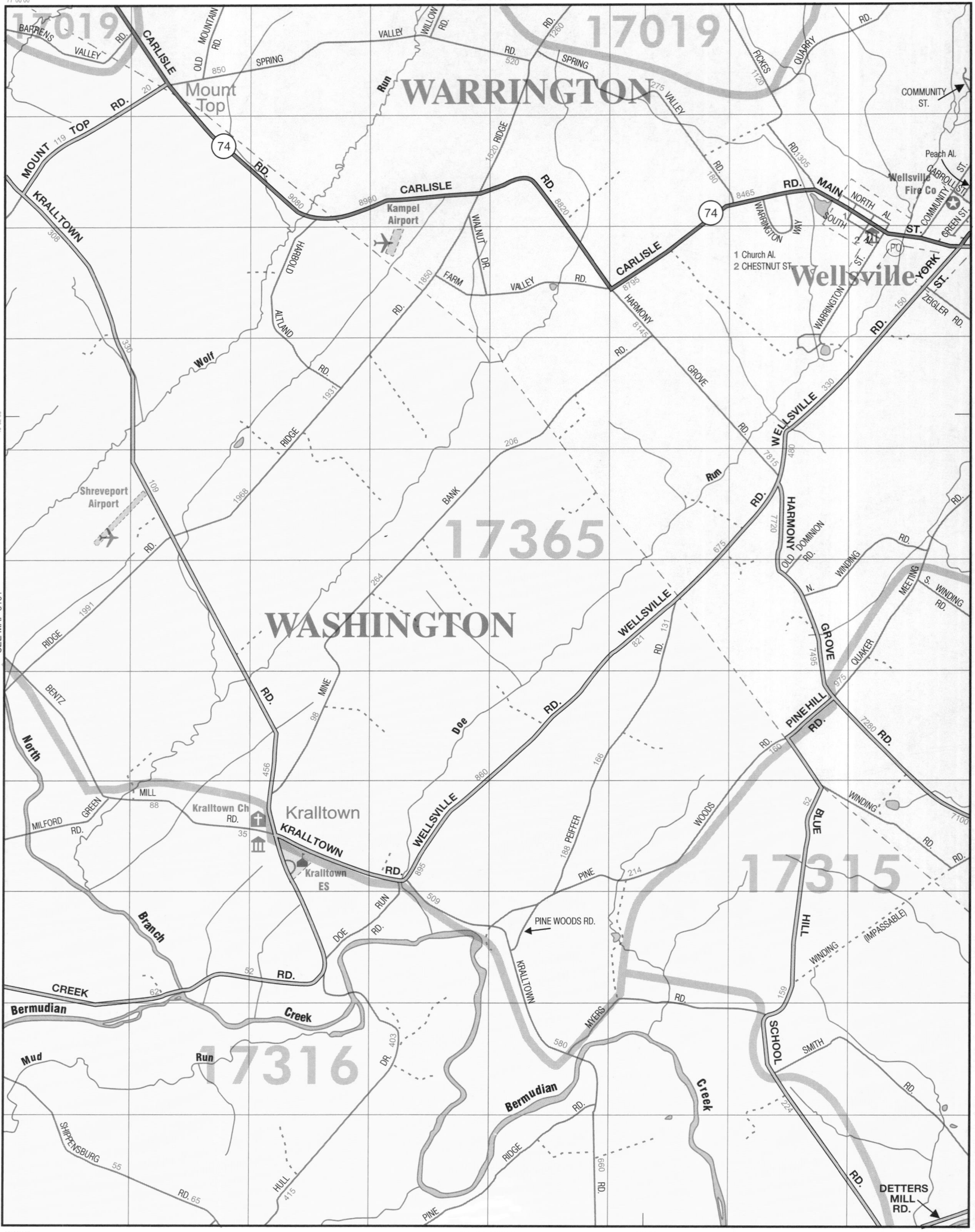

SEE MAP 3267

A B C D E F G H

THIS PAGE REPRESENTS THE SW QUARTER OF THE USGS WELLSVILLE QUAD

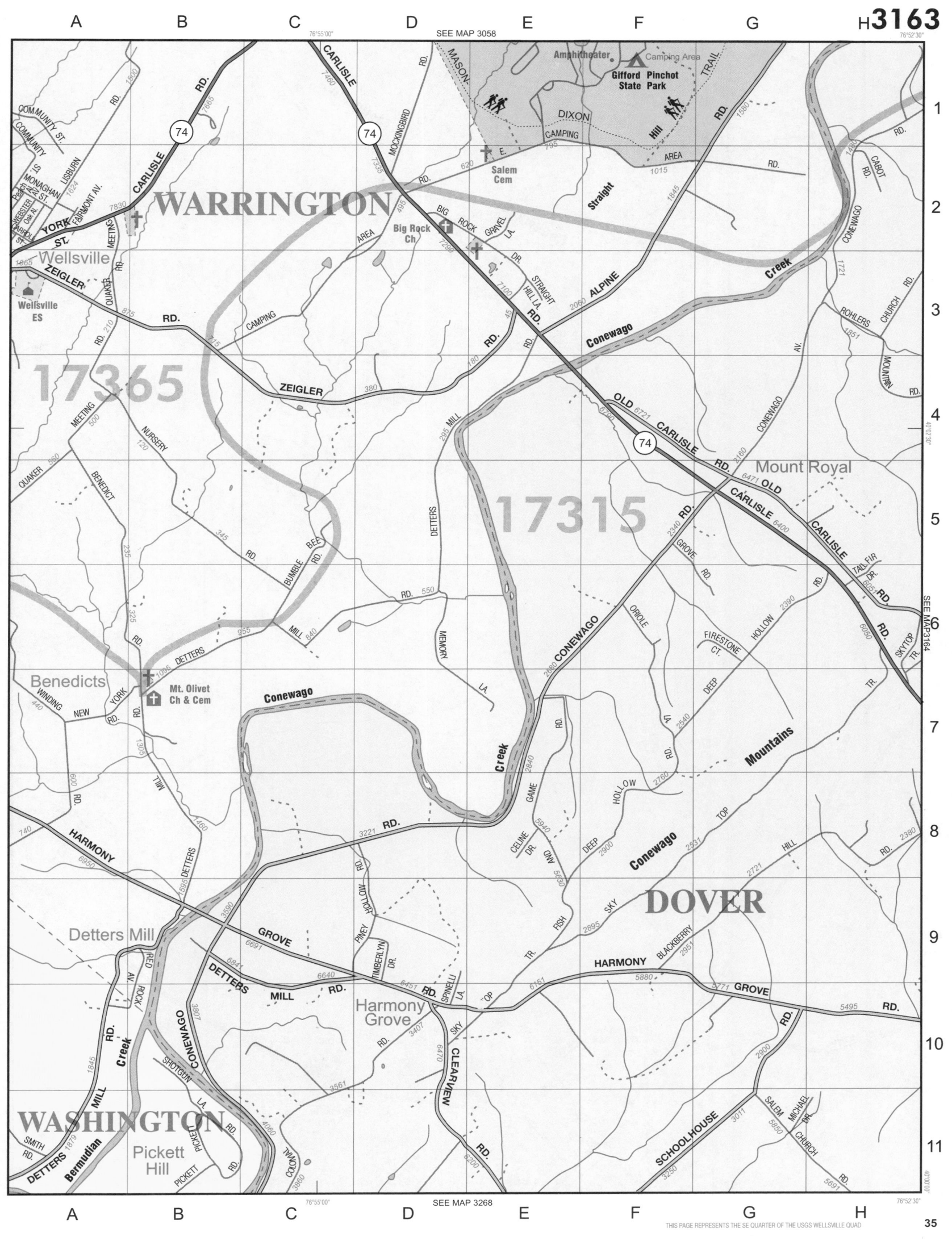

SEE MAP 3058

76°55'00"

76°52'30"

WARRINGTON

17365

WELLSVILLE
Wellsville ES

COMMUNITY RD.
COMMUNITY ST.
LISBURN ST.
MONAGHAN ST.
WEBSTER AV.
OAK AL.
FAIRMONT AV.
YORK ST.
MEETING RD.
CARLISLE RD.
7665
7830
1624
1065
1500

ZEIGLER RD.
QUAKER RD.
875
210
CARLISLE RD.
ZEIGLER
380
CAMPING AREA
715
180

74

MOCKINGBIRD RD.
7335
495
620
E. RD.
Salem Cem

Big Rock Ch
BIG ROCK
GRAVEL LA.
7290
7100
45

STRAIGHT HILL LA.
STRAIGHT HILL RD.
2060

ALPINE
Conewago
Creek

DIXON
CAMPING AREA
795
1015

Amphitheater
Gifford Pinchot State Park
Camping Area

Straight
Hill
1845

TRAIL RD.
1580

CONEWAGO
1721

CABOT RD.
1480

ROHLERS AV.
1851
CHURCH RD.
MOUNTAIN RD.

OLD CARLISLE RD.
6721
6790
6471

74

Mount Royal

17315

MEETING RD.
500
NURSERY RD.
120
QUAKER RD.
560
BENEDICT RD.
235
345
325

DETTERS RD.
MILL RD.
295
550
840
955
1096
DETTERS

BUMBLE BEE RD.

Benedicts
Mt. Olivet Ch & Cem
WINDING RD.
440
NEW RD.
YORK RD.
1305
MILL RD.
600
1460

MEMORY LA.

Conewago
Creek
2880
2840
GAME RD.

CONEWAGO RD.
2340
GROVE RD.
ORIOLE LA.
2390
DEEP LA.
2540
HOLLOW
2760
2531

FIRESTONE CT.
HOLLOW 2390

Mountains

OLD CARLISLE RD.
6400
TALL FIR DR.
905
6050
SKYTOP TR.

CELINE DR.
5940
DEEP AND 5630
2900
FISH TR.
6151
SKY TOP
2895

Conewago
2721
TOP
HILL
2380

DOVER

HARMONY RD.
6950
DETTERS RD.
1395
1460
13590

GROVE RD.
6691
6841
DETTERS MILL RD.
6640

PINEY HOLLOW RD.
TIMBERLYN DR.
6451
6470
SPINELLI LA.

Harmony Grove
3407
CLEARVIEW RD.
6200

HARMONY
5880
BLACKBERRY RD.
2951
GROVE RD.
6771
5495

SCHOOLHOUSE RD.
3011
SALEM RD.
MICHAEL DR.
5680
CHURCH RD.
2900
3250
5691

Detters Mill
RED ROCK AV.
Creek
SHOTGUN LA.
CONEWAGO RD.
1845
3807

WASHINGTON
Pickett Hill
SMITH RD.
DETTERS MILL RD.
1879
Bermudian
PICKETT RD.
TWIN COLONY RD.
3660
3561
4060

3221
RD.
3250

SEE MAP 3268

SEE MAP 3164

76°55'00"

76°52'30"

THIS PAGE REPRESENTS THE SE QUARTER OF THE USGS WELLSVILLE QUAD

35

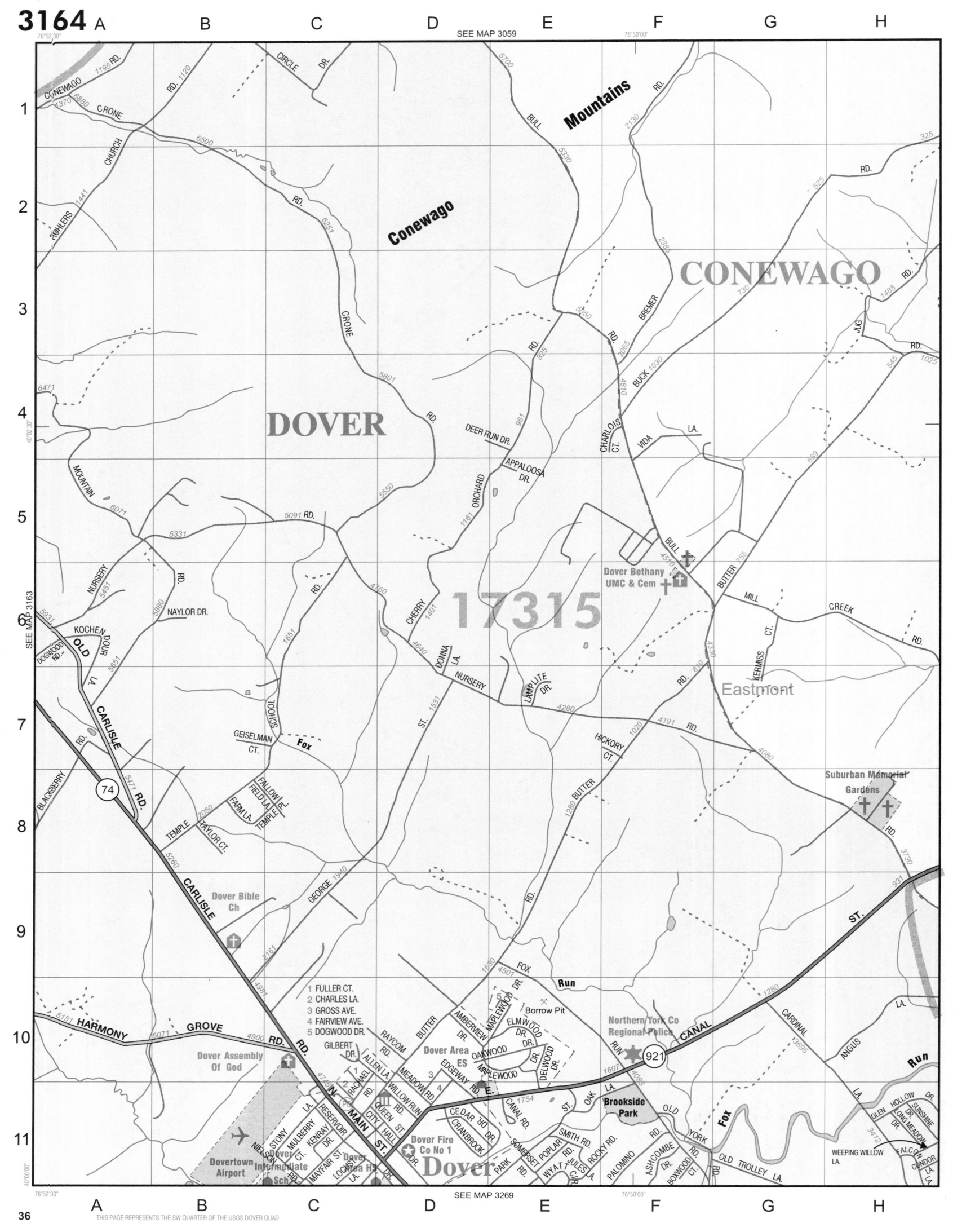

SEE MAP 3059

CONEWAGO

Mountains

Conewago

DOVER

17315

Eastmont

Dover Bethany
UMC & Cem

Suburban Memorial
Gardens

Dover Bible
Ch

1 FULLER CT.
2 CHARLES LA.
3 GROSS AVE.
4 FAIRVIEW AVE.
5 DOGWOOD DR.

Dover Assembly
Of God

HARMONY GROVE

Borrow Pit

Northern York Co
Regional Police

Dover Area
ES

Brookside
Park

Dover Fire
Co No 1

Dover

Dovertown
Airport

Dover Intermediate
Sch

SEE MAP 3269

THIS PAGE REPRESENTS THE SW QUARTER OF THE USGS DOVER QUAD

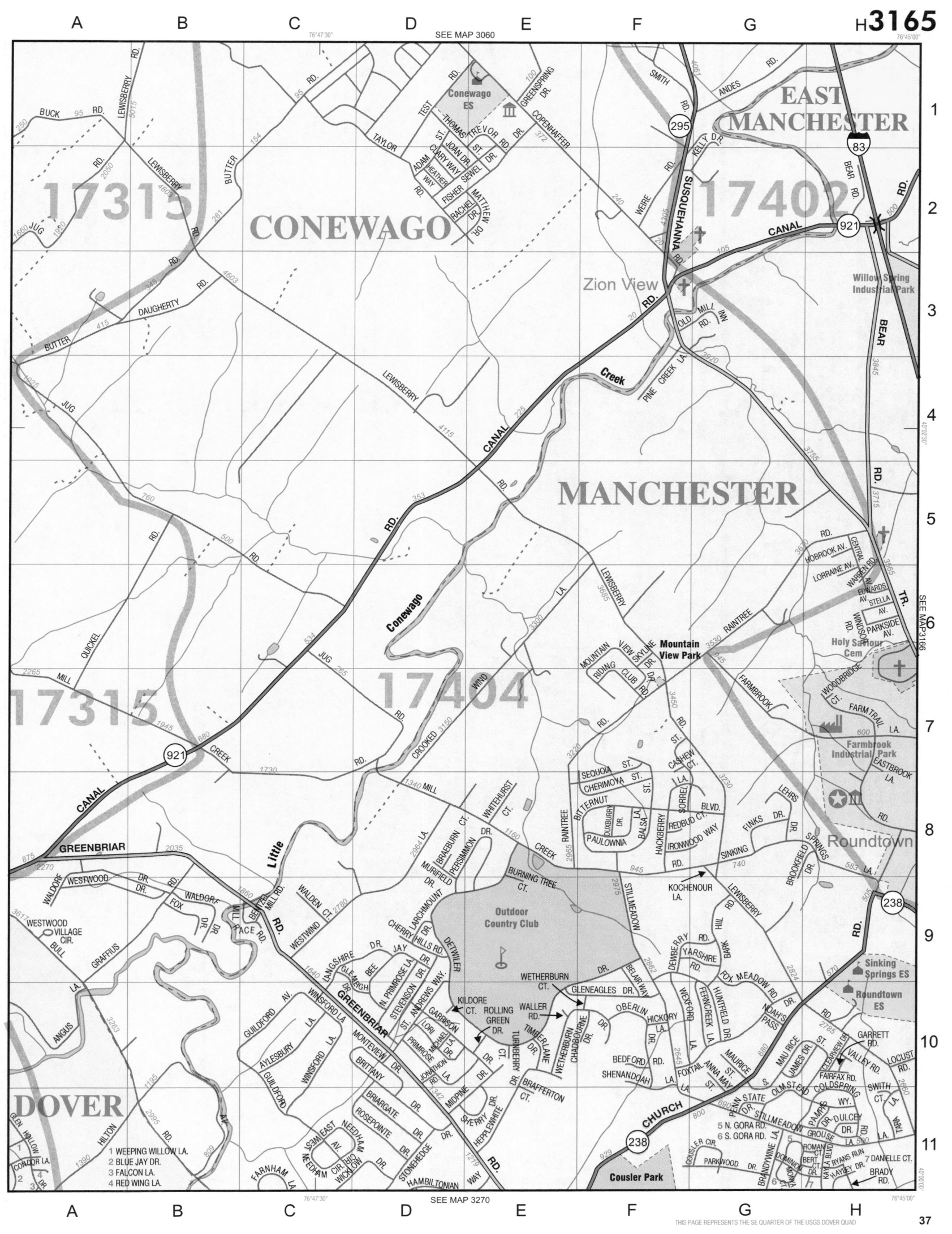

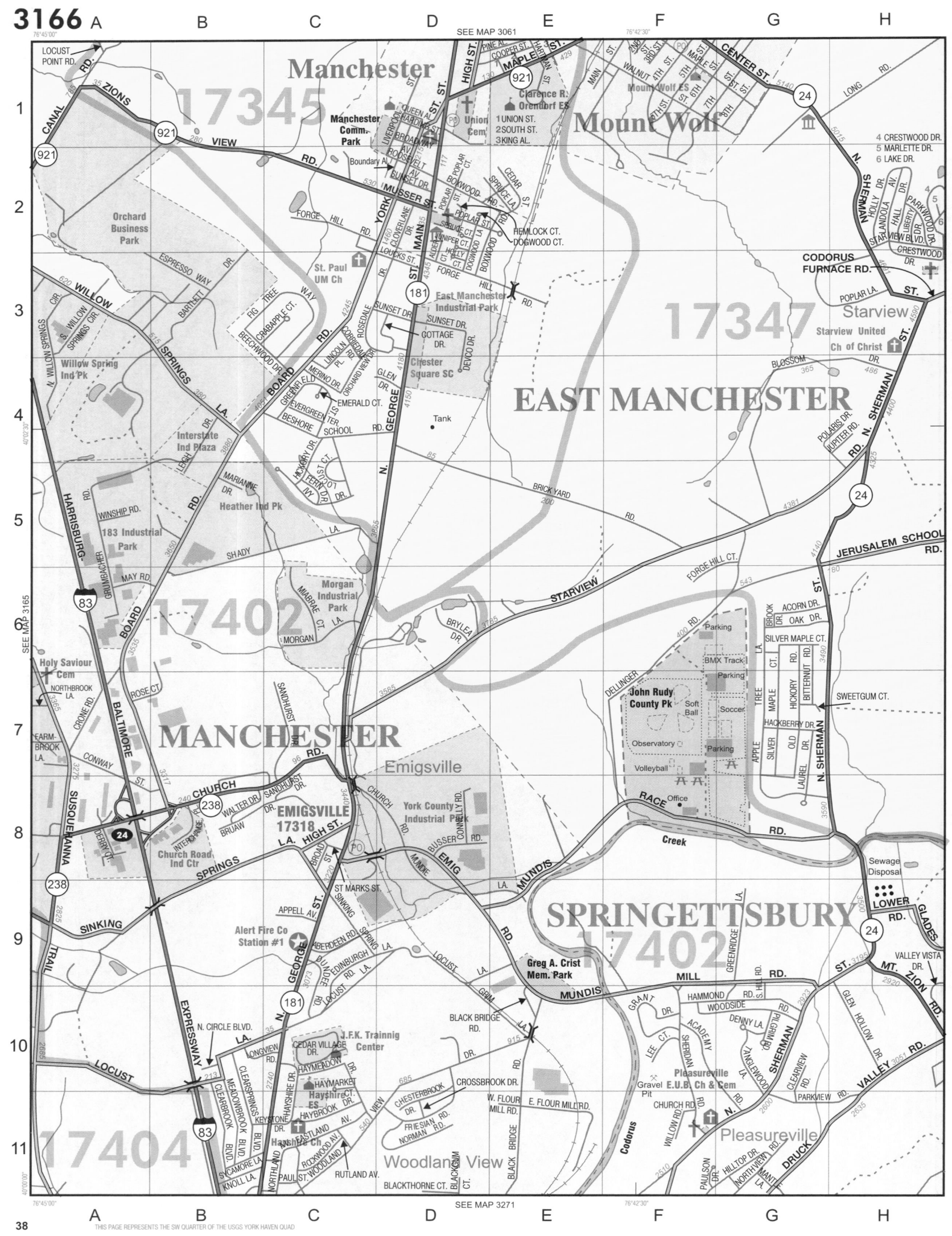

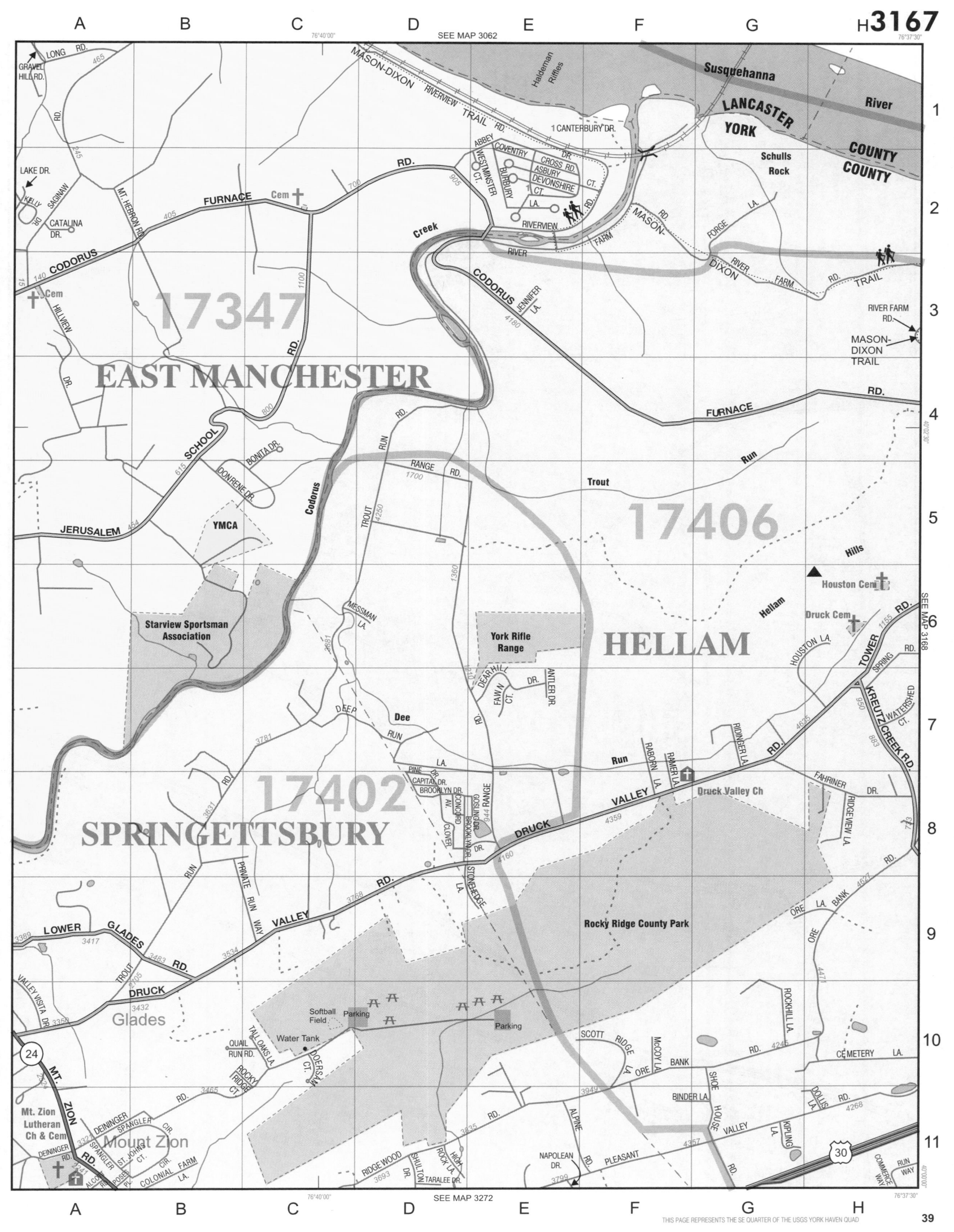

A B C 76°40'00" D SEE MAP 3062 E F G 76°37'30"

LONG RD.
GRAVEL HILL RD.
465
245
LAKE DR.
KELLY
SAGINAW
30
CATALINA DR.
Cem
FURNACE
405
CODORUS
15 140
Cem

Susquehanna
River
LANCASTER
YORK
Schulls Rock
COUNTY
COUNTY

1

Haldeman Riffles
1 CANTERBURY DR.
MASON-DIXON RIVERVIEW TRAIL RD.
COVENTRY
CROSS RD.
ABBEY
WESTMINSTER CT.
BURBURY
ASBURY
DEVONSHIRE CT.
LA.
RIVERVIEW
RIVER
MASON
FARM
FORGE
LA.
RD.

2

HILLVIEW DR.
MT. HEBRON RD.
700
RD.
905
Creek
RD.
1100

17347
CODORUS
JENNIFER LA.
4180
RIVER
DIXON
FARM RD. TRAIL

RIVER FARM RD.
MASON-DIXON TRAIL

3

EAST MANCHESTER
SCHOOL
615
BONITA DR.
DON RENE DR.
800
RD.
Codorus
RUN
RANGE
RD.
1700
TROUT
4250
FURNACE
Run
Trout
RD.

4

JERUSALEM
454
YMCA
3681
1360
MIESSMAN LA.
17406
Hills
Houston Cem
Druck Cem
Hellam
HOUSTON LA.
1155
TOWER RD.
SPRING RD.
SEE MAP 3168

5

Starview Sportsman Association
York Rifle Range
DEER HILL
FAWN CT.
ANTLER DR.
DR.
RD.
HELLAM
KREUTZ CREEK RD.
950
WATERSHED CT.
883

6

DEEP
3781
Dee
RUN
PINE DR.
CAPITAL DR.
BROOKLYN DR.
AV.
CONCORD RD.
GOSLING DR.
944 RANGE
Run
RABORN LA.
RAMER LA.
RIDINGER LA.
RD.
4625
FAHRINER DR.
RIDGEVIEW LA.
713

7

17402
RD.
3631
PRIVATE RUN WAY
CLOVER
BROOKLYN DR.
STONEHEDGE
LA.
DRUCK
VALLEY
4359
4160
Druck Valley Ch
Rocky Ridge County Park
ORE LA.
BANK
4627
RD.

8

SPRINGETTSBURY
RUN
VALLEY
3768
RD.
LOWER
GLADES
3389
3417
3483
3534
TROUT
3205
VALLEY VISTA DR.

9

DRUCK
3432
335N
Glades
QUAIL RUN RD.
TALL OAKS LA.
Water Tank
Softball Field
Parking
Parking
SCOTT
RIDGE LA.
McCOY LA.
ORE
RD.
4246
ROCKHILL LA.
CEMETERY LA.

10

24
MT. ZION RD.
2321
Mt. Zion Lutheran Ch & Cem
DEININGER
3324
SPANGLER
SPANGLER CIR.
ST. JOHN CT.
ROSE PL.
2341
ALCO
COLONIAL FARM LA.
RIDGEWOOD DR.
3693
ROCKY RIDGE CT.
3465
SHULTON
TARALEE DR.
ROCK LA.
HIGH
3635
NAPOLEAN DR.
3799
ALPINE RD.
PLEASANT
3949
4357
BINDER LA.
SHOE HOUSE RD.
VALLEY RD.
DOLLS RD.
KIPLING LA.
4268
30
COMMERCE WAY
RUN WAY

11

Mount Zion

A B C 76°40'00" D SEE MAP 3272 E F G H 76°37'30"
40°00'00"

THIS PAGE REPRESENTS THE SE QUARTER OF THE USGS YORK HAVEN QUAD

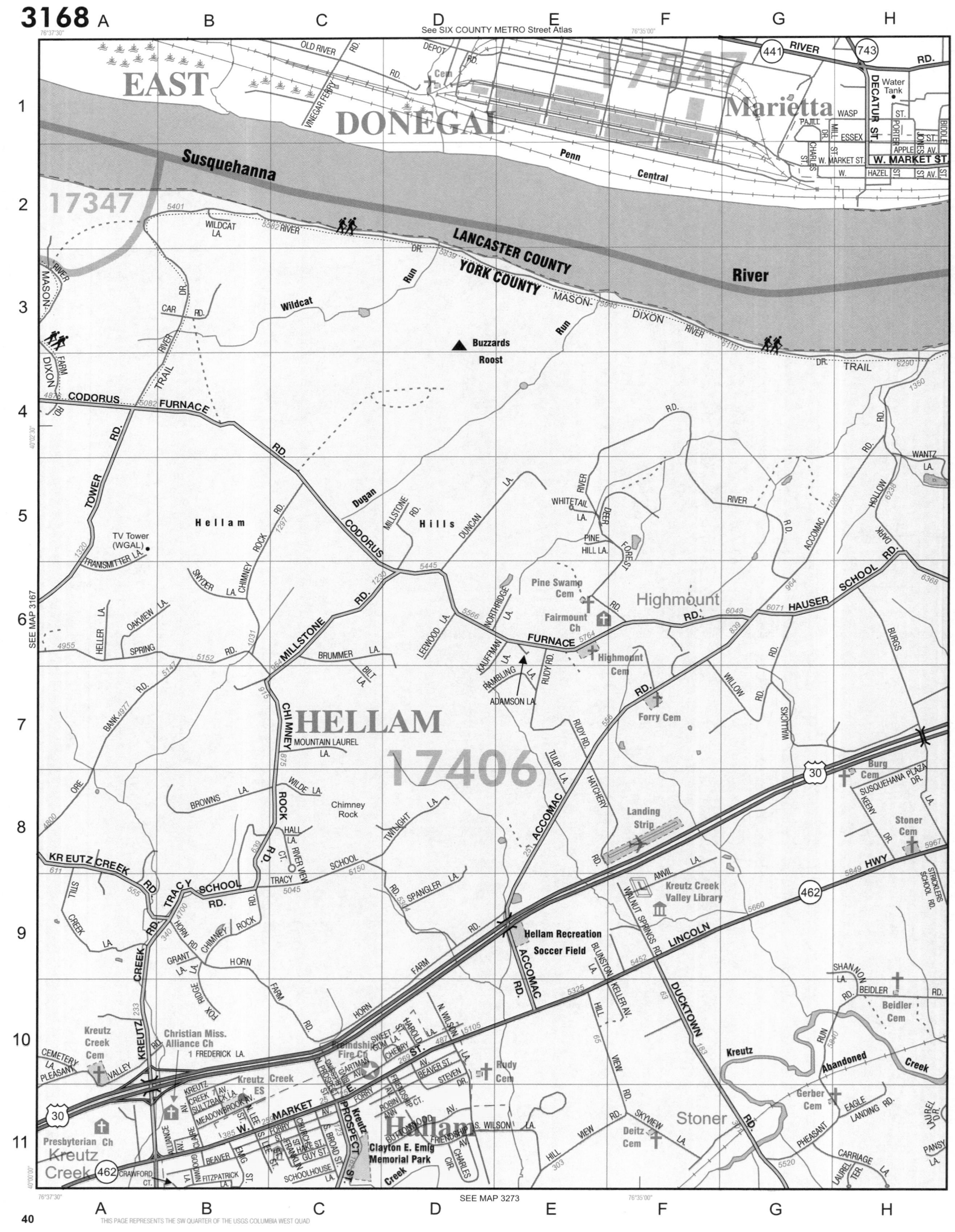

A B C D E F G H

EAST
DONEGAL

17347

Susquehanna

17347

WILDCAT LA.
VINEGAR FERRY RD.
OLD RIVER RD.
DEPOT
Cem
Marietta

Penn

LANCASTER COUNTY
YORK COUNTY
Central
River

MASON
RIVER DR.

WILDCAT RIVER
Run
Wildcat

CAR DR. RD.

▲ Buzzards
Roost

MASON DIXON RIVER

RIVER DR. TRAIL

FARM
DIXON

CODORUS
FURNACE
RD.

Hellam
TV Tower
(WGAL)
TRANSMITTER LA.

Dugan
CODORUS

Hills
Duncan

MILLSTONE RD.

WHITETAIL
LA.
DEER
PINE
HILL LA.

FOREST

RIVER

RD.

WANTZ
LA.

DARK HOLLOW RD.

TOWER RD.

SNYDER LA.
CHIMNEY ROCK LA.
OAKVIEW LA.
HELLER LA.
SPRING RD.
BANK RD.

MILLSTONE RD.
BRUMMER LA.
BILT LA.

Pine Swamp
Cem
Fairmount Ch
NORTHRIDGE LA.
LEEWOOD LA.
FURNACE
KAUFMAN LA.
RAMBLING LA.
ADAMSON LA.
RUDY RD.

Highmount
Highmount
Cem

HAUSER SCHOOL RD.

ACCOMAC RD.

WILLOW RD.

BURGS RD.

HELLAM

17406

CHIMNEY ROCK LA.
MOUNTAIN LAUREL LA.

Chimney
Rock

WILDE LA.
ROCK RD.
HALL LA.
RIVER VIEW
TWILIGHT LA.
SCHOOL

Forry Cem

RUDY RD.
TULIP LA.
HATCHERY RD.

Landing
Strip

30

Burg
Cem
SUSQUEHANNA PLAZA DR.
KEENY LA.
Stoner
Cem

ORE RD.

KREUTZ CREEK
TRACY SCHOOL RD.
BROWNS LA.

TRACY
SCHOOL RD.
GRANT LA.
HORN RD.
CHIMNEY ROCK LA.
HORN

FARM RD.

SPANGLER LA.

ACCOMAC RD.

Hellam Recreation
Soccer Field

ANVIL
WALNUT SPRINGS RD.
Kreutz Creek
Valley Library

LINCOLN

BLUNSTON LA.
KELLER AV.
HILL

DUCKTOWN RD.

462 HWY

STRICKLERS SCHOOL RD.

SHANNON
RD.
BEIDLER RD.
Beidler
Cem

STILL CREEK LA.
CREEK RD.
FOX RIDGE LA.

HORN
FARM RD.

Kreutz
Run

Kreutz

Abandoned Creek

Kreutz
Creek Cem
CEMETERY LA.
PLEASANT VALLEY

Christian Miss.
Alliance Ch
1 FREDERICK LA.

Kreutz Creek
KREUTZ RD.
SULTZBACK LA.
MEADOWBROOK LA.
ES

Friendship
Fire Co
GARTMAN AV.
N. WILSON ST.
SWEET GUM LA.
HAROLD ST.
CHERRY ST.
BEAVER ST.
STEVEN DR.
ANN
Rudy
Cem

VIEW RD.
SKYVIEW RD.
Deitz
Cem

Gerber
Cem

EAGLE LANDING RD.
PHEASANT LA.

30

Presbyterian Ch

Kreutz
Creek
462
CRAWFORD CT.

KREUTZ CREEK AV.
ALLIANCE AV.
W. MARKET
LEE
FRANKLIN
EMIG
BEAVER
GOODWIN
FITZPATRICK LA.
W. MARKET ST.
SCHOOLHOUSE LA.
CHURCH ST.
GUY ST.
BROAD ST.
PROSPECT ST.
KREUTZ
Hellam
Clayton E. Emig
Memorial Park
Creek
BUTTONWOOD AV.
FRIENDSHIP
S. WILSON LA.
CHARLES
ROBIN LA.
CT.

Stoner

HILL RD.

CARRIAGE TER.
LAUREL DR.
PANSY LA.

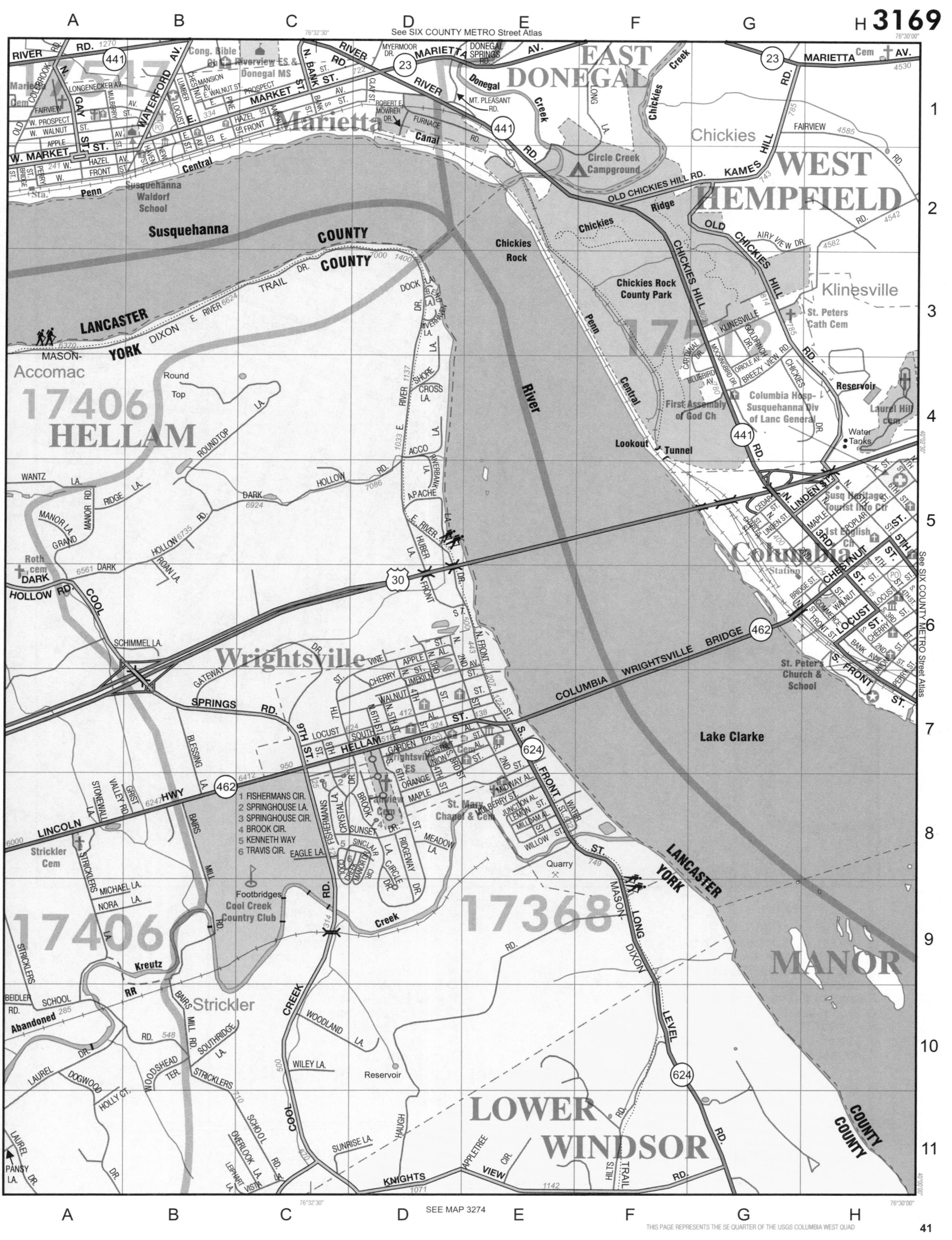

City of York

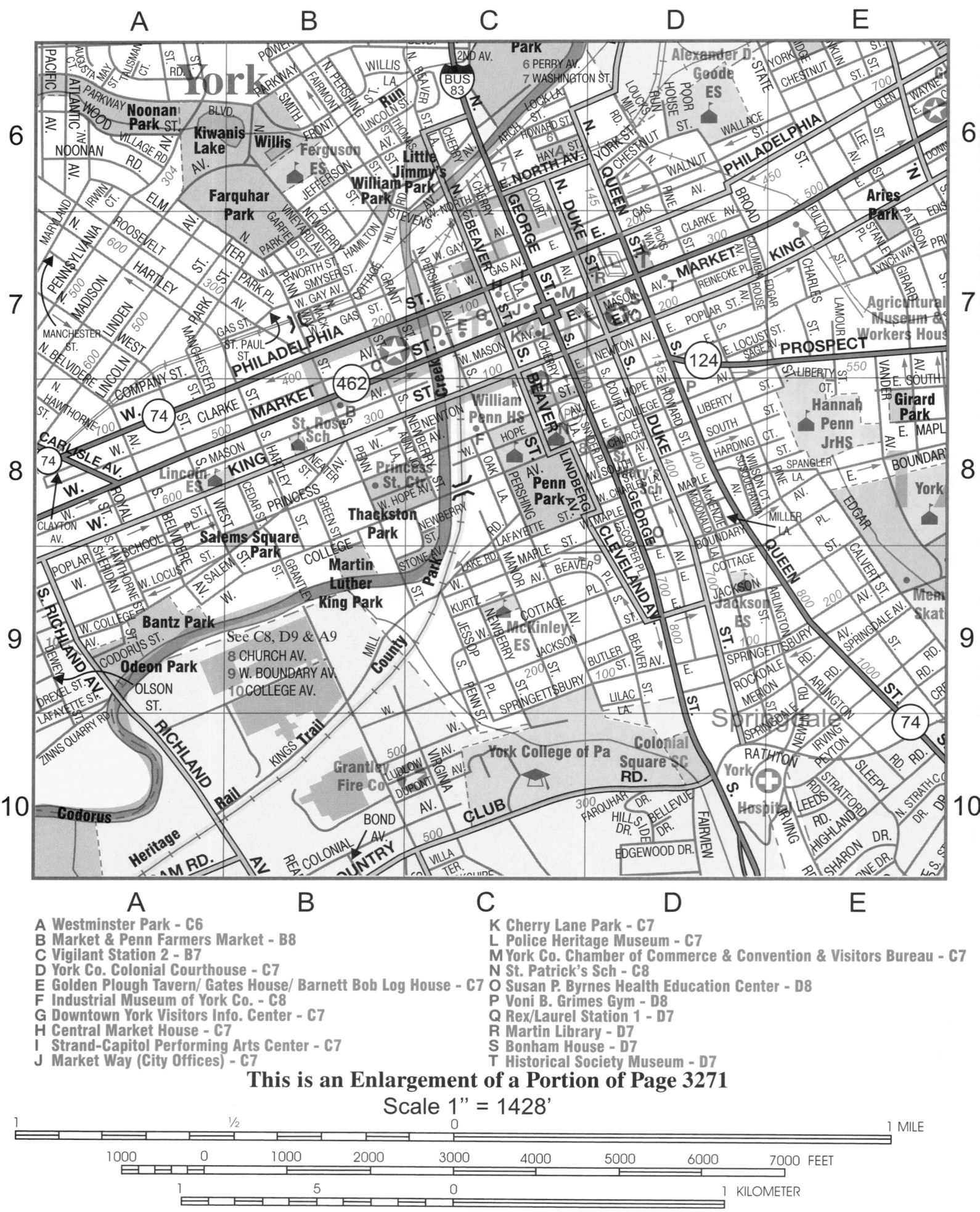

A **Westminster Park - C6**
B **Market & Penn Farmers Market - B8**
C **Vigilant Station 2 - B7**
D **York Co. Colonial Courthouse - C7**
E **Golden Plough Tavern/ Gates House/ Barnett Bob Log House - C7**
F **Industrial Museum of York Co. - C8**
G **Downtown York Visitors Info. Center - C7**
H **Central Market House - C7**
I **Strand-Capitol Performing Arts Center - C7**
J **Market Way (City Offices) - C7**

K **Cherry Lane Park - C7**
L **Police Heritage Museum - C7**
M **York Co. Chamber of Commerce & Convention & Visitors Bureau - C7**
N **St. Patrick's Sch - C8**
O **Susan P. Byrnes Health Education Center - D8**
P **Voni B. Grimes Gym - D8**
Q **Rex/Laurel Station 1 - D7**
R **Martin Library - D7**
S **Bonham House - D7**
T **Historical Society Museum - D7**

This is an Enlargement of a Portion of Page 3271
Scale 1" = 1428'

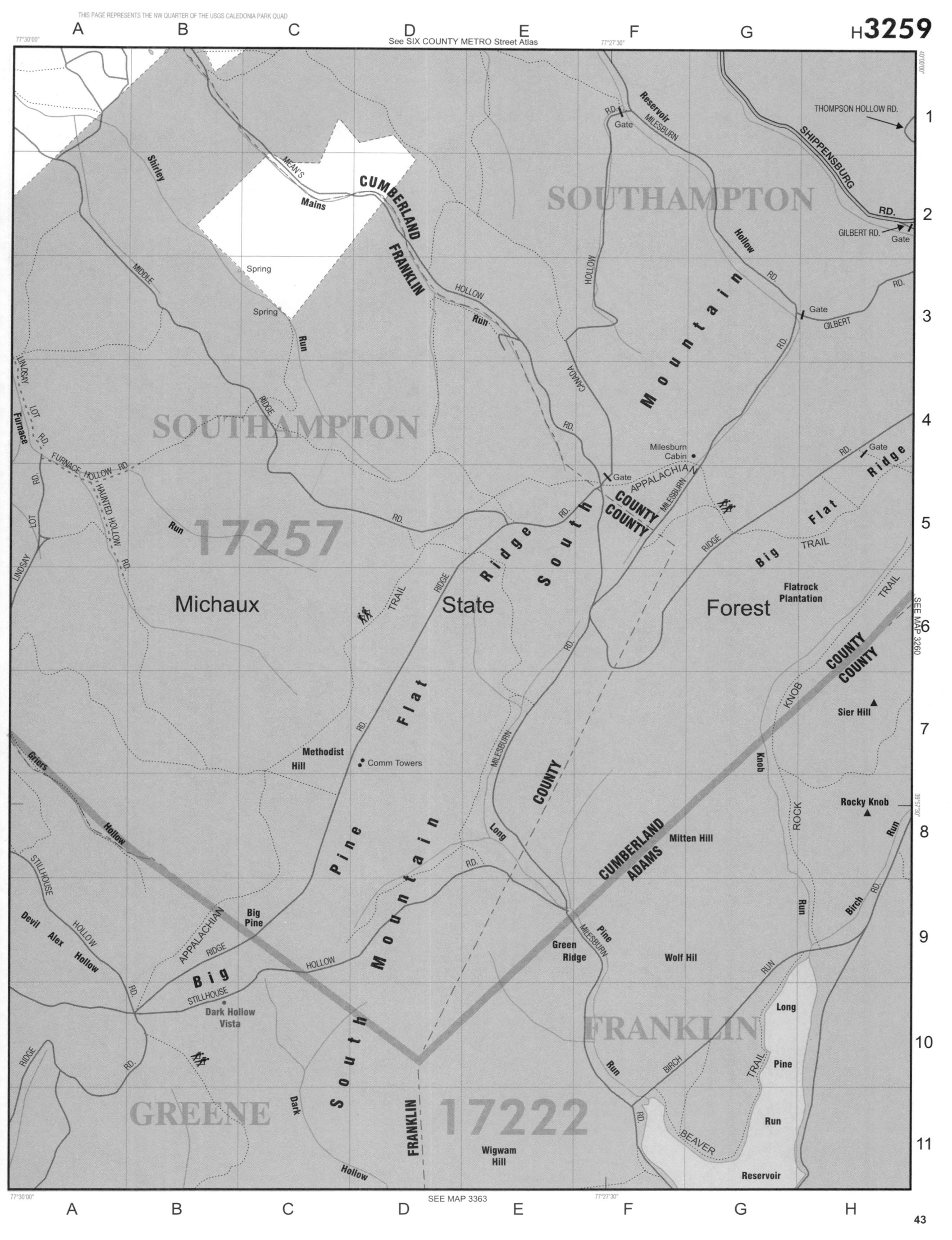

See SIX COUNTY METRO Street Atlas

H3259

77°30'00"

40°00'00"

A   B   C   D   E   F   G   H

1

THOMPSON HOLLOW RD.

Reservoir
RD.
Gate
MILESBURN

SHIPPENSBURG

SOUTHAMPTON

RD.

2

77°27'30"

GILBERT RD.   Gate

Shirley

MEAN'S

Mains

CUMBERLAND

FRANKLIN

HOLLOW

Hollow

RD.

Gate

GILBERT

3

MIDDLE

Spring

Run

HOLLOW

RD.

Mountain

Spring

CANADA

RD.

LINDSAY

LOT   RD.

Furnace

RIDGE

SOUTHAMPTON

RD.

4

RD.

Gate

Ridge

FURNACE HOLLOW   RD.

HAUNTED HOLLOW   RD.

Run

RD.

Milesburn
Cabin

APPALACHIAN

Gate

COUNTY
COUNTY

MILESBURN

RD.   Gate

Flat   Ridge

Big   Flat

TRAIL

5

17257

LOT

LINDSAY

TRAIL

RIDGE

State

Ridge

South

RD.

RIDGE

Flatrock
Plantation

Michaux

Forest

TRAIL

SEE MAP 3260

6

COUNTY
COUNTY

KNOB

Sier Hill

7

Pine   Flat

Methodist
Hill

Comm Towers

RD.

MILESBURN

COUNTY

Knob

ROCK

Rocky Knob

39°57'30"

8

Griers

Hollow

Long

RD.

CUMBERLAND
ADAMS

Mitten Hill

RD.

Run

Birch

Run

STILLHOUSE

Mountain

APPALACHIAN   RIDGE

Big
Pine

HOLLOW

South

MILESBURN

Pine

Green
Ridge

Wolf Hil

RUN

9

Devil   Alex
Hollow

HOLLOW

Hollow

Big

STILLHOUSE

Dark Hollow
Vista

Long

Pine

10

RIDGE

RD.

South

Dark

FRANKLIN

FRANKLIN

Run

BIRCH

TRAIL

Run

Mountain

17222

Run

BEAVER

11

77°30'00"

GREENE

Hollow

Wigwam
Hill

77°27'30"

Reservoir

A   B   C   D   E   F   G   H

SEE MAP 3363

43

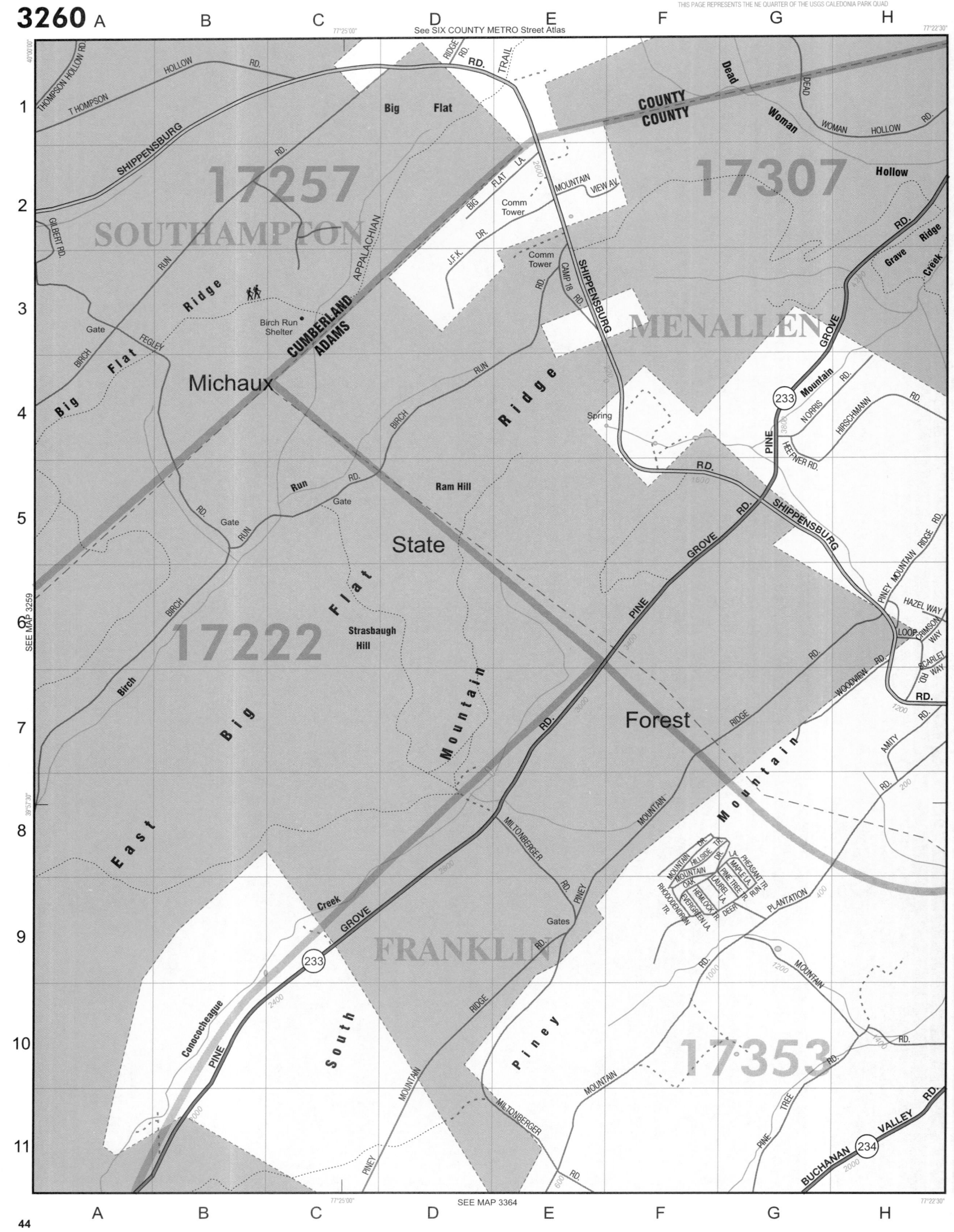

THIS PAGE REPRESENTS THE NE QUARTER OF THE USGS CALEDONIA PARK QUAD

See SIX COUNTY METRO Street Atlas

A B C D E F G H

1

THOMPSON HOLLOW RD.
T HOMPSON HOLLOW RD.
SHIPPENSBURG
RIDGE RD.
RD.
TRAIL
COUNTY COUNTY
Dead Woman
DEAD WOMAN HOLLOW RD.

Big Flat

17257

17307

Hollow

2

GILBERT RD.
RUN
Ridge
APPALACHIAN
BIG FLAT DR.
J.F.K.
MOUNTAIN VIEW AV.
Comm Tower
CAMP 18 RD.
SHIPPENSBURG

SOUTHAMPTON

RD.

3

Gate
Birch
Big Flat
FEGLEY
Birch Run Shelter
CUMBERLAND ADAMS
Michaux
RUN
Comm Tower
Ridge

MENALLEN

Grave Ridge Creek
GROVE
RD.

4

Big Flat
RUN
BIRCH
Ridge
Spring
RD.
233 Mountain RD.
NORRIS
HIRSCHMANN RD.
PINE
HEFNER RD.

5

RD.
Run RD.
Gate
Gate
Ram Hill
State
GROVE RD.
SHIPPENSBURG
PINEY MOUNTAIN RIDGE RD.
HAZEL WAY

6

SEE MAP 3259
BIRCH
17222
Flat
Strasbaugh Hill
PINE
RD.
LOOP
CRIMSON WAY
SCARLET WAY

7

Birch
Big
Mountain
Forest
RD.
RIDGE
RD.
WOODVIEW RD.
Mountain
AMITY
RD.

8

East
Mountain
MILTONBERGER RD.
PINEY RD.
Mountain
MOUNTAIN DR.
HILLSIDE TR.
LA.
PHEASANT TR.
MAPLE LA.
PINE TREE
OAK
RHODODENDRON
HEMLOCK TR.
LAUREL LA.
EVERGREEN LA.
DEER
PLANTATION
RD.

9

Creek
GROVE
233
Gates
FRANKLIN
RD.

17353

10

Conococheague
PINE
South
Mountain
PINEY
RIDGE
Piney
MOUNTAIN
PINE TREE
RD.

11

PINEY
MOUNTAIN
RD.
MILTONBERGER
VALLEY RD.
BUCHANAN
234

SEE MAP 3364

A B C D E F G H

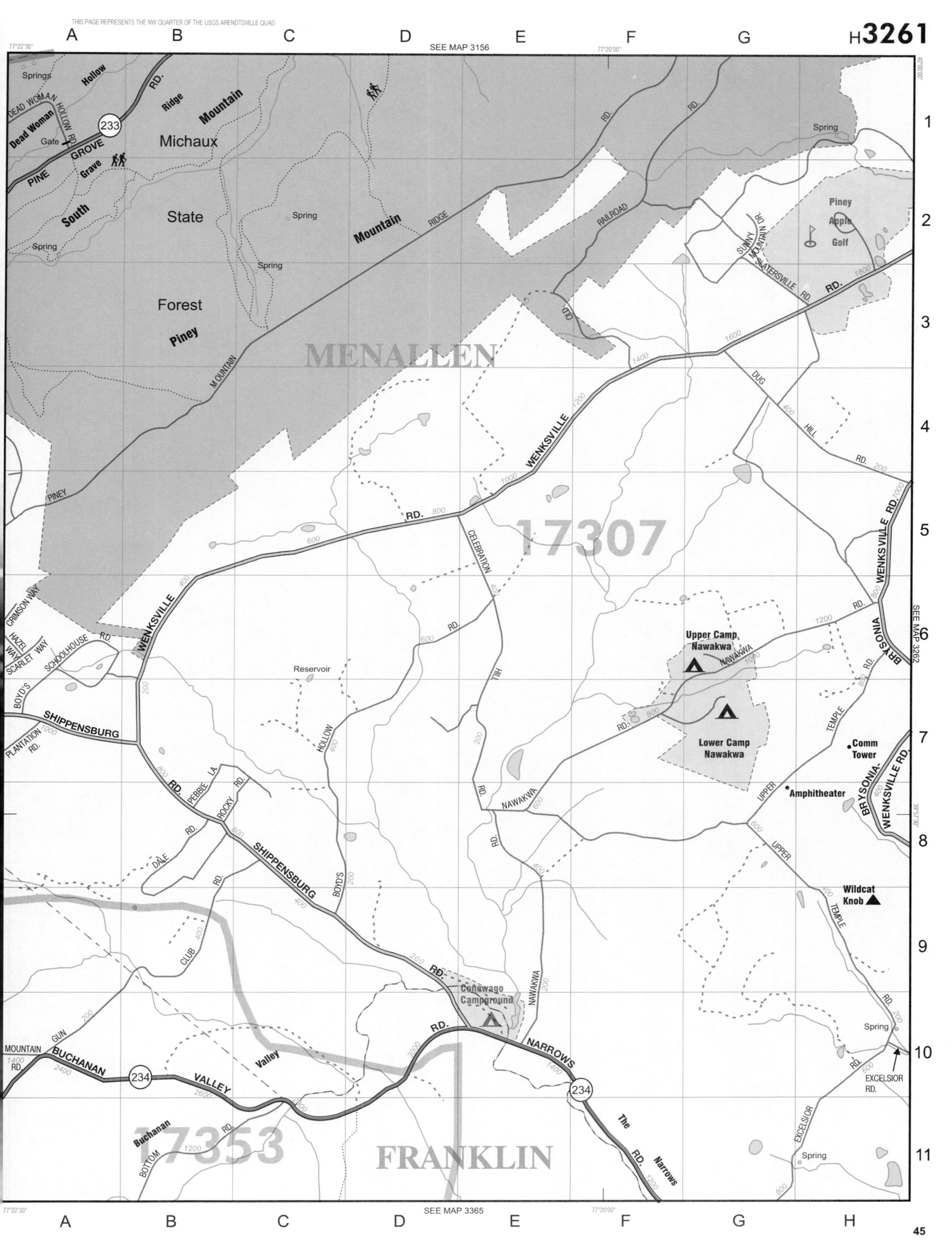

A B C D E F G H

1
2
3
4
5
6
7
8
9
10
11

77°22'30"
77°20'00"
40°00'00"
39°55'30"

SEE MAP 3156
SEE MAP 3262

Springs
Dead Woman Hollow
Ridge Mountain
Michaux
PINE GROVE RD.
Gate
Grave
South
State
Forest
Piney
Spring
Spring
Spring
Spring
PINEY
Mountain RIDGE
MOUNTAIN
RAILROAD
SUNNY MOUNTAIN DR.
SLAYERSVILLE RD.
Spring
Piney Apple Golf
1800
1600
1400
1200
1000
800
DUG HILL RD.
400

MENALLEN
17307

WENKSVILLE
RD. 800
600
400
200
CELEBRATION
1000

CRIMSON WAY
HAZEL WAY
SCARLET WAY
SCHOOLHOUSE RD.
WENKSVILLE
BOYD'S
SHIPPENSBURG
Reservoir
HOLLOW
HILL
RD.
NAWAKWA
RD.
Upper Camp Nawakwa
Lower Camp Nawakwa
WENKSVILLE RD.
BRYSONIA-
TEMPLE
Comm Tower
Amphitheater
UPPER
1200
800
600

PLANTATION RD.
1000
PEBBLE LA.
ROCKY RD.
DALE RD.
CLUB
BOYD'S
200
400
600
SHIPPENSBURG
NAWAKWA
RD.
UPPER
Wildcat Knob
TEMPLE

MOUNTAIN RD.
GUN RD.
BUCHANAN
234
VALLEY
BOTTOM RD.
Valley
200
400
600
1200
1400
2000
2400
2600
Conewago Campground
RD.
NARROWS
234
The Narrows RD.
1400
1200
Spring
EXCELSIOR RD.
600
800
Spring

17353
FRANKLIN

45

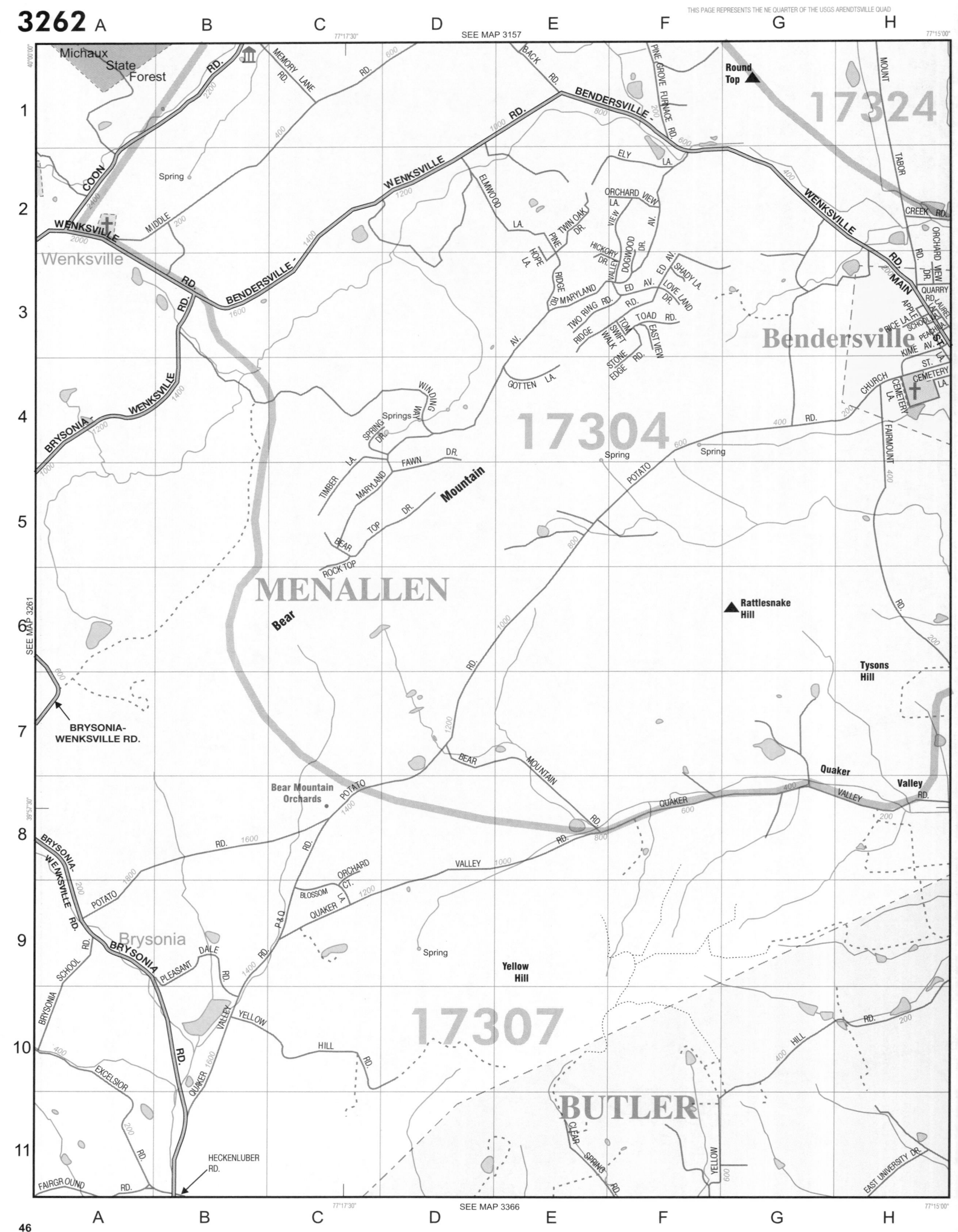

THIS PAGE REPRESENTS THE NE QUARTER OF THE USGS ARENDTSVILLE QUAD

A   B   C   D   E   F   G   H

77°17'30"   SEE MAP 3157   77°15'00"

40°00'00"

Michaux State Forest

MEMORY LANE
RD.
COON RD.

1

BENDERSVILLE RD.
Round Top
17324

Spring

WENKSVILLE RD.
WENKSVILLE
2

WENKSVILLE
MIDDLE
Wenksville
BENDERSVILLE RD.
ELMWOOD LA.
ELY LA.
ORCHARD VIEW
VIEW LA.
MAIN ST.
CREEK RD.
ORCHARD VIEW

3

BRYSONIA-WENKSVILLE RD.
WENKSVILLE
HOPE LA.
PINE RIDGE RD.
MARYLAND AV.
TWIN OAK DR.
HICKORY DR.
VALLEY DR.
DOGWOOD
ED AV.
SHADY LA.
LOVE LAND DR.
TWO RING RD.
ZION SWIFT WALK
TOAD RD.
EAST VIEW
STONE EDGE RD.
Bendersville
APPLE LA.
RICE LA.
KIME LA.
PEACH AV.
SCHOOL
QUARRY RD.
LAUREL
CEMETERY

4

WINDING WAY
SPRING DR.
Springs
FAWN DR.
Mountain
GOTTEN LA.
17304
Spring
Spring
CHURCH RD.
FAIRMOUNT
CEMETERY LA.

TIMBER LA.
MARYLAND
TOP DR.
BEAR
POTATO

5

ROCK TOP
MENALLEN

Bear

6
SEE MAP 3261

Rattlesnake Hill
17304

RD.
1000
800

Tysons Hill

7
BRYSONIA-WENKSVILLE RD.

RD.
1200

Quaker
Valley
VALLEY RD.

39°57'30"

BRYSONIA-WENKSVILLE
POTATO
Bear Mountain Orchards
POTATO
BEAR MOUNTAIN
QUAKER RD.

8
RD.
RD.
RD.
ORCHARD
BLOSSOM LA.
CT.
QUAKER
VALLEY

P&Q

9
BRYSONIA
SCHOOL RD.
BRYSONIA
PLEASANT
DALE
VALLEY
YELLOW
Spring
Yellow Hill

17307

10
EXCELSIOR
QUAKER RD.
YELLOW HILL RD.
YELLOW HILL RD.

BUTLER

11
FAIRGROUND RD.
HECKENLUBER RD.
CLEAR SPRING RD.
YELLOW
EAST UNIVERSITY DR.

A   B   C   D   E   F   G   H

77°17'30"   SEE MAP 3366   77°15'00"

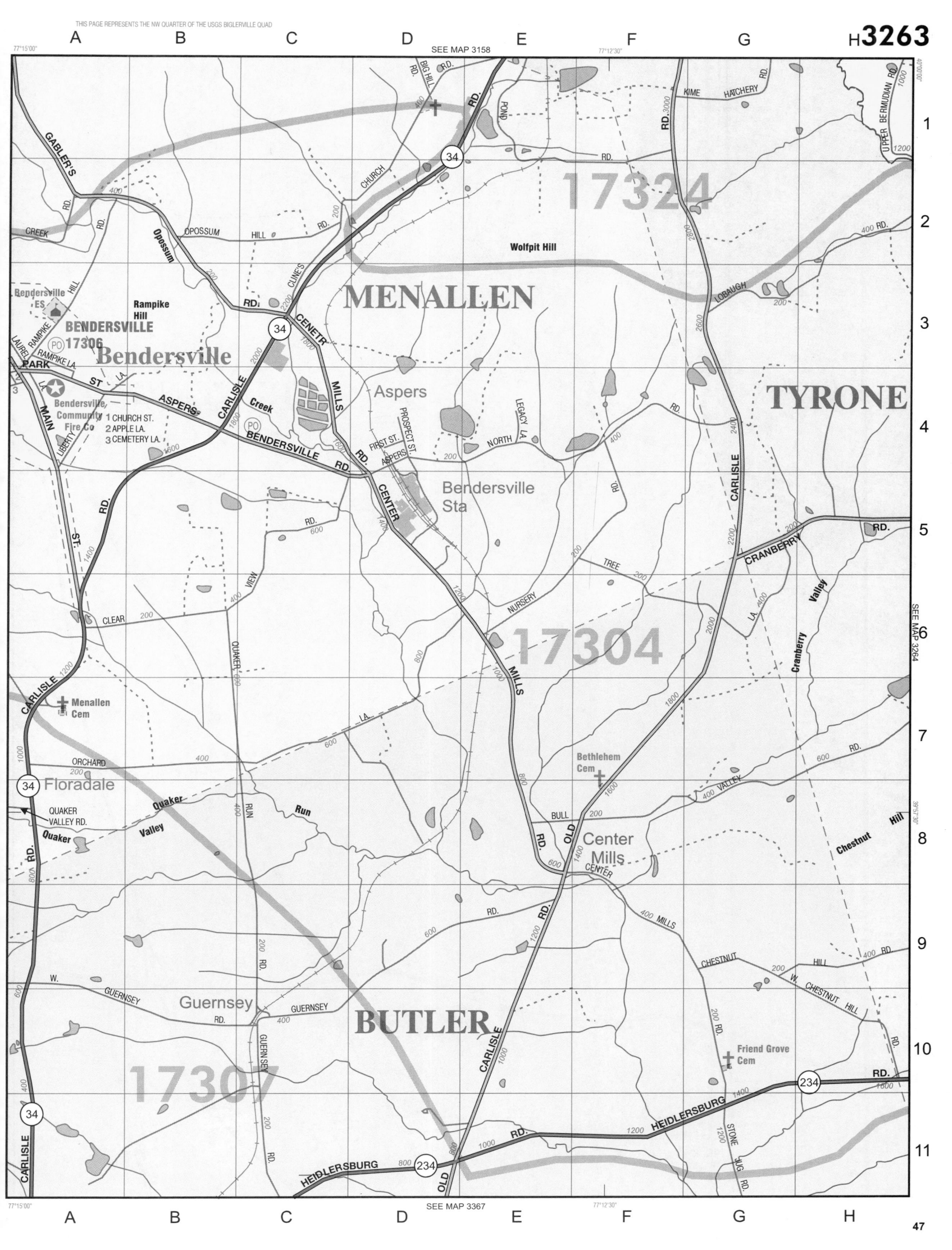

SEE MAP 3158

77°15'00"

77°12'30"

40°00'00"

1

2

3

4

5

SEE MAP 3264

6

7

8

9

10

11

MENALLEN

TYRONE

BUTLER

17324

17304

17307

Bendersville

1 CHURCH ST.
2 APPLE LA.
3 CEMETERY LA.

BENDERSVILLE
17306

Bendersville
ES

Rampike
Hill

Bendersville
Community
Fire Co

Floradale

Aspers

Bendersville
Sta

Wolfpit Hill

Menallen
Cem

Bethlehem
Cem

Center
Mills

Guernsey

Chestnut Hill

Friend Grove
Cem

34

34

34

34

234

234

A B C D E F G H

SEE MAP 3367

77°15'00"

77°12'30"

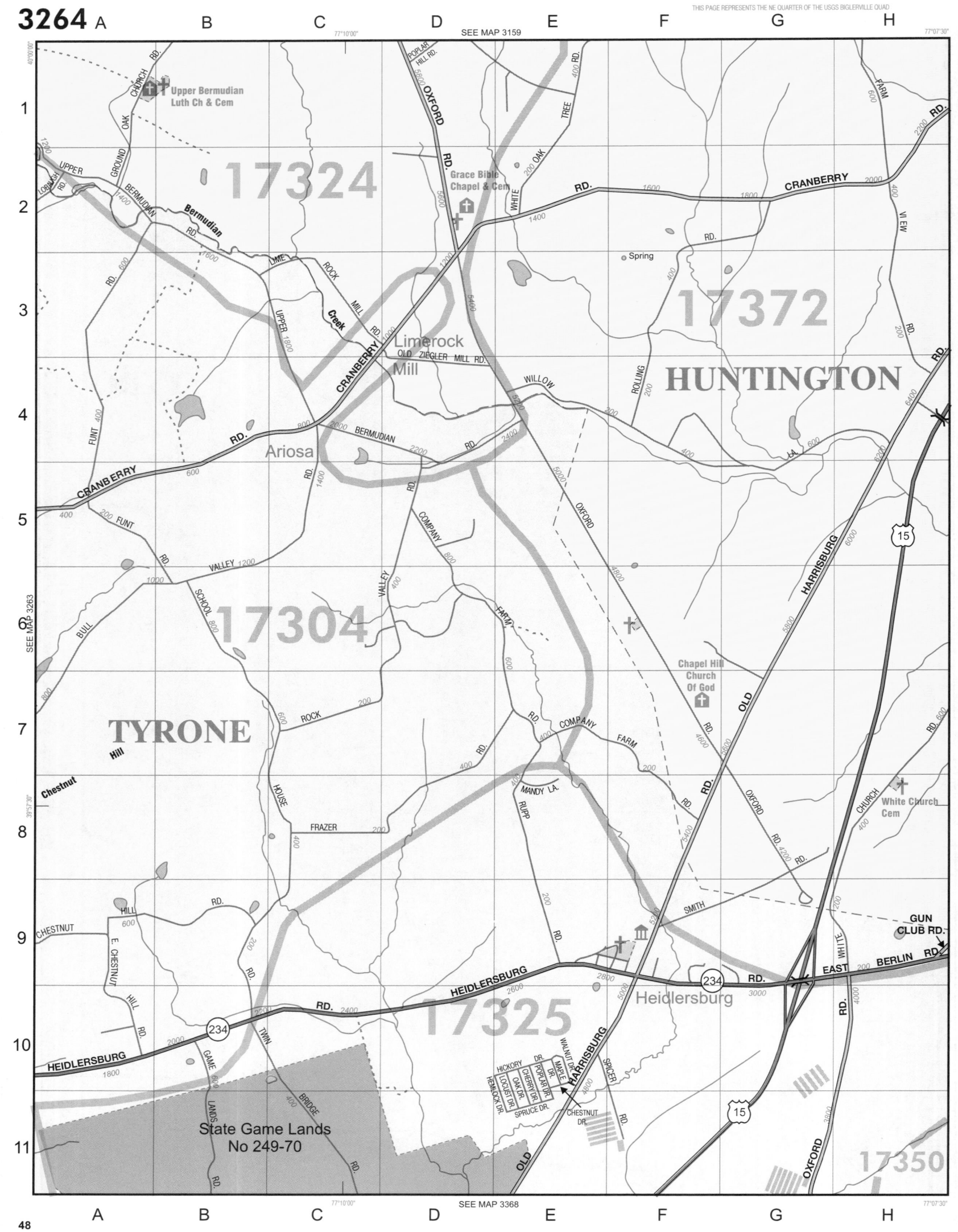

17324

17372

HUNTINGTON

17304

TYRONE

Upper Bermudian
Luth Ch & Cem

Bermudian

Grace Bible
Chapel & Cem

Limerock
Mill

OLD ZIEGLER MILL RD.

Ariosa

Spring

Chapel Hill
Church
Of God

White Church
Cem

Hill

Chestnut

MANDY LA.

RUPP

FRAZER

Heidlersburg

SMITH

GUN
CLUB RD.

EAST BERLIN RD.

17325

State Game Lands
No 249-70

HICKORY
WALNUT DR.
MAPLE DR.
POPLAR DR.
CHERRY DR.
OAK DR.
LOCUST DR.
HEMLOCK DR.
SPRUCE DR.
CHESTNUT DR.

17350

Heidlersburg

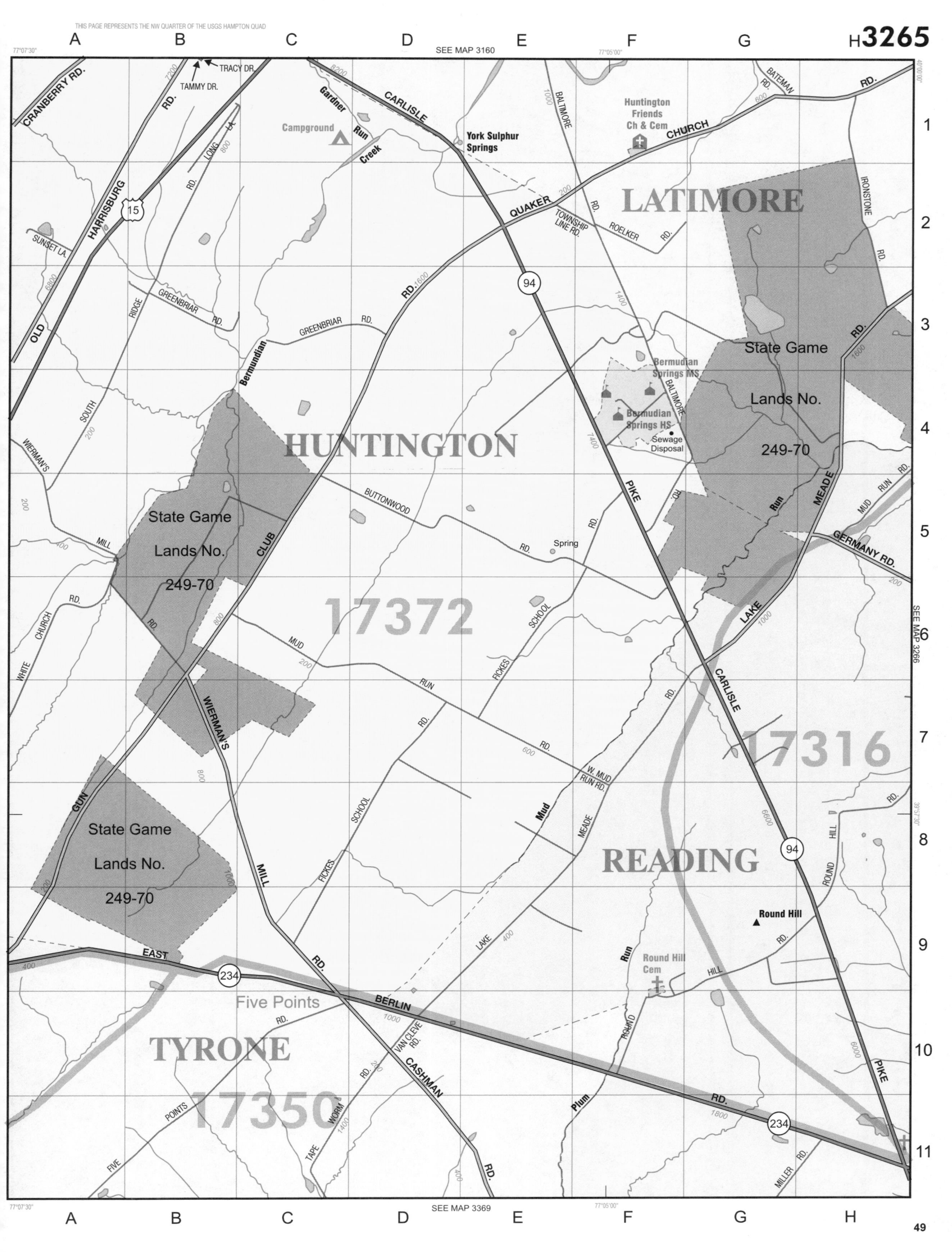

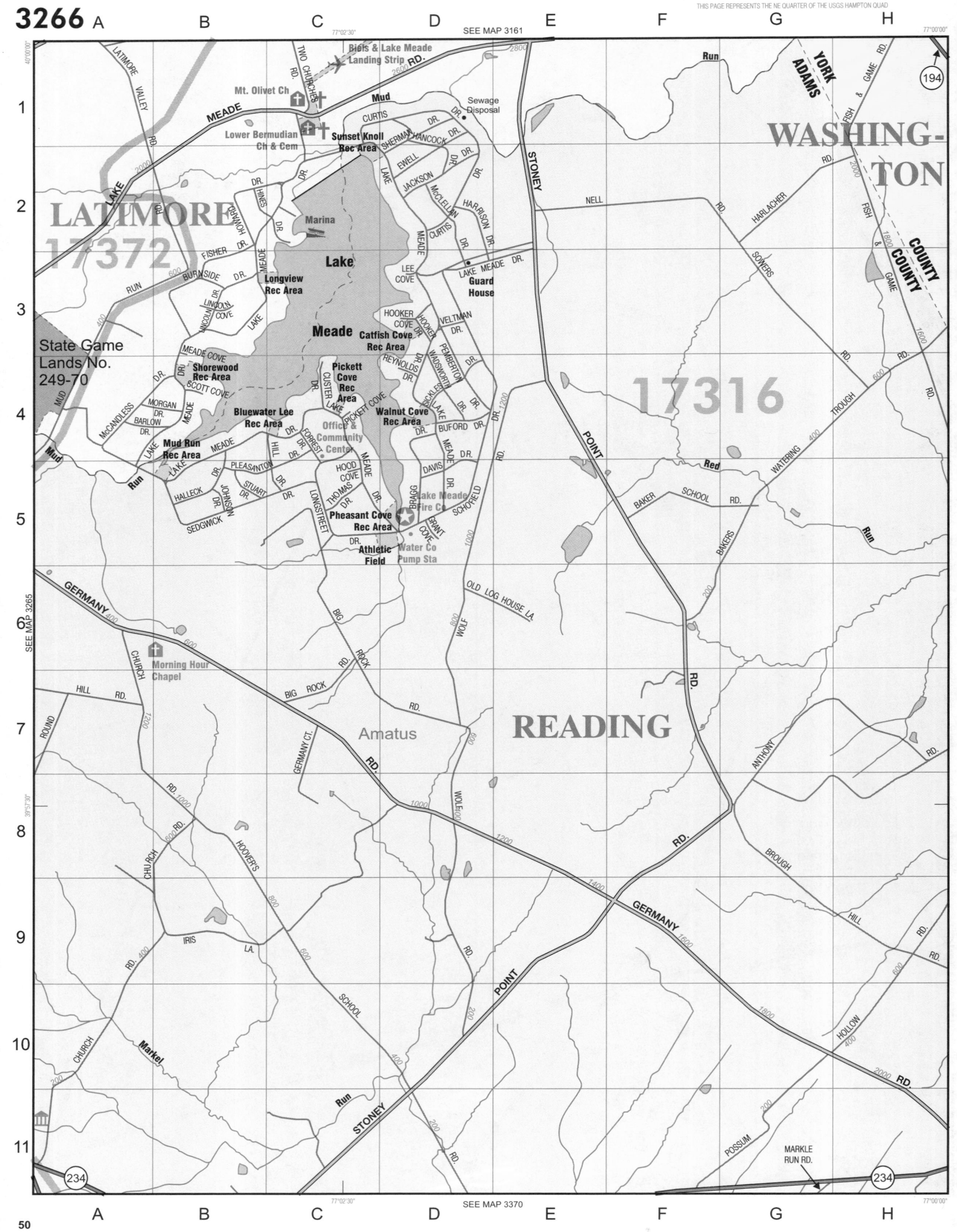

THIS PAGE REPRESENTS THE NE QUARTER OF THE USGS HAMPTON QUAD

WASHING-TON

LATIMORE 17372

State Game Lands No. 249-70

17316

READING

Amatus

Mt. Olivet Ch
Lower Bermudian Ch & Cem
Two Churches
Biels & Lake Meade Landing Strip
Sunset Knoll Rec Area
Sewage Disposal
Marina
Lake
Meade
Longview Rec Area
Guard House
Catfish Cove Rec Area
Shorewood Rec Area
Pickett Cove Rec Area
Bluewater Lee Rec Area
Walnut Cove Rec Area
Mud Run Rec Area
Office & Community Center
Pheasant Cove Rec Area
Lake Meade Fire Co.
Athletic Field
Water Co Pump Sta
Morning Hour Chapel

YORK ADAMS
COUNTY COUNTY

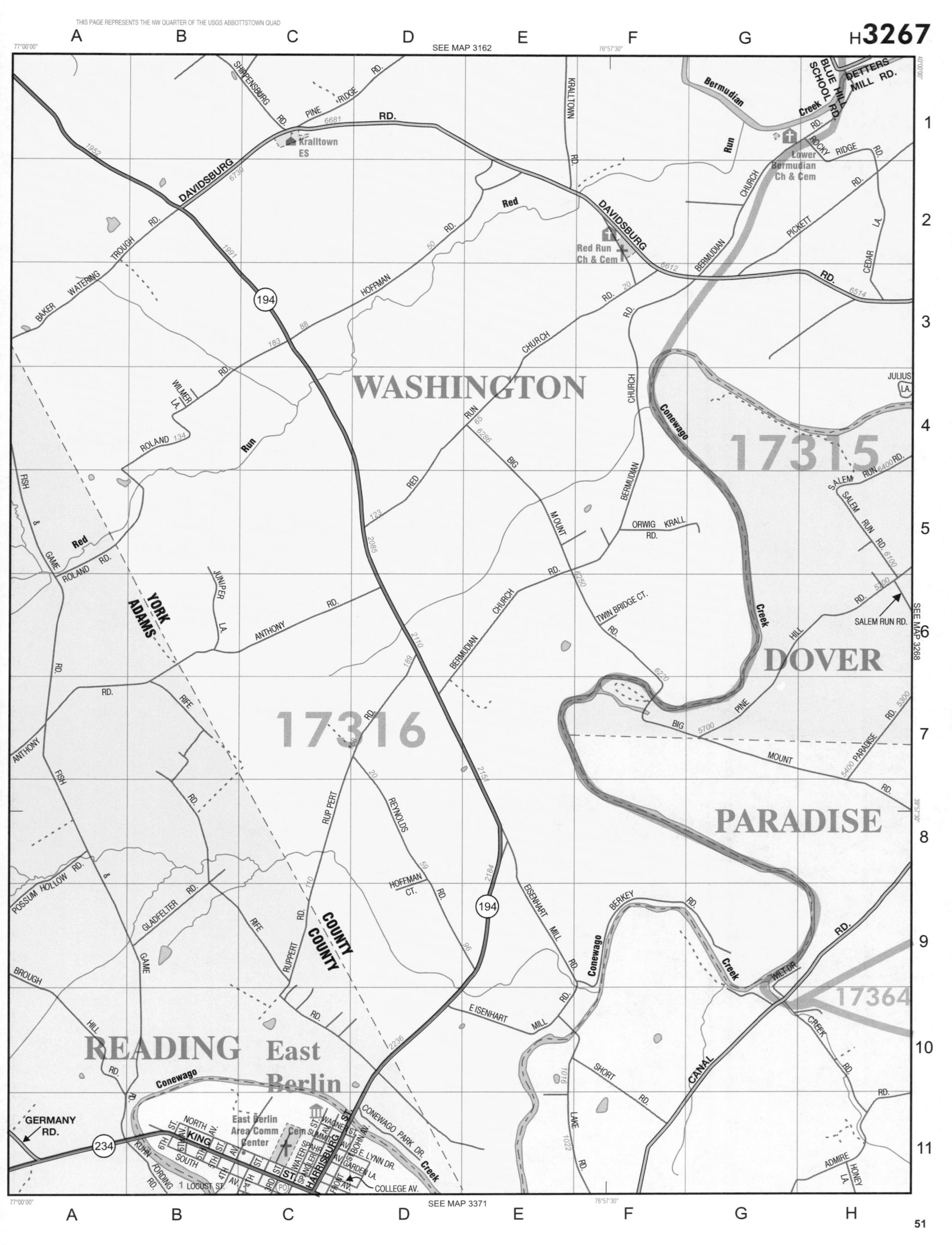

SEE MAP 3162

Bermudian

Creek

BLUE HILL SCHOOL RD.

DETTERS MILL RD.

Lower Bermudian Ch & Cem

ROCKY RIDGE RD.

PICKETT LA.

Run

Red

DAVIDSBURG

Kralltown ES

DAVIDSBURG

CEDAR LA.

Red Run Ch & Cem

WASHINGTON

17315

194

WATERING TROUGH RD.

BAKER

HOFFMAN RD.

CHURCH RD.

CHURCH RD.

Conewago

JULIUS LA.

WILMER LA.

ROLAND RD.

Run

RED RUN

BIG

BERMUDIAN

ORWIG RD.

KRALL RD.

SALEM RUN RD.

Creek

SALEM RUN RD.

Red

ROLAND RD.

FISH & GAME RD.

YORK ADAMS

JUNIPER LA.

MOUNT RD.

CHURCH RD.

TWIN BRIDGE CT.

DOVER

ANTHONY RD.

SEE MAP 3268

17316

BERMUDIAN RD.

BIG

PINE HILL

PARADISE

ANTHONY RD.

RIFE RD.

RUPPERT RD.

REYNOLDS RD.

MOUNT

PARADISE RD.

FISH & GAME RD.

HOFFMAN CT.

EISENHART MILL RD.

BERKEY RD.

17364

GLADFELTER RD.

RIFE RD.

COUNTY
COUNTY

Conewago

Creek

MILL CT.

POSSUM HOLLOW RD.

BROUGH

HILL RD.

GERMANY RD.

READING

East Berlin

RUPPERT RD.

E EISENHART MILL RD.

CONEWAGO PARK DR.

LAKE RD.

SHORT RD.

CANAL

234

Conewago

East Berlin Area Comm Center

Cem

NORTH ST.

KING ST.

SOUTH ST.

KUHN RD.

FORDING RD.

1 LOCUST ST.

WATER ST.

SPANGLER ST.

WAGNER ST.

SUMMIT ST.

BOHN AV.

HARRISBURG ST.

FRONT AV.

GARDEN LA.

E. LYNN DR.

COLLEGE AV.

Creek

ADMIRE LA.

HONEY LA.

SEE MAP 3371

51

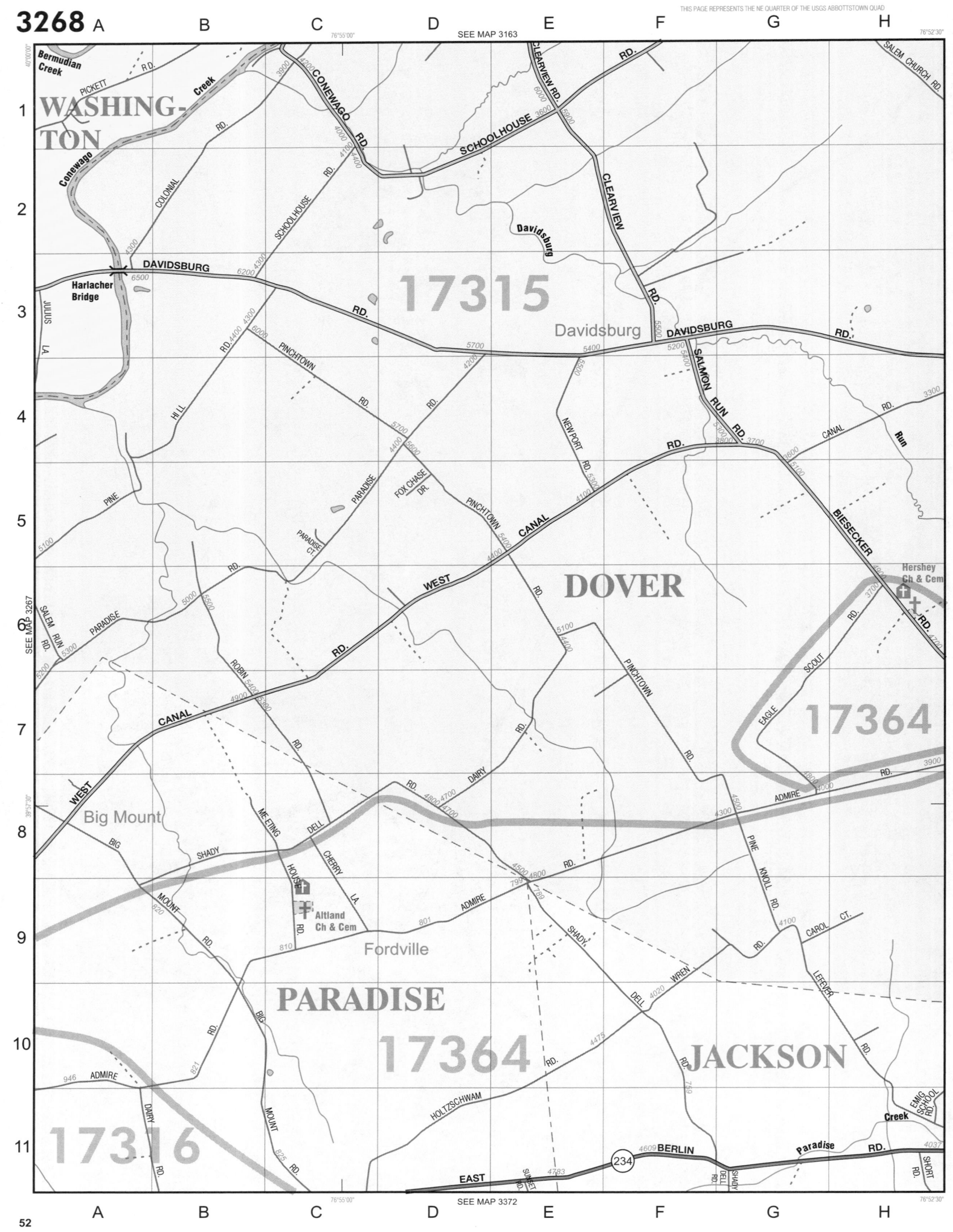

THIS PAGE REPRESENTS THE NE QUARTER OF THE USGS ABBOTTSTOWN QUAD

A   B   C   D   E   F   G   H

SEE MAP 3163

76°55'00"   76°52'30"

WASHING-TON

Bermudian Creek

PICKETT   RD.

Creek

Conewago

COLONIAL

CONEWAGO   RD.

SCHOOLHOUSE   RD.

CLEARVIEW RD.

RD.

CLEARVIEW

JULIUS   LA.

DAVIDSBURG

Harlacher Bridge

Davidsburg

17315

SCHOOLHOUSE

RD.

Davidsburg

Davidsburg   RD.

SALMON RUN RD.

RD.

PINCHTOWN

RD.

RD.

HILL

NEW PORT   RD.

Run

RD.

CANAL

PINE

PARADISE   CT.

FOX CHASE DR.

PARADISE

PINCHTOWN

CANAL

DOVER

BIESECKER

RD.

Hershey Ch & Cem

SALEM RUN   RD.

PARADISE

RD.

ROBIN   RD.

WEST   RD.

PINCHTOWN

RD.

SCOUT   RD.

EAGLE

17364

CANAL

RD.

WEST

Big Mount

BIG

SHADY

MOUNT

MEETING   DELL

CHERRY   LA.

DAIRY

RD.

RD.

ADMIRE

RD.

PINE

KNOLL   RD.

RD.

ADMIRE

RD.

CAROL   CT.

RD.

HOUSE   RD.

Altland Ch & Cem

Fordville

ADMIRE

SHADY

WREN

LEFEVER

RD.

PARADISE

RD.

BIG

MOUNT

17364

RD.

HOLTZSCHWAM

DELL

SHADY

JACKSON

RD.

ADMIRE

DAIRY

RD.

RD.

RD.

Creek

EMIG SCHOOL RD.

17316

EAST

SUNSET

234   BERLIN

Paradise   RD.

SHORT   RD.

DELL

SHADY RD.

SEE MAP 3372

76°55'00"   76°52'30"

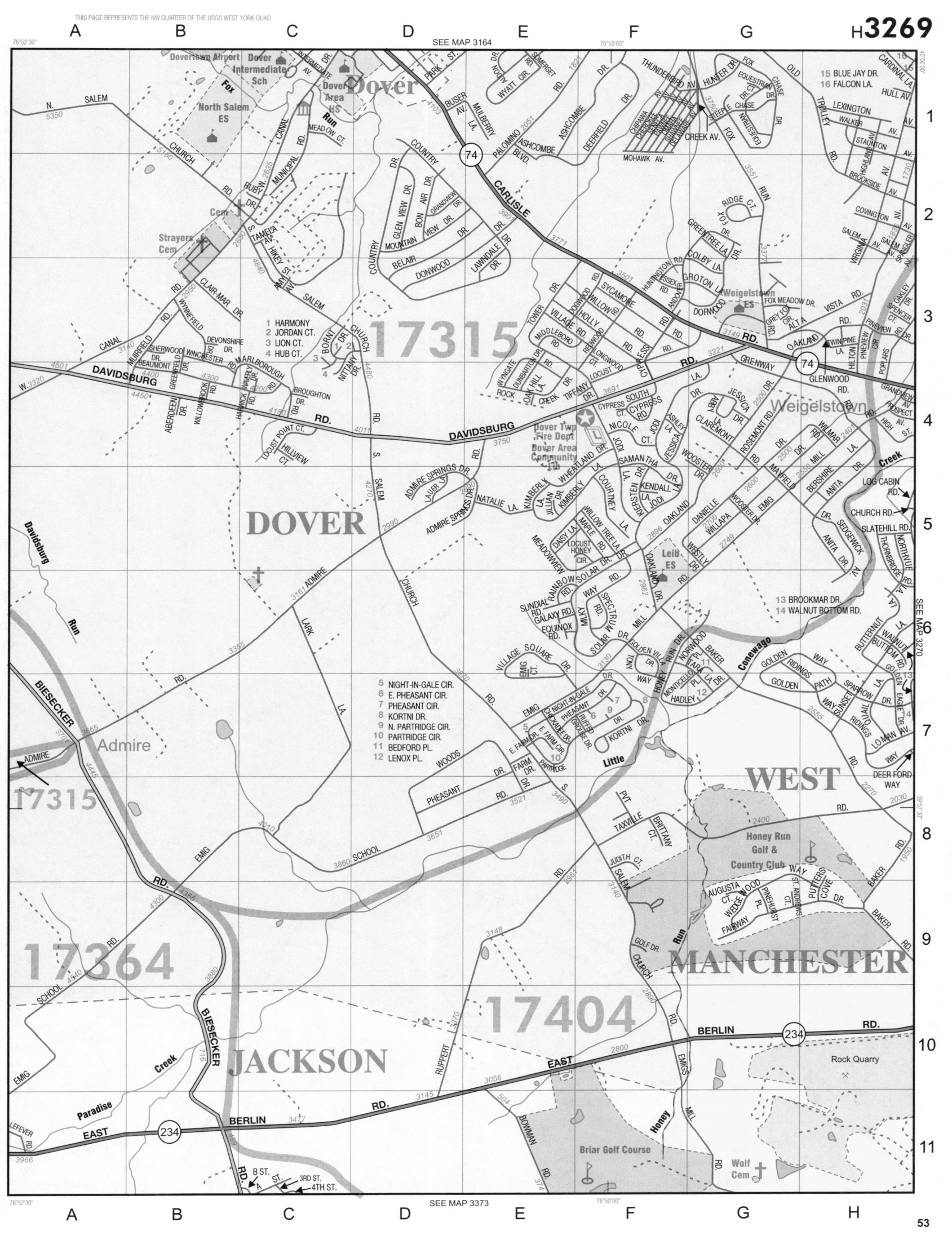

SEE MAP 3164

Dover

Dovertown Airport
Dover Intermediate Sch
Dover Area HS
North Salem ES

15 BLUE JAY DR.
16 FALCON LA.

17315

DOVER

1 HARMONY
2 JORDAN CT.
3 LION CT.
4 HUB CT.

Weigelstown

Weigelstown ES

Dover Twp Fire Dept
Dover Area Community FD

Leib ES

13 BROOKMAR DR.
14 WALNUT BOTTOM RD.

5 NIGHT-IN-GALE CIR.
6 E. PHEASANT CIR.
7 PHEASANT CIR.
8 KORTNI DR.
9 N. PARTRIDGE CIR.
10 PARTRIDGE CIR.
11 BEDFORD PL.
12 LENOX PL.

Little

WEST

Honey Run Golf & Country Club

17315

Admire

MANCHESTER

17364

17404

JACKSON

BERLIN RD. 234

Rock Quarry

Briar Golf Course

Wolf Cem

Paradise

EAST BERLIN 234

SEE MAP 3373

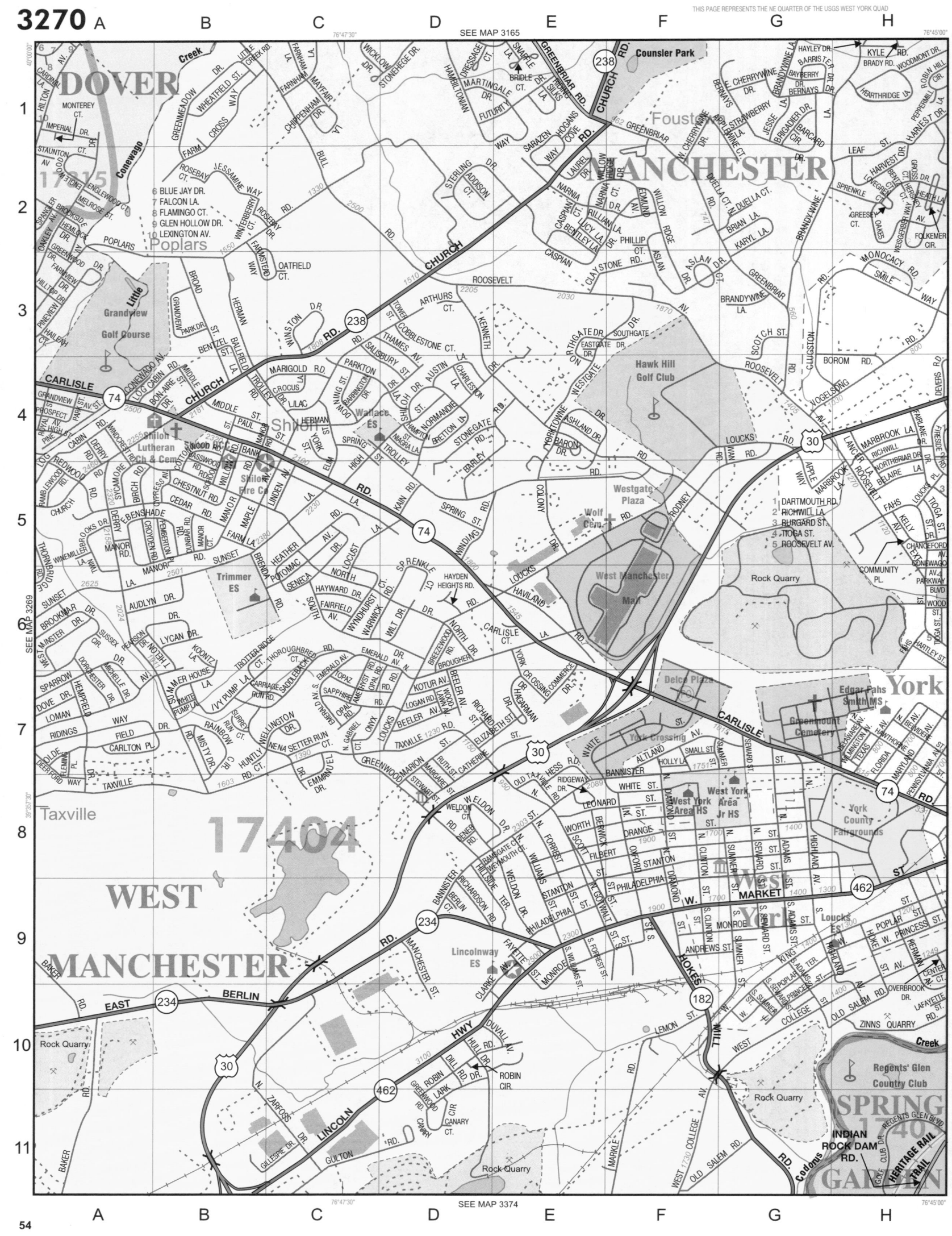

SEE MAP 3165

SEE MAP 3374

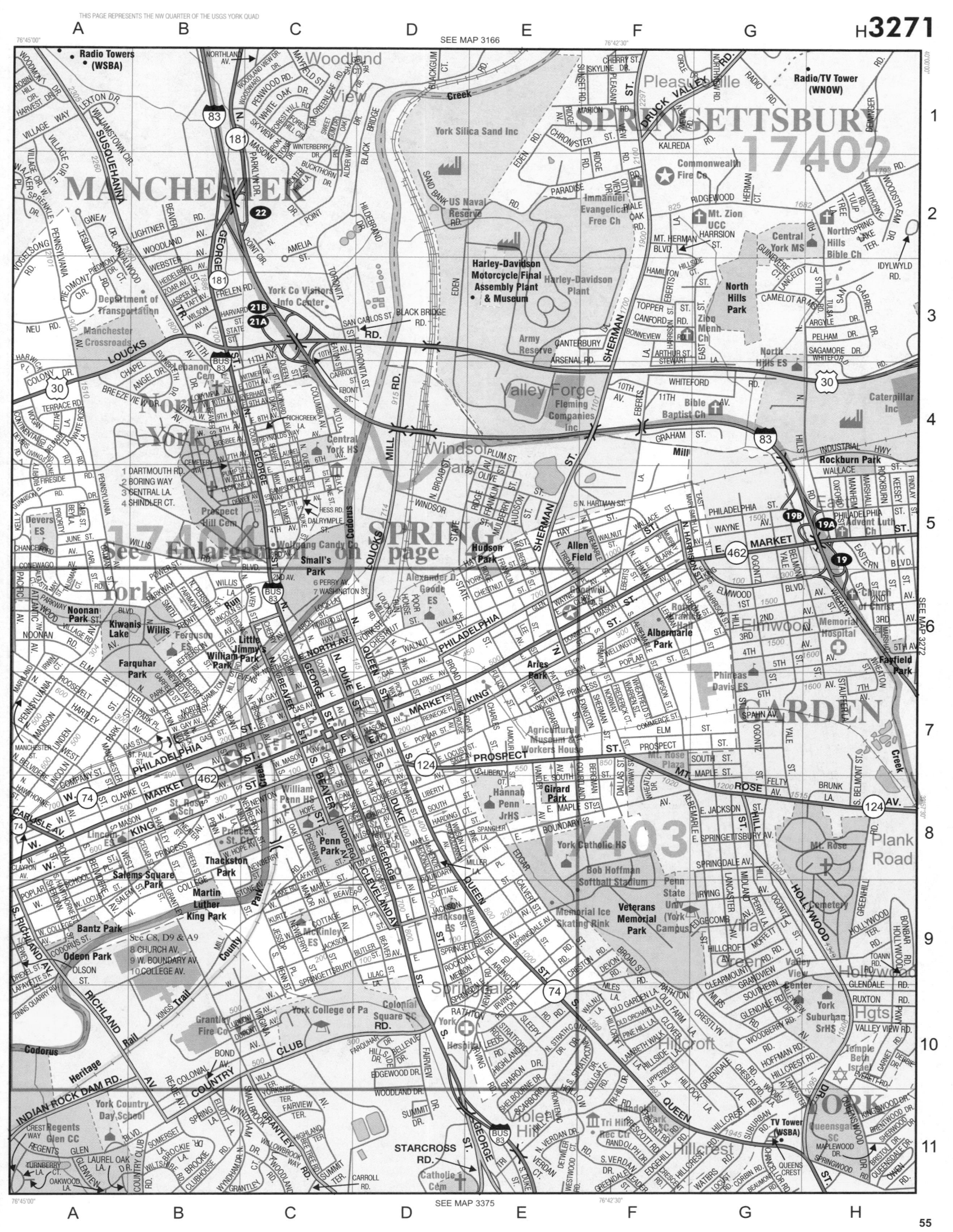

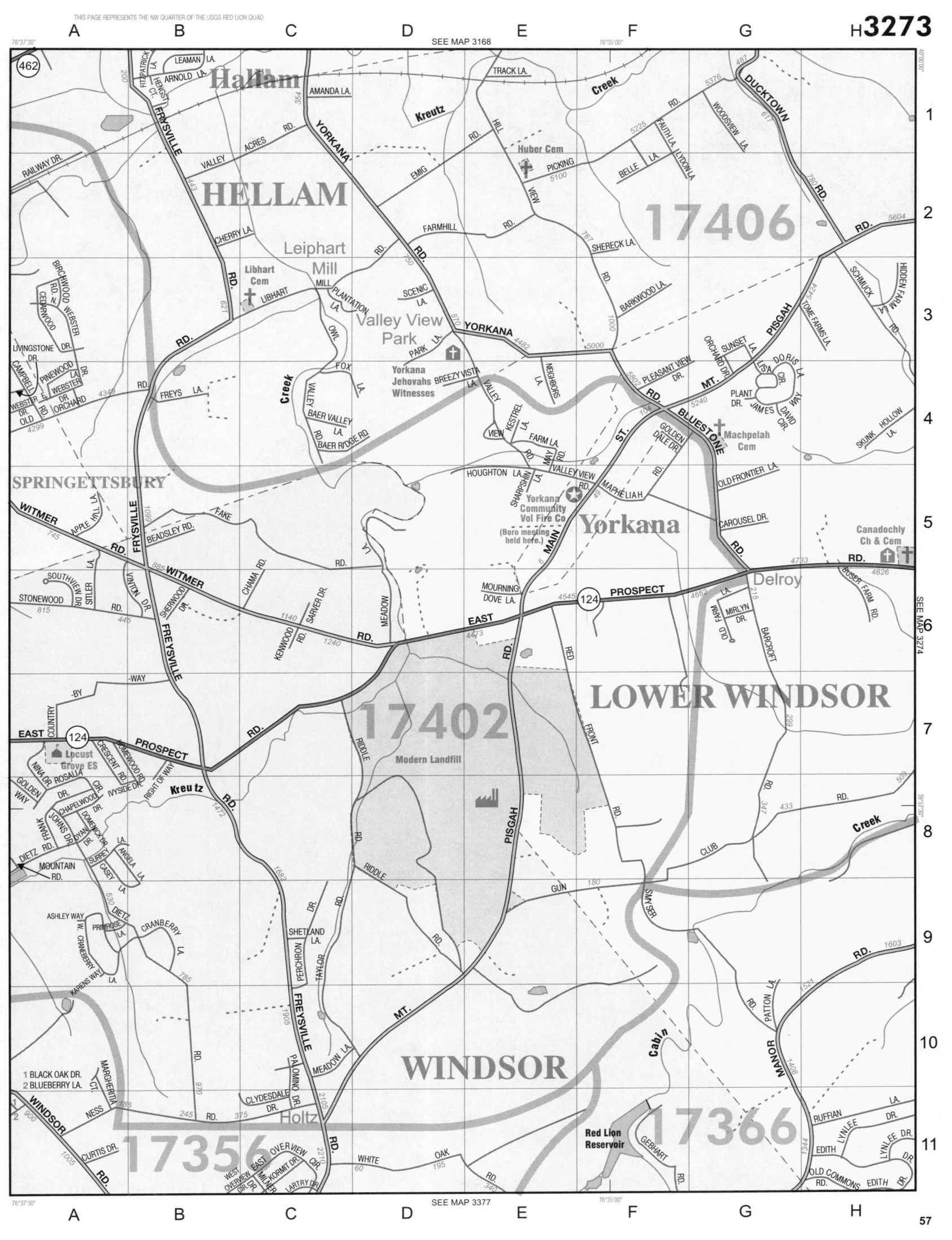

SEE MAP 3168

Hallam

Creek

DUCKTOWN

HELLAM

17406

Leiphart Mill

Libhart Cem

Huber Cem

Valley View Park

Yorkana Jehovahs Witnesses

Yorkana

SPRINGETTSBURY

Bluestone

Machpelah Cem

Yorkana Community Vol Fire Co
(Boro meeting held here.)

Canadochly Ch & Cem

Delroy

LOWER WINDSOR

PROSPECT

17402

Modern Landfill

Locust Grove ES

Kreutz

Creek

Red Lion Reservoir

1 BLACK OAK DR.
2 BLUEBERRY LA.

WINDSOR

Holtz

17356

17366

SEE MAP 3377

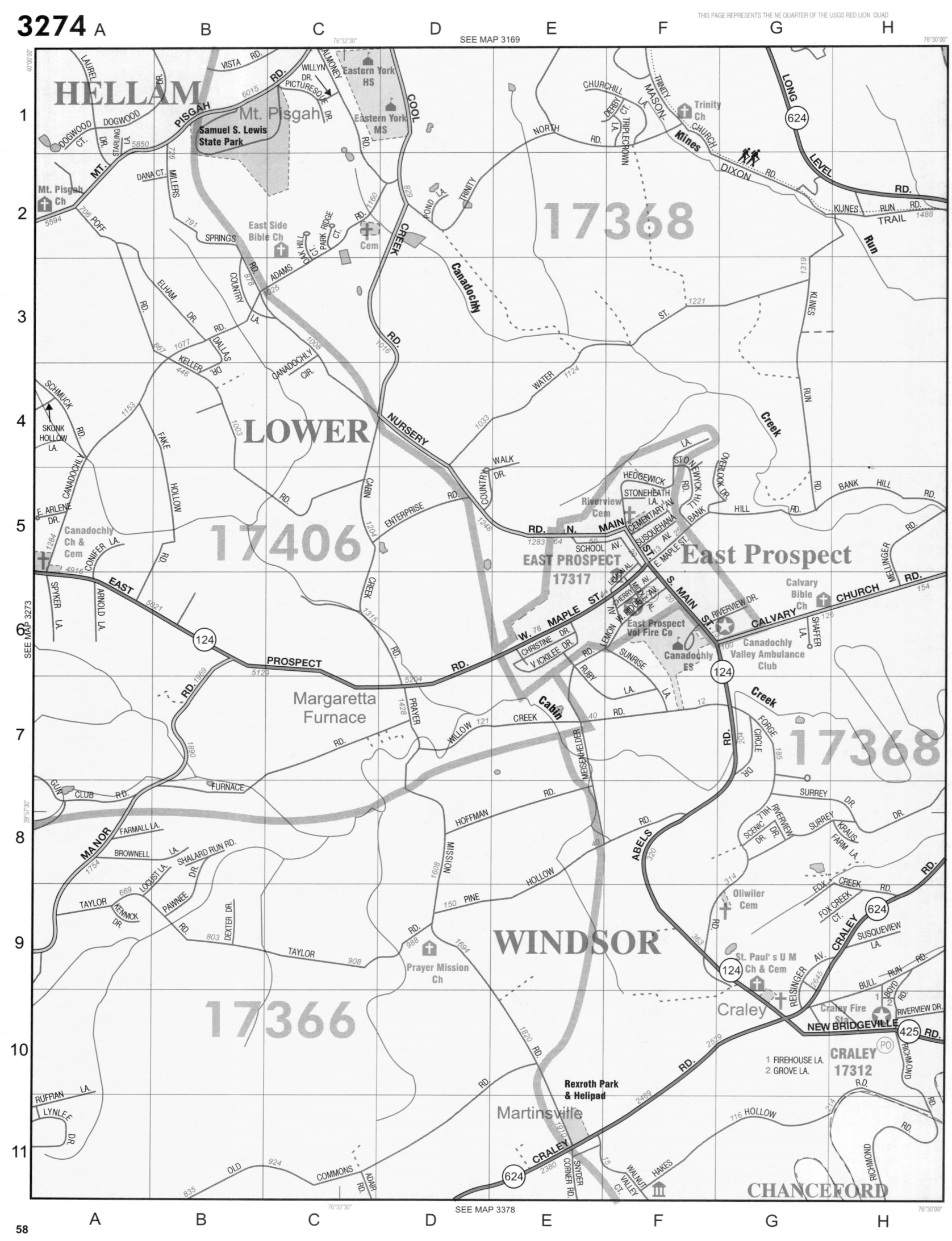

THIS PAGE REPRESENTS THE NE QUARTER OF THE USGS RED LION QUAD

SEE MAP 3169

HELLAM

Mt. Pisgah

Samuel S. Lewis
State Park

Eastern York
HS

Eastern York
MS

LAUREL LA.

DOGWOOD CT.

DOGWOOD DR.

STARLING LA.

VISTA RD.

WILLYN DR.

PICTURESQUE DR.

ALMONEY DR.

PISGAH RD.

MT.

DANA CT.

MILLERS

SPRINGS RD.

6015

5850

726

5594

706 POFF

PARK RIDGE CT.

OAK HILL CT.

Cem

East Side Bible Ch

ADAMS RD.

COUNTRY LA.

ELHAM DR.

DALLAS DR.

KELLER DR.

SCHMUCK RD.

SKUNK HOLLOW LA.

CANADOCHLY RD.

E. ARLENE DR.

Canadochly Ch & Cem

CONIFER LA.

SPYKER LA.

ARNOLD LA.

EAST

SEE MAP 3273

FAKE HOLLOW RD.

CANADOCHLY CIR.

CABIN

ENTERPRISE

CREEK RD.

NURSERY RD.

COOL CREEK RD.

CANADOCHLY RD.

POND LA.

TRINITY

WATER

WALK DR.

COUNTRY RD.

17368

17406

LOWER

829

1160

1016

1008

878

825

791

967

1077

446

1153

1003

4916

5921

1204

1315

1033

1248

1124

N. MAIN

SCHOOL AV.

RD.

EAST PROSPECT

17317

1283

64

50

CHURCHILL LA.

DERBY LA.

DIXON

MASON

TRINITY LA.

TRIPLECROWN

NORTH RD.

Trinity Ch

KLINES RD.

LONG LEVEL

624

KLINES RUN RD.

TRAIL

1488

ST.

1221

RUN

KLINES

Creek

1319

East Prospect

HEDGEWICK

STONEHEATH LA.

Riverview Cem

CEMENTARY AV.

SUSQUEHANA AV.

NEW YORK HILL

STO

BANK HILL

OVERLOOK DR.

BANK HILL RD.

MELLINGER RD.

Calvary Bible Ch

CALVARY CHURCH RD.

S. MAIN ST.

E. MAPLE ST.

RIVERVIEW DR.

CALVARY

SHAFFER LA.

Canadochly Valley Ambulance Club

Canadochly ES

East Prospect Vol Fire Co

124

W. MAPLE ST.

CHRISTINE DR.

V. VICKILEE DR.

LEMON AV.

CHERRY AV.

W. RIDGE AV.

SUNRISE

RUBY LA.

LA.

13

44

45

20

25

100

126

154

12

40

RD.

124

PROSPECT RD.

1969

5129

5204

Margaretta Furnace

PRAYER RD.

WILLOW

CREEK

CABIN CREEK

Creek

FORGE CIRCLE DR.

17368

1428

121

40

42

185

GUN CLUB RD.

FURNACE RD.

MANOR

FARMALL LA.

BROWNELL

SHALARD RUN RD.

LOCUST LA.

PAWNEE RD.

DEXTER DR.

TAYLOR

KENNICK DR.

1754

669

803

908

1608

1890

HOFFMAN RD.

MISSION HOLLOW

PINE RD.

150

988

1694

WINDSOR

MEISENHELDER DR.

ABELS

320

314

SCENIC DR.

7TH RIVERVIEW DR.

SURREY DR.

SURREY DR.

KRAUS FARM LA.

Oliwiler Cem

FOX CREEK CT.

FOX CREEK RD.

CRALEY

624

124

St. Paul's U M Ch & Cem

REISINGER AV.

SUSQUEVIEW LA.

363

2645

BULL RUN RD.

BOYD RD.

1

2

RIVERVIEW DR.

Craley

Craley Fire Sta.

NEW BRIDGEVILLE

425

RICHMOND RD.

PO

CRALEY

17312

1 FIREHOUSE LA.
2 GROVE LA.

17366

RUFFIAN LA.

LYNLEE DR.

TAYLOR RD.

OLD COMMONS RD.

ADAIR RD.

924

835

988

1820 RD.

Prayer Mission Ch

Rexroth Park & Helipad

Martinsville

CRALEY

624

SNYDER CORNER RD.

2380

2469

1910

116 HOLLOW

2579

214

WALNUT VALLEY CT.

HAKES

RICHMOND RD.

RD.

CHANCEFORD

75

SEE MAP 3378

76°32'30"

76°30'00"

40°00'00"

39°57'30"

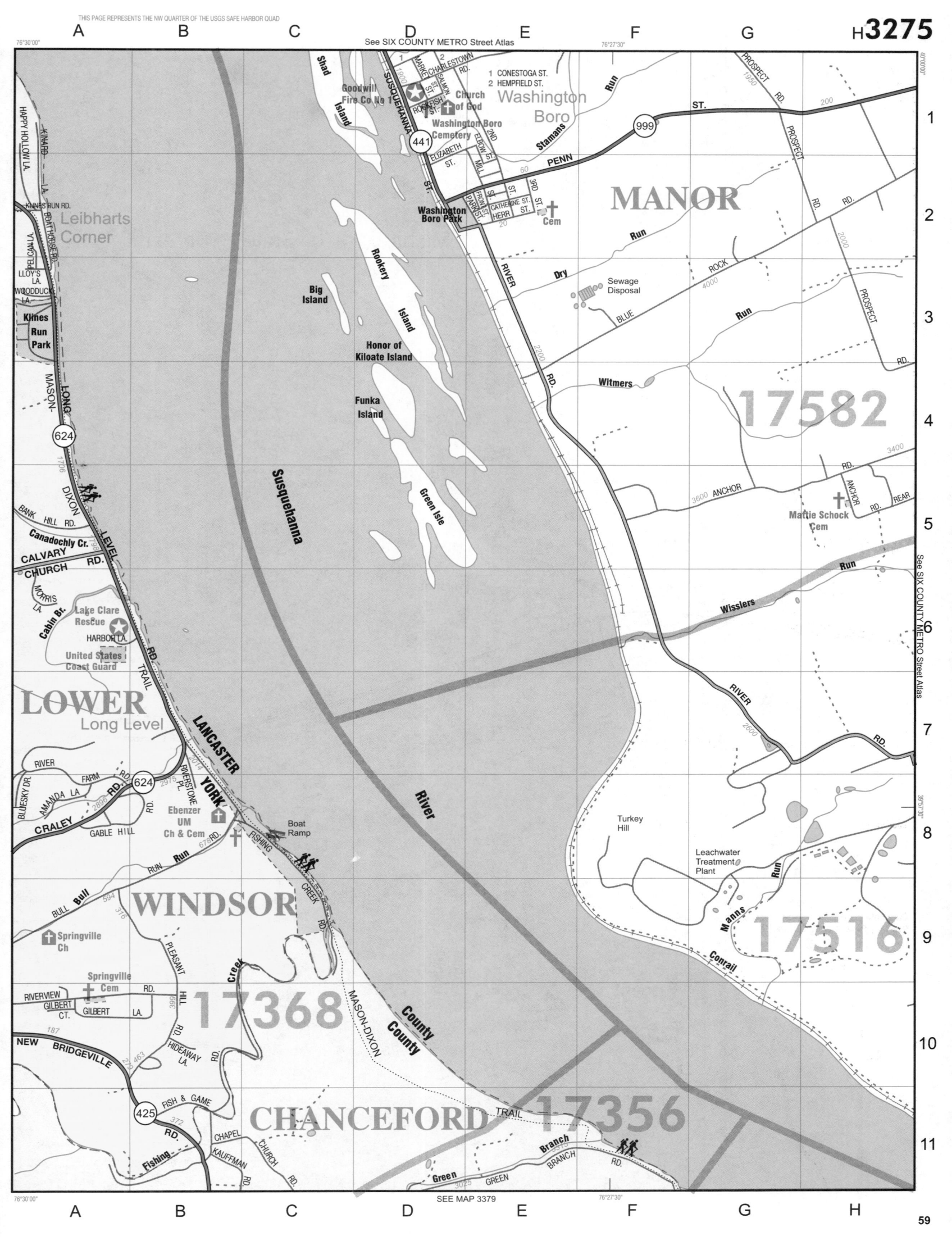

See SIX COUNTY METRO Street Atlas

1 CONESTOGA ST.
2 HEMPFIELD ST.

Goodwill
Fire Co No 1

Church
of God

Washington
Boro

Washington Boro
Cemetery

MANOR

Washington
Boro Park

17582

Leibharts
Corner

KINNES RUN RD.

Klines
Run
Park

Shad
Island

Rookery
Island

Big
Island

Honor of
Kiloate Island

Funka
Island

Green Isle

Sewage
Disposal

Witmers

Mattie Schock
Cem

BANK HILL RD.

Canadochly Cr.

CALVARY
CHURCH

Susquehanna

Wisslers

Lake Clare
Rescue

United States
Coast Guard

LOWER
Long Level

LANCASTER

YORK

River

Turkey
Hill

17516

Leachwater
Treatment
Plant

RIVER

RIVERSTONE
PL.

Ebenzer
UM
Ch & Cem

Boat
Ramp

Run

FISHING

WINDSOR

Bull

CREEK

Manns
Run

Conrail

Springville
Ch

Springville
Cem

RIVERVIEW
GILBERT
CT.

GILBERT
LA.

17368

Creek

PLEASANT

HIDEAWAY
LA.

MASON-DIXON

County
County

NEW
BRIDGEVILLE

FISH & GAME

CHANCEFORD

17356

TRAIL

CHAPEL

KAUFFMAN

CHURCH RD.

Fishing

Green

Branch

BRANCH

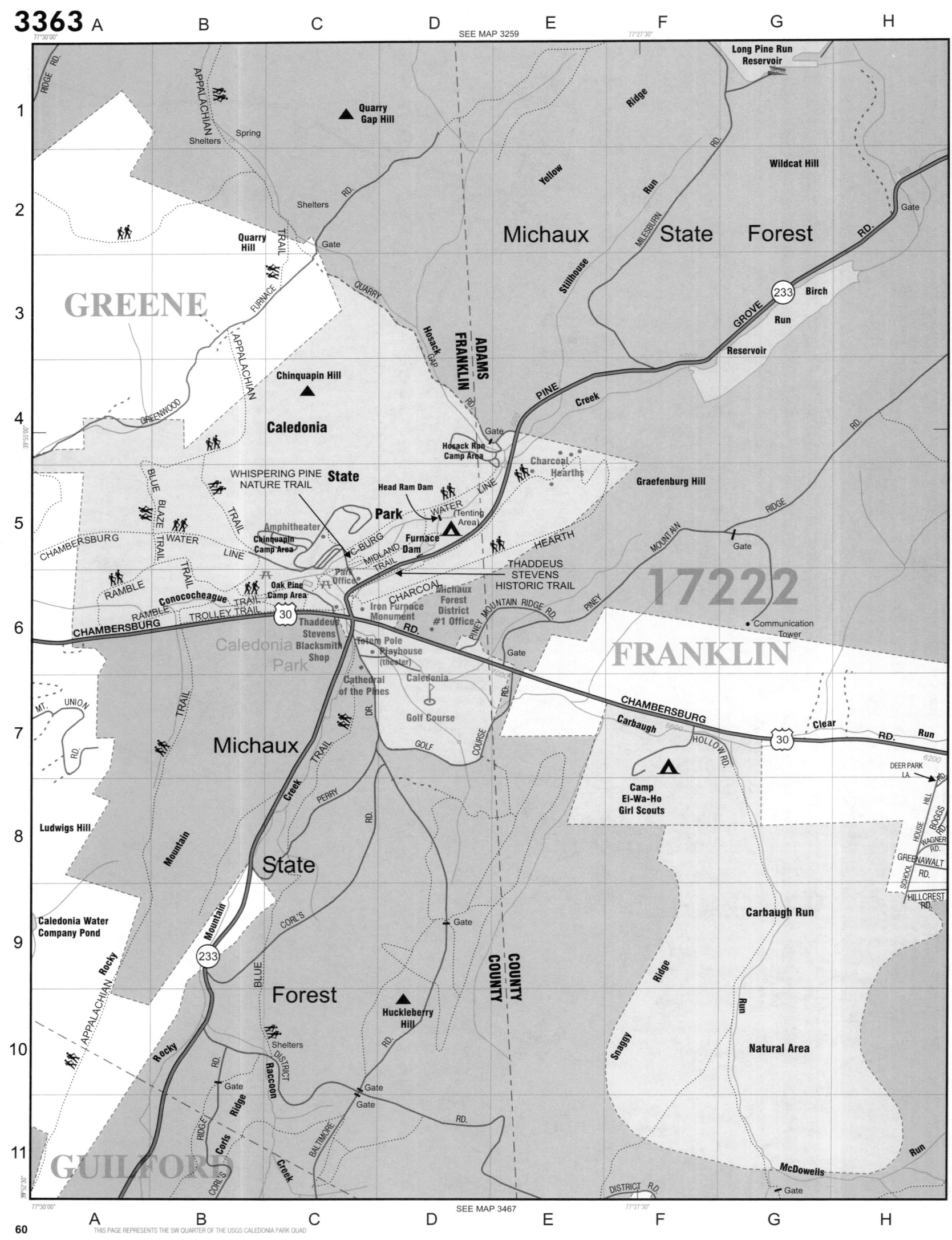

SEE MAP 3259

GREENE

Quarry Gap Hill

Shelters
Spring
APPALACHIAN
Quarry
Hill
Shelters
Gate
Quarry
Hill
TRAIL
FURNACE
QUARRY
Hosack GAP
RD.

Michaux **State** **Forest**

Ridge
Yellow
Run
MILESBURN
Stillhouse
Run

Long Pine Run Reservoir

Wildcat Hill

Gate
233
GROVE
Birch
Run
Reservoir
RD.

ADAMS FRANKLIN
LINE
PINE Creek

Chinquapin Hill

Caledonia

Gate
Hosack Run
Camp Area
Charcoal
Hearths
Graefenburg Hill
RIDGE
MOUNTAIN
Gate

WHISPERING PINE NATURE TRAIL
State **Park**
Head Ram Dam
WATER (Tenting Area)

BLUE BLAZE TRAIL
WATER LINE
TRAIL
Amphitheater
Chinquapin Camp Area
C.BURG
Furnace Dam
MIDLAND TRAIL
HEARTH

17222

CHAMBERSBURG
RAMBLE
TRAIL
RAMBLE
Conococheague
TROLLEY TRAIL
Park Office
CHARCOAL
Oak Pine Camp Area
Iron Furnace Monument
Michaux Forest District #1 Office
PINEY MOUNTAIN RIDGE RD.
PINEY

THADDEUS STEVENS HISTORIC TRAIL

FRANKLIN

Communication Tower

CHAMBERSBURG 30
Thaddeus Stevens Blacksmith Shop
Caledonia Park
Totem Pole Playhouse (theater)
Cathedral of the Pines
RD.
Caledonia
Golf Course
Gate

CHAMBERSBURG
Carbaugh
HOLLOW RD.
30
Clear RD. Run

MT. UNION RD.
TRAIL
DR.
GOLF
COURSE
Camp El-Wa-Ho Girl Scouts

DEER PARK LA.
HILL RD.
BOGGS RD.
WAGNER
GREENAWALT RD.
HOUSE
SCHOOL
HILLCREST RD.

Michaux
Creek
TRAIL
PERRY
Mountain
Ludwigs Hill

State
Mountain
CORL'S
RD.
Gate

Carbaugh Run

Caledonia Water Company Pond
233
BLUE
Ridge
Run

Forest
Huckleberry Hill
COUNTY COUNTY LINE
RD.
Snaggy
Ridge
Run
Natural Area

Rocky
APPALACHIAN
Shelters
DISTRICT
Raccoon
Gate
Gate
BALTIMORE
RD.

GUILFORD
Corls
RIDGE
Ridge
Creek
RD.
DISTRICT RD.
Gate
McDowells
Run

SEE MAP 3467

THIS PAGE REPRESENTS THE SW QUARTER OF THE USGS CALEDONIA PARK QUAD

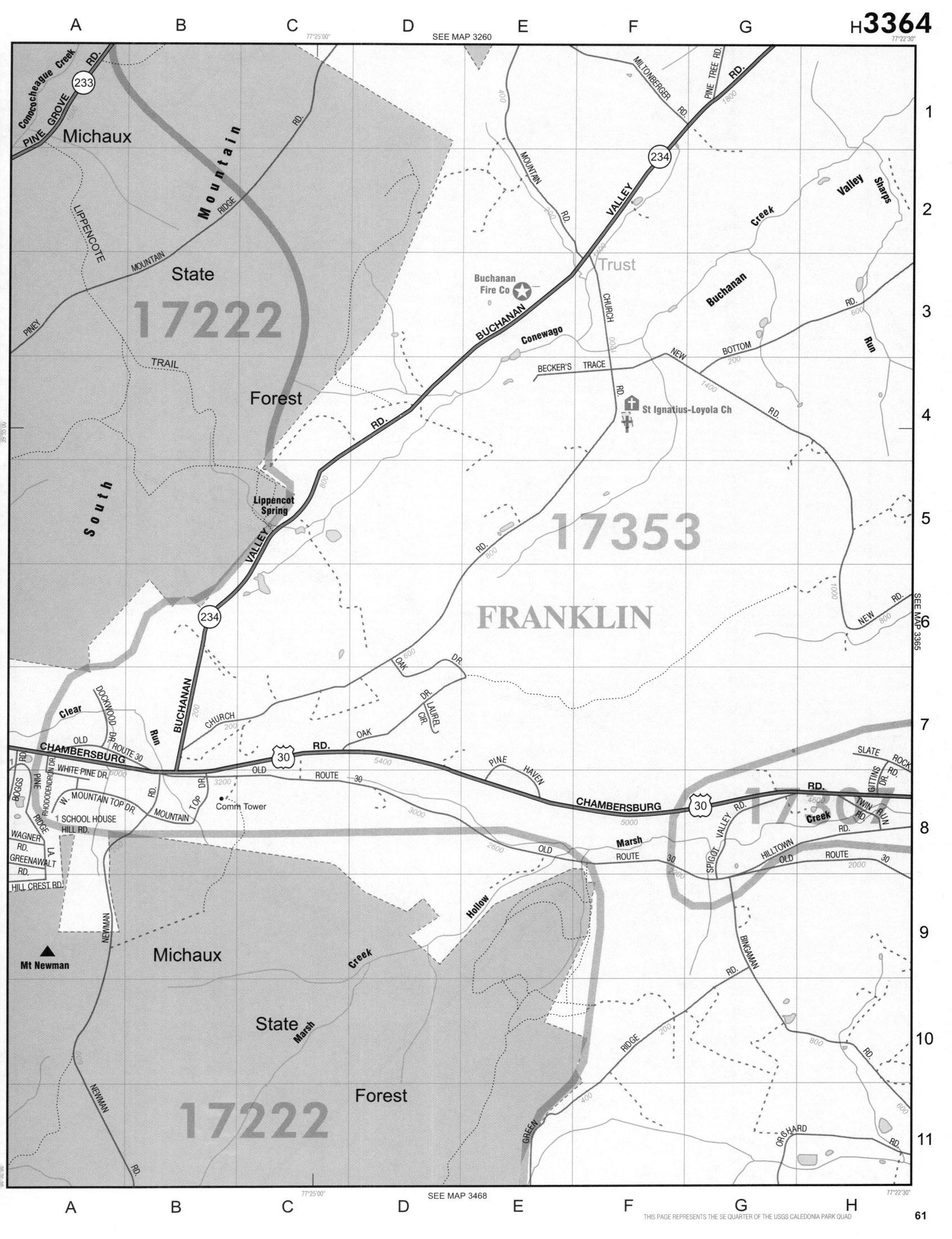

SEE MAP 3260

77°25'00"

77°22'30"

A B C D E F G H

Michaux

Conococheague Creek RD.

233

PINE GROVE

LIPPENCOTE

PINEY

Mountain

RIDGE

State

17222

Forest

MOUNTAIN TRAIL

South

VALLEY

Lippencot Spring

234

BUCHANAN

CHURCH 200

RD.

MOUNTAIN RD.

400

400

VALLEY

234

1800

PINE TREE RD.

MILTONBERGER RD.

Trust

Buchanan Fire Co

BUCHANAN

Conewago

BECKER'S TRACE

CHURCH RD.

St Ignatius-Loyola Ch

NEW

1400

BOTTOM 200

Buchanan

RD. 600

Sharps Valley

Creek

Run

17353

FRANKLIN

800

RD.

800 RD.

1000

NEW RD.

800

SEE MAP 3365

OAK

DR.

DR. LAUREL CIR.

600

Clear

Run

Buchanan 200

CHURCH 200

DOCKWOOD DR.

OLD ROUTE 30

CHAMBERSBURG

BOGGS

PINE RIDGE RD.

WHITE PINE DR.

W. MOUNTAIN TOP DR.

1 SCHOOL HOUSE HILL RD.

RHODODENDRON DR.

MOUNTAIN TOP DR.

1000

3200

Comm Tower

30

US 30

OLD ROUTE RD. OAK

5400

PINE HAVEN

ROUTE 30

3000

CHAMBERSBURG 30

5000

SLATE ROCK

GITTINS DR.

RD.

4600

TWIN RUN RD.

17

Creek

WAGNER RD.

GREENAWALT RD.

HILL CREST RD.

NEWMAN RD.

Mt Newman

Michaux

State

Marsh Creek

Forest

17222

2600

OLD

2500

Hollow

ROUTE 30 3200

Marsh

SPIGOT

VALLEY RD.

HILLTOWN

OLD ROUTE 30

2000

RIDGE 200

BINGAMAN RD.

RD.

GREEN

400

800

ORCHARD

RD.

77°25'00"

SEE MAP 3468

A B C D E F G H

1
2
3
4
5
6
7
8
9
10
11

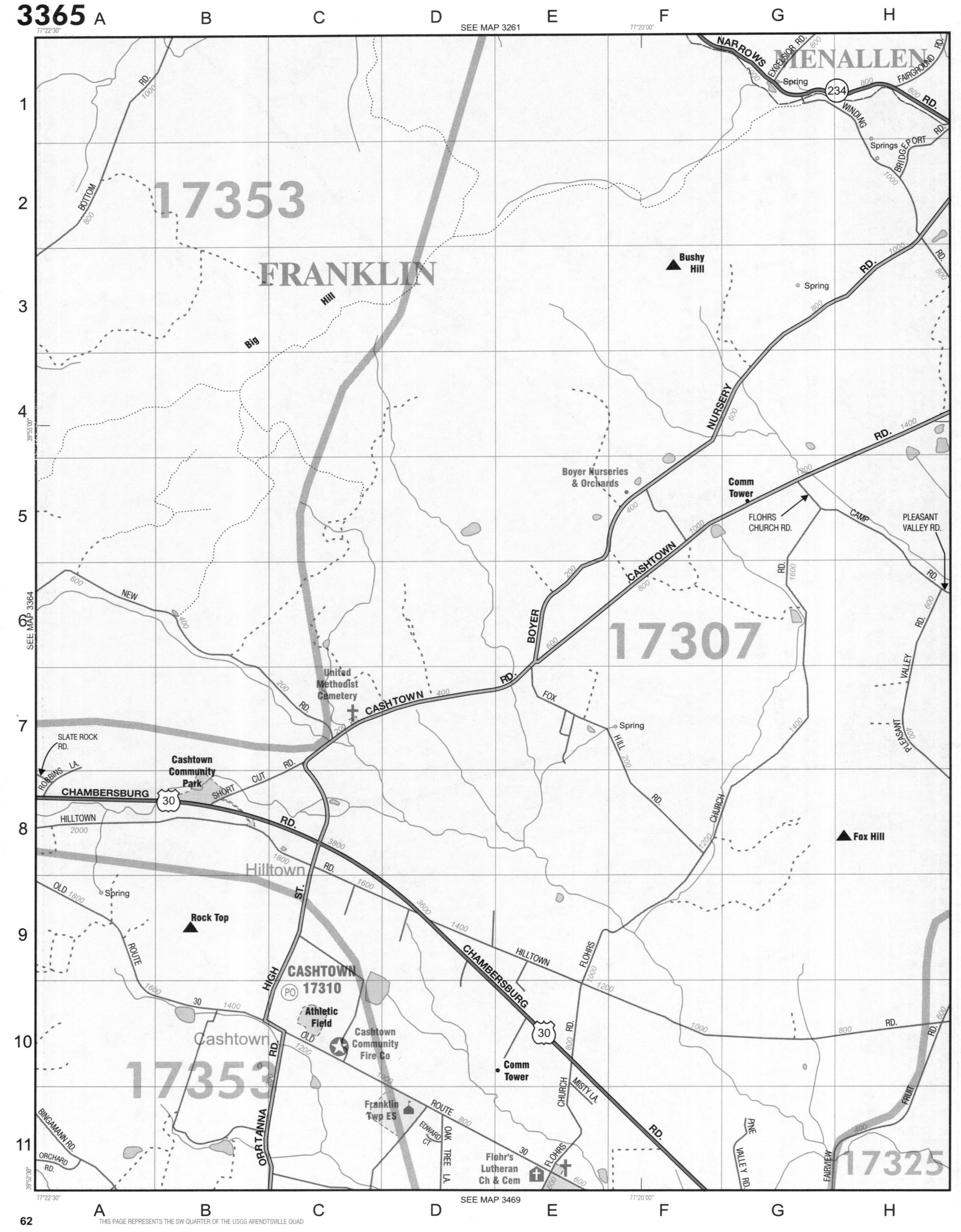

3365 A

77°22'30"   77°20'00"

MENALLEN

NARROWS

EXCELSIOR RD.

FAIRGROUND RD.

Spring

234

WINDING RD.

BRIDGEPORT RD.

Springs

17353

BOTTOM RD.

1000

800

FRANKLIN

Hill

Big

▲ Bushy Hill

Spring

NURSERY RD.

800

600

39°55'00"

Boyer Nurseries & Orchards

Comm Tower

1300

FLOHRS CHURCH RD.

CAMP RD.

PLEASANT VALLEY RD.

400

1600

600

RD.

600

NEW RD.

400

CASHTOWN

BOYER RD.

800

200

17307

SEE MAP 3364

600

United Methodist Cemetery

† CASHTOWN RD.

400

FOX HILL RD.

200

Spring

1400

PLEASANT VALLEY RD.

200

SLATE ROCK RD.

ROBINS LA.

Cashtown Community Park

SHORT CUT RD.

CHURCH RD.

1200

CHAMBERSBURG 30

HILLTOWN 2000

RD.

3800

Hilltown

ST. RD.

1800

1600

OLD 1800

Spring

▲ **Rock Top**

ROUTE 1600

3600

1400

CHAMBERSBURG

HILLTOWN RD.

FLOHRS RD.

1000

1200

▲ Fox Hill

800

RD.

CASHTOWN

PO **17310**

HIGH ST. RD.

30

1400

OLD 1200

Athletic Field

★ **Cashtown Community Fire Co**

30

800

Comm Tower

CHURCH RD.

MISTY LA.

PINE VALLEY RD.

FAIRVIEW RD.

FRUIT RD.

400

Cashtown

17353

BINGAMANN RD.

ORCHARD RD.

ORRTANNA RD.

Franklin Twp ES

ROUTE 800

EDWARD CT

OAK TREE LA.

Flohr's Lutheran Ch & Cem †

FLOHRS RD.

30

600

†

600

17325

39°52'30"

77°22'30"   77°20'00"

| A | B | C | D | E | F | G | H |

THIS PAGE REPRESENTS THE SW QUARTER OF THE USGS ARENDTSVILLE QUAD

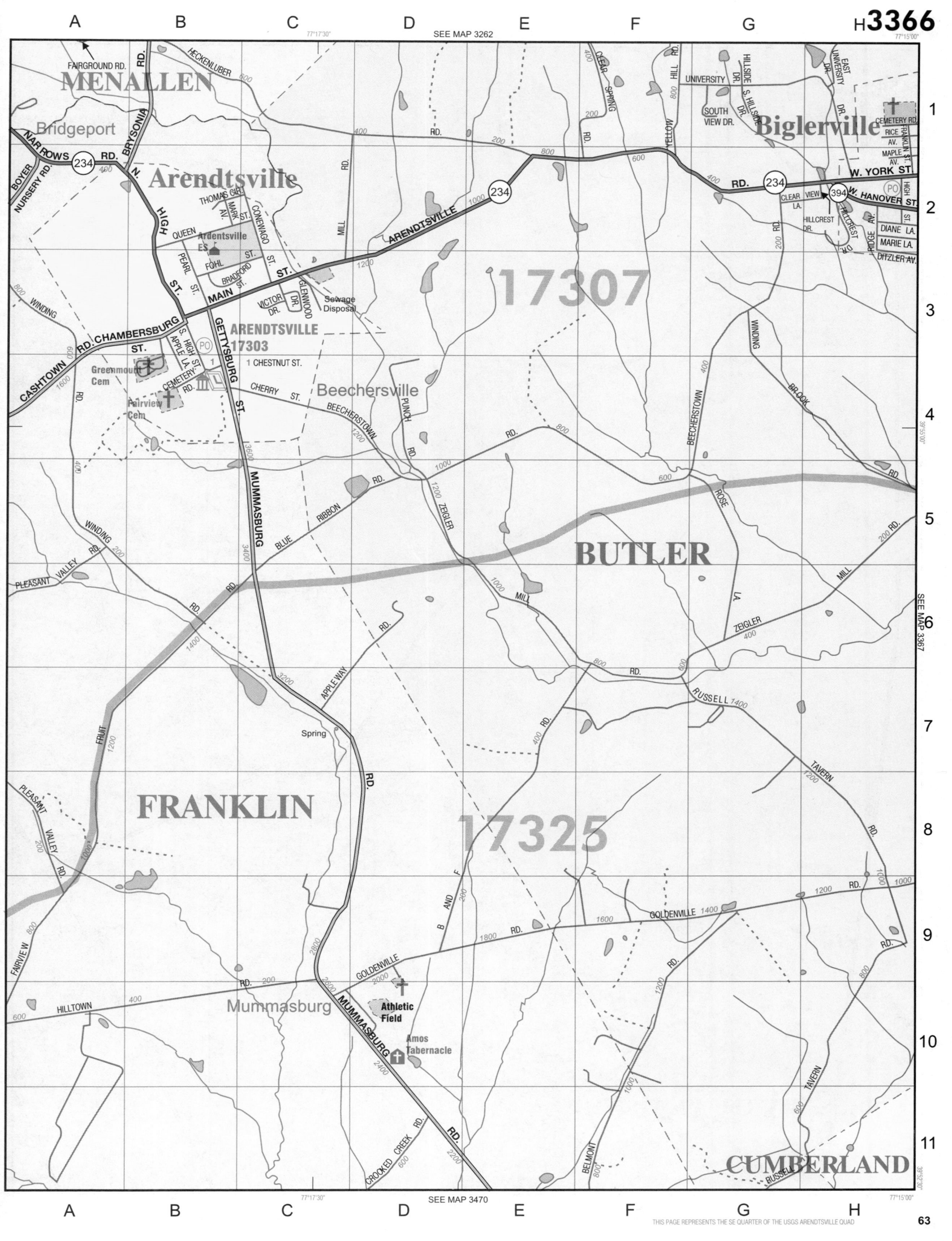

	A	B	C	D	E	F	G	H

SEE MAP 3262

MENALLEN

Bridgeport

Arendtsville

Biglerville

17307

ARENDTSVILLE
17303

Beechersville

BUTLER

FRANKLIN

17325

Mummasburg

Athletic
Field

Amos
Tabernacle

CUMBERLAND

SEE MAP 3470

THIS PAGE REPRESENTS THE SE QUARTER OF THE USGS ARENDTSVILLE QUAD

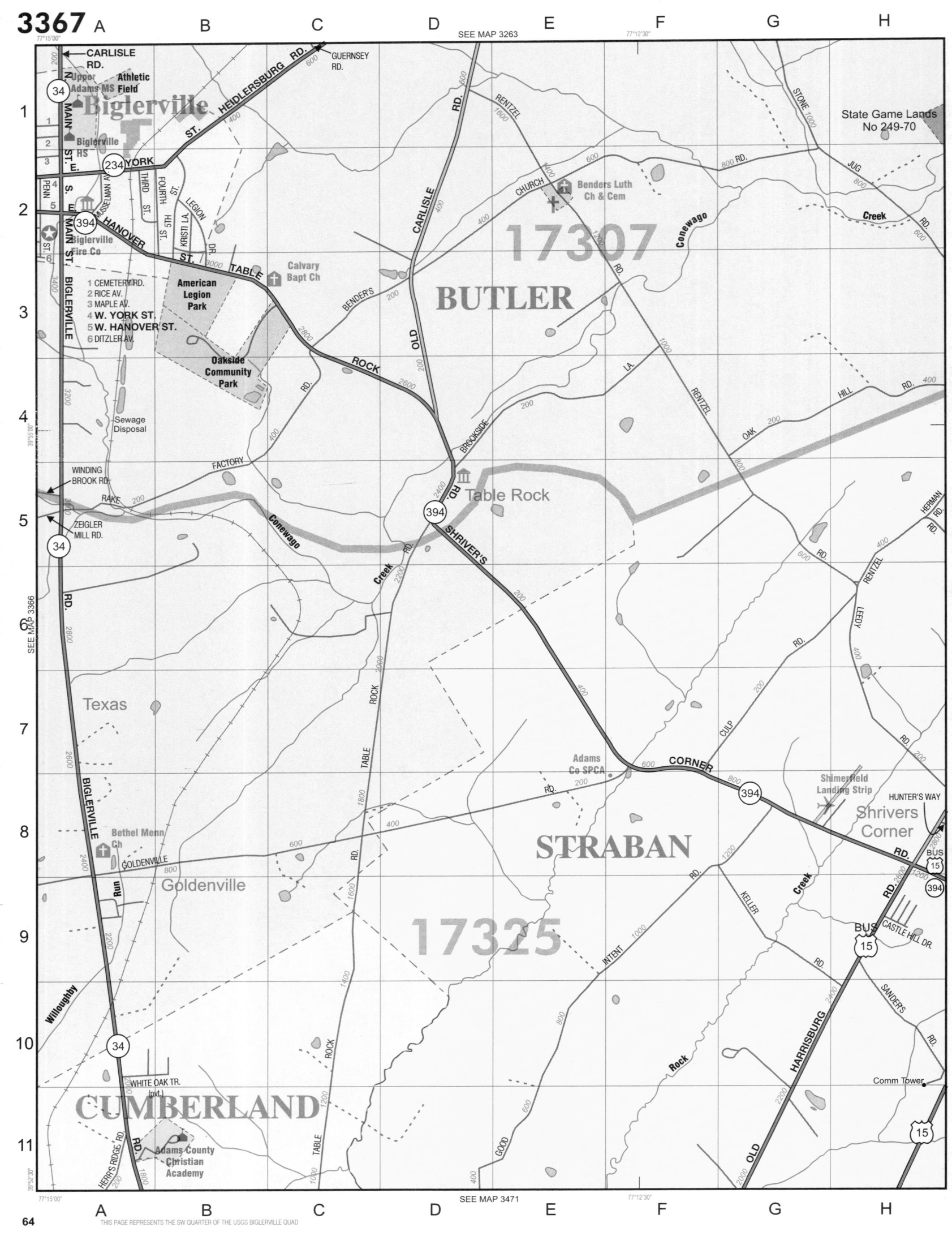

State Game Lands
No 249-70

CARLISLE
RD.

Upper
Adams MS
Athletic
Field

Biglerville

Biglerville HS

YORK

Benders Luth
Ch & Cem

Biglerville Fire Co

17307

BUTLER

Calvary
Bapt Ch

American
Legion
Park

1 CEMETERY RD.
2 RICE AV.
3 MAPLE AV.
4 W. YORK ST.
5 W. HANOVER ST.
6 DITZLER AV.

Oakside
Community
Park

Sewage
Disposal

WINDING
BROOK RD.

Table Rock

ZEIGLER
MILL RD.

Texas

Bethel Menn
Ch

GOLDENVILLE

Goldenville

Adams
Co SPCA

CORNER

STRABAN

Shimerfield
Landing Strip

HUNTER'S WAY

**Shrivers
Corner**

17325

CASTLE HILL DR.

Comm Tower

Willoughby

CUMBERLAND

WHITE OAK TR.
(pvt.)

Adams County
Christian
Academy

SEE MAP 3263

SEE MAP 3366

SEE MAP 3471

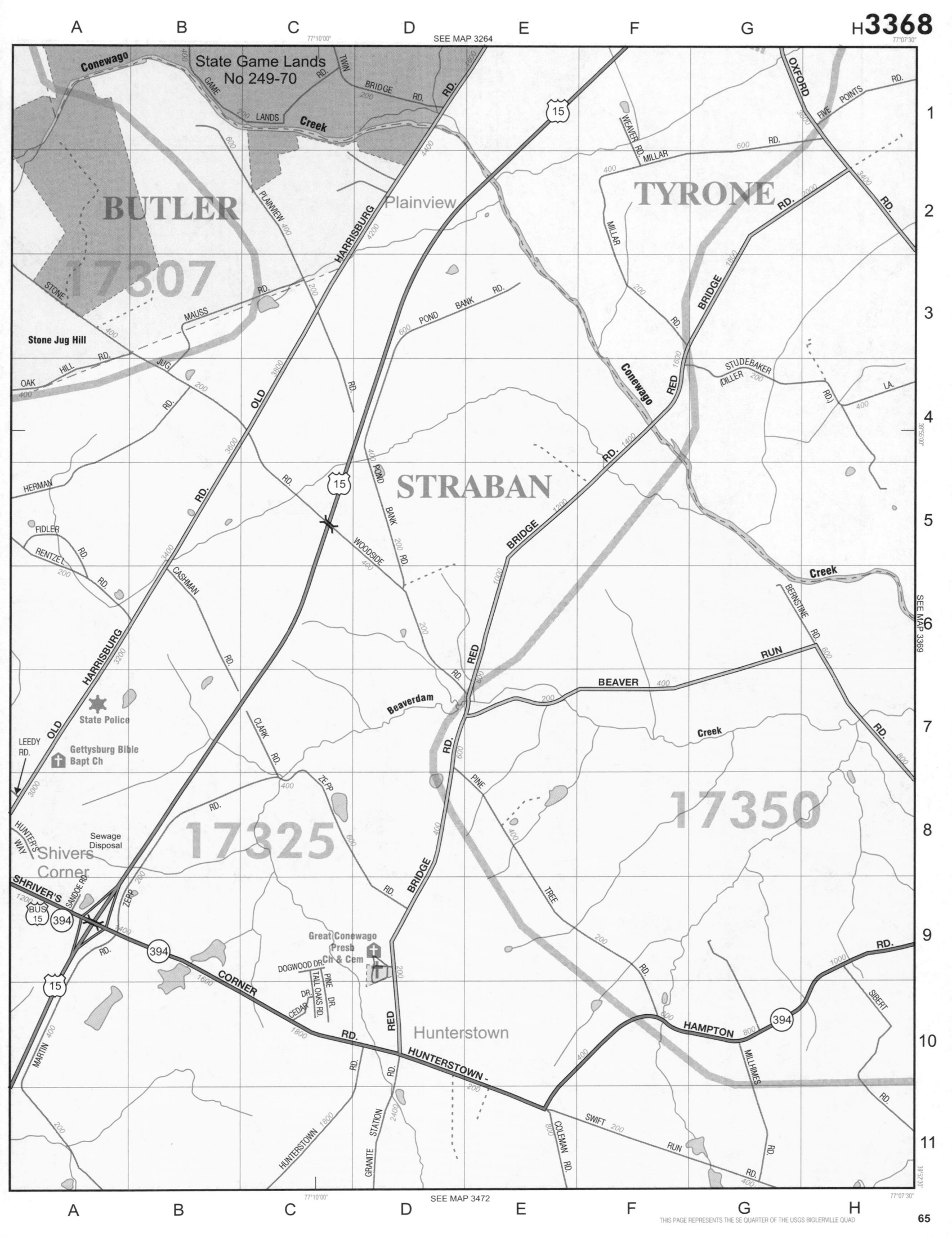

A B C D E F G

77°10'00"   SEE MAP 3264   77°07'30"

Conewago

State Game Lands
No 249-70

TWIN
BRIDGE
200

RD.

15

OXFORD

FIVE POINTS

RD.

1

BUTLER

17307

GAME

LANDS

Creek

Plainview

Plainview

WEAVER RD.

MILLAR

TYRONE

RD.

600

RD.

2

PLAINVIEW

HARRISBURG

4200

MILLAR

RD.

STONE

400

MAUSS
RD.

200

600

POND BANK

RD.

Conewago

RED

BRIDGE

STUDEBAKER
DILLER

200

RD.

LA.

3

Stone Jug Hill

OAK HILL
400

RD.

JUG

200

OLD

3800

RD.

1600

RD.

400

4

HERMAN

RD.

15

POND

STRABAN

BANK

RD.

200

4200

CONEWAGO
RD.
1400

5

FIDLER

RENTZEL RD.

200

CASHMAN

3400

RD.

WOODSIDE
400

200

RD.

BRIDGE

1000

Creek

BERNSTINE RD.
600

SEE MAP 3369

6

HARRISBURG
3200

RD.

400

200

RED

RD.

800

RUN

BEAVER
400

RD.

600

7

LEEDY
RD.

OLD
3000

State Police

Gettysburg Bible
Bapt Ch

CLARK RD.

400

RD.

ZEPP

400

Beaverdam

RD.
600

PINE

Creek

17350

RD.

8

HUNTER'S
WAY

Sewage
Disposal

17325

RD.

RD.

600

BRIDGE
400

RD.

TREE

Shivers
Corner

SHRIVER'S
1200

SANDOE RD.

ZEPP
400

200

200

9

BUS
15

394

394

CORNER

1600

Great Conewago
Presb
Ch & Cem

DOGWOOD DR.

PINE DR

TALL OAKS RD.

DR.

CEDAR

200

RD.

200

RED

RD.

200

HAMPTON

800

394

SIBERT

MILLHIMES

RD.

1000

15

MARTIN
400

RD.

1800

Hunterstown

HUNTERSTOWN

10

HUNTERSTOWN
1800

GRANITE
STATION

2400

RD.

200

SWIFT
200

RUN

COLEMAN RD.
800

RD.

RD.

400

11

77°10'00"   SEE MAP 3472   77°07'30"

A B C D E F G H

THIS PAGE REPRESENTS THE SE QUARTER OF THE USGS BIGLERVILLE QUAD

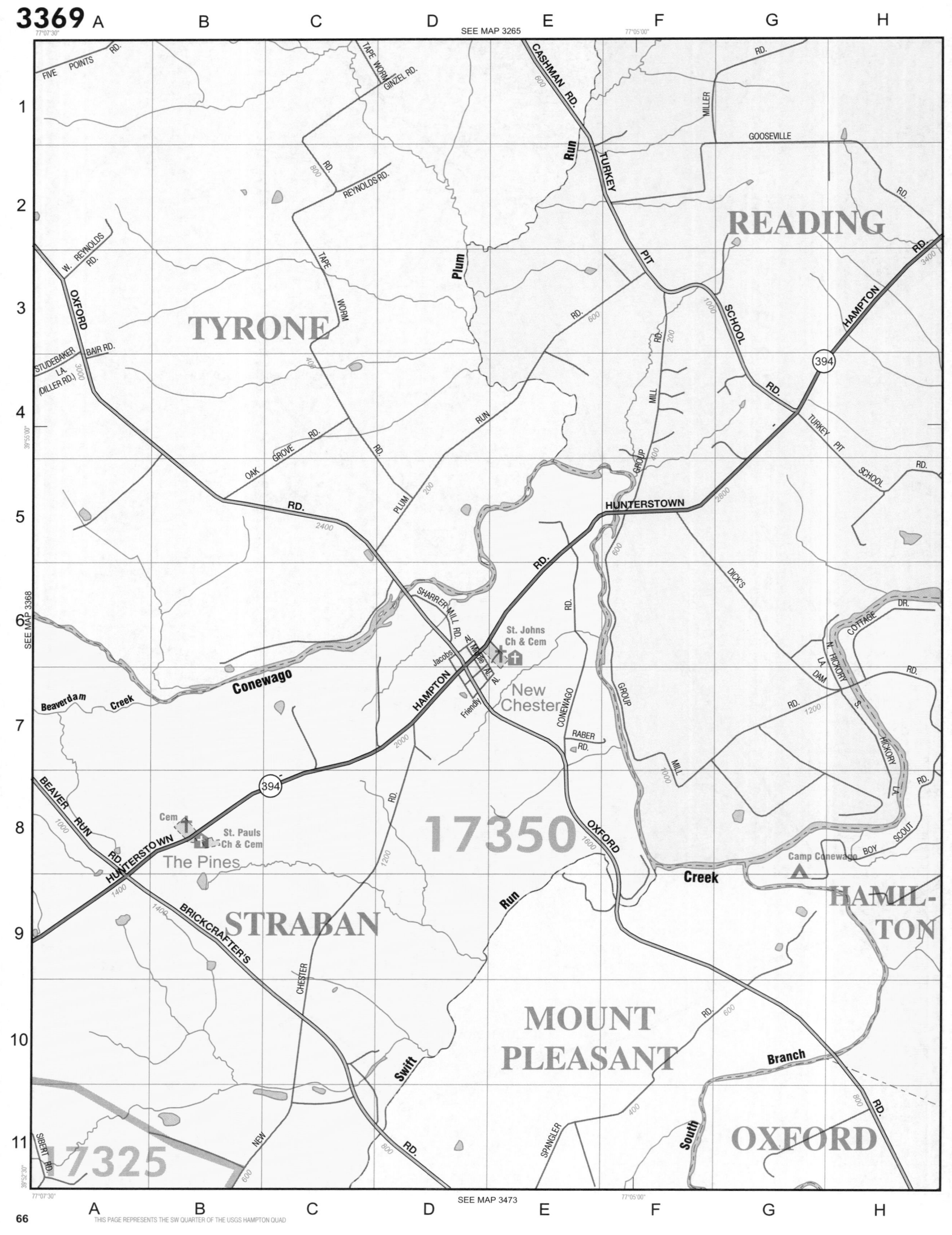

3369 A

REYNOLDS RD.

GINZEL RD.

CASHMAN RD.

FIVE POINTS RD.

W. REYNOLDS RD.

OXFORD

STUDEBAKER LA. (DILLER RD.)

BAIR RD.

TYRONE

TAPE WORM RD.

TAPE WORM

Plum

Run

Turkey Pit

READING

HAMPTON RD.

394

GOOSEVILLE

MILLER RD.

RD.

PLUM RUN RD.

OAK GROVE RD.

RD.

SCHOOL RD.

MILL RD.

GROUP RD.

HUNTERSTOWN

TURKEY PIT SCHOOL RD.

DICK'S

COTTAGE DR.

N. HICKORY LA.

RD.

DAM

Conewago

Beaverdam Creek

SHARRER MILL RD.

N. MOORE LA.

Jacobs

St. Johns
Ch & Cem

HAMPTON

Friendly

New Chester

CONEWAGO

RABER RD.

GROUP RD.

MILL RD.

S. HICKORY LA.

RD.

BOY SCOUT

Camp Conewago

17350

OXFORD RD.

Creek

HAMIL-TON

BEAVER RUN RD.

394

HUNTERSTOWN

Cem

St. Pauls
Ch & Cem

The Pines

BRICKCRAFTER'S

STRABAN

CHESTER

RD.

Run

Swift

MOUNT PLEASANT

Branch

South

OXFORD

NEW RD.

SPANGLER RD.

RD.

17325

SIBERT RD.

THIS PAGE REPRESENTS THE SW QUARTER OF THE USGS HAMPTON QUAD

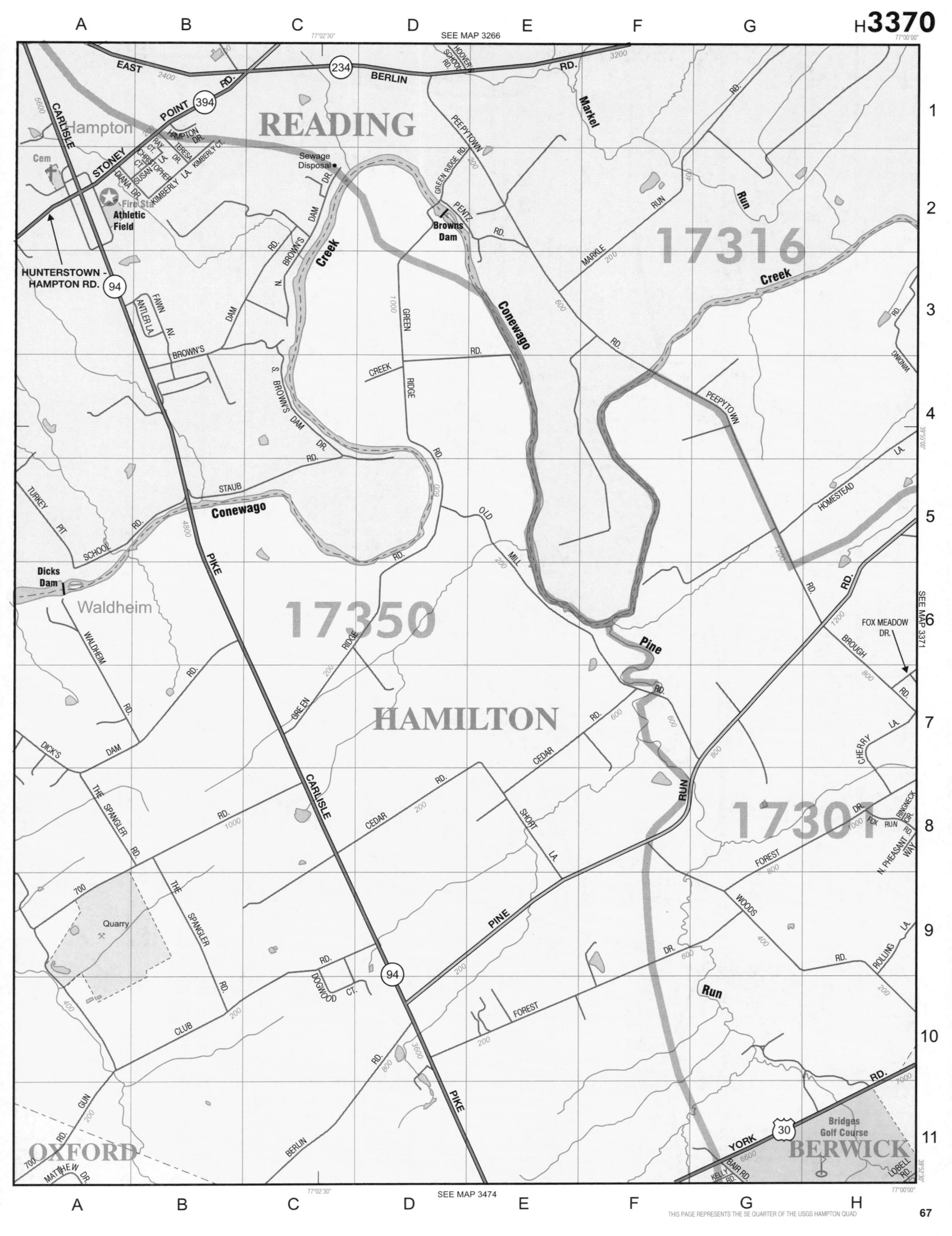

A B C D E F G

1

SEE MAP 3266

EAST

POINT

394

234 BERLIN RD.

Hampton

CARLISLE

Cem

STONEY

Fire Sta.

Athletic
Field

HUNTERSTOWN -
HAMPTON RD. 94

FAWN AV.
ANTLER LA.

BROWN'S

RAY LA.
CHRISTOPHER CT.
SUSAN LA.
KIMBERLY LA. KIMBERLY CT.
TERESA DR.
HAMPTON DR.
DIANA DR.

N. BROWN'S DAM RD.

S. BROWN'S DAM

RD. DAM

Creek

DAM RD.

STAUB

Conewago

READING

Sewage
Disposal

Browns
Dam

PENTZ RD.

GREEN RIDGE RD.

PEEPYTOWN

Markel

MARKLE RUN

17316

RUN

Creek

Conewago

GREEN

RD.

CREEK

RIDGE

RD.

RD.

PEEPYTOWN

WINDING RD.

RD.

HOMESTEAD

RD.

SEE MAP 3371

2

3

4

5

6

TURKEY PIT RD.

SCHOOL

Dicks
Dam

Waldheim

WALDHEIM

RD.

DICK'S RD.

17350

Conewago

PIKE

RIDGE

GREEN

DAM

RD.

OLD MILL RD.

Pine

RD.

RUN

Pine

FOX MEADOW
DR.

RD.

BROUGH

CHERRY LA.

7

HAMILTON

CARLISLE

CEDAR RD.

CEDAR

RD.

SHORT LA.

RD.

RUN

FOX RUN RD.

BINGNECK RD.

17301

8

THE SPANGLER RD.

THE SPANGLER RD.

700

Quarry

RD.

DOGWOOD CT.

94

PINE

DR.

FOREST

WOODS

N. PHEASANT WAY

FOREST RD.

ROLLINS LA.

RD.

9

CLUB

RD.

400

PIKE

BERLIN

3600

Run

94

Forest

RD.

10

GUN RD.

OXFORD

MATTHEW DR.

BERWICK

YORK

30

KELLY RD. BAIR RD.

Bridges
Golf Course

LOBELL
RD.

11

A B C D E F G H

SEE MAP 3474

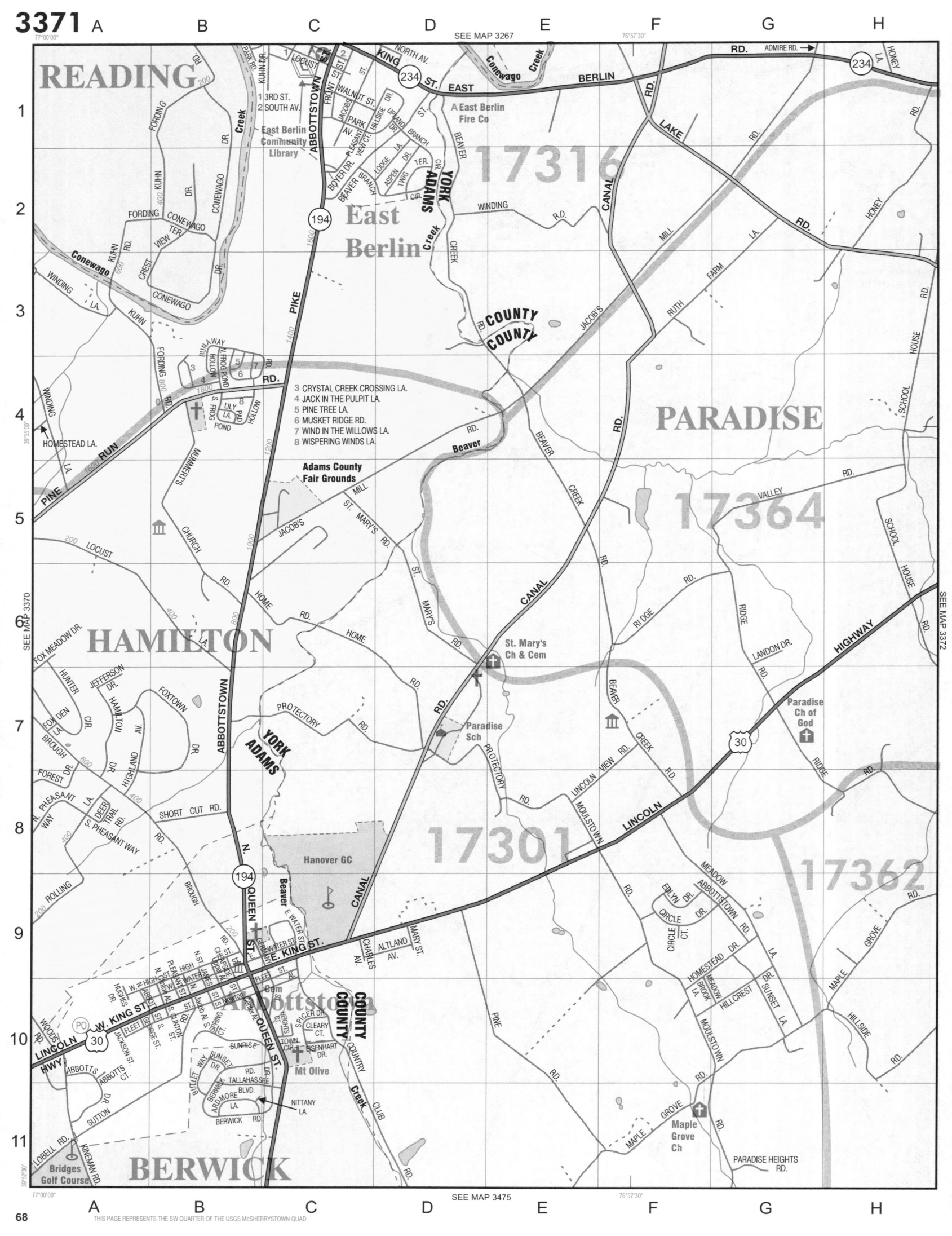

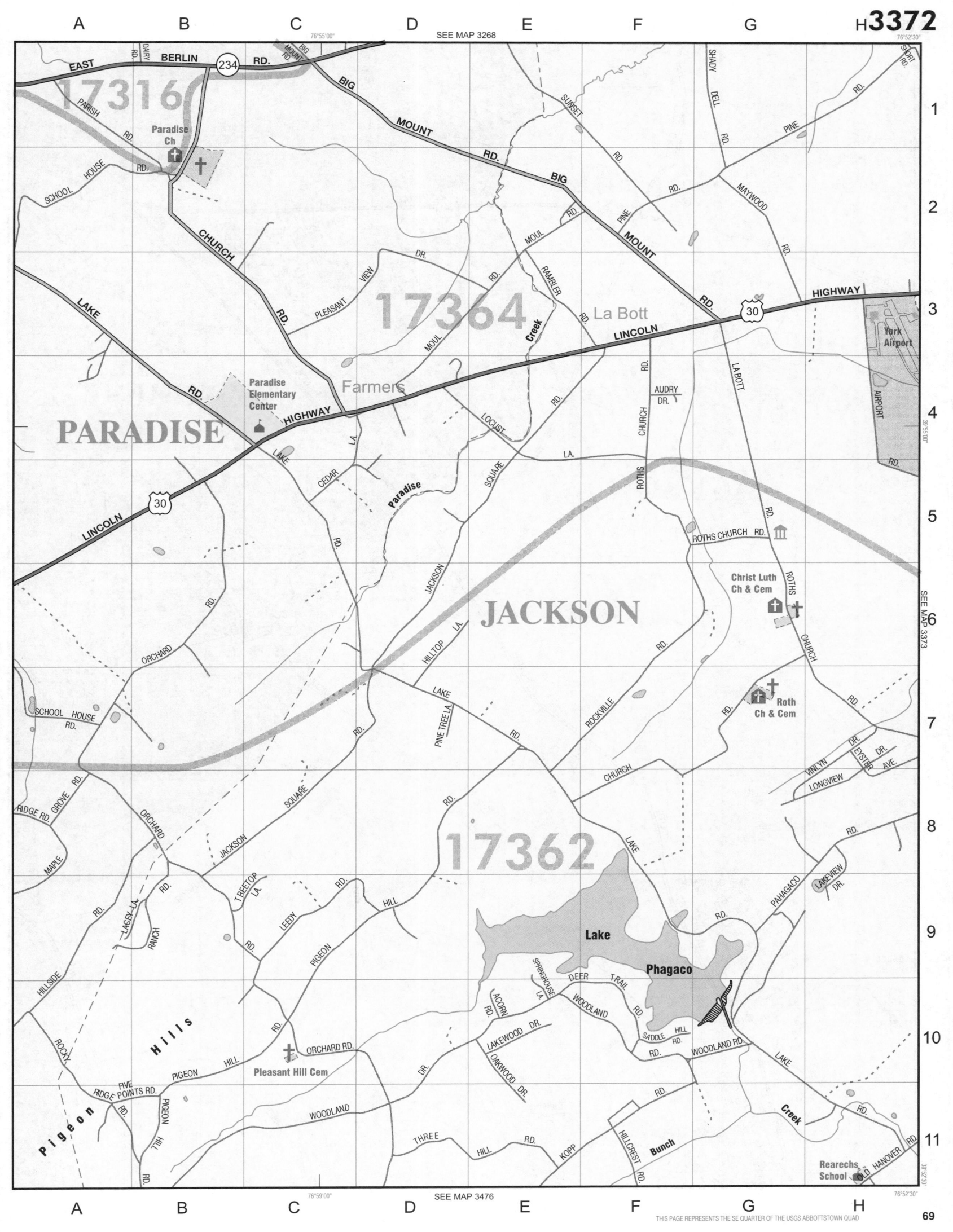

SEE MAP 3268

SEE MAP 3373

SEE MAP 3476

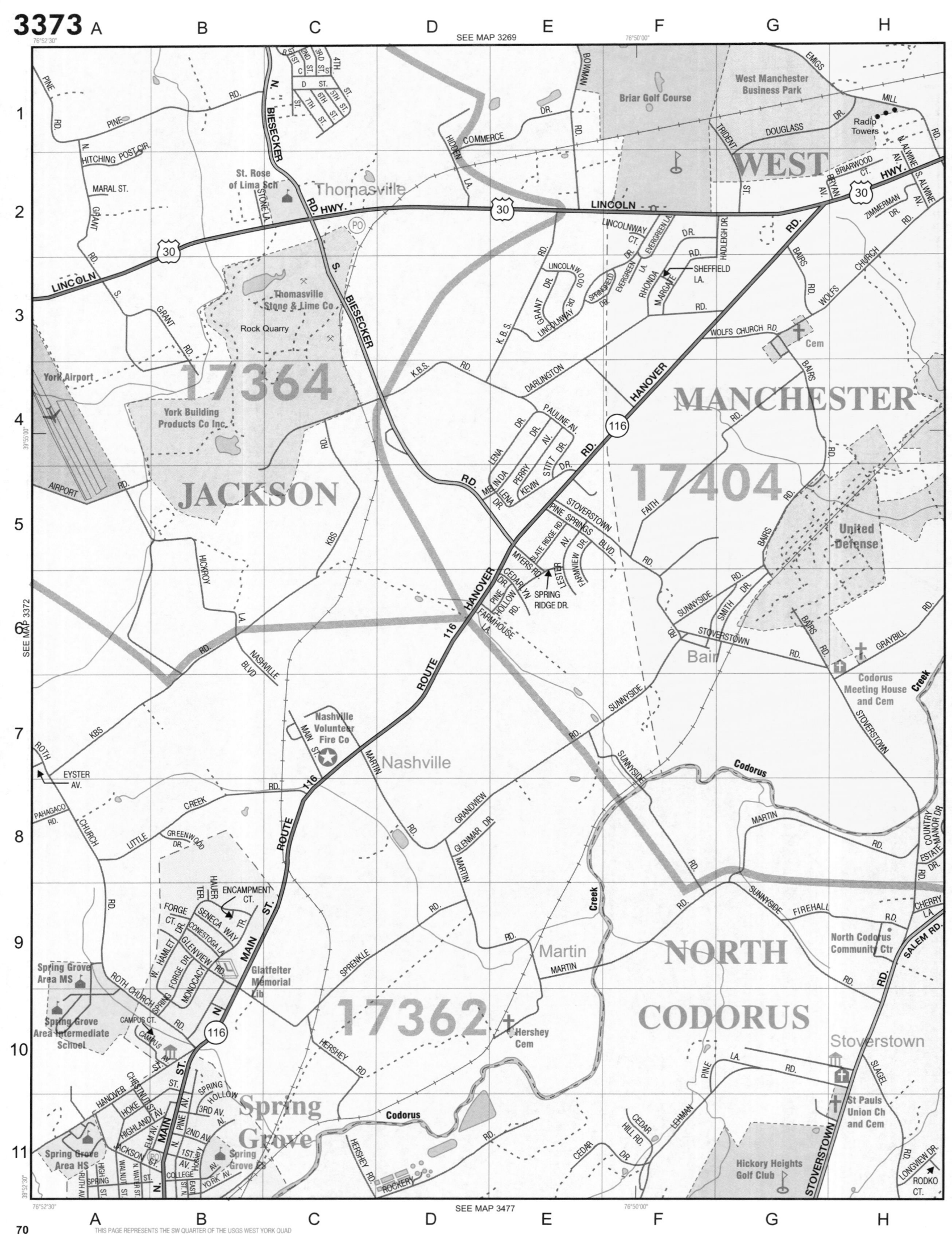

SEE MAP 3269

B C D E F G H

1

PINE RD.

HITCHING POST CIR.

MARAL ST.

GRANT RD.

PINE RD.

N. BIESECKER RD. HWY.

St. Rose of Lima Sch

STONE LA.

Thomasville

2ND ST. 3RD ST. 4TH ST.
D ST.
E ST.
5TH ST.
6TH ST.
7TH ST.

PO

COMMERCE

HIDEN LA.

DR.

BOWMAN

Briar Golf Course

West Manchester Business Park

EMIGS

DOUGLASS

MILL

TRIDENT

WEST

Radio Towers

BRIARWOOD CT.

N. ALWINE AV.

S. ALWINE AV.

30

30

LINCOLN

LINCOLN HWY.

2

LINCOLN

S. BIESECKER RD.

Thomasville Stone & Lime Co

Rock Quarry

GRANT RD.

17364

York Building Products Co Inc.

JACKSON

York Airport

AIRPORT RD.

3

4

HICKROY LA.

KBS RD.

NASHVILLE BLVD

KBS RD.

LINCOLNWAY CT.

EVERGREEN LA.

LINCOLNWAY

DR.

SPRINGFIELD DR.

RHONDA LA.

MARGATE

SHEFFIELD LA.

HADLEIGH DR.

DR.

RD.

LINCOLN WOOD

GRANT DR.

LINCOLNWAY RD.

K.B.S.

DARLINGTON DR.

K.B.S. RD.

RD.

RD.

MELINDA DR.

LENA DR.

PAULINE AV.

PERRY DR.

AV.

KEVIN

STITT DR.

STOVERSTOWN

PINE SPRINGS BLVD.

FARMVIEW DR.

LESTER AV.

MYERS RD.

SLATE RIDGE RD.

CEDARLYN DR.

PINE HOLLOW RD.

FARMHOUSE LA.

SPRING RIDGE DR.

HANOVER RD.

116

MANCHESTER

17404

FAITH RD.

WOLFS CHURCH RD.

WOLFS RD.

Cem

BAIRS RD.

CHURCH RD.

BAIRS RD.

United Defense

BAIRS RD.

SUNNYSIDE DR.

SMITH DR.

GRAYBILL

Codorus Meeting House and Cem

STOVERSTOWN

Creek

5

6

SEE MAP 3372

HANOVER

ROUTE 116

RD.

Bair

STOVERSTOWN RD.

SUNNYSIDE RD.

Codorus

MARTIN RD.

7

ROTH RD.

EYSTER AV.

PAHAGACO RD.

KBS RD.

CHURCH RD.

LITTLE

CREEK RD.

GREENWOOD DR.

Nashville Volunteer Fire Co

MAIN ST.

116

ROUTE 116

Nashville

MARTIN RD.

GRANDVIEW DR.

GLENMAR DR.

MARTIN

RD.

RD.

Creek

SUNNYSIDE RD.

MARTIN RD.

SUNNYSIDE RD.

Codorus

MARTIN

ESTATE MANOR DR.

COUNTRY

8

9

Spring Grove Area MS

Spring Grove Area Intermediate School

ROTH CHURCH RD.

RD.

CAMPUS CT.

HAVER TER.

FORGE CT.

SENECA WAY

CONESTOGA LA.

GLENVIEW RD.

HAMLET

FORGE DR.

MONOCACY

SPRING

ENCAMPMENT CT.

N. MAIN ST.

Glatfelter Memorial Lib

SPRENKLE RD.

RD.

MARTIN

Martin

17362

Hershey Cem

NORTH

CODORUS

FIREHALL RD.

North Codorus Community Ctr

SALEM RD.

CHERRY LA.

10

CAMPUS AV.

116

HANOVER ST.

CHESTNUT ST.

HOKE ST.

HIGHLAND AV.

ELM AV.

PINE AV.

N. MAIN ST.

SPRING

3RD AV.

SPRING HOLLOW

2ND AV.

HERSHEY RD.

Spring Grove

Spring Grove ES

PINE LA.

CEDAR HILL RD.

LEHMAN RD.

CEDAR DR.

Stoverstown

STOVERSTOWN

St Pauls Union Ch and Cem

SLAGEL RD.

LONGVIEW DR.

RODKO CT.

11

Spring Grove Area HS

JACKSON ST.

WALNUT ST.

RUTH AV.

SPRING

HIGH

1ST AV.

YORK AV.

COLLEGE

HERSHEY RD.

Codorus

ROCKERY

Hickory Heights Golf Club

SEE MAP 3477

A B C D E F G H

THIS PAGE REPRESENTS THE SW QUARTER OF THE USGS WEST YORK QUAD

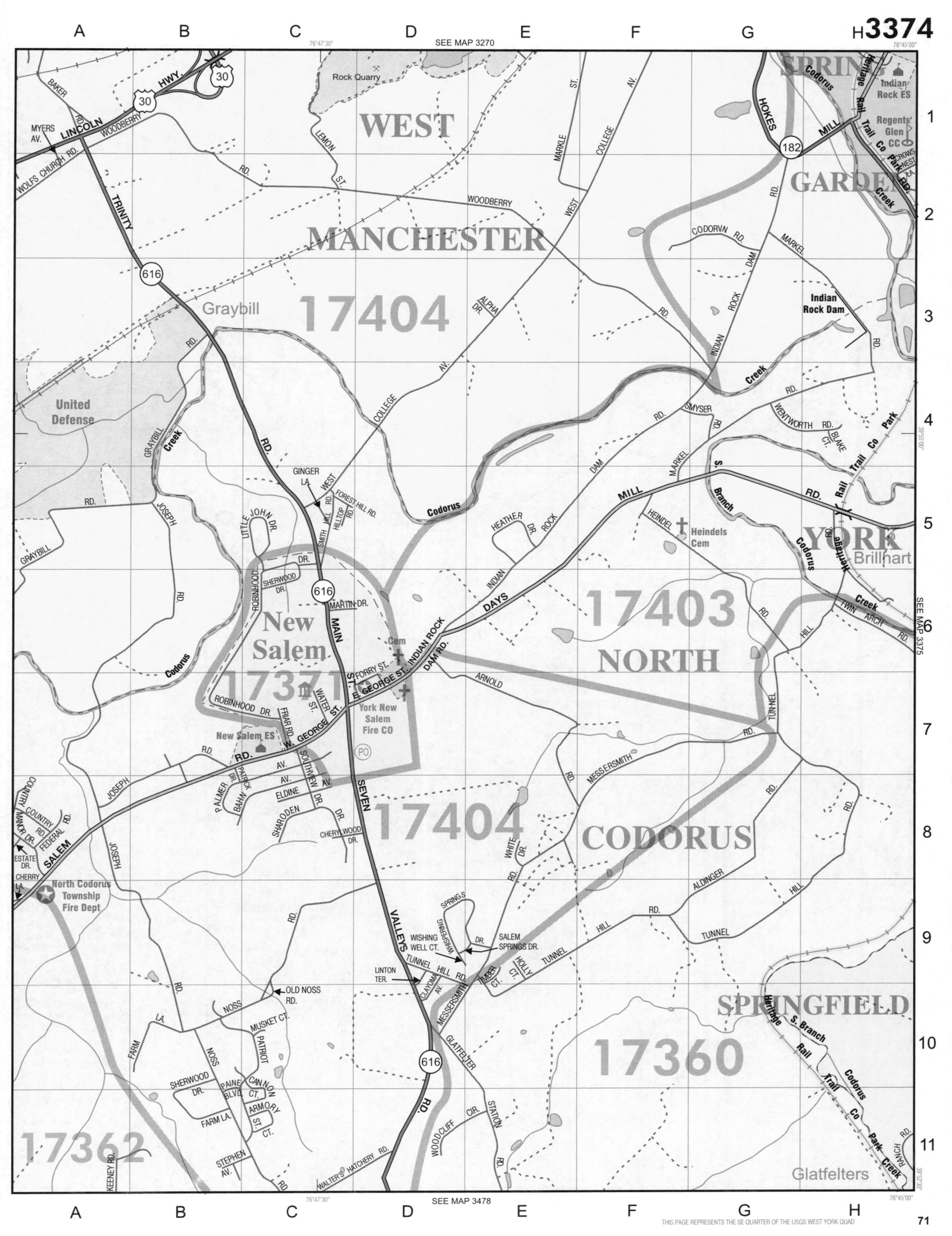

SEE MAP 3270

WEST

MANCHESTER

17404

Rock Quarry

SPRINGS

Indian Rock ES

Regents' Glen CC

Crows Nest

GARDE

Indian Rock Dam

United Defense

Graybill

Codorus Creek

New Salem

17371

York New Salem Fire CO

New Salem ES

PO

17404

17403

NORTH

CODORUS

Heindels Cem

YORK

Brillhart

North Codorus Township Fire Dept

SALEM SPRINGS DR.

WISHING WELL CT.

LINTON TER.

OLD NOSS RD.

SPRINGFIELD

17360

17362

Glatfelters

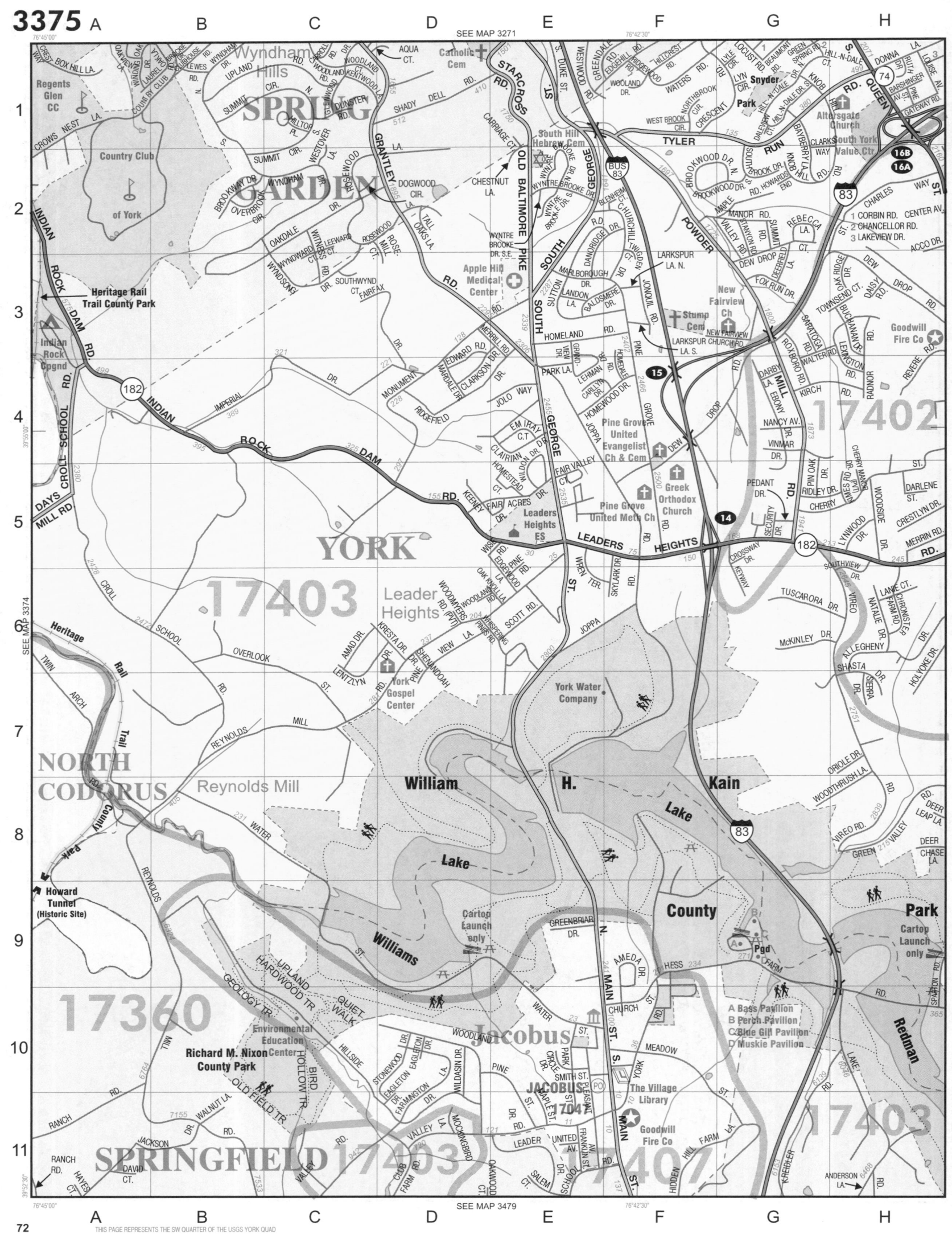

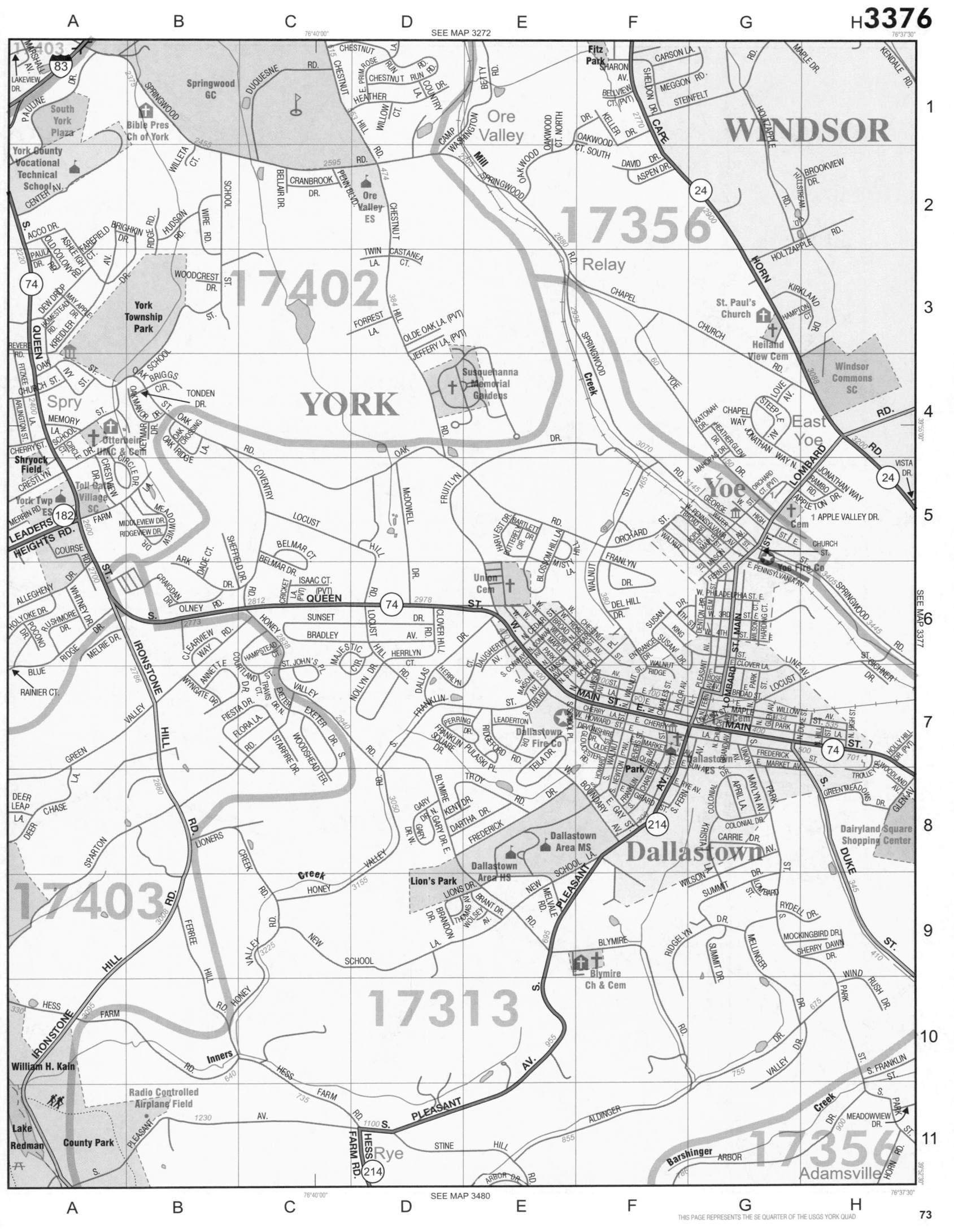

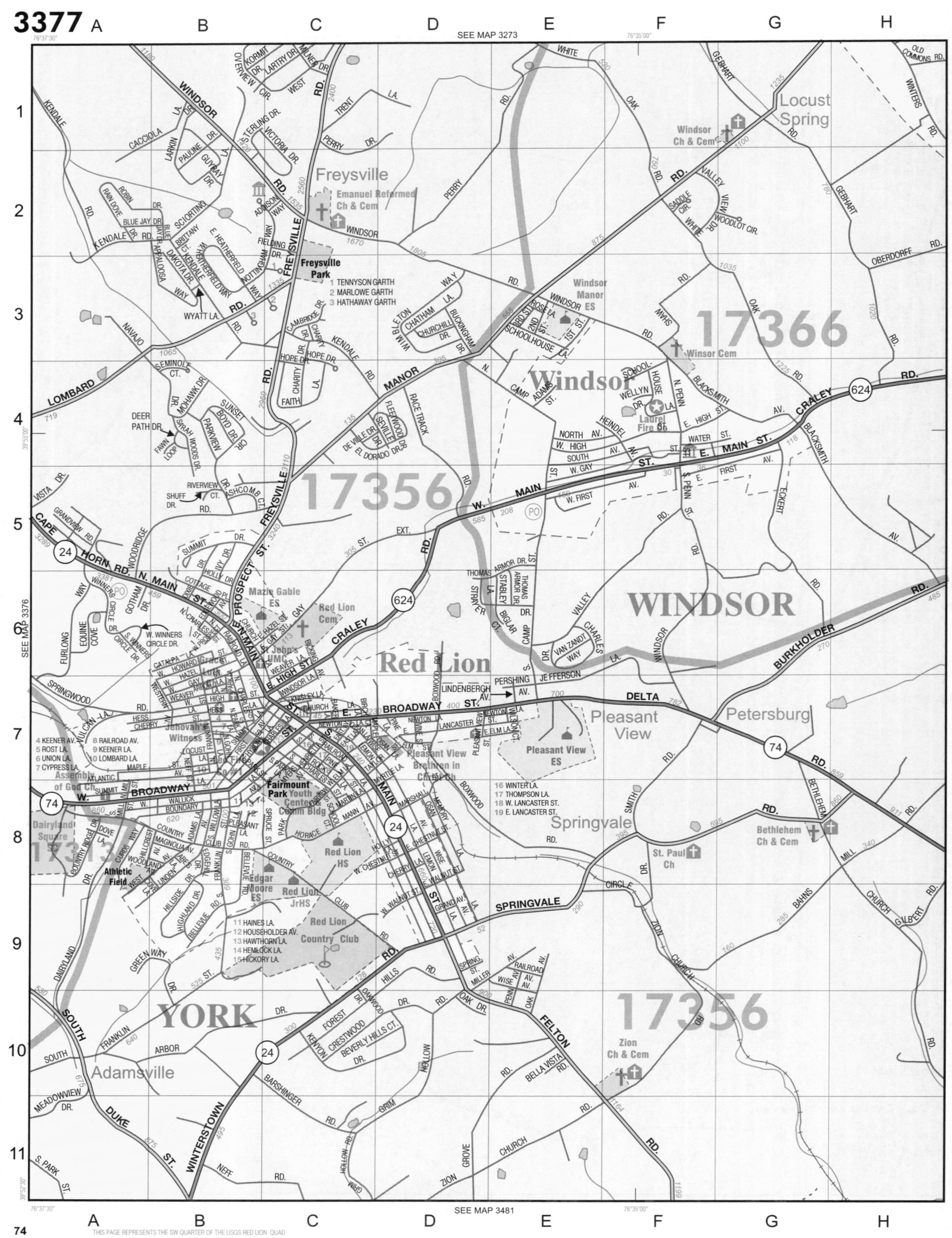

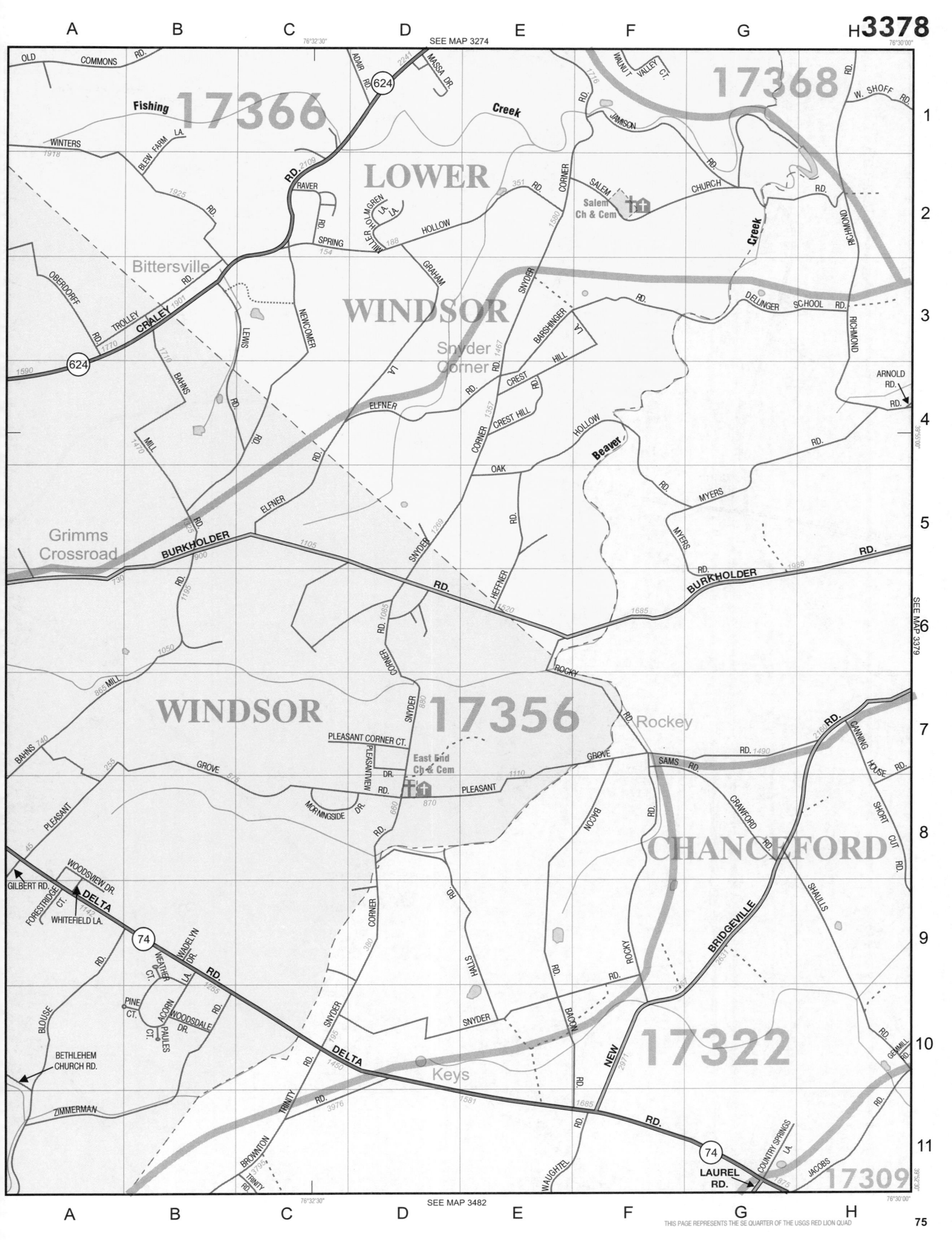

SEE MAP 3274

17366

17368

LOWER

Creek

Fishing

WINDSOR

Snyder
Corner

Bittersville

Grimms
Crossroad

WINDSOR

17356

Rockey

Pleasant Corner Ct.

East End
Ch & Cem

CHANCEFORD

Delta

BRIDGEVILLE

Keys

17322

17309

SEE MAP 3482

THIS PAGE REPRESENTS THE SE QUARTER OF THE USGS RED LION QUAD

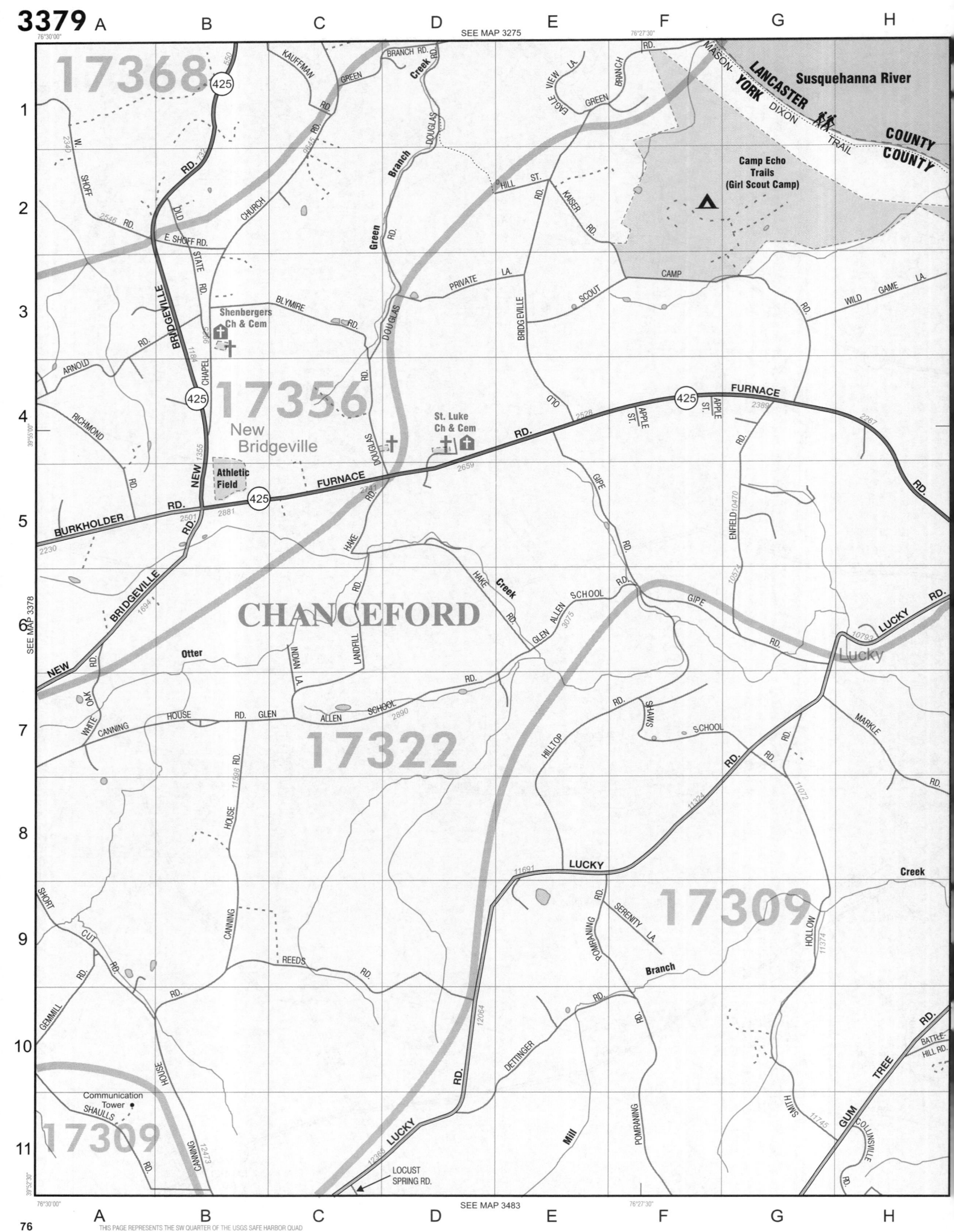

17368

425

SEE MAP 3275

KAUFFMAN

GREEN

BRANCH RD.

Creek RD.

DOUGLAS

EAGLE VIEW LA.

GREEN

BRANCH

MASON-DIXON

LANCASTER

Susquehanna River

YORK

DIXON

COUNTY

COUNTY

TRAIL

Camp Echo
Trails
(Girl Scout Camp)

W.

SHOFF

RD.

CHURCH

HILL ST.

Green Branch

RD.

KAISER RD.

E. SHOFF RD.

BRIDGEVILLE

OLD STATE RD.

Shenbergers
Ch & Cem

BLYMIRE

RD.

PRIVATE LA.

DOUGLAS

SCOUT

BRIDGEVILLE

CAMP

WILD GAME LA.

ARNOLD

CHAPEL

425

17356

New
Bridgeville

RICHMOND

NEW

DOUGLAS

St. Luke
Ch & Cem

Athletic
Field

FURNACE

425

FURNACE

425

APPLE ST.

APPLE ST.

RD.

OLD

RD.

ENFIELD

RD.

BURKHOLDER

RD.

HAKE

GIPE

RD.

NEW

BRIDGEVILLE

CHANCEFORD

Creek

HAKE

RD.

ALLEN SCHOOL

GLEN

GIPE

RD.

LUCKY RD.

SEE MAP 3378

Otter

INDIAN LA.

RD.

LANDFILL

RD.

SCHOOL

Lucky

WHITE OAK RD.

CANNING

HOUSE

RD.

GLEN

ALLEN

SCHOOL

RD.

SHAWS

MARKLE

17322

HILLTOP

SCHOOL

RD.

HOUSE

RD.

RD.

LUCKY

RD.

Creek

SHORT

CANNING

RD.

REEDS

RD.

LUCKY

POMRANING

SERENITY LA.

17309

HOLLOW

GEMMILL

CUT RD.

RD.

Branch

RD.

POMRANING

HOUSE

LUCKY

RD.

DETTINGER

GUM TREE

SMITH

BATTLE HILL RD.

Communication
Tower

SHAULLS

CANNING

RD.

Mill

POMRANING

COLLINSVILLE RD.

17309

LOCUST
SPRING RD.

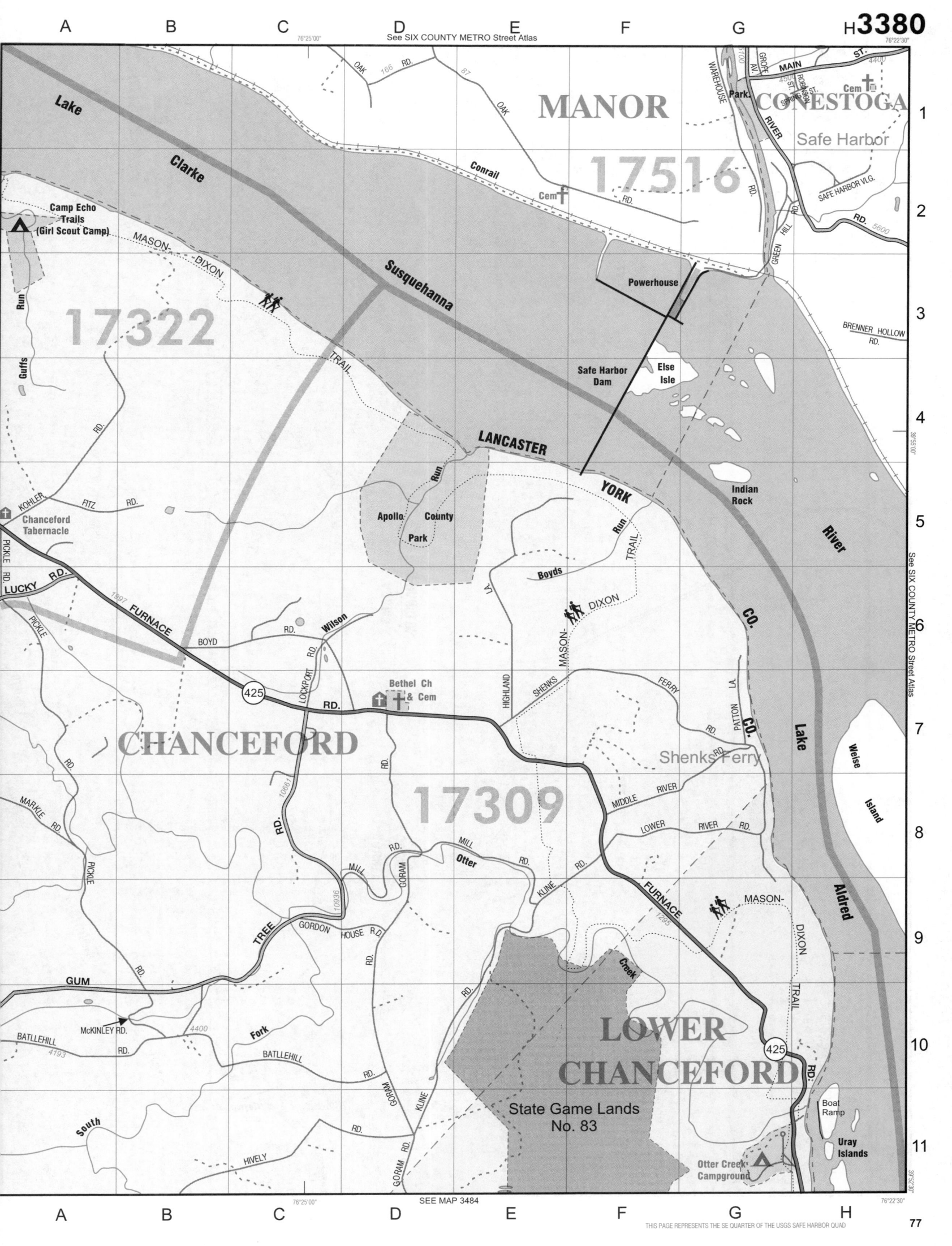

A   B   C   D   E   F   G

See SIX COUNTY METRO Street Atlas

76°25'00"

MANOR

17516

CONESTOGA

Safe Harbor

SAFE HARBOR VLG.

1

Lake

Clarke

Conrail

RD.

Cem

SAFE HARBOR RD. 5600

2

Camp Echo
Trails
(Girl Scout Camp)

MASON- DIXON

Susquehanna

Powerhouse

BRENNER HOLLOW
RD.

3

Run

17322

TRAIL

Safe Harbor
Dam

Else
Isle

4

Guffs

LANCASTER

YORK

Indian
Rock

River

39°55'00"

KOHLER

FITZ RD.

RD.

Run

Apollo County

Park

Boyds

Run

TRAIL

MASON- DIXON

5

Chanceford
Tabernacle

PICKLE RD.

Lucky RD.

FURNACE

Wilson
RD.

BOYD

LOCKPORT RD.

RD.

CO.

CO.

Lake

6

PICKLE

425

Bethel Ch
& Cem

HIGHLAND

SHENKS

MASON-

FERRY

PATTON LA.

RD.

Weise
Island

7

CHANCEFORD

RD.

Shenks Ferry

MARKLE
RD.

17309

MIDDLE

RIVER

LOWER RIVER RD.

8

PICKLE

MILL

GORAM

Otter

RD.

KLINE

RD.

FURNACE

MASON-

Aldred

9

TREE

GORDON HOUSE RD.

RD.

Creek

DIXON TRAIL

GUM

McKINLEY RD.

Fork

RD.

KLINE

LOWER

CHANCEFORD

425

10

BATTLEHILL

4193

RD.

BATTLEHILL

RD.

GORAM RD.

State Game Lands
No. 83

Boat
Ramp

11

South

HIVELY

GORAM RD.

Otter Creek
Campground

Uray
Islands

39°52'30"

A   B   C   D   E   F   G   H

76°25'00"

SEE MAP 3484

76°22'30"

See SIX COUNTY METRO Street Atlas

THIS PAGE REPRESENTS THE SE QUARTER OF THE USGS SAFE HARBOR QUAD

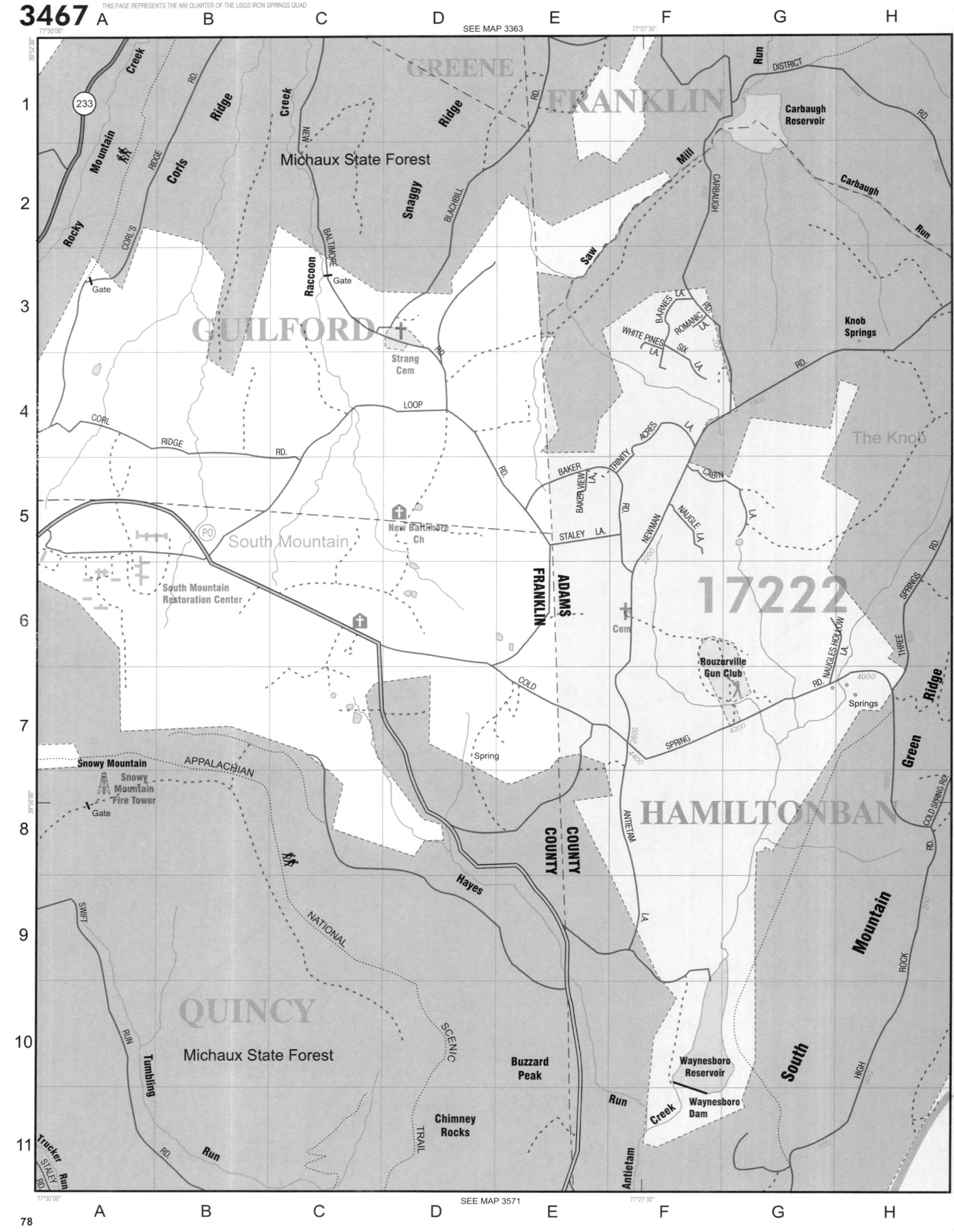

THIS PAGE REPRESENTS THE NW QUARTER OF THE USGS IRON SPRINGS QUAD

77°30'00"

SEE MAP 3363

77°27'30"

A · B · C · D · E · F · G · H

GREENE

FRANKLIN

Carbaugh Reservoir

233

Michaux State Forest

Mountain

Creek

Ridge

Corls

Creek

New

Snaggy

Ridge

BLACHBILL

Saw

Mill

CARBAUGH

Carbaugh Run

Run

District

RD.

RIDGE

CORL'S

Rocky

Gate

Raccoon

BALTIMORE

Gate

BARNES LA.

ROMANIC LA.

WHITE PINES LA.

SIX LA.

RD.

Knob Springs

GUILFORD

Strang Cem

RD.

LOOP

CORL

RIDGE

RD.

RD.

BAKER

BAKER VIEW LA.

TRINITY ACRES LA.

CABIN

NAUGLE LA

LA.

The Knob

PO

South Mountain

New Baltimore Ch

RD.

STALEY LA.

FRANKLIN

ADAMS

NEWMAN

17222

SPRINGS RD.

South Mountain Restoration Center

Cem

Rouzerville Gun Club

RD. NAUGLES HOLLOW LA.

Springs

THREE

4000

4200

COLD

Spring

Green Ridge

Snowy Mountain

APPALACHIAN

Snowy Mountain Fire Tower

Gate

Spring

ANTIETAM

LA.

HAMILTONBAN

COLD SPRING RD.

SWIFT

Hayes

COUNTY COUNTY

NATIONAL

QUINCY

Michaux State Forest

SCENIC

Buzzard Peak

Run

Creek

Waynesboro Reservoir

Waynesboro Dam

South Mountain

ROCK

HIGH

Tumbling

RUN

RD.

Run

Chimney Rocks

TRAIL

Antietam

Trucker Run

STALEY RD.

77°30'00"

SEE MAP 3571

77°27'30"

A · B · C · D · E · F · G · H

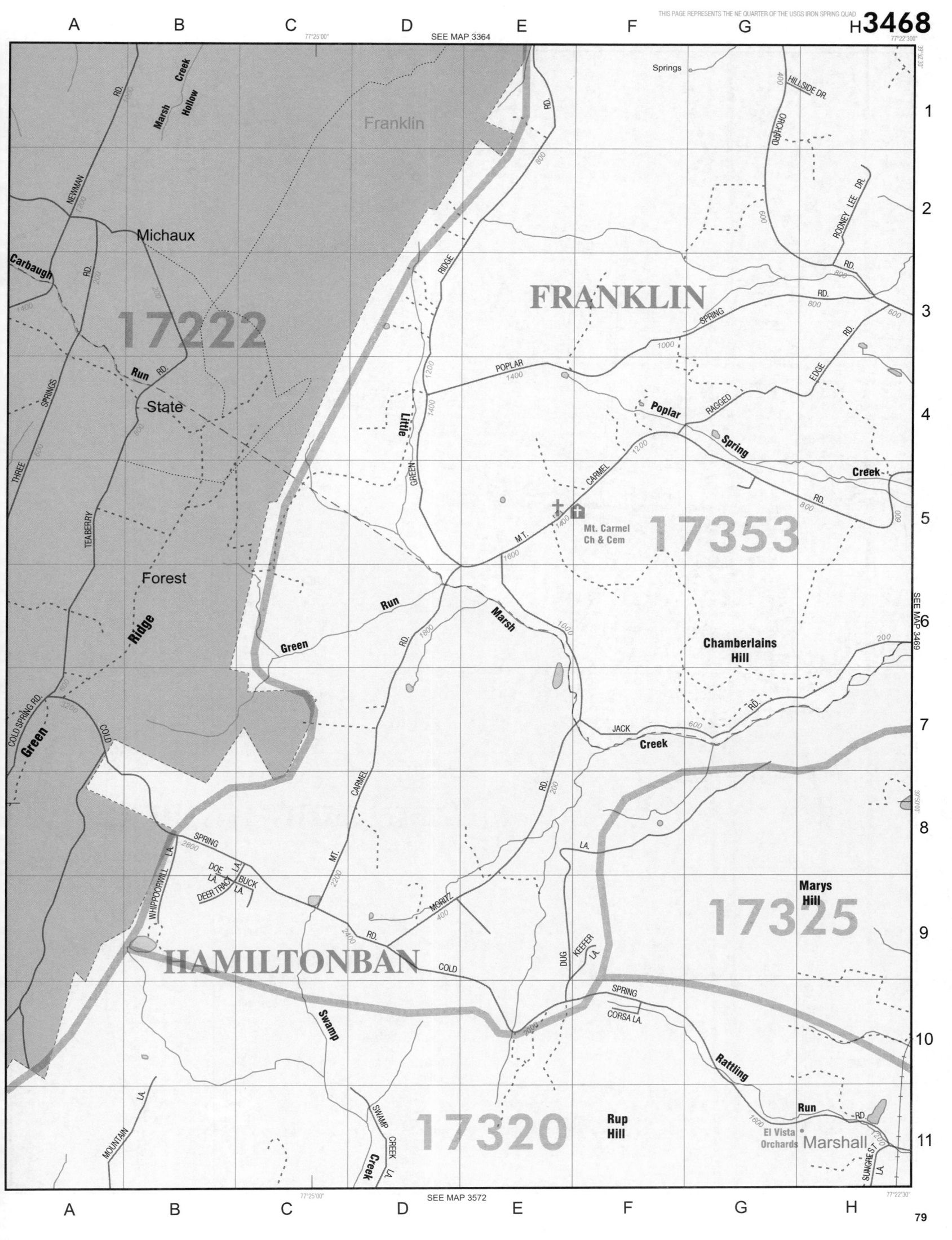

A   B   C   D   E   F   G   H

SEE MAP 3364

77°25'00"

77°22'300"

Springs

HILLSIDE DR.

1

Franklin

400

ORCHARD

600

RODNEY LEE DR.

2

Carbaugh

Michaux

NEWMAN

RD.

17222

FRANKLIN

RD.

800

RD.

800

600

3

RUN

RD.

SPRING

1000

RD.

EDGE

State

RIDGE

POPLAR

1400

Poplar

RAGGED

4

THREE

SPRINGS

TEABERRY

Little

GREEN

1200

1400

1200

CARMEL

Poplar

Spring

Creek

RD.

800

600

Forest

Mt. Carmel

17353

5

Ridge

MT.

1400

Ch & Cem

1600

COLD SPRING RD.

Green

Run

Marsh

1000

Chamberlains

Hill

200

6

Green

RD.

1800

RD.

600

Green

COLD

CARMEL

JACK

Creek

7

SPRING

LA.

RD.

200

8

WHIPPOORWILL LA.

2800

DOE

LA.

BUCK

LA.

MT.

LA.

Marys

Hill

DEER TRACT

LA.

2200

MORITZ

400

17325

9

HAMILTONBAN

2400

RD.

DUG

KEEFER

LA.

SPRING

SWAMP

COLD

SPRING

CORSA LA.

Rattling

10

2000

MOUNTAIN

LA.

SWAMP

CREEK

LA.

17320

Rup

Hill

Run

RD.

1600

El Vista

Orchards

Marshall

SUNCREST LA.

11

Creek

SEE MAP 3572

77°25'00"

77°22'30"

A   B   C   D   E   F   G   H

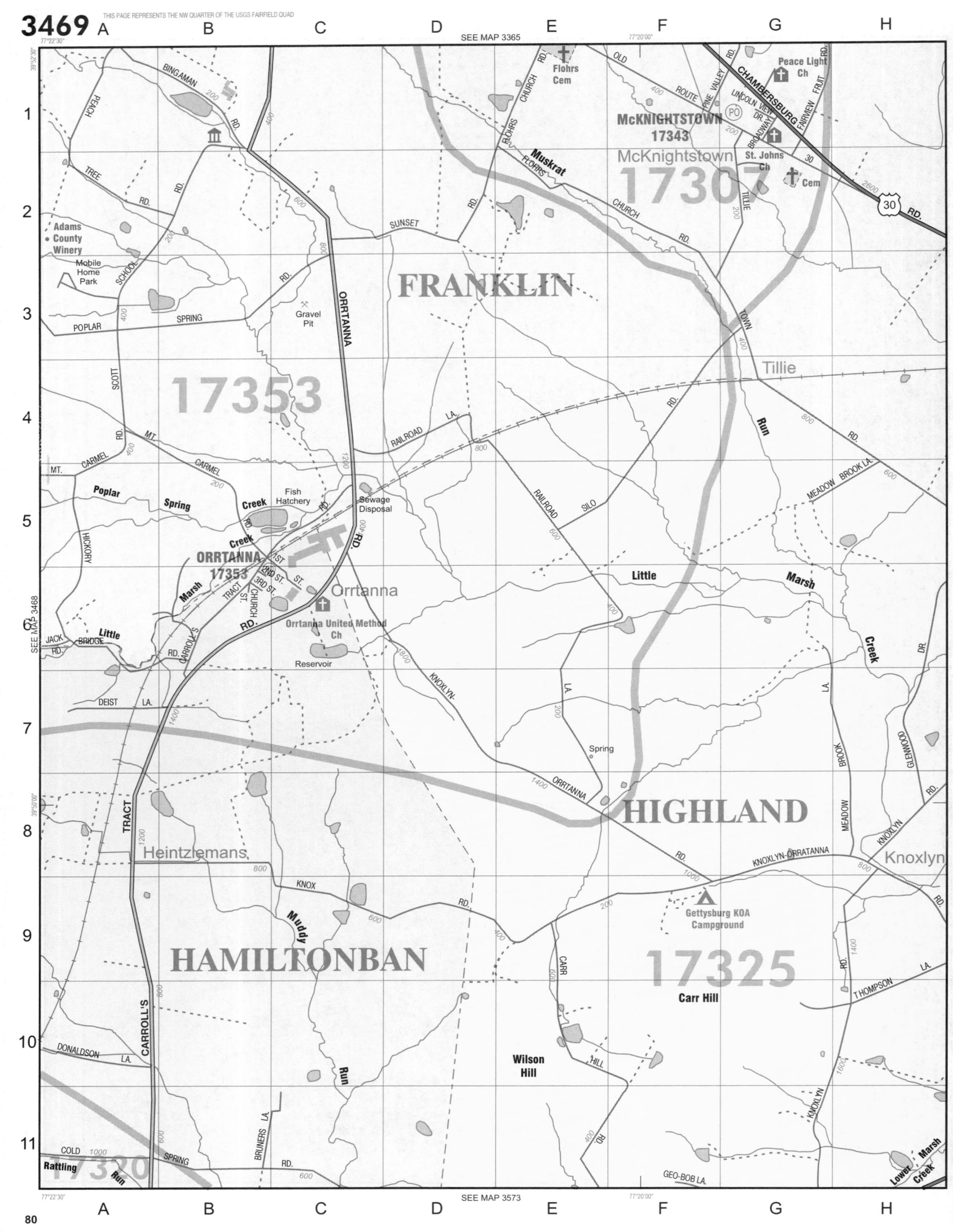

THIS PAGE REPRESENTS THE NW QUARTER OF THE USGS FAIRFIELD QUAD

SEE MAP 3365

A B C D E F G H

1
2
3
4
5
6
7
8
9
10
11

PEACH TREE RD.

BINGAMAN RD.

Adams County Winery

Mobile Home Park

SCHOOL RD.

POPLAR

SPRING

ORRTANNA RD.

Gravel Pit

SUNSET

FRANKLIN

17353

SCOTT RD.

MT. CARMEL RD.

CARMEL RD.

Poplar Spring

Creek

Fish Hatchery

Sewage Disposal

HICKORY

Creek

ORRTANNA 17353

Marsh

1ST ST.
2ND ST.
3RD ST.
CHURCH ST.
TRACT

Orrtanna

RD.

Orrtanna United Method Ch

Reservoir

Little

JACK RD.

BRIDGE

CARROLL'S RD.

DEIST LA.

RAILROAD LA.

RAILROAD RD.

SILO

KNOXLYN

LA.

ORRTANNA

Spring

HIGHLAND

Little

Marsh

Creek

MEADOW BROOK LA.

Run

Tillie

TOWN RD.

CHURCH RD.

FLOHRS

Flohrs Cem

Muskrat

OLD ROUTE 30

PINE VALLEY RD.

CHAMBERSBURG RD.

McKNIGHTSTOWN 17343

McKnightstown 17307

LINCOLN DR.
BROADWAY

PO

St. Johns Ch

Peace Light Ch

Cem

FAIRVIEW
FRUIT

30

2600

30 RD.

TILLIE

TRACT

HEINTZLEMANS

Muddy

KNOX

Run

HAMILTONBAN

800

600

KNOXLYN-ORRATANNA

Knoxlyn

Gettysburg KOA Campground

17325

CARR HILL

Carr Hill

Wilson Hill

MEADOW BROOK LA.

KNOXLYN RD.

GLENWOOD RD.

THOMPSON LA.

CARROLL'S

DONALDSON LA.

SPRING RD.

BRUNERS LA.

COLD SPRING

Rattling Run

17320

GEO-BOB LA.

Lower Marsh Creek

SEE MAP 3573

SEE MAP 3468

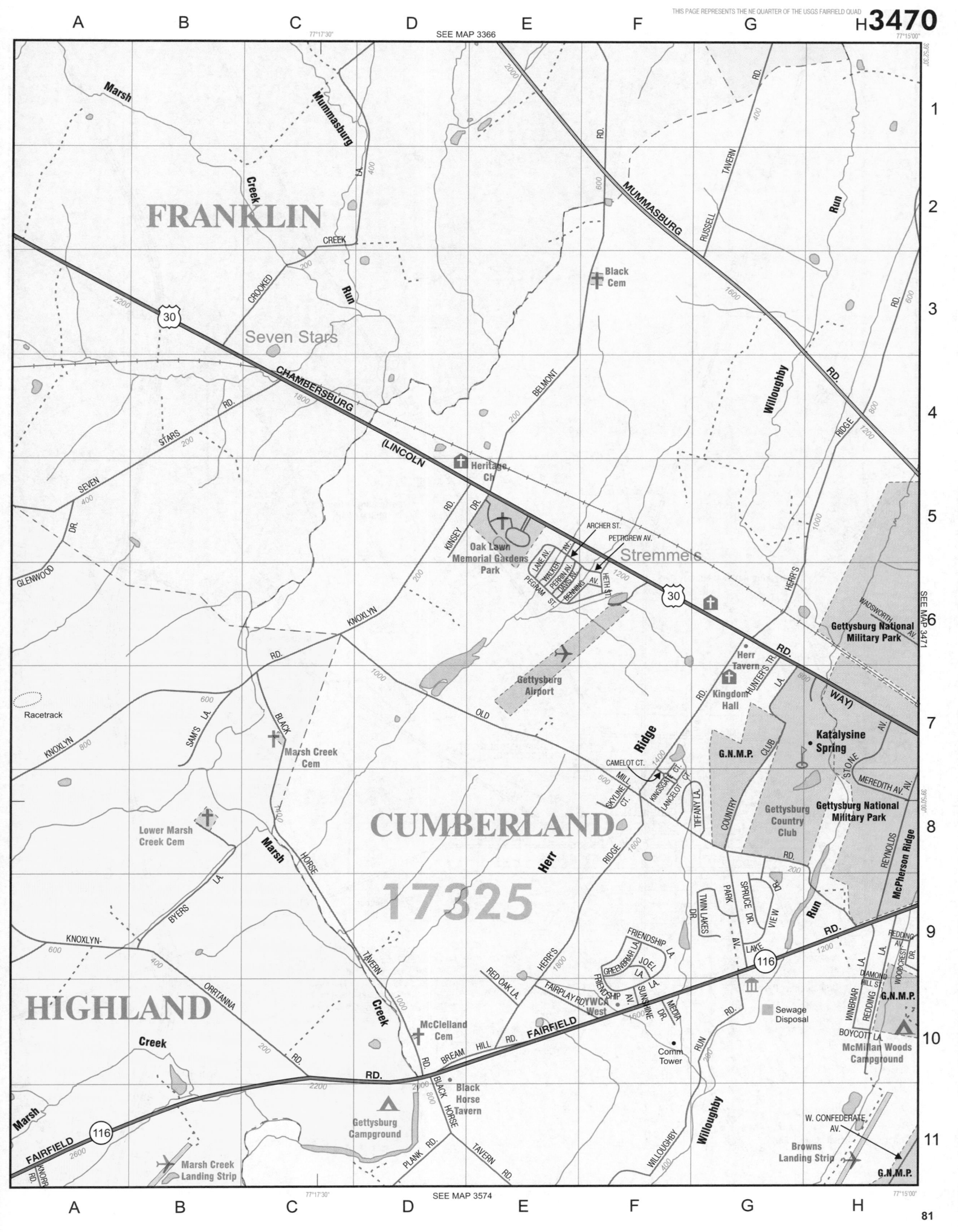

A B C D E F G H

SEE MAP 3366

77°17'30"   77°15'00"

1
2
3
4
5
6
7
8
9
10
11

FRANKLIN

Marsh
Creek
Mummasburg
CREEK
CROOKED
Run
Seven Stars
30
CHAMBERSBURG
STARS
SEVEN
DR.
GLENWOOD
KNOXLYN
RD.
KINSEY
DR.
Oak Lawn
Memorial Gardens
Park
Heritage
Ch.
(LINCOLN

MUMMASBURG
Black
Cem
RUSSELL
TAVERN
Willoughby
RD.
RIDGE
Run

Stremmels
ARCHER ST.
PETTIGREW AV.
LANE AV.
WALKER
AV.
PERRIN AV.
DOOSTAL
BENNING
PEGRAM
ST.
HETH ST.
30
AV.
Gettysburg
Airport
OLD
Ridge
Herr
Tavern
Kingdom
Hall
HUNTER'S TR.
RD.
LA.
WAY)
HERR'S
AV.
RD.
Gettysburg National
Military Park
WADSWORTH
AV.
SEE MAP 3471

**Katalysine
Spring**

G.N.M.P.
Gettysburg
Country
Club
Gettysburg National
Military Park
MEREDITH AV.
STONE
CLUB
COUNTRY
RD.
REYNOLDS
McPherson Ridge

CUMBERLAND
17325
Herr

Racetrack
KNOXLYN
SAM'S LA.
BLACK
Marsh Creek
Cem
Lower Marsh
Creek Cem
Marsh
HORSE
BYERS LA.
KNOXLYN-
ORRTANNA
TAVERN
Creek
McClelland
Cem
BREAM
CAMELOT CT.
MILL
SKYLINE CT.
KINGSGATE CT.
LANCELOT CT.
TIFFANY LA.
RIDGE
PARK
TWIN LAKES
SPRUCE DR.
VIEW DR.
LAKE
AV.
FRIENDSHIP LA.
GREENBRIAR LA.
JOEL
LA.
FRIENDSHIP
RED OAK LA.
FAIRPLAY RD.
YWCA
West
SUNSHINE
AV.
MEDIA
DR.
116
Run
RD.
Sewage
Disposal
Comm
Tower
HILL
RD.
FAIRFIELD
Run

HIGHLAND
Creek
Marsh
116
FAIRFIELD
KNOXLYN
RD.
PLANK RD.
BLACK HORSE
Black
Horse
Tavern
Gettysburg
Campground
Marsh Creek
Landing Strip
TAVERN
RD.
Willoughby
Willoughby

WINBRIAR
REDDING
LA.
REDDING
AV.
WOODCREST
DR.
DIAMOND
HILL ST.
BOYCOTT LA.
G.N.M.P.
McMillan Woods
Campground
W. CONFEDERATE
AV.
Browns
Landing Strip
G.N.M.P.

SEE MAP 3574

77°17'30"   77°15'00"

CUMBERLAND

STRABAN

Gettysburg National Military Park

Gettysburg

17325

See Enlargement on page 97

Gettysburg National Military Park

MOUNT JOY

See Grid C-8
1 MUMMASBURG ST.
2 CHAMBERSBURG ST.
3 LINCOLN SQ.

A Gettysburg Visitor Ctr.
B Lincoln Room Ctr.
C Gettysburg Battlefield Tape Tour
D Jennie Wade House Museum
E Soldier's National Museum
F Dobbin House Tavern Historical Site
G National Civil War Wax Museum

SEE MAP 3367
SEE MAP 3575
SEE MAP 3470

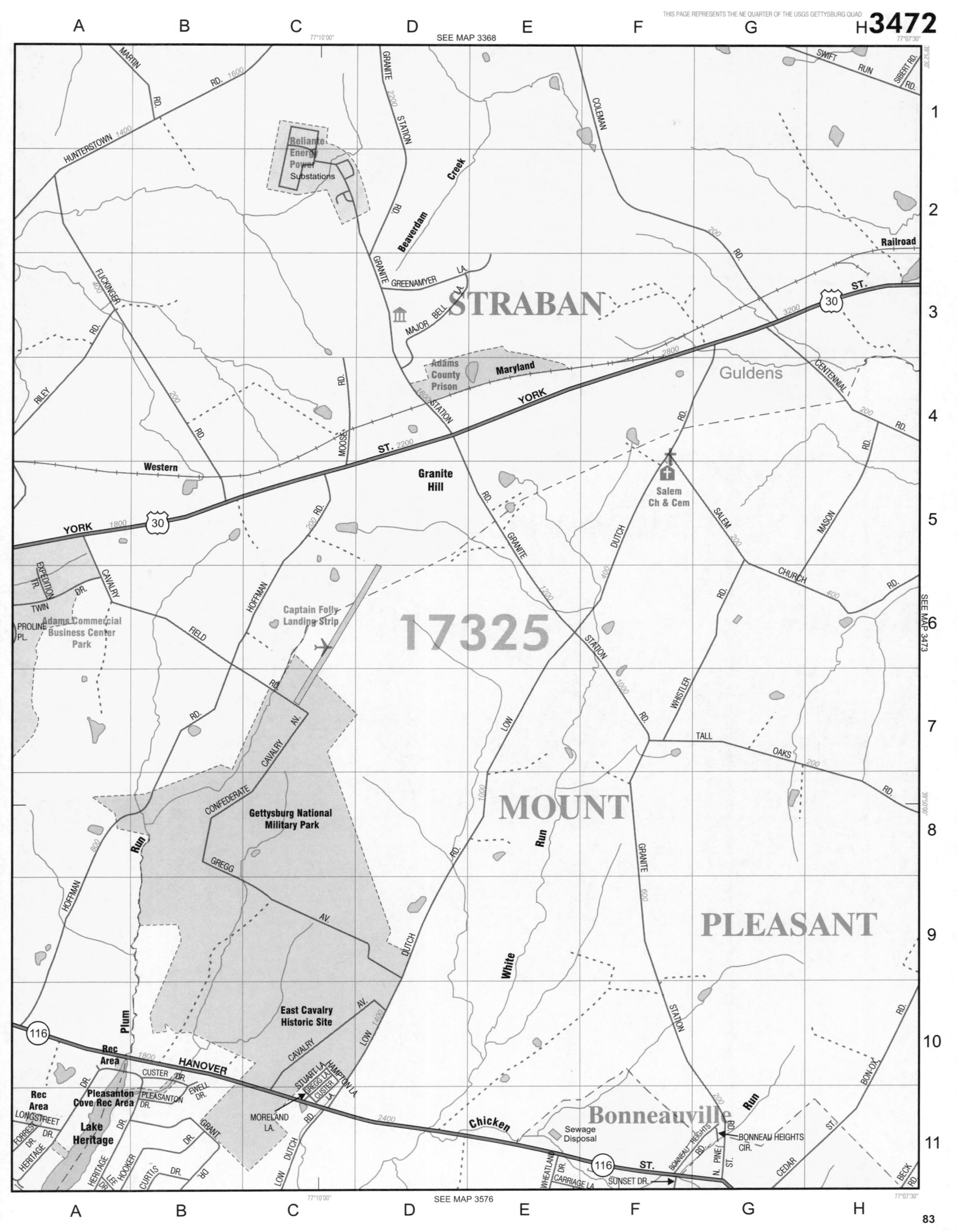

A   B   C   D   E   F   G   H

77°10'00"   SEE MAP 3368

STRABAN

Reliante
Energy
Power Substations

Beaverdam Creek

Railroad

30   ST.

Guldens

Adams
County
Prison

Maryland

YORK   ST.

Granite
Hill

Salem
Ch & Cem

Western

YORK   30

Adams Commercial
Business Center
Park

Captain Folly
Landing Strip

17325

MOUNT

Gettysburg National
Military Park

PLEASANT

East Cavalry
Historic Site

116

Rec
Area

HANOVER

Rec
Area

Pleasanton
Cove Rec Area

Lake
Heritage

Pleasanton

MORELAND
LA.

Chicken

Sewage
Disposal

Bonneauville

Bonneau Heights
CIR.

BONNEAU HEIGHTS

116   ST.

SUNSET DR.

77°10'00"   SEE MAP 3576

A   B   C   D   E   F   G   H

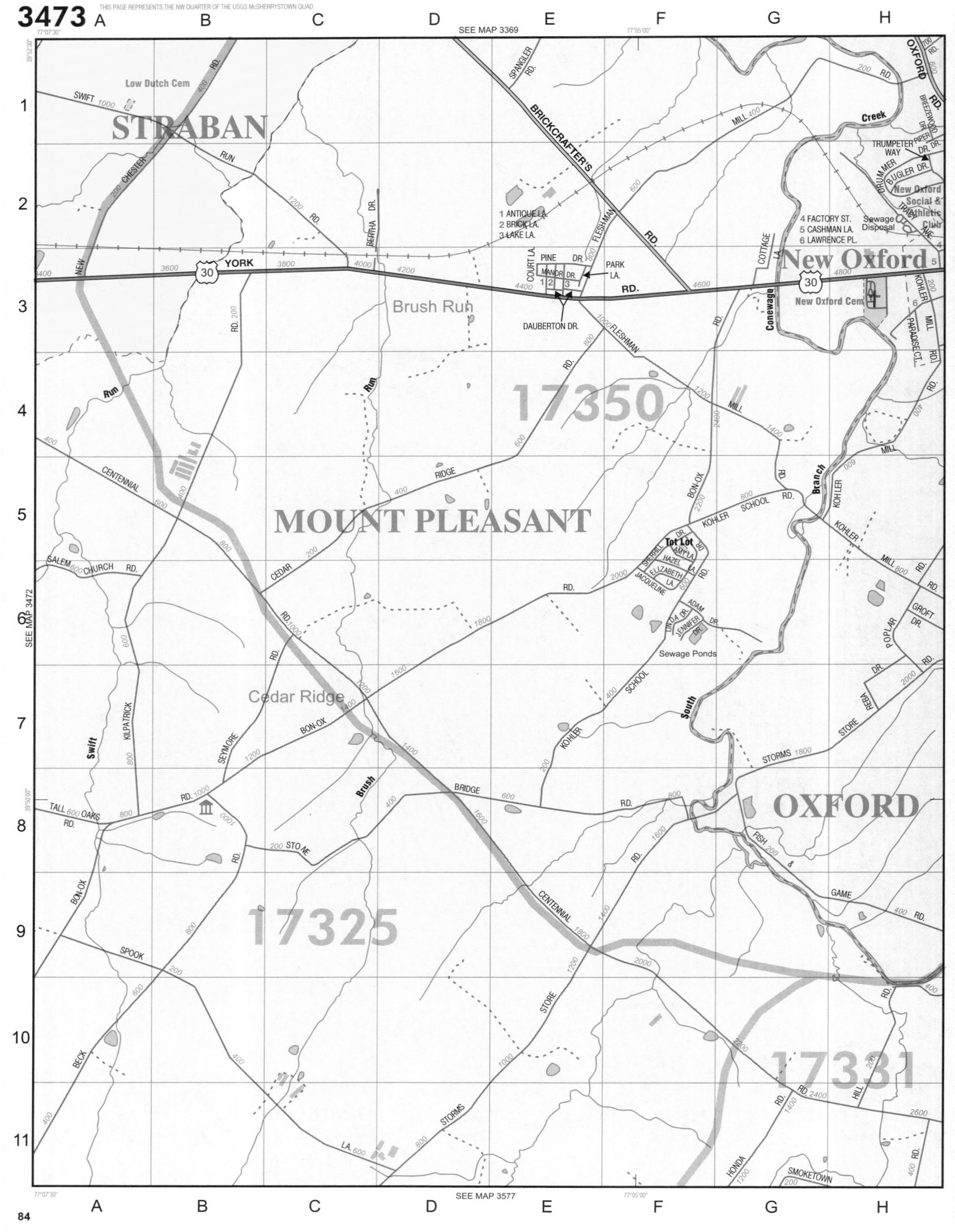

THIS PAGE REPRESENTS THE NW QUARTER OF THE USGS McSHERRYSTOWN QUAD

SEE MAP 3369

STRABAN

Low Dutch Cem

SWIFT 1000

CHESTER RUN

BERTHA DR.

BRICKCRAFTER'S

SPANGLER RD.

FLESHMAN RD.

MILL 400

Creek

TRUMPETER WAY

PIPER DR.
BREEZEWOOD DR.
BUGLER DR.
DRUMMER DR.

New Oxford Social & Athletic Club

OXFORD RD.

4 FACTORY ST.
5 CASHMAN LA.
6 LAWRENCE PL.

Sewage Disposal

NEW

YORK

30

1200 RD.

3600

3800

4000

4200

4400

1 ANTIQUE LA.
2 BRICK LA.
3 LAKE LA.

COURT LA.
PINE DR.
MAIN DR.
1 2 3
PARK LA.

RD.

4600

COTTAGE LA.

New Oxford

30

4800

Conewago

New Oxford Cem

KOHLER RD.

PARADISE CT.

Brush Run

DAUBERTON DR.

FLESHMAN

RD.

17350

MILL

MILL

Run

RIDGE

600

800

1200

1400

1000

BON-OX

KOHLER

SCHOOL RD.

Branch

KOHLER

MILL 800

RD.

CENTENNIAL

600

800

MOUNT PLEASANT

CEDAR

RD. 200

RD. 1000

RD.

2000

Tot Lot

AMY LA.

SHERRILL DR.

HAZEL LA.

ELIZABETH LA.

JACQUELINE LA.

KOHLER RD.

ADAM DR.

LINDA DR.

JENNIFER DR.

Sewage Ponds

SALEM CHURCH RD.

600

SEE MAP 3472

Cedar Ridge

KILPATRICK

SEYMORE

BON-OX

Swift

800

1200

1600

1400

RD. 1000

Brush

1800

SCHOOL

South

KOHLER

900

STORE

STORMS 1800

GROFT DR.

POPLAR

RD.

REBA DR.

2000

OXFORD

TALL OAKS RD.

600

RD. 1000

800

STONE

200

BRIDGE

RD.

600

400

1600

RD.

800

FISH & GAME

200

400 RD.

17325

BON-OX

SPOOK

600

200

800

CENTENNIAL

1800

STORE

1200

2000

RD.

1400

BECK

400

17331

STORMS

LA. 600

HONDA

SMOKETOWN

HILL

RD. 2400

2600

RD. 1400

2800

400 RD.

200

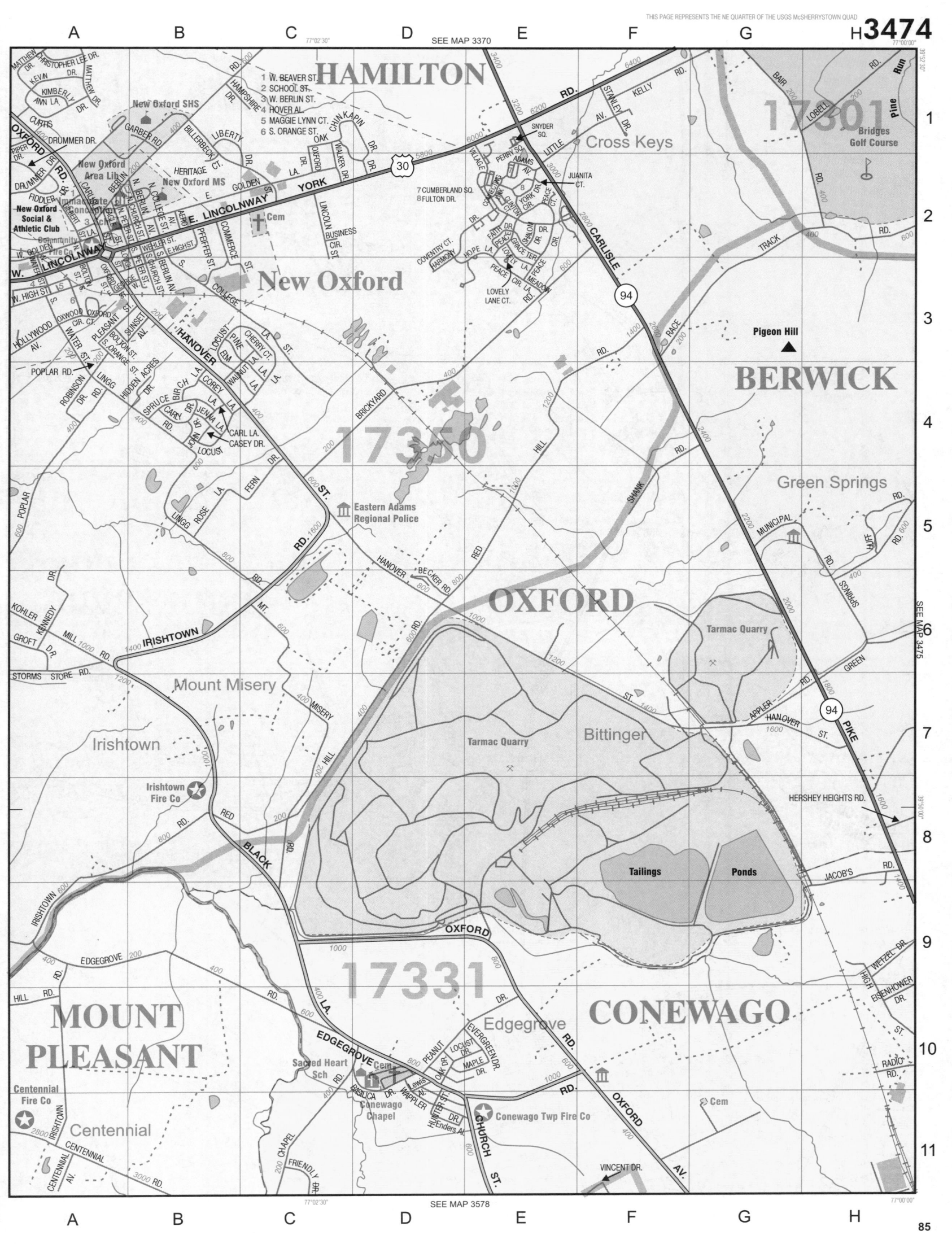

HAMILTON

1 W. BEAVER ST.
2 SCHOOL ST.
3 W. BERLIN ST.
4 HOVER AL.
5 MAGGIE LYNN CT.
6 S. ORANGE ST.

7 CUMBERLAND SQ.
8 FULTON DR.

Cross Keys

17301

Bridges
Golf Course

New Oxford SHS

New Oxford
Area Lib.

New Oxford
Social &
Athletic Club

New Oxford MS

Immaculate
Conception

Community
Fire Co.

New Oxford

Cem

BERWICK

Pigeon Hill

Green Springs

17350

Eastern Adams
Regional Police

OXFORD

Tarmac Quarry

IRISHTOWN

Mount Misery

Irishtown

Irishtown
Fire Co

Bittinger

Tarmac Quarry

Tailings

Ponds

HERSHEY HEIGHTS RD.

JACOB'S

MOUNT
PLEASANT

17331

Edgegrove

CONEWAGO

Centennial
Fire Co

Centennial

Sacred Heart
Sch

Cem

Conewago
Chapel

Conewago Twp Fire Co

Cem

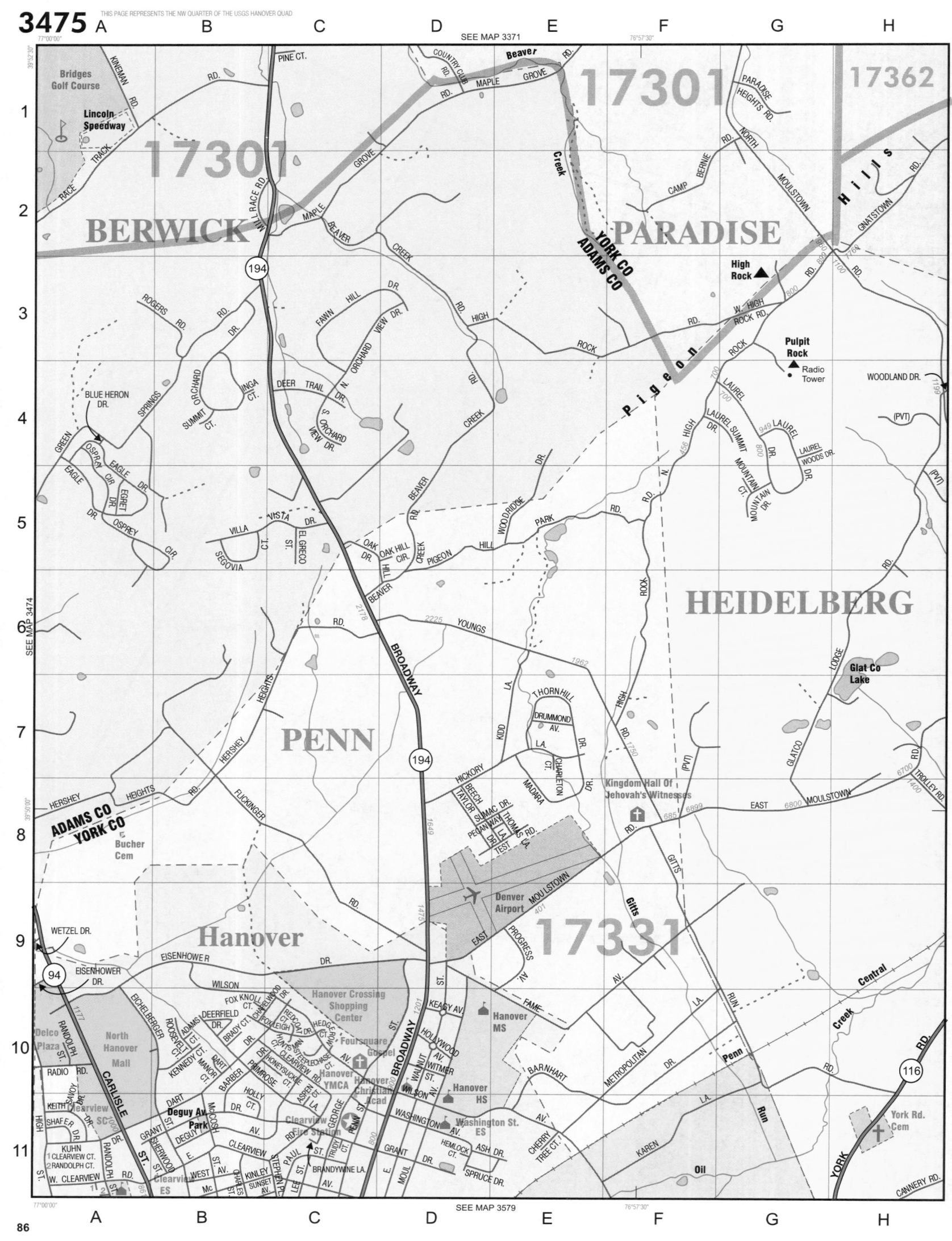

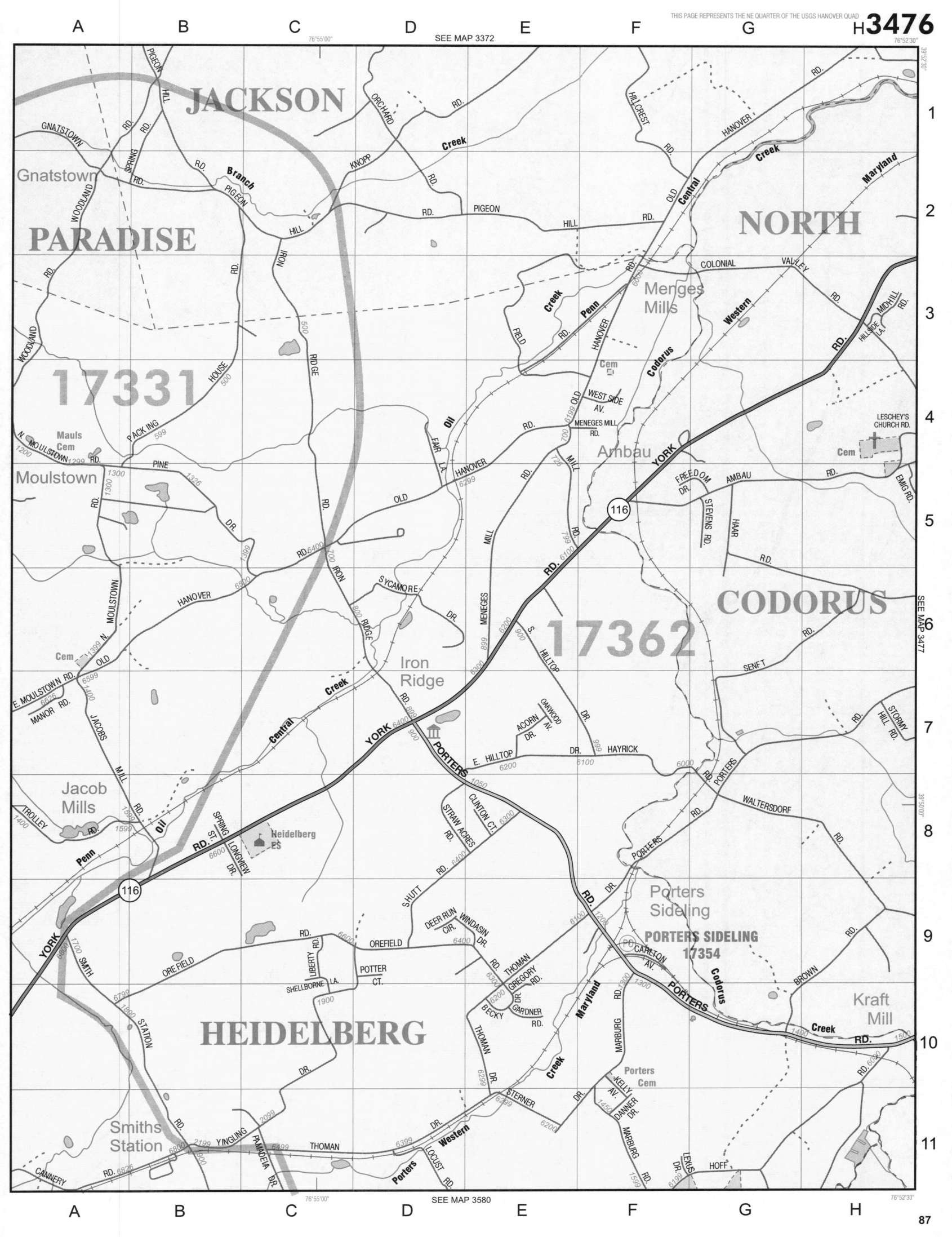

A B C D E F G H

SEE MAP 3372

76°55'00" 76°52'30"

39°52'30"

1

JACKSON

2

Gnatstown

PARADISE

NORTH

Menges
Mills

3

17331

Mauls
Cem

Moulstown

4

Amhau

LESCHEY'S
CHURCH RD.

Cem

5

116

Cem

CODORUS

6

Iron
Ridge

17362

7

Jacob
Mills

8

Heidelberg
ES

116

Porters
Sideling

9

PORTERS SIDELING
17354

Kraft
Mill

10

HEIDELBERG

Porters
Cem

Smiths
Station

11

A B C D E F G H

SEE MAP 3580

76°55'00" 76°52'30"

39°50'00"

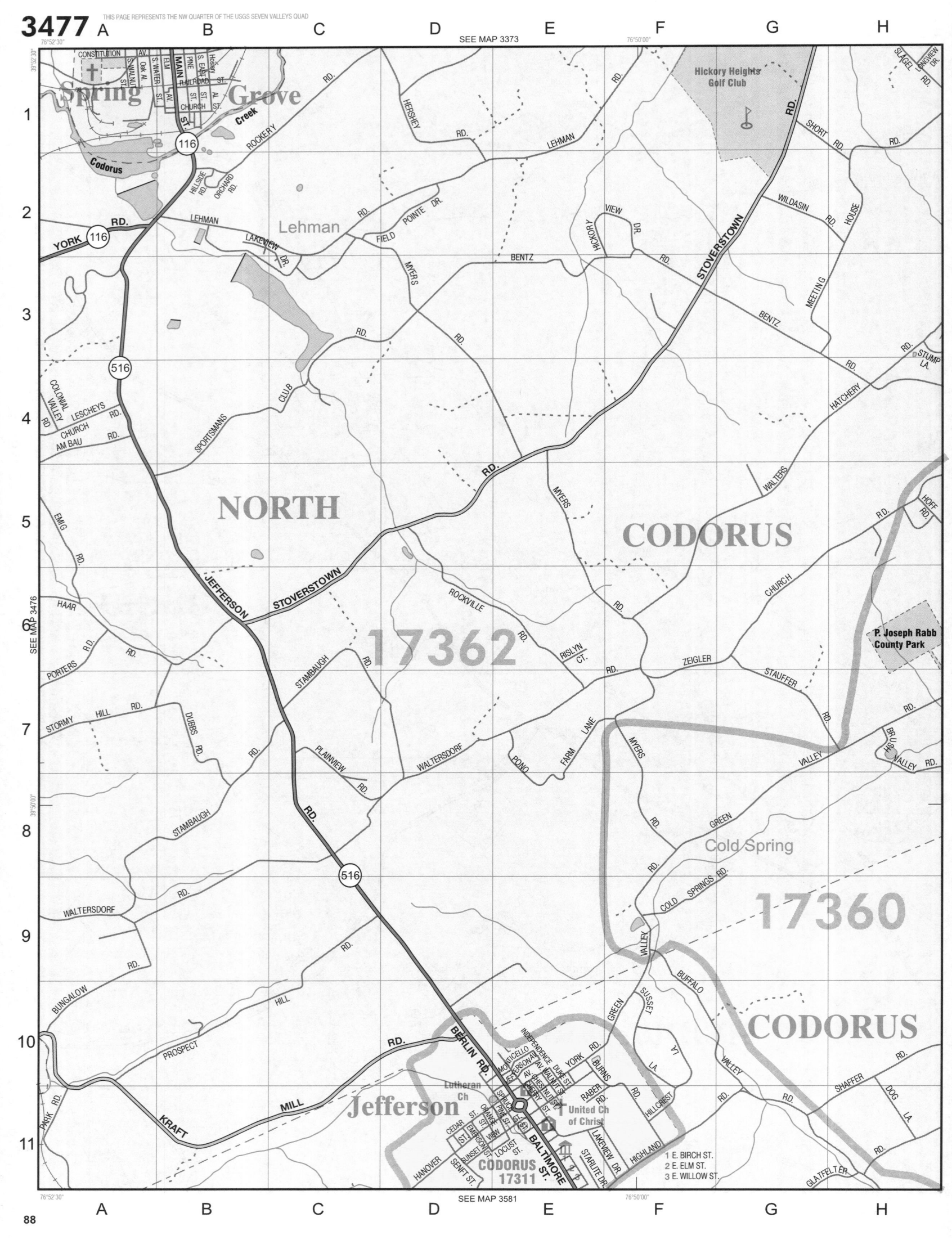

SEE MAP 3373

Spring Grove

Codorus Creek

Hickory Heights Golf Club

Lehman

NORTH CODORUS

17362

P. Joseph Rabb County Park

Cold Spring

17360

CODORUS

Jefferson

CODORUS 17311

1 E. BIRCH ST.
2 E. ELM ST.
3 E. WILLOW ST.

SEE MAP 3581

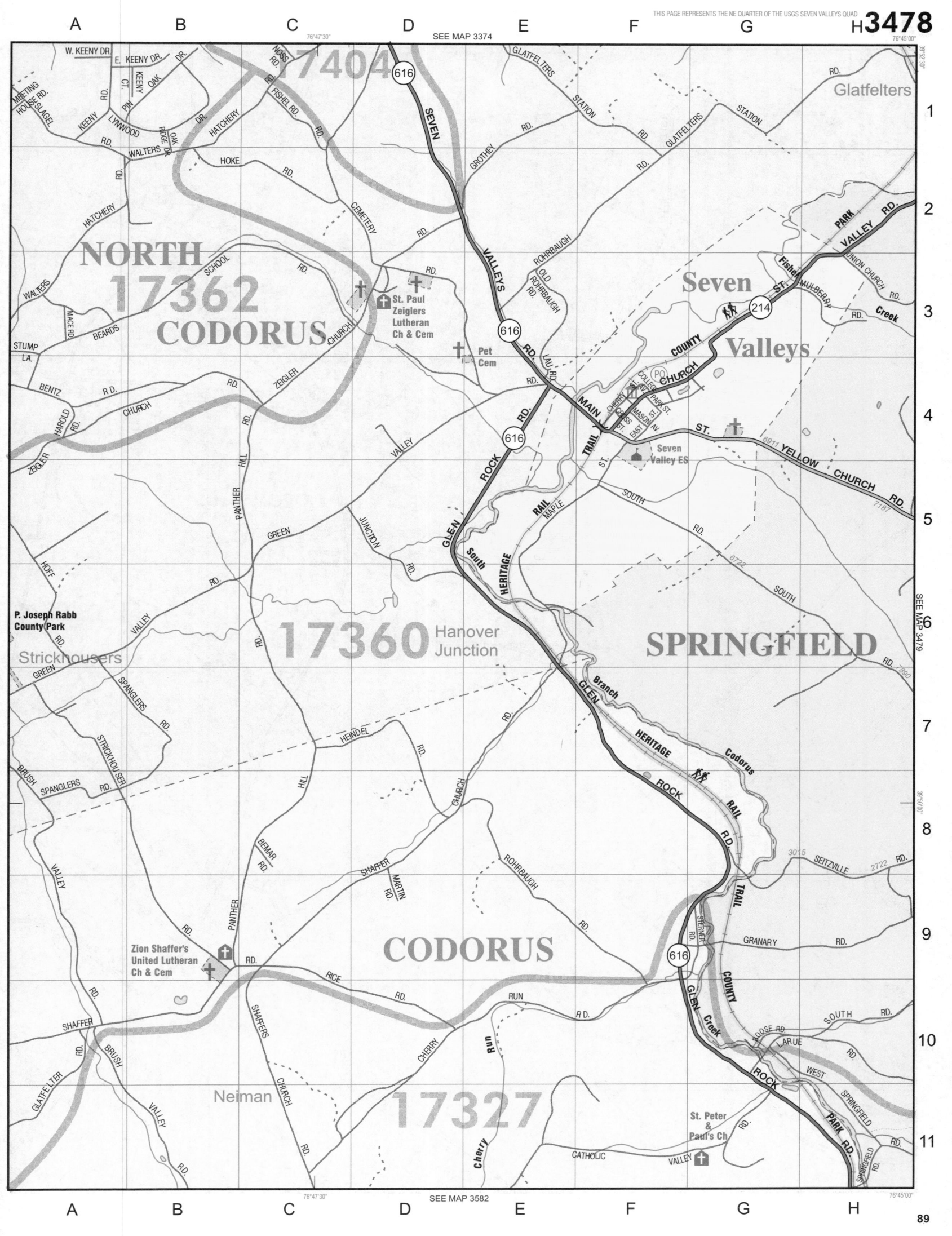

SEE MAP 3374

Glatfelters

NORTH
17362
CODORUS

Seven

Valleys

17404

St. Paul
Zeiglers
Lutheran
Ch & Cem

Pet
Cem

SPRINGFIELD

P. Joseph Rabb
County Park

Strickhousers

17360
Hanover
Junction

Seven
Valley ES

CODORUS

Zion Shaffer's
United Lutheran
Ch & Cem

Neiman

17327

St. Peter
&
Paul's Ch

SEE MAP 3582

SEE MAP 3479

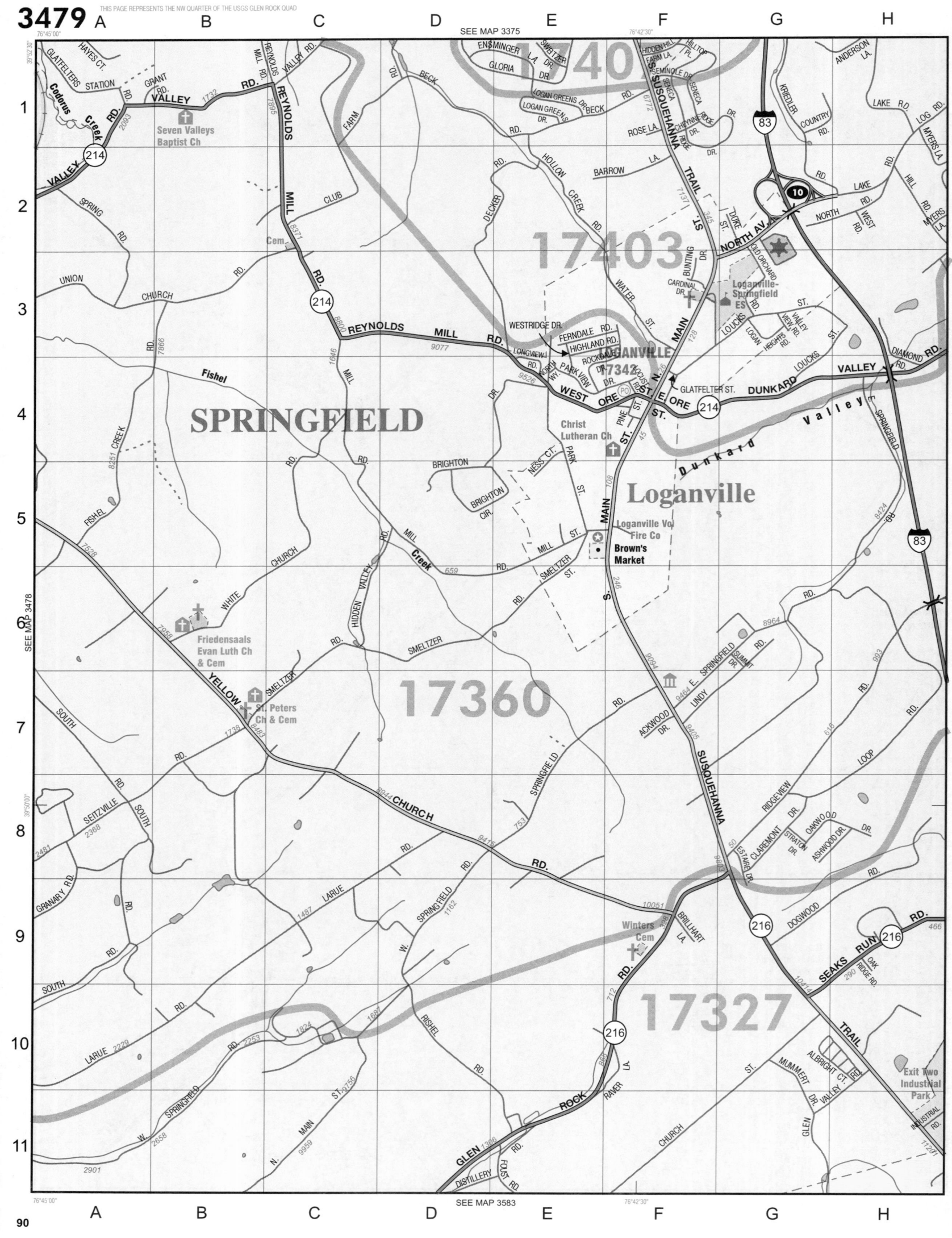

THIS PAGE REPRESENTS THE NW QUARTER OF THE USGS GLEN ROCK QUAD

SEE MAP 3375

17403

17360

17327

SPRINGFIELD

Loganville

Seven Valleys
Baptist Ch

Fishel

Friedensaals
Evan Luth Ch
& Cem

St. Peters
Ch & Cem

Christ
Lutheran Ch

Loganville Vo
Fire Co

Brown's
Market

Winters
Cem

Loganville-
Springfield
ES

Exit Two
Industrial
Park

SEE MAP 3478

SEE MAP 3583

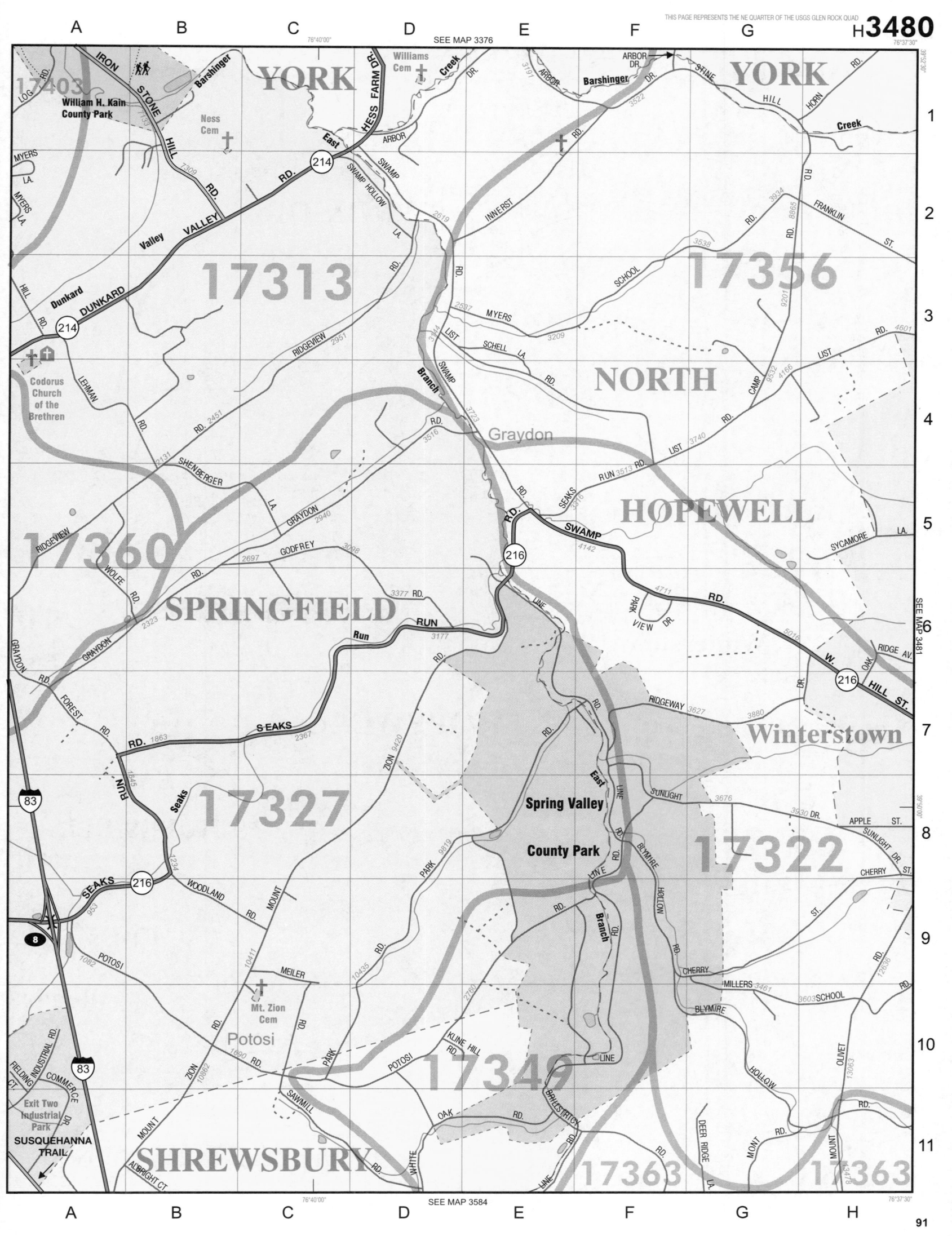

SEE MAP 3376

YORK

YORK

William H. Kain
County Park

ARBOR DR. →

Barshinger

Creek

17403

IRON STONE HILL RD.

Barshinger

Ness Cem

STINE HILL RD.

HORN RD.

Williams Cem

Creek

East RD.

214

MYERS LA.

MYERS LA.

VALLEY

Valley

FRANKLIN ST.

HESS FARM DR.

SWAMP HOLLOW

SWAMP RD.

ARBOR

INNERST RD.

SCHOOL RD.

CAMP RD.

17313

17356

HILL RD.

Dunkard

DUNKARD

214

Codorus
Church of
the Brethren

RIDGEVIEW

LEHMAN RD.

SHENBERGER

GRAYDON LA.

MYERS RD.

SCHELL LA.

LIST RD.

NORTH

LIST RD.

Graydon

Branch

SWAMP

RD.

HOPEWELL

RUN RD.

17360

RIDGEVIEW

WOLFE RD.

GODFREY RD.

RD.

SEAKS

SWAMP RD.

216

PARK VIEW DR.

RD.

SYCAMORE LA.

SPRINGFIELD

RUN

Run

LINE

RIDGEWAY

RIDGE AV.

216

W. OAK HILL ST.

DR.

SEAKS RD.

GRAYDON RD.

FOREST RD.

Seaks

RUN

17327

ZION RD.

East Line RD.

SUNLIGHT

Winterstown

SUNLIGHT DR.

17322

216

SEAKS

Seaks

WOODLAND RD.

MOUNT RD.

PARK RD.

Spring Valley

County Park

BLYMIRE

HOLLOW RD.

APPLE ST.

CHERRY ST.

8

83

POTOSI RD.

MEILER RD.

Branch

ST.

Cherry

MILLERS

SCHOOL RD.

RD.

Mt. Zion
Cem

ZION RD.

Line

BLYMIRE RD.

OLIVET RD.

Potosi

POTOSI RD.

17349

KLINE HILL RD.

HOLLOW RD.

MOUNT RD.

Exit Two
Industrial
Park

FIELDING INDUSTRIAL RD.

COMMERCE DR.

SAWMILL RD.

OAK RD.

BAHLSTRICK RD.

DEER RIDGE LA.

SUSQUEHANNA
TRAIL

83

AMBRIGHT CT.

WHITE RD.

Line

SHREWSBURY

17363

17363

SEE MAP 3584

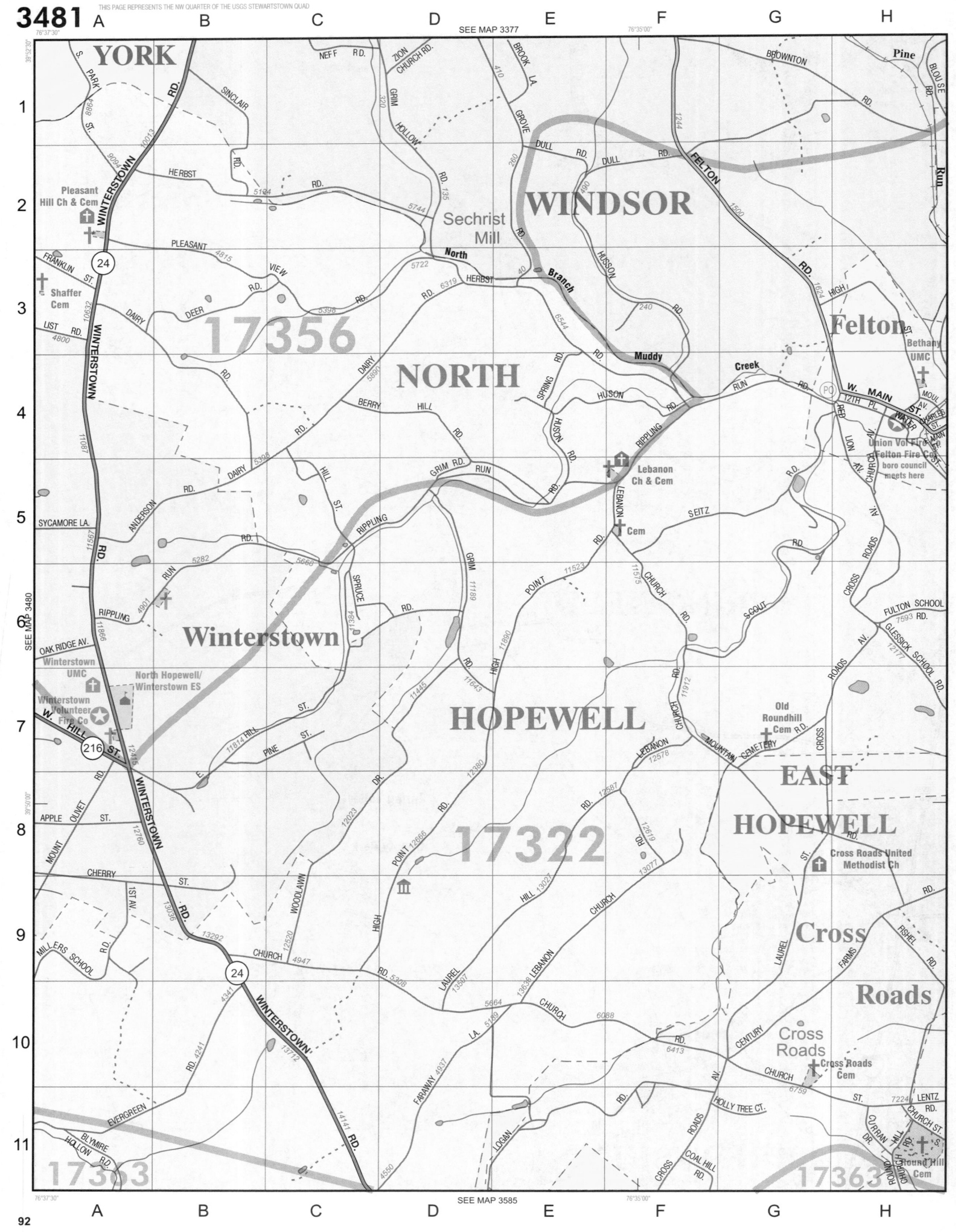

THIS PAGE REPRESENTS THE NW QUARTER OF THE USGS STEWARTSTOWN QUAD

SEE MAP 3377

YORK

WINDSOR

17356

NORTH

Sechrist Mill

Felton

Bethany UMC

Muddy

Creek

Pleasant Hill Ch & Cem

Shaffer Cem

Lebanon Ch & Cem

Cem

Winterstown

HOPEWELL

EAST

HOPEWELL

17322

Winterstown UMC

North Hopewell/ Winterstown ES

Winterstown Volunteer Fire Co

Old Roundhill Cem

Cross Roads United Methodist Ch

Cross

Roads

FULTON SCHOOL

MILLERS SCHOOL

Cross Roads

Cross Roads Cem

17363

17363

Round Hill Cem

SEE MAP 3585

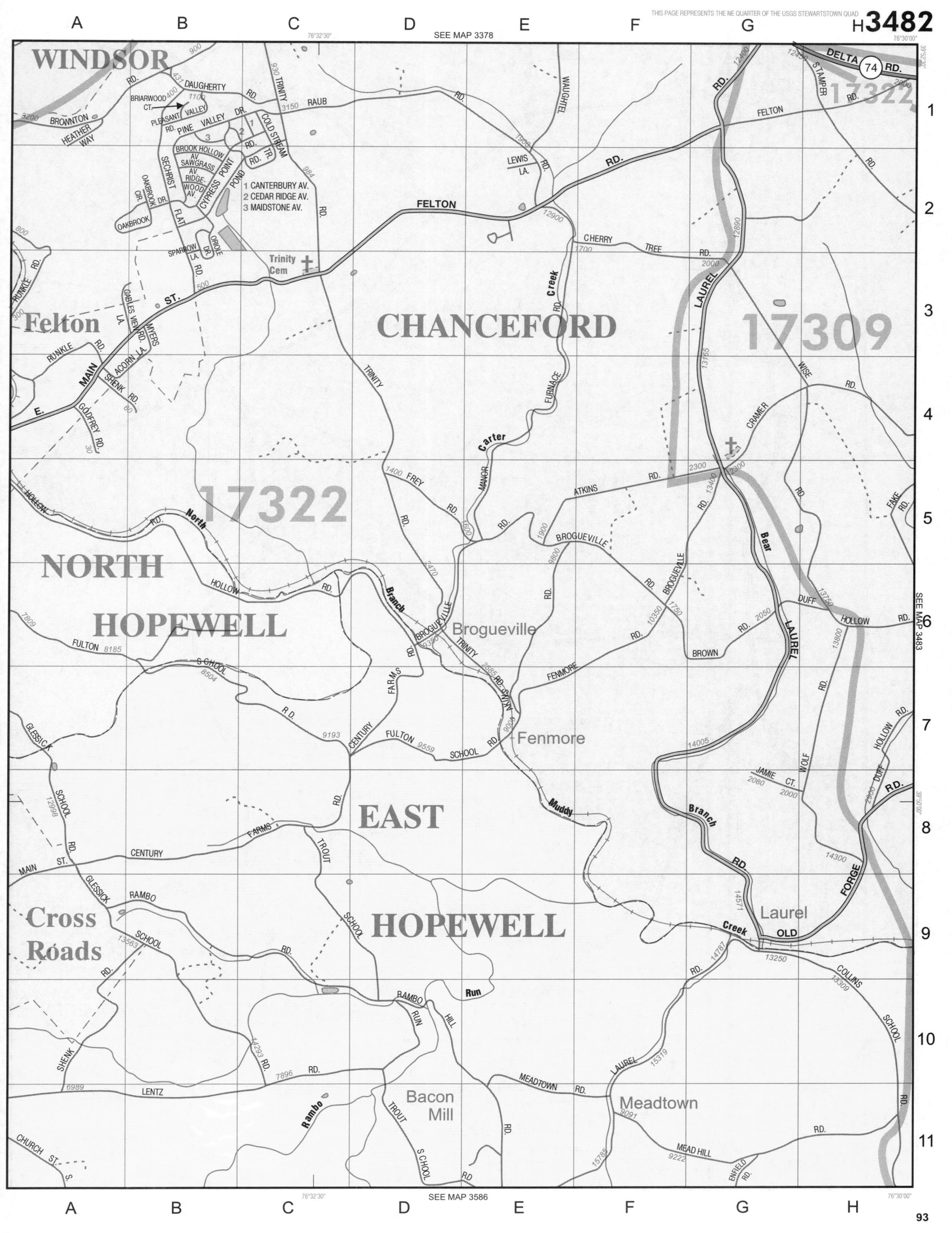

SEE MAP 3378

A   B   C   D   E   F   G   H

WINDSOR

DELTA 74 RD.
STAMPER RD.

17322

BROWNTON
HEATHER WAY
BRIARWOOD CT.
DAUGHERTY RD.
RAUB RD.
PLEASANT VALLEY RD.
PINE VALLEY DR.
COLD STREAM
TRINITY DR.

RUNKLE RD.
SECHRIST
OAKBROOK CIR.
OAKBROOK DR.
FLAT RD.
SPARROW LA.
ORIOLE DR.
BROOK HOLLOW AV
SAWGRASS AV
RIDGEWOOD AV
CYPRESS POINT RD.
POND
TR.

1 CANTERBURY AV.
2 CEDAR RIDGE AV.
3 MAIDSTONE AV.

WAUGHTEL RD.
LEWIS LA.

FELTON RD.

Trinity Cem

CHANCEFORD

17309

Felton

CHERRY TREE RD.

LAUREL

Creek

Furnace RD.

E. MAIN
SHENK RD.
GODFREY RD.
GABLES
MENARD LA.
MYERS
ACORN LA.
ST.

CRAMER

WISE RD.

Carter

MANOR RD.

17322

ATKINS RD.

FREY RD.

BROGUEVILLE

FAKE RD.

Bear

North HOLLOW RD.

NORTH

HOPEWELL

BROGUEVILLE RD.

Brogueville

DUFF HOLLOW RD.

LAUREL

FULTON

S SCHOOL RD.

FARMS RD

CENTURY RD.

FULTON SCHOOL RD.

BROGUEVILLE
TRINITY RD.

FENMORE

BROWN

GLESSICK RD.

SCHOOL RD.

RD

Fenmore

WOLF RD.

HOLLOW RD.

JAMIE CT.

EAST

FARMS

TROUT RD.

Muddy

Branch RD.

DUFF RD.

FORGE RD.

MAIN ST.
GLESSICK RD.
RAMBO
SCHOOL RD.
SCHOOL RD.
CENTURY

Cross Roads

HOPEWELL

Creek
Laurel
OLD

COLLINS RD.

SCHOOL RD.

SHENK RD.
LENTZ RD.

Run

RAMBO

RUN HILL

MEADTOWN RD.

LAUREL RD.

Rambo

TROUT SCHOOL RD.

Bacon Mill

Meadtown

MEAD HILL

ENFIELD RD.

SEE MAP 3586

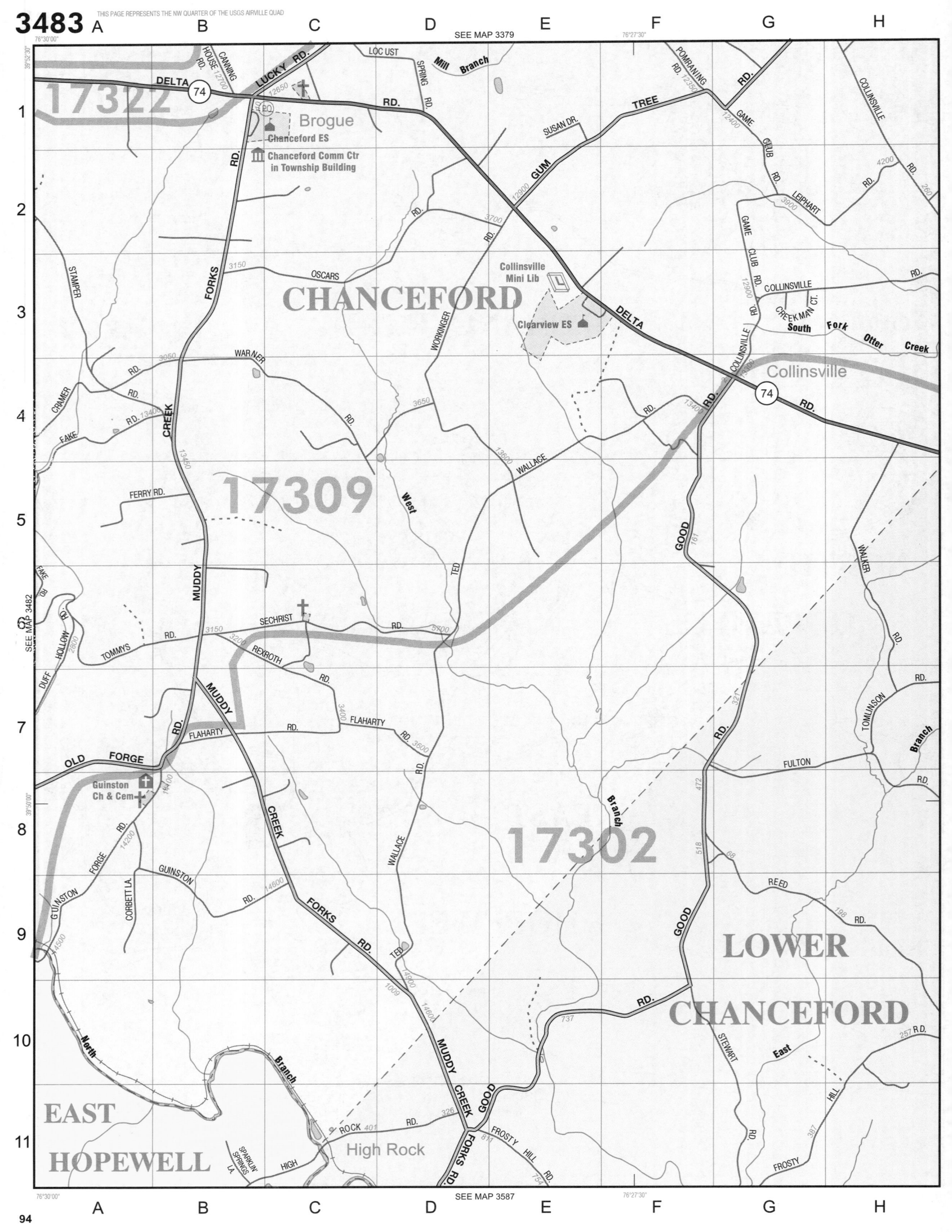

SEE MAP 3379

17322

DELTA 74

LUCKY RD.

LOCUST

Mill Branch

SPRING RD.

RD.

CANNING RD. 12700

HOUSE RD.

PO 12650

Brogue
Chanceford ES
Chanceford Comm Ctr
in Township Building

SUSAN DR.

POMRANING RD. 12350

GAME CLUB RD.

TREE

GUM RD. 12900

3700

GAME CLUB RD. 12400

COLLINSVILLE

4200

2600

FORKS 3150

OSCARS

CHANCEFORD

WORKINGER

Collinsville
Mini Lib

Clearview ES

DELTA

GAME CLUB RD. 12900

LEIPHART 3900

COLLINSVILLE

CREEKMAN CT.

South Fork Otter Creek

RD.

WARNER

CREEK RD. 3050

COLLINSVILLE RD.

Collinsville

74 RD.

CRAMER RD.

FAKE RD. 1340

CREEK 13450

3650

WALLACE 13600

RD.

GOOD 161

WALKER RD.

FERRY RD.

17309

West

TED RD.

RD. 13400

FANE RD.

HOLLOW RD. 2800

MUDDY 3150

SECHRIST

REXROTH RD.

RD. 5800

RD.

DUFF RD.

TOMMYS RD.

3200

3400

FLAHARTY RD. 3600

RD.

RD. 325

TOMLINSON RD.

Branch

MUDDY

FLAHARTY

RD. 3600

RD. 472

FULTON

RD.

OLD FORGE

Guinston
Ch & Cem

RD. 14000

CREEK 14200

Branch

17302

518 68

REED RD.

FORGE RD.

GUINSTON RD.

CORBETT LA.

GUINSTON RD.

RD. 14600

WALLACE

GOOD 198 RD.

GUINSTON 14500

FORKS RD.

TED 14900

GOOD RD.

LOWER

CHANCEFORD

STEWART RD.

East HILL

257 RD.

North Branch

1009 14600

737

RD.

EAST

MUDDY CREEK 326

GOOD FORKS RD.

FROSTY HILL RD. 617

754

FROSTY

ROCK 401 RD.

HOPEWELL

SPARLUN SPRINGS LA.

HIGH

High Rock

SEE MAP 3482

SEE MAP 3587

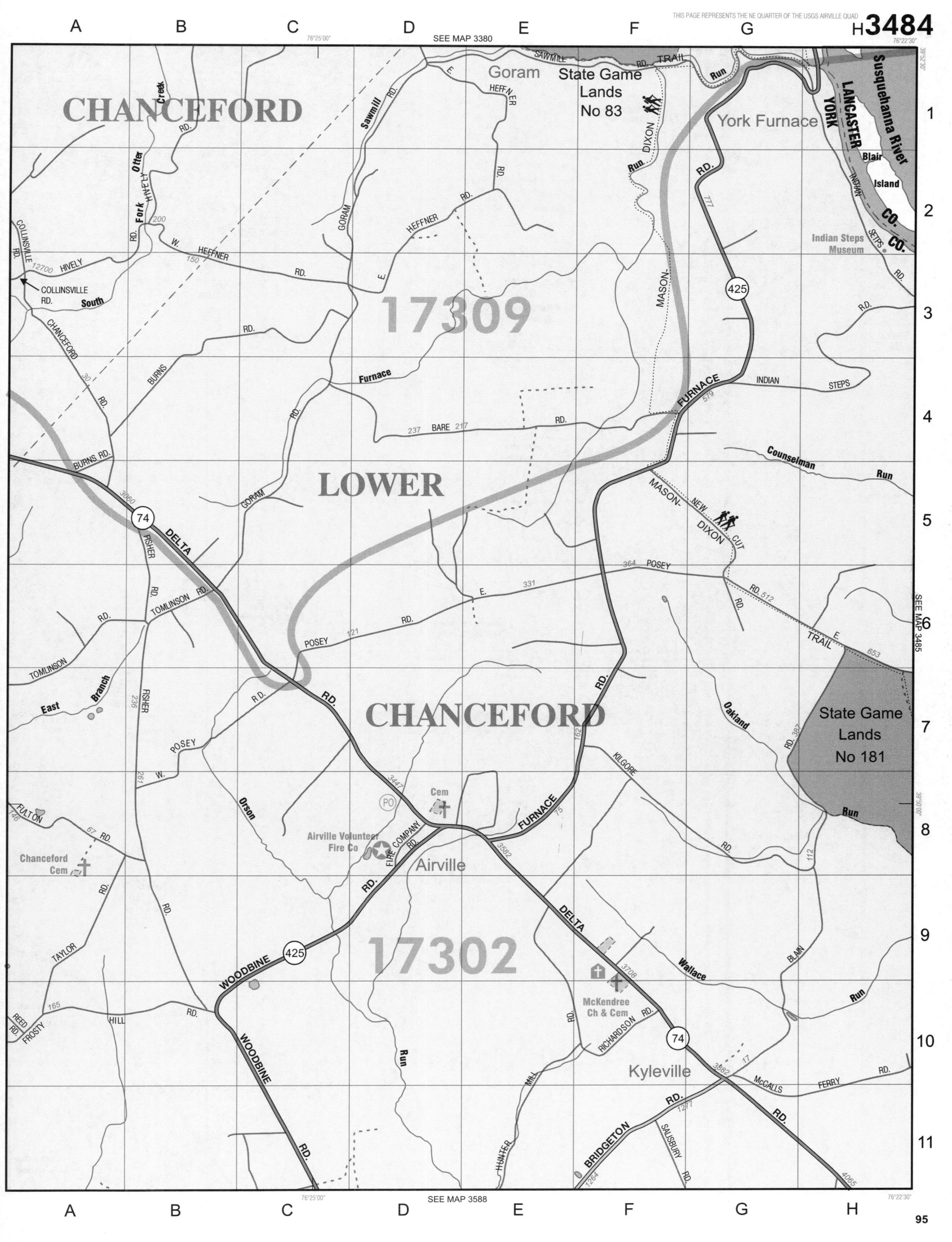

CHANCEFORD

Goram

State Game Lands No 83

York Furnace

Susquehanna River

YORK

LANCASTER

Blair

Island

York CO. CO. Lancaster

Indian Steps Museum

17309

LOWER

Furnace

Counselman Run

Indian Steps

Mason-Dixon

New Cut

Posey

CHANCEFORD

Oakland

State Game Lands No 181

Run

Cem

Airville Volunteer Fire Co

FIRE COMPANY

Kilgore

Furnace

Airville

17302

Chanceford Cem

McKendree Ch & Cem

Wallace

Blain Run

Kyleville

McCalls Ferry Rd.

Bridgeton

Salisbury

SEE MAP 3380

SEE MAP 3588

SEE MAP 3485

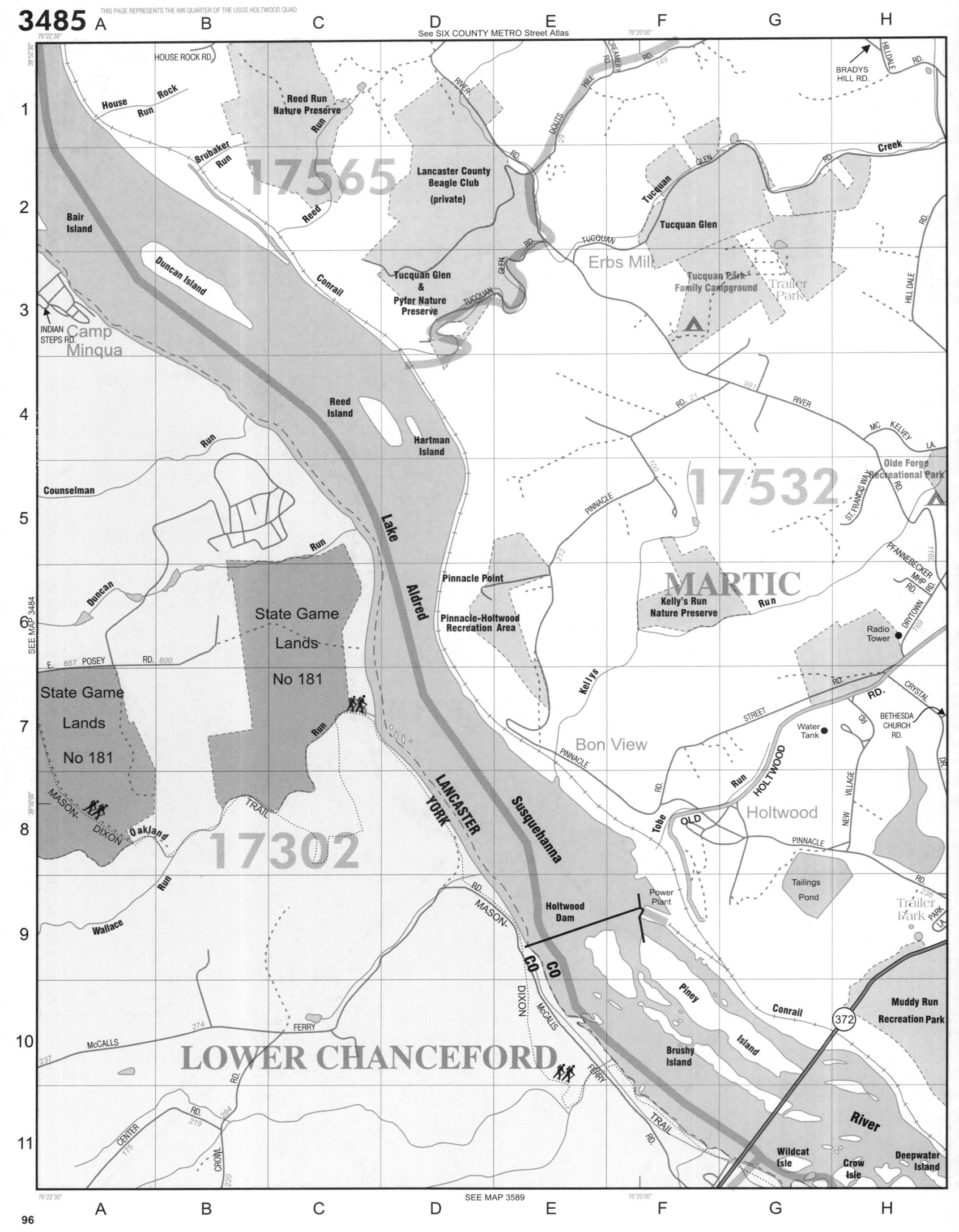

THIS PAGE REPRESENTS THE NW QUARTER OF THE USGS HOLTWOOD QUAD

See SIX COUNTY METRO Street Atlas

17565

17532

17302

Camp Minqua

Bair Island

Duncan Island

Reed Run Nature Preserve

Lancaster County Beagle Club (private)

Tucquan Glen & Pyfer Nature Preserve

Tucquan Glen

Erbs Mill

Tucquan Park Family Campground

Trailer Park

INDIAN STEPS RD.

House Rock

House Run

Rock

Brubaker Run

Reed

Conrail

Reed Island

Hartman Island

Counselman

Duncan Run

State Game Lands No 181

State Game Lands No 181

Pinnacle Point

Pinnacle-Holtwood Recreation Area

MARTIC

Kelly's Run Nature Preserve

Run

Radio Tower

Olde Forge Recreational Park

Lake Aldred

Run

Run

Kellys

Pinnacle

Bon View

Holtwood

Water Tank

BETHESDA CHURCH RD.

Tobe Run

OLD PINNACLE

Tailings Pond

Trailer Park

E. 657 POSEY RD. 800

MASON.

DIXON

Oakland

Run

Wallace

TRAIL

LANCASTER

YORK

Susquehanna

MASON.

RD.

DIXON

McCALLS

Holtwood Dam

Power Plant

CO

CO

LOWER CHANCEFORD

McCALLS

274

FERRY

CENTER RD. 219

284

CROM.

237

McCALLS

FERRY

Piney Island

Brushy Island

Conrail

372

Muddy Run Recreation Park

River

Wildcat Isle

Crow Isle

Deepwater Island

TRAIL

SEE MAP 3484

SEE MAP 3589

BRADYS HILL RD.

HILLDALE RD.

Creek

HILL DALE

CRYSTAL

DRYTOWN RD.

ST. FRANCIS WAY

PFANNEBECKER MHP RD.

NEW VILLAGE

HOLTWOOD

STREET

Borough of Gettysburg

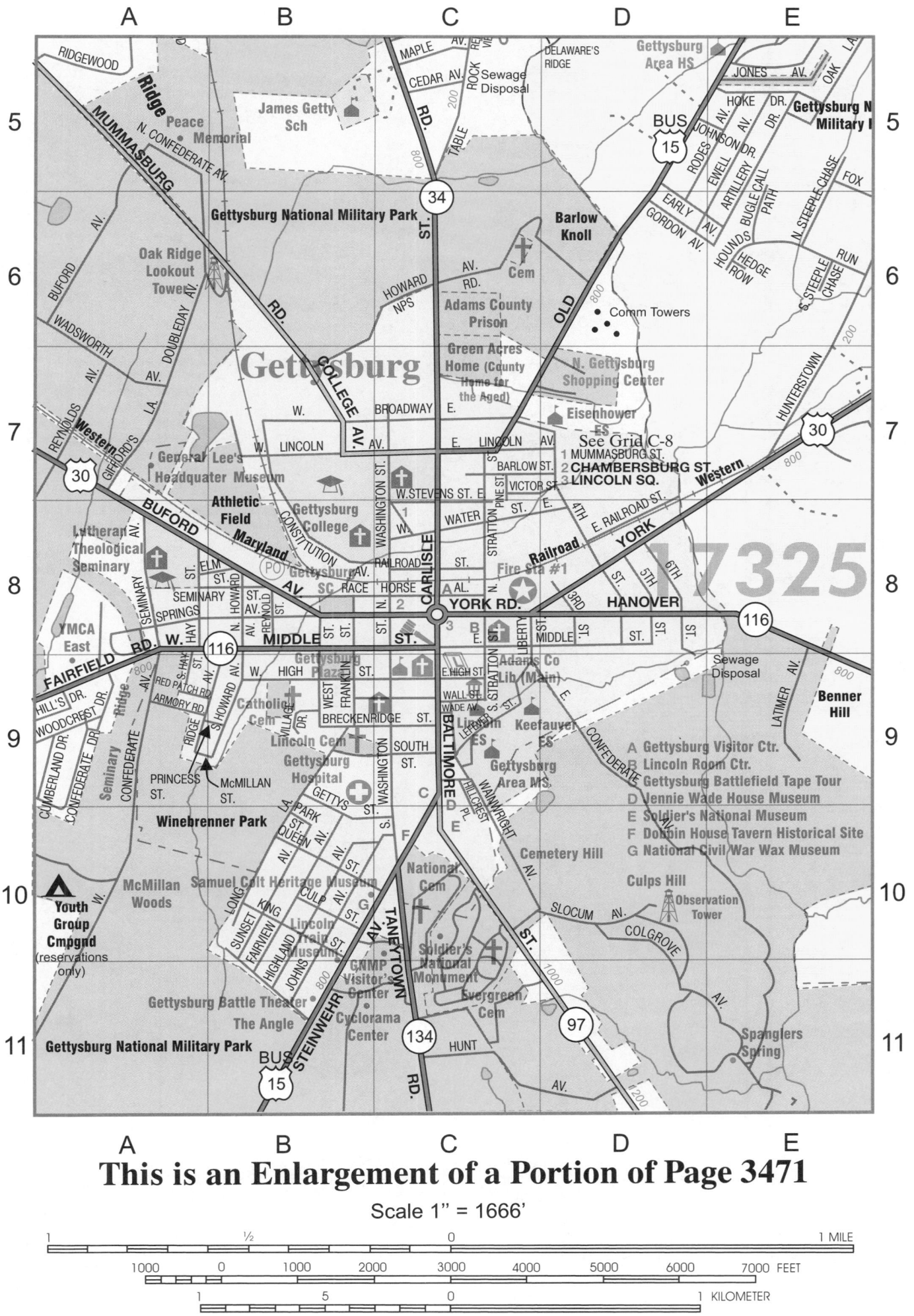

This is an Enlargement of a Portion of Page 3471

Scale 1" = 1666'

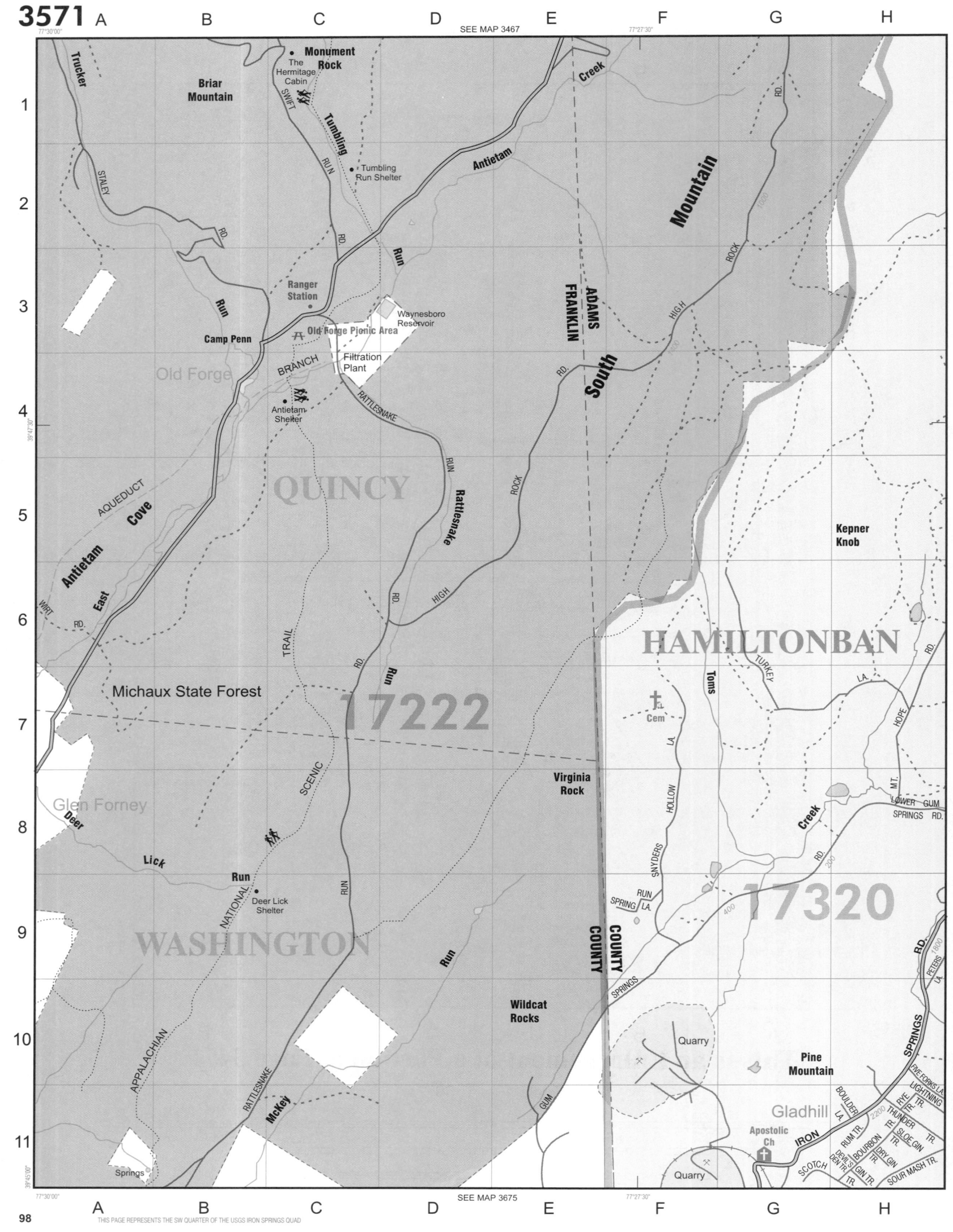

SEE MAP 3467

77°30'00"

77°27'30"

A   B   C   D   E   F   G   H

1

Trucker

Briar
Mountain

Monument
Rock

The Hermitage
Cabin

STALEY

Swift

Tumbling

2

Antietam

Creek

Mountain

RD.

RUN

RD.

Tumbling
Run Shelter

Run

ROCK

3

Run

Ranger
Station

Waynesboro
Reservoir

FRANKLIN

ADAMS

South

HIGH

Camp Penn

Old Forge Picnic Area

Old Forge

BRANCH

Filtration
Plant

RATTLESNAKE

4

Antietam
Shelter

RD.

39°47'30"

AQUEDUCT

Cove

5

Antietam

QUINCY

RUN

Rattlesnake

ROCK

Kepner
Knob

East

WIRT

RD.

6

Michaux State Forest

TRAIL

RD.

Run

HIGH

HAMILTONBAN

Toms

TURKEY

RD.

LA.

7

17222

SCENIC

Cem

LA.

HOPE

Virginia
Rock

8

Glen Forney

Deer

Lick

Run

NATIONAL

RUN

SNYDERS HOLLOW

Creek

LOWER GUM
SPRINGS RD.

M.T.

RD.

Deer Lick
Shelter

LA.

SPRING LA.

RUN LA.

9

WASHINGTON

Run

COUNTY

COUNTY

SPRINGS

17320

RD.

PETERS

10

APPALACHIAN

Wildcat
Rocks

GUM

Quarry

Pine
Mountain

SPRINGS

RD.

11

Springs

RATTLESNAKE

McKey

Gladhill

Apostolic
Ch

IRON

Quarry

BOULDER LA.

RUM LA.

SCOTCH TR.

DEVIL'S DEN TR.

GIN TR.

BOURBON TR.

DRY GIN TR.

SOUR MASH TR.

FIVE FORKS LA.

LIGHTNING TR.

THUNDER TR.

RYE TR.

SLOE GIN TR.

A   B   C   D   E   F   G   H

77°30'00"

SEE MAP 3675

77°27'30"

39°45'00"

THIS PAGE REPRESENTS THE SW QUARTER OF THE USGS IRON SPRINGS QUAD

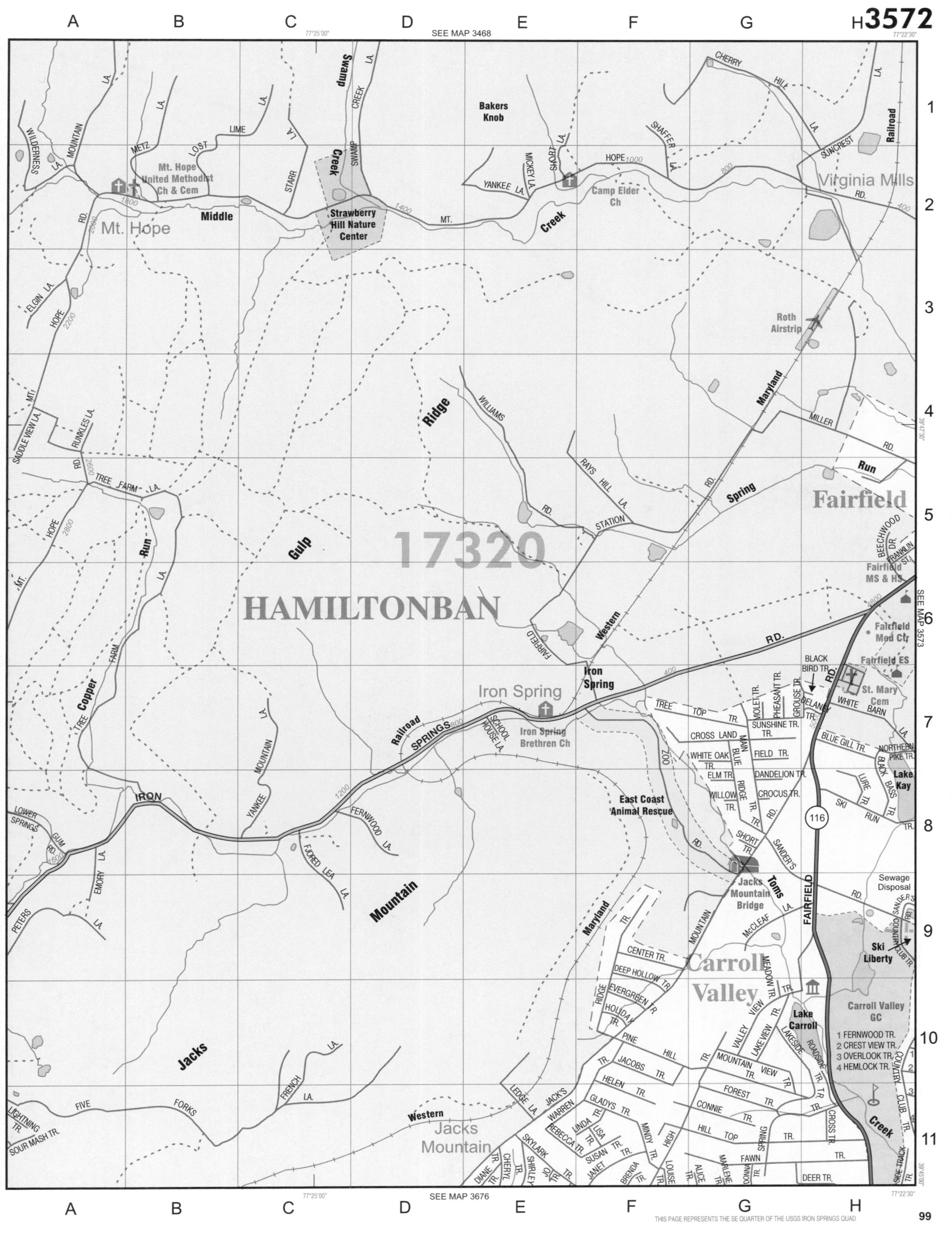

77°25'00"
SEE MAP 3468
Railroad
CHERRY HILL LA.
SUNCREST LA.
Railroad
Virginia Mills
Bakers Knob
SHAFFER LA.
HOPE 1000
SHORE LA.
MICKEY LA.
Camp Elder Ch
YANKEE LA.
Creek
WILDERNESS LA.
MOUNTAIN LA.
METZ LA.
LOST LA.
LIME LA.
STARR LA.
Mt. Hope United Methodist Ch & Cem
Swamp Creek
SWAMP CREEK
Strawberry Hill Nature Center
Middle
Mt. Hope
MT.
Creek
Roth Airstrip
ELGIN LA.
HOPE 2200
Maryland
Ridge
WILLIAMS
MILLER RD.
Run
Fairfield
SADDLE VIEW LA.
MT.
RUNKLES LA.
RD. 2600
TREE FARM LA.
RAYS HILL LA.
STATION
Spring
RD.
Beechwood Dr.
Fairfield MS & HS
FRANKLIN ST.
HOPE 2800
Run
Gulp
17320
HAMILTONBAN
Western
FAIRFIELD
SEE MAP 3573
Fairfield Med Ctr
Fairfield ES
BLACK BIRD TR.
DELANEY RD.
St. Mary Cem
BARN
WHITE LA.
Copper
TREE FARM LA.
Iron Spring
Iron Spring
TREE TOP TR.
MOLE TR.
PHEASANT TR.
GROUSE TR.
Railroad
SPRINGS 800
SCHOOL HOUSE LA.
Iron Spring Brethren Ch
CROSS LAND TR.
SUNSHINE TR.
MAIN TR.
BLUE GILL TR.
NORTHERN PIKE TR.
WHITE OAK TR.
BLUE RIDGE TR.
FIELD TR.
ELM TR.
DANDELION TR.
Lake Kay
MOUNTAIN LA.
YANKEE LA.
1200
RD. 200
WILLOW TR.
CROCUS TR.
LURE TR.
BLACK BASS TR.
IRON
FERNWOOD LA.
East Coast Animal Rescue
116
SKI RUN
LOWER SPRINGS
GUM RD. 1600
EMORY LA.
FJORD LEA LA.
RD.
SHORT TR.
SANDER'S RD.
Toms
Jacks Mountain Bridge
Sewage Disposal
Mountain
Maryland
MOUNTAIN LA.
McCLEAF
FAIRFIELD
Ski Liberty
WINWOOD SANDER'S RD.
CLUB RD.
PETERS LA.
Carroll Valley
CENTER TR.
DEEP HOLLOW TR.
RIDGE TR.
EVERGREEN TR.
HOLIDAY TR.
MEADOW TR.
VIEW TR.
Lake Carroll
ROADSIDE TR.
Carroll Valley GC
1 FERNWOOD TR.
2 CREST VIEW TR.
3 OVERLOOK TR.
4 HEMLOCK TR.
COUNTRY CLUB TR.
PINE TR.
JACOBS TR.
VALLEY VIEW TR.
MOUNTAIN VIEW TR.
LAKEVIEW TR.
LAKESIDE TR.
FOREST TR.
CONNIE TR.
SPRING TR.
CROSS TR.
Creek
Jacks
HELEN TR.
HILL TOP
HIGH TR.
FIVE FORKS
FRENCH LA.
LEDGE LA.
JACK'S TR.
WARREN TR.
GLADYS TR.
LINDA TR.
LISA TR.
MINDY TR.
FAWN TR.
MARLENE TR.
ALICE TR.
DONNA TR.
LIGHTNING TR.
SOUR MASH TR.
Western
Jacks Mountain
DIANE TR.
CHERYL
SHIRLEY TR.
SKYLARK TR.
REBECCA TR.
SUSAN TR.
JANET TR.
BRENDA TR.
LOUISE TR.
DEER TR.
SIDE TRACK TR.

77°25'00"
SEE MAP 3676

A B C D E F G H

39°47'30"
39°45'00"
77°22'30"

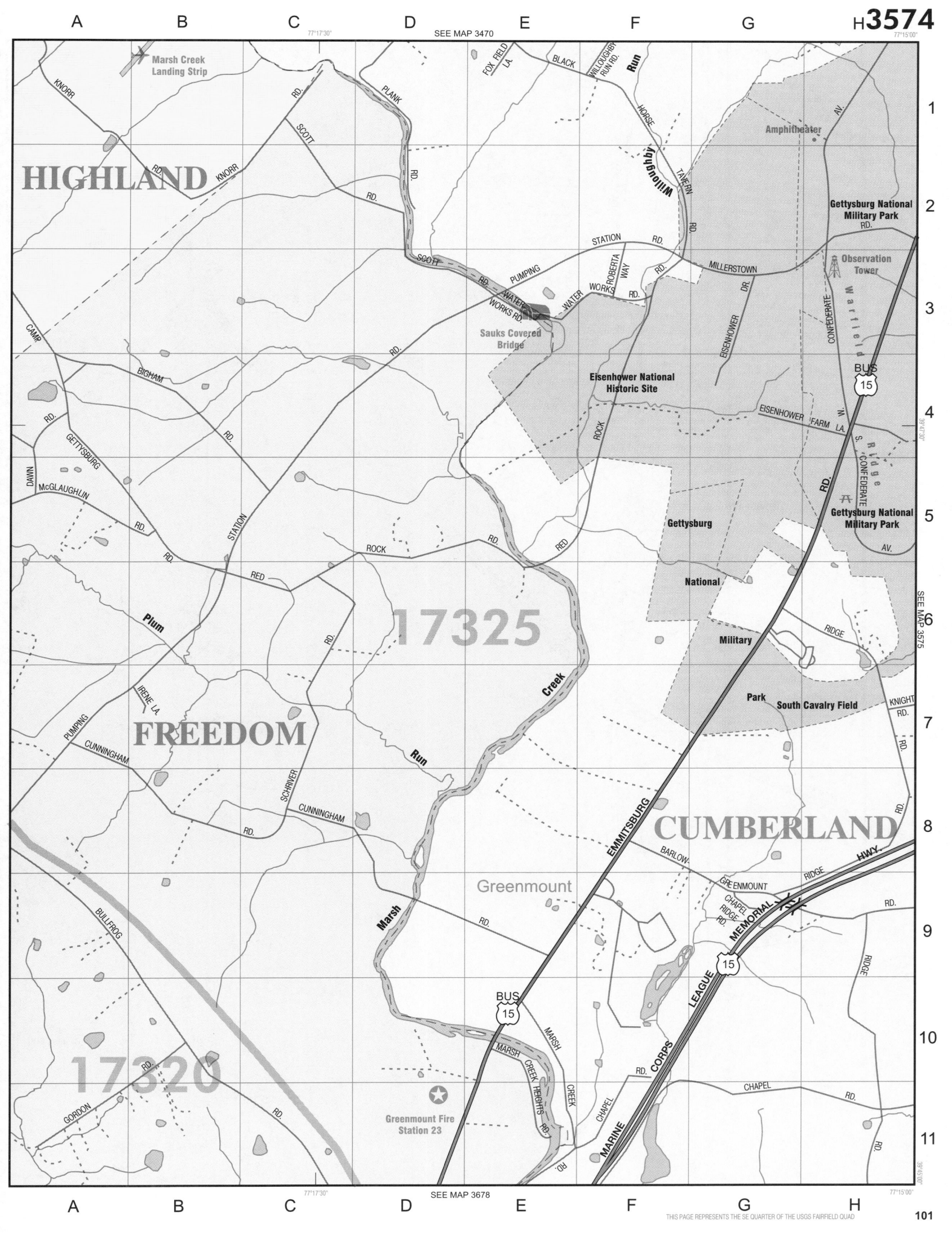

A   B   C   D   E   F   G

77°17'30"

SEE MAP 3470

77°15'00"

1

2

3

4

39°47'30"

5

SEE MAP 3575

6

7

8

9

10

11

39°45'00"

HIGHLAND

Marsh Creek
Landing Strip

KNORR

SCOTT

RD.

KNORR

PLANK

RD.

RD.

FOX FIELD LA.

BLACK

WILLOUGHBY
RUN RD.

Run

Willoughby

HORSE

TAVERN

RD.

Amphitheater

AV.

Gettysburg National
Military Park

RD.

Observation
Tower

Warfield

STATION

ROBERTA

WORKS

WAY

RD.

Millerstown

RD.

EISENHOWER
DR.

CONFEDERATE

SCOTT

RD.

PUMPING

WATER

WORKS RD.

WATER

RD.

Sauks Covered
Bridge

Eisenhower National
Historic Site

BUS
15

CAMP

BIGHAM

RD.

RD.

RD.

ROCK

EISENHOWER   FARM   LA.

W.

S.   CONFEDERATE

Ridge

RD.

Gettysburg National
Military Park

AV.

DAWN

GETTYSBURG

McGLAUGHLIN

RD.

STATION

RD.

RD.

ROCK

RED

RD.

RED

Gettysburg

National

RIDGE

Plum

RD.

17325

Creek

Military

Park

South Cavalry Field

KNIGHT
RD.

RD.

FREEDOM

IRENE LA.

PUMPING

CUNNINGHAM

SCHRIVER

CUNNINGHAM

RD.

RD.

Run

EMMITTSBURG

CUMBERLAND

BARLOW

HWY.

GREENMOUNT

RIDGE

CHAPEL
RIDGE
RD.

MEMORIAL

RD.

BULLFROG

RD.

Marsh

Greenmount

RD.

15

RIDGE

BUS
15

MARSH

CREEK HEIGHTS RD.

MARSH

CREEK

CHAPEL

MARINE

LEAGUE   CORPS

RD.

CHAPEL

RD.

RD.

17320

GORDON

RD.

RD.

Greenmount Fire
Station 23

A   B   C   D   E   F   G   H

77°17'30"

SEE MAP 3678

77°15'00"

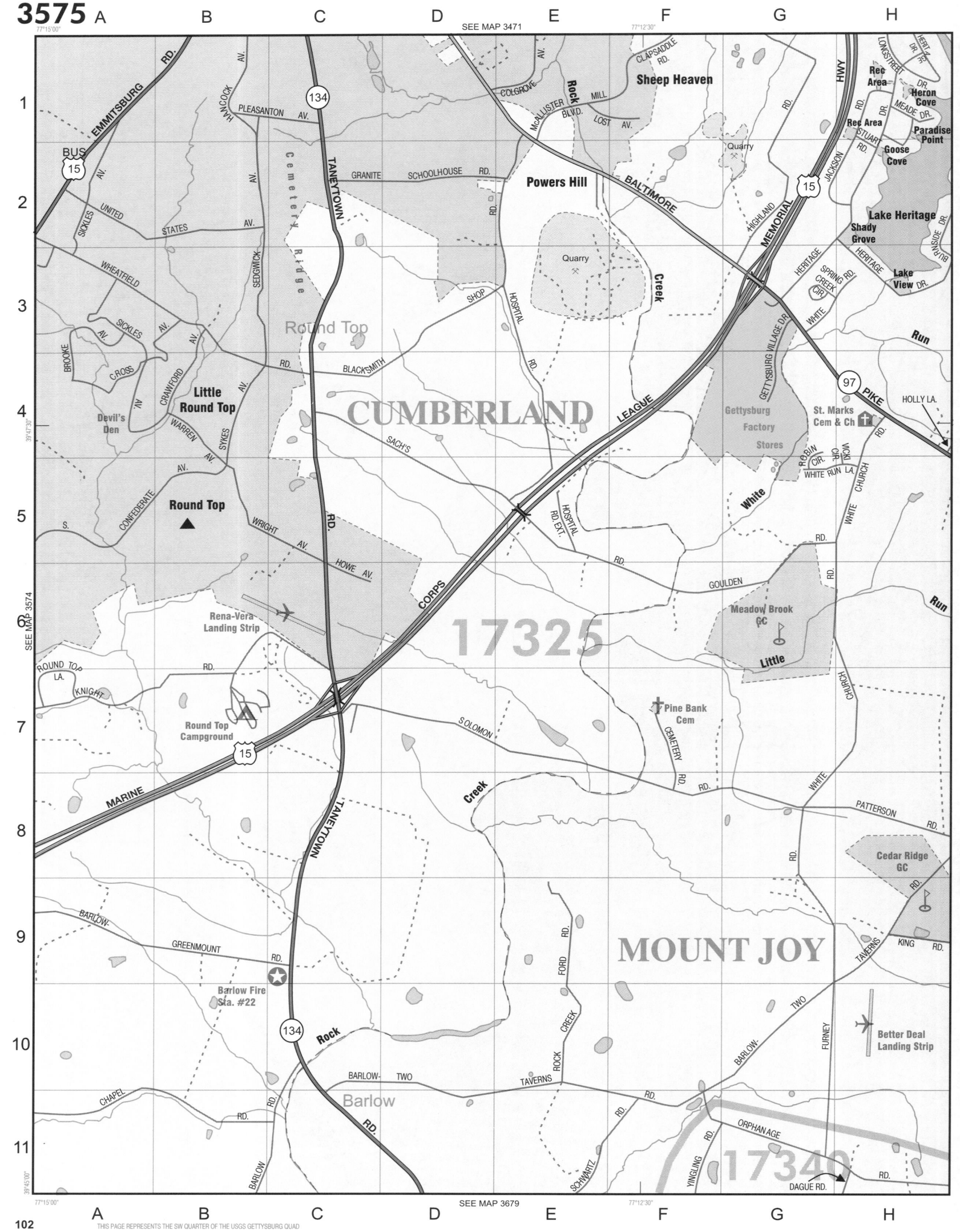

SEE MAP 3471

SEE MAP 3574

CUMBERLAND

17325

MOUNT JOY

17340

Sheep Heaven

Powers Hill

Round Top

Little
Round Top

Devil's
Den

Round Top ▲

Rena-Vera
Landing Strip

Round Top
Campground

Barlow Fire
Sta. #22

Barlow

Lake Heritage

Shady
Grove

Lake
View

Heron
Cove

Paradise
Point

Goose
Cove

Rec
Area

Rec Area

Gettysburg
Factory
Stores

St. Marks
Cem & Ch

Meadow Brook
GC

Little

Pine Bank
Cem

Cedar Ridge
GC

Better Deal
Landing Strip

SEE MAP 3679

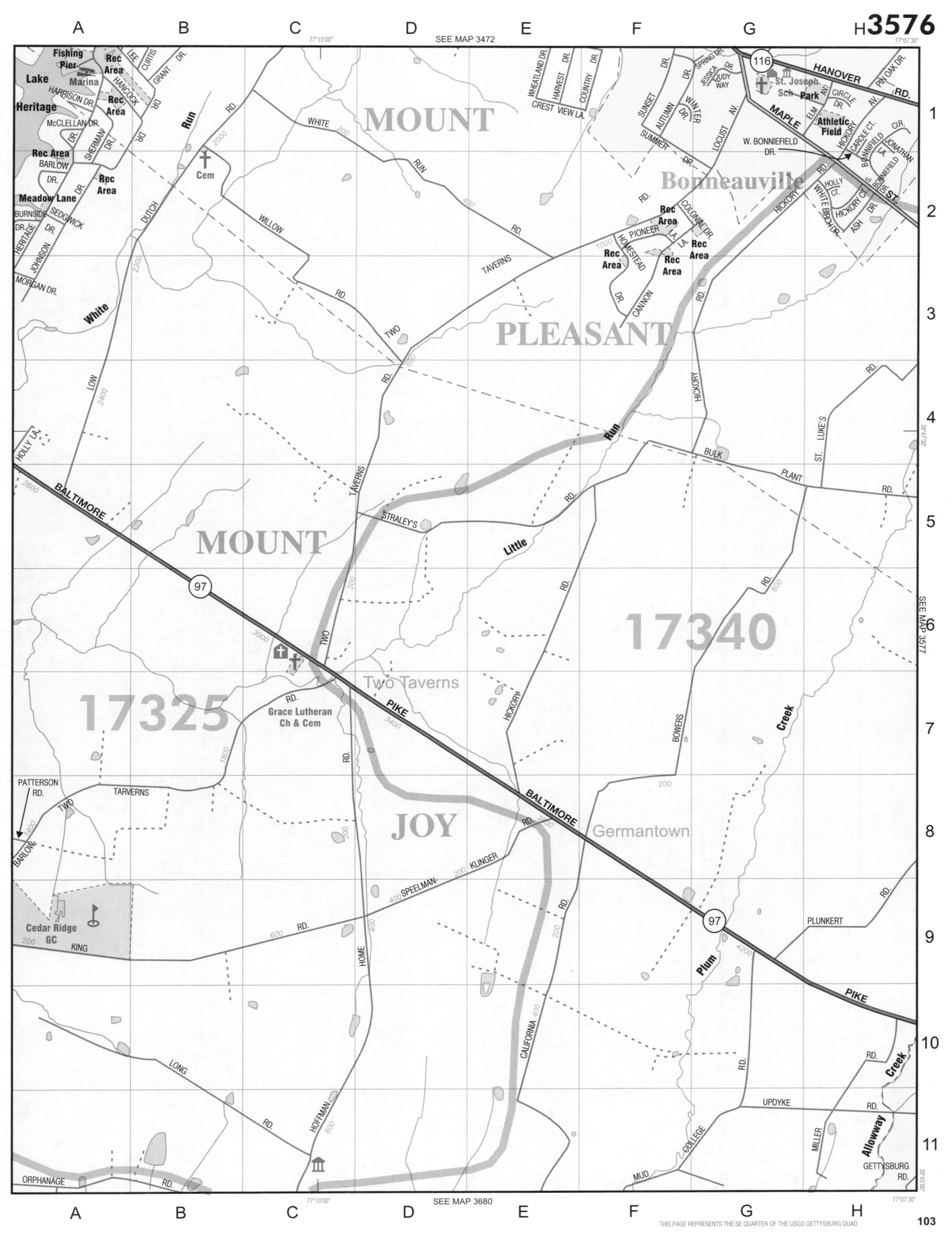

SEE MAP 3472

MOUNT

PLEASANT

Bonneauville

MOUNT

17340

17325

MOUNT

JOY

Two Taverns

Grace Lutheran
Ch & Cem

Germantown

Cedar Ridge
GC

SEE MAP 3680

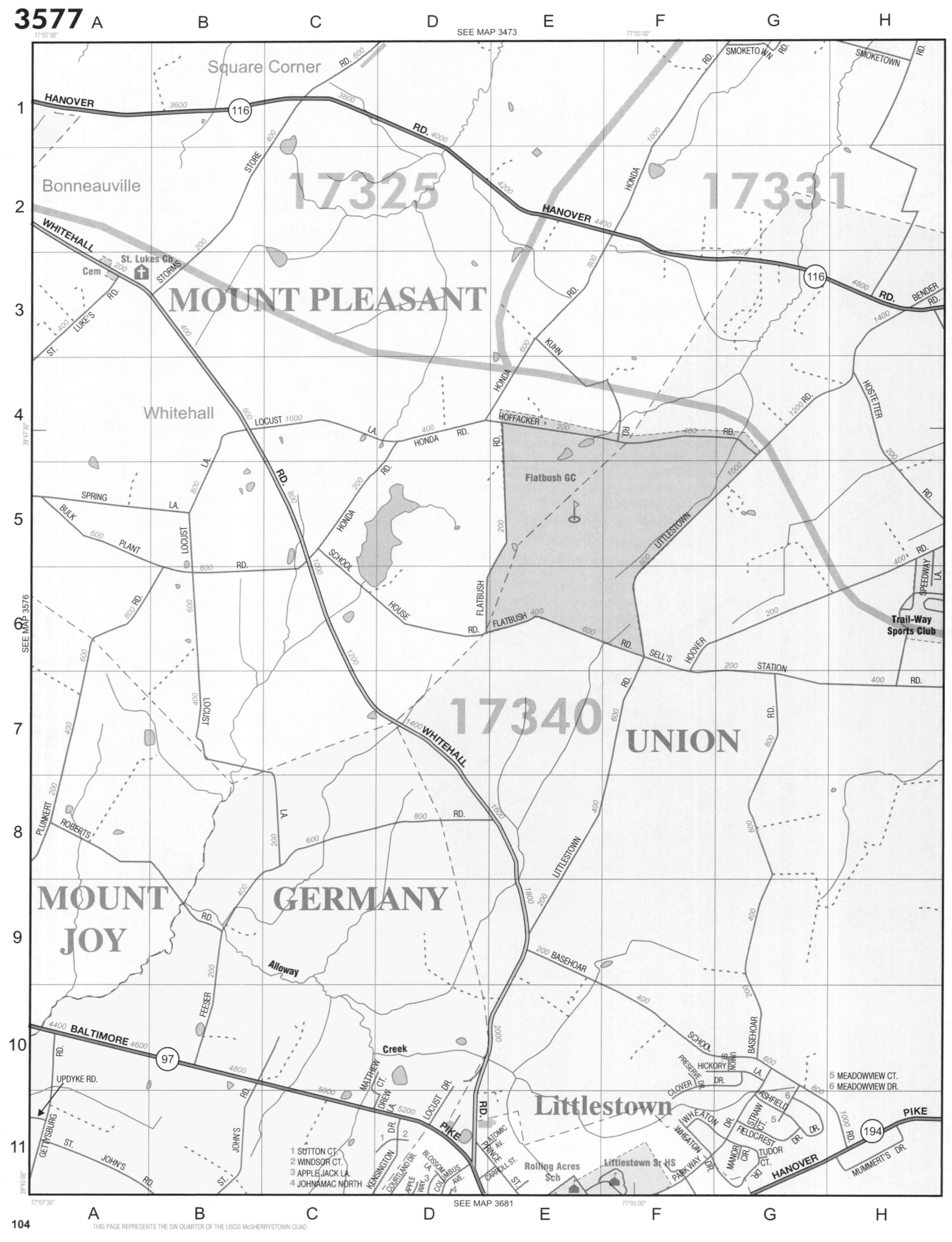

SEE MAP 3473

Square Corner

Bonneauville

17325

17331

HANOVER

116

WHITEHALL

St. Lukes Ch

Cem

MOUNT PLEASANT

HANOVER

116

RD.

BENDER RD.

STORMS

LUKE'S RD.

ST.

Whitehall

LOCUST

HONDA RD.

KUHN

HOFFACKER

HONDA RD.

Flatbush GC

HOSTETTER

SPRING LA.

BULK PLANT

LOCUST RD.

HONDA

SCHOOL HOUSE RD.

FLATBUSH

FLATBUSH

LITTLESTOWN

SPEEDWAY LA.

Trail-Way Sports Club

17340

UNION

SELL'S RD.

HOOVER

STATION RD.

LOCUST

WHITEHALL

RD.

LITTLESTOWN

MOUNT JOY

PLUMERT

ROBERTS

GERMANY

LA

RD.

BASEHOAR

FEESER

Alloway

Creek

BASEHOAR

SCHOOL

BALTIMORE

97

UPDYKE RD.

MATTHEW CT.

DREW LA.

LOCUST DR.

PRESERVE DR.

HICKORY DR.

CLOVER

UNION LA.

5 MEADOWVIEW CT.
6 MEADOWVIEW DR.

ASHFIELD

STRAW

FIELDCREST

WHEATON DR.

GETTYSBURG ST.

JOHN'S RD.

JOHN'S ST.

KENSINGTON DR.

COURTLAND DR.

APPLE WAY

BLOSSOM LA.

COLUMBUS AVE.

Littlestown

PATOMIC AV.

PRINCE ST.

CARROLL ST.

Rolling Acres Sch

Littlestown Sr HS

1 SUTTON CT.
2 WINDSOR CT.
3 APPLE JACK LA.
4 JOHNAMAC NORTH

WHEATON DR.

MANOR CIR.

TUDOR CT.

PARK WAY

HANOVER

MUMMERT'S DR.

PIKE

194

SEE MAP 3681

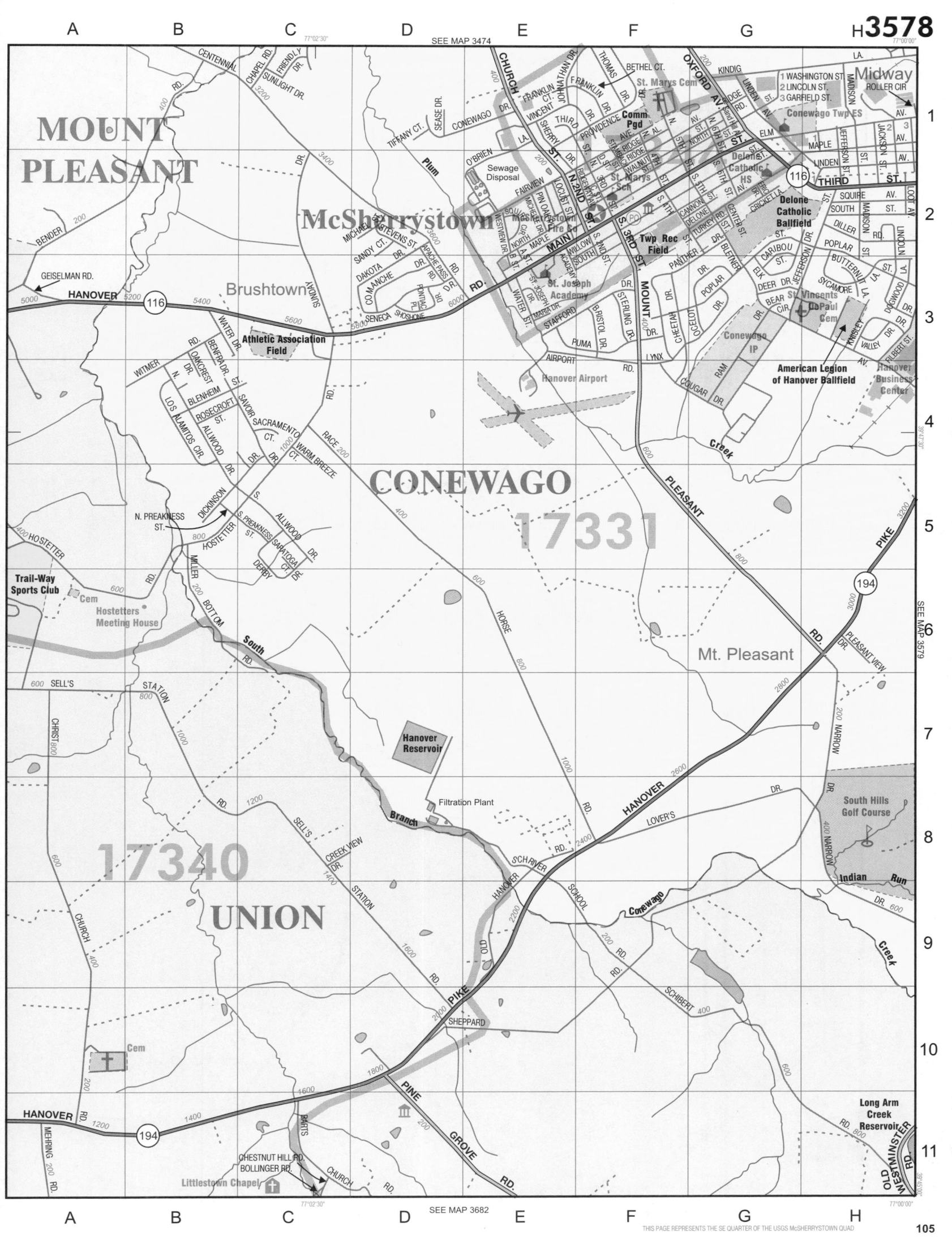

MOUNT PLEASANT

McSherrystown

Midway

Brushtown

CONEWAGO

17331

Mt. Pleasant

17340

UNION

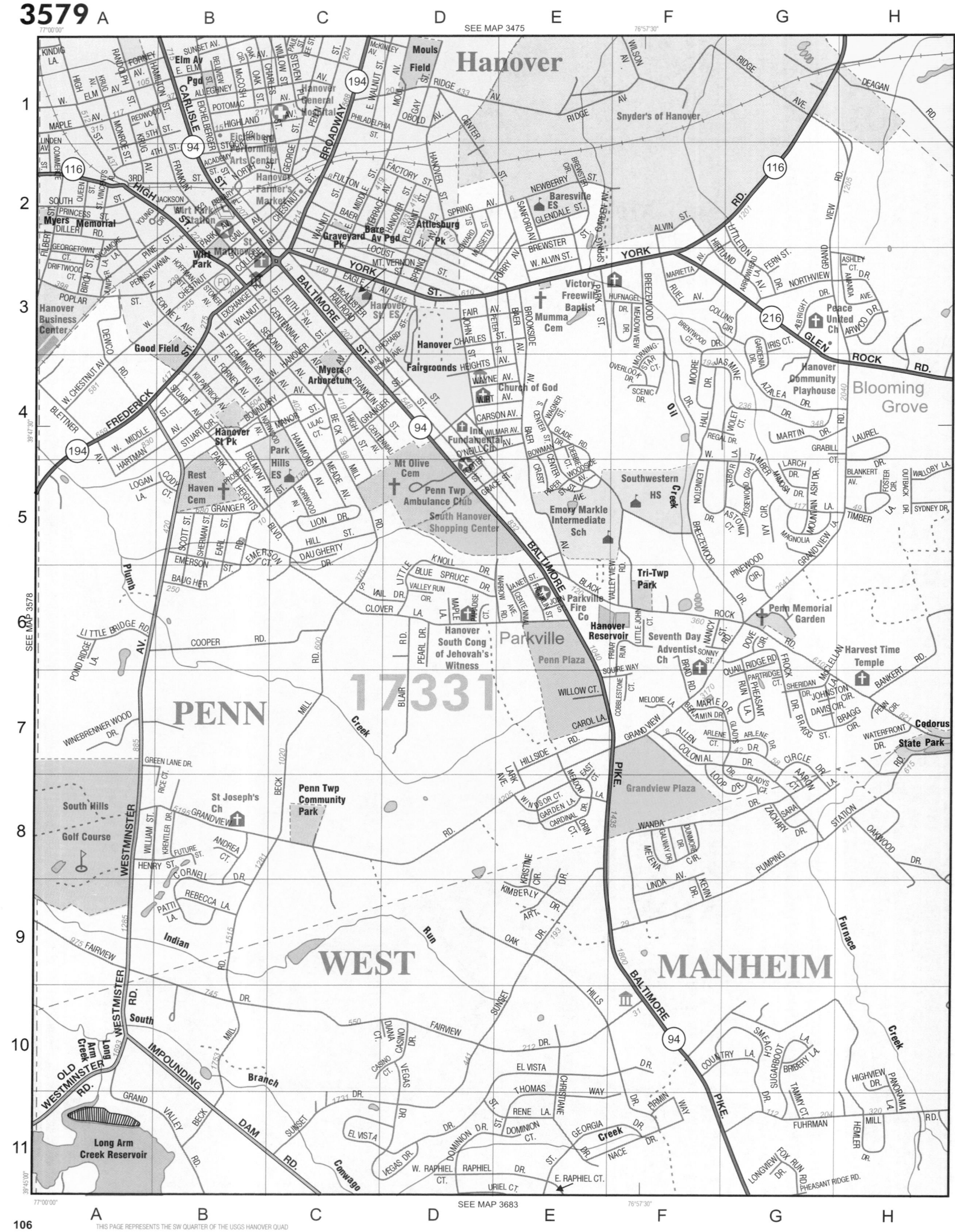

77°00'00"   76°57'30"

Hanover

Snyder's of Hanover

Hanover General Hospital

Eichelberger Performing Arts Center

Myers Memorial

Mouls Field

Baresville ES

Hanover Farmer's Market

Wirt Park Station

Wirt Market House Park

Graveyard Pk

Bare Av Pgd

Attlesburg Pk

Victory Freewill Baptist

Peace United Ch

Hanover Business Center

Good Field

Mumma Cem

Hanover St ES

Hanover Community Playhouse

Blooming Grove

Myers Arboretum

Hanover Fairgrounds

Church of God

Wirt

Southwestern HS

Hanover St Pk

Park Hills ES

Int'l Fundamental O'Neill Cir

Mt Olive Cem

Emory Markle Intermediate Sch

Rest Haven Cem

Penn Twp Ambulance Club

South Hanover Shopping Center

Tri-Twp Park

Penn Memorial Garden

Harvest Time Temple

Hanover South Cong of Jehovah's Witness

Parkville

Parkville Fire Co

Hanover Reservoir

Seventh Day Adventist Ch

PENN

Penn Plaza

17331

Codorus State Park

Winebrenner Wood Dr

St Joseph's Ch

Penn Twp Community Park

Grandview Plaza

South Hills Golf Course

WEST

MANHEIM

Indian

Long Arm Creek

South

Long Arm Creek Reservoir

Branch

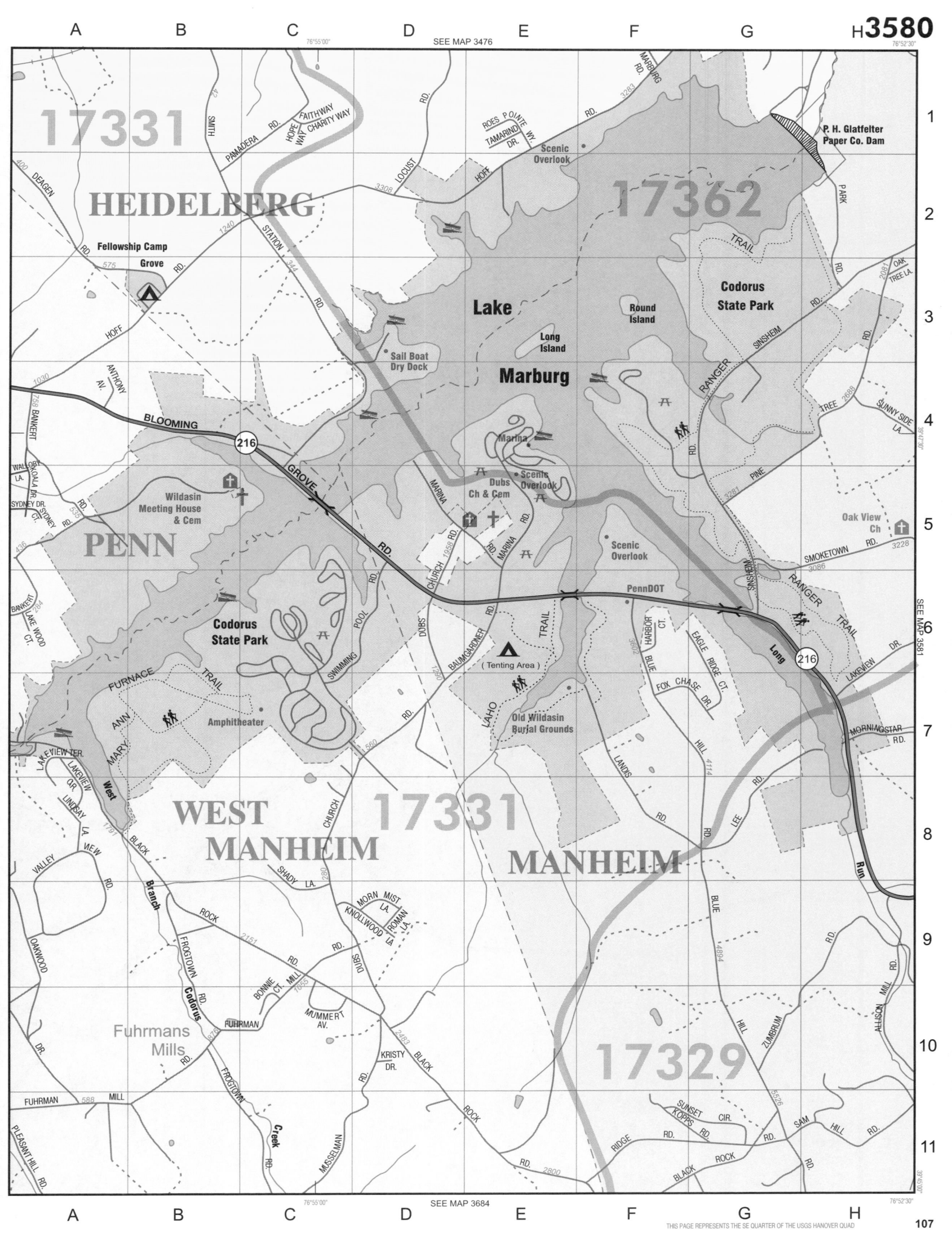

A B C D E F G

SEE MAP 3476

1

17331

2

HEIDELBERG

17362

Fellowship Camp
Grove

3

Codorus
State Park

Lake

Round
Island

Long
Island

Sail Boat
Dry Dock

Marburg

4

BLOOMING

216

Marina

Scenic
Overlook

PENN

Wildasin
Meeting House
& Cem

Dubs
Ch & Cem

GROVE

Scenic
Overlook

5

Oak View
Ch

RD.

PennDOT

6

Codorus
State Park

TRAIL

216

Long

Amphitheater

(Tenting Area)

7

Old Wildasin
Burial Grounds

MORNINGSTAR
RD.

WEST

17331

8

MANHEIM

MANHEIM

Branch

9

Fuhrmans
Mills

17329

10

11

A B C D E F G H

SEE MAP 3684

P. H. Glatfelter
Paper Co. Dam

SEE MAP 3581

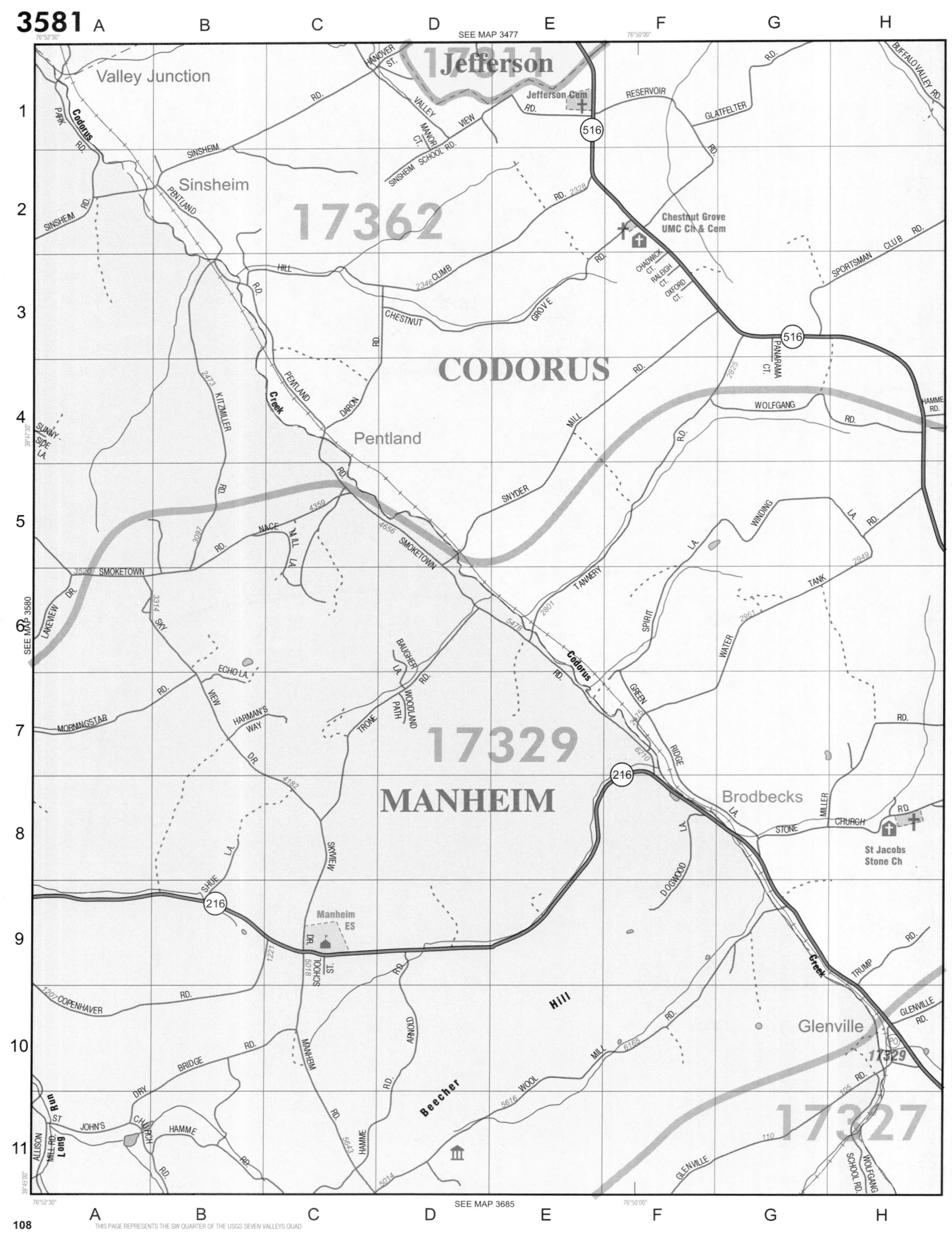

SEE MAP 3477

Valley Junction

Jefferson

17311

Jefferson Cem

RESERVOIR

BUFFALO VALLEY RD.

Sinsheim

Sinsheim

17362

516

GLATFELTER

Chestnut Grove
UMC Ch & Cem

SPORTSMAN CLUB RD.

CHESTNUT

CODORUS

516

PANARAMA

WOLFGANG

HAMME RD.

Pentland

Creek

Pentland

MILL

SNYDER

WINDING

RD.

SMOKETOWN

TANNERY

TANK

SMOKETOWN

SKY

Codorus

SPIRIT

WATER

GREEN

17329

MANHEIM

RIDGE

216

Brodbecks

MILLER

St Jacobs
Stone Ch

STONE

CHURCH

DOGWOOD

216

Manheim
ES

Hill

Creek

TRUMP

GLENVILLE RD.

COPENHAVER

Glenville

17329

60

BRIDGE

Beecher

MILL

WOOL

17327

DRY

ST JOHN'S

CHURCH

HAMME

GLENVILLE

WOLFGANG SCHOOL RD.

SEE MAP 3685

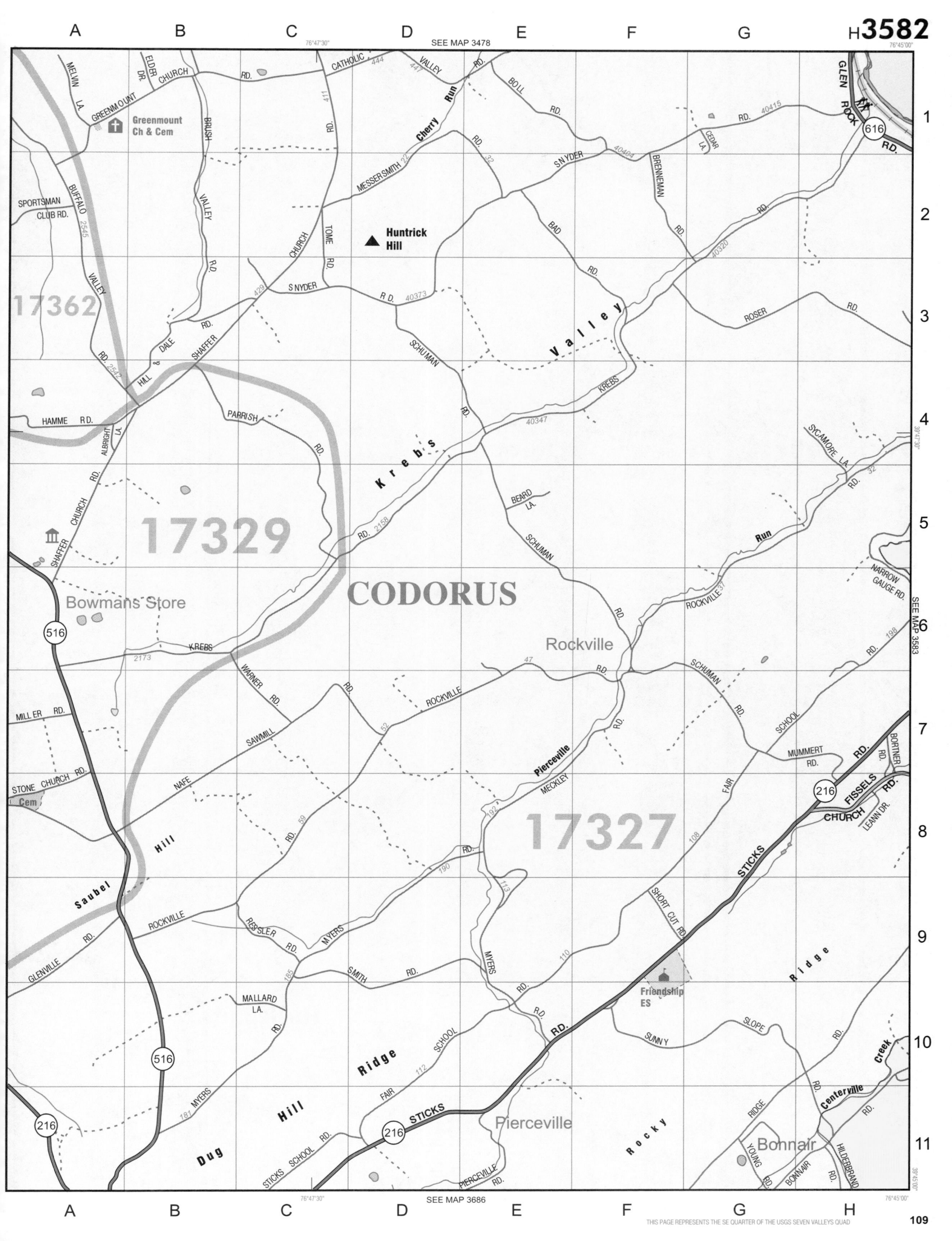

A B C D E F G H

76°47'30" SEE MAP 3478 76°45'00"

MELVIN LA.
ELDER DR.
CHURCH
GREENMOUNT
RD.
CATHOLIC
444
VALLEY
RD.
BOLL
RD.
GLEN ROCK RD.
616

Greenmount Ch & Cem

Cherry Run
411
BRUSH
VALLEY
RD.
MESSER SMITH 22
RD.
32
SNYDER
40404
BRENNEMAN RD.
CEDAR LA.
RD.
40415

SPORTSMAN CLUB RD.
BUFFALO 2545
VALLEY
TOME RD.
CHURCH 429
Huntrick Hill
RD.
BAD
RD.
40320

17362
RD. 2542
DALE
SHAFFER RD.
SNYDER
R D. 40373
SCHUMAN
Valley
ROSER
RD.

HILL &
HAMME RD.
ALBRIGHT LA.
CHURCH RD.
PARRISH RD.
RD.
Krebs
KREBS
RD. 40347
SYCAMORE LA.
RD. 32

17329
SHAFFER CHURCH
RD. 2158
Krebs
BEARD LA.
SCHUMAN
Run
NARROW GAUGE RD.
RD. 198

Bowmans Store
516
KREBS 2173
WARNER RD.
RD.
CODORUS
RD.
ROCKVILLE 37
Rockville
SCHUMAN RD.
SEE MAP 3583

MILLER RD.
SAWMILL
RD. 52
ROCKVILLE
47
RD.
SCHUMAN RD.
SCHOOL

STONE CHURCH RD.
Cem
NAFE
RD. 59
Pierceville
MECKLEY 192
RD.
FAIR
MUMMERT RD.
216
BORTNER RD.
FISSELS CHURCH RD.
LEANN DR.

HILL
RD.
RD. 190
17327
108
STICKS

Saubel
ROCKVILLE
RESSLER RD. 185
MYERS
SMITH RD.
MYERS RD.
110
SHORT CUT RD.
Ridge

GLENVILLE RD.
MALLARD LA.
RD.
Friendship ES
SUNNY
SLOPE RD.
Creek

516
Ridge
SCHOOL RD.
112
FAIR
MYERS RD. 181
STICKS 216
Pierceville
RIDGE RD.
Centerville RD.

216
Dug Hill
STICKS SCHOOL RD.
PIERCEVILLE RD.
Rocky
YOUNG RD.
Bonnair
BONNAIR RD.
HILDEBRAND

A B C D E F G H

76°47'30" SEE MAP 3686 76°45'00"

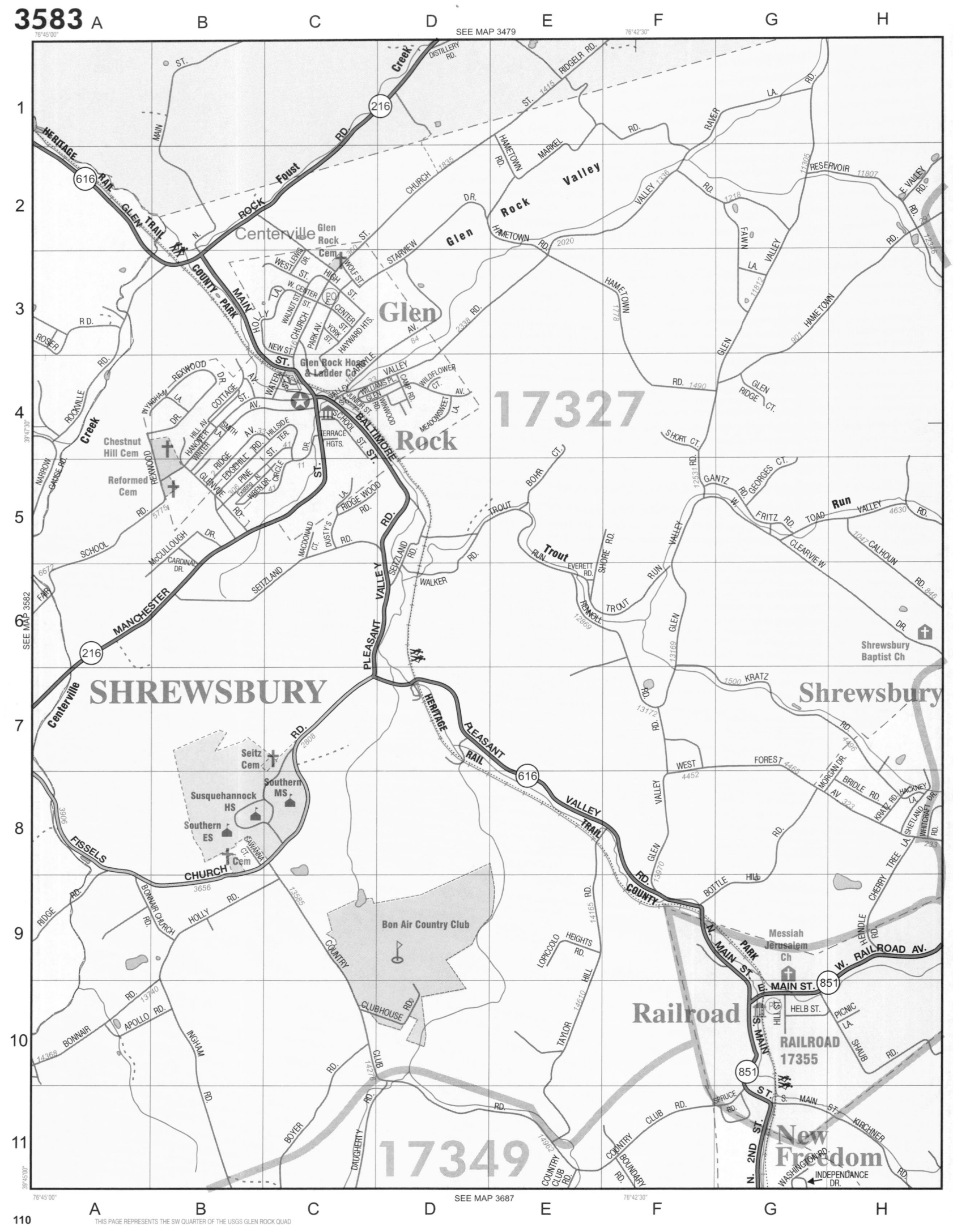

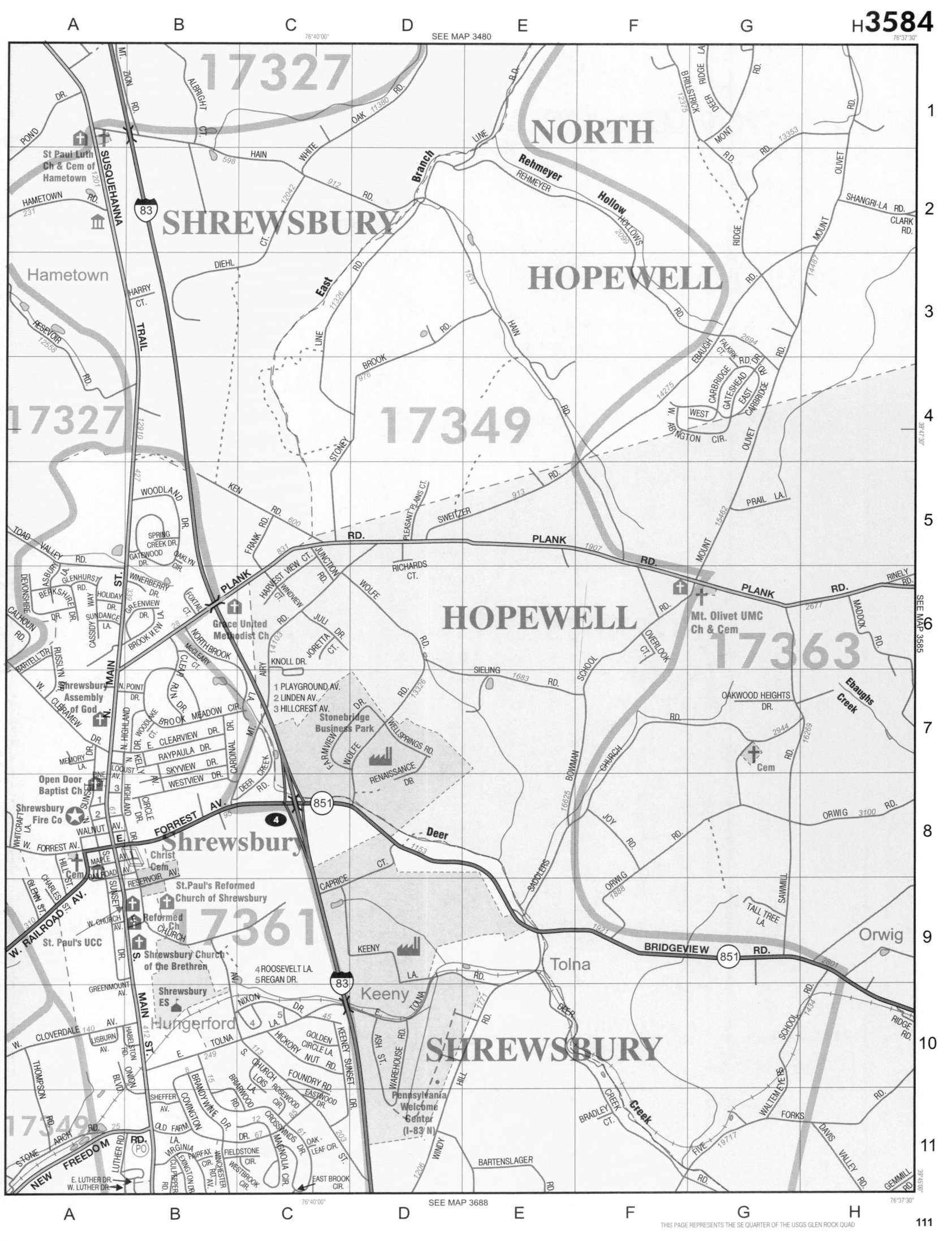

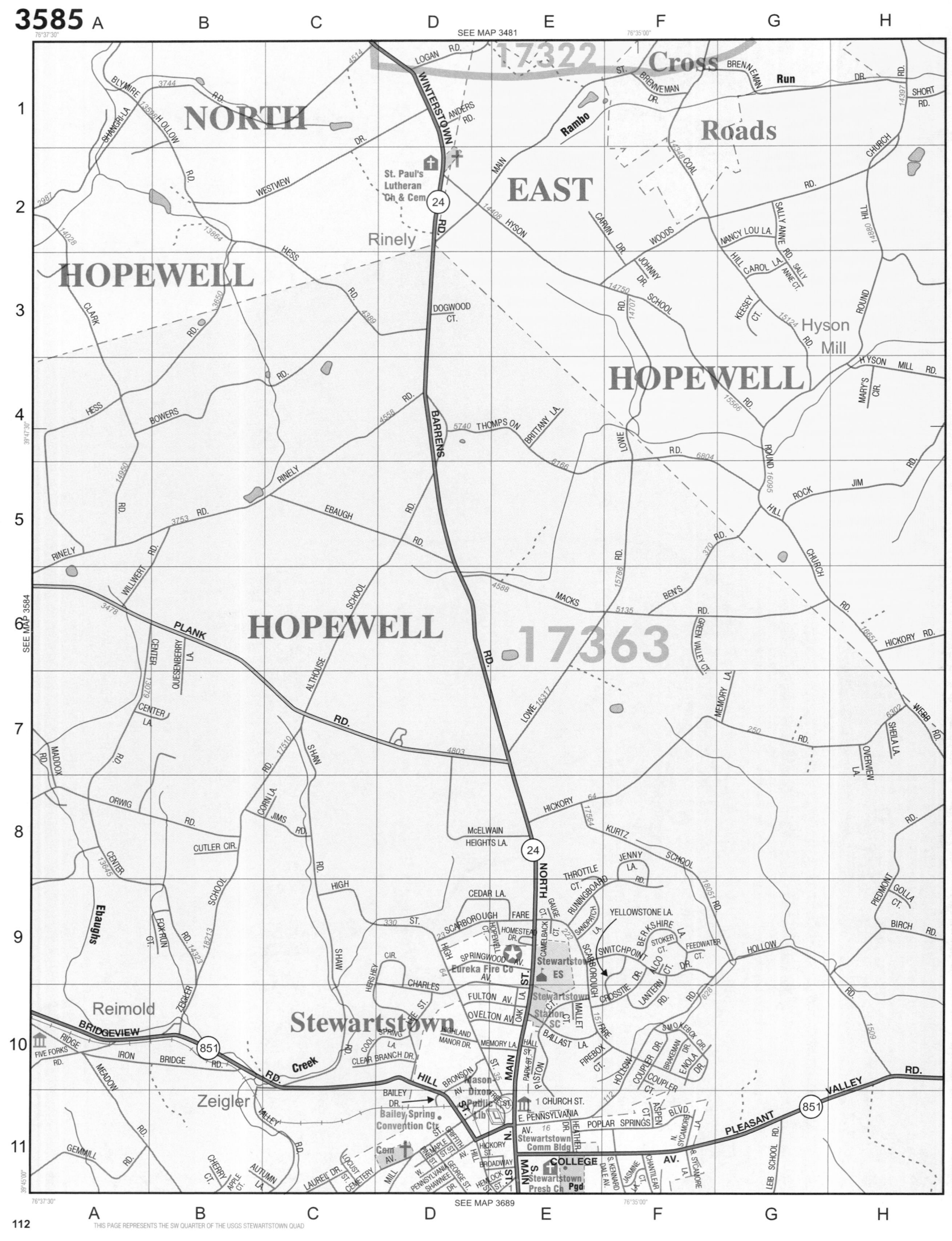

THIS PAGE REPRESENTS THE SW QUARTER OF THE USGS STEWARTSTOWN QUAD

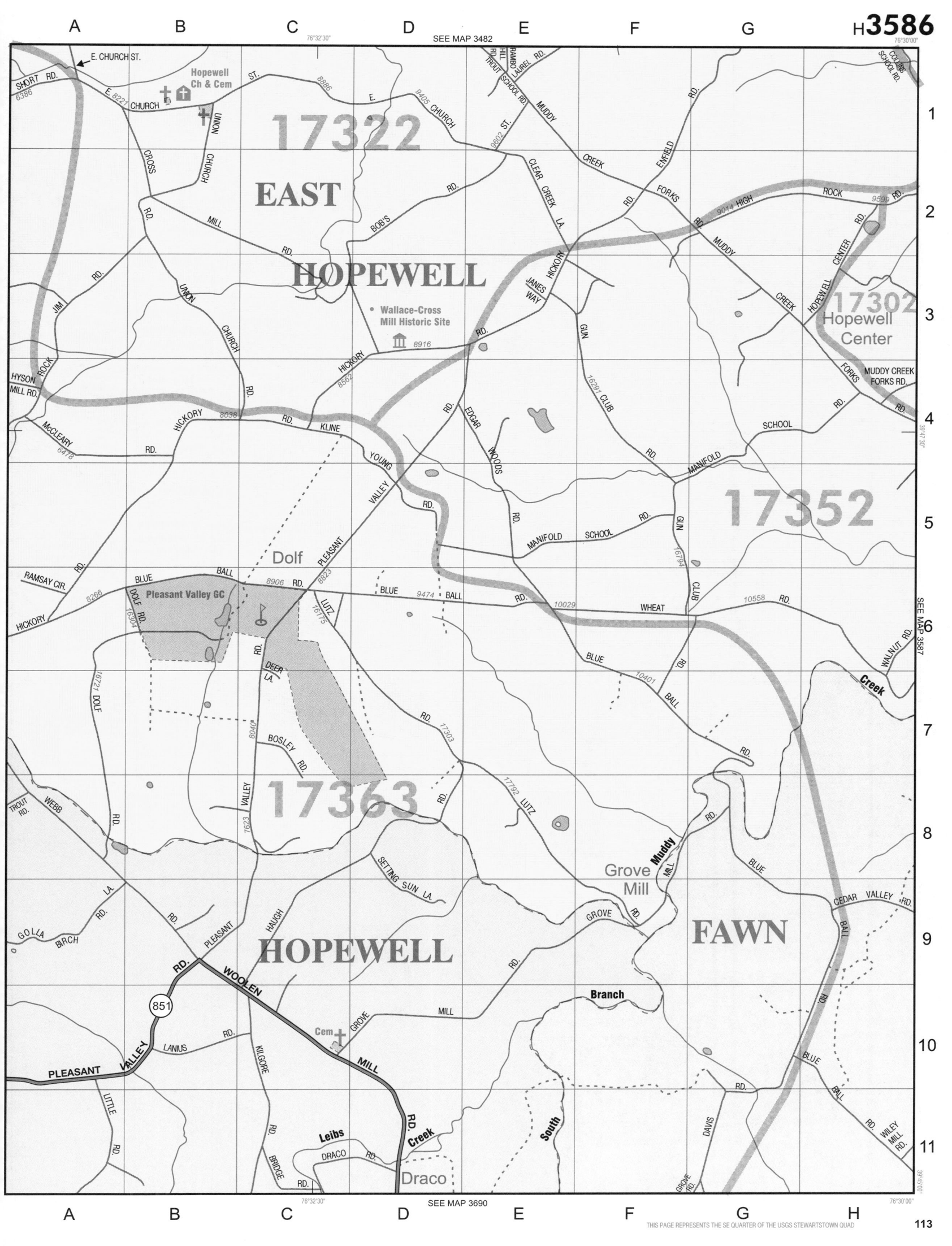

SEE MAP 3482

17322

EAST

HOPEWELL

• Wallace-Cross
Mill Historic Site

17302

Hopewell
Center

MUDDY CREEK
FORKS RD.

17352

Dolf

Pleasant Valley GC

17363

Grove
Mill

FAWN

Creek

HOPEWELL

851

Leibs

Draco

SEE MAP 3690

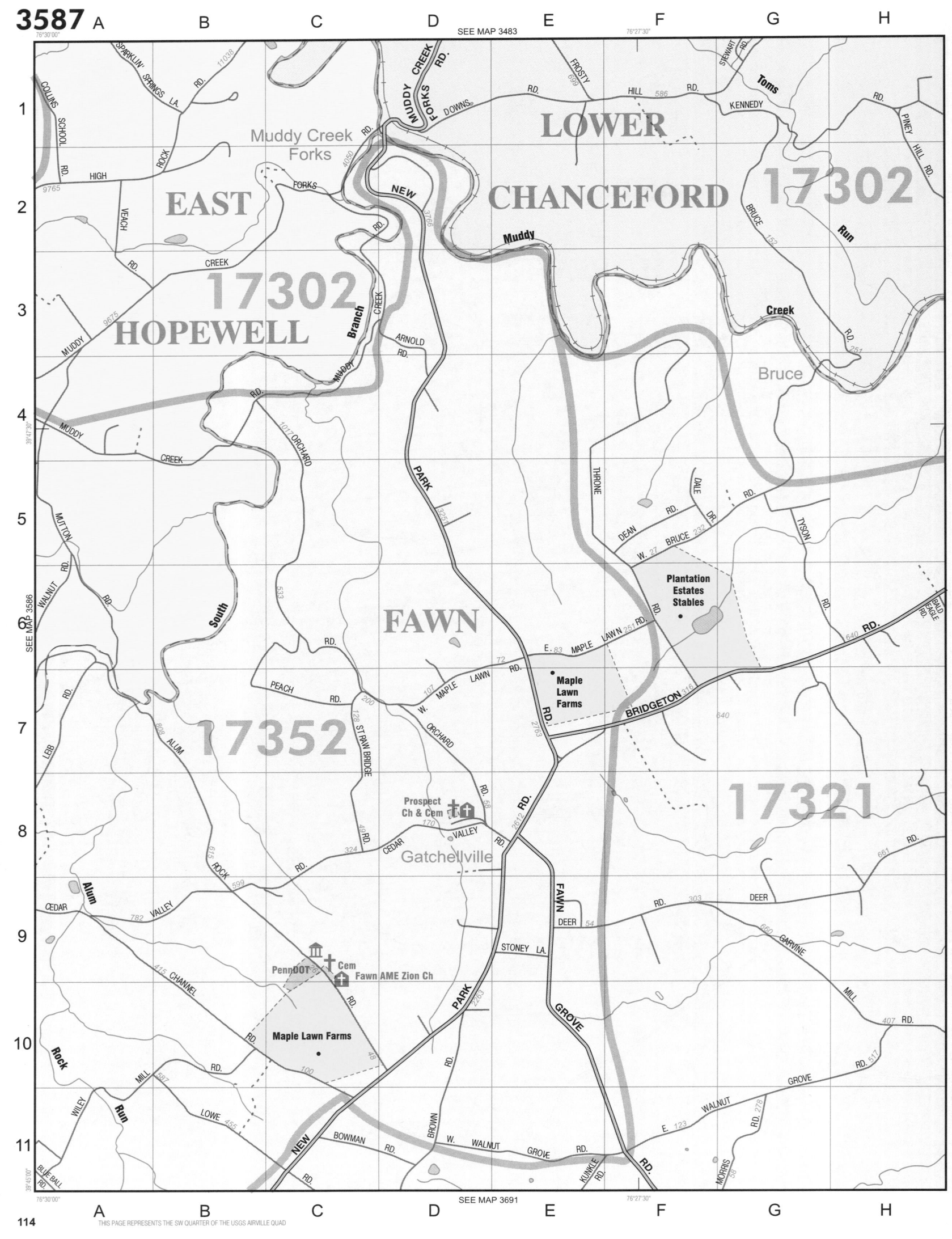

76°30'00"

B   C   D   SEE MAP 3483   E   76°27'30"   F   G   H

COLLINS
SCHOOL
RD.

SPARKLIN SPRINGS LA.

ROCK

HIGH

9765

VEACH

RD.

Muddy Creek
Forks

FORKS

RD.

110.38

4050

9766

MUDDY CREEK RD.

FORKS

NEW

DOWNS

RD.

FROSTY
699

RD.

HILL 586

KENNEDY

STEWART

Toms

RD.

PINEY HILL RD.

LOWER

CHANCEFORD

17302

Muddy

BRUCE 152

Run

EAST

17302

CREEK

Branch

CREEK

MUDDY

Arnold
RD.

9675

HOPEWELL

Creek

RD.

Creek

RD.
251

Bruce

MUDDY

RD.

CREEK

MUTTON

RD.

WALNUT RD.

9745.00

39745.00

PARK

1017 ORCHARD

533

125?

THRONE

DEAN

W. 27

DALE

BRUCE 232

RD.

RD.

DR.

RD.

TYSON RD.

SEE MAP 3586

South

FAWN

RD.

RD.

Plantation
Estates
Stables

E. 83 MAPLE LAWN

251 RD.

640 RD.

BALD EAGLE RD.

72 RD.

PEACH

RD.

107 W. MAPLE LAWN

200

808 ALUM

128 ST RAW BRIDGE

17352

ORCHARD

Maple
Lawn
Farms

640

LEIB RD.

RD.

2763

BRIDGETON 316

17321

RD. 58

Prospect
Ch & Cem

VALLEY

170

2612 RD.

RD.

RD.

Gatchellville

RD.

661 RD.

Alum

CEDAR

ROCK

615

782 VALLEY

324

599

CEDAR

FAWN

DEER

RD. 303

DEER

GARVINE

660

MILL

PennDOT

Cem

Fawn AME Zion Ch

415 CHANNEL

RD.

STONEY LA.

DEER 54

Maple Lawn Farms

48

100

PARK

2203

GROVE

0

Rock

MILL 587

LOWE 455

Run

WILEY RD.

BLUE BALL RD.

39745'00"

76°30'00"

NEW RD.

BOWMAN RD.

BROWN RD.

W. WALNUT

GROVE

RD.

KUNKLE RD.

RD.

E. 123

WALNUT RD. 278

MORRIS 58

GROVE RD. 517

407 RD.

A   B   C   SEE MAP 3691   D   E   76°27'30"   F   G   H

THIS PAGE REPRESENTS THE SW QUARTER OF THE USGS AIRVILLE QUAD

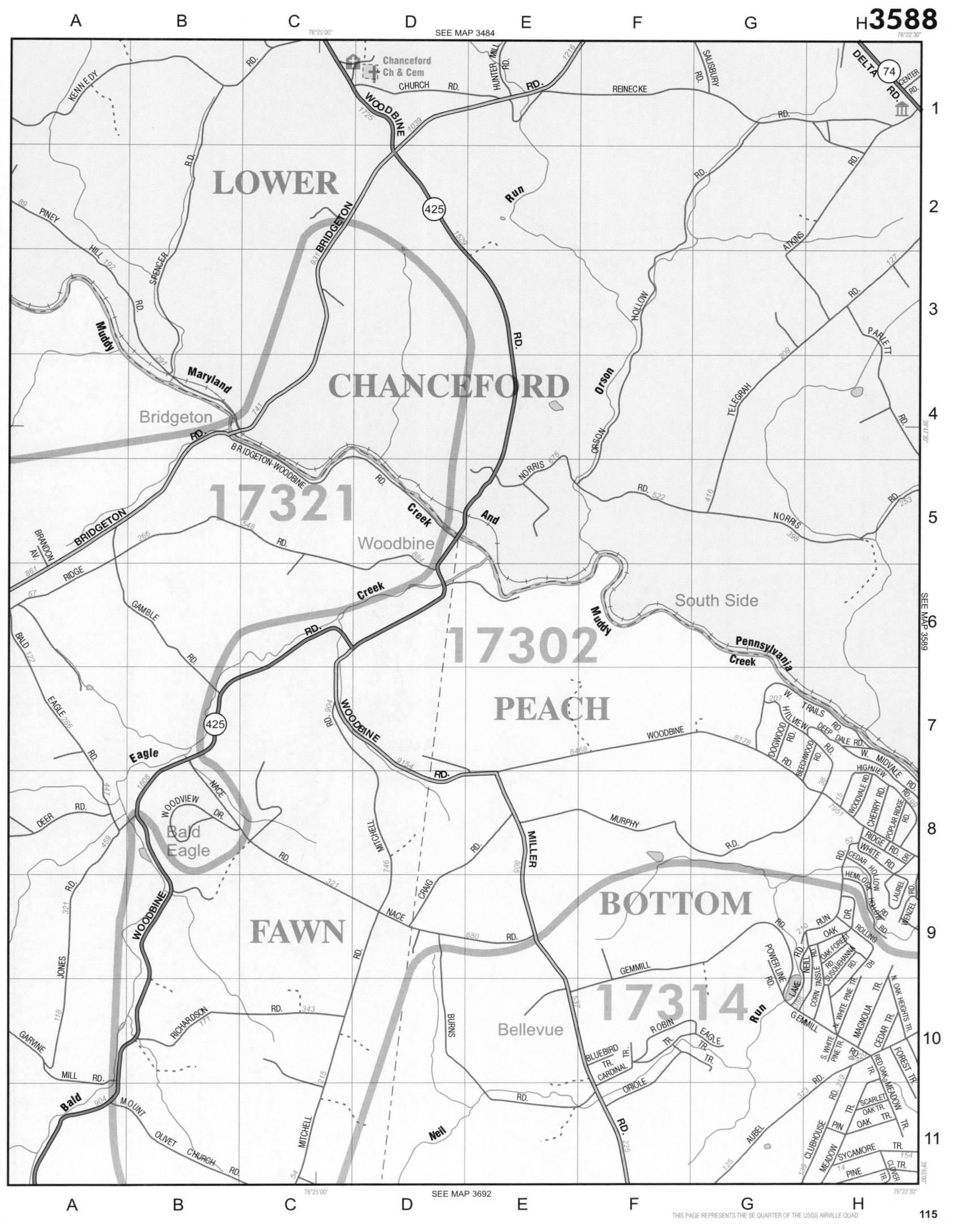

SEE MAP 3484

SEE MAP 3692

SEE MAP 3589

THIS PAGE REPRESENTS THE SE QUARTER OF THE USGS AIRVILLE QUAD

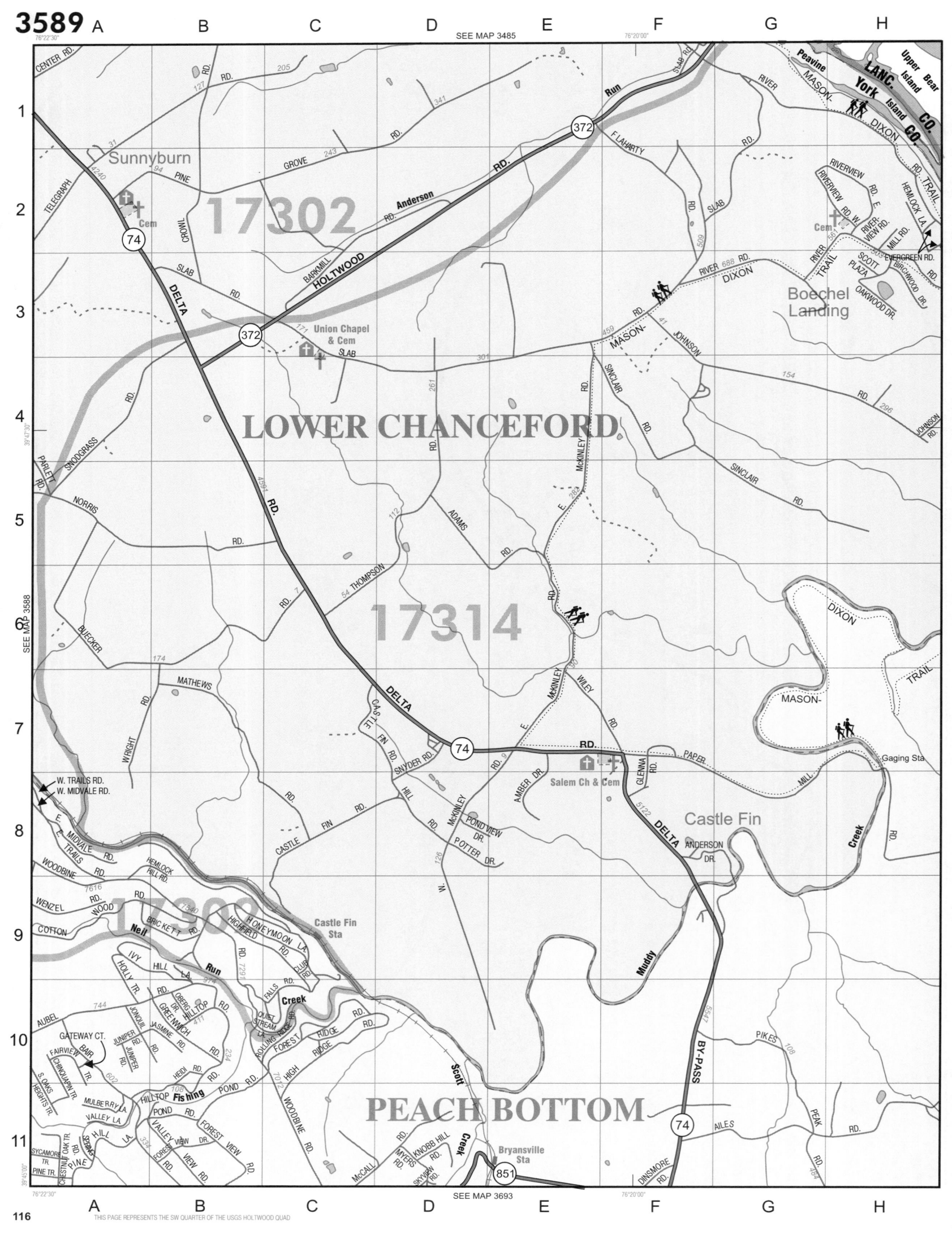

3589 A

LANC. CO.
York CO.

Upper Bear Island
Peavine
MASON-
DIXON

Sunnyburn

17302

Telegraph

CENTER RD.
127 RD.
RD.
205
GROVE 243
PINE
CROWL
94
Cem
31
4240
74
DELTA
SLAB
BARKMILL
HOLTWOOD
Anderson
RD.
341
RD.
RD.

372
Run
SLAB RD.
F.LAHARTY
RIVER
RIVERVIEW
RIVERVIEW RD. E.
RIVERVIEW RD. W.
RIVER VIEW RD.
661
MILL RD.
HEMLOCK LA.
DIXON RD. TRAIL
SCOTT PLAZA
EVERGREEN RD.
BIRCHWOOD DR.
OAKWOOD DR.
Cem

372
171
Union Chapel & Cem
SLAB
261
301
509
RIVER 688 RD.
MASON-
JOHNSON
SINCLAIR
459
41
154
RD. 296
JOHNSON RD.

LOWER CHANCEFORD

DELTA RD.
PARLETT RD.
SNODGRASS
NORRIS
RD.
RD.
ADAMS RD.
112
McKINLEY RD.
E. 282
SINCLAIR RD.
Boechel Landing

17314

BUECKER
174
MATHEWS RD.
WRIGHT RD.
54 THOMPSON
RD. 7
CASTLE FIN RD.
McKINLEY
WILEY
E. McKINLEY
RD.
RD.
DIXON
MASON-
TRAIL

74
SNYDER RD.
DELTA
HILL RD.
McKINLEY RD.
POTTER DR.
POND VIEW DR.
RD. 9
AMBER DR.
Salem Ch & Cem
GLENNA RD.
PAPER MILL RD.
5122
DELTA
Castle Fin
ANDERSON DR.
Gaging Sta
Creek
RD.

W. TRAILS RD.
W. MIDVALE RD.
E. MIDVALE TRAILS RD.
WOODBINE RD.
7616
WENZEL RD.
WOOD
COTTON
17309
HEMLOCK HILL RD.
7340
Neil
BRICKETT
HIGHFIELD RD.
HONEYMOON LA.
Castle Fin Sta
Run
IVY HILL LA.
HOLLY TR.
744
JONQUIL
JUNIPER
OBERG DR.
HILLTOP RD.
GREENWICH
JASMINE
YASMINE
HEIDI RD.
602
374
QUIET STREAM LA.
7291
BLUFF RD.
FALLS
ROLLING RIDGE RD.
Creek
FOREST RD.
RIDGE RD.
RD.
234
RD.
Muddy

GATEWAY CT.
FAIRVIEW
BAIR TR.
CHINQUAPIN TR.
S. OAKS HEIGHTS TR.
IVY
JONQUIL
JUNIPER
411
MULBERRY LA.
VALLEY LA.
HILL LA.
HILLTOP
Fishing
708
POND RD.
7072
HIGH
FOREST
WOODBINE RD.
Scott
PIKES
708
BY-PASS
554

SYCAMORE TR.
CHESTNUT OAK TR.
PINE TR.
SPRING HILL
VALLEY
FOREST VIEW DR.
VIEW RD.
336
McCALL
RD.
MYERS RD.
KNOBB HILL RD.
SKYVIEW RD.
Creek
Bryansville Sta
851
PEACH BOTTOM
74
AILES
DINSMORE RD.
PEAK RD.
404

THIS PAGE REPRESENTS THE SW QUARTER OF THE USGS HOLTWOOD QUAD

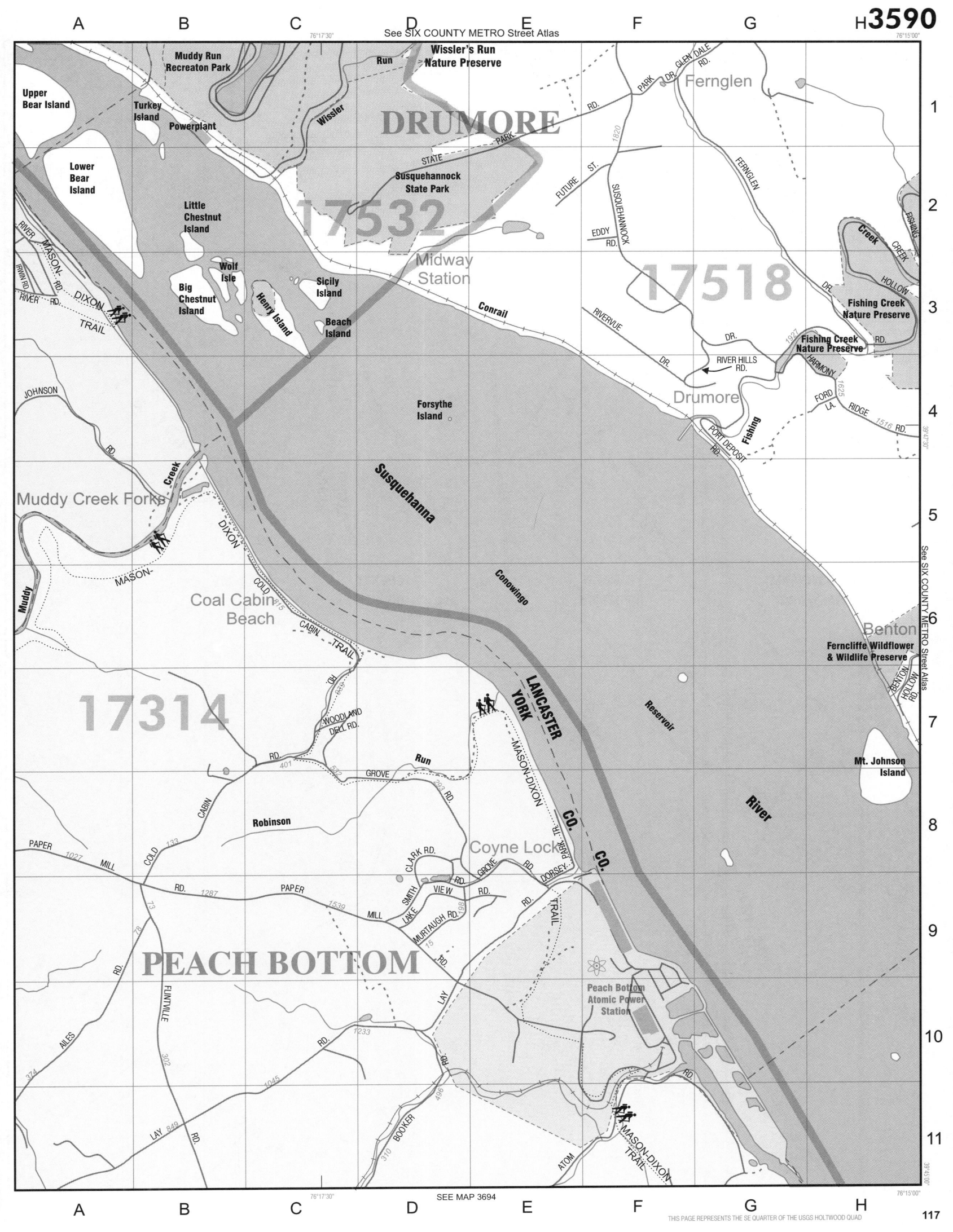

See SIX COUNTY METRO Street Atlas

A **B** **C** **D** **E** **F** **G**

Muddy Run
Recreaton Park

Wissler's Run
Nature Preserve

Fernglen

Upper
Bear Island

Turkey
Island

Powerplant

Wissler

Run

DRUMORE

1

Lower
Bear
Island

Little
Chestnut
Island

17532

Susquehannock
State Park

Creek

FISHING

2

RIVER RD.

MASON- RD.

IRWIN RD.

DIXON

TRAIL

Wolf
Isle

Big
Chestnut
Island

Henry Island

Sicily
Island

Beach
Island

Midway
Station

Conrail

17518

Fishing Creek
Nature Preserve

3

JOHNSON

RD

Creek

Muddy Creek Forks

Forsythe
Island

Susquehanna

RIVERVUE

DR.

DR.

Drumore

PORT DEPOSIT RD.

RIVER HILLS
RD.

Fishing

Fishing Creek
Nature Preserve

HARMONY

FORD
LA.

RIDGE

RD.

4

Muddy

DIXON

MASON-

COLD

CABIN TRAIL

RD.

Coal Cabin
Beach

Conowingo

5

17314

WOODLAND
DELL RD.

RD.
401

522

GROVE

Run

RD.

LANCASTER

YORK

MASON-DIXON

CO.

Reservoir

Benton

Ferncliffe Wildflower
& Wildlife Preserve

BENTON

6

7

Robinson

CABIN

COLD
133

CLARK RD.

GROVE

RD.

DORSEY

RD.

CO.

PARK

RD.

River

Mt. Johnson
Island

8

PAPER
1027

MILL

RD.
1287

PAPER

1539

MILL

SMITH

VIEW

LAKE

MURTAUGH RD.

RD.

15

RD.

Coyne Lock

TRAIL

9

73

78

FLINTVILLE

RD.

302

LAY

RD.

1233

BOOKER

RD.

ATOM

LAY

RD.

496

PEACH BOTTOM

Peach Bottom
Atomic Power
Station

MASON-DIXON

TRAIL

10

AILES

374

LAY 849 RD.

310

1045

11

A **B** **C** **D** **E** **F** **G** **H**

SEE MAP 3694

THIS PAGE REPRESENTS THE SE QUARTER OF THE USGS HOLTWOOD QUAD

See SIX COUNTY METRO Street Atlas

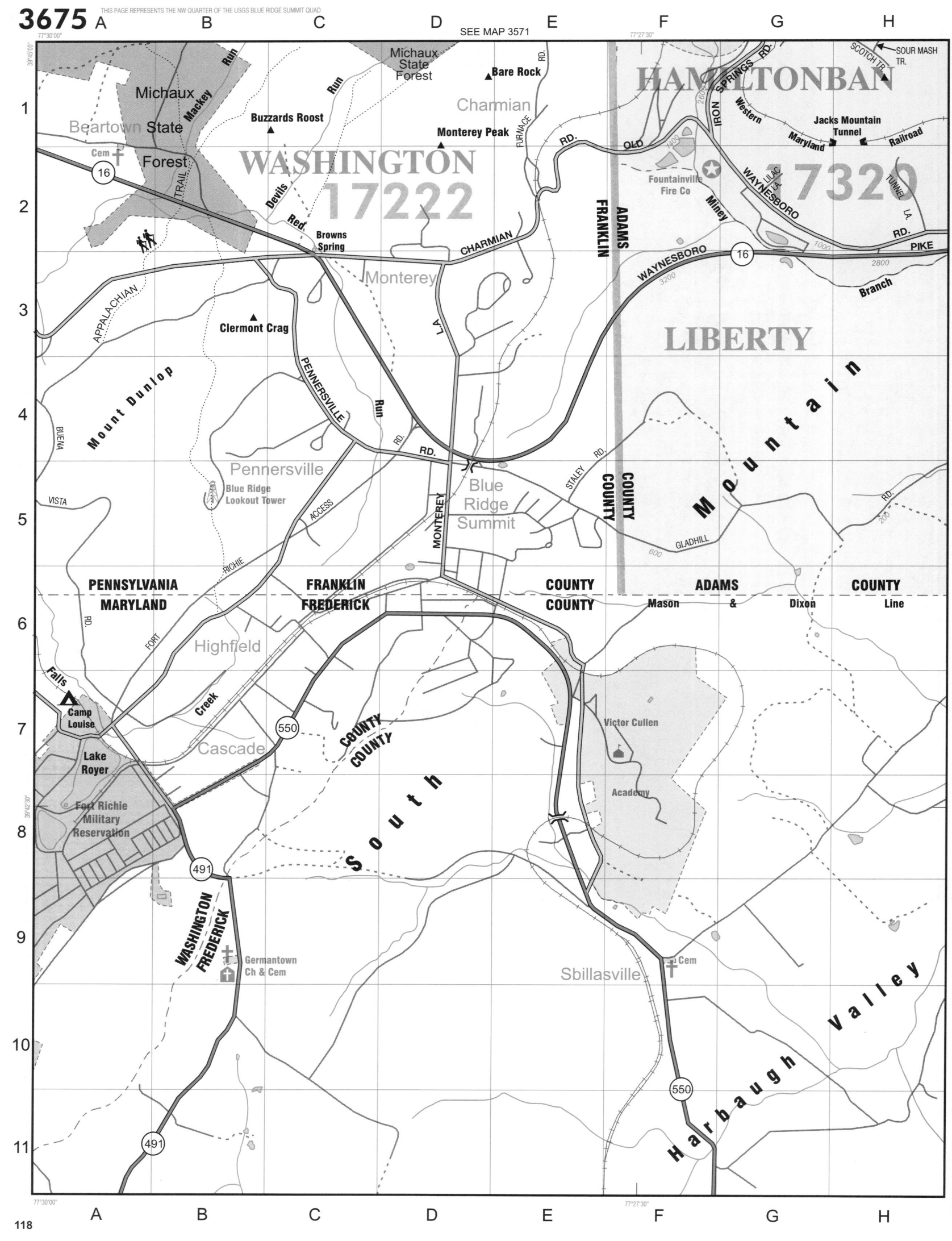

SEE MAP 3571

Michaux State Forest

Bare Rock

Charmian

HAMILTONBAN

SOUR MASH TR.

SCOTCH TR.

Michaux

Mackey Run

Buzzards Roost

Beartown State

Cem

Forest

16

WASHINGTON 17222

Monterey Peak

FURNACE RD.

OLD

1400

Fountainville Fire Co

Jacks Mountain Tunnel

Maryland

Railroad

Western

IRON SPRINGS RD.

WAYNESBORO

LILAC LA.

Miney

Tunnel

17320

LA.

Devils

Red

Browns Spring

CHARMIAN

FRANKLIN
ADAMS

WAYNESBORO

16

3200

Branch

2800

PIKE

RD.

1000

APPALACHIAN

Monterey

LIBERTY

Clermont Crag

Mount Dunlop

PENNERSVILLE

LA.

Run

Blue Ridge Summit

STALEY RD.

COUNTY
COUNTY

Mountain

BUENA

Pennersville

RD.

RD.

Monterey

RD.

200

VISTA

Blue Ridge Lookout Tower

ACCESS

GLADHILL

600

RICHIE

PENNSYLVANIA
MARYLAND

FRANKLIN
FREDERICK

COUNTY
COUNTY

ADAMS

COUNTY

Mason   &   Dixon   Line

FORT

RD.

Highfield

Falls

Creek

Camp Louise

550

COUNTY
COUNTY

Victor Cullen

Lake Royer

Cascade

South

Academy

Fort Richie Military Reservation

491

WASHINGTON
FREDERICK

Germantown Ch & Cem

Sbillasville

Cem

550

Harbaugh Valley

10

491

11

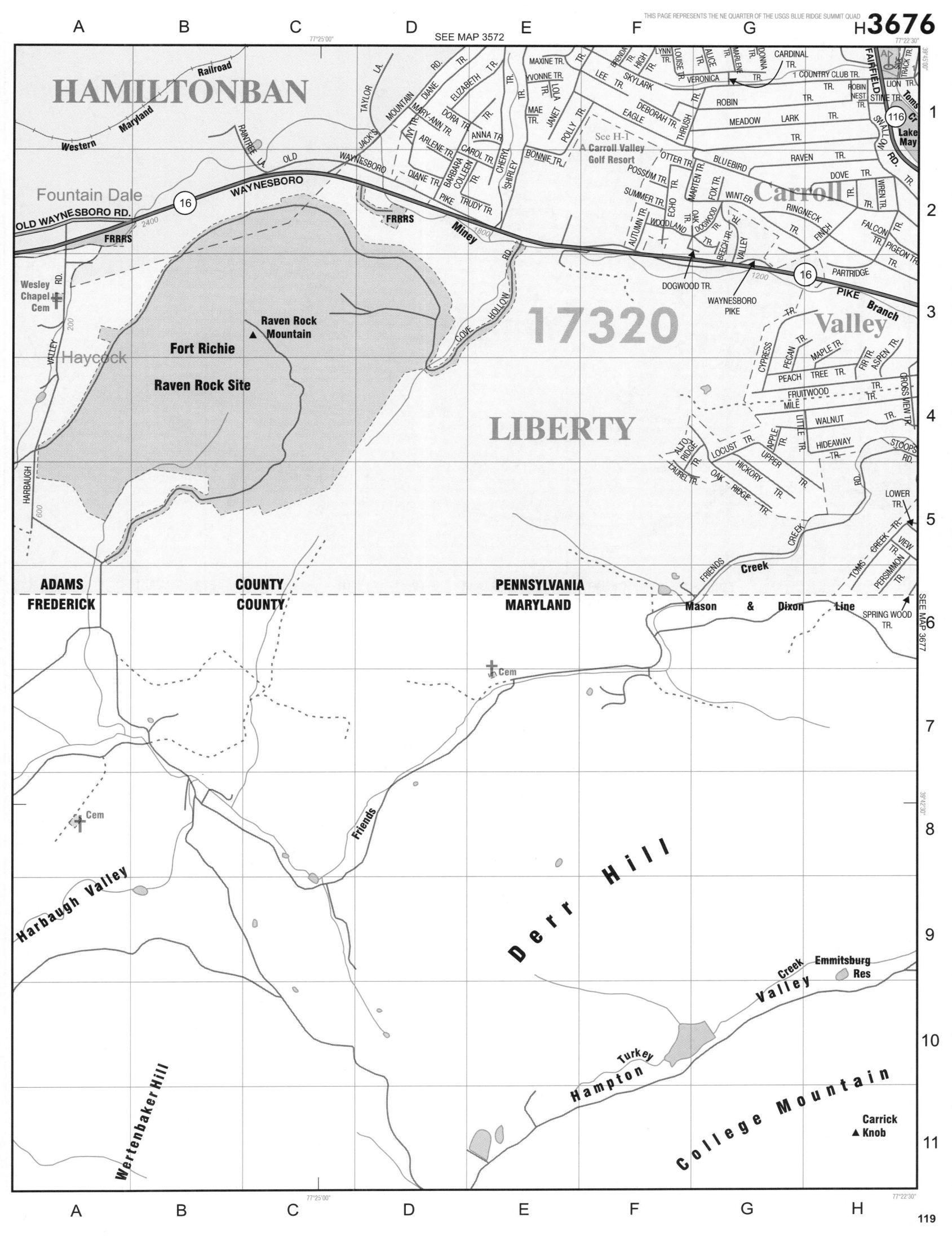

SEE MAP 3572

A B C D E F G H

1

HAMILTONBAN

Railroad

Maryland

Western

Fountain Dale

16

OLD WAYNESBORO RD.

FRRRS

Wesley
Chapel
Cem

Haycock

Fort Richie

Raven Rock Site

Raven Rock
Mountain

WAYNESBORO

OLD

FRRRS

Miney

17320

LIBERTY

See H-1
A Carroll Valley
Golf Resort

Carroll

Valley

DOGWOOD TR.

WAYNESBORO
PIKE

PIKE

Branch

16

1

2

3

4

FRIENDS CREEK

Creek

LOWER
TR.

SPRING WOOD
TR.

SEE MAP 3677

5

6

ADAMS

FREDERICK

COUNTY

COUNTY

PENNSYLVANIA

MARYLAND

Mason & Dixon Line

Cem

7

Friends

Cem

8

Harbaugh Valley

D e r r   H i l l

9

Creek

Valley

**Emmitsburg
Res**

10

Wertenbaker Hill

Turkey

Hampton

C o l l e g e   M o u n t a i n

**Carrick
▲ Knob**

11

A B C D E F G H

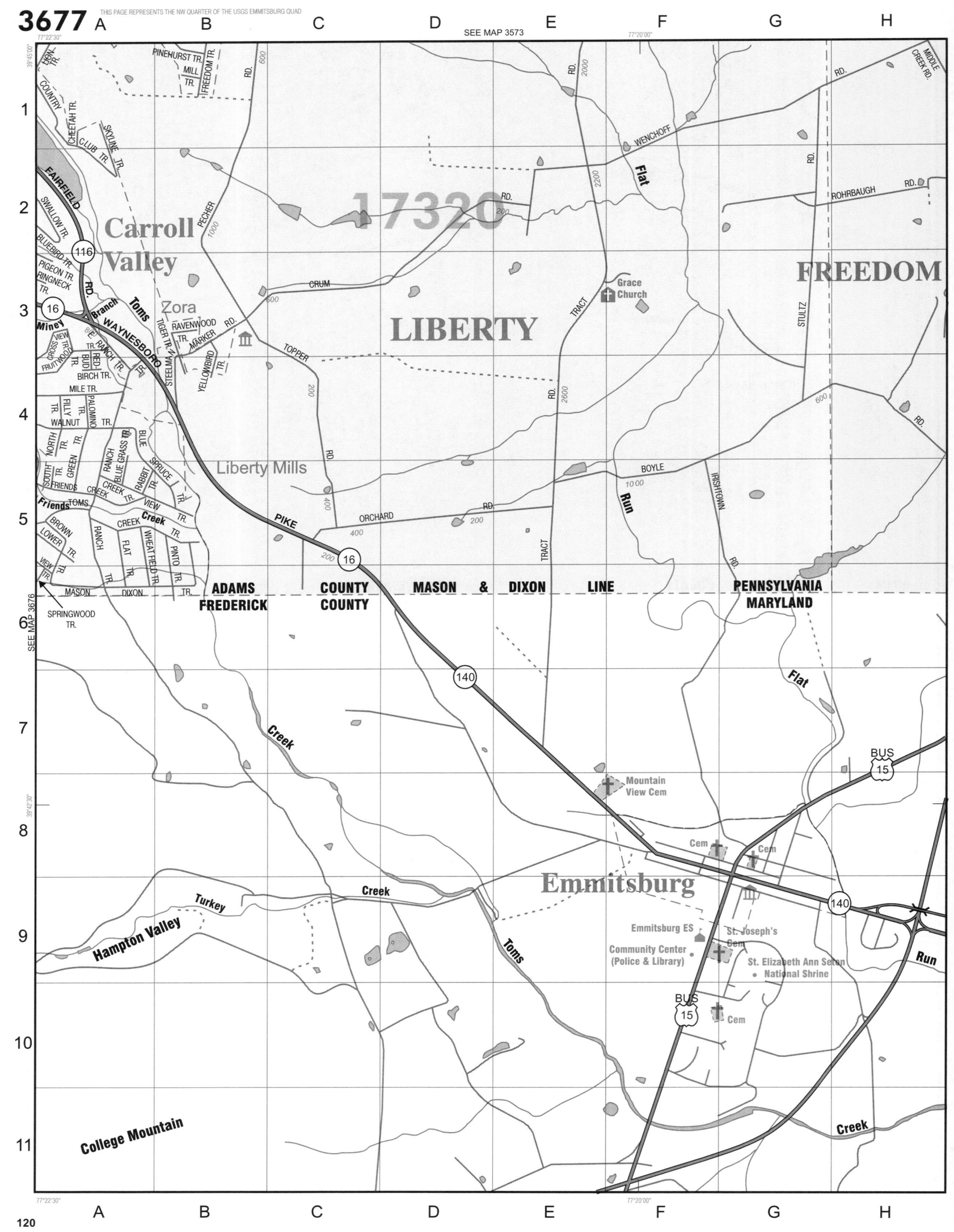

SEE MAP 3573

A B C D E F G H

77°22'30"
39°45'00"

1

PINEHURST TR.
MILL TR.
FREEDOM TR.
COUNTRY TR.
CHEETAH TR.
SKYLINE TR.
CLUB TR.
LION TR.

RD.
600

RD.
2000

WENCHOFF

MIDDLE CREEK RD.

2

FAIRFIELD
SWALLOW TR.
BLUEBIRD TR.
PECHER
1000

RD.
2200

Flat

RD.
2200

ROHRBAUGH RD.

17320

3

Carroll Valley
116
PIGEON TR.
RINGNECK TR.
Zora
CRUM
600

LIBERTY

Grace Church

FREEDOM

STULTZ
RD.

16
Miney
BRANCH
Toms
WAYNESBORO
RAVENWOOD RD.
TIGER TR.
MARKER
RAVENWOOD
STEELMAN
YELLOWBIRD TR.
TOPPER
RD.

TRACT

RD.

4

CROSS VIEW TR.
FRUITWOOD
RANCH TR.
RED TR.
BUD TR.
BIRCH TR.
MILE TR.
FILLY TR.
WALNUT TR.
PALOMINO TR.
NORTH TR.
200

RD.
2600

RD.
600

5

GREEN TR.
SOUTH TR.
FRIENDS
RANCH
BLUE GRASS RD.
SPRUCE TR.
RABBIT TR.
CREEK TR.
BLUE CREEK TR.
VIEW TR.
Liberty Mills
RD.
400

ORCHARD
RD.
400

BOYLE
1000

Run

IRISHTOWN RD.

Friends
Toms
Creek
BROWN TR.
LOWER TR.
VIEW TR.
RANCH
FLAT TR.
WHEATFIELD TR.
PINTO TR.
PIKE
200

16
200

TRACT

6

SEE MAP 3676
SPRINGWOOD TR.
MASON
DIXON
ADAMS COUNTY
FREDERICK COUNTY
MASON & DIXON LINE
PENNSYLVANIA
MARYLAND

39°42'30"

Flat

7

Creek

140

BUS 15

8

Mountain View Cem

Cem
Cem

9

Emmitsburg
Turkey
Creek
Toms
Hampton Valley
Emmitsburg ES
Community Center
(Police & Library)
St. Joseph's Cem
St. Elizabeth Ann Seton
National Shrine
140
Run

10

BUS 15
Cem

11

College Mountain
Creek

77°22'30"
A B C D E F G H
77°20'00"

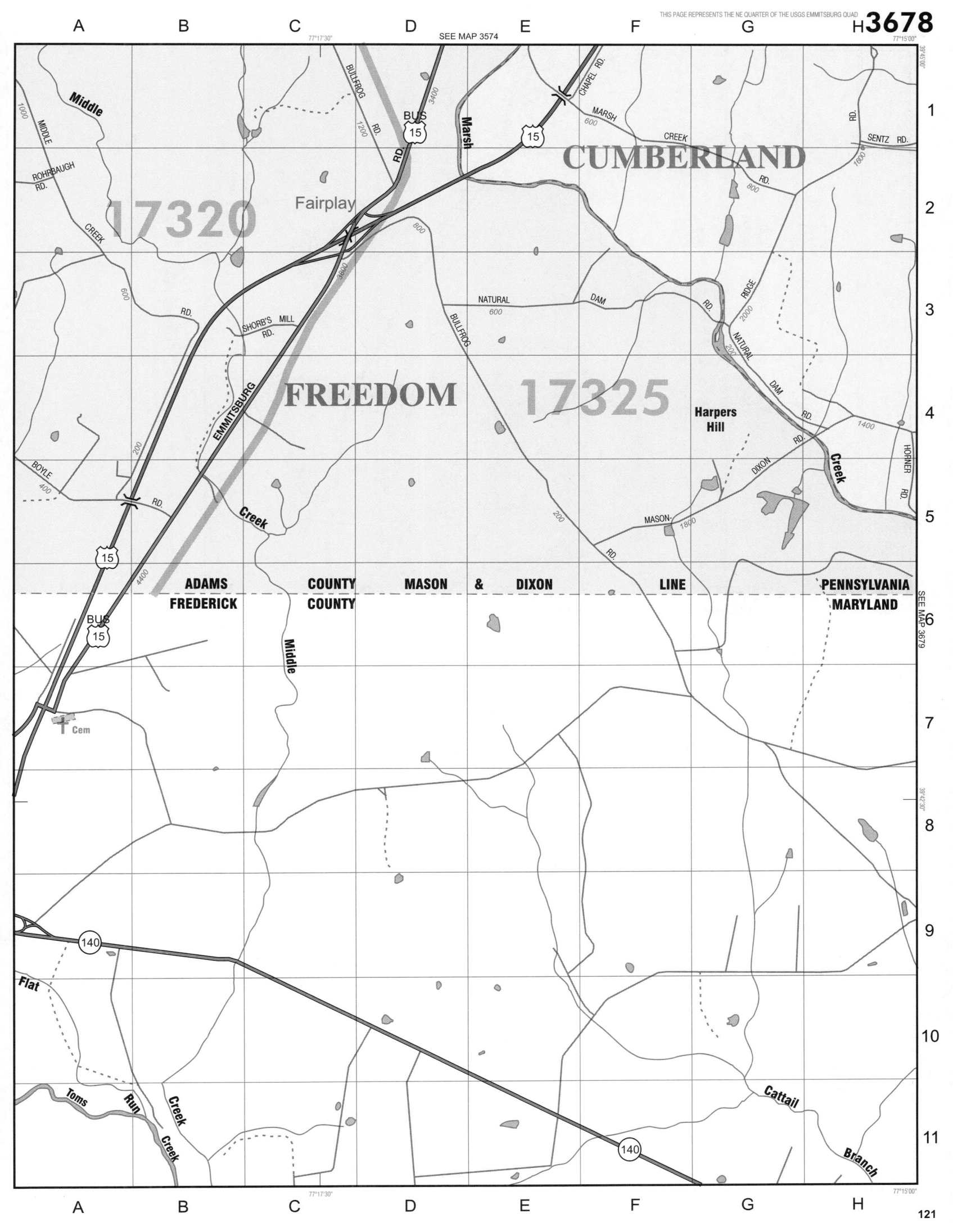

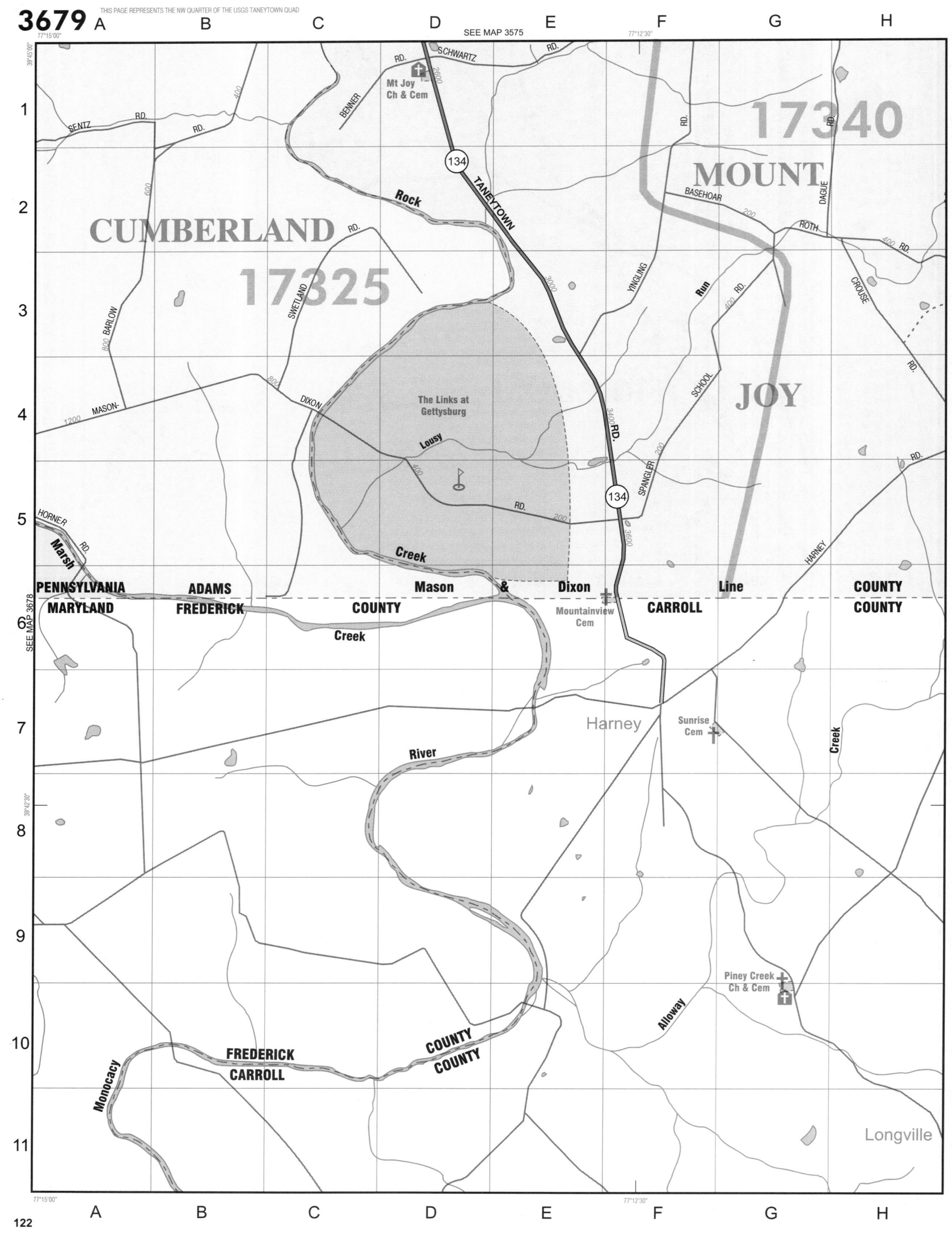

SEE MAP 3575

17340

MOUNT

CUMBERLAND

17325

JOY

The Links at
Gettysburg

134

PENNSYLVANIA
MARYLAND

ADAMS
FREDERICK

Mason   &   Dixon

Line

COUNTY
COUNTY

COUNTY

CARROLL

Mountainview
Cem

Harney

Sunrise
Cem

Piney Creek
Ch & Cem

FREDERICK
CARROLL

COUNTY
COUNTY

Alloway

Longville

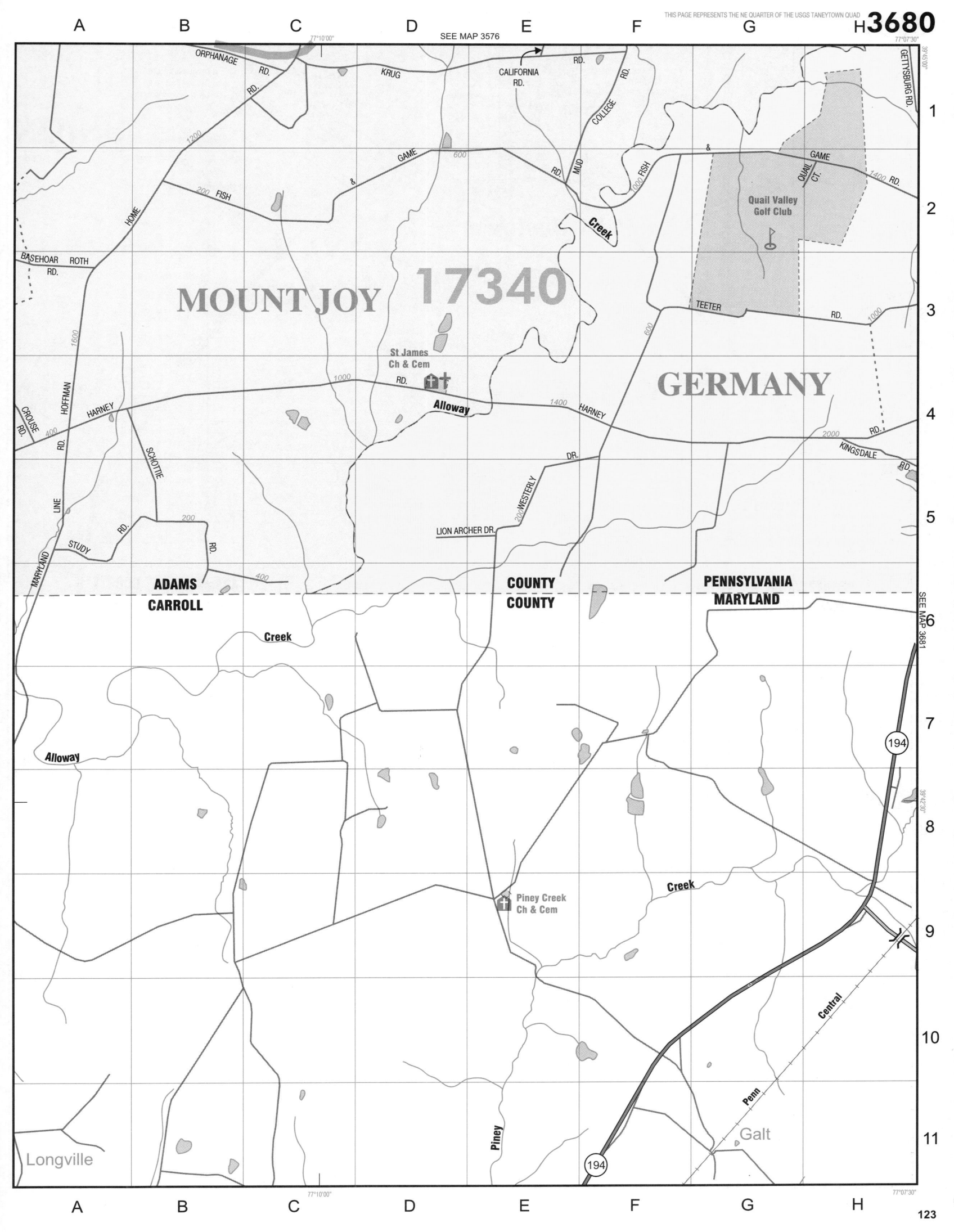

SEE MAP 3576

A   B   C   D   E   F   G   H

1
2
3
4
5
6
7
8
9
10
11

77°10'00"
77°07'30"
39°45'00"
39°42'30"

ORPHANAGE RD.
KRUG RD.
CALIFORNIA RD.
COLLEGE RD.
GETTYSBURG RD.
GAME
FISH
Creek
HOME
BASEHOAR ROTH RD.

MOUNT JOY **17340**

Quail Valley
Golf Club

TEETER RD.

GERMANY

St James
Ch & Cem
Alloway
HARNEY
HOFMAN
HARNEY
CROUSE RD.
SCHOTTIE RD.
LINE
STUDY RD.
DR.
WESTERLY
LION ARCHER DR.
KINGSDALE RD.

ADAMS   **COUNTY**   **PENNSYLVANIA**
CARROLL   **COUNTY**   **MARYLAND**

SEE MAP 3681

Creek

Alloway

Piney Creek
Ch & Cem

Creek

194

Central

Piney

Penn

194

Galt

Longville

A   B   C   D   E   F   G   H

77°10'00"
77°07'30"

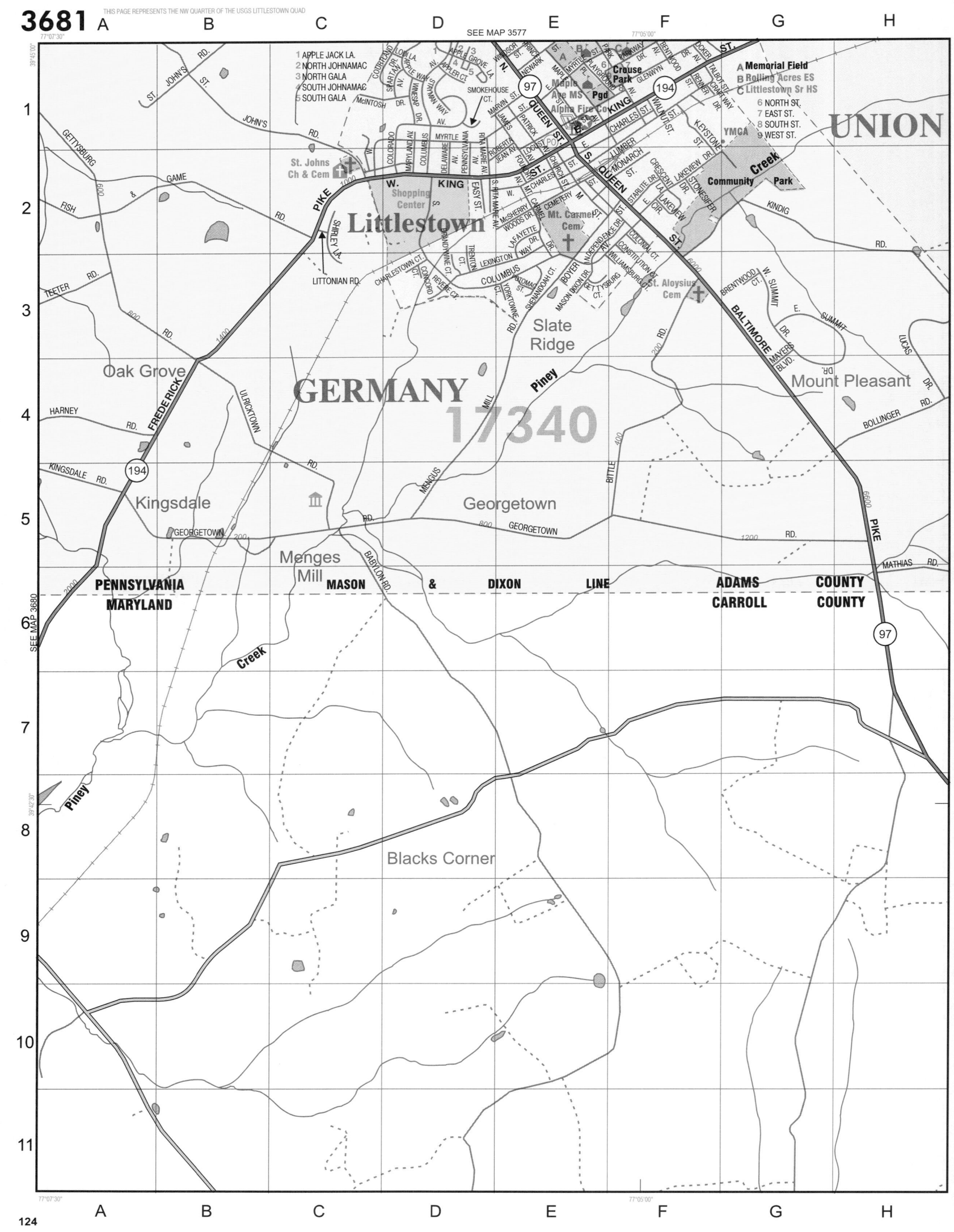

SEE MAP 3577

1 APPLE JACK LA.
2 NORTH JOHNAMAC
3 NORTH GALA
4 SOUTH JOHNAMAC
5 SOUTH GALA

A Memorial Field
B Rolling Acres ES
C Littlestown Sr HS

6 NORTH ST.
7 EAST ST.
8 SOUTH ST.
9 WEST ST.

UNION

Littlestown

GERMANY
17340

Slate
Ridge

Oak Grove

Piney

Mount Pleasant

Kingsdale

Georgetown

Menges
Mill

PENNSYLVANIA
MARYLAND

MASON & DIXON LINE

ADAMS
CARROLL

COUNTY
COUNTY

Piney

Blacks Corner

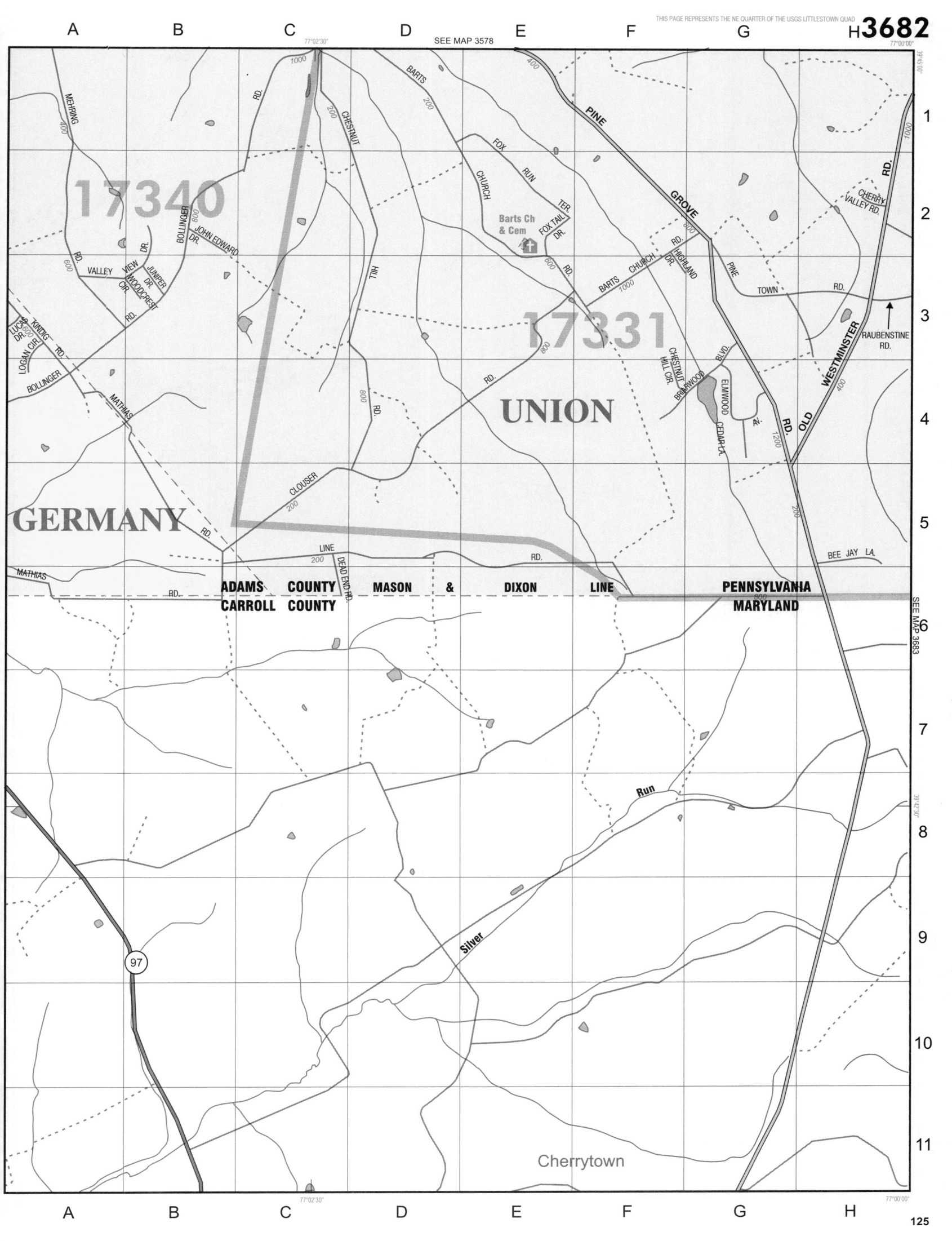

A B C D E F G H

77°02'30"

SEE MAP 3578

39°45'00"
77°00'00"

1

17340

BOLLINGER DR.
JOHN EDWARD
CHESTNUT
BARTS
PINE
GROVE
CHERRY VALLEY RD.
WESTMINSTER RD.

2

MEHRING

VALLEY VIEW DR.
JUNIPER DR.
WOODCREST CIR. RD.
FOX RUN TER.
FOX TAIL DR.
Barts Ch & Cem
CHURCH
BARTS CHURCH
HIGHLAND DR.
RD.
TOWN
RD.
RAUBENSTINE RD.

3

LUCAS DR. CIR.
KINDIG CIR.
LOGAN CIR.
BOLLINGER
17331
UNION
CHESTNUT HILL CIR.
BRIARWOOD BLVD.
ELMWOOD
CEDAR LA.
OLD RD.

4

MATHIAS
HILL RD.
RD.
RD.

5

GERMANY
CLOUSER
RD.
LINE
DEAD END RD.
RD.
BEE JAY LA.

39°42'30"

MATHIAS
RD.
ADAMS COUNTY
CARROLL COUNTY
MASON & DIXON LINE
PENNSYLVANIA
MARYLAND

6

SEE MAP 3683

7

Run

8

Silver

9

97

10

11

Cherrytown

A B C D E F G H

77°02'30"
77°00'00"

125

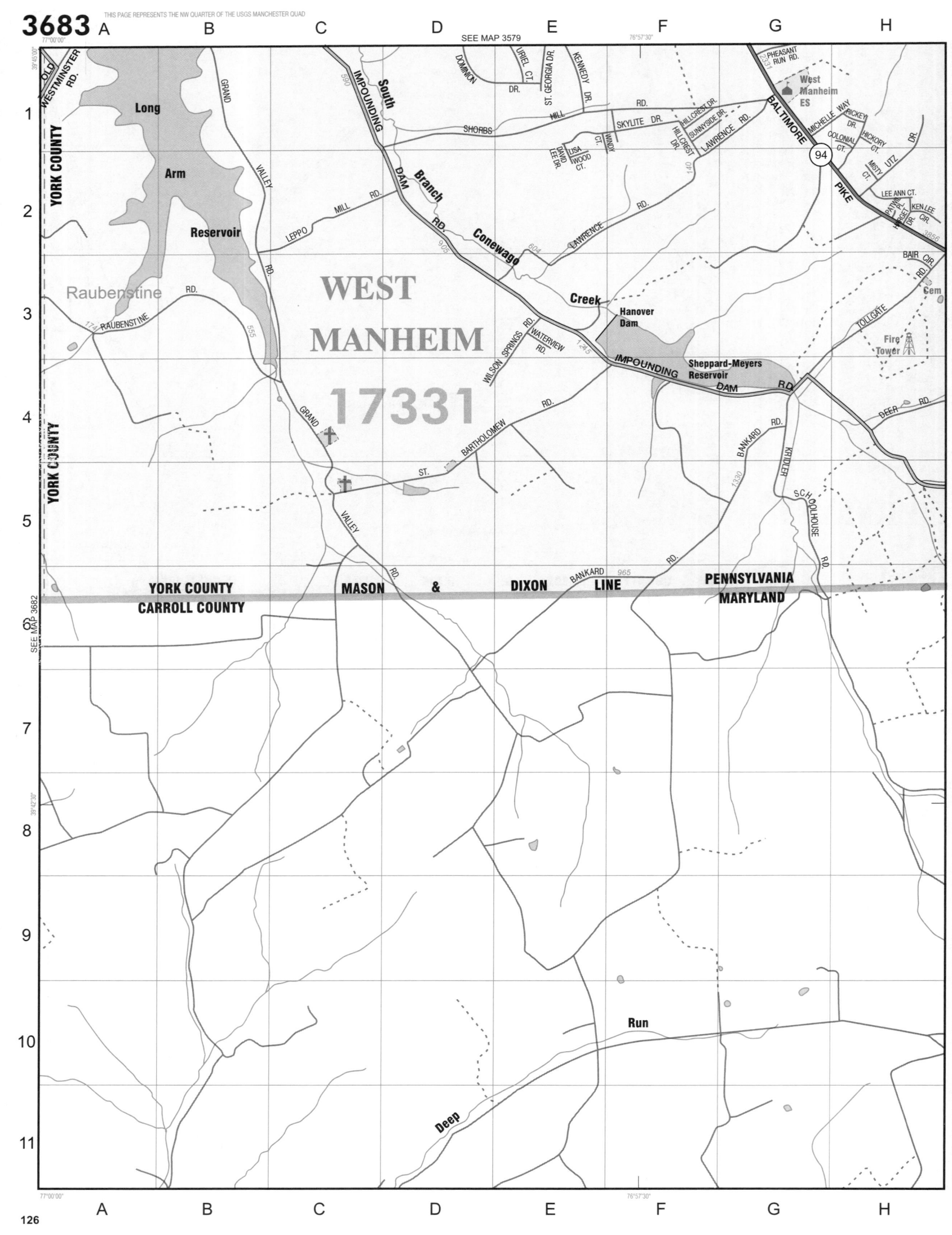

THIS PAGE REPRESENTS THE NW QUARTER OF THE USGS MANCHESTER QUAD

SEE MAP 3579

WEST

MANHEIM

17331

YORK COUNTY

YORK COUNTY

Long

Arm

Reservoir

Raubenstine

Raubenstine RD.

OLD WESTMINSTER RD.

GRAND VALLEY

MILL RD.

LEPPO RD.

South

Branch

Conewago

Creek

DOMINION

URIEL CT. DR.

ST. GEORGIA DR.

KENNEDY DR.

HILL

SHORBS RD.

SKYLITE DR.

DAVID LEE DR.

LISA CT.

WOOD CT.

WINDY CT.

HILLCREST DR.

SUNNYSIDE DR.

HILLCREST DR.

LAWRENCE RD.

LAWRENCE RD.

LAWRENCE

RD.

BALTIMORE

PIKE

West Manheim ES

PHEASANT RUN RD.

MICHELLE WAY

RICKEY DR.

HICKORY CT.

COLONIAL CT.

UTZ DR.

MISTY CT.

LEE ANN CT.

PATON PL.

TARGET DR.

KEN LEE CIR.

BAIR CIR.

RD.

Cem

TOLLGATE RD.

Fire Tower

Hanover Dam

Sheppard-Meyers Reservoir

IMPOUNDING DAM RD.

WILSON SPRINGS RD.

WATERVIEW RD.

BARTHOLOMEW ST.

GRAND VALLEY RD.

RD.

RD.

BANKARD RD.

KRIDLER RD.

SCHOOLHOUSE RD.

DEER RD.

BANKARD RD.

YORK COUNTY

CARROLL COUNTY

MASON & DIXON LINE

PENNSYLVANIA

MARYLAND

Run

Deep

SEE MAP 3682

94

580

RD.

905

604

245

174

555

747

2856

1330

965

2931

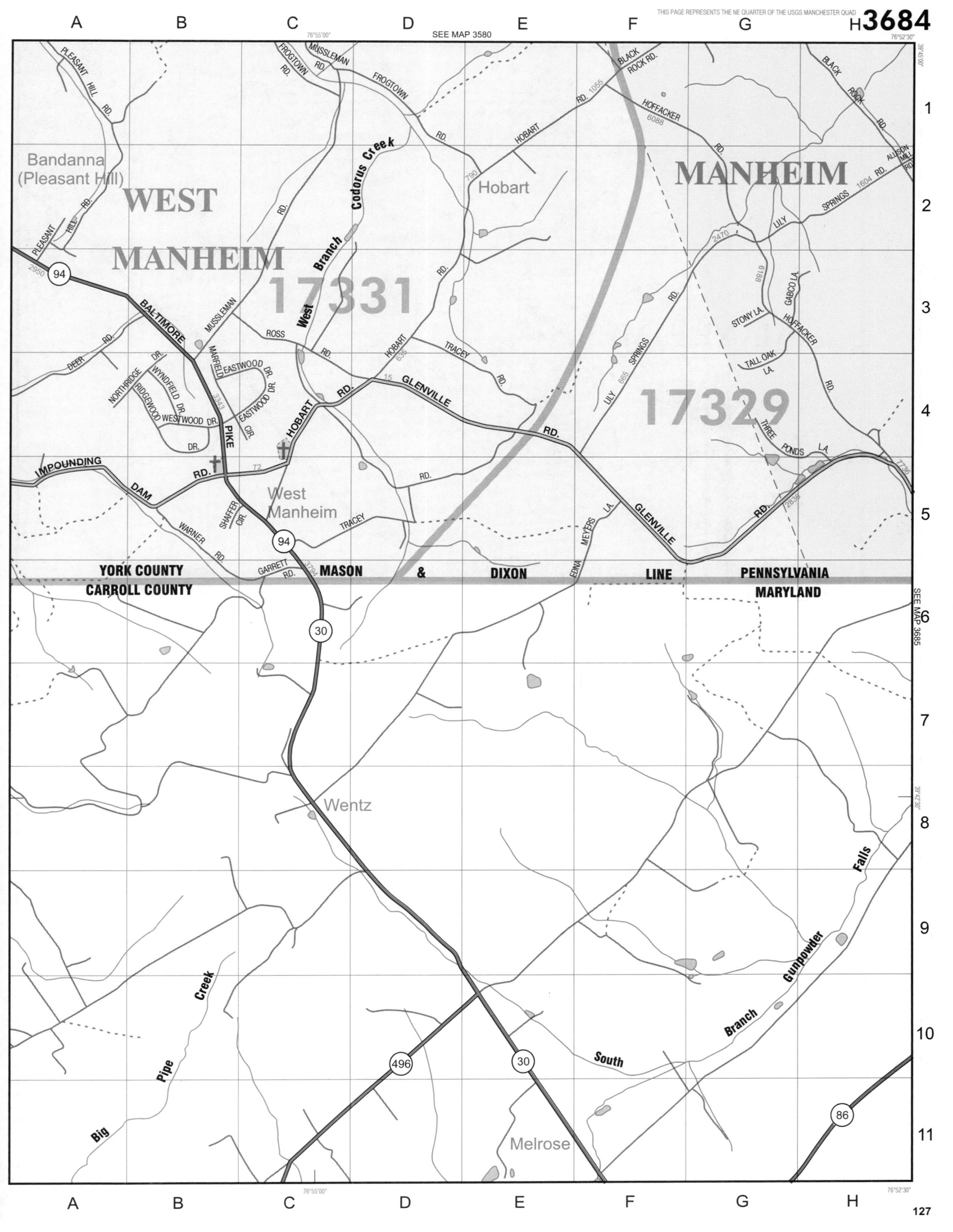

SEE MAP 3580

A B C D E F G H

76°55'00"

76°52'30"

39°45'00"

1

MANHEIM

Bandanna
(Pleasant Hill)

WEST

Hobart

2

MANHEIM

17331

3

4

17329

Codorus Creek

West Branch

PLEASANT HILL RD.

FROGTOWN RD.

MUSSLEMAN RD.

FROGTOWN RD.

BLACK ROCK RD.

HOFFACKER 6088

RD. 1055

HOBART RD.

790

BLACK ROCK RD.

ALLISON MILL RD.

SPRINGS 1604

LILY

GABCO LA.

STONY LA.

HOFFACKER RD.

TALL OAK LA.

LILY SPRINGS 665

RD.

THREE PONDS LA.

2470

6818

94

BALTIMORE

DEER RD.

MARFIELD

NORTHRIDGE DR.

WYNDFIELD DR.

RIDGEWOOD

WESTWOOD DR.

EASTWOOD DR.

EASTWOOD CIR.

DR.

MUSSLEMAN

ROSS RD.

RD.

HOBART RD.

15

HOBART RD. 635

TRACEY RD.

GLENVILLE

RD.

RD.

IMPOUNDING

DAM

RD.

PIKE

HOBART

72

West
Manheim

SHAFFER CIR.

WARNER RD.

TRACEY

RD.

RD.

GLENVILLE

RD.

EDNA LA.

MEYERS LA.

GLENVILLE RD.

2838

77735

5

2950

3843

94

GARRETT RD.

2794

YORK COUNTY   **MASON**   **&**   **DIXON**   **LINE**   **PENNSYLVANIA**

CARROLL COUNTY   **MARYLAND**

30

6

SEE MAP 3685

39°42'30"

7

Wentz

8

9

Creek

Pipe

Big

496

30

South

Melrose

Gunpowder

Branch

Falls

86

10

11

A B C D E F G H

76°55'00"

76°52'30"

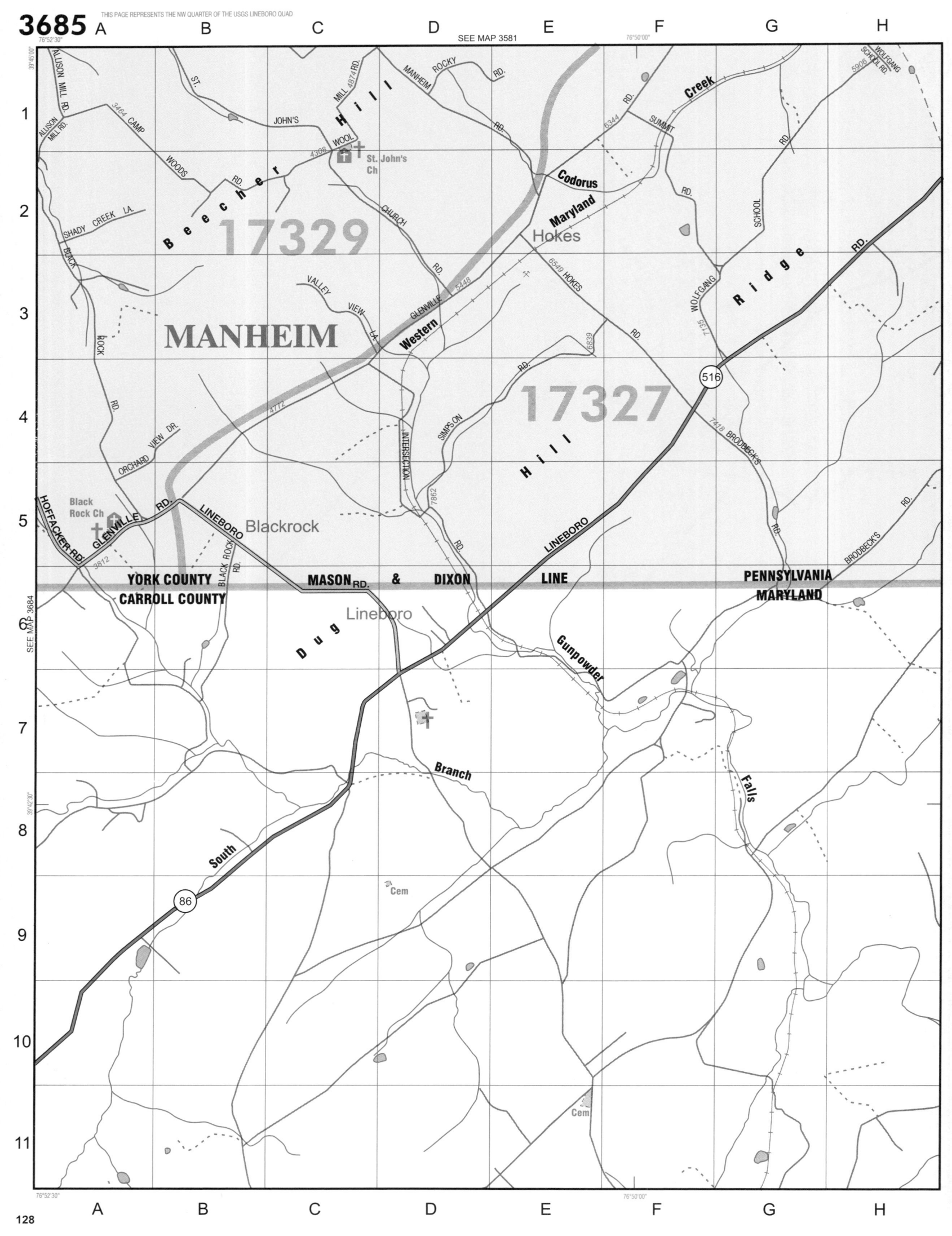

17329

MANHEIM

17327

Hill

Beecher Hill

Ridge

Codorus

Maryland

Hokes

Creek

Blackrock

Black Rock Ch

Glenville

Western

YORK COUNTY
CARROLL COUNTY

MASON RD. & DIXON LINE

PENNSYLVANIA
MARYLAND

Lineboro

Dug

Branch

Gunpowder

Falls

South

Cem

Cem

516

86

St. John's Ch

Hill

ALLISON MILL RD.

ALLISON MILL RD.

CAMP

WOODS

SHADY CREEK LA.

BLACK

ROCK

ORCHARD VIEW DR.

RD.

HOFFACKER RD.

LINEBORO RD.

BLACK ROCK RD.

ST.

JOHN'S

RD.

MILL RD.

WOOL

CHURCH

RD.

VALLEY VIEW LA.

GLENVILLE

RD.

INTERSECTION

SIMPSON

RD.

LINEBORO

MANHEIM

ROCKY

RD.

RD.

SUMMIT

WOLFGANG SCHOOL

RD.

HOKES

RD.

BRODBECK'S

RD.

BRODBECK'S

WOLFGANG SCHOOL RD.

Ridge RD.

3464

4308

4874

4112

3812

5906

5448

6344

6549

6839

7862

7335

7418

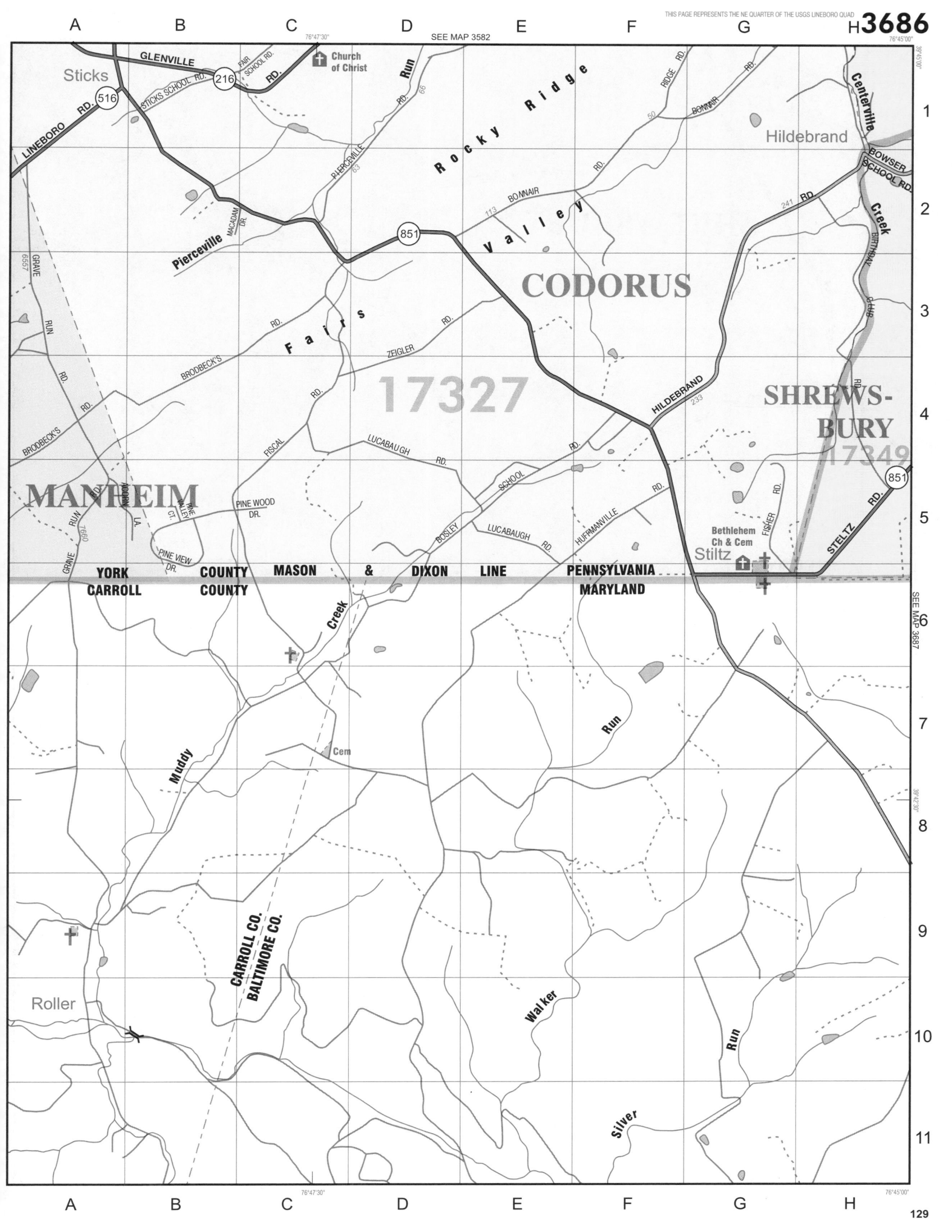

SEE MAP 3582

76°47'30"

76°45'00"

39°45'00"

Sticks

GLENVILLE

216

516

LINEBORO RD.

Church of Christ

FAIR SCHOOL RD.

STICKS SCHOOL RD.

Run

PIERCEVILLE 63

Rocky Ridge

RIDGE RD.

50

BONNAIR

Centerville

Hildebrand

BOWSER SCHOOL RD.

Creek

MACADAM DR.

Pierceville

851

Valley

BONNAIR 113

RD.

241 RD.

BIRTHDAY CLUB

GRAVE 6557

RUN

RD.

Fairs

RD.

ZEIGLER

CODORUS

17327

Hildebrand 233

SHREWS-BURY

17349

BRODBECK'S

RD.

FISCAL

PINE WOOD DR.

LUCABAUGH RD.

SCHOOL

RD.

RD.

FISHER RD.

851

BRODBECK'S

MANHEIM

ACORN LA.

PINE VALLEY CT.

GRAVE RUN RD. 7660

PINE VIEW DR.

BOSLEY

LUCABAUGH RD.

HUFFMANVILLE

STELTZ RD.

Bethlehem Ch & Cem

Stiltz

YORK COUNTY

CARROLL COUNTY

MASON   &   DIXON   LINE

PENNSYLVANIA

MARYLAND

SEE MAP 3687

Creek

Cem

Run

Muddy

CARROLL CO.

BALTIMORE CO.

Roller

Walker

Run

Silver

Run

39°42'30"

76°45'00"

SEE MAP 3687

76°47'30"

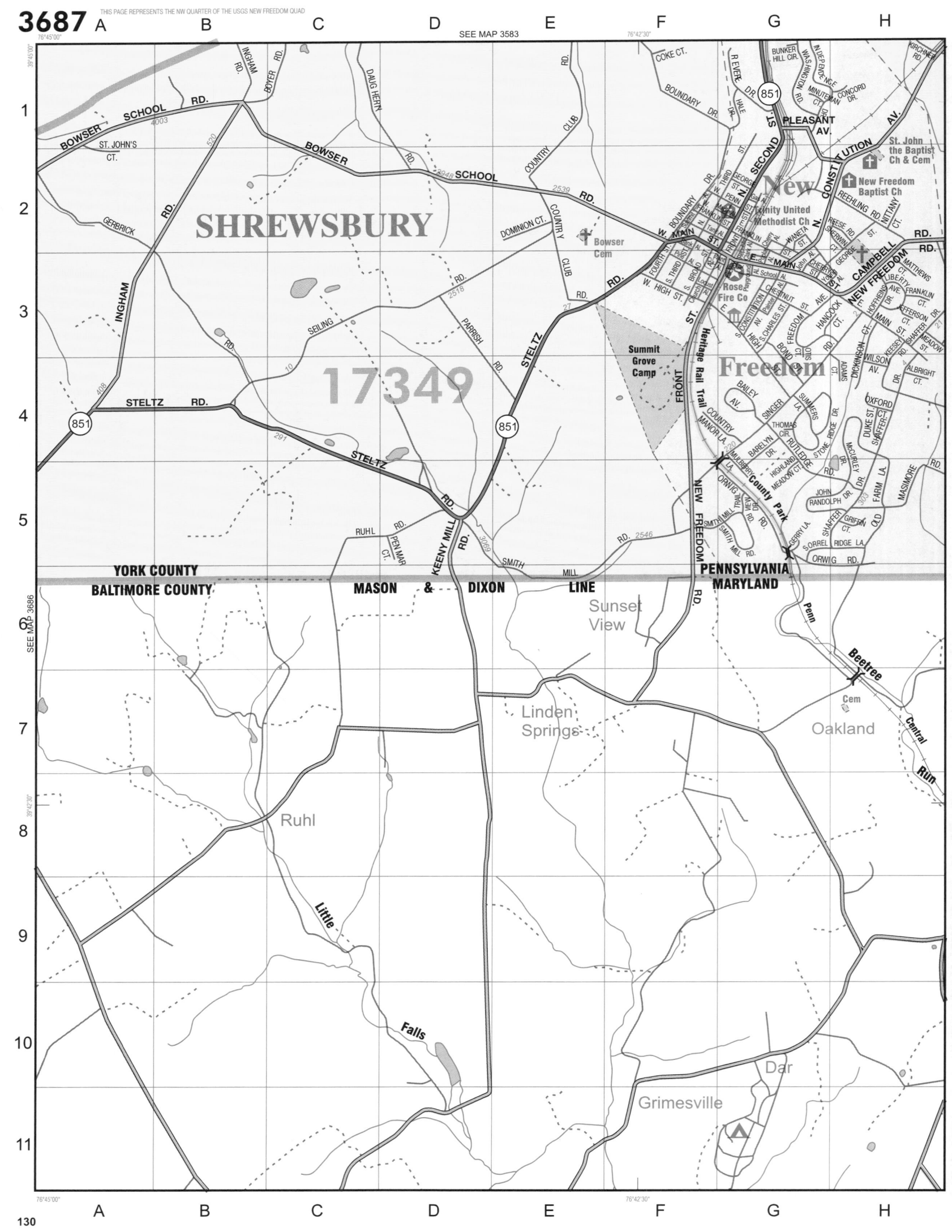

SEE MAP 3583

SHREWSBURY

17349

New
Freedom

Summit
Grove
Camp

Heritage Rail Trail Country

County Park

YORK COUNTY
BALTIMORE COUNTY

MASON   &   DIXON   LINE

PENNSYLVANIA
MARYLAND

Sunset
View

Linden
Springs

Oakland

Beetree

Cem

Ruhl

Little

Falls

Dar

Grimesville

St. John
the Baptist
Ch & Cem

New Freedom
Baptist Ch

Trinity United
Methodist Ch

Rose
Fire Co

Bowser
Cem

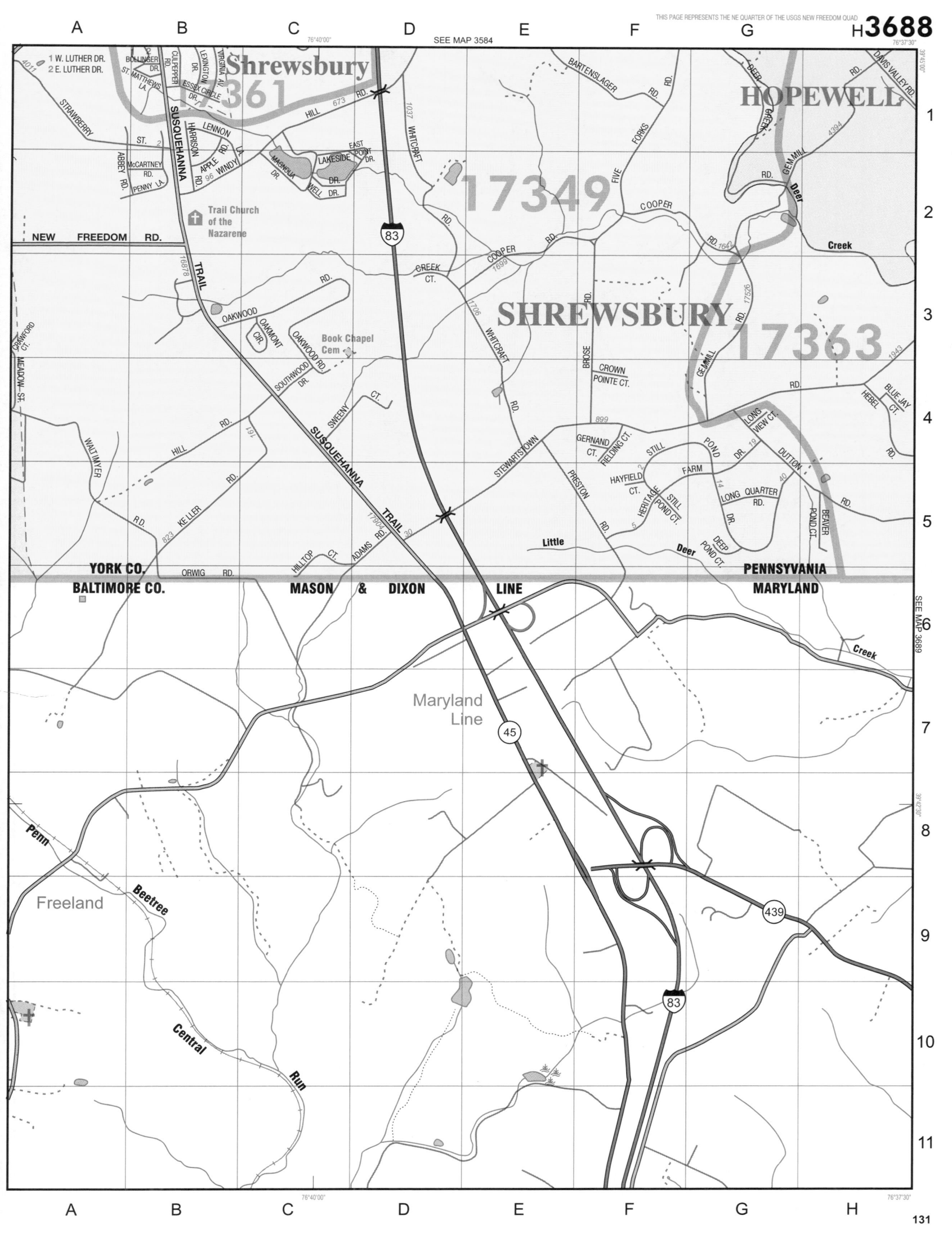

1 W. LUTHER DR.
2 E. LUTHER DR.

Shrewsbury
17361

HOPEWELL

SEE MAP 3584

NEW FREEDOM RD.

Trail Church
of the Nazarene

17349

SHREWSBURY

17363

Book Chapel
Cem

YORK CO.
BALTIMORE CO.

MASON & DIXON LINE

PENNSYLVANIA
MARYLAND

Maryland
Line

Penn

Freeland

Beetree

Central

Run

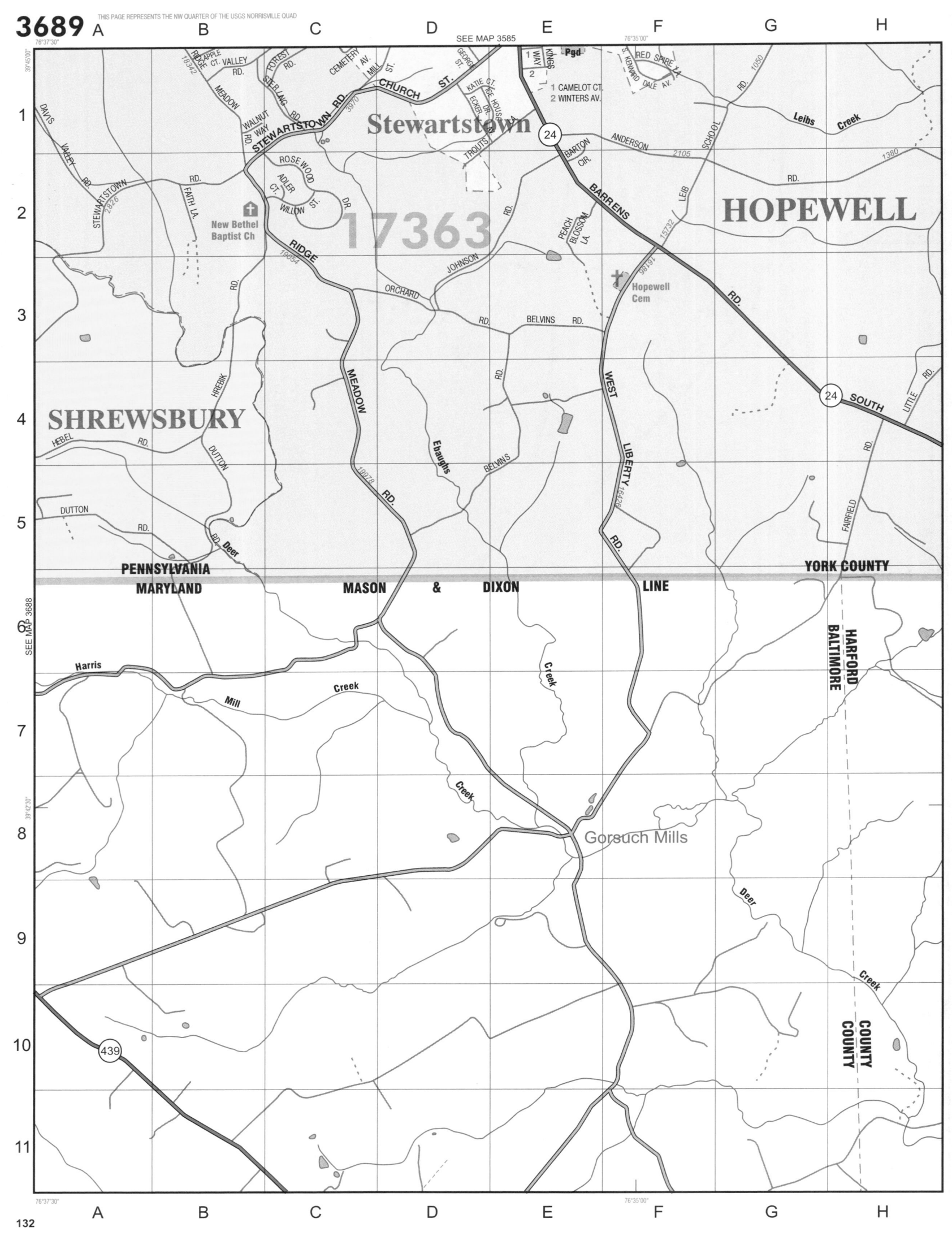

76°37'30"

SEE MAP 3585

B   C   D   E   F   G   H

76°35'00"

Stewartstown

17363

HOPEWELL

Pgd
1 Camelot Ct.
2 Winters Av.

Hopewell Cem

Leibs Creek

SHREWSBURY

New Bethel Baptist Ch

1 Camelot Ct.
2 Winters Av.

PENNSYLVANIA
MARYLAND
MASON & DIXON LINE
YORK COUNTY

Harris

Mill

Creek

Creek

Creek

Gorsuch Mills

Deer

HARFORD
BALTIMORE

Creek

COUNTY
COUNTY

439

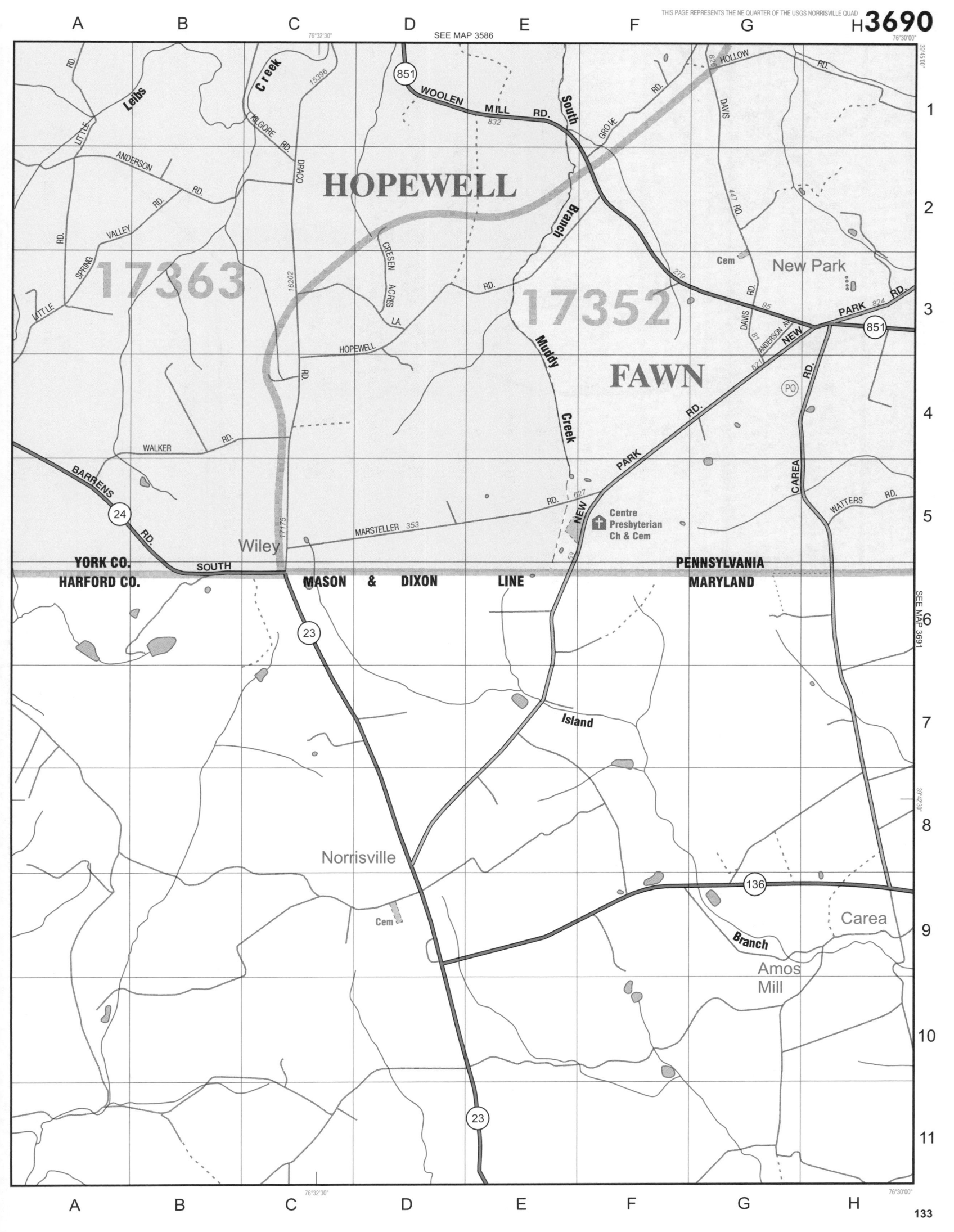

A B C D E F G H

1
2
3
4
5
6
7
8
9
10
11

HOPEWELL

17363

17352

FAWN

Leibs

Creek

WOOLEN MILL RD.

South Branch

New Park

Cem

NEW PARK RD.

PO

Muddy Creek

NEW PARK RD.

CAREA

WATTERS RD.

Centre
Presbyterian
Ch & Cem

MARSTELLER

Wiley

YORK CO.
HARFORD CO.

SOUTH

MASON & DIXON LINE

PENNSYLVANIA
MARYLAND

BARRENS RD.

WALKER RD.

ANDERSON RD.

VALLEY RD.

SPRING RD.

LITTLE

Island

Norrisville

Cem

Carea

Branch

Amos
Mill

SEE MAP 3586

SEE MAP 3691

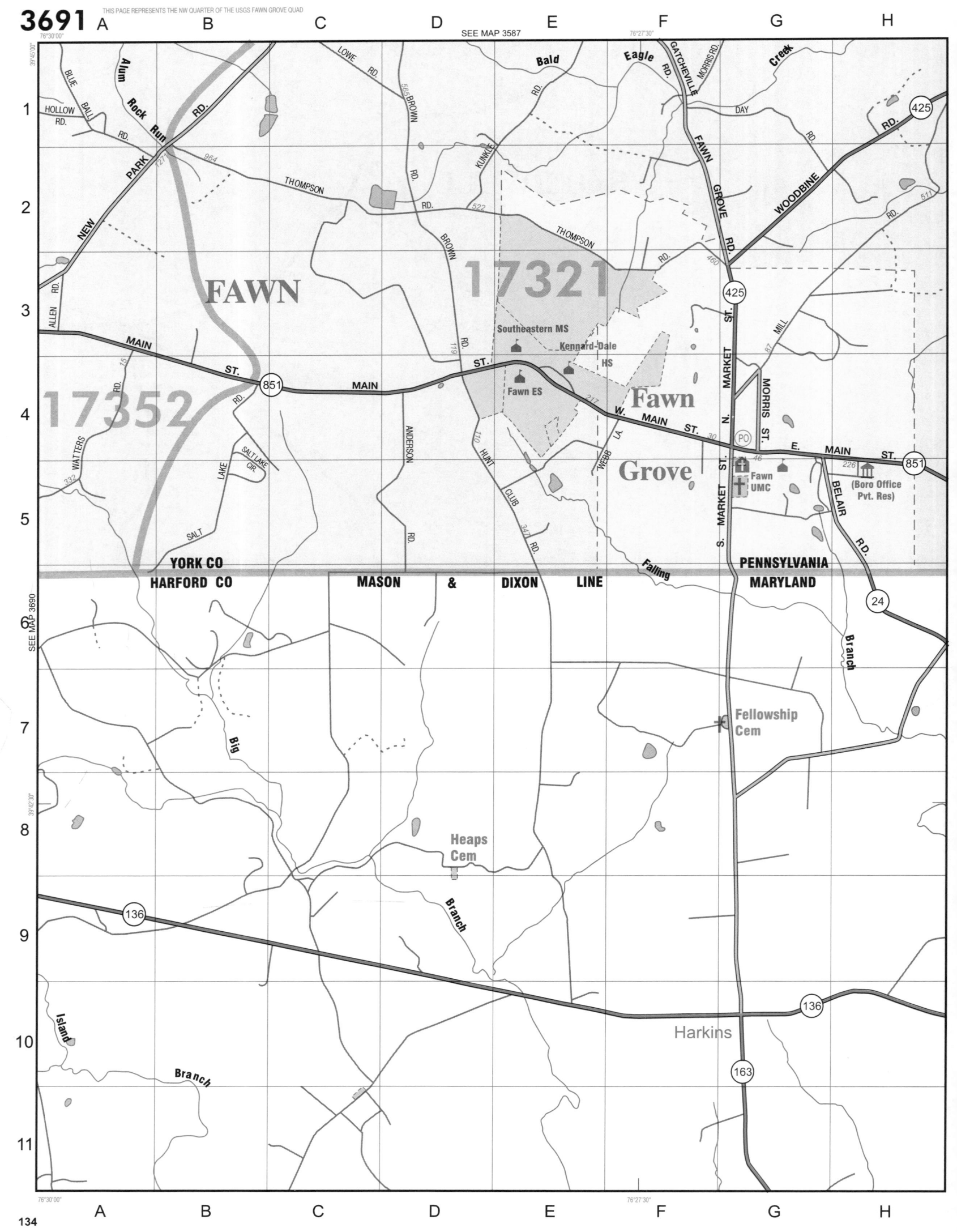

FAWN

17321

17352

Southeastern MS

Kennard-Dale HS

Fawn ES

Fawn

Grove

Fawn UMC

(Boro Office Pvt. Res)

YORK CO

HARFORD CO

MASON & DIXON LINE

PENNSYLVANIA

MARYLAND

Fellowship Cem

Heaps Cem

Harkins

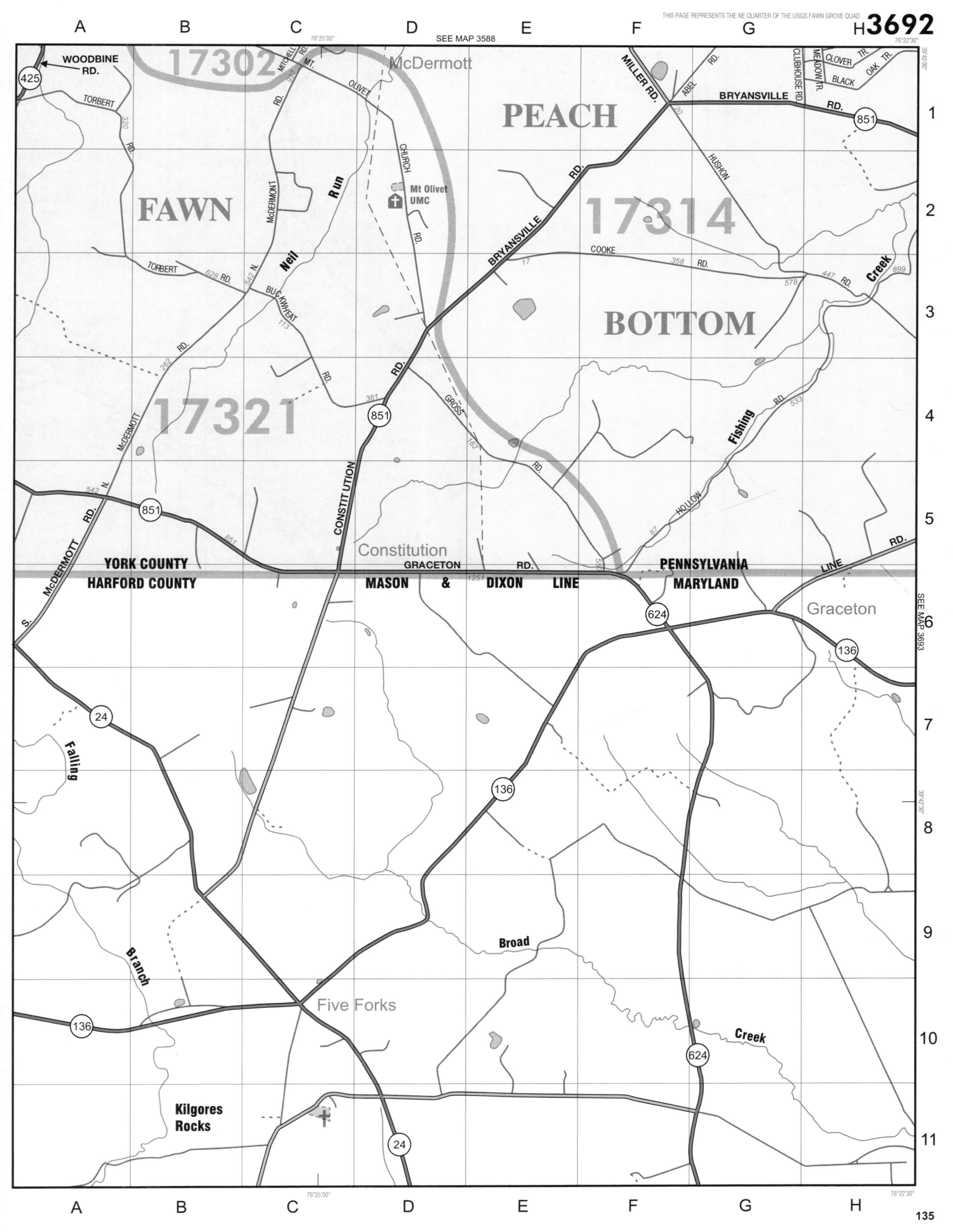

A B C D SEE MAP 3588 E F G H

76°25'00" 76°22'30"
39°45'00"

WOODBINE RD.
425
TORBERT
17302
McDermott
PEACH
MILLER RD.
ABEL
BRYANSVILLE RD.
CLUBHOUSE RD.
MEADOW TR.
CLOVER TR.
OAK TR.
BLACK
851
1

FAWN
McDERMONT
MT. OLIVET
CHURCH RD.
Mt Olivet UMC
BRYANSVILLE RD.
17314
HUSHON
2

Run
TORBERT 628 RD.
542 N.
Neil
BUCKWHEAT 773
COOKE 358 RD.
17
578 447 RD. Creek 899
3

17321
262 RD.
McDERMOTT
381
RD.
851
GROSS 162
BOTTOM
RD.
Fishing RD. 533
4

542 N.
851
851
CONSTITUTION
RD.
HOLLOW
87
RD.
5

YORK COUNTY
HARFORD COUNTY
S. McDERMOTT RD.
Constitution
GRACETON
MASON & 1251 DIXON LINE
PENNSYLVANIA
MARYLAND
LINE
SEE MAP 3693
6

624
Graceton
136

24
Falling
136
136
7

39°42'30"

8

Broad
9

Branch
136
Five Forks
Creek
624
10

Kilgores Rocks
24
11

76°25'00" 76°22'30"

A B C D E F G H

135

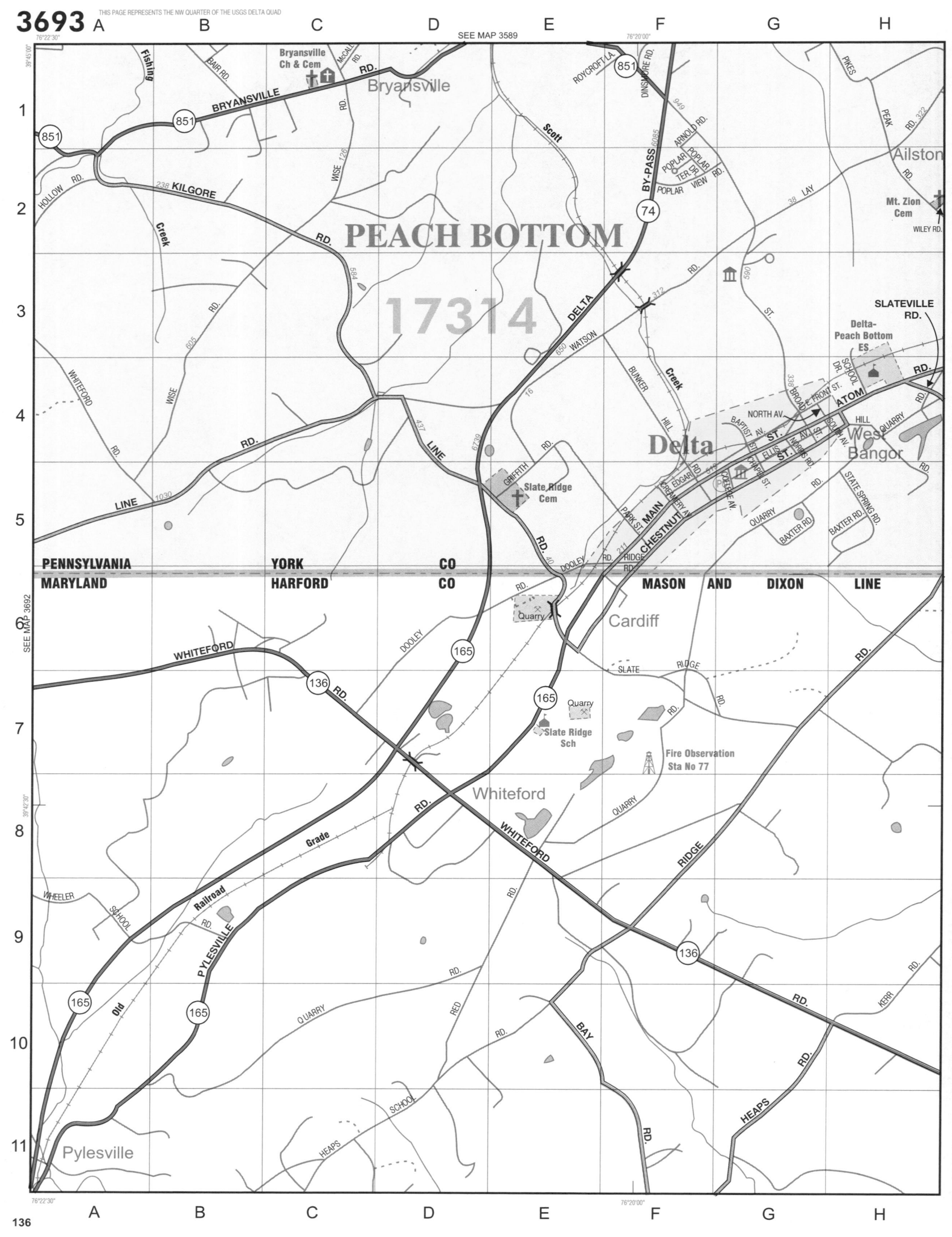

PEACH BOTTOM

17314

Bryansville Ch & Cem
Bryansville

BRYANSVILLE

851

851

HOLLOW RD.
KILGORE
238
Creek
Fishing
BAIR RD.
McCALL
WISE 126
RD.
Scott

SEE MAP 3589

851
74
BY-PASS
DINSMORE RD.
ROYCROFT LA.
POPLAR
POPLAR
TER. DR
POPLAR VIEW RD.
ARNOLD RD.
949
6086
LAY
38
590

Ailston

Mt. Zion
Cem
WILEY RD.
PIKES
PEAK
RD. 322

DELTA
WATSON
650
BUNKER
Creek
312
590

SLATEVILLE
RD.
Delta-
Peach Bottom
ES
SCHOOL DR.
RD.

WHITEFORD
RD.
WISE
605
584
437
LINE
6739
16
RD.
GRIFFITH
Slate Ridge
Cem
NORTH AV.
BAPTIST AV.
CREAMERY AV.
EDGAR
CHAPEL ST.
COLLEGE AV.
ELLIS ST.
INNS RD.
E FRONT ST.
BROAD ST.
338
ATOM
HILL
West
Bangor
QUARRY
Delta
MAIN
PARK ST.
CHESTNUT
211
RIDGE RD.
DOOLEY
RD.
40
QUARRY
BAXTER RD.
BAXTER RD.
STATE SPRING RD.
HILL

LINE 1030

PENNSYLVANIA
MARYLAND

YORK
HARFORD

CO
CO

MASON AND DIXON LINE

SEE MAP 3692

WHITEFORD
136 RD.
DOOLEY
165
Quarry
Cardiff
SLATE RIDGE
RD.
RD.

165
Quarry
Slate Ridge
Sch
QUARRY
Fire Observation
Sta No 77
RIDGE
RD.

WHEELER
School
Railroad
Grade
RD.
PYLESVILLE
Whiteford
WHITEFORD
RD.
BAY
136

165
Old
165
QUARRY
HEAPS
SCHOOL
RED
RD.
RD.
RD.
RD.
KERR
HEAPS

Pylesville

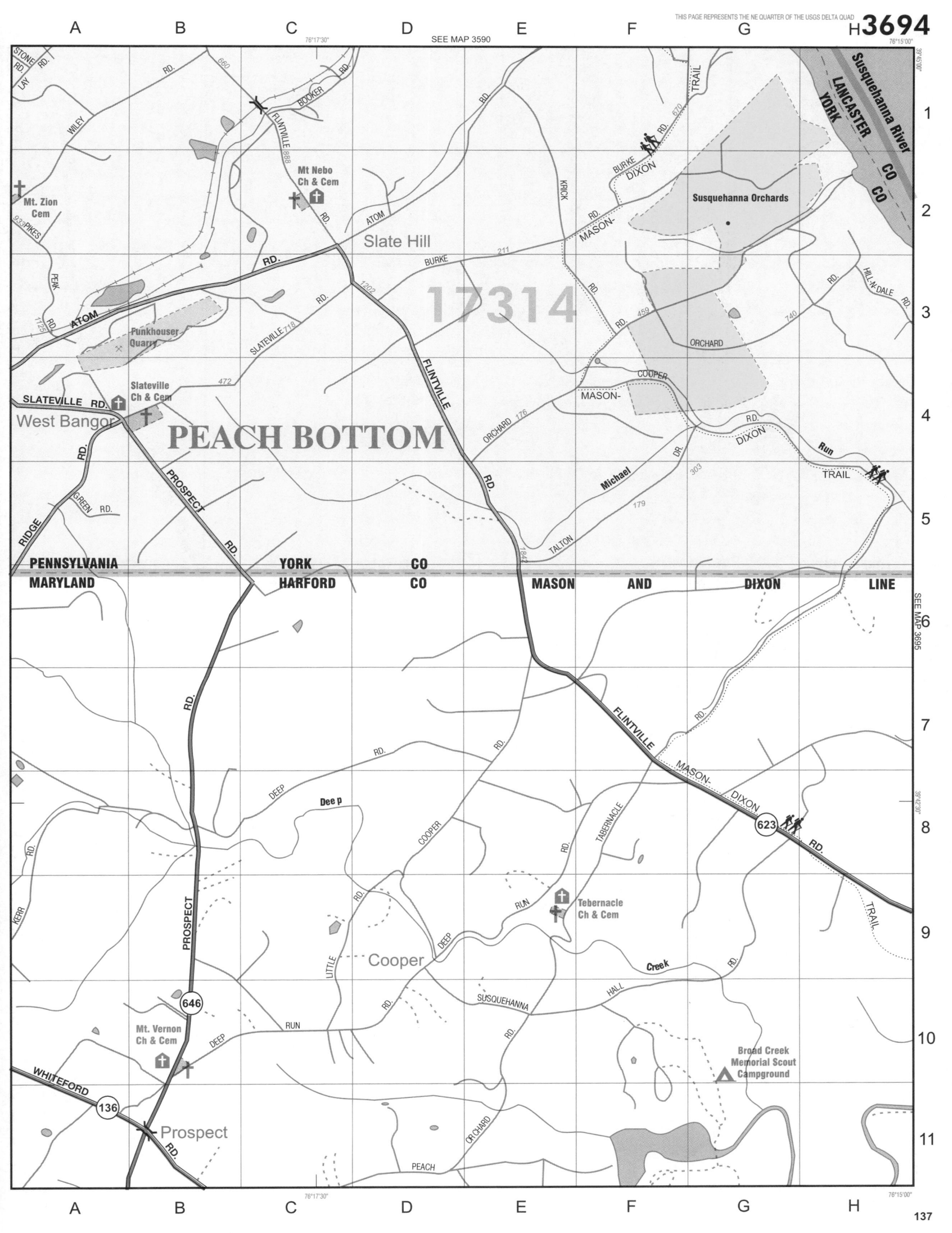

A B C D E F G H

76°17'30" SEE MAP 3590 76°15'00"

39°45'00"

Susquehanna River

LANCASTER CO

YORK CO

STONE RD.

WILEY

LAY

RD.

BOOKER

FLINTVILLE 888

Mt Nebo
Ch & Cem

Mt. Zion
Cem

PIKES 933

PEAK

ATOM

RD. 1125

Slate Hill

Punkhouser
Quarry

SLATEVILLE 718

SLATE HILL RD.

BURKE

211

1202

KRICK RD.

BURKE RD. 670

DIXON

Susquehanna Orchards

MASON- RD.

459

ORCHARD

740

HILL-N-DALE RD.

Slateville
Ch & Cem

472

FLINTVILLE RD.

ORCHARD 176

COOPER

MASON-

DIXON RD.

Run

TRAIL

SLATEVILLE RD.

West Bangor

PEACH BOTTOM

17314

PROSPECT RD.

GREEN RD.

RIDGE RD.

303

179

Michael

DR

TALTON

1844

PENNSYLVANIA **YORK** **CO**

MARYLAND **HARFORD** **CO** **MASON** **AND** **DIXON** **LINE**

SEE MAP 3695

39°42'30"

PROSPECT RD.

DEEP

Dee p

COOPER

RD.

RD.

RD.

FLINTVILLE

MASON- DIXON RD.

623

KERR RD.

LITTLE

DEEP

RD.

Cooper

RUN

TABERNACLE

RD.

Tebernacle
Ch & Cem

Creek

HALL

RD.

TRAIL

646

Mt. Vernon
Ch & Cem

DEEP

RUN

SUSQUEHANNA

RD.

Broad Creek
Memorial Scout
Campground

WHITEFORD

136

Prospect RD.

OR CHARD

PEACH

76°17'30"

76°15'00"

A B C D E F G H

1 2 3 4 5 6 7 8 9 10 11

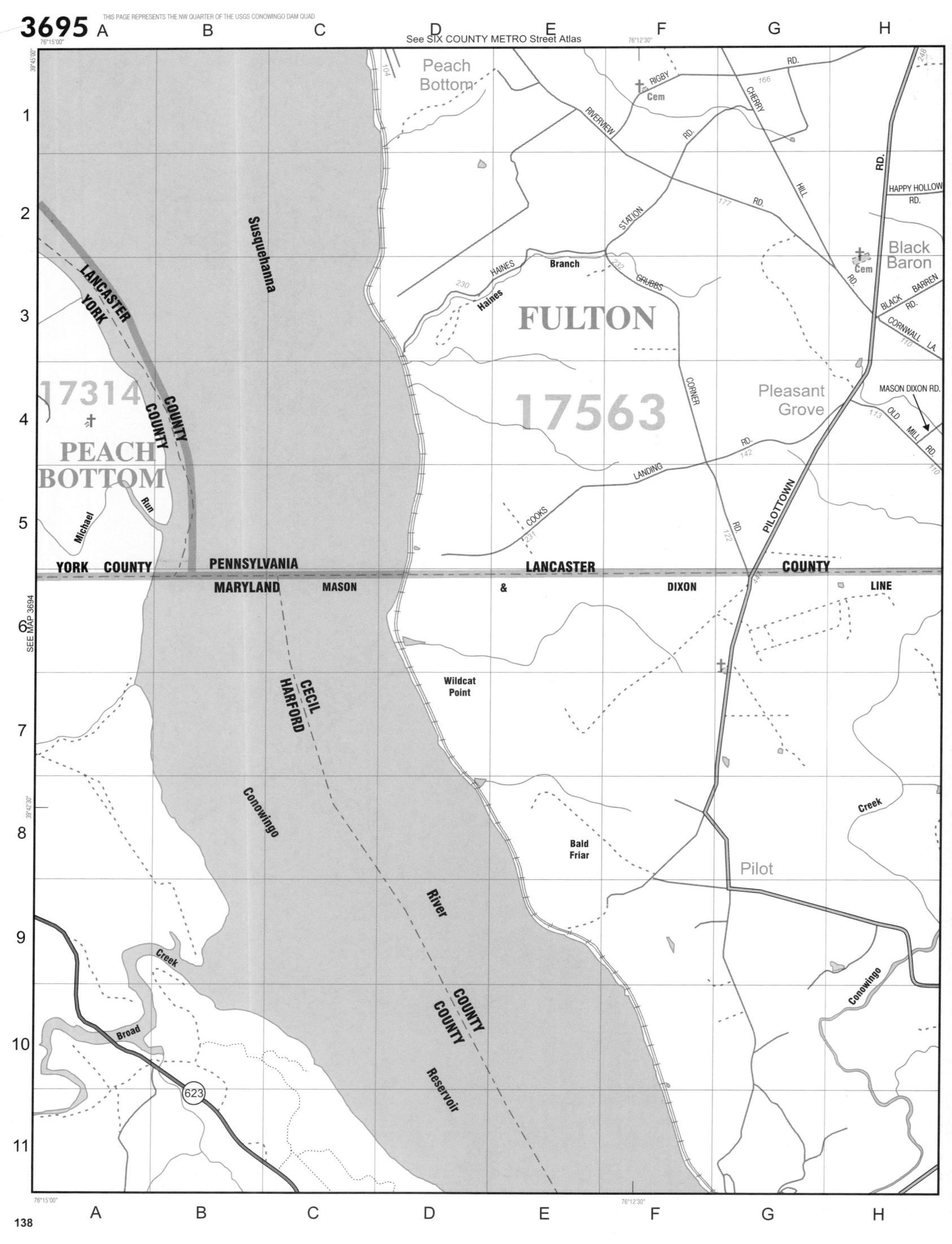

See SIX COUNTY METRO Street Atlas

Peach Bottom

76°15'00"
39°45'00"

RIGBY
Cem

CHERRY

RD.

RD.

166

RD.

246

HAPPY HOLLOW
RD.

RIVERVIEW

STATION

HAINES

Branch

230

Haines

GRUBBS

177

RD.

HILL

RD.

Cem

Black
Baron

BLACK BARREN
RD.

LANCASTER
YORK
COUNTY
COUNTY

Susquehanna

FULTON

17563

CORNER

232

CORNWALL LA.

110

MASON DIXON RD.

17314

PEACH
BOTTOM

Pleasant
Grove

OLD
113

MILL
RD.
110

Michael

Run

LANDING

COOKS

231

RD.
142

PILOTTOWN

RD.
122

44

YORK   COUNTY   PENNSYLVANIA

MARYLAND   MASON

LANCASTER   &   DIXON   COUNTY   LINE

SEE MAP 3694

39°42'30"

CECIL
HARFORD

Wildcat
Point

Conowingo

Bald
Friar

Creek

River

Pilot

Creek

Broad

COUNTY
COUNTY

Conowingo

623

Reservoir

76°15'00"

76°12'30"

76°12'30"

COUNTY ABBREVIATIONS

Ad .... Adams
Yk .... York

A

Street	County	ZIP	Grid	Map
A ST. N., York Spring	Ad	17372	B11	3160
A ST. S., York Spring	Ad	17372	B11	3160
A ST., Jackson	Yk	17364	C11	3269
A ST., McSherrystown	Ad	17344	E2	3578
A ST., Newberry	Yk	17315	E3	3059
AARON CT., Penn	Yk	17331	G8	3579
AARON CT., West Manheim	Yk	17331	G8	3579
ABBEY DR., East Manchester	Yk	17347	E1	3167
ABBEY LA., Springettsbury	Yk	17402	H4	3272
ABBEY RD., Shrewsbury Twp	Yk	17349	A2	3688
ABBOT ST. N., Abbottstown	Ad	17301	A10	3371
ABBOT ST. S., Abbottstown	Ad	17301	A10	3371
ABBOTTS CT., Abbottstown	Ad	17301	A10	3371
ABBOTTS DR., Abbottstown	Ad	17301	A10	3371
ABBOTTSTOWN PIKE, Hamilton	Ad	17301	B7	3371
ABBOTTSTOWN ST., East Berlin	Ad	17316	C1	3371
ABBY LA., Dover Twp	Yk	17315	G4	3269
ABEL RD., Peach Bottom	Yk	17314	F1	3692
ABERDEEN DR., Dover Twp	Yk	17315	B4	3269
ABERDEEN RD., Manchester Twp	Yk	17402	C9	3166
ABE'S LA., Red Lion	Yk	17356	B8	3377
ABINGTON CIR. W., Hopewell	Yk	17363	F4	3584
ABINGTON CIR. W., North Hopewell	Yk	17363	F4	3584
ABLES RD., Lower Windsor	Yk	17368	F8	3274
ABOTTSTOWN RD., Paradise	Yk	17301	F9	3371
ACADEMY RD., Springettsbury	Yk	17402	F10	3166
ACADEMY ST., Hanover	Yk	17331	B2	3579
ACADEMY ST., McSherrystown	Ad	17344	E2	3578
ACCO DR., York Twp	Yk	17402	A2	3376
ACCO DR., York Twp	Yk	17402	H2	3375
ACCO LA., Hellam	Yk	17368	D4	3169
ACCOMAC RD., Hellam	Yk	17406	E8	3168
ACCOMAC RD., Hellam	Yk	17406	G5	3168
ACKWOOD DR., Springfield	Yk	17360	F7	3479
ACOMO DR., Franklin	Yk	17019	B11	3055
ACORN DR., East Manchester	Yk	17347	G6	3166
ACORN DR., Heidelberg	Yk	17362	E7	3476
ACORN LA., Felton	Yk	17322	A4	3482
ACORN LA., Manheim	Yk	17327	A5	3686
ACORN LA., Windsor Twp	Yk	17356	B9	3378
ACORN RD., Jackson	Yk	17362	E10	3372
ADAIR RD., Lower Windsor	Yk	17366	C11	3274
ADAIR RD., Lower Windsor	Yk	17366	D1	3378
ADAM DR., Mount Pleasant	Ad	17350	F6	3473
ADAM ST., Conewago	Yk	17404	D2	3165
ADAMS AV., Oxford	Ad	17350	E2	3474
ADAMS CT., Hanover	Yk	17331	B10	3475
ADAMS CT., New Freedom	Yk	17349	H4	3687
ADAMS LA., Red Lion	Yk	17356	B8	3377
ADAMS RD., Lower Chanceford	Yk	17314	D5	3589
ADAMS RD., Lower Windsor	Yk	17368	C3	3274
ADAMS RD., Shrewsbury Twp	Yk	17349	D5	3688
ADAMS ST. N., West York	Yk	17404	G8	3270
ADAMS ST. S., West York	Yk	17404	G9	3270
ADAMS ST., Windsor Boro	Yk	17366	E4	3377
ADAMSON LA., Hellam	Yk	17406	E7	3168
ADDISON CT., Manchester Twp	Yk	17404	D2	3270
ADDISON WAY, Windsor Twp	Yk	17356	B2	3377
ADERLY CT., Springettsbury	Yk	17402	F6	3272
ADLER CT., Hopewell	Yk	17363	C2	3689
ADMIRE RD., Dover Twp	Yk	17315	G8	3268
ADMIRE RD., Dover Twp	Yk	17315	A7	3269
ADMIRE RD., Paradise	Yk	17316	H11	3267
ADMIRE RD., Paradise	Yk	17316	A10	3268
ADMIRE RD., Paradise	Yk	17316	G1	3371
ADMIRE RD., Paradise	Yk	17364	A10	3268
ADMIRE SPRINGS DR., Dover Twp	Yk	17315	D5	3269
AERO AV., New Oxford	Ad	17350	B2	3474
AFFIRMED DR., Carroll	Yk	17019	G1	3056
AILES RD., Peach Bottom	Yk	17314	G11	3589
AILES RD., Peach Bottom	Yk	17314	A10	3590
AIREDALE TR., Liberty	Ad	17320	E9	3573
AIRPORT ACCESS RD., Fairview	Yk	17070	C6	2849
AIRPORT DR., Fairview	Yk	17070	C8	2849
AIRPORT GLIDE PATH, Liberty	Ad	17320	C9	3573
AIRPORT RD., Conewago	Ad	17331	E3	3578
AIRPORT RD., Jackson	Yk	17364	H4	3372
AIRPORT RD., Jackson	Yk	17364	A5	3373
AKINS RD., Chanceford	Yk	17322	E7	3482
ALANA DR., York Twp	Yk	17402	C10	3272
ALBEMARLE ST. N., York City	Yk	17403	F5	3271
ALBEMARLE ST. S., York City	Yk	17403	F6	3271
ALBEMARLE ST., Spring Garden	Yk	17403	G8	3271
ALBERT LA., Franklin	Yk	17019	H4	3055
ALBRIGHT CT., New Freedom	Yk	17349	H4	3687
ALBRIGHT CT., Shrewsbury Twp	Yk	17327	B11	3480
ALBRIGHT CT., Shrewsbury Twp	Yk	17327	B1	3584
ALBRIGHT CT., Springfield	Yk	17327	G10	3479
ALBRIGHT DR., Penn	Yk	17331	G3	3579
ALBRIGHT LA., Codorus	Yk	17329	A4	3582
ALCO CT., Hopewell	Yk	17363	F9	3585
ALCOTT RD., Springettsbury	Yk	17402	A11	3167
ALCOTT RD., Springettsbury	Yk	17402	A1	3272
ALDER CT., Manchester Boro	Yk	17345	D3	3166
ALDER WAY, Manchester Twp	Yk	17402	C2	3271
ALDINGER DR., York Twp	Yk	17313	F11	3376
ALDINGER RD., North Codorus	Yk	17360	G9	3374
ALDON DR., Dover Twp	Yk	17315	E1	3269
ALEXANDER CT., Springettsbury	Yk	17402	E1	3272
ALFRED DR., Fairview	Yk	17339	E5	2954
ALICE TR., Carroll Valley	Ad	17320	G11	3572
ALICE TR., Carroll Valley	Ad	17320	G1	3676
ALLEGHENY AV., Hanover	Yk	17331	B1	3579
ALLEGHENY DR., York Twp	Yk	17402	A6	3376
ALLEGHENY DR., York Twp	Yk	17402	H6	3375
ALLEN DR., Newberry	Yk	17319	C9	2955
ALLEN DR., Penn	Yk	17331	F7	3579
ALLEN LA., Dover Boro	Yk	17315	C10	3164
ALLEN RD., Fawn	Yk	17352	A3	3691
ALLIANCE AV., Hellam	Yk	17406	B11	3168
ALLISON DR., Springettsbury	Yk	17402	G4	3272
ALLISON MILL RD., Manheim	Yk	17329	H10	3580
ALLISON MILL RD., Manheim	Yk	17329	A11	3581
ALLISON MILL RD., Manheim	Yk	17329	H2	3684
ALLISON MILL RD., Manheim	Yk	17329	A1	3685
ALLWOOD DR. N., Conewago	Ad	17331	B4	3578
ALLWOOD DR. S., Conewago	Ad	17331	C5	3578
ALMONEY RD., Lower Windsor	Yk	17368	C1	3274
ALMSBURY WAY, Springettsbury	Yk	17402	F5	3272
ALNWICK CIR., Springettsbury	Yk	17402	F5	3272
ALOE CT., Hellam	Yk	17402	H2	3272
ALPAT DR., Carroll	Yk	17019	H8	2951
ALPAT DR., Monaghan	Yk	17019	A7	2952
ALPAT DR., Washington	Yk	17019	F6	3161
ALPHA DR., West Manchester	Yk	17404	E3	3374
ALPINE RD., Springettsbury	Yk	17402	E11	3167
ALPINE RD., Warrington	Yk	17315	F3	3163
ALPINE RD., Warrington	Yk	17339	H10	3058
ALPINE RD., Warrington	Yk	17339	A7	3059
ALPINE RD., Warrington	Yk	17365	H10	3058
ALPINE RD., Warrington	Yk	17365	F3	3163
ALTA VISTA RD., Dover Twp	Yk	17315	G3	3269
ALTHOUSE SCHOOL RD., Hopewell	Yk	17363	C7	3585
ALTLAND AV., Paradise	Yk	17301	D9	3371
ALTLAND AV., West Manchester	Yk	17404	F7	3270
ALTO LA., North York	Yk	17404	C4	3271
ALTO RIDGE TR., Carroll Valley	Ad	17320	F4	3676
ALTON LA., Springettsbury	Yk	17402	B7	3272
ALUM ROCK RD., Fawn	Yk	17352	B7	3587
ALVIN ST, W., Penn	Yk	17331	E3	3579
ALVIN ST., Penn	Yk	17331	F2	3579
ALWINE AV. N., West Manchester	Yk	17404	H1	3373
ALWINE AV. S., West Manchester	Yk	17404	H2	3373
ALYCE CIR., York Twp	Yk	17402	B9	3272
ALYDAR BLVD., Carroll	Yk	17019	G11	2951
ALYDER BLVD., Carroll	Yk	17019	F1	3056
AMAD DR., York Twp	Yk	17403	C6	3375
AMANDA AV., Penn	Yk	17331	H3	3579
AMANDA LA., Hellam	Yk	17406	C1	3273
AMANDA LA., Lower Windsor	Yk	17368	A8	3275
AMBAU RD., North Codorus	Yk	17362	G5	3476
AMBAU RD., North Codorus	Yk	17362	A4	3477
AMBER DR., Lower Chanceford	Yk	17314	E8	3589
AMBERVIEW DR., Dover Boro	Yk	17315	D10	3164
AMEDA DR., Jacobus	Yk	17407	F9	3375
AMELIA ST., Manchester Twp	Yk	17402	C2	3271
AMETHYST RD., West Manchester	Yk	17404	C7	3270
AMITY RD., Menallen	Ad	17307	H7	3260
AMVET'S RD., Highland	Ad	17325	E2	3573
AMY AV., Dover Twp	Yk	17315	C3	3269
AMY LA., Mount Pleasant	Ad	17350	F5	3473
ANDERS RD., North Hopewell	Yk	17363	D1	3585
ANDERSON AV., Fawn	Yk	17352	G3	3690
ANDERSON DR., Lower Chanceford	Yk	17314	F8	3589
ANDERSON LA., Springfield	Yk	17403	H11	3375
ANDERSON LA., Springfield	Yk	17403	H1	3479
ANDERSON RD., Fawn	Yk	17321	D4	3691
ANDERSON RD., Hopewell	Yk	17363	F1	3689
ANDERSON RD., Hopewell	Yk	17363	A2	3690
ANDERSON RD., Winterstown	Yk	17356	A5	3481
ANDERSONTOWN RD EXT., Conewago	Yk	17315	E10	3059
ANDERSONTOWN RD., Monaghan	Yk	17055	A8	2953
ANDES RD., Conewago	Yk	17402	H11	3060
ANDES RD., Conewago	Yk	17402	G1	3165
ANDOVER DR., Dover Twp	Yk	17315	F3	3269
ANDREA CT., Penn	Yk	17331	B8	3579
ANDREWS ST., West Manchester	Yk	17404	F9	3270
ANDREWS ST., West York	Yk	17404	F9	3270
ANGEL DR., Manchester Twp	Yk	17404	B4	3271
ANGELA LA., Windsor Twp	Yk	17402	A8	3273
ANGUS LA., Dover Twp	Yk	17315	H11	3164
ANITA DR., Dover Twp	Yk	17315	H5	3269
ANN DR., Fairview	Yk	17070	C10	2849
ANNA TR., Carroll Valley	Ad	17320	E1	3676
ANNAMAY ST., Manchester Twp	Yk	17404	G10	3165
ANNETTE DR., York Twp	Yk	17403	B7	3376
ANTHONY AV., Penn	Yk	17331	A4	3580
ANTHONY RD., Reading	Ad	17316	G7	3266
ANTHONY RD., Reading	Ad	17316	A7	3267
ANTHONY RD., Washington	Yk	17316	C6	3267
ANTIETAM DR., Warrington	Yk	17339	B3	3059
ANTIETAM LA., Hamiltonban	Ad	17222	F8	3467
ANTIQUE LA., Mount Pleasant	Ad	17350	E2	3473
ANTLER DR., Hellam	Yk	17402	E7	3167
ANTLER LA., Reading	Ad	17350	B3	3370
ANTLER RD., Fairview	Yk	17339	C2	2954
ANVIL LA., Hellam	Yk	17406	F9	3168
APACHE LA., Hellam	Yk	17368	D5	3169
APACHE PASS RD., Conewago	Ad	17331	D2	3578
APACHE TR., Liberty	Ad	17320	C9	3573
APOLLO RD., Shrewsbury Twp	Yk	17327	A10	3583
APPACHE TR., Newberry	Yk	17370	A10	2956
APPALOOSA AV., Carroll	Yk	17019	B4	3057
APPALOOSA DR., Dover Twp	Yk	17315	E5	3164
APPALOOSA WAY, Fairview	Yk	17319	G2	2954
APPALOOSA WAY, Windsor Twp	Yk	17356	B2	3377
APPELL AV., Manchester Twp	Yk	17402	C9	3166
APPLE AL., Wrightsville	Yk	17368	D7	3169
APPLE AV., Cumberland	Ad	17325	C4	3471
APPLE CT., Hopewell	Yk	17363	B11	3585
APPLE GROVE LA., Littlestown	Ad	17340	D1	3681
APPLE HILL LA., Springettsbury	Yk	17402	A5	3273
APPLE JACK LA., Littlestown	Ad	17340	C11	3577
APPLE JACK LA., Littlestown	Ad	17340	C1	3681
APPLE LA., Arendtsville	Ad	17307	B3	3366
APPLE LA., Bendersville	Ad	17304	G3	3262
APPLE LA., Bendersville	Ad	17304	A4	3263
APPLE RD., Shrewsbury Twp	Yk	17349	B2	3688
APPLE ST., Chanceford	Yk	17322	F4	3379
APPLE ST., Winterstown	Yk	17322	H8	3480
APPLE ST., Winterstown	Yk	17322	A8	3481
APPLE TR., Carroll Valley	Ad	17320	G4	3676
APPLE TREE CIR., Lower Windsor	Yk	17368	E11	3169
APPLE TREE LA., East Manchester	Yk	17347	G7	3166
APPLE VALLEY DR., York Twp	Yk	17356	H5	3376
APPLE WAY, Littlestown	Ad	17340	D11	3577
APPLE WAY, Littlestown	Ad	17340	D1	3681
APPLE WAY, York Twp	Yk	17404	G5	3270
APPLEFORD WAY, Springettsbury	Yk	17402	D5	3272
APPLER CT., Littlestown	Ad	17340	D1	3681
APPLER RD., Oxford	Ad	17331	G7	3474
APPLETON DR., York Twp	Yk	17356	G5	3376
APPLEWAY RD., Franklin	Ad	17325	C7	3366
APPLEWINE CT., Manchester Twp	Yk	17404	G1	3270
APRIL LA., Dallastown	Yk	17313	G8	3376
AQUA CT., Spring Garden	Yk	17403	D1	3375
ARBOR DR., North Hopewell	Yk	17313	D1	3480
ARBOR DR., North Hopewell	Yk	17313	E1	3480
ARBOR DR., North Hopewell	Yk	17356	F1	3480
ARBOR DR., York Twp	Yk	17313	E11	3376
ARBOR DR., York Twp	Yk	17356	G11	3376
ARBOR DR., York Twp	Yk	17356	B10	3377
ARBOR LA., Penn	Yk	17331	G5	3579
ARBOR LA., Red Lion	Yk	17356	B7	3377
ARBOR LA., Springettsbury	Yk	17402	E1	3272
ARCH ST., York City	Yk	17403	C6	3271
ARCHER ST., Cumberland	Ad	17325	F5	3470
ARDMORE LA., Berwick	Ad	17301	B10	3371
ARDMORE LA., Springettsbury	Yk	17402	C6	3272
ARENDTSVILLE RD., Butler	Ad	17307	D2	3366
ARGYLE AV., Glen Rock	Yk	17327	C4	3583
ARGYLE AV., Shrewsbury Twp	Yk	17327	C3	3583
ARGYLE DR., Springettsbury	Yk	17402	H3	3271
ARK DR., York Twp	Yk	17313	B5	3376
ARLENE CT., Penn	Yk	17331	F7	3579
ARLENE DR. E., Lower Windsor	Yk	17406	A5	3274
ARLENE DR., Penn	Yk	17331	G7	3579
ARLENE TR., Carroll Valley	Ad	17320	D1	3676
ARLINGTON RD., Spring Garden	Yk	17403	E9	3271
ARLINGTON RD., York City	Yk	17403	E9	3271
ARLINGTON ST., York City	Yk	17403	E9	3271
ARLINGTON ST., York Twp	Yk	17402	A4	3376
ARMORY CT., North Codorus	Yk	17404	C11	3374
ARMORY RD., Gettysburg	Ad	17325	A9	3471
ARNOLD LA., Hallam	Yk	17406	B1	3273
ARNOLD LA., Lower Windsor	Yk	17406	A6	3274
ARNOLD RD., Chanceford	Yk	17356	H4	3378
ARNOLD RD., Chanceford	Yk	17356	A4	3379
ARNOLD RD., Fawn	Yk	17352	D3	3587
ARNOLD RD., Manheim	Yk	17329	D10	3581
ARNOLD RD., North Codorus	Yk	17404	E7	3374
ARNOLD RD., Peach Bottom	Yk	17314	F1	3693
ARROWHEAD LA., Penn	Yk	17331	G3	3579
ARSENAL RD., Springettsbury	Yk	17402	E3	3271
ART DR., West Manheim	Yk	17331	E9	3579
ARTHUR ST., Springettsbury	Yk	17402	F3	3271
ARTHURS CT., West Manchester	Yk	17404	D3	3270
ARTILLERY DR., Straban	Ad	17325	E6	3471
ARTMAN AV., Hallam	Yk	17406	C10	3168
ARWCO DR., Penn	Yk	17331	H3	3579
ASBURY CT., East Manchester	Yk	17347	E2	3167
ASBURY LA., Shrewsbury Boro	Yk	17361	A6	3584
ASH DR., Bonneauville	Ad	17340	H2	3576
ASH DR., Hanover	Yk	17331	D11	3475
ASH ST., Shrewsbury Twp	Yk	17349	D10	3584
ASHCOMB CT., Windsor Twp	Yk	17356	B5	3377
ASHCOMBE DR., Dover Twp	Yk	17315	F11	3164
ASHFIELD DR., Union	Ad	17340	G11	3577
ASHLAND DR., West Manchester	Yk	17404	E4	3270
ASHLEIGH DR., York Twp	Yk	17402	A2	3376
ASHLEY CT., Penn	Yk	17331	H3	3579
ASHLEY DR., Carroll	Yk	17019	E8	2951
ASHLEY LA., Dover Twp	Yk	17315	F4	3269
ASHOMBE DR., Dover Twp	Yk	17315	E1	3269
ASHTON DR., Newberry	Yk	17319	E10	2955
ASHWOOD DR., Springfield	Yk	17360	G8	3479
ASLAN CT., Manchester Twp	Yk	17404	F3	3270
ASLAN DR., Manchester Twp	Yk	17404	F3	3270
ASPEN CT., Hanover	Yk	17331	C11	3475
ASPEN CT., Stewartstown	Yk	17363	F11	3585
ASPEN DR., Dillsburg	Yk	17019	E5	3056
ASPEN DR., East Berlin	Ad	17316	D2	3371
ASPEN DR., Newberry	Yk	17319	A6	2955
ASPEN DR., Warrington	Yk	17019	G3	3057
ASPEN DR., York Twp	Yk	17356	F2	3376
ASPEN TR., Carroll Valley	Ad	17320	H4	3676
ASPERS NORTH RD., Menallen	Ad	17304	D4	3263
ASPERS-BENDERSVILLE RD., Menallen	Ad	17304	B2	3263
ASTONIA CT., Penn	Yk	17331	G5	3579
ATKINS RD., Chanceford	Yk	17322	F5	3482
ATKINS RD., Lower Chanceford	Yk	17302	G2	3588
ATLANTHIA LA., Fairview	Yk	17319	C3	2955
ATLANTIC AV., Red Lion	Yk	17356	A8	3377
ATLANTIC AV., York City	Yk	17404	A6	3271
ATLANTIC AV., York Spring	Ad	17372	A10	3160
ATOM RD., Peach Bottom	Yk	17314	E11	3590
ATOM RD., Peach Bottom	Yk	17314	H4	3693
ATOM RD., Peach Bottom	Yk	17314	D2	3694
ATOM RD., Peach Bottom	Yk	17314	A3	3694
ATOMIC AV., Littlestown	Ad	17340	E11	3577
AUBEL RD., Peach Bottom	Yk	17314	G11	3588
AUBEL RD., Peach Bottom	Yk	17314	A10	3589
AUBURN RD., Springettsbury	Yk	17402	A7	3272
AUCTION DR., Latimore	Ad	17372	D8	3160
AUDLYN DR., West Manchester	Yk	17404	A6	3270
AUDRY DR., Jackson	Yk	17364	F4	3372
AUGUSTA CIR., York Twp	Yk	17402	C9	3272
AUGUSTA CT., West Manchester	Yk	17404	G9	3269
AUGUSTA CT., York City	Yk	17404	A6	3271
AUNTO JO LA., York City	Yk	17404	B8	3271
AUSTIN LA., West Manchester	Yk	17404	D4	3270
AUTUMN DR., Bonneauville	Ad	17325	F1	3576
AUTUMN DR., Monaghan	Yk	17019	A9	2952
AUTUMN DR., Newberry	Yk	17319	E9	2955
AUTUMN LA., Hopewell	Yk	17363	B11	3585
AUTUMN TR., Carroll Valley	Ad	17320	F2	3676
AUTUMN WOODS CT., Dillsburg	Yk	17019	F3	3056
AYLESBURY LA., Manchester Twp	Yk	17404	C10	3165
AZALEA DR., Franklin	Yk	17019	A1	3161
AZALEA DR., Penn	Yk	17331	G4	3579

B

Street	County	ZIP	Grid	Map
B & F RD., Butler	Ad	17325	D9	3366
B & F RD., Franklin	Ad	17325	D9	3366
B ST. S., York Spring	Ad	17372	B11	3160
B ST., Jackson	Yk	17364	C11	3269
B ST., Jackson	Yk	17364	C1	3373
B ST., McSherrystown	Ad	17344	E3	3578
B ST., Newberry	Yk	17315	E4	3059
BABYLON RD., Germany	Ad	17340	C5	3681
BACK RD., Menallen	Ad	17304	C11	3157
BACK RD., Menallen	Ad	17304	E1	3262
BACON RD., Chanceford	Yk	17322	E10	3378
BACON RD., Chanceford	Yk	17356	F8	3378
BAD RD., Codorus	Yk	17327	E2	3582
BAER AV., Hanover	Yk	17331	C2	3579
BAER AV., Penn	Yk	17331	C2	3579
BAER AV., Penn	Yk	17331	E3	3579
BAER RIDGE RD., Hellam	Yk	17406	C4	3273
BAER VALLEY RD., Hellam	Yk	17406	C4	3273
BAHN AV., North Codorus	Yk	17404	B8	3374
BAHNS MILL RD., Windsor Twp	Yk	17356	G9	3377
BAHNS MILL RD., Windsor Twp	Yk	17356	A7	3378
BAHNS MILL RD., Windsor Twp	Yk	17366	B4	3378
BAILEY AV., New Freedom	Yk	17349	G4	3687
BAILEY DR., Stewartstown	Yk	17363	D11	3585
BAIR CIR., West Manheim	Yk	17331	H3	3683
BAIR RD., Berwick	Ad	17301	G11	3370
BAIR RD., Berwick	Ad	17301	G1	3474
BAIR RD., Peach Bottom	Yk	17314	A10	3589
BAIR RD., Peach Bottom	Yk	17314	B1	3693
BAIR RD., Tyrone	Ad	17350	A3	3369
BAIRS MILL RD., Hellam	Yk	17368	B10	3169
BAIRS RD., West Manchester	Yk	17404	G2	3373
BAIRS RD., West Manchester	Yk	17404	G5	3373
BAIRS RD., West Manchester	Yk	17404	G6	3373
BAKER LA., Red Lion	Yk	17356	C7	3377
BAKER RD., Hamiltonban	Ad	17222	E5	3467
BAKER RD., West Manchester	Yk	17404	H9	3269
BAKER RD., West Manchester	Yk	17404	A11	3270
BAKER RD., West Manchester	Yk	17404	A9	3270
BAKER RD., West Manchester	Yk	17404	A1	3374
BAKER SCHOOL RD., Reading	Ad	17316	F5	3266
BAKER VIEW LA., Hamiltonban	Ad	17222	E5	3467
BAKERS WATERING TROUGH RD., Reading	Ad	17316	G5	3266
BAKERS WATERING TROUGH RD., Washington	Yk	17316	A3	3267
BALD EAGLE RD., Fawn	Yk	17321	H6	3587
BALD EAGLE RD., Fawn	Yk	17321	A6	3588
BALDER ST. N., Fairfield	Ad	17320	A5	3573
BALDER ST. S., Fairfield	Ad	17320	A5	3573
BALDSMERE DR., York Twp	Yk	17403	E3	3375
BALLAST LA., Hopewell	Yk	17363	E10	3585
BALLAST LA., Stewartstown	Yk	17363	E10	3585
BALLFIED LA., West Manchester	Yk	17404	B3	3270
BALLTOWN RD., Huntington	Ad	17324	B11	3159
BALLTOWN RD., Huntington	Ad	17372	B11	3159
BALSA ST., Manchester Twp	Yk	17404	F8	3165
BALTIMORE PIKE , Mount Joy	Ad	17325	A5	3576
BALTIMORE PIKE , Mount Joy	Ad	17340	E8	3576
BALTIMORE PIKE , Washington	Yk	17019	E1	3161
BALTIMORE PIKE, Cumberland	Ad	17325	F2	3575
BALTIMORE PIKE, Germany	Ad	17340	A10	3577
BALTIMORE PIKE, Germany	Ad	17340	G3	3681
BALTIMORE PIKE, Littlestown	Ad	17340	A10	3577
BALTIMORE PIKE, Mount Joy	Ad	17325	F2	3575
BALTIMORE PIKE, Penn	Yk	17331	E6	3579
BALTIMORE PIKE, Union	Ad	17340	A10	3577
BALTIMORE PIKE, West Manheim	Yk	17331	F9	3579
BALTIMORE PIKE, West Manheim	Yk	17331	G1	3683
BALTIMORE PIKE, West Manheim	Yk	17331	B3	3684
BALTIMORE RD., Franklin	Yk	17019	E9	3056
BALTIMORE RD., Franklin	Yk	17019	E1	3161
BALTIMORE RD., Franklintown	Yk	17323	E9	3056
BALTIMORE RD., Latimore	Ad	17372	E1	3265
BALTIMORE RD., Latimore	Ad	17372	E11	3160
BALTIMORE ST N., Dillsburg	Yk	17019	D2	3056
BALTIMORE ST. S., Carroll	Yk	17019	D4	3056
BALTIMORE ST. S., Dillsburg	Yk	17019	D4	3056
BALTIMORE ST. S., Franklin	Yk	17019	D4	3056
BALTIMORE ST. S., Franklintown	Yk	17323	D4	3056
BALTIMORE ST., Cumberland	Ad	17325	C9	3471
BALTIMORE ST., Gettysburg	Ad	17325	C9	3471
BALTIMORE ST., Glen Rock	Yk	17327	C4	3583
BALTIMORE ST., Hanover	Yk	17331	C3	3579
BALTIMORE ST., Jefferson	Yk	17362	E11	3477
BAMBERGER RD., Fairview	Yk	17319	C3	2955
BAMBERGER RD., Newberry	Yk	17319	G7	2954
BANK AL., New Freedom	Yk	17349	F2	3687
BANK HILL RD., Lower Windsor	Yk	17368	H5	3274

BANK HILL RD., Lower Windsor	Yk	17368	A5	3275
BANK LA., West Manchester	Yk	17404	B4	3270
BANKARD RD., West Manheim	Yk	17331	G4	3683
BANKERT RD., Penn	Yk	17331	H7	3579
BANKERT RD., Penn	Yk	17331	A4	3580
BANNISTER ST., West Manchester	Yk	17404	D9	3270
BANTY LA., Hamiltonban	Ad	17320	A7	3573
BAPTIST ST., Delta	Yk	17314	G4	3693
BARACHEL DR., Windsor Twp	Yk	17402	F7	3272
BARBARA LA., Newberry	Yk	17370	H10	2955
BARBARA TR., Carroll Valley	Ad	17320	D2	3676
BARBER DR., Hanover	Yk	17331	B10	3475
BARCARD CIR., Manchester Twp	Yk	17404	G1	3270
BARCROFT RD., Lower Windsor	Yk	17406	G6	3273
BARE RD., Lower Chanceford	Yk	17309	D4	3484
BARELYN DR., New Freedom	Yk	17349	G4	3687
BARK HILL RD., Manchester Twp	Yk	17404	G9	3165
BARKMILL RD., Lower Chanceford	Yk	17302	C3	3589
BARKWOOD LA., Hellam	Yk	17406	F3	3273
BARLEY RD., West Manchester	Yk	17404	D5	3270
BARLOW CIR., Carroll	Yk	17019	C2	3056
BARLOW DR., Latimore	Ad	17316	A4	3266
BARLOW DR., Mount Joy	Ad	17325	A2	3576
BARLOW RD., Cumberland	Ad	17325	B11	3575
BARLOW RD., Cumberland	Ad	17325	A3	3679
BARLOW ST., Gettysburg	Ad	17325	C7	3471
BARLOW-GREENMOUNT RD., Cumberland	Ad	17325	F8	3574
BARLOW-GREENMOUNT RD., Cumberland	Ad	17325	A9	3575
BARLOW-TWO TAVERNS RD., Mount Joy	Ad	17325	C10	3575
BARLOW-TWO TAVERNS RD., Mount Joy	Ad	17325	A8	3576
BARNES LA., Hamiltonban	Ad	17222	F3	3467
BARNHART DR., Hanover	Yk	17331	E10	3475
BARNHART DR., Penn	Yk	17331	E10	3475
BARON DR., West Manchester	Yk	17404	E4	3270
BARRENS CHURCH RD., Washington	Yk	17019	G10	3056
BARRENS CHURCH RD., Washington	Yk	17019	D7	3161
BARRENS RD. N., Hopewell	Yk	17363	D4	3585
BARRENS RD. S., Hopewell	Yk	17363	E2	3689
BARRENS RD. S., Hopewell	Yk	17363	A5	3690
BARRENS VALLEY RD., Franklin	Yk	17019	F9	3056
BARRENS VALLEY RD., Warrington	Yk	17019	F9	3056
BARRENS VALLEY RD., Washington	Yk	17019	A1	3162
BARRENS VALLEY RD., Washington	Yk	17365	H1	3161
BARRINGTON DR., West Manchester	Yk	17404	C4	3270
BARRISTER DR., Manchester Twp	Yk	17404	G1	3270
BARROW LA., Springfield	Yk	17403	E2	3479
BARSHINGER AV., York Twp	Yk	17403	H1	3375
BARSHINGER RD., Lower Windsor	Yk	17356	E3	3378
BARSHINGER RD., Windsor Twp	Yk	17356	C10	3377
BARTELL DR., Shrewsbury Boro	Yk	17361	A6	3584
BARTENSLAGER RD., Shrewsbury Twp	Yk	17349	E11	3584
BARTENSLAGER RD., Shrewsbury Twp	Yk	17349	E1	3688
BARTLETT DR., Manchester Twp	Yk	17402	B3	3166
BARTLETT DR., York Twp	Yk	17313	E5	3376
BARTON CIR., Hopewell	Yk	17363	E2	3689
BARTS CHURCH RD., Union	Ad	17331	C11	3578
BARTS CHURCH RD., Union	Ad	17331	F3	3682
BARTS CHURCH RD., Union	Ad	17331	D1	3682
BARTS CHURCH RD., Union	Ad	17340	C11	3578
BARWOOD RD., Springettsbury	Yk	17402	B1	3272
BASEHOAR RD., Union	Ad	17340	G10	3577
BASEHOAR RD., Union	Ad	17340	E9	3577
BASEHOAR ROTH RD., Mount Joy	Ad	17340	F2	3679
BASEHOAR ROTH RD., Mount Joy	Ad	17340	A3	3680
BASIL CT., Hellam	Yk	17402	H2	3272
BASILICA DR., Conewago	Ad	17331	D10	3474
BASIN TR., Liberty	Ad	17320	E7	3573
BASS LAKE RD., Newberry	Yk	17319	D8	2955
BASSWOOD RD., West Manchester	Yk	17404	B4	3270
BATEMAN RD., Latimore	Ad	17372	G1	3265
BATEMAN RD., Latimore	Ad	17372	F11	3160
BATTLEHILL RD., Chanceford	Yk	17309	H10	3379
BATTLEHILL RD., Chanceford	Yk	17309	A10	3380
BAUGHER LA., Manheim	Yk	17329	D6	3581
BAUGHER RD., Penn	Yk	17331	B6	3579
BAUMGARDNER RD., Manheim	Yk	17331	D6	3580
BAXTER RD., Peach Bottom	Yk	17314	G5	3693
BAXTER RD., Peach Bottom	Yk	17314	G5	3693
BAYBERRY DR., Manchester Twp	Yk	17404	G1	3270
BAYBERRY LA., York Twp	Yk	17403	G1	3375
BEACON HILL BLVD., Fairview	Yk	17070	H6	2848
BEACON RD., Springettsbury	Yk	17402	C6	3272
BEADSLEY RD., Windsor Twp	Yk	17402	B5	3273
BEAR CIR., Conewago	Ad	17331	G3	3578
BEAR DR., Menallen	Ad	17304	C5	3262
BEAR MOUNTAIN RD., Menallen	Ad	17304	D7	3262
BEAR RD., East Manchester	Yk	17402	H2	3165
BEAR RD., Manchester Twp	Yk	17402	H3	3165
BEARD LA., Codorus	Yk	17327	E5	3582
BEARDS SCHOOL RD., North Codorus	Yk	17362	A3	3478
BEAUMONT RD., Dover Twp	Yk	17315	B4	3269
BEAUMONT RD., York Twp	Yk	17403	G11	3271
BEAUMONT RD., York Twp	Yk	17403	G1	3375
BEAVER CREEK RD., Berwick	Ad	17331	C2	3475
BEAVER CREEK RD., Paradise	Yk	17301	F7	3371
BEAVER CREEK RD., Paradise	Yk	17316	D1	3371
BEAVER CREEK RD., Paradise	Yk	17364	E4	3371
BEAVER CREEK RD., Penn	Yk	17331	C6	3475
BEAVER CREEK RD., Warrington	Yk	17019	A8	3058
BEAVER PL., York City	Yk	17403	C9	3271
BEAVER POND CT., Shrewsbury Twp	Yk	17349	H5	3688
BEAVER RD., Newberry	Yk	17315	D6	3059
BEAVER RD., Warrington	Yk	17315	D6	3059
BEAVER RUN RD., Straban	Ad	17350	E7	3368
BEAVER RUN RD., Straban	Ad	17350	A8	3369
BEAVER ST. N., York City	Yk	17401	C7	3271
BEAVER ST. N., York City	Yk	17404	C6	3271
BEAVER ST. N., York City	Yk	17404	C7	3271
BEAVER ST. S., York City	Yk	17403	C8	3271
BEAVER ST. S., York City	Yk	17403	D9	3271
BEAVER ST. W., New Oxford	Ad	17350	C1	3474
BEAVER ST., Dillsburg	Yk	17019	C3	3056
BEAVER ST., East Berlin	Ad	17316	C2	3371
BEAVER ST., Hallam	Yk	17406	D10	3168
BEAVER ST., Hallam	Yk	17406	B11	3168
BEAVER ST., Manchester Twp	Yk	17404	B2	3271
BEAVER ST., North York	Yk	17404	B4	3271
BEAVERTON DR., Windsor Twp	Yk	17402	F6	3272
BECK MILL RD., Penn	Yk	17331	C4	3579
BECK MILL RD., West Manheim	Yk	17331	B11	3579
BECK RD., Mount Pleasant	Ad	17325	H11	3472
BECK RD., Mount Pleasant	Ad	17325	A10	3473
BECK RD., Springfield	Yk	17403	D1	3479
BECKER RD., Oxford	Ad	17350	D6	3474
BECKER'S TRACE, Franklin	Ad	17353	E4	3364
BECKET RD., Springettsbury	Yk	17402	E6	3272
BECKY DR., East Manchester	Yk	17347	E10	3061
BECKY DR., Heidelberg	Yk	17362	E10	3476
BEDFORD PL., Dover Twp	Yk	17404	D7	3269
BEDFORD RD., Manchester Twp	Yk	17404	F10	3165
BEE JAY DR., Manchester Twp	Yk	17404	D9	3165
BEE JAY LA., Union	Ad	17331	H5	3682
BEE TREE RD., Spring Garden	Yk	17403	C11	3271
BEECH LA., Penn	Yk	17331	D8	3475
BEECH TR., Carroll Valley	Ad	17320	G3	3676
BEECHERSTOWN RD., Butler	Ad	17307	C4	3366
BEECHWOOD DR., Dillsburg	Yk	17019	E5	3056
BEECHWOOD DR., Hamiltonban	Ad	17320	H5	3572
BEECHWOOD DR., Manchester Twp	Yk	17402	B3	3166
BEECHWOOD RD., Peach Bottom	Yk	17302	G8	3588
BEELER AV., West Manchester	Yk	17404	D7	3270
BEIDLER RD., Hellam	Yk	17406	H10	3168
BEIDLER RD., Hellam	Yk	17406	A10	3169
BEINHOWER RD., Fairview	Yk	17319	H4	2954
BELAIR DR., Dillsburg	Yk	17019	D2	3056
BELAIR DR., Dover Twp	Yk	17315	D3	3269
BELAIR RD., Fawn Grove	Yk	17321	H5	3691
BELAIRE LA., York Twp	Yk	17404	H5	3270
BELLA VISTA RD., Windsor Twp	Yk	17356	E10	3377
BELLAIR DR., York Twp	Yk	17402	C2	3376
BELLE LA., Hellam	Yk	17406	F2	3273
BELLE RD., York Twp	Yk	17356	E11	3272
BELLEVUE DR., Spring Garden	Yk	17403	D10	3271
BELLEVUE RD., Red Lion	Yk	17356	B9	3377
BELLVIEW CT., York Twp	Yk	17356	F1	3376
BELLVIEW ST., Hanover	Yk	17331	B1	3579
BELMAR CT., York Twp	Yk	17313	C5	3376
BELMAR DR., York Twp	Yk	17313	C5	3376
BELMONT AV., Penn	Yk	17331	B4	3579
BELMONT RD., Butler	Ad	17325	F11	3366
BELMONT RD., Cumberland	Ad	17325	E4	3470
BELMONT RD., Franklin	Ad	17325	F11	3366
BELMONT RD., Franklin	Ad	17325	E5	3470
BELMONT ST. S., Spring Garden	Yk	17403	H8	3271
BELMONT ST., Spring Garden	Yk	17403	G5	3271
BELVIDERE AV. N., York City	Yk	17404	A7	3271
BELVIDERE AV. S., York City	Yk	17404	A8	3271
BELVIDERE ST. N., York Twp	Yk	17404	H7	3270
BELVINS RD., Hopewell	Yk	17363	E3	3689
BEMAR RD., Codorus	Yk	17360	C8	3478
BEN HOGAN DR., Newberry	Yk	17319	E6	2955
BEND LA., Hellam	Yk	17368	D3	3169
BENDER RD., Mount Pleasant	Ad	17331	A2	3578
BENDER RD., Union	Ad	17331	H3	3577
BENDER'S CHURCH RD., Butler	Ad	17307	C3	3367
BENDERSVILLE-WENKSVILLE RD., Menallen	Ad	17304	E1	3262
BENEDICT RD., Warrington	Yk	17365	B5	3163
BENFRA DR., Conewago	Ad	17331	B3	3578
BENJAMIN DR., Penn	Yk	17331	F7	3579
BENNER RD., Mount Joy	Ad	17325	C1	3679
BENNING AV., Cumberland	Ad	17325	E6	3470
BEN'S RD., East Hopewell	Yk	17363	F6	3585
BEN'S RD., Hopewell	Yk	17363	F6	3585
BENTLEY LA., Manchester Twp	Yk	17404	E2	3270
BENTWOOD AV., Littlestown	Ad	17340	F1	3681
BENTZ CT., Manchester Twp	Yk	17404	H2	3270
BENTZ MILL RD., Washington	Yk	17316	C9	3162
BENTZ MILL RD., Washington	Yk	17365	G4	3161
BENTZ MILL RD., Washington	Yk	17365	A7	3162
BENTZ RD., North Codorus	Yk	17362	E3	3477
BENTZ RD., North Codorus	Yk	17362	A4	3478
BENTZEL MILL RD., Manchester Twp	Yk	17404	C9	3165
BENTZEL RD., Warrington	Yk	17339	G5	3058
BENTZEL RD., Warrington	Yk	17339	A3	3059
BENYOU LA., Fairview	Yk	17070	C1	2954
BENZEL ST., West Manchester	Yk	17404	B3	3270
BERGMAN ST., York City	Yk	17403	F7	3271
BERKEY RD., Washington	Yk	17316	F9	3267
BERKLEY RD., Springettsbury	Yk	17402	B7	3272
BERKSHIRE DR., Shrewsbury Boro	Yk	17361	A6	3584
BERKSHIRE LA., Hopewell	Yk	17363	F9	3585
BERLIN AV. N., New Oxford	Ad	17350	B2	3474
BERLIN AV. S., New Oxford	Ad	17350	B3	3474
BERLIN CT., West Manchester	Yk	17404	D9	3270
BERLIN RD., Hamilton	Ad	17350	C11	3370
BERLIN RD. E., Huntington	Ad	17372	B9	3265
BERLIN RD. E., Reading	Ad	17316	A1	3370
BERLIN RD. E., Tyrone	Ad	17372	H9	3264
BERLIN RD. E., West Manchester	Yk	17404	G10	3269
BERLIN RD. E., West Manchester	Yk	17404	A10	3270
BERLIN RD., Jefferson	Yk	17362	D10	3477
BERLIN RD., New Oxford	Ad	17350	A2	3474
BERLIN RD., Oxford	Ad	17350	A2	3474
BERLIN ST. W., New Oxford	Ad	17350	C1	3474
BERMUDIAN CHURCH RD., Washington	Yk	17316	E6	3267
BERMUDIAN CREEK RD., Latimore	Ad	17372	B11	3161
BERNAYS DR., Manchester Twp	Yk	17404	F1	3270
BERRY HILL RD., North Hopewell	Yk	17356	C4	3481
BERSHIRE LA., Dover Twp	Yk	17315	H5	3269
BERT CT., Manchester Twp	Yk	17404	H11	3165
BERTHA DR., Mount Pleasant	Ad	17350	C2	3473
BERWICK RD., Berwick	Ad	17301	B10	3371
BERWICK ST., West Manchester	Yk	17404	E8	3270
BESHORE SCHOOL RD., East Manchester	Yk	17345	C4	3166
BETHEL CHURCH RD., Fairview	Yk	17070	F11	2848
BETHEL CHURCH RD., Fairview	Yk	17070	F1	2953
BETHEL CHURCH RD., Franklin	Yk	17019	C11	3055
BETHEL CT., Conewago	Ad	17344	F1	3578
BETHEL RD., Warrington	Yk	17339	A9	3059
BETHLEHEM CHURCH RD., Windsor Twp	Yk	17356	G8	3377
BETHLEHEM CHURCH RD., Windsor Twp	Yk	17356	A10	3378
BEVERLY HILLS CT., Windsor Twp	Yk	17356	C10	3377
BEY LA., York City	Yk	17404	A5	3271
BICKING AV., Red Lion	Yk	17356	C6	3377
BICKING AV., Windsor Twp	Yk	17356	C6	3377
BIESECKER RD. N., Jackson	Yk	17364	C1	3373
BIESECKER RD. S., Jackson	Yk	17364	C3	3373
BIESECKER RD. S., Jackson	Yk	17404	C3	3373
BIESECKER RD., Dover Twp	Yk	17315	H5	3268
BIESECKER RD., Jackson	Yk	17364	B10	3269
BIG CONEWAGO AV., Conewago	Yk	17345	G7	3060
BIG CONEWAGO RD., East Manchester	Yk	17345	D7	3061
BIG CREEK RD., Conewago	Yk	17315	A5	3060
BIG DAM RD., Washington	Yk	17019	C6	3161
BIG FLAT LA., Menallen	Ad	17307	D2	3260
BIG HILL RD., Menallen	Ad	17324	B10	3158
BIG HILL RD., Menallen	Ad	17324	D1	3263
BIG MOUNT RD., Dover Twp	Yk	17315	F7	3267
BIG MOUNT RD., Paradise	Yk	17315	F7	3267
BIG MOUNT RD., Paradise	Yk	17315	A8	3268
BIG MOUNT RD., Paradise	Yk	17364	A8	3268
BIG MOUNT RD., Paradise	Yk	17316	C1	3372
BIG MOUNT RD., Paradise	Yk	17364	C1	3372
BIG MOUNT RD., Washington	Yk	17316	E4	3267
BIG OAK RD., Monaghan	Yk	17019	C2	3057
BIG ROCK DR., Warrington	Yk	17315	D2	3163
BIG ROCK RD., Reading	Ad	17316	C6	3266
BIG SKY DR., Goldsboro	Yk	17319	H6	2955
BIG SPRING RD., Fairview	Yk	17070	E1	2954
BIG SPRING RD., Fairview	Yk	17319	A2	2955
BIG SPRINGS RD., Fairview	Yk	17319	G1	2954
BIGHAM RD., Freedom	Ad	17325	B4	3574
BIGLAR CT., Windsor Twp	Yk	17356	E6	3377
BIGLERVILLE RD., Butler	Ad	17307	A3	3367
BIGLERVILLE RD., Butler	Ad	17325	A8	3367
BIGLERVILLE RD., Cumberland	Ad	17325	B3	3471
BILL DUGAN DR., Newberry	Yk	17319	H6	2954
BILLERBECK ST., Oxford	Ad	17350	B1	3474
BILLET DR., Fairview	Yk	17055	C7	2953
BILT LA., Hellam	Yk	17406	C7	3168
BINDER LA., Hellam	Yk	17406	F11	3167
BINGAMAN RD., Franklin	Ad	17353	G9	3364
BINGAMAN RD., Franklin	Ad	17353	A11	3365
BINGAMAN RD., Franklin	Ad	17353	B1	3469
BIRCH LA., Oxford	Ad	17350	B4	3474
BIRCH LA., Red Lion	Yk	17356	C7	3377
BIRCH RD., Hopewell	Yk	17363	H9	3585
BIRCH RD., Hopewell	Yk	17363	A9	3586
BIRCH RD., West Manchester	Yk	17404	A5	3270
BIRCH RUN RD., Franklin	Ad	17222	F10	3259
BIRCH RUN RD., Franklin	Ad	17222	B6	3260
BIRCH RUN RD., Menallen	Ad	17307	D4	3260
BIRCH ST. E., Codorus	Yk	17362	F11	3477
BIRCH ST., Hanover	Yk	17331	A3	3579
BIRCH TR., Carroll Valley	Ad	17320	A4	3677
BIRCHWOOD DR., Lower Chanceford	Yk	17314	H3	3589
BIRCHWOOD RD., Hellam	Yk	17402	A3	3273
BIRTHDAY CLUB RD., Codorus	Yk	17327	H2	3686
BIRTHDAY CLUB RD., Shrewsbury Twp	Yk	17349	H2	3686
BISHOP RD., Monaghan	Yk	17055	C6	2952
BISHOPS CIR., Windsor Twp	Yk	17402	F8	3272
BITTER SWEET LA., Newberry	Yk	17319	F7	2955
BITTERNUT BLVD., Manchester Twp	Yk	17404	F8	3165
BITTERNUT RD., East Manchester	Yk	17347	G7	3166
BITTLE RD., Germany	Ad	17340	F5	3681
BLACHBILL RD., Franklin	Ad	17222	D2	3467
BLACK BASS TR., Carroll Valley	Ad	17320	H7	3572
BLACK BIRD TR., Carroll Valley	Ad	17320	H6	3572
BLACK BRIDGE RD., Manchester Twp	Yk	17402	E11	3166
BLACK BRIDGE RD., Manchester Twp	Yk	17402	D10	3166
BLACK BRIDGE RD., Manchester Twp	Yk	17402	D1	3271
BLACK BRIDGE RD., Manchester Twp	Yk	17402	D3	3271
BLACK HORSE TAVERN RD., Cumberland	Ad	17325	D11	3470
BLACK HORSE TAVERN RD., Cumberland	Ad	17325	E1	3574
BLACK HORSE TAVERN RD., Highland	Ad	17325	C7	3470
BLACK LA., Conewago	Ad	17331	C8	3474
BLACK LA., Oxford	Ad	17331	C8	3474
BLACK OAK CT., Windsor Twp	Yk	17356	H11	3272
BLACK OAK DR., Windsor Twp	Yk	17356	H11	3272
BLACK OAK DR., Windsor Twp	Yk	17356	A10	3273
BLACK OAK TR., Peach Bottom	Yk	17314	H1	3692
BLACK POWDER DR., Fairview	Yk	17319	C3	2954
BLACK ROCK RD., Manheim	Yk	17327	B6	3685
BLACK ROCK RD., Manheim	Yk	17329	F11	3580
BLACK ROCK RD., Manheim	Yk	17329	F1	3684
BLACK ROCK RD., Manheim	Yk	17329	H1	3684
BLACK ROCK RD., Manheim	Yk	17329	A2	3685
BLACK ROCK RD., Penn	Yk	17331	E6	3579
BLACK ROCK RD., West Manheim	Yk	17331	B8	3580
BLACK WALNUT DR., Newberry	Yk	17319	C5	2955
BLACKBERRY HILL RD., Dover Twp	Yk	17315	F9	3163
BLACKBERRY RD., Dover Twp	Yk	17315	A8	3164
BLACKBERRY SCHOOL RD., Latimore	Ad	17372	A2	3160
BLACKBIRD LA., Dover Twp	Yk	17315	C9	3059
BLACKFRIAR LA., Springettsbury	Yk	17402	E6	3272
BLACKGUM CT., Manchester Twp	Yk	17402	D11	3166
BLACKGUM CT., Manchester Twp	Yk	17402	D1	3271
BLACKSMITH AV., Windsor Boro	Yk	17366	F4	3377
BLACKSMITH AV., Windsor Twp	Yk	17366	G4	3377
BLACKSMITH SHOP RD., Cumberland	Ad	17325	C4	3575
BLACKTHORNE CT., Manchester Twp	Yk	17402	D11	3166
BLAIN RD., Lower Chanceford	Yk	17302	G9	3484
BLAIR HOLLOW RD., Carroll	Yk	17019	A5	3057
BLAIR MOUNTAIN RD., Carroll	Yk	17019	H6	3056
BLAIR MOUNTAIN RD., Carroll	Yk	17019	A5	3057
BLAIR RD., Penn	Yk	17331	D7	3579
BLAKE CT., North Codorus	Yk	17403	H4	3374
BLANKERT AV., Penn	Yk	17331	H5	3579
BLENHEIM CT., York Twp	Yk	17403	F2	3375
BLENHEIM ST., Conewago	Ad	17331	B4	3578
BLESSING BLVD., Hallam	Yk	17406	C10	3168
BLESSING LA., Hellam	Yk	17368	B7	3169
BLETNER AV., Conewago	Ad	17331	G2	3578
BLETNER AV., Penn	Yk	17331	A4	3579
BLEW FARM LA., Lower Windsor	Yk	17366	B2	3378
BLIZZARD TR., Carroll Valley	Ad	17320	A8	3573
BLOOMING GROVE RD., Penn	Yk	17331	B4	3580
BLOSSOM DR., East Manchester	Yk	17347	G4	3166
BLOSSOM HILL LA., York Twp	Yk	17313	E6	3376
BLOSSOM LA., Littlestown	Ad	17340	D11	3577
BLOSSOM LA., Menallen	Ad	17307	C9	3262
BLOUSE RD., Windsor Twp	Yk	17356	A10	3378
BLOUSE RD., Windsor Twp	Yk	17356	H1	3481
BLUE BALL RD., East Hopewell	Yk	17363	B6	3586
BLUE BALL RD., East Hopewell	Yk	17363	F6	3586
BLUE BALL RD., Fawn	Yk	17352	H10	3586
BLUE BALL RD., Fawn	Yk	17352	A11	3587
BLUE BALL RD., Fawn	Yk	17352	A1	3691
BLUE BALL RD., Fawn	Yk	17363	G9	3586
BLUE GILL TR., Carroll Valley	Ad	17320	H7	3572
BLUE GRASS TR., Carroll Valley	Ad	17320	A5	3677
BLUE HERON DR., Berwick	Ad	17331	A4	3475
BLUE HILL RD., Manheim	Yk	17329	G9	3580
BLUE HILL RD., Manheim	Yk	17331	D6	3580
BLUE HILL SCHOOL RD., Washington	Yk	17315	G8	3162
BLUE HILL SCHOOL RD., Washington	Yk	17316	G8	3162
BLUE HILL SCHOOL RD., Washington	Yk	17316	H1	3267
BLUE JAY CT., Shrewsbury Twp	Yk	17363	H4	3688
BLUE JAY DR., Conewago	Yk	17315	A11	3165
BLUE JAY DR., Dover Twp	Yk	17315	H1	3269
BLUE JAY DR., Dover Twp	Yk	17315	B2	3270
BLUE JAY DR., Windsor Twp	Yk	17356	A2	3377
BLUE RIBBON RD., Franklin	Ad	17307	C5	3366
BLUE RIDGE DR., York Twp	Yk	17402	A7	3376
BLUE RIDGE TR., Carroll Valley	Ad	17320	G7	3572
BLUE SKY DR., Lower Windsor	Yk	17368	A8	3275
BLUE SPRUCE DR., Penn	Yk	17331	D6	3579
BLUE SPRUCE TR., Carroll Valley	Ad	17320	A4	3677
BLUEBERRY LA., Windsor Twp	Yk	17356	H11	3272
BLUEBERRY LA., Windsor Twp	Yk	17356	A10	3273
BLUEBERRY RD., Huntington	Ad	17324	C11	3159
BLUEBILL DR., Fairview	Yk	17319	G3	2954
BLUEBIRD LA., Dover Twp	Yk	17315	B9	3059
BLUEBIRD TR., Carroll Valley	Ad	17320	G2	3676
BLUEBIRD TR., Carroll Valley	Ad	17320	A2	3677
BLUEBIRD TR., Peach Bottom	Yk	17314	F10	3588
BLUNSTON LA., Hellam	Yk	17406	E9	3168
BLYMIRE HOLLOW RD., North Hopewell	Yk	17322	F8	3480
BLYMIRE HOLLOW RD., North Hopewell	Yk	17363	G10	3480
BLYMIRE HOLLOW RD., North Hopewell	Yk	17363	A11	3481
BLYMIRE HOLLOW RD., North Hopewell	Yk	17363	A1	3585
BLYMIRE RD., Chanceford	Yk	17356	C3	3379
BLYMIRE RD., York Twp	Yk	17313	D8	3376
BOARD RD., East Manchester	Yk	17345	C4	3166
BOARD RD., East Manchester	Yk	17347	F9	3061
BOARD RD., Manchester Twp	Yk	17402	A6	3166
BOAT LANDING AV., Newberry	Yk	17345	D8	3061
BOATHOUSE RD., Lower Windsor	Yk	17368	A2	3275
BOBBY JONES DR., Newberry	Yk	17319	C7	2955
BOB'S RD., East Hopewell	Yk	17322	D2	3586
BODDINGTON PL., York Twp	Yk	17402	E9	3272
BOEING RD., Fairview	Yk	17070	C8	2849
BOGGS RD., Franklin	Ad	17222	H8	3363
BOGGS RD., Franklin	Ad	17222	A8	3364
BOHN AV., East Berlin	Ad	17316	D11	3267
BOHR CT., Shrewsbury Twp	Yk	17327	E5	3583
BOLD RULER CIR., Carroll	Yk	17019	G11	2951
BOLL RD., Codorus	Yk	17327	E1	3582
BOLLINGER DR., Shrewsbury Twp	Yk	17361	A1	3688
BOLLINGER RD., Germany	Ad	17340	H4	3681
BOLLINGER RD. W., Germany	Ad	17340	A4	3682
BOLLINGER RD., Union	Ad	17331	C11	3578
BOLLINGER RD., Union	Ad	17340	B2	3682
BOLTON ST. N., New Oxford	Ad	17350	A3	3474
BOLTON ST. S., New Oxford	Ad	17350	A3	3474
BON AIR DR., Dover Twp	Yk	17315	D2	3269
BON AIRE DR., West Manchester	Yk	17404	B4	3270
BONBAR RD., Spring Garden	Yk	17403	H9	3271
BOND AV., Spring Garden	Yk	17403	B10	3271
BOND ST., New Freedom	Yk	17349	G3	3687
BONITA DR., East Manchester	Yk	17347	C5	3167
BONNAIR CHURCH RD., Shrewsbury Twp	Yk	17327	A9	3583
BONNAIR RD., Codorus	Yk	17327	G11	3582
BONNAIR RD., Codorus	Yk	17327	E2	3686
BONNAIR RD., Shrewsbury Twp	Yk	17327	G11	3582
BONNAIR RD., Shrewsbury Twp	Yk	17327	A10	3583
BONNEAU HEIGHTS CIR., Mount Pleasant	Ad	17325	G11	3472
BONNEAU HEIGHTS RD., Mount Pleasant	Ad	17325	F11	3472
BONNERS HILL RD., Latimore	Ad	17372	C6	3160
BONNEVIEW RD., Springettsbury	Yk	17402	F3	3271
BONNIE TR., Carroll Valley	Ad	17320	E2	3676
BONNIEFIELD CIR., Bonneauville	Ad	17325	H2	3576
BONNIEFIELD DR. S., Bonneauville	Ad	17325	H2	3576
BONNIEFIELD DR. W., Bonneauville	Ad	17325	G1	3576
BONNINE CT., West Manheim	Yk	17331	C10	3580
BON-OX RD., Mount Pleasant	Ad	17325	H10	3472
BON-OX RD., Mount Pleasant	Ad	17325	A9	3473

BON-OX RD. CANADOCHLY CIR.

BON-OX RD., Mount Pleasant	Ad	17350	C7	3473
BON-OX RD., Mount Pleasant	Ad	17350	F5	3473
BOOKER RD., Peach Bottom	Yk	17314	D11	3590
BOOKER RD., Peach Bottom	Yk	17314	C1	3694
BOOSE RD., Springfield	Yk	17360	G10	3478
BORING BRIDGE RD., Warrington	Yk	17339	A8	3059
BORING WAY, North York	Yk	17404	B5	3271
BORNT DR., Dover Twp	Yk	17315	C3	3269
BOROM RD., York Twp	Yk	17404	G4	3270
BORTNER RD., Codorus	Yk	17327	H7	3582
BOSLEY RD., East Hopewell	Yk	17363	C7	3586
BOSLEY SCHOOL RD., Codorus	Yk	17327	D5	3686
BOTTLE HILL RD., Shrewsbury Twp	Yk	17327	F9	3583
BOTTOM RD., Franklin	Ad	17353	B11	3261
BOTTOM RD., Franklin	Ad	17353	G3	3364
BOTTOM RD., Franklin	Ad	17353	A2	3365
BOULDER LA., Hamiltonban	Ad	17320	H11	3571
BOUNDARY AL., Manchester Boro	Yk	17345	C2	3166
BOUNDARY AV. E., Spring Garden	Yk	17403	E8	3271
BOUNDARY AV. E., York City	Yk	17403	E8	3271
BOUNDARY AV. W., Dallastown	Yk	17313	F8	3376
BOUNDARY AV. W., York City	Yk	17403	B9	3271
BOUNDARY AV. W., York Twp	Yk	17313	F8	3376
BOUNDARY AV., Hanover	Yk	17331	B4	3579
BOUNDARY AV., Newberry	Yk	17345	D7	3061
BOUNDARY AV., Red Lion	Yk	17356	B8	3377
BOUNDARY DR., New Freedom	Yk	17349	F2	3687
BOUNDARY DR., Shrewsbury Twp	Yk	17349	F1	3687
BOUNDARY RD., Shrewsbury Twp	Yk	17349	F11	3583
BOURBON TR., Hamiltonban	Ad	17320	H11	3571
BOVARY DR., Hellam	Yk	17402	H1	3272
BOWERS BRIDGE RD., Conewago	Yk	17345	H9	3060
BOWERS BRIDGE RD., Conewago	Yk	17345	A7	3061
BOWERS DR., Carroll	Yk	17019	F11	2951
BOWERS RD., Hopewell	Yk	17363	B4	3585
BOWERS RD., Mount Joy	Ad	17340	F7	3576
BOWERS RD., Mount Pleasant	Ad	17340	F7	3576
BOWMAN AV., Fairview	Yk	17339	D2	2954
BOWMAN DR., Penn	Yk	17331	E4	3579
BOWMAN RD., Fawn	Yk	17321	C11	3587
BOWMAN RD., Jackson	Yk	17364	E11	3269
BOWMAN RD., Jackson	Yk	17404	E1	3373
BOWMAN SCHOOL RD., Hopewell	Yk	17349	E8	3584
BOWSER SCHOOL RD., Shrewsbury Twp	Yk	17349	H2	3686
BOWSER SCHOOL RD., Shrewsbury Twp	Yk	17349	C2	3687
BOX HILL LA., Spring Garden	Yk	17403	A1	3375
BOXWOOD CT., Dover Twp	Yk	17315	F11	3164
BOXWOOD LA., Springettsbury	Yk	17402	G2	3272
BOXWOOD RD., East Manchester	Yk	17345	D3	3166
BOXWOOD RD., Manchester Boro	Yk	17345	D2	3166
BOXWOOD RD., Red Lion	Yk	17356	D7	3377
BOXWOOD RD., Windsor Twp	Yk	17356	D8	3377
BOYCOTT LA., Cumberland	Ad	17325	H10	3470
BOYD DR., Windsor Twp	Yk	17356	B4	3377
BOYD RD., Chanceford	Yk	17309	B6	3380
BOYD RD., Lower Windsor	Yk	17368	H10	3274
BOYD'S HOLLOW RD., Menallen	Ad	17307	C9	3261
BOYD'S SCHOOL RD., Cumberland	Ad	17325	B3	3471
BOYD'S SCHOOLHOUSE RD., Menallen	Ad	17307	A7	3261
BOYELS DR., Newberry	Yk	17370	D3	3060
BOYER DR., East Berlin	Ad	17316	C2	3371
BOYER NURSERY RD., Franklin	Ad	17307	E6	3365
BOYER NURSERY RD., Franklin	Ad	17307	A2	3366
BOYER RD., Shrewsbury Twp	Yk	17327	C11	3583
BOYER RD., Shrewsbury Twp	Yk	17349	C1	3687
BOYER ST., Germany	Ad	17340	E3	3681
BOYLE RD., Freedom	Ad	17320	F5	3677
BOYLE RD., Freedom	Ad	17320	A5	3678
BOYLE RD., Liberty	Ad	17320	F5	3677
BOYSCOUT RD., Hamilton	Ad	17350	H8	3369
BRAD RD., Penn	Yk	17331	F6	3579
BRADDOCK DR., Fairview	Yk	17319	H2	2954
BRADFORD DR., Springettsbury	Yk	17402	B6	3272
BRADFORD ST., Arendtsville	Ad	17307	B3	3366
BRADLEY AV., York Twp	Yk	17313	C6	3376
BRADLEY CIR., Fairview	Yk	17070	F11	2848
BRADLEY CT., Shrewsbury Twp	Yk	17349	F11	3584
BRADY RD., Manchester Twp	Yk	17404	H11	3165
BRAEBURN CT., Manchester Twp	Yk	17404	D8	3165
BRAEBURN DR., Fairview	Yk	17319	A2	2955
BRAFFERTON CT., Manchester Twp	Yk	17404	E11	3165
BRAGG CIR., Penn	Yk	17331	H7	3579
BRAGG DR., Reading	Ad	17316	D5	3266
BRAGG ST., Penn	Yk	17331	G7	3579
BRAGGTOWN RD., Latimore	Ad	17316	D9	3161
BRAGGTOWN RD., Latimore	Ad	17372	G7	3160
BRAKEMAN DR., Hopewell	Yk	17363	F10	3585
BRAMBLEWOOD LA., Fairview	Yk	17339	B1	2953
BRANCH CIR., East Berlin	Ad	17316	D1	3371
BRANDON AV., Fawn	Yk	17321	A5	3588
BRANDON DR., York Twp	Yk	17313	D9	3376
BRANDON LA., Carroll	Yk	17019	G5	3056
BRANDY CT., Hanover	Yk	17331	B10	3475
BRANDYWINE CT., Littlestown	Ad	17340	D2	3681
BRANDYWINE DR., Shrewsbury Boro	Yk	17361	B10	3584
BRANDYWINE DR., Shrewsbury Twp	Yk	17361	B10	3584
BRANDYWINE LA., Hanover	Yk	17331	C11	3475
BRANDYWINE LA., Manchester Twp	Yk	17404	G11	3165
BRANDYWINE LA., Manchester Twp	Yk	17404	G1	3270
BRANT DR., York Twp	Yk	17313	E9	3376
BREAM HILL RD., Cumberland	Ad	17325	D10	3470
BRECKENRIDGE ST., Gettysburg	Ad	17325	B9	3471
BREEZEWOOD DR., Manchester Twp	Yk	17404	A4	3271
BREEZEWOOD DR., Oxford	Ad	17350	H1	3473
BREEZEWOOD DR., Penn	Yk	17331	F3	3579
BREEZEWOOD DR., Penn	Yk	17331	F5	3579
BREEZEWOOD RD., West Manchester	Yk	17404	D6	3270
BREEZY VISTA LA., Hellam	Yk	17406	D4	3273
BREMER RD., Conewago	Yk	17315	F11	3059
BREMER RD., Conewago	Yk	17315	A7	3060
BREMER RD., Conewago	Yk	17315	F3	3164
BRENDA RD., West Manchester	Yk	17404	B5	3270
BRENDA TR., Carroll Valley	Ad	17320	F11	3572
BRENDA TR., Carroll Valley	Ad	17320	F1	3676
BRENNEMAN DR., Cross Roads	Yk	17363	F1	3585
BRENNEMAN DR., Cross Roads	Yk	17363	G1	3585
BRENNEMAN DR., East Hopewell	Yk	17363	G1	3585
BRENNEMAN DR., Fairview	Yk	17055	C5	2953
BRENNEMAN DR., Fairview	Yk	17339	F7	2953
BRENNEMAN RD., Codorus	Yk	17327	F2	3582
BRENT RD., Liberty	Ad	17320	C8	3573
BRENTWOOD CT., Germany	Ad	17340	G3	3681
BRENTWOOD CT., Penn	Yk	17331	F3	3579
BRENTWOOD DR., York Twp	Yk	17403	H11	3271
BRETON LA., Carroll	Yk	17019	G9	2951
BRETTON LA., West Manchester	Yk	17404	D4	3270
BREWSTER CIR., Penn	Yk	17331	E2	3579
BREWSTER ST., Penn	Yk	17331	E3	3579
BRIAN LA., Manchester Twp	Yk	17404	G2	3270
BRIAR CT., Dillsburg	Yk	17019	E2	3056
BRIARWOOD BLVD., Union	Ad	17331	F4	3682
BRIARWOOD CT., Chanceford	Yk	17322	B1	3482
BRIARWOOD CT., West Manchester	Yk	17404	H2	3373
BRIARWOOD RD., Shrewsbury Twp	Yk	17361	B10	3584
BRIBERY LA., West Manheim	Yk	17331	G10	3579
BRICK LA., Mount Pleasant	Ad	17350	E2	3473
BRICK YARD RD., East Manchester	Yk	17345	E5	3166
BRICK YARD RD., East Manchester	Yk	17347	E5	3166
BRICKCRAFTER'S RD., Mount Pleasant	Ad	17350	E1	3473
BRICKCRAFTER'S RD., Straban	Ad	17350	B9	3369
BRICKETT RD., Peach Bottom	Yk	17302	B9	3589
BRICKYARD RD., Oxford	Ad	17350	D4	3474
BRIDGE RD., Hopewell	Yk	17363	C11	3586
BRIDGEPORT RD., Franklin	Ad	17307	H2	3365
BRIDGETON RD., Fawn	Yk	17321	F7	3587
BRIDGETON RD., Fawn	Yk	17321	A5	3588
BRIDGETON RD., Fawn	Yk	17352	F7	3587
BRIDGETON RD., Lower Chanceford	Yk	17302	F11	3484
BRIDGETON RD., Lower Chanceford	Yk	17302	C2	3588
BRIDGETON RD., Lower Chanceford	Yk	17321	C2	3588
BRIDGETON-WOODBINE RD., Fawn	Yk	17321	B4	3588
BRIDGEVIEW RD., Hopewell	Yk	17349	F9	3584
BRIDGEVIEW RD., Hopewell	Yk	17363	F9	3584
BRIDGEVIEW RD., Hopewell	Yk	17363	A10	3585
BRIDLE CT., Manchester Twp	Yk	17404	E1	3270
BRIDLE CT., Newberry	Yk	17319	F10	2955
BRIDLE RD., Shrewsbury Boro	Yk	17327	H8	3583
BRIDLEWOOD WAY, Springettsbury	Yk	17402	A8	3272
BRIGADIER DR., Manchester Twp	Yk	17404	G1	3270
BRIGGS CIR., York Twp	Yk	17402	B4	3376
BRIGHKIN DR., York Twp	Yk	17402	A2	3376
BRIGHTON CIR., Springfield	Yk	17360	D5	3479
BRIGHTON DR., Springettsbury	Yk	17402	B7	3272
BRIGHTON DR., Springfield	Yk	17360	D5	3479
BRILLHART LA., Springfield	Yk	17327	F9	3479
BRILLSTRICK RD., North Hopewell	Yk	17363	E11	3480
BRILLSTRICK RD., North Hopewell	Yk	17363	F1	3584
BRILLSTRICK RD., Shrewsbury Twp	Yk	17349	E11	3480
BRISTOL DR., Conewago	Ad	17331	F3	3578
BRISTOL DR., York Twp	Yk	17403	H11	3271
BRITTANY CT., Dover Twp	Yk	17404	F8	3269
BRITTANY CT., Windsor Twp	Yk	17356	B2	3377
BRITTANY DR., Manchester Twp	Yk	17404	D10	3165
BRITTANY LA., Franklin	Yk	17019	C4	3161
BRITTANY LA., Hopewell	Yk	17363	E4	3585
BRITTANY LA., Washington	Yk	17019	C4	3161
BROAD ST. E., Dallastown	Yk	17313	G7	3376
BROAD ST. N., Spring Garden	Yk	17403	D5	3271
BROAD ST. S., Hallam	Yk	17406	C11	3168
BROAD ST. S., New Freedom	Yk	17349	F3	3687
BROAD ST. W., Dallastown	Yk	17313	E6	3376
BROAD ST., Manchester Twp	Yk	17402	C8	3166
BROAD ST., Peach Bottom	Yk	17314	G3	3693
BROAD ST., Spring Garden	Yk	17403	F9	3271
BROAD ST., West Manchester	Yk	17404	B3	3270
BROAD ST., Yoe	Yk	17313	G5	3376
BROAD ST., York City	Yk	17403	D6	3271
BROADWAY AV., Manchester Boro	Yk	17345	D1	3166
BROADWAY E., Gettysburg	Ad	17325	C7	3471
BROADWAY ST. E., Red Lion	Yk	17356	D7	3377
BROADWAY ST. W., Goldsboro	Yk	17319	G7	2955
BROADWAY ST. W., Red Lion	Yk	17356	A8	3377
BROADWAY ST., Goldsboro	Yk	17319	A7	2956
BROADWAY W., Gettysburg	Ad	17325	C7	3471
BROADWAY, Franklin	Ad	17307	G1	3469
BROADWAY, Hanover	Yk	17331	D10	3475
BROADWAY, Hanover	Yk	17331	C2	3579
BROADWAY, Penn	Yk	17331	D6	3475
BROADWAY, Stewartstown	Yk	17363	D11	3585
BROCKIE DR., Spring Garden	Yk	17403	B11	3271
BROCKIE DR., Spring Garden	Yk	17403	B1	3375
BROCKIE LA., Spring Garden	Yk	17403	B11	3271
BRODBECKS RD., Codorus	Yk	17327	B4	3686
BRODBECKS RD., Manheim	Yk	17327	G4	3685
BRODBECKS RD., Manheim	Yk	17327	A4	3686
BROGUEVILLE RD., Chanceford	Yk	17322	D6	3482
BROGUEVILLE RD., Chanceford	Yk	17322	F6	3482
BRONSON AV., Stewartstown	Yk	17363	D10	3585
BROOK CIR. W., York Twp	Yk	17403	F1	3375
BROOK CIR., Hellam	Yk	17368	C8	3169
BROOK CIR., Newberry	Yk	17319	E10	2955
BROOK DR., East Manchester	Yk	17347	G6	3166
BROOK HOLLOW AV., Chanceford	Yk	17322	B2	3482
BROOK LA., Hellam	Yk	17368	D8	3169
BROOK LA., Windsor Twp	Yk	17356	E1	3481
BROOK MEADOW CIR., Shrewsbury Boro	Yk	17361	B7	3584
BROOKE AV., Cumberland	Ad	17325	A4	3575
BROOKEDGE LA., Springettsbury	Yk	17402	F5	3272
BROOKFIELD DR., Manchester Twp	Yk	17404	G8	3165
BROOKLYN DR., Hellam	Yk	17402	D8	3167
BROOKMAR DR., West Manchester	Yk	17404	A6	3270
BROOKSIDE AV., Dover Twp	Yk	17315	H2	3269
BROOKSIDE AV., Dover Twp	Yk	17315	A2	3270
BROOKSIDE AV., Dover Twp	Yk	17404	A2	3270
BROOKSIDE AV., Penn	Yk	17331	E3	3579
BROOKSIDE CIR., Carroll	Yk	17019	E3	3056
BROOKSIDE LA., Butler	Ad	17307	D4	3367
BROOKSIDE LA., Springettsbury	Yk	17402	B7	3272
BROOKVIEW DR., Windsor Twp	Yk	17356	H2	3376
BROOKVIEW LA., Shrewsbury Boro	Yk	17361	B6	3584
BROOKWAY DR., Spring Garden	Yk	17403	B2	3375
BROOKWOOD DR. N., York Twp	Yk	17403	F2	3375
BROOKWOOD DR. S., York Twp	Yk	17403	F2	3375
BROSE RD., Shrewsbury Twp	Yk	17349	F11	3584
BROSE RD., Shrewsbury Twp	Yk	17349	F4	3688
BROUGH HILL RD., Reading	Ad	17316	G8	3266
BROUGH HILL RD., Reading	Ad	17316	A9	3267
BROUGH RD., Hamilton	Ad	17301	H6	3370
BROUGH RD., Hamilton	Ad	17301	A7	3371
BROUGH RD., Latimore	Ad	17372	B4	3160
BROUGHER LA., West Manchester	Yk	17404	D6	3270
BROUGHTON DR., Dover Twp	Yk	17315	C4	3269
BROWN DR., Fairfield	Ad	17320	B6	3573
BROWN RD., Chanceford	Yk	17322	G6	3482
BROWN RD., Fawn	Yk	17321	D11	3587
BROWN RD., Fawn	Yk	17321	D2	3691
BROWN RD., Fawn	Yk	17352	D11	3587
BROWN RD., North Codorus	Yk	17362	G10	3476
BROWN TR., Carroll Valley	Ad	17320	A5	3677
BROWNELL LA., Lower Windsor	Yk	17366	A8	3274
BROWN'S DAM DR. N., Reading	Ad	17350	C3	3370
BROWN'S DAM DR. S., Reading	Ad	17350	C4	3370
BROWN'S DAM RD., Reading	Ad	17350	B4	3370
BROWNS LA., Hellam	Yk	17406	B8	3168
BROWNTON RD., Chanceford	Yk	17322	C11	3378
BROWNTON RD., Chanceford	Yk	17322	A1	3482
BROWNTON RD., Windsor Twp	Yk	17356	G1	3481
BROXTON LA., Springettsbury	Yk	17402	C7	3272
BRUAW DR., Manchester Twp	Yk	17404	B8	3166
BRUCE RD. W., Fawn	Yk	17302	F5	3587
BRUCE RD. W., Fawn	Yk	17321	F5	3587
BRUCE RD., Lower Chanceford	Yk	17302	G2	3587
BRUMMER LA., Hellam	Yk	17406	C6	3168
BRUNERS LA., Hamiltonban	Ad	17353	B11	3469
BRUNK LA., Spring Garden	Yk	17403	H8	3271
BRUSH CIR., Newberry	Yk	17319	C7	2955
BRUSH VALLEY RD., Codorus	Yk	17327	A10	3478
BRUSH VALLEY RD., Codorus	Yk	17327	B1	3582
BRUSH VALLEY RD., Codorus	Yk	17360	A8	3478
BRUSH VALLEY RD., North Codorus	Yk	17360	H7	3477
BRUSH VALLEY RD., North Codorus	Yk	17360	A8	3478
BRYAN AV., West Manchester	Yk	17404	H2	3373
BRYANSVILLE RD., Peach Bottom	Yk	17314	E3	3692
BRYANSVILLE RD., Peach Bottom	Yk	17314	B1	3693
BRYLEA DR., East Manchester	Yk	17402	D6	3166
BRYSONIA RD., Menallen	Ad	17307	A9	3262
BRYSONIA RD., Menallen	Ad	17307	B1	3366
BRYSONIA SCHOOL RD., Menallen	Ad	17307	A10	3262
BRYSONIA-WENKSVILLE RD., Menallen	Ad	17307	H6	3261
BRYSONIA-WENKSVILLE RD., Menallen	Ad	17307	A4	3262
BRYSONIA-WENKSVILLE RD., Menallen	Ad	17307	A8	3262
BUCHANAN DR., York Twp	Yk	17402	H3	3375
BUCHANAN VALLEY RD., Franklin	Ad	17353	G11	3260
BUCHANAN VALLEY RD., Franklin	Ad	17353	A10	3261
BUCHANAN VALLEY RD., Franklin	Ad	17353	E3	3364
BUCK LA., Hamiltonban	Ad	17353	C9	3468
BUCK RD., Conewago	Yk	17315	F4	3164
BUCK RD., Conewago	Yk	17315	A1	3165
BUCK RD., Newberry	Yk	17315	D3	3059
BUCKHORN CT., Fairview	Yk	17339	C3	2954
BUCKINGHAM DR., Windsor Twp	Yk	17356	D3	3377
BUCKTHORN DR., Manchester Twp	Yk	17402	C2	3271
BUCKWHEAT RD., Fawn	Yk	17321	C3	3692
BUECKER RD., Lower Chanceford	Yk	17314	A6	3589
BUFFALO TR., Carroll Valley	Ad	17320	B11	3573
BUFFALO VALLEY RD., Codorus	Yk	17362	F9	3477
BUFFALO VALLEY RD., Codorus	Yk	17362	H1	3581
BUFFALO VALLEY RD., Codorus	Yk	17362	A2	3582
BUFORD AV., Cumberland	Ad	17325	A6	3471
BUFORD AV., Cumberland	Ad	17325	A8	3471
BUFORD AV., Gettysburg	Ad	17325	A8	3471
BUFORD DR., Reading	Ad	17316	D4	3266
BUGLE CALL PATH, Straban	Ad	17325	E6	3471
BUGLER DR., Oxford	Ad	17350	H2	3473
BULK PLANT RD., Mount Pleasant	Ad	17340	G4	3576
BULK PLANT RD., Mount Pleasant	Ad	17340	A5	3577
BULL RD., Conewago	Yk	17315	D6	3059
BULL RD., Conewago	Yk	17315	E1	3164
BULL RD., Conewago	Yk	17404	A9	3165
BULL RD., Dover Twp	Yk	17315	D6	3059
BULL RD., Manchester Twp	Yk	17404	C2	3270
BULL RD., Newberry	Yk	17339	B2	3059
BULL RD., Warrington	Yk	17339	B2	3059
BULL RD., West Manchester	Yk	17404	C2	3270
BULL RUN RD., Lower Windsor	Yk	17368	H9	3274
BULL RUN RD., Lower Windsor	Yk	17368	A9	3275
BULL VALLEY RD., Butler	Ad	17304	E8	3263
BULL VALLEY RD., Tyrone	Ad	17304	A6	3264
BULLET WAY, Berwick	Ad	17301	B11	3371
BULLFROG RD., Freedom	Ad	17320	G7	3573
BULLFROG RD., Freedom	Ad	17320	A9	3574
BULLFROG RD., Freedom	Ad	17320	C1	3678
BULLFROG RD., Freedom	Ad	17325	D3	3678
BULLFROG RD., Hamiltonban	Ad	17320	B3	3573
BULLFROG RD., Liberty	Ad	17320	D5	3573
BUMBLE BEE RD., Lower Windsor	Yk	17365	C6	3163
BUNGALOW RD., North Codorus	Yk	17362	A10	3477
BUNKER HILL CIR., New Freedom	Yk	17349	G1	3687
BUNKER HILL RD., Delta	Yk	17314	E4	3693
BUNKER HILL RD., Fairview	Yk	17070	F11	2848
BUNKER HILL RD., Peach Bottom	Yk	17314	F4	3693
BUNKER LA., Newberry	Yk	17319	D6	2955
BUNNY LA. , Hellam	Yk	17406	H1	3272
BUNNY TR., Carroll Valley	Ad	17320	A8	3573
BUNTING DR., Loganville	Yk	17403	F3	3479
BURBURY LA., East Manchester	Yk	17347	E2	3167
BURGARD ST., York Twp	Yk	17404	G5	3270
BURGS LA., Hellam	Yk	17406	H6	3168
BURKE RD., Peach Bottom	Yk	17314	D3	3694
BURKHOLDER RD., Chanceford	Yk	17356	G6	3378
BURKHOLDER RD., Chanceford	Yk	17356	A5	3379
BURKHOLDER RD., Lower Windsor	Yk	17356	B5	3378
BURKHOLDER RD., Windsor Twp	Yk	17356	G6	3377
BURKHOLDER RD., Windsor Twp	Yk	17356	B5	3378
BURNING BRUSH CIR., Newberry	Yk	17319	C5	2955
BURNNING TREE CT., Manchester Twp	Yk	17404	E8	3165
BURNS RD., Jefferson	Yk	17362	E10	3477
BURNS RD., Lower Chanceford	Yk	17309	A5	3484
BURNS RD., Lower Chanceford	Yk	17309	B4	3484
BURNS RD., Peach Bottom	Yk	17314	D10	3588
BURNSIDE DR., Latimore	Ad	17316	B3	3266
BURNSIDE DR., Mount Joy	Ad	17325	H3	3575
BURNSIDE DR., Mount Joy	Ad	17325	A2	3576
BUSER AV., Dover Twp	Yk	17315	D1	3269
BUSER FARM RD., Lower Windsor	Yk	17406	H6	3273
BUSHEY SCHOOL RD., Latimore	Ad	17372	B5	3160
BUSINESS CIR., Oxford	Ad	17350	C2	3474
BUSSER RD., Manchester Twp	Yk	17402	D8	3166
BUTCHER AV., Goldsboro	Yk	17319	G7	2955
BUTCHER AV., Goldsboro	Yk	17319	A6	2956
BUTLER ST., York City	Yk	17403	D9	3271
BUTTER RD., Conewago	Yk	17315	G6	3164
BUTTER RD., Conewago	Yk	17402	D6	3060
BUTTER RD., Conewago	Yk	17404	D9	3060
BUTTER RD., Conewago	Yk	17404	B2	3165
BUTTERFLY CIR., York Twp	Yk	17313	E5	3376
BUTTERNUT AV., Conewago	Ad	17331	H3	3578
BUTTERNUT LA., West Manchester	Yk	17404	H6	3269
BUTTLER RD., Dover Twp	Yk	17315	D10	3164
BUTTONWOOD AV., Hallam	Yk	17406	D11	3168
BUTTONWOOD CT., Fairview	Yk	17011	E8	2848
BUTTONWOOD DR., Dillsburg	Yk	17019	E5	3056
BUTTONWOOD RD., Huntington	Ad	17372	D5	3265
BYERS LA., Highland	Ad	17325	B9	3470
BYERS RD., Warrington	Yk	17019	A10	3057
BYPASS RD., Franklin	Yk	17019	D7	3056
BYRON NELSON CIR., Newberry	Yk	17319	D6	2955

C

C ST., Jackson	Yk	17364	C1	3373
C ST., McSherrystown	Ad	17344	F2	3578
CABIN CREEK RD., Lower Windsor	Yk	17406	C5	3274
CABIN HOLLOW RD., Carroll	Yk	17019	B9	3056
CABIN HOLLOW RD., Franklin	Yk	17019	B9	3056
CABIN HOLLOW RD., Warrington	Yk	17019	B9	3056
CABIN HOLLOW RD., Warrington	Yk	17019	A9	3057
CABIN LA., Hamiltonban	Ad	17222	F5	3467
CABOT RD., Dover Twp	Yk	17315	H2	3163
CACCIOLA LA., Windsor Twp	Yk	17356	A1	3377
CALDWELL DR., Springettsbury	Yk	17402	H4	3272
CALHOUN RD., Shrewsbury Twp	Yk	17327	H5	3583
CALHOUN RD., Shrewsbury Twp	Yk	17327	A6	3584
CALIFORNIA RD., Mount Joy	Ad	17340	E10	3576
CALIFORNIA RD., Mount Joy	Ad	17340	E1	3680
CALVARY CHURCH RD., East Prospect	Yk	17317	G6	3274
CALVARY CHURCH RD., Lower Windsor	Yk	17368	G6	3274
CALVARY CHURCH RD., Lower Windsor	Yk	17368	A5	3275
CALVERT ST., York City	Yk	17403	E9	3271
CAMBERLAY DR., Springettsbury	Yk	17402	H4	3272
CAMBRIDGE DR., Windsor Twp	Yk	17366	C3	3377
CAMBRIDGE RD., Springettsbury	Yk	17402	B6	3272
CAMELBACK CT., Hopewell	Yk	17363	E9	3585
CAMELOT ARMS, Springettsbury	Yk	17402	G3	3271
CAMELOT CT., Cumberland	Ad	17325	F7	3470
CAMELOT CT., Stewartstown	Yk	17363	E1	3689
CAMERON ST., Fairview	Yk	17319	H4	2954
CAMP 18 RD., Menallen	Ad	17307	E3	3260
CAMP BERNIE RD., Paradise	Yk	17301	F2	3475
CAMP BETTY WASHINGTON RD., York Twp	Yk	17356	C10	3272
CAMP BETTY WASHINGTON RD., York Twp	Yk	17356	E1	3376
CAMP BETTY WASHINGTON RD., York Twp	Yk	17402	A9	3272
CAMP GETTYSBURG RD., Freedom	Ad	17325	A3	3574
CAMP GETTYSBURG RD., Highland	Ad	17325	H1	3573
CAMP GETTYSBURG RD., Highland	Ad	17325	A3	3574
CAMP GROUND RD., Carroll	Yk	17019	C11	2951
CAMP GROUND RD., Carroll	Yk	17019	B2	3056
CAMP LESTERMAN RD., Straban	Ad	17325	F7	3471
CAMP RD., Franklin	Ad	17307	H5	3365
CAMP RD., Glen Rock	Yk	17327	D4	3583
CAMP RD., North Hopewell	Yk	17356	G4	3480
CAMP ST. N., Windsor Boro	Yk	17366	E4	3377
CAMP ST. N., Windsor Twp	Yk	17366	E4	3377
CAMP ST. S., Windsor Boro	Yk	17366	E6	3377
CAMP ST. S., Windsor Twp	Yk	17356	E6	3377
CAMP ST. S., Windsor Twp	Yk	17366	E6	3377
CAMP WOODS RD., Manheim	Yk	17329	A1	3685
CAMPBELL RD., Hellam	Yk	17402	H2	3272
CAMPBELL RD., New Freedom	Yk	17349	H3	3687
CAMPBELL RD., Springettsbury	Yk	17402	G2	3272
CAMPBELL RD., Springettsbury	Yk	17402	A4	3273
CAMPING AREA RD., Warrington	Yk	17315	C3	3163
CAMPING AREA RD. E., Warrington	Yk	17365	E2	3163
CAMPUS AV., Spring Grove	Yk	17362	A10	3373
CAMPUS CT., Manchester Boro	Yk	17345	E11	3061
CAMPUS CT., Spring Grove	Yk	17362	A10	3373
CANADA DR., Springettsbury	Yk	17402	F6	3272
CANADA DR., Windsor Twp	Yk	17402	F6	3272
CANADOCHLY CIR., Lower Windsor	Yk	17406	C4	3274

CANADOCHLY RD., Lower Windsor	Yk	17406	A5	3274
CANAL RD., Dover Twp	Yk	17315	G4	3268
CANAL RD. E., Dover Twp	Yk	17315	F10	3164
CANAL RD. Ext., East Manchester	Yk	17345	B11	3061
CANAL RD. W., Dover Twp	Yk	17315	D6	3268
CANAL RD. W., Dover Twp	Yk	17315	A4	3269
CANAL RD., Conewago	Yk	17315	A8	3165
CANAL RD., Conewago	Yk	17402	G2	3165
CANAL RD., Conewago	Yk	17404	E4	3165
CANAL RD., Dover Twp	Yk	17315	E11	3164
CANAL RD., East Manchester	Yk	17345	A3	3166
CANAL RD., East Manchester	Yk	17402	A1	3166
CANAL RD., Paradise	Yk	17301	C9	3371
CANAL RD., Paradise	Yk	17316	G10	3267
CANAL RD., Paradise	Yk	17316	G10	3267
CANAL RD., Paradise	Yk	17316	F2	3371
CANAL RD., Paradise	Yk	17364	E6	3371
CANARY CIR., West Manchester	Yk	17404	D11	3270
CANARY CT., West Manchester	Yk	17404	D11	3270
CANDLELIGHT DR., York Twp	Yk	17402	C9	3272
CANDLEWYCK CT., Springettsbury	Yk	17402	E4	3272
CANFORD RD., Springettsbury	Yk	17402	F3	3271
CANNERY RD., Heidelberg	Yk	17331	H11	3475
CANNERY RD., Heidelberg	Yk	17331	A11	3476
CANNING HOUSE RD., Chanceford	Yk	17322	H7	3378
CANNING HOUSE RD., Chanceford	Yk	17322	B11	3379
CANNING HOUSE RD., Chanceford	Yk	17322	A7	3379
CANNING HOUSE RD., Chanceford	Yk	17322	B1	3483
CANNON CT., North Codorus	Yk	17404	C10	3374
CANNON LA., Mount Pleasant	Ad	17325	F3	3576
CANNON ST., McSherrystown	Ad	17344	F2	3578
CANTERBURY AV., Chanceford	Yk	17322	C2	3482
CANTERBURY DR., East Manchester	Yk	17347	E1	3167
CANTERBURY LA., Springettsbury	Yk	17402	E3	3271
CANVASBACH DR., Fairview	Yk	17319	G4	2954
CAPE HORN RD., Windsor Twp	Yk	17356	E9	3272
CAPE HORN RD., Windsor Twp	Yk	17356	F1	3376
CAPE HORN RD., Windsor Twp	Yk	17356	A5	3377
CAPE HORN RD., Windsor Twp	Yk	17402	D8	3272
CAPE HORN RD., York Twp	Yk	17356	E9	3272
CAPE HORN RD., York Twp	Yk	17356	F1	3376
CAPE HORN RD., York Twp	Yk	17356	A5	3377
CAPE HORN RD., York Twp	Yk	17402	D8	3272
CAPITAL DR., Hellam	Yk	17402	D8	3167
CAPITOL HILL RD., Franklin	Yk	17019	A11	3056
CAPITOL HILL RD., Franklin	Yk	17019	A1	3131
CAPITOL HILL RD., Franklin	Yk	17019	G5	3160
CAPRI CIR., Fairview	Yk	17070	H2	2953
CAPRI CIR., Fairview	Yk	17070	A2	2954
CAPRICE CT., Shrewsbury Twp	Yk	17349	C9	3584
CAR RD., Hellam	Yk	17406	B3	3168
CARBAUGH RD., Hamiltonban	Ad	17222	F2	3467
CARBRIDGE RD. E., North Hopewell	Yk	17363	G4	3584
CARBRIDGE RD. W., North Hopewell	Yk	17363	G4	3584
CARDINAL DR., Loganville	Yk	17403	F3	3479
CARDINAL DR., Newberry	Yk	17319	G8	2954
CARDINAL DR., Penn	Yk	17331	E8	3579
CARDINAL DR., Shrewsbury Boro	Yk	17361	B7	3584
CARDINAL DR., Shrewsbury Twp	Yk	17327	B5	3583
CARDINAL LA., Dover Twp	Yk	17315	G10	3164
CARDINAL LA., Dover Twp	Yk	17315	H1	3269
CARDINAL LA., Dover Twp	Yk	17315	A1	3270
CARDINAL LA., Fairview	Yk	17339	A10	2954
CARDINAL TR., Carroll Valley	Ad	17320	G1	3676
CARDINAL TR., Peach Bottom	Yk	17314	F10	3588
CAREA RD., Fawn	Yk	17352	G5	3690
CARIBOU ST., Conewago	Ad	17331	G3	3578
CARL LA., Oxford	Ad	17350	B4	3474
CARL ST., York City	Yk	17404	A5	3271
CARLISLE AV., York City	Yk	17404	A8	3271
CARLISLE CT., West Manchester	Yk	17404	E6	3270
CARLISLE PIKE, Berwick	Ad	17331	F2	3474
CARLISLE PIKE, Berwick	Ad	17350	F2	3474
CARLISLE PIKE, Conewago	Ad	17331	F2	3474
CARLISLE PIKE, Hamilton	Ad	17350	C8	3370
CARLISLE PIKE, Hamilton	Ad	17350	F2	3474
CARLISLE PIKE, Huntington	Ad	17372	F5	3159
CARLISLE PIKE, Huntington	Ad	17372	D1	3265
CARLISLE PIKE, Latimore	Ad	17324	E1	3159
CARLISLE PIKE, Latimore	Ad	17372	E1	3159
CARLISLE PIKE, Latimore	Ad	17372	D1	3265
CARLISLE PIKE, Oxford	Ad	17331	F2	3474
CARLISLE PIKE, Oxford	Ad	17350	F2	3474
CARLISLE PIKE, Reading	Ad	17316	G7	3265
CARLISLE PIKE, Reading	Ad	17350	A1	3370
CARLISLE RD., Butler	Ad	17307	A11	3263
CARLISLE RD., Butler	Ad	17307	A1	3367
CARLISLE RD., Carroll	Yk	17019	E6	3056
CARLISLE RD., Dover Twp	Yk	17315	B9	3164
CARLISLE RD., Dover Twp	Yk	17315	E2	3269
CARLISLE RD., Dover Twp	Yk	17365	G5	3163
CARLISLE RD., Dover Twp	Yk	17404	A4	3270
CARLISLE RD., Huntington	Ad	17324	F9	3158
CARLISLE RD., Menallen	Ad	17304	B4	3263
CARLISLE RD., Tyrone	Ad	17324	E11	3158
CARLISLE RD., Warrington	Yk	17019	E6	3056
CARLISLE RD., Warrington	Yk	17019	A10	3057
CARLISLE RD., Warrington	Yk	17365	C11	3058
CARLISLE RD., Warrington	Yk	17365	B2	3163
CARLISLE RD., Warrington	Yk	17365	D2	3612
CARLISLE RD., Washington	Yk	17365	B1	3162
CARLISLE RD., West Manchester	Yk	17404	A4	3270
CARLISLE ST., Cumberland	Ad	17325	C8	3471
CARLISLE ST., Gettysburg	Ad	17325	C8	3471
CARLISLE ST., Hanover	Yk	17331	A10	3475
CARLISLE ST., Hanover	Yk	17331	B1	3579
CARLISLE ST., New Oxford	Ad	17350	A2	3474
CARLLYN DR., York Twp	Yk	17403	E4	3375
CARLTON AV., Heidelberg	Yk	17362	F9	3476
CARLTON CT., Springettsbury	Yk	17402	B7	3272
CARLTON PL., West Manchester	Yk	17404	A7	3270
CARLY DR., Oxford	Ad	17350	B4	3474
CARNEGIE RD., Springettsbury	Yk	17402	B6	3272
CAROL AV., Springettsbury	Yk	17402	D7	3272
CAROL AV., Windsor Twp	Yk	17402	D7	3272
CAROL CT., Dover Twp	Yk	17364	G9	3268
CAROL LA., East Hopewell	Yk	17363	G3	3585
CAROL LA., Penn	Yk	17331	E7	3579
CAROL RD., Springettsbury	Yk	17402	C7	3272
CAROL TR., Carroll Valley	Ad	17320	D1	3676
CAROLE CT., Bonneauville	Ad	17325	H1	3576
CAROUSEL DR., Lower Windsor	Yk	17406	G5	3273
CARR HILL RD., Highland	Ad	17325	E9	3469
CARR HILL RD., Highland	Ad	17325	F1	3573
CARRIAGE CT., Spring Garden	Yk	17403	D1	3375
CARRIAGE HILL LA., Springettsbury	Yk	17402	C1	3272
CARRIAGE LA., Hellam	Yk	17406	H11	3168
CARRIAGE LA., Mount Pleasant	Ad	17325	E11	3472
CARRIAGE RD., Fairview	Yk	17070	F10	2848
CARRIAGE RUN RD., West Manchester	Yk	17404	B7	3270
CARRIE DR., Dallastown	Yk	17313	G8	3376
CARRIE DR., York Twp	Yk	17313	G8	3376
CARROLL DR, Carroll	Yk	17019	G10	2951
CARROLL RD., Spring Garden	Yk	17403	C1	3375
CARROLL ST., Littlestown	Ad	17340	E11	3577
CARROLL ST., Warrington	Yk	17365	A2	3163
CARROLL ST., Wellsville	Yk	17365	H2	3162
CARROLL'S TRACT RD., Fairfield	Ad	17320	B1	3573
CARROLL'S TRACT RD., Franklin	Ad	17353	B6	3469
CARROLL'S TRACT RD., Hamiltonban	Ad	17320	A10	3469
CARROLL'S TRACT RD., Hamiltonban	Ad	17320	B1	3573
CARROLL'S TRACT RD., Hamiltonban	Ad	17325	A10	3469
CARROLL'S TRACT RD., Hamiltonban	Ad	17353	B6	3469
CARROLL'S TRACT RD., Hamiltonban	Ad	17353	A10	3469
CARSON AV., Penn	Yk	17331	D4	3579
CARSON LA., Windsor Twp	Yk	17356	F1	3376
CARTREF RD., Newberry	Yk	17319	H8	2954
CARTREF RD., Newberry	Yk	17319	A8	2955
CARTREF RD., Newberry	Yk	17319	C7	2955
CARVIN DR., East Hopewell	Yk	17363	E2	3585
CASEY DR., Oxford	Ad	17350	B4	3474
CASEY LA., Windsor Twp	Yk	17402	A8	3273
CASHMAN LA., New Oxford	Ad	17350	G2	3473
CASHMAN RD., Straban	Ad	17325	B6	3368
CASHMAN RD., Tyrone	Ad	17350	D10	3265
CASHMAN RD., Tyrone	Ad	17350	E1	3369
CASHTOWN RD., Franklin	Ad	17307	F6	3365
CASHTOWN RD., Franklin	Ad	17307	A4	3366
CASINO CT., West Manheim	Yk	17331	C10	3579
CASINO DR., West Manheim	Yk	17331	D10	3579
CASPIAN CT., Manchester Twp	Yk	17404	E2	3270
CASPIAN DR., Manchester Twp	Yk	17404	E3	3270
CASSEL RD., Newberry	Yk	17345	D7	3061
CASSIDY WAY, Shrewsbury Boro	Yk	17361	A6	3584
CASTANEA CT., York Twp	Yk	17402	D3	3376
CASTLE FIN RD., Lower Chanceford	Yk	17314	C7	3589
CASTLE FIN RD., Lower Chanceford	Yk	17314	C8	3589
CASTLE HILL DR., Straban	Ad	17325	H9	3367
CASTLE POND DR., Windsor Twp	Yk	17402	F8	3272
CATALINA DR., East Manchester	Yk	17347	A2	3167
CATALPA LA., Red Lion	Yk	17356	B6	3377
CATALPA LA., Warrington	Yk	17019	B9	3057
CATHERINE CT., Fairview	Yk	17339	E5	2954
CATHERINE ST., West Manchester	Yk	17404	D7	3270
CATHOLIC VALLEY RD., Codorus	Yk	17327	F11	3478
CATHOLIC VALLEY RD., Codorus	Yk	17327	C1	3582
CAVALRY AV., Mount Pleasant	Ad	17325	C10	3472
CAVALRY FIELD RD., Straban	Ad	17325	A6	3472
CAYUGA LA., Springettsbury	Yk	17402	E7	3272
CEDAR AV., Cumberland	Ad	17325	C5	3471
CEDAR CIR., Newberry	Yk	17315	E3	3059
CEDAR DR., Dover Boro	Yk	17315	D11	3164
CEDAR DR., Newberry	Yk	17370	D1	3059
CEDAR DR., North Codorus	Yk	17362	E11	3373
CEDAR DR., Straban	Ad	17325	C10	3368
CEDAR HILL DR., Newberry	Yk	17315	E5	3059
CEDAR HILL RD., North Codorus	Yk	17362	F11	3373
CEDAR HOLLOW RD., Peach Bottom	Yk	17302	H8	3588
CEDAR LA., Codorus	Yk	17327	G1	3582
CEDAR LA., Hopewell	Yk	17363	D9	3585
CEDAR LA., Paradise	Yk	17364	C5	3372
CEDAR LA., Union	Ad	17331	G4	3682
CEDAR LA., Washington	Yk	17315	H3	3267
CEDAR RD., Hamilton	Ad	17350	E7	3370
CEDAR RD., Hamilton	Ad	17350	D8	3370
CEDAR RD., Warrington	Yk	17019	B9	3057
CEDAR RD., West Manchester	Yk	17404	B5	3270
CEDAR RIDGE AV., Chanceford	Yk	17322	C2	3482
CEDAR RIDGE RD., Mount Pleasant	Ad	17350	C6	3473
CEDAR ST., York City	Yk	17404	B8	3271
CEDAR ST. N., Dallastown	Yk	17313	E6	3376
CEDAR ST., Bonneauville	Ad	17325	G11	3472
CEDAR ST., Jefferson	Yk	17362	D11	3477
CEDAR ST., Manchester Boro	Yk	17345	E2	3166
CEDAR ST., Mount Pleasant	Ad	17325	G11	3472
CEDAR TR., Peach Bottom	Yk	17314	H10	3588
CEDAR VALLEY RD., Fawn	Yk	17352	H9	3586
CEDAR VALLEY RD., Fawn	Yk	17352	A9	3587
CEDAR VILLAGE DR., Manchester Twp	Yk	17402	C10	3166
CEDARLYN DR., Jackson	Yk	17404	E6	3373
CEDARS RD., Fairview	Yk	17339	E4	2953
CEDARWOOD DR., Hellam	Yk	17402	A3	3273
CEEJAY DR., Fairview	Yk	17319	C3	2955
CELEBRATION HILL RD., Menallen	Ad	17307	E5	3261
CELINE DR., Dover Twp	Yk	17315	E8	3163
CEMETERY AV., East Prospect	Yk	17317	F5	3274
CEMETERY AV., East Prospect	Yk	17368	F5	3274
CEMETERY AV., Stewartstown	Yk	17363	C11	3585
CEMETERY AV., Stewartstown	Yk	17363	C1	3689
CEMETERY LA., Bendersville	Ad	17304	H4	3262
CEMETERY LA., Bendersville	Ad	17304	A4	3263
CEMETERY LA., Hellam	Yk	17406	H10	3167
CEMETERY LA., Hellam	Yk	17406	A10	3168
CEMETERY RD., Arendtsville	Ad	17307	B4	3366
CEMETERY RD., Biglerville	Ad	17307	H1	3366
CEMETERY RD., Biglerville	Ad	17307	A3	3367
CEMETERY RD., Conewago	Yk	17345	F6	3060
CEMETERY RD., Mount Joy	Ad	17325	F7	3575
CEMETERY RD., North Codorus	Yk	17360	D2	3478
CEMETERY RD., North Codorus	Yk	17404	D2	3478
CEMETERY RD., North Hopewell	Yk	17322	G7	3481
CEMETERY ST., Littlestown	Ad	17340	E2	3681
CEMETERY WAY, North York	Yk	17404	B4	3271
CENTENNIAL AV., Hanover	Yk	17331	C3	3579
CENTENNIAL AV., Mount Pleasant	Ad	17331	A11	3474
CENTENNIAL AV., Penn	Yk	17331	C4	3579
CENTENNIAL AV., Penn	Yk	17331	E6	3579
CENTENNIAL RD., Conewago	Ad	17331	B1	3578
CENTENNIAL RD., Mount Pleasant	Ad	17325	H4	3472
CENTENNIAL RD., Mount Pleasant	Ad	17325	A5	3473
CENTENNIAL RD., Mount Pleasant	Ad	17331	E9	3473
CENTENNIAL RD., Mount Pleasant	Ad	17331	A11	3474
CENTENNIAL RD., Mount Pleasant	Ad	17331	B1	3578
CENTENNIAL RD., Mount Pleasant	Ad	17350	E9	3473
CENTENNIAL RD., Straban	Ad	17325	H4	3472
CENTENNIAL ST., Fairfield	Ad	17320	B5	3573
CENTER AV., York Twp	Yk	17402	A2	3376
CENTER AV., York Twp	Yk	17402	H2	3375
CENTER CT., Newberry	Yk	17370	F11	2955
CENTER CT., West Manchester	Yk	17404	H9	3270
CENTER LA., Hopewell	Yk	17363	A7	3585
CENTER MILLS RD., Butler	Ad	17304	D5	3263
CENTER MILLS RD., Butler	Ad	17304	E8	3263
CENTER MILLS RD., Menallen	Ad	17304	C3	3263
CENTER RD., Hopewell	Yk	17363	A8	3585
CENTER RD., Lower Chanceford	Yk	17302	A1	3589
CENTER RD., Lower Chanceford	Yk	17302	A11	3485
CENTER RD., Lower Chanceford	Yk	17302	H1	3588
CENTER ST. E., Glen Rock	Yk	17327	C3	3583
CENTER ST. S., Penn	Yk	17331	E4	3579
CENTER ST. W., Glen Rock	Yk	17327	C3	3583
CENTER ST., East Manchester	Yk	17347	G1	3166
CENTER ST., Hanover	Yk	17331	D1	3579
CENTER ST., McSherrystown	Ad	17331	G2	3578
CENTER ST., Penn	Yk	17331	D1	3579
CENTER ST., Penn	Yk	17331	E5	3579
CENTER TR., Carroll Valley	Ad	17320	F10	3572
CENTERVIEW AV., Fairview	Yk	17070	D1	2954
CENTRAL AV., Manchester Twp	Yk	17404	H5	3165
CENTRAL LA., North York	Yk	17404	B5	3271
CENTRAL VIEW RD., Franklin	Yk	17019	G9	3055
CENTURY FARMS RD., Cross Roads	Yk	17322	G10	3481
CENTURY FARMS RD., East Hopewell	Yk	17322	B8	3482
CENTURY LA., Franklin	Yk	17019	H8	3055
CENTURY LA., Franklin	Yk	17019	A9	3056
CESSINA TR. N., Liberty	Ad	17320	C10	3573
CESSINA TR. S., Liberty	Ad	17320	C10	3573
CHADWICK CT., Codorus	Yk	17362	F3	3581
CHAIN SAW RD., Franklin	Yk	17019	D5	3055
CHALET AV., Carroll	Yk	17019	C4	3056
CHALET AV., Dillsburg	Yk	17019	C4	3056
CHAMA RD., Windsor Twp	Yk	17402	C6	3273
CHAMBERS RD., York Twp	Yk	17402	C10	3272
CHAMBERS RIDGE , York Twp	Yk	17402	D8	3272
CHAMBERSBURG RD., Cumberland	Ad	17325	C4	3470
CHAMBERSBURG RD., Franklin	Ad	17222	F7	3363
CHAMBERSBURG RD., Franklin	Ad	17307	A8	3365
CHAMBERSBURG RD., Franklin	Ad	17307	G1	3469
CHAMBERSBURG RD., Franklin	Ad	17325	G1	3469
CHAMBERSBURG RD., Franklin	Ad	17325	C4	3470
CHAMBERSBURG RD., Franklin	Ad	17353	A7	3364
CHAMBERSBURG ST., Arendtsville	Ad	17307	A3	3366
CHAMBERSBURG ST., Gettysburg	Ad	17325	D7	3471
CHAMPION TR., Carroll Valley	Ad	17320	A10	3573
CHANCEFORD AV., York City	Yk	17404	A5	3271
CHANCEFORD AV., York Twp	Yk	17404	H5	3270
CHANCEFORD RD., Chanceford	Yk	17309	A3	3484
CHANCEFORD RD., Lower Chanceford	Yk	17309	A3	3484
CHANCELLOR RD., York Twp	Yk	17403	G11	3271
CHANCELLOR RD., York Twp	Yk	17403	H2	3375
CHANNEL RD., Fawn	Yk	17352	B9	3587
CHANTILEAR CT., Stewartstown	Yk	17363	F11	3585
CHAPEL CHURCH RD., Chanceford	Yk	17356	B4	3379
CHAPEL CHURCH RD., Chanceford	Yk	17368	B11	3275
CHAPEL CHURCH RD., Chanceford	Yk	17368	B4	3379
CHAPEL CHURCH RD., York Twp	Yk	17356	F3	3376
CHAPEL DR., Manchester Twp	Yk	17404	A4	3271
CHAPEL RD., Conewago	Ad	17331	C11	3474
CHAPEL RD., Conewago	Ad	17331	C1	3578
CHAPEL RD., Cumberland	Ad	17325	G11	3574
CHAPEL RD., Cumberland	Ad	17325	F11	3574
CHAPEL RD., Cumberland	Ad	17325	A11	3575
CHAPEL RD., Cumberland	Ad	17325	F1	3678
CHAPEL RIDGE RD., Cumberland	Ad	17325	G9	3574
CHAPEL ST., Delta	Yk	17314	G5	3693
CHAPEL WAY, York Twp	Yk	17356	G4	3376
CHAPELWOOD DR., Hanover	Yk	17331	B10	3475
CHAPELWOOD DR., Windsor Twp	Yk	17402	A8	3273
CHARITY DR., Windsor Twp	Yk	17356	C4	3377
CHARITY DR., Windsor Twp	Yk	17366	C3	3377
CHARITY WAY, Heidelberg	Yk	17331	C1	3580
CHARLES AL., Fairview	Yk	17070	C5	2849
CHARLES AV., Hopewell	Yk	17363	D10	3585
CHARLES AV., Paradise	Yk	17301	C9	3371
CHARLES AV., Stewartstown	Yk	17363	D10	3585
CHARLES CIR., Hellam	Yk	17406	D11	3168
CHARLES DR., Windsor Twp	Yk	17366	E6	3377
CHARLES LA. W., York City	Yk	17403	D8	3271
CHARLES LA., Dover Twp	Yk	17315	C10	3164
CHARLES LA., Red Lion	Yk	17356	C7	3377
CHARLES RD., Franklin	Yk	17019	E10	3056
CHARLES ST. E., Littlestown	Ad	17340	F1	3681
CHARLES ST. N., Dallastown	Yk	17313	F7	3376
CHARLES ST. N., Red Lion	Yk	17356	B7	3377
CHARLES ST. S., Dallastown	Yk	17313	F8	3376
CHARLES ST. S., Red Lion	Yk	17356	C7	3377
CHARLES ST. W., Littlestown	Ad	17340	E2	3681
CHARLES ST., Felton	Yk	17322	H4	3481
CHARLES ST., Hanover	Yk	17331	B11	3475
CHARLES ST., Hanover	Yk	17331	B1	3579
CHARLES ST., Penn	Yk	17331	D3	3579
CHARLES ST., Shrewsbury Boro	Yk	17361	A9	3584
CHARLES ST., York City	Yk	17403	E7	3271
CHARLESTON LA., West Manchester	Yk	17404	D4	3270
CHARLESTOWN CT., Littlestown	Ad	17340	C3	3681
CHARLETON CT., Penn	Yk	17331	E7	3475
CHARLOIS CT., Dover Twp	Yk	17315	F4	3164
CHARMED CIRCLE DR., Straban	Ad	17325	F3	3471
CHATBOURNE DR., Manchester Twp	Yk	17404	F10	3165
CHATHAM LA., Windsor Twp	Yk	17356	D3	3377
CHEAPSIDE ST., Abbottstown	Ad	17301	B9	3371
CHEETAH DR., Conewago	Ad	17331	F3	3578
CHEETAH TR., Carroll Valley	Ad	17320	A1	3677
CHELTENHAM RD., Springettsbury	Yk	17402	E5	3272
CHERIMOYA ST., Manchester Twp	Yk	17404	F8	3165
CHEROKEE AV., Dover Twp	Yk	17315	F1	3269
CHEROKEE TR., Newberry	Yk	17370	A8	2956
CHERRY AL., New Freedom	Yk	17349	G2	3687
CHERRY AV., East Prospect	Yk	17317	F6	3274
CHERRY AV., East Prospect	Yk	17368	F6	3274
CHERRY AV., Newberry	Yk	17345	D7	3061
CHERRY CT., Hopewell	Yk	17363	B11	3585
CHERRY CT., Oxford	Ad	17350	C3	3474
CHERRY DR., Tyrone	Ad	17325	E10	3264
CHERRY HILL DR., Fairview	Yk	17070	B8	2849
CHERRY HILL LA., Hamiltonban	Ad	17320	G1	3572
CHERRY HILL RD., Huntington	Ad	17372	F6	3159
CHERRY HILLS RD., Manchester Twp	Yk	17404	D9	3165
CHERRY LA. E., Dallastown	Yk	17313	F7	3376
CHERRY LA. W., Dallastown	Yk	17313	F7	3376
CHERRY LA., Dillsburg	Yk	17019	E4	3056
CHERRY LA., Hallam	Yk	17406	D10	3168
CHERRY LA., Hamilton	Ad	17301	H7	3370
CHERRY LA., Hellam	Yk	17406	B2	3273
CHERRY LA., North Codorus	Yk	17362	G9	3373
CHERRY LA., North Codorus	Yk	17362	A8	3374
CHERRY LA., Paradise	Yk	17364	C8	3268
CHERRY LA., Red Lion	Yk	17356	D8	3377
CHERRY LA., York City	Yk	17401	C6	3271
CHERRY LA., York City	Yk	17403	C8	3271
CHERRY LA., York City	Yk	17404	C6	3271
CHERRY MANOR DR. (PVT), York Twp	Yk	17402	H4	3375
CHERRY ORCHARD RD., Dover Twp	Yk	17315	D6	3164
CHERRY RD., Peach Bottom	Yk	17302	H8	3588
CHERRY RUN RD., Codorus	Yk	17327	D10	3478
CHERRY ST., Arendtsville	Ad	17307	C4	3366
CHERRY ST., Goldsboro	Yk	17319	G7	2955
CHERRY ST., Goldsboro	Yk	17319	A6	2956
CHERRY ST., Jefferson	Yk	17362	E11	3477
CHERRY ST., New Freedom	Yk	17349	G3	3687
CHERRY ST., North Hopewell	Yk	17322	G9	3480
CHERRY ST., Red Lion	Yk	17356	A7	3377
CHERRY ST., Seven Valleys	Yk	17360	F4	3478
CHERRY ST., Springettsbury	Yk	17402	F1	3271
CHERRY ST., Winterstown	Yk	17322	H8	3480
CHERRY ST., Winterstown	Yk	17322	A8	3481
CHERRY ST., Wrightsville	Yk	17368	D7	3169
CHERRY ST., York Haven	Yk	17370	E3	3061
CHERRY ST., York Twp	Yk	17402	A4	3376
CHERRY ST., York Twp	Yk	17402	G5	3375
CHERRY TREE CT., Hanover	Yk	17331	E11	3475
CHERRY TREE LA., Shrewsbury Twp	Yk	17327	H9	3583
CHERRY TREE RD., Chanceford	Yk	17322	F2	3482
CHERRY VALLEY RD., Union	Ad	17331	H2	3682
CHERRYWINE DR. E., Manchester Twp	Yk	17404	G1	3270
CHERRYWINE DR. W., Manchester Twp	Yk	17404	F1	3270
CHERYL TR., Carroll Valley	Ad	17320	E11	3572
CHERYL TR., Carroll Valley	Ad	17320	E2	3676
CHERYLWOOD DR., North Codorus	Yk	17404	C8	3374
CHESAPEAKE RD., Springettsbury	Yk	17402	C7	3272
CHESLEY RD., Spring Garden	Yk	17403	G10	3271
CHESTERBROOK DR., Manchester Twp	Yk	17402	D11	3166
CHESTNUT AV. W., Penn	Yk	17331	A4	3579
CHESTNUT CIR., Newberry	Yk	17319	E9	2955
CHESTNUT DR., Tyrone	Ad	17325	E11	3264
CHESTNUT GROVE RD., Carroll	Yk	17019	H7	2951
CHESTNUT GROVE RD., Carroll	Yk	17019	A2	3057
CHESTNUT GROVE RD., Codorus	Yk	17362	D3	3581
CHESTNUT HILL CIR., Union	Ad	17331	F3	3682
CHESTNUT HILL RD. E., Tyrone	Ad	17304	A9	3264
CHESTNUT HILL RD. W., Butler	Ad	17304	G9	3263
CHESTNUT HILL RD., Butler	Ad	17304	G9	3263
CHESTNUT HILL RD., Franklin	Yk	17019	F1	3160
CHESTNUT HILL RD., Tyrone	Ad	17304	A9	3264
CHESTNUT HILL RD., Union	Ad	17331	C11	3578
CHESTNUT HILL RD., Union	Ad	17331	C1	3682
CHESTNUT HILL RD., York Twp	Yk	17313	D2	3376
CHESTNUT HILL RD., York Twp	Yk	17402	C11	3272
CHESTNUT HILL RD., York Twp	Yk	17402	C1	3376
CHESTNUT LA., York Twp	Yk	17403	D2	3375
CHESTNUT OAK TR., Peach Bottom	Yk	17314	A11	3589
CHESTNUT RD., West Manchester	Yk	17404	B5	3270
CHESTNUT RUN RD., York Twp	Yk	17402	D1	3376
CHESTNUT ST. E., Hanover	Yk	17331	C2	3579
CHESTNUT ST. E., Red Lion	Yk	17356	D8	3377
CHESTNUT ST. E., Windsor Twp	Yk	17356	D8	3377
CHESTNUT ST. N., Dillsburg	Yk	17019	D3	3056
CHESTNUT ST. S., Carroll	Yk	17019	E4	3056
CHESTNUT ST. S., Dillsburg	Yk	17019	E4	3056
CHESTNUT ST. W., Dallastown	Yk	17313	F6	3376
CHESTNUT ST. W., Hanover	Yk	17331	B3	3579
CHESTNUT ST. W., Red Lion	Yk	17356	C8	3377
CHESTNUT ST. W., York Twp	Yk	17313	F6	3376
CHESTNUT ST. W., York Twp	Yk	17356	C8	3377

CHESTNUT ST., Arendtsville	Ad	17307	C4	3366
CHESTNUT ST., East Manchester	Yk	17347	E10	3061
CHESTNUT ST., Jefferson	Yk	17362	E10	3477
CHESTNUT ST., Mount Wolf	Yk	17347	F11	3061
CHESTNUT ST., New Freedom	Yk	17349	G3	3687
CHESTNUT ST., Peach Bottom	Yk	17314	F5	3693
CHESTNUT ST., Spring Grove	Yk	17362	A10	3373
CHESTNUT ST., Wellsville	Yk	17365	G3	3162
CHESTNUT ST., Wrightsville	Yk	17368	D7	3169
CHESTNUT ST., York City	Yk	17403	D6	3271
CHESTNUT ST., York City	Yk	17403	E6	3271
CHESTNUT WAY, Fairview	Yk	17070	B1	2954
CHEYENNE CT., Newberry	Yk	17370	A9	2956
CHEYNNE DR., Springfield	Yk	17403	F1	3479
CHICK A DEER DR., Dover Twp	Yk	17315	E7	3269
CHIMNEY ROCK RD., Hellam	Yk	17406	C7	3168
CHIMNEY ROCK RD., Hellam	Yk	17406	B6	3168
CHIMNEY ROCK RD., Hellam	Yk	17406	B9	3168
CHINKAPIN DR., Oxford	Ad	17350	C1	3474
CHINQUAPIN TR., Peach Bottom	Yk	17314	A10	3589
CHIPAWA AV., Dover Twp	Yk	17315	F1	3269
CHIPPENHAM DR., Manchester Twp	Yk	17404	C1	3270
CHRIST CHURCH RD., Union	Ad	17340	A7	3578
CHRISTENSEN RD., Windsor Twp	Yk	17402	G8	3272
CHRISTIANE DR., West Manheim	Yk	17331	E10	3579
CHRISTINE DR., East Prospect	Yk	17317	E6	3274
CHRISTINE DR., East Prospect	Yk	17368	E6	3274
CHRISTOPHER CT., Reading	Ad	17316	B2	3370
CHRISTOPHER LEE DR., Oxford	Ad	17350	A1	3474
CHRONISTER FARM RD., York Twp	Yk	17402	H6	3375
CHRONISTER ST., Springettsbury	Yk	17402	E1	3271
CHURCH AL., New Freedom	Yk	17349	F3	3687
CHURCH AL., Wellsville	Yk	17365	G3	3162
CHURCH AV. E., Shrewsbury Boro	Yk	17361	B9	3584
CHURCH AV. E., Shrewsbury Twp	Yk	17361	B9	3584
CHURCH AV. E., York City	Yk	17403	D8	3271
CHURCH AV. N., Dallastown	Yk	17313	G7	3376
CHURCH AV. W., Shrewsbury Boro	Yk	17361	A9	3584
CHURCH AV., Felton	Yk	17322	H5	3481
CHURCH AV., North Hopewell	Yk	17322	H5	3481
CHURCH AV., York City	Yk	17403	B9	3271
CHURCH LA., Red Lion	Yk	17356	B6	3377
CHURCH LA., Red Lion	Yk	17356	C7	3377
CHURCH RD., Cross Roads	Yk	17322	E10	3481
CHURCH RD., Franklin	Ad	17353	F3	3364
CHURCH RD., Jackson	Yk	17362	F8	3372
CHURCH RD., Lower Chanceford	Yk	17302	D1	3588
CHURCH RD., Manchester Twp	Yk	17402	B8	3166
CHURCH RD., Manchester Twp	Yk	17402	C8	3166
CHURCH RD., Manchester Twp	Yk	17404	F11	3165
CHURCH RD., Manchester Twp	Yk	17404	E1	3270
CHURCH RD., Newberry	Yk	17319	C9	2955
CHURCH RD., North Hopewell	Yk	17322	B9	3481
CHURCH RD., Paradise	Yk	17364	B2	3372
CHURCH RD., Reading	Ad	17316	A6	3266
CHURCH RD., Springettsbury	Yk	17402	F11	3166
CHURCH RD., Warrington	Yk	17339	A5	3059
CHURCH RD., West Manchester	Yk	17404	H5	3269
CHURCH RD., West Manchester	Yk	17404	A5	3270
CHURCH RD., West Manchester	Yk	17404	B4	3270
CHURCH ST. E., Dillsburg	Yk	17019	F3	3056
CHURCH ST. E., East Hopewell	Yk	17322	A1	3586
CHURCH ST. E., East Hopewell	Yk	17322	D1	3586
CHURCH ST. N., New Oxford	Ad	17350	B2	3474
CHURCH ST. S., East Hopewell	Yk	17322	H11	3481
CHURCH ST. S., East Hopewell	Yk	17322	A11	3482
CHURCH ST. S., New Oxford	Ad	17350	B3	3474
CHURCH ST. S., Shrewsbury Twp	Yk	17361	B9	3584
CHURCH ST. W., Dillsburg	Yk	17019	F3	3056
CHURCH ST., Bendersville	Ad	17304	H4	3262
CHURCH ST., Bendersville	Ad	17304	A4	3263
CHURCH ST., Conewago	Ad	17331	E11	3474
CHURCH ST., Conewago	Ad	17331	E1	3578
CHURCH ST., Conewago	Ad	17344	E1	3578
CHURCH ST., Cross Roads	Yk	17322	G10	3481
CHURCH ST., Franklintown	Yk	17323	D9	3056
CHURCH ST., Glen Rock	Yk	17327	C3	3583
CHURCH ST., Hallam	Yk	17406	C11	3168
CHURCH ST., Hamiltonban	Ad	17353	B6	3469
CHURCH ST., Jacobus	Yk	17407	F10	3375
CHURCH ST., Littlestown	Ad	17340	E2	3681
CHURCH ST., Seven Valleys	Yk	17360	F4	3478
CHURCH ST., Shrewsbury Twp	Yk	17327	D2	3583
CHURCH ST., Spring Grove	Yk	17362	B1	3477
CHURCH ST., Springfield	Yk	17327	F11	3479
CHURCH ST., Springfield	Yk	17327	D2	3583
CHURCH ST., Stewartstown	Yk	17363	E11	3585
CHURCH ST., Stewartstown	Yk	17363	D1	3689
CHURCH ST., Yoe	Yk	17313	H5	3376
CHURCH ST., York Haven	Yk	17370	E3	3061
CHURCH ST., York Twp	Yk	17402	A4	3376
CHURCHILL DR., Windsor Twp	Yk	17356	D3	3377
CHURCHILL DR., York Twp	Yk	17403	F2	3375
CHURCHILL LA., Lower Windsor	Yk	17368	E1	3274
CIDER DR., York Spring	Ad	17372	A10	3160
CIDER PRESS RD., Fairview	Yk	17055	B9	2953
CIMMERON RD., Springettsbury	Yk	17402	E6	3272
CIRCLE BLVD. N., Manchester Twp	Yk	17402	B10	3166
CIRCLE CT., Paradise	Yk	17301	F9	3371
CIRCLE CT., York Twp	Yk	17402	A4	3376
CIRCLE DR., Bonneauville	Ad	17325	H1	3576
CIRCLE DR., Chanceford	Yk	17322	B2	3482
CIRCLE DR., Dover Twp	Yk	17314	C1	3164
CIRCLE DR., Dover Twp	Yk	17315	C11	3059
CIRCLE DR., East Manchester	Yk	17345	C10	3061
CIRCLE DR., Franklin	Yk	17019	D11	3055
CIRCLE DR., Franklin	Yk	17019	D1	3160
CIRCLE DR., Glen Rock	Yk	17327	C5	3583
CIRCLE DR., Hellam	Yk	17368	D8	3169
CIRCLE DR., Jacobus	Yk	17407	E10	3375
CIRCLE DR., Lower Windsor	Yk	17368	G7	3274
CIRCLE DR., Paradise	Yk	17301	F9	3371
CIRCLE DR., Penn	Yk	17331	G7	3579
CIRCLE DR., Shrewsbury Boro	Yk	17361	B8	3584
CIRCLE DR., Springettsbury	Yk	17402	F1	3271
CIRCLE DR., West Manheim	Yk	17331	G7	3579
CIRCLE DR., Windsor Twp	Yk	17356	F9	3377
CIRCLE DR., York Twp	Yk	17402	A5	3376
CITY HALL DR., Dover Boro	Yk	17315	D11	3164
CITY VIEW RD., Springettsbury	Yk	17402	F2	3271
CLAIRE AV., Hellam	Yk	17406	B11	3168
CLAIRIAN DR., York Twp	Yk	17403	E4	3375
CLAIR-MAR DR., Dover Twp	Yk	17315	B3	3269
CLAPSADDLE RD., Mount Joy	Ad	17325	F11	3471
CLAPSADDLE RD., Mount Joy	Ad	17325	F11	3575
CLARATON DR., Newberry	Yk	17370	F11	2955
CLARE LA., Windsor Twp	Yk	17402	D7	3272
CLAREMONT DR., Springfield	Yk	17360	G8	3479
CLAREMONT RD., Dover Twp	Yk	17315	G4	3269
CLARK RD., Hopewell	Yk	17363	A3	3585
CLARK RD., North Hopewell	Yk	17363	H2	3584
CLARK RD., North Hopewell	Yk	17363	A3	3585
CLARK RD., Peach Bottom	Yk	17314	D8	3590
CLARK RD., Straban	Ad	17325	C7	3368
CLARKE AV. E., York City	Yk	17401	D7	3271
CLARKE AV. E., York City	Yk	17403	D7	3271
CLARKE AV. E., York City	Yk	17403	F5	3271
CLARKE AV. E., York City	Yk	17403	F6	3271
CLARKE AV. W., York City	Yk	17401	A8	3271
CLARKE AV. W., York City	Yk	17404	A8	3271
CLARKE AV., West Manchester	Yk	17404	D10	3270
CLARK'S WAY, York Twp	Yk	17403	G1	3375
CLARKSON DR., York Twp	Yk	17403	D4	3375
CLARY WAY, Conewago	Yk	17404	D2	3165
CLAYOMA AV., North Codorus	Yk	17404	D10	3374
CLAYSTONE RD., Manchester Twp	Yk	17404	E3	3270
CLAYTON AV., York City	Yk	17404	A8	3271
CLEAR BRANCH DR., Hopewell	Yk	17363	C10	3585
CLEAR CREEK LA., East Hopewell	Yk	17322	E2	3586
CLEAR RUN DR., Shrewsbury Boro	Yk	17361	B6	3584
CLEAR SPRING RD., Butler	Ad	17307	E11	3262
CLEAR SPRING RD., Butler	Ad	17307	F1	3366
CLEAR SPRING RD., Franklin	Yk	17019	D10	3055
CLEAR SPRING RD., Franklin	Yk	17019	A1	3161
CLEAR SPRING RD., Franklin	Yk	17019	F1	3160
CLEAR SPRINGS BLVD., Manchester Twp	Yk	17402	B10	3166
CLEAR VIEW LA., Butler	Ad	17307	G2	3366
CLEAR VIEW RD., Menallen	Ad	17304	A6	3263
CLEARBROOK BLVD, Manchester Twp	Yk	17402	B10	3166
CLEARMOUNT RD., Spring Garden	Yk	17403	G9	3271
CLEARVIEW CT., Hanover	Yk	17331	A11	3475
CLEARVIEW DR. E., Shrewsbury Boro	Yk	17361	B7	3584
CLEARVIEW DR. W., Shrewsbury Boro	Yk	17361	A7	3584
CLEARVIEW DR., Manchester Twp	Yk	17404	H10	3165
CLEARVIEW RD. E., Hanover	Yk	17331	B11	3475
CLEARVIEW RD. W., Hanover	Yk	17331	A11	3475
CLEARVIEW RD. W., Shrewsbury Twp	Yk	17327	G5	3583
CLEARVIEW RD., Dover Twp	Yk	17315	D10	3163
CLEARVIEW RD., Dover Twp	Yk	17315	E1	3268
CLEARVIEW RD., Fairview	Yk	17070	B9	2849
CLEARVIEW RD., Franklin	Yk	17019	B10	3056
CLEARVIEW RD., Hanover	Yk	17331	C10	3475
CLEARVIEW RD., Springettsbury	Yk	17402	G10	3166
CLEARVIEW WAY, York Twp	Yk	17403	B6	3376
CLEARY CT., Abbottstown	Ad	17301	C10	3371
CLEMENS DR., Carroll	Yk	17019	E3	3056
CLEMENS DR., Dillsburg	Yk	17019	E3	3056
CLEVELAND AV., York City	Yk	17403	D8	3271
CLIFFSIDE DR., Fairview	Yk	17070	H6	2848
CLINE'S CHURCH RD., Menallen	Ad	17304	D2	3263
CLINE'S CHURCH RD., Menallen	Ad	17324	D2	3263
CLINTON AL. N., Abbottstown	Ad	17301	B9	3371
CLINTON CT., Heidelberg	Yk	17362	E8	3476
CLINTON CT., Oxford	Ad	17350	E2	3474
CLINTON ST. N., West York	Yk	17404	F8	3270
CLINTON ST. S., Abbottstown	Ad	17301	B10	3371
CLINTON ST. S., West York	Yk	17404	F9	3270
CLIPPER TR., Carroll Valley	Ad	17320	B11	3573
CLOISTERS WAY, Newberry	Yk	17319	E6	2955
CLOUSER RD., Germany	Ad	17340	C5	3682
CLOUSER RD., Union	Ad	17331	C5	3682
CLOUSER RD., Union	Ad	17340	C5	3682
CLOVER DR., Hellam	Yk	17402	D8	3167
CLOVER DR., Union	Ad	17340	F11	3577
CLOVER HILL RD., York Twp	Yk	17313	D6	3376
CLOVER LA. E., Dallastown	Yk	17313	G7	3376
CLOVER LA., Penn	Yk	17331	C6	3579
CLOVER LA., Spring Garden	Yk	17403	F10	3271
CLOVER RD., Goldsboro	Yk	17319	H5	2955
CLOVER ST., Fairview	Yk	17319	G4	2954
CLOVER TR., Peach Bottom	Yk	17314	H11	3588
CLOVER TR., Peach Bottom	Yk	17314	H1	3692
CLOVERDALE AV. W., Shrewsbury Boro	Yk	17361	A10	3584
CLOVERDALE FARM DR., Latimore	Ad	17372	A5	3160
CLOVERDALE RD., Huntington	Ad	17372	G6	3159
CLOVERDALE RD., Latimore	Ad	17372	G6	3159
CLOVERDALE RD., Shrewsbury Twp	Yk	17349	A10	3584
CLOVERLANE DR., East Manchester	Yk	17345	D2	3166
CLOVERLANE DR., Manchester Boro	Yk	17345	D2	3166
CLOVERLEAF RD., Conewago	Yk	17402	E7	3060
CLUB FARM RD., Springfield	Yk	17360	C2	3479
CLUB FARM RD., Springfield	Yk	17403	D11	3375
CLUB FARM RD., Springfield	Yk	17403	C1	3479
CLUB HOUSE RD., Shrewsbury Twp	Yk	17327	C10	3583
CLUB RD., Peach Bottom	Yk	17302	C9	3589
CLUBHOUSE RD., Peach Bottom	Yk	17314	H11	3588
CLUBHOUSE RD., Peach Bottom	Yk	17314	G1	3692
CLUBHOUSE RD., Spring Garden	Yk	17403	B11	3271
CLUBHOUSE RD., Spring Garden	Yk	17403	B1	3375
CLUGSTON RD., York Twp	Yk	17404	G4	3270
CLY RD., Newberry	Yk	17319	A8	2956
CLY RD., Newberry	Yk	17370	H8	2955
CLY RD., Newberry	Yk	17370	A11	2956
CLY RD., Newberry	Yk	17370	A3	3061
CLY RD., Newberry	Yk	17370	B1	3061
CLYDESDALE CT., Fairview	Yk	17319	H3	2954
CLYDESDALE DR., Windsor Twp	Yk	17402	C11	3273
COACH LA., Fairview	Yk	17011	F8	2848
COAL HILL RD., Cross Roads	Yk	17322	F11	3481
COAL HILL RD., Cross Roads	Yk	17363	F2	3585
COAL HILL RD., East Hopewell	Yk	17363	F2	3585
COBBLESTONE CT., Penn	Yk	17331	F7	3579
COBBLESTONE CT., West Manchester	Yk	17404	D3	3270
CODORUS FURNACE RD., East Manchester	Yk	17347	G3	3166
CODORUS FURNACE RD., East Manchester	Yk	17347	A3	3167
CODORUS FURNACE RD., Hellam	Yk	17406	E3	3167
CODORUS FURNACE RD., Hellam	Yk	17406	A4	3168
CODORUS ST., York City	Yk	17404	A9	3271
CODORVN RD., West Manchester	Yk	17403	G2	3374
CODY CT., Penn	Yk	17331	B5	3579
COFFEETOWN RD., Franklin	Yk	17019	A9	3055
COKE CT., Shrewsbury Twp	Yk	17349	F1	3687
COLBY LA., Dover Twp	Yk	17315	G3	3269
COLD CABIN RD., Peach Bottom	Yk	17314	B8	3590
COLD CABIN RD., Peach Bottom	Yk	17314	C6	3590
COLD SPRING RD., Hamiltonban	Ad	17222	E7	3467
COLD SPRING RD., Hamiltonban	Ad	17222	A7	3468
COLD SPRING RD., Hamiltonban	Ad	17320	D9	3468
COLD SPRING RD., Hamiltonban	Ad	17320	A11	3469
COLD SPRING RD., Hamiltonban	Ad	17325	C1	3573
COLD SPRING RD., Hamiltonban	Ad	17353	D9	3468
COLD SPRING RD., Hamiltonban	Ad	17353	A11	3469
COLD SPRING RD., Highland	Ad	17325	C1	3573
COLD SPRINGS RD., Carroll	Yk	17019	A2	3056
COLD SPRINGS RD., North Codorus	Yk	17360	F9	3477
COLD STREAM TR., Chanceford	Yk	17322	C1	3482
COLDSPRING RD., Manchester Twp	Yk	17404	H11	3165
COLEMAN RD., Straban	Ad	17325	E11	3368
COLEMAN RD., Straban	Ad	17325	F11	3472
COLGROVE AV., Cumberland	Ad	17325	D10	3471
COLGROVE AV., Cumberland	Ad	17325	E1	3575
COLLEEN TR., Carroll Valley	Ad	17320	D2	3676
COLLEGE AV. E., York City	Yk	17403	D8	3271
COLLEGE AV. W., York City	Yk	17403	B9	3271
COLLEGE AV. W., York City	Yk	17404	A9	3271
COLLEGE AV. W., York City	Yk	17404	B9	3271
COLLEGE AV., Delta	Yk	17314	G5	3693
COLLEGE AV., East Berlin	Ad	17316	D11	3267
COLLEGE AV., Gettysburg	Ad	17325	B7	3471
COLLEGE AV., Hanover	Yk	17331	B3	3579
COLLEGE AV., Seven Valleys	Yk	17360	F4	3478
COLLEGE AV., Spring Grove	Yk	17362	B11	3373
COLLEGE AV., Stewartstown	Yk	17363	E11	3585
COLLEGE AV., West Manchester	Yk	17404	B9	3271
COLLEGE ST. N., New Oxford	Ad	17350	B2	3474
COLLEGE ST. S., New Oxford	Ad	17350	B3	3474
COLLEGE ST. S., Oxford	Ad	17350	B3	3474
COLLIE TR., Liberty	Ad	17320	E9	3573
COLLINA DR., Fairview	Yk	17339	H3	2953
COLLINA DR., Fairview	Yk	17339	A2	2954
COLLINS CIR., Penn	Yk	17331	F3	3579
COLLINS SCHOOL RD., East Hopewell	Yk	17302	A1	3587
COLLINS SCHOOL RD., East Hopewell	Yk	17309	H9	3482
COLLINS SCHOOL RD., East Hopewell	Yk	17322	H9	3482
COLLINS SCHOOL RD., East Hopewell	Yk	17322	H1	3586
COLLINSVILLE RD., Chanceford	Yk	17309	H11	3379
COLLINSVILLE RD., Chanceford	Yk	17309	G3	3483
COLLINSVILLE RD., Chanceford	Yk	17309	H1	3483
COLLINSVILLE RD., Chanceford	Yk	17309	A2	3484
COLONIAL AV., Spring Garden	Yk	17403	B10	3271
COLONIAL CT., Littlestown	Ad	17340	F2	3681
COLONIAL CT., West Manheim	Yk	17331	H1	3683
COLONIAL DR., Dallastown	Yk	17313	G8	3376
COLONIAL DR., Mount Pleasant	Ad	17325	F2	3576
COLONIAL DR., Penn	Yk	17331	F7	3579
COLONIAL FARM LA., Springettsbury	Yk	17402	B11	3167
COLONIAL RD., Dover Twp	Yk	17315	C11	3163
COLONIAL RD., Dover Twp	Yk	17315	B2	3268
COLONIAL RD., Springettsbury	Yk	17402	A1	3272
COLONIAL VALLEY RD., Heidelberg	Yk	17362	G3	3476
COLONIAL VALLEY RD., North Codorus	Yk	17362	G3	3476
COLONIAL VALLEY RD., North Codorus	Yk	17362	A4	3477
COLONY DR., West Manchester	Yk	17404	E5	3270
COLONY DR., York City	Yk	17404	A4	3271
COLORADO AV., Littlestown	Ad	17340	D2	3681
COLUMBIA AV., North York	Yk	17404	C4	3271
COLUMBIA AV., York City	Yk	17403	D7	3271
COLUMBUS AV. S., Littlestown	Ad	17340	D3	3681
COLUMBUS AV., Littlestown	Ad	17340	D11	3577
COLUMBUS AV., Littlestown	Ad	17340	D2	3681
COMANCHE DR., Conewago	Ad	17331	D3	3578
COMANCHE TR., Liberty	Ad	17320	C9	3573
COMETLIGHT DR., York Twp	Yk	17402	D9	3272
COMMERCE DR., Fairview	Yk	17070	G7	2848
COMMERCE DR., Jackson	Yk	17364	D1	3373
COMMERCE DR., Jackson	Yk	17404	D1	3373
COMMERCE DR., Springfield	Yk	17327	A10	3480
COMMERCE DR., West Manchester	Yk	17404	E7	3270
COMMERCE ST., Hanover	Yk	17331	A2	3579
COMMERCE ST., New Oxford	Ad	17350	B2	3474
COMMERCE ST., York City	Yk	17403	F7	3271
COMMERCE WAY, Hellam	Yk	17406	H11	3167
COMMERCE WAY, Hellam	Yk	17406	H1	3272
COMMUNITY PL., York Twp	Yk	17404	H6	3270
COMMUNITY ST., Warrington	Yk	17365	H1	3162
COMMUNITY ST., Warrington	Yk	17365	A1	3163
COMMUNITY ST., Wellsville	Yk	17365	H2	3162
COMPANY FARM RD., Huntington	Ad	17372	E7	3264
COMPANY FARM RD., Tyrone	Ad	17304	D5	3264
COMPANY FARM RD., Tyrone	Ad	17372	E7	3264
COMPANY ST., York City	Yk	17404	A8	3271
COMPTON LA., Springettsbury	Yk	17402	E7	3272
CONCORD AV., Hellam	Yk	17402	D8	3167
CONCORD CT., Littlestown	Ad	17340	D3	3681
CONCORD DR., New Freedom	Yk	17349	H1	3687
CONCORD RD., Springettsbury	Yk	17402	E1	3272
CONCORD RD., Springettsbury	Yk	17402	D3	3272
CONDOR LA., Dover Twp	Yk	17315	H11	3164
CONDOR LA., Dover Twp	Yk	17315	A11	3165
CONESTOGA LA., Spring Grove	Yk	17362	B9	3373
CONEWAGO AV., Dover Twp	Yk	17365	G4	3163
CONEWAGO AV., Newberry	Yk	17345	D8	3061
CONEWAGO AV., Newberry	Yk	17345	E7	3061
CONEWAGO AV., Warrington	Yk	17365	H10	3058
CONEWAGO AV., West Manchester	Yk	17404	A4	3270
CONEWAGO AV., York City	Yk	17404	A5	3271
CONEWAGO AV., York Twp	Yk	17404	H5	3270
CONEWAGO CREEK RD., Conewago	Yk	17345	G7	3060
CONEWAGO CREEK RD., Conewago	Yk	17345	A9	3061
CONEWAGO CREEK RD., East Manchester	Yk	17345	A9	3061
CONEWAGO DR., Conewago	Ad	17331	D1	3578
CONEWAGO DR., Conewago	Ad	17344	D1	3578
CONEWAGO DR., Newberry	Yk	17315	E8	3059
CONEWAGO DR., Reading	Ad	17316	B2	3371
CONEWAGO PARK DR., Reading	Ad	17316	D11	3267
CONEWAGO RD., Dover Twp	Yk	17315	B11	3059
CONEWAGO RD., Dover Twp	Yk	17315	E6	3163
CONEWAGO RD., Dover Twp	Yk	17315	A1	3164
CONEWAGO RD., Dover Twp	Yk	17315	C1	3268
CONEWAGO RD., Straban	Ad	17350	E7	3369
CONEWAGO ST., Arendtsville	Ad	17307	C2	3366
CONEWAGO TER., Reading	Ad	17316	B2	3371
CONFEDERATE AV. E., Cumberland	Ad	17325	D9	3471
CONFEDERATE AV. E., Gettysburg	Ad	17325	D9	3471
CONFEDERATE AV. N., Cumberland	Ad	17325	A5	3471
CONFEDERATE AV. S., Cumberland	Ad	17325	H5	3574
CONFEDERATE AV. S., Cumberland	Ad	17325	A5	3575
CONFEDERATE AV. W., Cumberland	Ad	17325	H11	3470
CONFEDERATE AV. W., Cumberland	Ad	17325	A9	3471
CONFEDERATE AV. W., Cumberland	Ad	17325	H3	3574
CONFEDERATE AV. W., Gettysburg	Ad	17325	A9	3471
CONFEDERATE CAVALRY AV., Mount Pleasant	Ad	17325	B8	3472
CONFEDERATE DR., Cumberland	Ad	17325	A10	3471
CONGRESS AV., Fairview	Yk	17070	A9	2849
CONIFER LA., Lower Windsor	Yk	17406	A5	3274
CONLEY LA., Newberry	Yk	17319	H7	2954
CONLEY LA., Newberry	Yk	17319	H6	2954
CONLEY RD., Warrington	Yk	17339	A6	3059
CONNECTING LINK, Oxford	Ad	17350	E2	3474
CONNELLY RD., Manchester Twp	Yk	17402	D8	3166
CONNIE TR., Carroll Valley	Ad	17320	G11	3572
CONRAD LA., Menallen	Ad	17324	E10	3158
CONRAD LA., Tyrone	Ad	17324	E10	3158
CONSTITUTION AV. N., New Freedom	Yk	17349	G2	3687
CONSTITUTION AV. S., New Freedom	Yk	17349	G3	3687
CONSTITUTION AV., Gettysburg	Ad	17325	B8	3471
CONSTITUTION AV., Spring Grove	Yk	17362	A1	3477
CONSTITUTION CT., Littlestown	Ad	17340	F2	3681
CONSTITUTION RD., Fawn	Yk	17321	C5	3692
CONTINENTAL RD., York City	Yk	17404	A4	3271
CONWAY AV. N., Dallastown	Yk	17313	E6	3376
CONWAY AV. S., Dallastown	Yk	17313	E7	3376
CONWAY ST., Manchester Twp	Yk	17402	A7	3166
COOKE RD., Peach Bottom	Yk	17314	F2	3692
COOL CREEK MANOR DR., Hellam	Yk	17368	C8	3169
COOL CREEK RD., Hellam	Yk	17368	C11	3169
COOL CREEK RD., Lower Windsor	Yk	17368	D1	3274
COOL CREEK RD., Wrightsville	Yk	17368	C11	3169
COOL SPRING LA., Hopewell	Yk	17363	C10	3585
COOL SPRINGS RD., Hellam	Yk	17368	A6	3169
COOL SPRINGS RD., Wrightsville	Yk	17368	A6	3169
COON RD., Menallen	Ad	17304	C11	3157
COON RD., Menallen	Ad	17304	A2	3262
COON RD., Menallen	Ad	17324	F8	3157
COON RD., Tyrone	Ad	17324	A8	3158
COOPER PL., York City	Yk	17403	D8	3271
COOPER RD., Peach Bottom	Yk	17314	F4	3694
COOPER RD., Penn	Yk	17331	B6	3579
COOPER RD., Shrewsbury Twp	Yk	17349	F2	3688
COOPER ST., Manchester Boro	Yk	17345	E1	3166
COOVER CT., Carroll	Yk	17019	C2	3056
COPENHAFFER RD., Conewago	Yk	17315	G7	3059
COPENHAFFER RD., Conewago	Yk	17315	A7	3060
COPENHAFFER RD., Conewago	Yk	17404	D11	3060
COPENHAFFER RD., Conewago	Yk	17404	E1	3165
COPENHAVER RD., Manheim	Yk	17329	A10	3581
COPPER CIR., Fairview	Yk	17339	E3	2954
CORBETT LA., Chanceford	Yk	17302	A9	3483
CORBIN RD., York Twp	Yk	17403	G11	3271
CORBIN RD., York Twp	Yk	17403	H2	3375
CORDYBEN RD., West Manchester	Yk	17404	A5	3270
COREY LA., Oxford	Ad	17350	B4	3474
CORN HILL RD., Newberry	Yk	17319	A5	2955
CORN LA., Hopewell	Yk	17363	C8	3585
CORN TASSLE RD., Peach Bottom	Yk	17314	H10	3588
CORNELL DR., Penn	Yk	17331	B8	3579
CORPORATE CIR., Fairview	Yk	17070	G8	2848
CORRIEDALE RD., East Manchester	Yk	17345	C3	3166
CORSA LA., Hamiltonban	Ad	17320	F10	3468
CORTLEIGH DR., Springettsbury	Yk	17402	C5	3272
CORVAIR DR., Dillsburg	Yk	17019	D2	3056
COTTAGE AV., Glen Rock	Yk	17327	B4	3583
COTTAGE DR., East Manchester	Yk	17345	D3	3166
COTTAGE DR., Hamilton	Ad	17350	H6	3369
COTTAGE HILL RD., Menallen	Ad	17324	A9	3158
COTTAGE HILL RD., York City	Yk	17404	B7	3271
COTTAGE LA., Mount Pleasant	Ad	17350	G3	3473
COTTAGE PL. E., York City	Yk	17403	D9	3271
COTTAGE PL. W., York City	Yk	17403	C9	3271
COTTAGE PL., Red Lion	Yk	17356	B6	3377

COTTON WOOD RD., Peach Bottom	Yk	17302	A9	3589
COTTONWOOD RD., West Manchester	Yk	17404	B4	3270
COUGAR DR., Conewago	Ad	17331	F4	3578
COUNTRY BY WAY, Windsor Twp	Yk	17402	A7	3273
COUNTRY CLUB RD., Berwick	Ad	17331	D1	3475
COUNTRY CLUB LA., Cumberland	Ad	17325	G8	3470
COUNTRY CLUB RD., Paradise	Ad	17301	C10	3371
COUNTRY CLUB RD., Paradise	Ad	17301	D1	3475
COUNTRY CLUB RD., Red Lion	Yk	17356	B8	3377
COUNTRY CLUB RD., Shrewsbury Twp	Yk	17327	C9	3583
COUNTRY CLUB RD., Shrewsbury Twp	Yk	17349	F11	3583
COUNTRY CLUB RD., Shrewsbury Twp	Yk	17349	E2	3687
COUNTRY CLUB RD., Spring Garden	Yk	17403	B11	3271
COUNTRY CLUB RD., Spring Garden	Yk	17403	B11	3271
COUNTRY CLUB RD., Spring Garden	Yk	17403	A1	3375
COUNTRY CLUB RD., York Twp	Yk	17356	C8	3377
COUNTRY CLUB TR., Carroll Valley	Ad	17320	H10	3572
COUNTRY CLUB TR., Carroll Valley	Ad	17320	H9	3572
COUNTRY CLUB TR., Carroll Valley	Ad	17320	A9	3573
COUNTRY CLUB TR., Carroll Valley	Ad	17320	A11	3573
COUNTRY CLUB TR., Carroll Valley	Ad	17320	G1	3676
COUNTRY CLUB TR., Carroll Valley	Ad	17320	A1	3677
COUNTRY DR., Dover Twp	Yk	17315	D1	3269
COUNTRY DR., Mount Pleasant	Ad	17325	F11	3576
COUNTRY LA., Lower Windsor	Yk	17406	B3	3274
COUNTRY LA., West Manheim	Yk	17331	F10	3579
COUNTRY LA., York Twp	Yk	17402	D1	3376
COUNTRY MANOR DR., North Codorus	Yk	17404	A8	3374
COUNTRY MANOR LA., New Freedom	Yk	17349	F4	3687
COUNTRY MANOR DR., North Codorus	Yk	17404	H8	3373
COUNTRY RD., North Codorus	Yk	17404	A8	3374
COUNTRY RD., Springfield	Yk	17403	G1	3479
COUNTRY RIDGE DR., York Twp	Yk	17313	A8	3377
COUNTRY SPRINGS LA., Chanceford	Yk	17322	G11	3378
COUNTRY WALK DR., Lower Windsor	Yk	17368	D5	3274
COUNTY LINE RD., Franklin	Yk	17019	G10	3054
COUNTY LINE RD., Franklin	Yk	17019	A7	3161
COUNTY LINE RD., Franklin	Yk	17019	B1	3160
COUNTY LINE RD., Latimore	Ad	17372	B1	3160
COUPLER CT., Hopewell	Yk	17363	F10	3585
COUPLER DR., Hopewell	Yk	17363	F10	3585
COURSE RD., York Twp	Yk	17402	A5	3376
COURT AV. N., York City	Yk	17401	C6	3271
COURT AV. N., York City	Yk	17403	C6	3271
COURT AV. S., York City	Yk	17403	D8	3271
COURT LA., Mount Pleasant	Ad	17350	E3	3473
COURT ST., North York	Yk	17404	C4	3271
COURTLAND DR., Littlestown	Ad	17340	D11	3577
COURTLAND DR., Littlestown	Ad	17340	C1	3681
COURTLAND ST., York City	Yk	17403	F7	3271
COURTLAND ST., York Twp	Yk	17403	B6	3376
COUSLER CIR., Manchester Twp	Yk	17404	G11	3165
COVE HOLLOW RD., Liberty	Ad	17320	D3	3676
COVE LA., Red Lion	Yk	17356	B9	3377
COVENTRY CROSS RD., East Manchester	Yk	17347	E2	3167
COVENTRY CT., Oxford	Ad	17350	D3	3474
COVENTRY CT., Springettsbury	Yk	17402	D1	3272
COVENTRY RD., York Twp	Yk	17313	C5	3376
COVINGTON AV., Dover Twp	Yk	17315	H2	3269
COVINGTON DR., Manchester Boro	Yk	17345	E10	3061
COVINGTON DR., Shrewsbury Boro	Yk	17361	B11	3584
COVINGTON DR., Shrewsbury Twp	Yk	17361	B11	3584
CRABAPPLE CT., Manchester Twp	Yk	17402	B3	3166
CRAFTWAY DR., Littlestown	Ad	17340	F1	3681
CRAGMOOR RD., Newberry	Yk	17370	G4	3060
CRAGMOOR RD., Newberry	Yk	17370	A2	3061
CRAIG RD., Peach Bottom	Yk	17302	D9	3588
CRAIGDAN DR., York Twp	Yk	17313	B6	3376
CRALEY RD., Lower Windsor	Yk	17366	E11	3274
CRALEY RD., Lower Windsor	Yk	17366	B3	3378
CRALEY RD., Lower Windsor	Yk	17368	H9	3274
CRALEY RD., Lower Windsor	Yk	17368	A8	3275
CRALEY RD., Windsor Twp	Yk	17356	C6	3377
CRALEY RD., Windsor Twp	Yk	17366	G4	3377
CRALEY RD., Windsor Twp	Yk	17366	B3	3378
CRAMER RD., Chanceford	Yk	17309	G4	3482
CRAMER RD., Chanceford	Yk	17309	A4	3483
CRANBERRY LA., Windsor Twp	Yk	17402	A9	3273
CRANBERRY LA., Windsor Twp	Yk	17402	B9	3273
CRANBERRY RD., Huntington	Ad	17372	A11	3160
CRANBERRY RD., Huntington	Ad	17372	G2	3264
CRANBERRY RD., Huntington	Ad	17372	A1	3265
CRANBERRY RD., Tyrone	Ad	17304	G5	3263
CRANBERRY RD., Tyrone	Ad	17304	A5	3264
CRANBROOK DR., Dover Boro	Yk	17315	D11	3164
CRANBROOK DR., York Twp	Yk	17402	C2	3376
CRANE RD., Warrington	Yk	17019	B9	3057
CRANMERE LA., Springettsbury	Yk	17402	D5	3272
CRAWFORD AV., Cumberland	Ad	17325	B4	3575
CRAWFORD CT., Hallam	Yk	17406	A11	3168
CRAWFORD CT., New Freedom	Yk	17349	A3	3688
CRAWFORD RD., Chanceford	Yk	17322	G8	3378
CREAMERY AV., Delta	Yk	17314	E5	3693
CREEK AV., Dover Twp	Yk	17315	G1	3269
CREEK BOTTOM CIR., Carroll	Yk	17019	E3	3056
CREEK BOTTOM RD., East Manchester	Yk	17345	E8	3061
CREEK CT., Shrewsbury Twp	Yk	17349	D3	3688
CREEK RD., Carroll	Yk	17019	E8	2951
CREEK RD., Hamilton	Ad	17350	D4	3370
CREEK RD., Menallen	Ad	17304	H2	3262
CREEK RD., Menallen	Ad	17304	A2	3263
CREEK RD., Newberry	Yk	17345	D5	3061
CREEK RD., Paradise	Yk	17316	H10	3267
CREEK RD., Washington	Yk	17316	G10	3161
CREEK RD., Washington	Yk	17316	A9	3162
CREEK VIEW DR., Union	Ad	17340	C8	3578
CREEK VIEW TR., Carroll Valley	Ad	17320	A5	3677
CREEKMAN CT., Chanceford	Yk	17309	G3	3483
CREEKSIDE CT., Cumberland	Ad	17325	C4	3471
CRESCENT DR., Fairview	Yk	17070	H9	2848
CRESCENT LA., Littlestown	Ad	17340	F2	3681
CRESCENT RD., Spring Garden	Yk	17403	F11	3271
CRESCENT RD., Windsor Twp	Yk	17402	A7	3273
CRESCENT RD., York Twp	Yk	17403	F11	3271
CRESCENT RD., York Twp	Yk	17403	F1	3375
CRESEN ACRES LA., Hopewell	Yk	17352	D2	3690
CREST AV., Penn	Yk	17331	E5	3579
CREST HILL RD., Lower Windsor	Yk	17356	E4	3378
CREST HILL RD., Lower Windsor	Yk	17356	E4	3378
CREST VIEW DR., Reading	Ad	17316	A3	3371
CREST VIEW LA., Mount Pleasant	Ad	17325	E1	3576
CREST VIEW TR., Carroll Valley	Ad	17320	H10	3572
CREST VIEW TR., Carroll Valley	Ad	17320	A10	3573
CREST WAY, Spring Garden	Yk	17403	A11	3271
CREST WAY, Spring Garden	Yk	17403	A1	3375
CRESTLINE DR., East Manchester	Yk	17345	C10	3061
CRESTLYN DR., York Twp	Yk	17402	A4	3376
CRESTLYN DR., York Twp	Yk	17402	H5	3375
CRESTLYN RD., Spring Garden	Yk	17403	G10	3271
CRESTON RD., Spring Garden	Yk	17403	E9	3271
CRESTON RD., York City	Yk	17403	E9	3271
CRESTVIEW CT., Newberry	Yk	17370	E11	2955
CRESTVIEW DR., York Twp	Yk	17402	A5	3376
CRESTWOOD DR., East Manchester	Yk	17347	H3	3166
CRESTWOOD DR., East Manchester	Yk	17347	H1	3166
CRESTWOOD DR., Windsor Twp	Yk	17356	C10	3377
CRICKET LA., McSherrystown	Ad	17331	G2	3578
CRICKET LA., York Twp	Yk	17313	C6	3376
CRIMSON WAY, Menallen	Ad	17307	H6	3260
CRIMSON WAY, Menallen	Ad	17307	A6	3261
CROCUS LA., West Manchester	Yk	17404	C4	3270
CROCUS TR., Carroll Valley	Ad	17320	G8	3572
CROLL SCHOOL RD., Spring Garden	Yk	17403	A5	3375
CROLL SCHOOL RD., York Twp	Yk	17403	A5	3375
CROLL SCHOOL RD., York Twp	Yk	17403	A6	3375
CRONE RD., Dover Twp	Yk	17315	A1	3164
CRONE RD., Manchester Twp	Yk	17402	A7	3166
CROOKED CREEK LA., Franklin	Ad	17325	C3	3470
CROOKED CREEK RD., Franklin	Ad	17325	D11	3366
CROOKED WIND LA., Manchester Twp	Yk	17404	D7	3165
CROSS AV., Cumberland	Ad	17325	A4	3575
CROSS LA., Hellam	Yk	17368	D4	3169
CROSS LAND TR., Carroll Valley	Ad	17320	G7	3572
CROSS MILL RD., East Hopewell	Yk	17322	B2	3586
CROSS ROADS AV., Cross Roads	Yk	17322	F11	3481
CROSS ROADS AV., East Hopewell	Yk	17322	G7	3481
CROSS ROADS AV., North Hopewell	Yk	17322	G7	3481
CROSS ROADS AV., North Hopewell	Yk	17322	H6	3481
CROSS ST., Seven Valleys	Yk	17360	F4	3478
CROSS TR., Carroll Valley	Ad	17320	H11	3572
CROSS VIEW TR., Carroll Valley	Ad	17320	H4	3676
CROSS VIEW TR., Carroll Valley	Ad	17320	A4	3677
CROSSBROOK DR., Manchester Twp	Yk	17402	D10	3166
CROSSFIELD LA., Springettsbury	Yk	17402	E1	3272
CROSSING WAY, Manchester Boro	Yk	17345	D10	3061
CROSSTIE DR., Hopewell	Yk	17363	F10	3585
CROSSWAY DR., York Twp	Yk	17402	G5	3375
CROSSWINDS DR., Shrewsbury Boro	Yk	17361	C11	3584
CROSSWINDS DR., Shrewsbury Twp	Yk	17361	C11	3584
CROSSWINDS TR., Liberty	Ad	17320	D10	3573
CROUSE RD., Mount Joy	Ad	17340	H3	3679
CROUSE RD., Mount Joy	Ad	17340	A4	3680
CROWL RD., Lower Chanceford	Yk	17302	B11	3485
CROWN POINTE CT., Shrewsbury Twp	Yk	17349	F4	3688
CROWN POINTE DR., Springettsbury	Yk	17402	B9	3272
CROWS NEST LA., Spring Garden	Yk	17403	H2	3374
CROWS NEST LA., Spring Garden	Yk	17403	A1	3375
CRULL RD., Newberry	Yk	17370	H9	2955
CRUM RD., Liberty	Ad	17320	C3	3677
CRYSTAL CREEK CROSSING LA., Hamilton	Ad	17301	C4	3371
CRYSTAL CREEK CROSSING LA., Hamilton	Ad	17316	C4	3371
CRYSTAL DR., Hellam	Yk	17368	C8	3169
CRYSTAL DR., Wrightsville	Yk	17368	C8	3169
CRYSTAL LA., Springettsbury	Yk	17402	B6	3272
CULHANE RD., Newberry	Yk	17370	C11	2955
CULHANE RD., Newberry	Yk	17370	B1	3060
CULP RD., Straban	Ad	17325	G7	3367
CULP ST., Gettysburg	Ad	17325	B10	3471
CULPEPPER RD., Shrewsbury Boro	Yk	17361	B11	3584
CULPEPPER RD., Shrewsbury Boro	Yk	17361	B1	3688
CUMBERLAND DR., Cumberland	Ad	17325	A10	3471
CUMBERLAND SQ., Oxford	Ad	17350	D2	3474
CUNNINGHAM RD., Cumberland	Ad	17325	C8	3574
CUNNINGHAM RD., Freedom	Ad	17325	A7	3574
CURRAN DR., Cross Roads	Yk	17322	H11	3481
CURTIS DR., Mount Pleasant	Ad	17325	B11	3472
CURTIS DR., Mount Pleasant	Ad	17325	B1	3576
CURTIS DR., Oxford	Ad	17350	A1	3474
CURTIS DR., Reading	Ad	17316	C1	3266
CURTIS DR., Windsor Twp	Yk	17356	A11	3273
CUSTER DR., Mount Pleasant	Ad	17325	B10	3472
CUSTER DR., Reading	Ad	17316	C4	3266
CUSTER LA., Mount Pleasant	Ad	17325	C11	3472
CUTLER CIR., Hopewell	Yk	17363	B8	3585
CYPRESS AV., West Manchester	Yk	17404	B5	3270
CYPRESS CT., Dover Twp	Yk	17315	F4	3269
CYPRESS LA., Red Lion	Yk	17356	A7	3377
CYPRESS PL., Fairview	Yk	17011	F6	2848
CYPRESS POINT RD., Chanceford	Yk	17322	B2	3482
CYPRESS RD. S., Dover Twp	Yk	17315	F4	3269
CYPRESS RD., Dover Twp	Yk	17315	F3	3269
CYPRESS TR., Carroll Valley	Ad	17320	G4	3676

D

D ST. N., York Spring	Ad	17372	B10	3160
D ST. S., York Spring	Ad	17372	B10	3160
D ST., Jackson	Yk	17364	C1	3373
D ST., McSherrystown	Ad	17344	F2	3578
DADE CT., York Twp	Yk	17313	B6	3376
DAGUE RD., Mount Joy	Ad	17340	G11	3575
DAGUE RD., Mount Joy	Ad	17340	G2	3679
DAIRY RD., Dover Twp	Yk	17315	D8	3268
DAIRY RD., North Hopewell	Yk	17356	A3	3481
DAIRY RD., North Hopewell	Yk	17356	C4	3481
DAIRY RD., Paradise	Yk	17316	A11	3268
DAIRY RD., Paradise	Yk	17316	B1	3372
DAIRYLAND DR., York Twp	Yk	17313	A9	3377
DAISY LA., Dover Twp	Yk	17315	E5	3269
DAISY RD., York Twp	Yk	17402	H3	3375
DAKOTA DR., Conewago	Ad	17331	D3	3578
DAKOTA DR., Windsor Twp	Yk	17356	B3	3377
DALE DR., Fawn	Yk	17321	F5	3587
DALE RD., Menallen	Ad	17307	B8	3261
DALEVIEW CT., York Twp	Yk	17403	G1	3375
DALLAS DR., Lower Windsor	Yk	17406	B3	3274
DALLAS DR., York Twp	Yk	17313	D7	3376
DALLAS ST., York City	Yk	17403	F8	3271
DALRYMPLE ST., North York	Yk	17404	C5	3271
DANA CT., Lower Windsor	Yk	17406	A2	3274
DANDELION TR., Carroll Valley	Ad	17320	G8	3572
DANDRIDGE DR., York Twp	Yk	17403	E3	3375
DANE DR., Fairview	Yk	17319	A3	2955
DANIELLE CT., Manchester Twp	Yk	17404	H11	3165
DANIELLE DR., Dover Twp	Yk	17315	G5	3269
DANNER DR., Heidelberg	Yk	17362	F11	3476
DANNER LA., Fairview	Yk	17070	B2	2954
DARBY LA., York Twp	Yk	17402	G4	3375
DARK HOLLOW RD., Hellam	Yk	17368	A6	3169
DARK HOLLOW RD., Hellam	Yk	17368	C5	3169
DARK HOLLOW RD., Hellam	Yk	17406	H5	3168
DARK HOLLOW RD., Hellam	Yk	17406	A6	3169
DARLENE ST., York Twp	Yk	17402	H5	3375
DARLINGTON RD., Jackson	Yk	17404	E4	3373
DARLINGTON RD., West Manchester	Yk	17404	E4	3373
DARON RD., Codorus	Yk	17362	C4	3581
DART DR., Hanover	Yk	17331	B11	3475
DART MANOR CT., Hanover	Yk	17331	B10	3475
DARTHA DR., York Twp	Yk	17313	D8	3376
DARTMOUTH RD., York City	Yk	17404	B5	3271
DARTMOUTH RD., York Twp	Yk	17404	G5	3270
DAUBERTON DR., Mount Pleasant	Ad	17350	E3	3473
DAUGHERTY AV., Dallastown	Yk	17313	E6	3376
DAUGHERTY AV., York Twp	Yk	17313	E6	3376
DAUGHERTY DR., Penn	Yk	17331	C5	3579
DAUGHERTY RD., Chanceford	Yk	17322	B1	3482
DAUGHERTY RD., Shrewsbury Twp	Yk	17349	C11	3583
DAUGHERTY RD., Shrewsbury Twp	Yk	17349	C1	3687
DAVID CIR., Lower Windsor	Yk	17406	G4	3273
DAVID CT., Springfield	Yk	17360	A11	3375
DAVID DR., Fairview	Yk	17319	A4	2955
DAVID DR., York Twp	Yk	17356	F2	3376
DAVID LEE DR., West Manheim	Yk	17331	E2	3683
DAVIDSBURG RD., Dover Twp	Yk	17315	B3	3268
DAVIDSBURG RD., Dover Twp	Yk	17315	A4	3269
DAVIDSBURG RD., Washington	Yk	17316	B2	3267
DAVIDSON DR., Springettsbury	Yk	17402	G4	3272
DAVIES DR., Springettsbury	Yk	17402	E2	3272
DAVIS AV., Cumberland	Ad	17325	E6	3470
DAVIS CIR., Penn	Yk	17331	G7	3579
DAVIS DR., Reading	Ad	17316	D5	3266
DAVIS RD., Fawn	Yk	17352	G3	3690
DAVIS RD., Fawn	Yk	17363	G11	3586
DAVIS VALLEY RD., Hopewell	Yk	17363	H11	3584
DAVIS VALLEY RD., Hopewell	Yk	17363	H1	3688
DAVIS VALLEY RD., Hopewell	Yk	17363	A1	3689
DAWN RD., Freedom	Ad	17325	A5	3574
DAWNLIGHT DR., York Twp	Yk	17402	D8	3272
DAY RD., Fawn	Yk	17321	G1	3691
DAYLIGHT DR., York Twp	Yk	17402	D9	3272
DAYS MILL RD., North Codorus	Yk	17403	E6	3374
DAYS MILL RD., York Twp	Yk	17403	E6	3374
DAYS MILL RD., York Twp	Yk	17403	A5	3375
DEAD END RD., Union	Ad	17340	C5	3682
DEAD WOMAN HOLLOW RD., Menallen	Ad	17307	G1	3260
DEAD WOMAN HOLLOW RD., Menallen	Ad	17307	A1	3261
DEAGAN RD., Heidelberg	Yk	17331	H1	3579
DEAGEN RD., Heidelberg	Yk	17331	A2	3580
DEAGY AV., Hanover	Yk	17331	D10	3475
DEAMERLYN DR., Springettsbury	Yk	17402	C1	3272
DEAN RD., Fawn	Yk	17321	F5	3587
DEARBORN LA., Springettsbury	Yk	17402	C7	3272
DEARDORFF DR., Newberry	Yk	17319	H9	2954
DEARDORFF RD., Warrington	Yk	17019	G11	3056
DEARDORFF RD., Washington	Yk	17019	G11	3056
DEARDORFF RD., Washington	Yk	17019	F1	3161
DEARHILL DR., Hellam	Yk	17402	E7	3168
DEBBIE CT., Penn	Yk	17331	E4	3579
DEBBIE DR., Spring Garden	Yk	17403	H10	3271
DEBBIE DR., Spring Garden	Yk	17403	A10	3272
DEBORAH TR., Carroll Valley	Ad	17320	F1	3676
DEBRA DR., Newberry	Yk	17370	H10	2955
DEBRA LA., Franklin	Yk	17019	B9	3056
DECKER RD., Springfield	Yk	17403	D2	3479
DEEP DALE RD., Peach Bottom	Yk	17302	H7	3588
DEEP HOLLOW RD., Dover Twp	Yk	17315	F8	3163
DEEP HOLLOW TR., Carroll Valley	Ad	17320	F10	3572
DEEP POND CT., Shrewsbury Twp	Yk	17349	G5	3688
DEEP POWDER TR., Carroll Valley	Ad	17320	A8	3573
DEEP RUN LA., Hellam	Yk	17402	C8	3167
DEEP RUN LA., Springettsbury	Yk	17402	C8	3167
DEER CHASE LA., York Twp	Yk	17403	A8	3376
DEER CHASE LA., York Twp	Yk	17403	H8	3375
DEER CREEK RD., Hopewell	Yk	17349	G1	3688
DEER CREEK RD., Shrewsbury Boro	Yk	17349	C8	3584
DEER CREEK RD., Shrewsbury Twp	Yk	17349	E10	3584
DEER CREEK RD., Shrewsbury Twp	Yk	17349	G1	3688
DEER CT., Fairview	Yk	17339	C2	2954
DEER DR., Conewago	Ad	17331	G3	3578
DEER FORD WAY, West Manchester	Yk	17404	H8	3269
DEER FORD WAY, West Manchester	Yk	17404	A7	3270
DEER FOREST RD., Hellam	Yk	17406	E5	3168
DEER LA., East Hopewell	Yk	17363	C6	3586
DEER LEAP LA., York Twp	Yk	17403	A8	3376
DEER LEAP LA., York Twp	Yk	17403	H8	3375
DEER PARK LA., Franklin	Ad	17222	H7	3363
DEER PATH DR., Windsor Twp	Yk	17356	A4	3377
DEER RD, West Manheim	Yk	17331	A4	3684
DEER RD., Fawn	Yk	17321	G9	3587
DEER RD., Fawn	Yk	17321	A8	3588
DEER RD., Fawn	Yk	17352	E9	3587
DEER RD., North Hopewell	Yk	17356	B3	3481
DEER RD., West Manheim	Yk	17331	H4	3683
DEER RIDGE LA., North Hopewell	Yk	17322	G11	3480
DEER RIDGE LA., North Hopewell	Yk	17363	G11	3480
DEER RIDGE LA., North Hopewell	Yk	17363	G1	3584
DEER RUN CIR., Heidelberg	Yk	17362	D9	3476
DEER RUN DR., Dover Twp	Yk	17315	E4	3164
DEER RUN DR., Newberry	Yk	17319	E10	2955
DEER RUN, Franklin	Ad	17353	G9	3260
DEER TR., Carroll Valley	Ad	17320	H11	3572
DEER TRACT LA., Hamiltonban	Ad	17353	B9	3468
DEER TRAIL DR., Berwick	Ad	17331	C4	3475
DEER TRAIL RD., Hamilton	Ad	17301	A8	3371
DEER TRAIL RD., Jackson	Yk	17362	F10	3372
DEERFIELD DR., Dover Twp	Yk	17315	F1	3269
DEERFIELD DR., Hanover	Yk	17331	B10	3475
DEERFIELD LA., York Twp	Yk	17403	G3	3375
DEGUY AV., Hanover	Yk	17331	B11	3475
DEININGER RD., Springettsbury	Yk	17402	A11	3167
DEININGER RD., Springettsbury	Yk	17402	H1	3271
DEIST LA., Hamiltonban	Ad	17353	A7	3469
DEL HILL RD., York Twp	Yk	17313	F6	3376
DELANEY TR., Carroll Valley	Ad	17320	H7	3572
DELAWARE AV., Dover Twp	Yk	17315	F1	3269
DELAWARE AV., Littlestown	Ad	17340	D2	3681
DELAWARE AV., York Twp	Yk	17404	H7	3270
DELAWARE DR., Newberry	Yk	17370	A9	2956
DELAWARE'S RIDGE, Cumberland	Ad	17325	D5	3471
DELLINGER RD., East Manchester	Yk	17347	F7	3166
DELLINGER RD., East Manchester	Yk	17402	F7	3166
DELLINGER SCHOOL RD., Chanceford	Yk	17356	G3	3378
DELONE AV., McSherrystown	Ad	17344	F2	3578
DELPARK LA., York City	Yk	17404	A4	3271
DELTA BY-PASS, Lower Chanceford	Yk	17314	F8	3589
DELTA BY-PASS, Peach Bottom	Yk	17314	F8	3589
DELTA BY-PASS, Peach Bottom	Yk	17314	E3	3693
DELTA RD., Chanceford	Yk	17302	F3	3483
DELTA RD., Chanceford	Yk	17309	F3	3483
DELTA RD., Chanceford	Yk	17322	C10	3378
DELTA RD., Chanceford	Yk	17322	H1	3482
DELTA RD., Chanceford	Yk	17322	B1	3483
DELTA RD., Chanceford	Yk	17356	C10	3378
DELTA RD., Lower Chanceford	Yk	17302	B3	3589
DELTA RD., Lower Chanceford	Yk	17314	D7	3589
DELTA RD., Lower Chanceford	Yk	17302	E9	3484
DELTA RD., Lower Chanceford	Yk	17302	H1	3588
DELTA RD., Lower Chanceford	Yk	17309	B5	3484
DELTA RD., Windsor Twp	Yk	17356	F7	3377
DELTA RD., Windsor Twp	Yk	17356	A9	3378
DELWOOD DR., Dover Boro	Yk	17315	E10	3164
DENEB RD., West Manchester	Yk	17404	D8	3270
DENISE DR., Franklin	Yk	17019	B9	3056
DENNY LA., Springettsbury	Yk	17402	G10	3166
DENTON DR., Yoe	Yk	17313	G6	3376
DENTON DR., York Twp	Yk	17313	G6	3376
DERBY AV., Fairview	Yk	17011	E8	2848
DERBY CT., Lower Windsor	Yk	17368	F1	3274
DERBY DR., Conewago	Ad	17331	C5	3578
DERRY CT., Manchester Twp	Yk	17402	A8	3166
DERRY RD., Manchester Twp	Yk	17404	A5	3270
DERRY RD., West Manchester	Yk	17404	A4	3270
DETTERS MILL RD., Dover Twp	Yk	17315	B9	3163
DETTERS MILL RD., Dover Twp	Yk	17315	B9	3163
DETTERS MILL RD., Warrington	Yk	17315	B8	3163
DETTERS MILL RD., Warrington	Yk	17315	B9	3163
DETTERS MILL RD., Washington	Yk	17315	H11	3162
DETTERS MILL RD., Washington	Yk	17315	A11	3163
DETTERS MILL RD., Washington	Yk	17315	H1	3267
DETTINGER RD., Chanceford	Yk	17309	E10	3379
DETWILER CT., Spring Garden	Yk	17403	E11	3271
DETWILER DR., Manchester Twp	Yk	17404	D9	3165
DEVCO DR., East Manchester	Yk	17345	D4	3166
DEVERS RD., York City	Yk	17404	A4	3271
DEVERS RD., York Twp	Yk	17404	H4	3270
DEVERS ST., Dallastown	Yk	17313	F7	3376
DEVILLE DR., Windsor Twp	Yk	17356	D4	3377
DEVIL'S DEN TR., Hamiltonban	Ad	17320	H11	3571
DEVON RD., Spring Garden	Yk	17403	F9	3271
DEVONSHIRE CT., East Manchester	Yk	17347	E2	3167
DEVONSHIRE DR., Dover Twp	Yk	17315	B3	3269
DEVONSHIRE DR., Shrewsbury Boro	Yk	17361	A6	3584
DEVONSHIRE DR., York Twp	Yk	17313	F7	3376
DEW DROP CT., York Twp	Yk	17403	G3	3375
DEW DROP RD., York Twp	Yk	17402	A3	3376
DEW DROP RD., York Twp	Yk	17402	H3	3375
DEW DROP RD., York Twp	Yk	17403	F3	3375
DEWBERRY RD., Manchester Twp	Yk	17404	F9	3165
DEWCO RD., Penn	Yk	17331	A3	3579
DEWEY AV., North York	Yk	17404	B5	3271
DEWEY ST., Mount Wolf	Yk	17347	F11	3061
DEWEY ST., West Manchester	Yk	17404	A9	3271
DEXTER DR., Lower Windsor	Yk	17366	B9	3274
DIAMOND HILL ST., Cumberland	Ad	17325	H9	3470
DIAMOND RD., Springfield	Yk	17403	H4	3479
DIAMOND ST. N., West Manchester	Yk	17404	F8	3270
DIANA CT., West Manheim	Yk	17331	D10	3579
DIANA DR., Reading	Ad	17350	A2	3370
DIANE CT., Newberry	Yk	17370	H10	2955

Street	County	ZIP	Grid	Map
DIANE LA., Biglerville	Ad	17307	H2	3366
DIANE TR., Carroll Valley	Ad	17320	E11	3572
DIANE TR., Carroll Valley	Ad	17320	D1	3676
DIANE TR., Carroll Valley	Ad	17320	D2	3676
DICKINSON CT., New Freedom	Yk	17349	H4	3687
DICKINSON DR., Conewago	Ad	17331	B5	3578
DICK'S DAM RD., Reading	Ad	17350	G6	3369
DICK'S DAM RUN, Hamilton	Ad	17350	A7	3370
DIEHL CT., Shrewsbury Twp	Yk	17349	B3	3584
DIETZ RD., Windsor Twp	Yk	17402	H9	3272
DIETZ RD., Windsor Twp	Yk	17402	A9	3273
DIETZ RD., Windsor Twp	Yk	17402	A8	3273
DILL RD., West Manchester	Yk	17404	D10	3270
DILLER RD., Conewago	Ad	17331	H2	3578
DILLER RD., Fairview	Yk	17070	E10	2848
DILLER RD., Hanover	Yk	17331	A2	3579
DILLER RD., Tyrone	Ad	17350	G4	3368
DILLER RD., Tyrone	Ad	17350	A4	3369
DINSMORE RD., Peach Bottom	Yk	17314	F11	3589
DINSMORE RD., Peach Bottom	Yk	17314	F1	3693
DINWIDDIES TRACT, Cumberland	Ad	17325	C4	3471
DISTILLERY RD., Springfield	Yk	17327	D11	3479
DISTILLERY RD., Springfield	Yk	17327	D1	3583
DISTRICT RD., Franklin	Ad	17222	F11	3363
DISTRICT RD., Franklin	Ad	17222	G1	3467
DITZLER AV., Biglerville	Ad	17307	H3	3366
DITZLER AV., Biglerville	Ad	17307	A3	3367
DIVEN DR., Newberry	Yk	17370	A2	3061
DIXIE DR., Red Lion	Yk	17356	B6	3377
DIXIE DR., Springettsbury	Yk	17402	A5	3272
DOCK LA., Hellam	Yk	17368	D3	3169
DOCKWOOD DR., Franklin	Ad	17353	A7	3364
DOE LA., Fairview	Yk	17339	C3	2954
DOE LA., Hamiltonban	Ad	17353	B9	3468
DOE RUN RD., Washington	Yk	17316	C9	3162
DOERSAM CT., Springettsbury	Yk	17402	C10	3167
DOG LA., Codorus	Yk	17360	H11	3477
DOGWOOD CIR., Spring Garden	Yk	17403	D2	3375
DOGWOOD CT., East Manchester	Yk	17345	E2	3166
DOGWOOD CT., Hamilton	Ad	17350	C10	3370
DOGWOOD CT., Hellam	Yk	17406	A1	3274
DOGWOOD CT., Hopewell	Yk	17363	D3	3585
DOGWOOD DR., Dover Twp	Yk	17315	C10	3164
DOGWOOD DR., Hellam	Yk	17406	A10	3169
DOGWOOD DR., Hellam	Yk	17406	A1	3274
DOGWOOD DR., Menallen	Ad	17304	F3	3262
DOGWOOD DR., Straban	Ad	17325	C9	3368
DOGWOOD LA., Carroll	Yk	17019	B3	3056
DOGWOOD LA., Conewago	Ad	17331	H3	3578
DOGWOOD LA., East Manchester	Yk	17345	D3	3166
DOGWOOD LA., Manheim	Yk	17329	F9	3581
DOGWOOD LA., Newberry	Yk	17315	E3	3059
DOGWOOD RD., Dover Twp	Yk	17315	A6	3164
DOGWOOD RD., Dover Twp	Yk	17315	E3	3269
DOGWOOD RD., Peach Bottom	Yk	17302	G7	3588
DOGWOOD RD., Springfield	Yk	17327	G9	3479
DOGWOOD ST., Newberry	Yk	17370	G1	3060
DOGWOOD TER., Carroll	Yk	17019	B3	3056
DOGWOOD TR., Carroll Valley	Ad	17320	G2	3676
DOGWOOD TR., Carroll Valley	Ad	17320	F3	3676
DOLF RD., East Hopewell	Yk	17363	A7	3586
DOLLIS LA., Hellam	Yk	17406	H11	3167
DOMENICK DR., Windsor Twp	Yk	17402	A8	3273
DOMINION CT., Shrewsbury Twp	Yk	17349	E2	3687
DOMINION CT., West Manheim	Yk	17331	E11	3579
DOMINION DR., Manchester Twp	Yk	17404	G11	3165
DOMINION DR., West Manheim	Yk	17331	D11	3579
DOMINON DR., West Manheim	Yk	17331	D1	3683
DONALDSON LA., Hamiltonban	Ad	17353	A10	3469
DONNA LA., Conewago	Yk	17345	G8	3060
DONNA LA., Dover Twp	Yk	17315	D6	3164
DONNA LA., York Twp	Yk	17403	H1	3375
DONNA TR., Carroll Valley	Ad	17320	G11	3572
DONNA TR., Carroll Valley	Ad	17320	G1	3676
DONNELLY ST., York City	Yk	17403	E6	3271
DONRENE DR., East Manchester	Yk	17347	B5	3167
DONWOOD DR., Dover Twp	Yk	17315	D3	3269
DOOLEY RD., Delta	Yk	17314	E5	3693
DOOLEY RD., Peach Bottom	Yk	17314	E6	3693
DORA TR., Carroll Valley	Ad	17320	D1	3676
DORCHESTER DR., West Manchester	Yk	17404	A6	3270
DORIS LA., Lower Windsor	Yk	17406	G4	3273
DORSETT LA., Springettsbury	Yk	17402	C6	3272
DORSEY LA., Carroll	Yk	17019	A1	3057
DORSEY LA. (EXT.), Carroll	Yk	17019	A11	2952
DORSEY LA. (EXT.), Carroll	Yk	17019	A1	3057
DORSEY LA. (EXT.), Monaghan	Yk	17019	A1	3057
DORSEY LA., Carroll	Yk	17019	H2	3056
DORSEY LA., Monaghan	Yk	17019	A1	3057
DORSEY PARK TR., Peach Bottom	Yk	17314	E9	3590
DORWART CIR., Fairview	Yk	17319	A3	2955
DORWOOD DR., Dover Twp	Yk	17315	G3	3269
DOUBLEDAY AV., Cumberland	Ad	17325	A7	3471
DOUBLEDAY AV., Gettysburg	Ad	17325	A7	3471
DOUGLAS DR., West Manchester	Yk	17404	G1	3373
DOUGLAS RD., Chanceford	Yk	17356	C5	3379
DOUGLAS RD., Chanceford	Yk	17356	D1	3379
DOVE CIR., Penn	Yk	17331	G6	3579
DOVE CT., Dillsburg	Yk	17019	E4	3056
DOVE DR., West Manchester	Yk	17404	A7	3270
DOVE LA., York Twp	Yk	17313	A8	3377
DOVE TR., Carroll Valley	Ad	17320	H2	3676
DOWNING ST., West Manchester	Yk	17404	C4	3270
DOWNS RD., Lower Chanceford	Yk	17302	D1	3587
DRACO RD., Hopewell	Yk	17352	C2	3690
DRACO RD., Hopewell	Yk	17363	C11	3586
DRACO RD., Hopewell	Yk	17363	C2	3690
DRESSAGE CT., Manchester Twp	Yk	17404	D1	3270
DREW LA., Germany	Ad	17340	D11	3577
DREXEL ST., West Manchester	Yk	17404	A9	3271
DRIFTWOOD CT., Hanover	Yk	17331	A3	3579
DRUCK VALLEY RD., Hellam	Yk	17402	E8	3167
DRUCK VALLEY RD., Hellam	Yk	17406	E8	3167
DRUCK VALLEY RD., Springettsbury	Yk	17402	G11	3166
DRUCK VALLEY RD., Springettsbury	Yk	17402	B10	3167
DRUCK VALLEY RD., Springettsbury	Yk	17402	F1	3271
DRUMMER DR., Oxford	Ad	17350	H2	3473
DRUMMER DR., Oxford	Ad	17350	A1	3474
DRUMMOND AV., Penn	Yk	17331	E7	3475
DRY BRIDGE RD., Manheim	Yk	17329	A11	3581
DRY GIN TR., Hamiltonban	Ad	17320	H11	3571
DUBBERS DR., Newberry	Yk	17319	D5	2955
DUBBS RD., North Codorus	Yk	17362	B7	3477
DUBS CHURCH RD., Manheim	Yk	17331	D6	3580
DUBS CHURCH RD., West Manheim	Yk	17331	D9	3580
DUCKTOWN RD., Hellam	Yk	17406	F10	3168
DUCKTOWN RD., Hellam	Yk	17406	G1	3273
DUELLA CT. N., Manchester Twp	Yk	17404	F2	3270
DUELLA CT., Manchester Twp	Yk	17404	G2	3270
DUFF HOLLOW RD., Chanceford	Yk	17309	H6	3482
DUFF HOLLOW RD., Chanceford	Yk	17309	H8	3482
DUFF HOLLOW RD., Chanceford	Yk	17309	A7	3483
DUFF HOLLOW RD., Chanceford	Yk	17322	H6	3482
DUG HILL RD., Menallen	Ad	17307	G4	3261
DUG LA., Hamiltonban	Ad	17320	E9	3468
DUG LA., Hamiltonban	Ad	17353	E9	3468
DUKE ST. N., Dallastown	Yk	17313	H7	3376
DUKE ST. N., North York	Yk	17404	C4	3271
DUKE ST. N., York City	Yk	17401	C6	3271
DUKE ST. N., York City	Yk	17403	C7	3271
DUKE ST. S., Dallastown	Yk	17313	H8	3376
DUKE ST. S., North York	Yk	17404	C5	3271
DUKE ST. S., Spring Garden	Yk	17403	E11	3271
DUKE ST. S., Spring Garden	Yk	17403	E1	3375
DUKE ST. S., York City	Yk	17403	D8	3271
DUKE ST. S., York Twp	Yk	17313	H8	3376
DUKE ST. S., York Twp	Yk	17313	A11	3377
DUKE ST. S., York Twp	Yk	17356	A11	3377
DUKE ST., Jefferson	Yk	17362	E10	3477
DUKE ST., Loganville	Yk	17403	G2	3479
DUKE ST., New Freedom	Yk	17349	H4	3687
DULCEY DR., Manchester Twp	Yk	17404	H11	3165
DULL RD., Windsor Twp	Yk	17322	E2	3481
DUNBAR RD., West Manchester	Yk	17404	B5	3270
DUNBARTON DR., Dover Twp	Yk	17315	E4	3269
DUNCAN LA., Hellam	Yk	17406	D5	3168
DUNDEE RD., Manchester Twp	Yk	17402	C9	3166
DUNKARD VALLEY RD., Springfield	Yk	17313	A3	3480
DUNKARD VALLEY RD., Springfield	Yk	17403	G4	3479
DUNKLEY AV., York Haven	Yk	17370	E4	3061
DUNMORE DR., West Manheim	Yk	17331	F8	3579
DUNSTER RD., Spring Garden	Yk	17403	C1	3375
DUPONT AV., Spring Garden	Yk	17403	B10	3271
DUQUESNE RD., York Twp	Yk	17402	C1	3376
DURHAM DR., Carroll	Yk	17019	D9	2951
DURHAM RD., Springettsbury	Yk	17402	B7	3272
DUSTIN RD., York Twp	Yk	17402	C10	3272
DUSTYS LA., Shrewsbury Twp	Yk	17327	C5	3583
DUTTON CT., Springettsbury	Yk	17402	G1	3272
DUTTON RD., Shrewsbury Twp	Yk	17349	G4	3688
DUTTON RD., Shrewsbury Twp	Yk	17363	G4	3688
DUTTON RD., Shrewsbury Twp	Yk	17363	A5	3689
DUVALL AV., West Manchester	Yk	17404	E10	3270
DUXBURRY DR., Manchester Twp	Yk	17404	F8	3165
DYAN DR., Windsor Twp	Yk	17402	A8	3273

E

Street	County	ZIP	Grid	Map
EAGAS DR., West Manheim	Yk	17331	D10	3579
EAGLE AV., Hanover	Yk	17331	C3	3579
EAGLE DR., Berwick	Ad	17331	A5	3475
EAGLE LA., Hellam	Yk	17368	C8	3169
EAGLE LA., Newberry	Yk	17319	C6	2955
EAGLE LANDING RD., Hellam	Yk	17406	H11	3168
EAGLE RIDGE CT., Manheim	Yk	17331	G6	3580
EAGLE SCOUT RD., Dover Twp	Yk	17364	G7	3268
EAGLE ST., New Oxford	Ad	17350	A2	3474
EAGLE TR., Carroll Valley	Ad	17320	F1	3676
EAGLE TR., Peach Bottom	Yk	17314	G10	3588
EAGLE VIEW LA., Chanceford	Yk	17356	E1	3379
EAGLETON DR., Jacobus	Yk	17407	D10	3375
EARL ST., Penn	Yk	17331	B5	3579
EARLY AV., Straban	Ad	17325	D6	3471
EAST ARLENE DR., Lower Windsor	Yk	17406	A5	3274
EAST AV., Red Lion	Yk	17356	C7	3377
EAST BERLIN RD., Huntington	Ad	17372	B9	3265
EAST BERLIN RD., Jackson	Yk	17364	D11	3268
EAST BERLIN RD., Jackson	Yk	17364	A11	3269
EAST BERLIN RD., Paradise	Yk	17316	D1	3371
EAST BERLIN RD., Paradise	Yk	17364	D11	3268
EAST BERLIN RD., Paradise	Yk	17316	A1	3372
EAST BERLIN RD., Reading	Ad	17316	A1	3370
EAST BERLIN RD., Tyrone	Ad	17372	H9	3264
EAST BERLIN RD., West Manchester	Yk	17404	G10	3269
EAST BERLIN RD., West Manchester	Yk	17404	A10	3270
EAST BIRCH ST., Codorus	Yk	17362	F11	3477
EAST BOUNDARY AV., Spring Garden	Yk	17403	E8	3271
EAST BOUNDARY AV., York City	Yk	17403	E8	3271
EAST BROAD ST., Dallastown	Yk	17313	G7	3376
EAST BROADWAY ST., Red Lion	Yk	17356	D7	3377
EAST BROADWAY, Gettysburg	Ad	17325	C7	3471
EAST CAMPING AREA RD., Warrington	Yk	17365	E2	3163
EAST CANAL ST., Dover Twp	Yk	17315	F10	3164
EAST CARBRIDGE RD., North Hopewell	Yk	17363	G4	3584
EAST CENTER ST., Glen Rock	Yk	17327	C3	3583
EAST CHARLES ST., Littlestown	Ad	17340	F1	3681
EAST CHERRY LA., Dallastown	Yk	17313	F7	3376
EAST CHERRYWINE DR., Manchester Twp	Yk	17404	G1	3270
EAST CHESTNUT HILL RD., Tyrone	Ad	17304	A9	3264
EAST CHESTNUT ST., Hanover	Yk	17331	C2	3579
EAST CHESTNUT ST., Red Lion	Yk	17356	D8	3377
EAST CHESTNUT ST., Windsor Twp	Yk	17356	D8	3377
EAST CHURCH AV., Shrewsbury Boro	Yk	17361	B9	3584
EAST CHURCH AV., Shrewsbury Twp	Yk	17361	B9	3584
EAST CHURCH AV., York City	Yk	17403	D8	3271
EAST CHURCH ST., Dillsburg	Yk	17019	F3	3056
EAST CHURCH ST., East Hopewell	Yk	17322	A1	3586
EAST CHURCH ST., East Hopewell	Yk	17322	D1	3586
EAST CLARK AV., York City	Yk	17401	D7	3271
EAST CLARK AV., York City	Yk	17403	D7	3271
EAST CLARK AV., York City	Yk	17403	F5	3271
EAST CLARK AV., York City	Yk	17403	F6	3271
EAST CLEARVIEW DR., Shrewsbury Boro	Yk	17361	B7	3584
EAST CLEARVIEW RD., Hanover	Yk	17331	B11	3475
EAST CLOVER LA., Dallastown	Yk	17313	G7	3376
EAST COLLEGE AV., York City	Yk	17403	D8	3271
EAST CONFEDERATE AV., Cumberland	Ad	17325	D9	3471
EAST CONFEDERATE AV., Gettysburg	Ad	17325	D9	3471
EAST COTTAGE PL., York City	Yk	17403	D9	3271
EAST CT., Penn	Yk	17331	E8	3579
EAST DR., Newberry	Yk	17370	F11	2955
EAST DR., Newberry	Yk	17370	F1	3060
EAST ELM AV., Hanover	Yk	17331	B1	3579
EAST ELM ST., Codorus	Yk	17362	F11	3477
EAST ELM ST., Red Lion	Yk	17356	D7	3377
EAST FARM CIR., Dover Twp	Yk	17315	D7	3269
EAST FARM DR., Dover Twp	Yk	17315	D7	3269
EAST FLOUR MILL RD., Manchester Twp	Yk	17402	E11	3166
EAST FORREST AV., Shrewsbury Boro	Yk	17361	B8	3584
EAST FRANKLIN ST., New Freedom	Yk	17349	G2	3687
EAST FRONT ST., Delta	Yk	17314	G4	3693
EAST GARY DR., York Twp	Yk	17313	D8	3376
EAST GAS AV., York City	Yk	17401	D7	3271
EAST GAS AV., York City	Yk	17403	D7	3271
EAST GAY ST., Dallastown	Yk	17313	F8	3376
EAST GAY ST., Red Lion	Yk	17356	C6	3377
EAST GEORGE ST., New Oxford	Ad	17350	A3	3474
EAST GEORGE ST., New Salem	Yk	17371	D7	3374
EAST GIRARD ST., Dallastown	Yk	17313	F8	3376
EAST GOLDEN LA., Oxford	Ad	17350	B2	3474
EAST HANOVER ST., Biglerville	Ad	17307	A2	3367
EAST HAZEL ST., Red Lion	Yk	17356	C6	3377
EAST HEATHERFIELD WAY, Windsor Twp	Yk	17356	B2	3377
EAST HEFFNER RD., Lower Chanceford	Yk	17309	D1	3484
EAST HIGH ST., Gettysburg	Ad	17325	C9	3471
EAST HIGH ST., New Freedom	Yk	17349	G3	3687
EAST HIGH ST., New Oxford	Ad	17350	B2	3474
EAST HIGH ST., Red Lion	Yk	17356	C7	3377
EAST HIGH ST., Windsor Boro	Yk	17366	F4	3377
EAST HIGH ST., Yoe	Yk	17313	G5	3376
EAST HILL ST., Winterstown	Yk	17322	B7	3481
EAST HILLTOP DR., Heidelberg	Yk	17362	E7	3476
EAST HOLLY LA., Newberry	Yk	17319	F7	2955
EAST HOPE AV., York City	Yk	17403	D8	3271
EAST JACKSON ST., Spring Garden	Yk	17403	G8	3271
EAST JACKSON ST., York City	Yk	17403	D9	3271
EAST KEENY DR., North Codorus	Yk	17362	A1	3478
EAST KING ST., Abbottstown	Ad	17301	C9	3371
EAST KING ST., Littlestown	Ad	17340	F1	3681
EAST KING ST., Spring Garden	Yk	17403	G6	3271
EAST KING ST., York City	Yk	17401	E7	3271
EAST KING ST., York City	Yk	17403	E7	3271
EAST LA., Red Lion	Yk	17356	C7	3377
EAST LAKEVIEW DR., Littlestown	Ad	17340	F2	3681
EAST LANCASTER ST., Red Lion	Yk	17356	D7	3377
EAST LANCASTER ST., Red Lion	Yk	17356	E8	3377
EAST LANDIS DR., Fairfield	Ad	17320	A5	3573
EAST LINCOLNWAY, New Oxford	Ad	17350	B2	3474
EAST LINCOLNWAY, Oxford	Ad	17350	B2	3474
EAST LINCON AV., Gettysburg	Ad	17325	C7	3471
EAST LOCUST ST., York City	Yk	17403	D7	3271
EAST LUTHER DR., Shrewsbury Boro	Yk	17361	A11	3584
EAST LUTHER DR., Shrewsbury Twp	Yk	17361	A1	3688
EAST LYNN DR., East Berlin	Ad	17316	D11	3267
EAST MAIN ST., Dallastown	Yk	17313	G7	3376
EAST MAIN ST., Fairfield	Ad	17320	A5	3573
EAST MAIN ST., Fawn Grove	Yk	17321	G4	3691
EAST MAIN ST., Felton	Yk	17322	H4	3481
EAST MAIN ST., Felton	Yk	17322	A4	3482
EAST MAIN ST., New Freedom	Yk	17349	G3	3687
EAST MAIN ST., New Freedom	Yk	17349	H3	3687
EAST MAIN ST., Railroad	Yk	17355	G10	3583
EAST MAIN ST., Windsor Boro	Yk	17366	G4	3377
EAST MAPLE LAWN RD., Fawn	Yk	17352	E6	3587
EAST MAPLE ST., Dallastown	Yk	17313	G7	3376
EAST MAPLE ST., East Prospect	Yk	17317	F5	3274
EAST MAPLE ST., East Prospect	Yk	17368	F5	3274
EAST MAPLE ST., York City	Yk	17403	D8	3271
EAST MAPLE ST., York City	Yk	17403	E8	3271
EAST MARKET AV., Dallastown	Yk	17313	G7	3376
EAST MARKET AV., Dallastown	Yk	17313	F7	3376
EAST MARKET ST., Hallam	Yk	17406	C11	3168
EAST MARKET ST., Spring Garden	Yk	17403	G5	3271
EAST MARKET ST., Springettsbury	Yk	17402	G5	3271
EAST MARKET ST., Springettsbury	Yk	17402	B5	3272
EAST MARKET ST., York City	Yk	17401	D7	3271
EAST MARKET ST., York City	Yk	17403	D7	3271
EAST MASON AV., York City	Yk	17401	D7	3271
EAST MASON AV., York City	Yk	17403	D7	3271
EAST MASON AV., York City	Yk	17403	F6	3271
EAST McKINLEY RD., Lower Chanceford	Yk	17314	E7	3589
EAST MIDDLE ST., Gettysburg	Ad	17325	D8	3471
EAST MIDDLE ST., Hanover	Yk	17331	C2	3579
EAST MIDVALE RD., Peach Bottom	Yk	17302	A8	3589
EAST MOULSTOWN RD., Hanover	Yk	17331	D9	3475
EAST MOULSTOWN RD., Heidelberg	Yk	17331	G8	3475
EAST MOULSTOWN RD., Heidelberg	Yk	17331	A7	3476
EAST MOULSTOWN RD., Penn	Yk	17331	E9	3475
EAST MT. AIRY RD., Monaghan	Yk	17019	G10	2952
EAST MT. AIRY RD., Monaghan	Yk	17019	A1	3058
EAST MYRTLE ST., Littlestown	Ad	17340	E1	3681
EAST NEEDHAM CIR., Manchester Twp	Yk	17404	C11	3165
EAST NEWTON AV., York City	Yk	17403	D7	3271
EAST NORTH AV., York City	Yk	17403	C6	3271
EAST ORE ST., Loganville	Yk	17403	F4	3479
EAST OVERVIEW CIR., Windsor Twp	Yk	17356	C11	3273
EAST PARK LA., Dallastown	Yk	17313	G7	3376
EAST PENNSYLVANIA AV., Stewartstown	Yk	17363	E11	3585
EAST PENNSYLVANIA AV., Yoe	Yk	17313	G6	3376
EAST PHEASANT CIR., Dover Twp	Yk	17315	D7	3269
EAST PHILADELPHIA ST., York City	Yk	17401	D6	3271
EAST PHILADELPHIA ST., York City	Yk	17403	D6	3271
EAST PHILADELPHIA ST., Yoe	Yk	17313	G6	3376
EAST POINT DR., Shrewsbury Twp	Yk	17349	C1	3688
EAST POPLAR ST., York City	Yk	17403	D7	3271
EAST POPLAR ST., York City	Yk	17403	F6	3271
EAST POSEY RD., Lower Chanceford	Yk	17302	F6	3484
EAST POSEY RD., Lower Chanceford	Yk	17302	A6	3485
EAST PRINCESS ST., West York	Yk	17404	G10	3270
EAST PRINCESS ST., York City	Yk	17403	E7	3271
EAST PROSPECT RD., Lower Windsor	Yk	17402	F6	3273
EAST PROSPECT RD., Lower Windsor	Yk	17406	F6	3273
EAST PROSPECT RD., Lower Windsor	Yk	17406	C6	3274
EAST PROSPECT RD., Windsor Twp	Yk	17402	G8	3272
EAST PROSPECT RD., Windsor Twp	Yk	17402	B7	3273
EAST PROSPECT ST., Red Lion	Yk	17356	B6	3377
EAST PROSPECT ST., Windsor Twp	Yk	17356	B6	3377
EAST QUEEN ST., Dallastown	Yk	17313	F7	3376
EAST RAILROAD ST., Gettysburg	Ad	17325	D8	3471
EAST RANCH TR., Carroll Valley	Ad	17320	A3	3677
EAST RAPHIEL CT., West Manheim	Yk	17331	E11	3579
EAST RIDGE RD., Monaghan	Yk	17019	H11	2952
EAST RIVER DR., Hellam	Yk	17368	D4	3169
EAST RIVER DR., Hellam	Yk	17368	D5	3169
EAST RIVER DR., Hellam	Yk	17406	B3	3169
EAST RIVER VIEW RD., Lower Chanceford	Yk	17314	H2	3589
EAST ROSE AV., Dallastown	Yk	17313	G7	3376
EAST RYE ST., Dallastown	Yk	17313	F8	3376
EAST SHOFF RD., Chanceford	Yk	17356	B2	3379
EAST SIDDONSBURG RD., Monaghan	Yk	17019	E8	2952
EAST SIDDONSBURG RD., Monaghan	Yk	17055	G7	2952
EAST SIDDONSBURG RD., Monaghan	Yk	17055	A6	2953
EAST SKYLIGHT DR., York Twp	Yk	17402	D9	3272
EAST SOUTH ST., York City	Yk	17403	D8	3271
EAST SOUTH ST., York City	Yk	17403	E8	3271
EAST SPRINGETTSBURY ST., Spring Garden	Yk	17403	G8	3271
EAST SPRINGETTSBURY ST., York City	Yk	17403	D9	3271
EAST SPRINGFIELD RD., Springfield	Yk	17360	F7	3479
EAST SPRINGFIELD RD., Springfield	Yk	17360	H4	3479
EAST ST. N., Spring Grove	Yk	17362	B11	3373
EAST ST. S., Spring Grove	Yk	17362	B1	3477
EAST ST., Littlestown	Ad	17340	G1	3681
EAST ST., Seven Valleys	Yk	17360	F4	3478
EAST ST., Springettsbury	Yk	17402	G3	3271
EAST ST., York City	Yk	17403	G5	3271
EAST STEVENS ST., Gettysburg	Ad	17325	C7	3471
EAST SUMMIT DR., Germany	Ad	17340	G3	3681
EAST SUN AV., Dallastown	Yk	17313	G7	3376
EAST TOLNA LA., Shrewsbury Boro	Yk	17361	B10	3584
EAST TOLNA LA., Shrewsbury Twp	Yk	17349	D10	3584
EAST TOLNA LA., Shrewsbury Twp	Yk	17361	B10	3584
EAST TRAILS RD., Peach Bottom	Yk	17302	A8	3589
EAST UNIVERSITY DR., Butler	Ad	17307	H11	3262
EAST UNIVERSITY DR., Butler	Ad	17307	H1	3366
EAST VALLEY RD., Shrewsbury Twp	Yk	17327	H2	3583
EAST VIEW, Menallen	Ad	17304	F3	3262
EAST VILLAGE CIR., Manchester Twp	Yk	17404	A1	3271
EAST WALNUT GROVE RD., Fawn	Yk	17321	F11	3587
EAST WALNUT ST., Hanover	Yk	17331	D10	3475
EAST WALNUT ST., Hanover	Yk	17331	C1	3579
EAST WALNUT ST., Red Lion	Yk	17356	D8	3377
EAST WALNUT ST., Windsor Twp	Yk	17356	D8	3377
EAST WATER ST., Abbottstown	Ad	17301	C9	3371
EAST WATER ST., Gettysburg	Ad	17325	C8	3471
EAST WEBSTER DR., Hellam	Yk	17402	A4	3273
EAST WEBSTER DR., Springettsbury	Yk	17402	A4	3273
EAST WILLOW AV., Dallastown	Yk	17313	G7	3376
EAST WILLOW ST., Codorus	Yk	17362	F11	3477
EAST WIND TR., Carroll Valley	Ad	17320	B10	3573
EAST YORK ST., Biglerville	Ad	17307	A2	3367
EAST YORK ST., Dillsburg	Yk	17019	F3	3056
EASTBROOK CIR., Shrewsbury Twp	Yk	17361	C11	3584
EASTBROOK LA., Manchester Twp	Yk	17402	H7	3165
EASTERN BLVD., Springettsbury	Yk	17402	H5	3271
EASTERN BLVD., Springettsbury	Yk	17402	A5	3272
EASTERN BLVD., Springettsbury	Yk	17402	D4	3272
EASTGATE DR., Springettsbury	Yk	17402	G2	3272
EASTGATE DR., West Manchester	Yk	17404	E3	3270
EASTLAND AV., Manchester Twp	Yk	17402	C11	3166
EASTWOOD DR., Shrewsbury Twp	Yk	17361	C11	3584
EASTWOOD DR., Springettsbury	Yk	17402	B8	3272
EASTWOOD DR., West Manheim	Yk	17331	B4	3684
EASY ST., Littlestown	Ad	17340	D2	3681
EATON ST., Manchester Twp	Yk	17402	C3	3271
EBAUGH RD., Hopewell	Yk	17363	C5	3585
EBAUGH RD., North Hopewell	Yk	17363	G3	3584
EBERTS LA., Springettsbury	Yk	17402	F3	3271
EBERTS LA., Springettsbury	Yk	17402	F4	3271
EBERTS LA., York City	Yk	17403	F6	3271
EBONY DR., York Twp	Yk	17402	G4	3375
ECHO LA., Manheim	Yk	17329	B7	3581
ECHO TR., Carroll Valley	Ad	17320	F2	3676
ECKER AV., Stewartstown	Yk	17363	D1	3689
ECKERT RD., Windsor Boro	Yk	17366	G5	3377
ECKERT RD., Windsor Twp	Yk	17366	G5	3377
EDEN RD., Newberry	Yk	17319	C6	2955
EDEN RD., Springettsbury	Yk	17402	D3	3271
EDEN RD., Springettsbury	Yk	17402	E2	3271
EDENRIDGE RD., Springettsbury	Yk	17402	D5	3272

EDGAR AV., Delta	Yk	17314	E5	3693
EDGAR ROUSE AV., York City	Yk	17403	E7	3271
EDGAR ST., Spring Garden	Yk	17403	E8	3271
EDGAR ST., York City	Yk	17403	E8	3271
EDGAR WOODS RD., East Hopewell	Yk	17352	E4	3586
EDGEBORO DR., Manchester Boro	Yk	17345	D10	3061
EDGECOMB AV., Spring Garden	Yk	17403	G9	3271
EDGEGROVE RD., Conewago	Ad	17331	A9	3474
EDGEGROVE RD., Conewago	Ad	17331	C10	3474
EDGEGROVE RD., Conewago	Ad	17331	A9	3474
EDGEGROVE RD., Mount Pleasant	Ad	17331	A9	3474
EDGEGROVE RD., Mount Pleasant	Ad	17331	A9	3474
EDGEHILL DR., Red Lion	Yk	17356	B8	3377
EDGEHILL RD., Glen Rock	Yk	17327	B5	3583
EDGEHILL RD., Shrewsbury Twp	Yk	17327	B5	3583
EDGEHILL RD., Spring Garden	Yk	17403	F11	3271
EDGEHILL RD., Spring Garden	Yk	17403	F1	3375
EDGEWAY RD. , Dover Boro	Yk	17315	D10	3164
EDGEWOOD AV., Red Lion	Yk	17356	B6	3377
EDGEWOOD DR., Spring Garden	Yk	17403	D10	3271
EDGEWOOD LA., York Twp	Yk	17403	E5	3375
EDGEWOOD RD., Springettsbury	Yk	17402	D4	3272
EDGEWOOD RD., Windsor Twp	Yk	17402	D4	3272
EDGEWOOD RD., York Twp	Yk	17402	D4	3272
EDINBURGH RD., Manchester Twp	Yk	17402	C9	3166
EDISON ST., York City	Yk	17403	E7	3271
EDITH DR., Lower Windsor	Yk	17366	H11	3273
EDLYN DR., Paradise	Yk	17301	F9	3371
EDMUND AV., Manchester Twp	Yk	17404	F2	3270
EDNA MEYERS LA., West Manheim	Yk	17329	F6	3684
EDWARD AV., Manchester Twp	Yk	17402	H6	3165
EDWARD CT., Franklin	Ad	17307	D11	3365
EDWARD RD., York Twp	Yk	17403	D4	3375
EDWARD ST., Penn	Yk	17331	D3	3579
EDWARDS AL., Conewago	Ad	17331	D11	3474
EGRET DR., Berwick	Ad	17331	A5	3475
EICHELBERGER ST., Hanover	Yk	17331	A10	3475
EICHELBERGER ST., Hanover	Yk	17331	B1	3579
EISENHART DR., Abbottstown	Ad	17301	C10	3371
EISENHART MILL RD., Washington	Yk	17316	E9	3267
EISENHOWER DR., Conewago	Ad	17331	H10	3474
EISENHOWER DR., Cumberland	Ad	17325	G4	3574
EISENHOWER DR., Hanover	Yk	17331	B9	3475
EISENHOWER DR., Penn	Yk	17331	A9	3475
EISENHOWER FARM LA., Cumberland	Ad	17325	G4	3574
EL DORADO DR., Windsor Twp	Yk	17356	C4	3377
EL GRECO ST., Berwick	Ad	17331	C5	3475
EL VISTA DR., West Manheim	Yk	17331	E10	3579
ELDER DR., Codorus	Yk	17327	B1	3582
ELDER TRAIL, Fairview	Yk	17070	F1	2954
ELDINE AV., North Codorus	Yk	17404	C8	3374
ELFNER RD., Lower Windsor	Yk	17356	D4	3378
ELFNER RD., Windsor Twp	Yk	17356	C5	3378
ELGIN LA., Hamiltonban	Ad	17320	A3	3572
ELHAM DR., Lower Windsor	Yk	17406	B3	3274
ELICKER RD., Monaghan	Yk	17019	G10	2952
ELIM ST., West Manchester	Yk	17404	C5	3270
ELIZABETH LA., Mount Pleasant	Ad	17350	F6	3473
ELIZABETH ST., West Manchester	Yk	17404	D7	3270
ELIZABETH TR., Carroll Valley	Ad	17320	D1	3676
ELK DR., Conewago	Ad	17331	G3	3578
ELK LA., North York	Yk	17404	C5	3271
ELK RUN TR., Liberty	Ad	17320	E7	3573
ELLENCROFT RD., Fairview	Yk	17339	D2	2954
ELLIOT DR., Fairview	Yk	17339	H6	2953
ELLIOTT LA., Spring Garden	Yk	17403	B11	3271
ELLIS AV., Delta	Yk	17314	G4	3693
ELM AV. E., Hanover	Yk	17331	B1	3579
ELM AV. W., Hanover	Yk	17331	A1	3579
ELM AV., Bonneauville	Ad	17325	H1	3576
ELM AV., Conewago	Ad	17331	G1	3578
ELM AV., Conewago	Ad	17344	G1	3578
ELM AV., Spring Grove	Yk	17362	A11	3373
ELM AV., Spring Grove	Yk	17362	B1	3477
ELM LA., Oxford	Ad	17350	B3	3474
ELM ST. E., Codorus	Yk	17362	F11	3477
ELM ST. E., Red Lion	Yk	17356	D7	3377
ELM ST. W., Red Lion	Yk	17356	C7	3377
ELM ST., Gettysburg	Ad	17325	A8	3471
ELM ST., Yoe	Yk	17313	G6	3376
ELM ST., York City	Yk	17403	F7	3271
ELM TER., York City	Yk	17404	A6	3271
ELM TR., Carroll Valley	Ad	17320	G8	3572
ELMER AV., Newberry	Yk	17315	G3	3059
ELMWOOD AV., Union	Ad	17331	G4	3682
ELMWOOD BLVD., Spring Garden	Yk	17403	G6	3271
ELMWOOD DR., Dover Boro	Yk	17315	E10	3164
ELMWOOD LA., Menallen	Ad	17304	D2	3262
ELY LA., Menallen	Ad	17304	F2	3262
EMANUEL RD., Fairview	Yk	17339	H11	2953
EMANUEL RD., Fairview	Yk	17339	A11	2954
EMANUEL RD., Fairview	Yk	17339	H1	3058
EMERALD AV. S., West Manchester	Yk	17404	C7	3270
EMERALD AV., West Manchester	Yk	17404	C6	3270
EMERALD CT., East Manchester	Yk	17345	C4	3166
EMERALDEW LA., Carroll	Yk	17019	G2	3056
EMERSON CT., Penn	Yk	17331	B5	3579
EMERSON ST., Jefferson	Yk	17362	D11	3477
EMERSON ST., Penn	Yk	17331	B5	3579
EMIG MILL RD., Dover Twp	Yk	17315	E7	3269
EMIG RD., Hellam	Yk	17406	D2	3273
EMIG RD., Manchester Twp	Yk	17402	D8	3166
EMIG RD., North Codorus	Yk	17362	H5	3476
EMIG RD., North Codorus	Yk	17362	A5	3477
EMIG SCHOOL RD., Jackson	Yk	17364	H11	3268
EMIG SCHOOL RD., Jackson	Yk	17364	A10	3269
EMIG ST., Hallam	Yk	17406	B11	3168
EMIGS MILL RD., West Manchester	Yk	17404	F10	3269
EMIGS MILL RD., West Manchester	Yk	17404	G1	3373
EMIGS SCHOOL RD., Dover Twp	Yk	17315	B8	3269
EMILY LA., Fairview	Yk	17070	E1	2954
EMIRAY CT., York Twp	Yk	17403	E4	3375
EMMANUEL DR., West Manchester	Yk	17404	C8	3270
EMMITSBURG RD., Cumberland	Ad	17325	F8	3574
EMMITSBURG RD., Cumberland	Ad	17325	A1	3575
EMMITSBURG RD., Freedom	Ad	17320	B4	3678
EMMITSBURG RD., Freedom	Ad	17325	F8	3574
EMMITSBURG RD., Freedom	Ad	17325	B4	3678
EMORY LA., Hamiltonban	Ad	17320	A9	3572
ENCAMPMENT CT., Spring Grove	Yk	17362	B9	3373
ENFIELD RD., Chanceford	Yk	17322	G5	3379
ENFIELD RD., East Hopewell	Yk	17322	G11	3482
ENFIELD RD., East Hopewell	Yk	17322	F2	3586
ENGLEWOOD CT., Dover Twp	Yk	17315	A2	3270
ENOLA DR., Hopewell	Yk	17363	F10	3585
ENSMINGER LA., Springfield	Yk	17407	D1	3479
ENTERPRISE RD., Lower Windsor	Yk	17406	D5	3274
ENTRANCE DR., York Twp	Yk	17313	F6	3376
ENTRY LA., Fairview	Yk	17011	E8	2848
EQUESTRIAN CT., Dover Twp	Yk	17315	G1	3269
EQUESTRIAN DR., York Twp	Yk	17402	C11	3272
EQUINE COVE, York Twp	Yk	17356	A6	3377
EQUINOX RD., Dover Twp	Yk	17315	E6	3269
EQUUS DR., Fairview	Yk	17011	E7	2848
ERIC DR., McSherrystown	Ad	17331	G2	3578
ERLEN DR., Springettsbury	Yk	17402	A7	3272
ERNEY RD., Newberry	Yk	17315	F2	3059
ERNST MILL RD., Latimore	Ad	17372	A5	3160
ESBENSHADE RD., West Manchester	Yk	17404	A5	3270
ESPRESSO WAY, Manchester Twp	Yk	17402	B3	3166
ESSEX CIRCLE DR., Shrewsbury Boro	Yk	17361	B1	3688
ESSEX RD., Dover Twp	Yk	17315	F3	3269
ESTAIRE DR., Springfield	Yk	17360	G8	3479
ESTATE DR., North Codorus	Yk	17404	H8	3373
ESTATE DR., North Codorus	Yk	17404	A8	3374
ESTHER LA., Carroll	Yk	17019	C11	2951
ETHAN ALLEN DR., Fairview	Yk	17070	F1	2954
ETON LA., Springettsbury	Yk	17402	E6	3272
EVERETT RD., Shrewsbury Twp	Yk	17327	E6	3583
EVERETT RD., York Twp	Yk	17403	H10	3271
EVERGREEN DR., Conewago	Ad	17331	D10	3474
EVERGREEN DR., York Twp	Yk	17402	D11	3272
EVERGREEN LA., Franklin	Ad	17353	F9	3260
EVERGREEN LA., West Manchester	Yk	17404	F3	3373
EVERGREEN RD., Fairview	Yk	17070	B8	2849
EVERGREEN RD., Lower Chanceford	Yk	17314	H3	3589
EVERGREEN RD., North Hopewell	Yk	17322	A11	3481
EVERGREEN RD., North Hopewell	Yk	17363	A11	3481
EVERGREEN TER., East Manchester	Yk	17345	C4	3166
EVERGREEN TR., Carroll Valley	Ad	17320	F10	3572
EVERHART ST., North York	Yk	17404	C4	3271
EVUNBRETH DR., Manchester Twp	Yk	17404	B3	3271
EWELL AV., Straban	Ad	17325	E5	3471
EWELL DR., Mount Pleasant	Ad	17325	B11	3472
EWELL DR., Reading	Ad	17316	D2	3266
EXCELSIOR RD., Menallen	Ad	17307	H11	3261
EXCELSIOR RD., Menallen	Ad	17307	A10	3262
EXCELSIOR RD., Menallen	Ad	17307	G1	3365
EXCHANGE PL., Hanover	Yk	17331	B3	3579
EXETER DR. N., York Twp	Yk	17403	C7	3376
EXETER DR. S., York Twp	Yk	17403	C7	3376
EXISTING AL., Glen Rock	Yk	17327	B5	3583
EXISTING AL., Shrewsbury Twp	Yk	17327	B5	3583
EXPEDITION TR., Straban	Ad	17325	A6	3472
EXTON LA., Springettsbury	Yk	17402	H3	3272
EYSTER RD., Jackson	Yk	17362	A7	3373

F

F ST. S., York Spring	Ad	17372	B10	3160
FACTORY AL., New Freedom	Yk	17349	G3	3687
FACTORY ST., Hanover	Yk	17331	D2	3579
FACTORY ST., New Oxford	Ad	17350	G2	3473
FAHRINER DR., Hellam	Yk	17406	H8	3167
FAHS ST., York Twp	Yk	17402	H5	3270
FAIR ACRES DR., York Twp	Yk	17403	E5	3375
FAIR AV., Penn	Yk	17331	D3	3579
FAIR LA., Heidelberg	Yk	17362	D4	3476
FAIR SCHOOL RD., Codorus	Yk	17327	D11	3582
FAIR SCHOOL RD., Codorus	Yk	17327	G8	3582
FAIR SCHOOL RD., Codorus	Yk	17327	C1	3686
FAIR SCHOOL RD., Shrewsbury Twp	Yk	17327	A6	3583
FAIR VALLEY CT., York Twp	Yk	17403	E5	3375
FAIRFAX CIR., Shrewsbury Boro	Yk	17361	B11	3584
FAIRFAX DR., York Twp	Yk	17403	C3	3375
FAIRFAX RD., Manchester Twp	Yk	17404	H10	3165
FAIRFIELD AV., West Manchester	Yk	17404	C6	3270
FAIRFIELD RD., Carroll Valley	Ad	17320	H9	3572
FAIRFIELD RD., Carroll Valley	Ad	17320	H1	3676
FAIRFIELD RD., Carroll Valley	Ad	17320	A2	3677
FAIRFIELD RD., Cumberland	Ad	17325	E9	3470
FAIRFIELD RD., Cumberland	Ad	17325	A9	3471
FAIRFIELD RD., Hamiltonban	Ad	17320	H9	3572
FAIRFIELD RD., Hamiltonban	Ad	17320	C3	3573
FAIRFIELD RD., Highland	Ad	17325	A11	3470
FAIRFIELD RD., Highland	Ad	17325	C3	3573
FAIRFIELD RD., Hopewell	Yk	17363	H5	3689
FAIRFIELD STATION RD., Hamiltonban	Ad	17320	E6	3572
FAIRGROUND RD., Menallen	Ad	17307	A11	3262
FAIRGROUND RD., Menallen	Ad	17307	H1	3365
FAIRGROUND RD., Menallen	Ad	17307	A1	3366
FAIRLANE DR., York Twp	Yk	17404	H4	3270
FAIRMONT AV., Fairview	Yk	17070	D1	2954
FAIRMONT AV., Warrington	Yk	17365	A2	3163
FAIRMONT ST., York City	Yk	17404	B6	3271
FAIRMOUNT AV., Newberry	Yk	17345	D7	3061
FAIRMOUNT RD., Bendersville	Ad	17304	H4	3262
FAIRMOUNT RD., Menallen	Ad	17304	H4	3262
FAIRPLAY RD., Cumberland	Ad	17325	E10	3470
FAIRVIEW AV., Conewago	Ad	17331	E2	3578
FAIRVIEW AV., Conewago	Ad	17344	E2	3578
FAIRVIEW AV., Dover Twp	Yk	17315	C10	3164
FAIRVIEW AV., Gettysburg	Ad	17325	B10	3471
FAIRVIEW AV., McSherrystown	Ad	17344	E2	3578
FAIRVIEW DR., Dover Twp	Yk	17404	A3	3270
FAIRVIEW DR., Penn	Yk	17331	A9	3579
FAIRVIEW DR., Spring Garden	Yk	17403	D10	3271
FAIRVIEW DR., West Manheim	Yk	17331	D10	3579
FAIRVIEW FRUIT RD., Franklin	Ad	17307	G11	3365
FAIRVIEW FRUIT RD., Franklin	Ad	17307	G1	3469
FAIRVIEW FRUIT RD., Franklin	Ad	17325	A9	3366
FAIRVIEW JUNIPER DR., Fairview	Yk	17011	E6	2848
FAIRVIEW RD., Fairview	Yk	17070	B7	2849
FAIRVIEW RD., Straban	Ad	17325	G4	3471
FAIRVIEW ST., Red Lion	Yk	17356	C8	3377
FAIRVIEW TER., Spring Garden	Yk	17403	C11	3271
FAIRVIEW TR., Peach Bottom	Yk	17314	A10	3589
FAIRWAY DR., Carroll	Yk	17019	B4	3056
FAIRWAY DR., Newberry	Yk	17319	C7	2955
FAIRWAY DR., Springettsbury	Yk	17402	B9	3272
FAIRWAY DR., West Manchester	Yk	17404	G9	3269
FAIRWAY DR., York Twp	Yk	17402	B9	3272
FAITH DR., Oxford	Ad	17350	E2	3474
FAITH LA., Hopewell	Yk	17363	B2	3689
FAITH LA., Windsor Twp	Yk	17356	C4	3377
FAITH RD., West Manchester	Yk	17404	F5	3373
FAITH WAY, Heidelberg	Yk	17331	C1	3580
FAKE HOLLOW RD., Lower Windsor	Yk	17406	B4	3274
FAKE RD., Chanceford	Yk	17309	H5	3482
FAKE RD., Chanceford	Yk	17309	A4	3483
FAKE RD., Chanceford	Yk	17309	A6	3483
FAKE RD., Hellam	Yk	17402	B6	3273
FAKE RD., Windsor Twp	Yk	17402	B6	3273
FALCON LA., Conewago	Yk	17315	A11	3165
FALCON LA., Dover Twp	Yk	17315	H11	3164
FALCON LA., Dover Twp	Yk	17315	H1	3269
FALCON LA., Dover Twp	Yk	17315	B2	3270
FALCON TR., Carroll Valley	Ad	17320	H2	3676
FALKIRK CT., North Hopewell	Yk	17363	G3	3584
FALLOW FIELD LA., Dover Twp	Yk	17315	B8	3164
FALLS RD., Peach Bottom	Yk	17302	C10	3589
FALLSVIEW AV., Newberry	Yk	17345	E5	3061
FAME AV., Hanover	Yk	17331	E10	3475
FAME AV., Penn	Yk	17331	E10	3475
FARAWAY LA., North Hopewell	Yk	17322	D11	3481
FAREFIELD CT., York Twp	Yk	17402	A2	3376
FARHAM LA., Manchester Twp	Yk	17404	C11	3165
FARM CIR. E., Dover Twp	Yk	17315	D7	3269
FARM CROSS WAY, West Manchester	Yk	17404	B2	3270
FARM DR. E., Dover Twp	Yk	17315	E7	3269
FARM DR. , Dover Twp	Yk	17315	E7	3269
FARM DR., Dover Twp	Yk	17315	B8	3164
FARM DR., Windsor Twp	Yk	17402	F7	3272
FARM HOUSE LA., Fairview	Yk	17011	F6	2848
FARM LA., Lower Windsor	Yk	17402	E4	3273
FARM LA., Manchester Boro	Yk	17345	D10	3061
FARM LA., North Codorus	Yk	17404	B10	3374
FARM LA., West Manchester	Yk	17404	B5	3270
FARM LA., York Twp	Yk	17402	A5	3376
FARM VALLEY RD., Warrington	Yk	17365	D3	3162
FARM VIEW RD., Huntington	Ad	17372	F9	3159
FARM VIEW RD., Huntington	Ad	17372	H1	3264
FARMALL LA., Lower Windsor	Yk	17366	A8	3274
FARMBROOK LA., Manchester Twp	Yk	17402	G7	3165
FARMBROOK LA., Manchester Twp	Yk	17402	A7	3166
FARMHILL RD., Hellam	Yk	17406	D2	3273
FARMHOUSE LA., Jackson	Yk	17404	D6	3373
FARMINGTON DR., Jacobus	Yk	17407	D11	3375
FARMSTEAD WAY, West Manchester	Yk	17404	B3	3270
FARMTRAIL RD., Manchester Twp	Yk	17402	H7	3165
FARMVIEW DR., Hopewell	Yk	17349	C7	3584
FARMVIEW DR., Jackson	Yk	17404	E6	3373
FARNHAM LA., Manchester Twp	Yk	17404	C1	3270
FARQUHAR DR., Spring Garden	Yk	17403	D10	3271
FAUERSHAM WAY, Windsor Twp	Yk	17402	F8	3272
FAUST RD., Washington	Yk	17019	F11	3056
FAUTH LA., Hellam	Yk	17406	F11	3273
FAWN AV., Reading	Ad	17350	B3	3370
FAWN CT., Fairview	Yk	17339	C3	2954
FAWN CT., Hellam	Yk	17402	E7	3167
FAWN DR., Menallen	Ad	17304	D5	3262
FAWN GROVE RD., Fawn	Yk	17321	E10	3587
FAWN GROVE RD., Fawn	Yk	17321	F1	3691
FAWN GROVE RD., Fawn	Yk	17352	E9	3587
FAWN HILL DR., Berwick	Ad	17331	C3	3475
FAWN LA., Shrewsbury Twp	Yk	17327	G2	3583
FAWN LOOP, Windsor Twp	Yk	17356	B4	3377
FAWN TR., Carroll Valley	Ad	17320	G11	3572
FAYETTE ST., West Manchester	Yk	17404	E9	3270
FEDERAL RD., North Codorus	Yk	17404	A8	3374
FEEDWATER CT., Hopewell	Yk	17363	F9	3585
FEESER RD., Germany	Ad	17340	B10	3577
FEESER RD., Union	Ad	17340	B10	3577
FELTON RD., Chanceford	Yk	17309	G1	3482
FELTON RD., Chanceford	Yk	17322	D2	3482
FELTON RD., Felton	Yk	17322	F2	3481
FELTON RD., Windsor Twp	Yk	17322	F2	3481
FELTON RD., Windsor Twp	Yk	17356	E10	3377
FELTON RD., Windsor Twp	Yk	17356	F2	3481
FELTY AV., Spring Garden	Yk	17403	G8	3271
FENMORE RD., Chanceford	Yk	17322	E7	3482
FENWICK DR., Manchester Boro	Yk	17345	E10	3061
FERN AV. N., Dallastown	Yk	17313	G7	3376
FERN AV. S., Dallastown	Yk	17313	F8	3376
FERN DR., East Manchester	Yk	17345	C5	3166
FERN DR., Oxford	Ad	17350	C5	3474
FERN ST., Penn	Yk	17331	G3	3579
FERN ST., Yoe	Yk	17313	G6	3376
FERNCREEK LA., Manchester Twp	Yk	17404	G10	3165
FERNDALE RD., Loganville	Yk	17360	E3	3479
FERNWOOD LA., Hamiltonban	Ad	17320	D8	3572
FERNWOOD TR., Carroll Valley	Ad	17320	H10	3572
FERNWOOD TR., Carroll Valley	Ad	17320	A10	3573
FERREE HILL RD., York Twp	Yk	17403	B9	3376
FERRY RD., Chanceford	Yk	17309	A5	3483
FETROW LA., Fairview	Yk	17070	D1	2954
FICKEL HILL RD., Latimore	Ad	17372	E3	3159
FICKES RD., Warrington	Yk	17019	F11	3057
FICKES RD., Warrington	Yk	17019	G1	3162
FICKES RD., Warrington	Yk	17365	G1	3162
FICKES SCHOOL RD., Huntington	Ad	17372	E6	3265
FIDDLER DR., Oxford	Ad	17350	A2	3474
FIDLER RD., Straban	Ad	17325	A5	3368
FIELD POINTE DR., North Codorus	Yk	17362	D2	3477
FIELD RD., Heidelberg	Yk	17362	E3	3476
FIELD TR., Carroll Valley	Ad	17320	G7	3572
FIELDCREST DR., Union	Ad	17340	G11	3577
FIELDING CT., Shrewsbury Twp	Yk	17349	F4	3688
FIELDING CT., Springfield	Yk	17327	A10	3480
FIELDING DR., Windsor Twp	Yk	17356	B2	3377
FIELDING WAY, Newberry	Yk	17319	A6	2955
FIELDSTONE CIR., Shrewsbury Twp	Yk	17361	B11	3584
FIESTA DR., York Twp	Yk	17403	B7	3376
FIG TREE WAY, Manchester Twp	Yk	17402	B3	3166
FILBERT ST., Conewago	Ad	17331	H3	3578
FILBERT ST., Hanover	Yk	17331	A3	3579
FILBERT ST., West Manchester	Yk	17404	E8	3270
FILBERT ST., West York	Yk	17404	D8	3270
FILEYS RD. N., Monaghan	Yk	17019	B7	2952
FILEYS RD. S., Monaghan	Yk	17019	B9	2952
FILEYS RD., Carroll	Yk	17019	B2	3057
FILEYS RD., Monaghan	Yk	17019	B2	3057
FILLY TR., Carroll Valley	Ad	17320	A4	3677
FINCH TR., Carroll Valley	Ad	17320	H2	3676
FINDLAY ST., Springettsbury	Yk	17402	H5	3271
FINDLAY ST., Springettsbury	Yk	17402	A6	3272
FINEVIEW RD., Springettsbury	Yk	17402	F1	3271
FINKS DR., East Manchester	Yk	17345	B8	3061
FINKS DR., Manchester Twp	Yk	17404	G8	3165
FIR TR., Carroll Valley	Ad	17320	H4	3676
FIRE COMPANY RD., Lower Chanceford	Yk	17302	D8	3484
FIRE HOUSE, York Spring	Ad	17372	B10	3160
FIREBOX CT., Hopewell	Yk	17363	E10	3585
FIREHALL RD., North Codorus	Yk	17362	G9	3373
FIREHOUSE LA., Lower Windsor	Yk	17368	G10	3274
FIRESIDE RD., York City	Yk	17404	A5	3271
FIRESIDE RD., York Twp	Yk	17404	H4	3270
FIRESTONE CT., Dover Twp	Yk	17315	G6	3163
FIRMIN WAY, West Manheim	Yk	17331	F11	3579
FISCAL RD., Codorus	Yk	17327	C4	3686
FISH & GAME RD., Dover Twp	Yk	17315	E9	3163
FISH & GAME RD., Germany	Ad	17340	F2	3680
FISH & GAME RD., Germany	Ad	17340	A2	3681
FISH & GAME RD., Lower Windsor	Yk	17368	B11	3275
FISH & GAME RD., Mount Joy	Ad	17340	B2	3680
FISH & GAME RD., Oxford	Ad	17350	G8	3473
FISH & GAME RD., Reading	Ad	17316	H2	3266
FISH & GAME RD., Reading	Ad	17316	A5	3267
FISH & GAME RD., Washington	Yk	17316	H11	3161
FISH & GAME RD., Washington	Yk	17316	H1	3266
FISHEL CREEK RD., Springfield	Yk	17360	A5	3479
FISHEL RD., Cross Roads	Yk	17322	H9	3481
FISHEL RD., North Codorus	Yk	17360	C1	3478
FISHER DR., Conewago	Yk	17404	D2	3165
FISHER DR., Latimore	Ad	17316	B3	3266
FISHER RD., Codorus	Yk	17327	G5	3686
FISHER RD., Fairview	Yk	17319	B4	2955
FISHER RD., Lower Chanceford	Yk	17302	B7	3484
FISHER RD., Newberry	Yk	17319	B4	2955
FISHER RD., Newberry	Yk	17370	E1	3060
FISHER RUN RD., Monaghan	Yk	17019	D11	2952
FISHER RUN RD., Monaghan	Yk	17019	D1	3057
FISHERMANS CIR., Hellam	Yk	17368	C8	3169
FISHERMANS LA., Hellam	Yk	17368	C8	3169
FISHING CREEK AV., Goldsboro	Yk	17319	H7	2955
FISHING CREEK RD. W., Newberry	Yk	17319	A6	2955
FISHING CREEK RD., Fairview	Yk	17070	H2	2953
FISHING CREEK RD., Fairview	Yk	17070	A1	2954
FISHING CREEK RD., Fairview	Yk	17319	A1	2954
FISHING CREEK RD., Fairview	Yk	17339	A1	2954
FISHING CREEK RD., Lower Windsor	Yk	17368	C8	3275
FISSELS CHURCH RD., Codorus	Yk	17327	H8	3582
FISSELS CHURCH RD., Shrewsbury Twp	Yk	17327	A8	3583
FITZ RD., Chanceford	Yk	17322	A5	3380
FITZKEE LA., York Twp	Yk	17402	A4	3376
FITZPATRICK LA., Hallam	Yk	17406	B11	3168
FITZPATRICK LA., Hallam	Yk	17406	B1	3273
FIVE FORKS LA., Hamiltonban	Ad	17320	H10	3571
FIVE FORKS LA., Hamiltonban	Ad	17320	A11	3572
FIVE FORKS RD., Hopewell	Yk	17349	G11	3584
FIVE FORKS RD., Hopewell	Yk	17363	G11	3584
FIVE FORKS RD., Hopewell	Yk	17363	A10	3585
FIVE FORKS RD., Shrewsbury Twp	Yk	17349	F2	3688
FIVE POINT RD., Jackson	Yk	17362	A11	3372
FIVE POINTS RD., Tyrone	Ad	17350	A11	3265
FIVE POINTS RD., Tyrone	Ad	17350	H1	3368
FIVE POINTS RD., Tyrone	Ad	17350	A1	3369
FJORED LEA LA, Hamiltonban	Ad	17320	C8	3572
FLAHARTY RD., Chanceford	Yk	17302	B7	3483
FLAHARTY RD., Lower Chanceford	Yk	17314	F1	3589
FLAMINGO CT., Dover Twp	Yk	17315	B2	3270
FLAT TR., Carroll Valley	Ad	17320	A5	3677
FLATBUSH RD., Mount Pleasant	Ad	17340	D6	3577
FLATBUSH RD., Union	Ad	17340	E6	3577
FLEET ST., Abbottstown	Ad	17301	A10	3371
FLEETWOOD DR., Windsor Twp	Yk	17356	D4	3377
FLEMMING AV., Hanover	Yk	17331	B3	3579
FLEMMING PL., West Manchester	Yk	17404	A7	3270
FLENNER TR., Liberty	Ad	17320	F5	3573
FLESHMAN MILL RD., Mount Pleasant	Ad	17350	E2	3473
FLESHMAN MILL RD., Mount Pleasant	Ad	17350	F3	3473
FLESHMAN MILL RD., Oxford	Ad	17350	E2	3473

FLICK HILL RD., Menallen	Ad	17304	B10	3157
FLICKINGER RD., Hanover	Yk	17331	B8	3475
FLICKINGER RD., Penn	Yk	17331	B8	3475
FLICKINGER RD., Straban	Ad	17325	A3	3472
FLINTVILLE RD., Peach Bottom	Yk	17314	B10	3590
FLINTVILLE RD., Peach Bottom	Yk	17314	C1	3694
FLINTVILLE RD., Peach Bottom	Yk	17314	D4	3694
FLOHRS CHURCH RD., Franklin	Ad	17307	G5	3365
FLOHRS CHURCH RD., Franklin	Ad	17307	E2	3469
FLORA LA., York Twp	Yk	17403	C8	3376
FLORIDA AV., York Twp	Yk	17404	H7	3270
FLOUR MILL RD. E., Manchester Twp	Yk	17402	E11	3166
FLOUR MILL RD. W., Manchester Twp	Yk	17402	E11	3166
FOHL ST., Arendtsville	Ad	17307	B3	3366
FOLKEMER CIR., Manchester Twp	Yk	17404	H2	3270
FOLKSTONE CT., Springettsbury	Yk	17402	D6	3272
FOLKSTONE WAY, Springettsbury	Yk	17402	D6	3272
FOOTER ST., Penn	Yk	17331	D5	3579
FOREST AV. W., Shrewsbury Boro	Yk	17327	G7	3583
FOREST AV. W., Shrewsbury Boro	Yk	17361	A8	3584
FOREST AV. W., Shrewsbury Twp	Yk	17327	G7	3583
FOREST DR., Fairview	Yk	17011	F6	2848
FOREST DR., Hamilton	Ad	17301	G8	3370
FOREST DR., Hamilton	Ad	17301	A8	3371
FOREST DR., Hamilton	Ad	17350	E10	3370
FOREST DR., Newberry	Yk	17319	E9	2955
FOREST HILL CIR., Manchester Twp	Yk	17402	C1	3271
FOREST HILL RD., Manchester Twp	Yk	17402	C1	3271
FOREST HILL RD., North Codorus	Yk	17404	C5	3374
FOREST HILLS RD., Windsor Twp	Yk	17356	C10	3377
FOREST RD., Hopewell	Yk	17363	C1	3689
FOREST RD., Springfield	Yk	17327	A7	3480
FOREST RIDGE RD., Peach Bottom	Yk	17314	C10	3589
FOREST TR., Carroll Valley	Ad	17320	G11	3572
FOREST TR., Peach Bottom	Yk	17314	H10	3588
FOREST VIEW DR., Peach Bottom	Yk	17314	B11	3589
FOREST VIEW RD., Peach Bottom	Yk	17314	B11	3589
FORESTRIDGE CT., Windsor Twp	Yk	17356	A9	3378
FORGE CT., Spring Grove	Yk	17362	B9	3373
FORGE HILL CT., East Manchester	Yk	17347	F6	3166
FORGE HILL RD., East Manchester	Yk	17345	C2	3166
FORGE HILL RD., Lower Windsor	Yk	17368	G7	3274
FORGE HILL RD., Manchester Boro	Yk	17345	D3	3166
FORGE LA., Hellam	Yk	17347	G2	3167
FORNEY AV. N., Hanover	Yk	17331	B3	3579
FORNEY AV. S., Hanover	Yk	17331	B4	3579
FORNEY AV., Hanover	Yk	17331	A1	3579
FORREST AV. E., Shrewsbury Boro	Yk	17361	B8	3584
FORREST DR., Mount Joy	Ad	17325	H11	3471
FORREST DR., Reading	Ad	17316	C4	3266
FORREST DR., Straban	Ad	17325	H11	3471
FORREST DR., Straban	Ad	17325	A11	3472
FORREST LA., Springettsbury	Yk	17402	C7	3272
FORREST LA., York Twp	Yk	17402	D3	3376
FORREST ST. N., West Manchester	Yk	17404	E8	3270
FORREST ST. S., West Manchester	Yk	17404	E9	3270
FORRY AV., Hallam	Yk	17406	C11	3168
FORRY AV., Penn	Yk	17331	E3	3579
FORRY ST., New Salem	Yk	17371	D7	3374
FORRY'S CT., Warrington	Yk	17339	A9	3059
FOSTER CIR., Penn	Yk	17331	H5	3579
FOUNDRY AV., Littlestown	Ad	17340	E2	3681
FOUNDRY RD., Shrewsbury Twp	Yk	17361	C10	3584
FOUR LEAF LA., Fairview	Yk	17319	G4	2954
FOUST RD., Springfield	Yk	17327	D11	3479
FOX CHASE DR., Dover Twp	Yk	17315	D5	3268
FOX CHASE DR., Dover Twp	Yk	17315	G1	3269
FOX CHASE DR., Manheim	Yk	17331	D7	3580
FOX CREEK CT., Lower Windsor	Yk	17368	G9	3274
FOX CREEK RD., Lower Windsor	Yk	17368	G9	3274
FOX DEN LA., Hamilton	Ad	17301	A7	3371
FOX DR., Conewago	Yk	17404	B9	3165
FOX FIELD RD., Cumberland	Ad	17325	E1	3574
FOX HILL RD., Franklin	Ad	17307	E7	3365
FOX KNOLL CT., Hanover	Yk	17331	B10	3475
FOX LA., Hellam	Yk	17406	C4	3273
FOX MEADOW DR., Dover Twp	Yk	17315	G3	3269
FOX MEADOW DR., Hamilton	Ad	17301	H6	3370
FOX MEADOW DR., Hamilton	Ad	17301	A6	3371
FOX MEADOW RD., Manchester Twp	Yk	17404	G10	3165
FOX RIDGE CT., Dover Twp	Yk	17315	G2	3269
FOX RIDGE LA., Hellam	Yk	17406	B10	3168
FOX RUN CIR., Fairview	Yk	17319	A2	2955
FOX RUN CT., Hopewell	Yk	17363	B9	3585
FOX RUN DR., York Twp	Yk	17403	G3	3375
FOX RUN RD., Dover Twp	Yk	17315	E9	3164
FOX RUN RD., Dover Twp	Yk	17315	G1	3269
FOX RUN RD., Hamilton	Ad	17301	H8	3370
FOX RUN RD., West Manheim	Yk	17331	G11	3579
FOX RUN TER., Union	Ad	17331	E1	3682
FOX TAIL DR., Union	Ad	17331	E2	3682
FOX TR., Carroll Valley	Ad	17320	G2	3676
FOX TR., Straban	Ad	17325	E5	3471
FOXFIRE LA., Fairview	Yk	17339	B1	2953
FOXLEIGH DR., Hanover	Yk	17331	C10	3475
FOXSHIRE DR., York Twp	Yk	17402	C11	3272
FOXTAIL CT., Shrewsbury Boro	Yk	17361	B6	3584
FOXTAIL DR., Manchester Twp	Yk	17404	G10	3165
FOXTOWN DR., Hamilton	Ad	17301	B7	3371
FOXWALD AV., Springettsbury	Yk	17402	E1	3272
FRANK DR., Windsor Twp	Yk	17402	A8	3273
FRANK RD., Shrewsbury Twp	Yk	17349	C5	3584
FRANKLIN AV., Dallastown	Yk	17313	F8	3376
FRANKLIN CHURCH RD., Franklin	Yk	17019	A10	3056
FRANKLIN CHURCH RD., Franklin	Yk	17019	A2	3161
FRANKLIN CHURCH RD., Washington	Yk	17019	C6	3161
FRANKLIN CT., Conewago	Ad	17344	E1	3578
FRANKLIN CT., New Freedom	Yk	17349	H3	3687
FRANKLIN DR., Conewago	Ad	17344	E1	3578
FRANKLIN HILLS RD., Franklin	Yk	17019	G5	3160
FRANKLIN SQUARE DR., York Twp	Yk	17313	D7	3376
FRANKLIN ST. E., New Freedom	Yk	17349	G2	3687
FRANKLIN ST. N., Red Lion	Yk	17356	B7	3377
FRANKLIN ST. S., Dallastown	Yk	17313	D7	3376
FRANKLIN ST. S., Hanover	Yk	17331	C4	3579
FRANKLIN ST. S., Penn	Yk	17331	C4	3579
FRANKLIN ST. S., Red Lion	Yk	17356	B8	3377
FRANKLIN ST. S., York Twp	Yk	17313	D7	3376
FRANKLIN ST. S., York Twp	Yk	17356	H10	3376
FRANKLIN ST. S., York Twp	Yk	17356	A10	3377
FRANKLIN ST. W., New Freedom	Yk	17349	F2	3687
FRANKLIN ST., Biglerville	Ad	17307	H1	3366
FRANKLIN ST., Dillsburg	Yk	17019	D4	3056
FRANKLIN ST., Fairfield	Ad	17320	A5	3573
FRANKLIN ST., Gettysburg	Ad	17325	B9	3471
FRANKLIN ST., Hallam	Yk	17406	C11	3168
FRANKLIN ST., Hamiltonban	Ad	17320	H5	3572
FRANKLIN ST., Hanover	Yk	17331	B2	3579
FRANKLIN ST., Jacobus	Yk	17407	E11	3375
FRANKLIN ST., North Hopewell	Yk	17356	H2	3480
FRANKLIN ST., North Hopewell	Yk	17356	A3	3481
FRANKLIN ST., Penn	Yk	17331	E6	3579
FRANKLIN ST., Spring Garden	Yk	17403	E5	3271
FRANKLIN ST., York City	Yk	17403	E5	3271
FRANKLINTOWN RD., Franklin	Yk	17019	D11	3056
FRANKLINTOWN RD., Franklin	Yk	17019	C2	3161
FRANKLINTOWN RD., Franklin	Yk	17019	H4	3160
FRANLYN DR., York Twp	Yk	17313	F5	3376
FRASER ST., Goldsboro	Yk	17319	H7	2955
FRASER ST., Goldsboro	Yk	17319	A7	2956
FRAZER RD., Tyrone	Ad	17304	C8	3264
FREDERICK CT., York City	Yk	17403	F7	3271
FREDERICK DR., York Twp	Yk	17313	E8	3376
FREDERICK LA., Hellam	Yk	17406	B10	3168
FREDERICK PIKE, Germany	Ad	17340	A4	3681
FREDERICK ST., Dallastown	Yk	17313	G7	3376
FREDERICK ST., Hanover	Yk	17331	A4	3579
FREDERICK ST., Penn	Yk	17331	A4	3579
FREE ST., Stewartstown	Yk	17363	E11	3585
FREEDOM AV., New Freedom	Yk	17349	G3	3687
FREEDOM DR., North Codorus	Yk	17362	F5	3476
FREEDOM TR., Carroll Valley	Ad	17320	B11	3573
FREEDOM TR., Carroll Valley	Ad	17320	B1	3677
FRENCH LA., Hamiltonban	Ad	17320	C11	3572
FRENLEN RD., Manchester Twp	Yk	17404	B3	3271
FREY RD., Chanceford	Yk	17322	D5	3482
FREYS LA., Hellam	Yk	17406	B4	3273
FREYSVILLE RD., Hellam	Yk	17402	B5	3273
FREYSVILLE RD., Hellam	Yk	17406	B1	3273
FREYSVILLE RD., Windsor Twp	Yk	17356	C10	3273
FREYSVILLE RD., Windsor Twp	Yk	17356	C5	3377
FREYSVILLE RD., Windsor Twp	Yk	17402	B6	3273
FRIAR RD., New Salem	Yk	17371	C6	3374
FRIAR RUN, Penn	Yk	17331	F6	3579
FRIENDLY AL., Straban	Ad	17350	D7	3369
FRIENDLY DR., Conewago	Ad	17331	C11	3474
FRIENDLY DR., Conewago	Ad	17331	C1	3578
FRIENDS CREEK RD., Liberty	Ad	17320	G6	3676
FRIENDS CREEK TR., Carroll Valley	Ad	17320	A5	3677
FRIENDSHIP AV., Hallam	Yk	17406	D10	3168
FRIENDSHIP AV., Hallam	Yk	17406	D11	3168
FRIENDSHIP LA., Cumberland	Ad	17325	F9	3470
FRIESIAN RD., Manchester Twp	Yk	17402	D11	3166
FRITZ RD., Shrewsbury Twp	Yk	17327	G5	3583
FROCK DR., Penn	Yk	17331	G6	3579
FROG POND HOLLOW N., Hamilton	Ad	17301	B3	3371
FROG POND HOLLOW, Hamilton	Ad	17316	B3	3371
FROG POND HOLLOW S., Hamilton	Ad	17301	B3	3371
FROGTOWN RD., West Manheim	Yk	17331	B9	3580
FROGTOWN RD., West Manheim	Yk	17331	C1	3684
FROGTOWN RD., West Manheim	Yk	17331	D1	3684
FRONT AL., Franklintown	Yk	17323	E9	3056
FRONT ST. E., Delta	Yk	17314	G4	3693
FRONT ST. N., Wrightsville	Yk	17368	E6	3169
FRONT ST. S., Wrightsville	Yk	17368	E7	3169
FRONT ST., East Berlin	Ad	17316	C11	3267
FRONT ST., East Berlin	Ad	17316	C1	3371
FRONT ST., Hellam	Yk	17368	D6	3169
FRONT ST., Lewisberry	Yk	17339	B10	2954
FRONT ST., Manchester Twp	Yk	17402	C4	3271
FRONT ST., Mount Wolf	Yk	17347	F11	3061
FRONT ST., New Freedom	Yk	17349	F4	3687
FRONT ST., New Freedom	Yk	17349	G2	3687
FRONT ST., Newberry	Yk	17339	B10	2954
FRONT ST., York City	Yk	17404	B6	3271
FRONT ST., York Haven	Yk	17370	E3	3061
FRONTENAC CT., Spring Garden	Yk	17403	E11	3271
FROST LA., Carroll	Yk	17019	G9	2951
FROSTY HILL RD., Lower Chanceford	Yk	17302	E11	3483
FROSTY HILL RD., Lower Chanceford	Yk	17302	G11	3483
FROSTY HILL RD., Lower Chanceford	Yk	17302	A10	3484
FROSTY HILL RD., Lower Chanceford	Yk	17302	E1	3587
FRUITLYN DR., York Twp	Yk	17313	D5	3376
FRUITWOOD TR., Carroll Valley	Ad	17320	G4	3676
FRUITWOOD TR., Carroll Valley	Ad	17320	A4	3677
FUHRMAN MILL RD., West Manheim	Yk	17331	G11	3579
FUHRMAN MILL RD., West Manheim	Yk	17331	B10	3580
FULLER CT., Dover Twp	Yk	17315	C10	3164
FULTON AV., Stewartstown	Yk	17363	D10	3585
FULTON DR., Oxford	Ad	17350	D2	3474
FULTON RD., Lower Chanceford	Yk	17302	G7	3483
FULTON RD., Lower Chanceford	Yk	17302	A8	3484
FULTON SCHOOL RD., Chanceford	Yk	17322	D7	3482
FULTON SCHOOL RD., East Hopewell	Yk	17322	A6	3482
FULTON SCHOOL RD., East Hopewell	Yk	17322	D7	3482
FULTON SCHOOL RD., North Hopewell	Yk	17322	H6	3481
FULTON SCHOOL RD., North Hopewell	Yk	17322	A6	3482
FULTON ST., Hanover	Yk	17331	C2	3579
FULTON ST., Penn	Yk	17331	C2	3579
FULTON ST., York City	Yk	17403	E7	3271
FUNT RD., Tyrone	Ad	17304	A4	3264
FURLONG LA., Fairview	Yk	17011	F8	2848
FURLONG WAY, York Twp	Yk	17356	A6	3377
FURMAN RD., Franklin	Yk	17019	A6	3056
FURNACE RD., Chanceford	Yk	17309	F9	3380
FURNACE RD., Chanceford	Yk	17322	G4	3379
FURNACE RD., Chanceford	Yk	17322	B6	3380
FURNACE RD., Chanceford	Yk	17356	C5	3379
FURNACE RD., Lower Chanceford	Yk	17302	E8	3484
FURNACE RD., Lower Chanceford	Yk	17302	F4	3484
FURNACE RD., Lower Chanceford	Yk	17309	F9	3380
FURNACE RD., Lower Windsor	Yk	17406	B8	3274
FURNEY RD., Mount Joy	Ad	17325	G10	3575
FURNLEY RD., Mount Joy	Ad	17340	G10	3575
FUTURE ST., Penn	Yk	17331	B8	3579
FUTURITY DR., Fairview	Yk	17011	E8	2848
FUTURITY DR., Manchester Twp	Yk	17404	D1	3270

G

G ST. S., York Spring	Ad	17372	B10	3160
GABCO LA., Manheim	Yk	17329	G3	3684
GABLE HILL RD., Lower Windsor	Yk	17368	A8	3275
GABLERS RD., Menallen	Ad	17324	A10	3158
GABLER'S RD., Menallen	Ad	17304	A1	3263
GABLER'S RD., Menallen	Ad	17324	A1	3263
GABLERS RD., Tyrone	Ad	17324	A10	3158
GABLES VIEW LA., Chanceford	Yk	17322	A3	3482
GABLES VIEW LA., Felton	Yk	17322	A3	3482
GAIL AV., Hanover	Yk	17331	B2	3579
GALA N., Littlestown	Ad	17340	C1	3681
GALA S., Littlestown	Ad	17340	C1	3681
GALAXY RD., Dover Twp	Yk	17315	E6	3269
GALTEE CT., York Twp	Yk	17402	E10	3272
GALWAY DR., West Manheim	Yk	17331	F8	3579
GAMBLE RD., Fawn	Yk	17321	B6	3588
GAME CLUB RD., Chanceford	Yk	17309	G1	3483
GAME LANDS RD., Tyrone	Ad	17325	B10	3264
GAME LANDS RD., Tyrone	Ad	17325	B1	3368
GAME RD., Warrington	Yk	17019	F6	3057
GAMELAND RD., Franklin	Yk	17019	B10	3056
GANTZ RD., Shrewsbury Twp	Yk	17327	F5	3583
GAP RD., Fairview	Yk	17339	B5	2954
GARBER RD., Oxford	Ad	17350	B1	3474
GARDEN AL., Wrightsville	Yk	17368	D7	3169
GARDEN LA., East Berlin	Ad	17316	D11	3267
GARDEN LA., Penn	Yk	17331	E8	3579
GARDENIA DR., Penn	Yk	17331	G3	3579
GARDNER RD., Heidelberg	Yk	17362	E10	3476
GARDNERS STATION RD., Tyrone	Ad	17324	G10	3158
GARDNERS STATION RD., Tyrone	Ad	17324	E11	3158
GARFIELD ST., Conewago	Ad	17331	G1	3578
GARFIELD ST., York City	Yk	17404	B7	3271
GARNET RD., Spring Garden	Yk	17403	H10	3271
GARRETT RD., Manchester Twp	Yk	17404	H10	3165
GARRETT RD., West Manheim	Yk	17331	C6	3684
GARRISON DR., Manchester Twp	Yk	17404	D10	3165
GARRISTON RD., Newberry	Yk	17339	D2	3059
GARRISTON RD., Newberry	Yk	17370	F11	2954
GARRISTON RD., Newberry	Yk	17370	D2	3059
GARVINE MILL RD., Fawn	Yk	17321	G10	3587
GARVINE MILL RD., Fawn	Yk	17321	A10	3588
GARY DR. E., York Twp	Yk	17313	D8	3376
GARY DR. N., York Twp	Yk	17313	D8	3376
GARY DR. W., York Twp	Yk	17313	D8	3376
GARY PLAYER DR., Newberry	Yk	17319	E6	2955
GAS AL., New Freedom	Yk	17349	G2	3687
GAS AV. E., York City	Yk	17401	D7	3271
GAS AV. W., York City	Yk	17401	C7	3271
GAS AV. W., York City	Yk	17403	D7	3271
GAS ST. W., York City	Yk	17404	B7	3271
GAS ST., York City	Yk	17404	B7	3271
GATEHOUSE LA. W., Springettsbury	Yk	17402	D6	3272
GATEHOUSE LA., Springettsbury	Yk	17402	D6	3272
GATESHEAD DR., North Hopewell	Yk	17363	G4	3584
GATEWAY CT., Peach Bottom	Yk	17314	A10	3589
GATEWAY DR., Hellam	Yk	17368	B7	3169
GATEWAY DR., Wrightsville	Yk	17368	B7	3169
GATEWAY RD., York Twp	Yk	17403	H1	3375
GATEWOOD DR., Shrewsbury Boro	Yk	17361	B5	3584
GAUGE CT., Hopewell	Yk	17363	E9	3585
GAUMER RD., Fairview	Yk	17070	A8	2849
GAY AL., York Haven	Yk	17370	E4	3061
GAY AV. W., York City	Yk	17401	C7	3271
GAY AV. W., York City	Yk	17404	B7	3271
GAY AV. W., York City	Yk	17404	B7	3271
GAY ST. E., Dallastown	Yk	17313	F8	3376
GAY ST. E., Red Lion	Yk	17356	C6	3377
GAY ST. EXT., Windsor Twp	Yk	17356	C6	3377
GAY ST. W., Red Lion	Yk	17356	B7	3377
GAY ST. W., Windsor Boro	Yk	17366	E5	3377
GAY ST. W., York City	Yk	17404	C7	3271
GAY ST., Hanover	Yk	17331	D1	3579
GEBHART RD., Windsor Twp	Yk	17366	F11	3273
GEBHART RD., Windsor Twp	Yk	17366	F11	3273
GEBHART RD., Windsor Twp	Yk	17366	G1	3377
GEISELMAN CT. , Dover Twp	Yk	17315	B7	3164
GEISELMAN RD., Mount Pleasant	Ad	17331	A3	3578
GEISELMAN RD., Union	Ad	17331	A3	3578
GEMMILL RD., Chanceford	Yk	17322	H10	3378
GEMMILL RD., Chanceford	Yk	17322	A10	3379
GEMMILL RD., Hopewell	Yk	17363	H11	3584
GEMMILL RD., Hopewell	Yk	17363	A11	3585
GEMMILL RD., Hopewell	Yk	17363	G2	3688
GEMMILL RD., Peach Bottom	Yk	17314	G10	3588
GEMMILL RD., Peach Bottom	Yk	17314	F9	3588
GEMMILL RD., Shrewsbury Twp	Yk	17349	G4	3688
GEMMILL RD., Shrewsbury Twp	Yk	17363	G4	3688
GEO-BOB LA., Highland	Ad	17325	F11	3469
GEO-BOB LA., Highland	Ad	17325	G1	3573
GEORGE ST. E., New Oxford	Ad	17350	A3	3474
GEORGE ST. E., New Salem	Yk	17371	D7	3374
GEORGE ST. N., East Manchester	Yk	17345	D4	3166
GEORGE ST. N., Manchester Twp	Yk	17402	C9	3166
GEORGE ST. N., Manchester Twp	Yk	17402	B2	3271
GEORGE ST. N., Manchester Twp	Yk	17404	B2	3271
GEORGE ST. N., North York	Yk	17404	C4	3271
GEORGE ST. N., York City	Yk	17401	C6	3271
GEORGE ST. N., York City	Yk	17403	C6	3271
GEORGE ST. N., York City	Yk	17404	C6	3271
GEORGE ST. S., Spring Garden	Yk	17403	E11	3271
GEORGE ST. S., Spring Garden	Yk	17403	E2	3375
GEORGE ST. S., York City	Yk	17401	D8	3271
GEORGE ST. S., York City	Yk	17403	D8	3271
GEORGE ST. S., York Twp	Yk	17403	E2	3375
GEORGE ST. W., New Oxford	Ad	17350	A3	3474
GEORGE ST. W., New Salem	Yk	17371	C7	3374
GEORGE ST., Abbottstown	Ad	17301	A10	3371
GEORGE ST., Dover Twp	Yk	17315	C9	3164
GEORGE ST., East Manchester	Yk	17345	D10	3061
GEORGE ST., Hanover	Yk	17331	C11	3475
GEORGE ST., Hanover	Yk	17331	C2	3579
GEORGE ST., New Freedom	Yk	17349	G2	3687
GEORGE ST., New Freedom	Yk	17349	H3	3687
GEORGE ST., Stewartstown	Yk	17363	D11	3585
GEORGE ST., Stewartstown	Yk	17363	D1	3689
GEORGE ST., Yoe	Yk	17313	G5	3376
GEORGES CT., Shrewsbury Twp	Yk	17327	G5	3583
GEORGETOWN CT., Hanover	Yk	17331	A3	3579
GEORGETOWN RD., Germany	Ad	17340	B5	3681
GEORGETOWN RD., Huntington	Ad	17324	E6	3158
GERBRICK RD., Shrewsbury Twp	Yk	17349	A2	3687
GERMAN ST., Abbottstown	Ad	17301	C9	3371
GERMANY CT., Reading	Ad	17316	C7	3266
GERMANY RD., Reading	Ad	17316	H5	3265
GERMANY RD., Reading	Ad	17316	A6	3266
GERMANY RD., Reading	Ad	17316	A11	3267
GERNAND CT., Shrewsbury Twp	Yk	17349	F4	3688
GERRY LA., New Freedom	Yk	17349	G5	3687
GETTYS ST., Gettysburg	Ad	17325	B9	3471
GETTYSBURG CT., Littlestown	Ad	17340	E3	3681
GETTYSBURG RD., Germany	Ad	17340	H11	3576
GETTYSBURG RD., Germany	Ad	17340	A11	3577
GETTYSBURG RD., Germany	Ad	17340	H1	3680
GETTYSBURG RD., Germany	Ad	17340	A1	3681
GETTYSBURG ST., Arendtsville	Ad	17307	B3	3366
GETTYSBURG ST., Carroll	Yk	17019	C4	3056
GETTYSBURG ST., Dillsburg	Yk	17019	C4	3056
GETTYSBURG VILLAGE DR., Mount Joy	Ad	17325	G4	3575
GICHNER DR., York Twp	Yk	17313	H7	3376
GIFFORD'S LA., Cumberland	Ad	17325	A7	3471
GILBERT CT., Lower Windsor	Yk	17368	A10	3275
GILBERT DR., Dover Twp	Yk	17315	C10	3164
GILBERT LA., Lower Windsor	Yk	17368	A10	3275
GILBERT RD., Monaghan	Yk	17019	C7	2952
GILBERT RD., Windsor Twp	Yk	17356	H9	3377
GILBERT RD., Windsor Twp	Yk	17356	A9	3378
GILBERT ST., Oxford	Ad	17350	A2	3474
GILLESPIE DR., West Manchester	Yk	17404	C11	3270
GIN TR., Hamiltonban	Ad	17320	H11	3571
GINGER CIR., Hellam	Yk	17402	H2	3272
GINGER LA., North Codorus	Yk	17404	C5	3374
GINZEL RD., Tyrone	Ad	17350	D1	3369
GIPE RD., Chanceford	Yk	17309	F6	3379
GIPE RD., Chanceford	Yk	17322	E5	3379
GIRARD AV., York City	Yk	17403	E7	3271
GIRARD ST. E., Dallastown	Yk	17313	F8	3376
GIRL SCOUT RD., Liberty	Ad	17320	E6	3573
GITTINS DR., Franklin	Ad	17307	H8	3364
GITTS RUN RD., Heidelberg	Yk	17331	F8	3475
GITTS RUN RD., Penn	Yk	17331	F8	3475
GLADE RD., Penn	Yk	17331	E4	3579
GLADFELTER RD., Reading	Ad	17316	B9	3267
GLADFELTER ST., Loganville	Yk	17403	F4	3479
GLADHILL RD., Liberty	Ad	17320	F5	3675
GLADSTONE DR., Springettsbury	Yk	17402	F5	3272
GLADSTONE DR., Windsor Twp	Yk	17402	F5	3272
GLADYS CT., Penn	Yk	17331	G8	3579
GLADYS DR., Penn	Yk	17331	G7	3579
GLADYS TR., Carroll Valley	Ad	17320	F11	3572
GLATCO LODGE RD., Heidelberg	Yk	17331	G7	3475
GLATFELTER RD., Codorus	Yk	17360	G11	3477
GLATFELTER RD., Codorus	Yk	17360	A11	3478
GLATFELTER RD., Codorus	Yk	17362	G11	3477
GLATFELTER RD., Codorus	Yk	17362	F1	3581
GLATFELTERS STATION RD., North Codorus	Yk	17360	D10	3374
GLATFELTERS STATION RD., North Codorus	Yk	17360	E1	3478
GLATFELTERS STATION RD., Springfield	Yk	17360	A1	3479
GLEN ALLEN SCHOOL RD., Chanceford	Yk	17322	B7	3379
GLEN AV. N., Dallastown	Yk	17313	G7	3376
GLEN AV., Glen Rock	Yk	17327	C4	3583
GLEN AV., York Twp	Yk	17313	H8	3376
GLEN DR., East Manchester	Yk	17345	D4	3166
GLEN EAGLE DR., Manchester Twp	Yk	17404	F10	3165
GLEN HOLLOW DR., Dover Twp	Yk	17315	H11	3164
GLEN HOLLOW DR., Dover Twp	Yk	17315	A11	3165
GLEN HOLLOW DR., Dover Twp	Yk	17315	B2	3270
GLEN HOLLOW DR., Springettsbury	Yk	17402	H10	3166
GLEN PL., York City	Yk	17403	E6	3271
GLEN RIDGE CT., Shrewsbury Twp	Yk	17327	G4	3583
GLEN ROCK RD., Codorus	Yk	17327	G10	3478
GLEN ROCK RD., Codorus	Yk	17327	H1	3582
GLEN ROCK RD., Codorus	Yk	17327	A2	3583
GLEN ROCK RD., Codorus	Yk	17360	F7	3478
GLEN ROCK RD., North Codorus	Yk	17360	D5	3478
GLEN ROCK RD., Penn	Yk	17331	G3	3579
GLEN ROCK RD., Shrewsbury Twp	Yk	17327	A2	3583
GLEN ROCK RD., Springfield	Yk	17327	D11	3479
GLEN ROCK RD., Springfield	Yk	17327	A2	3583
GLEN VALLEY RD., Shrewsbury Twp	Yk	17327	F8	3583

Street	Co.	ZIP	Grid	Page
GLEN VALLEY RD., Shrewsbury Twp	Yk	17327	G3	3583
GLEN VALLEY RD., Springfield	Yk	17327	G11	3479
GLEN VIEW DR., Dover Twp	Yk	17315	D2	3269
GLENARDEN DR., Fairview	Yk	17339	E9	2953
GLENDALE RD., Spring Garden	Yk	17403	G10	3271
GLENDALE RD., Spring Garden	Yk	17403	H10	3271
GLENDALE RD., Spring Garden	Yk	17403	A10	3272
GLENDALE ST., Penn	Yk	17331	E2	3579
GLENHURST RD., Shrewsbury Boro	Yk	17361	A6	3584
GLENLEIGH DR., Manchester Twp	Yk	17404	C9	3165
GLENMAR DR., Jackson	Yk	17362	D8	3373
GLENMORE WAY, York Twp	Yk	17356	E10	3272
GLENN CARON CT., Carroll	Yk	17019	D3	3057
GLENNA RD., Lower Chanceford	Yk	17314	F8	3589
GLENVIEW CIR., Franklintown	Yk	17323	D9	3056
GLENVIEW DR., Franklintown	Yk	17323	E9	3056
GLENVIEW DR., Spring Garden	Yk	17403	A11	3271
GLENVIEW RD., Spring Grove	Yk	17362	B9	3373
GLENVILLE RD., Codorus	Yk	17327	H10	3581
GLENVILLE RD., Codorus	Yk	17327	A9	3582
GLENVILLE RD., Codorus	Yk	17327	B1	3686
GLENVILLE RD., Manheim	Yk	17327	F11	3581
GLENVILLE RD., Manheim	Yk	17327	D3	3685
GLENVILLE RD., Manheim	Yk	17329	F5	3684
GLENVILLE RD., Manheim	Yk	17329	A5	3685
GLENVILLE RD., West Manheim	Yk	17329	F5	3684
GLENVILLE RD., West Manheim	Yk	17331	D4	3684
GLENVUE RD., Glen Rock	Yk	17327	B5	3583
GLENVUE RD., Shrewsbury Twp	Yk	17327	B5	3583
GLENWOOD DR., Arendtsville	Ad	17307	C3	3366
GLENWOOD DR., Franklin	Ad	17325	A6	3470
GLENWOOD DR., Highland	Ad	17325	H7	3469
GLENWOOD DR., Highland	Ad	17325	A6	3470
GLENWOOD DR., Spring Garden	Yk	17403	C1	3375
GLENWOOD RD., Dover Twp	Yk	17315	H4	3269
GLENWOOD RD., Franklin	Yk	17019	C7	3056
GLENWOOD RD., Franklintown	Yk	17323	C7	3056
GLENWYN DR., Littlestown	Ad	17340	F1	3681
GLESSICK SCHOOL RD., Cross Roads	Yk	17322	A9	3482
GLESSICK SCHOOL RD., East Hopewell	Yk	17322	A7	3482
GLESSICK SCHOOL RD., North Hopewell	Yk	17322	H6	3481
GLESSICK SCHOOL RD., North Hopewell	Yk	17322	A7	3482
GLORIA DR., Springfield	Yk	17407	D1	3479
GNATSTOWN RD., Jackson	Yk	17331	A1	3476
GNATSTOWN RD., Paradise	Yk	17331	H2	3475
GNATSTOWN RD., Paradise	Yk	17331	A1	3476
GODFREY RD., Chanceford	Yk	17322	A4	3482
GODFREY RD., Felton	Yk	17322	A4	3482
GODFREY RD., Springfield	Yk	17327	C5	3480
GOETZ TR., Liberty	Ad	17320	F5	3573
GOHN LA. N., Red Lion	Yk	17356	B7	3377
GOHN LA. S., Red Lion	Yk	17356	B8	3377
GOLDEN CIRCLE LA., Shrewsbury Twp	Yk	17361	C10	3584
GOLDEN DALE DR., Lower Windsor	Yk	17402	F4	3273
GOLDEN DALE DR., Yorkana	Yk	17402	F4	3273
GOLDEN DR., Newberry	Yk	17319	E9	2955
GOLDEN EAGLE DR., West Manchester	Yk	17404	H7	3269
GOLDEN LA. E., New Oxford	Ad	17350	B2	3474
GOLDEN LA. W., New Oxford	Ad	17350	A2	3474
GOLDEN VILLA DR., Dover Twp	Yk	17315	F6	3269
GOLDEN WAY, West Manchester	Yk	17404	G6	3269
GOLDEN WAY, Windsor Twp	Yk	17402	H7	3272
GOLDEN WAY, Windsor Twp	Yk	17402	A8	3273
GOLDENVILLE RD., Butler	Ad	17325	F9	3366
GOLDENVILLE RD., Butler	Ad	17325	A8	3367
GOLDENVILLE RD., Franklin	Ad	17325	D9	3366
GOLDENVILLE RD., Straban	Ad	17325	A8	3367
GOLF CLUB AV., Carroll	Yk	17019	B4	3056
GOLF CLUB DR., Spring Garden	Yk	17403	H11	3270
GOLF COURSE RD., Carroll	Yk	17019	C5	3056
GOLF COURSE RD., Franklin	Ad	17222	D7	3363
GOLF DR., Dover Twp	Yk	17404	F9	3269
GOLF VIEW TR., Carroll Valley	Ad	17320	A10	3573
GOLLA CT., Hopewell	Yk	17363	H9	3585
GOOD INTENT RD., Straban	Ad	17325	E11	3367
GOOD INTENT RD., Straban	Ad	17325	D2	3471
GOOD RD., Chanceford	Yk	17302	F5	3483
GOOD RD., Lower Chanceford	Yk	17302	D11	3483
GOOD RD., Lower Chanceford	Yk	17302	F9	3483
GOODWIN LA., Hallam	Yk	17406	B11	3168
GOODYEAR RD., Huntington	Ad	17324	A4	3159
GOODYEAR RD., Huntington	Ad	17372	A4	3159
GOOSEVILLE RD., Reading	Ad	17350	G1	3369
GORA RD. N., Manchester Twp	Yk	17404	G11	3165
GORA RD. S., Manchester Twp	Yk	17404	G11	3165
GORAM RD., Chanceford	Yk	17309	D11	3380
GORAM RD., Chanceford	Yk	17309	D9	3380
GORAM RD., Lower Chanceford	Yk	17309	C5	3484
GORDON AV., Straban	Ad	17325	D6	3471
GORDON HOUSE RD., Chanceford	Yk	17309	C9	3380
GORDON RD., Freedom	Ad	17320	A11	3574
GOSLING DR., Hellam	Yk	17402	E8	3167
GOTHAM DR., York Twp	Yk	17356	A6	3377
GOTTEN LA., Menallen	Ad	17304	E4	3262
GOULDEN RD., Mount Joy	Ad	17325	F6	3575
GRABILL CT., Penn	Yk	17331	G4	3579
GRACE ST., Penn	Yk	17331	D5	3579
GRACE TER., Oxford	Ad	17350	E2	3474
GRACETON RD., Fawn	Yk	17321	D5	3692
GRACETON RD., Peach Bottom	Yk	17321	D5	3692
GRAFFIUS LA., Carroll	Yk	17019	G10	2951
GRAFFIUS RD., Conewago	Yk	17404	A9	3165
GRAHAM LA., Lower Windsor	Yk	17366	D3	3378
GRAHAM ST., Springettsbury	Yk	17403	F4	3271
GRANARY RD., Codorus	Yk	17327	G9	3478
GRANARY RD., Springfield	Yk	17360	G9	3478
GRANARY RD., Springfield	Yk	17360	A9	3479
GRAND AV. S., Dallastown	Yk	17313	G7	3376
GRAND AV., Red Lion	Yk	17356	D9	3377
GRAND MANOR RD., Hellam	Yk	17368	A5	3169
GRAND VALLEY RD., West Manheim	Yk	17331	A11	3579
GRAND VALLEY RD., West Manheim	Yk	17331	B1	3683
GRANDVIEW AV., Dover Twp	Yk	17404	H4	3269
GRANDVIEW AV., Dover Twp	Yk	17404	A4	3270
GRANDVIEW DR., Dover Twp	Yk	17315	D2	3269
GRANDVIEW DR., Newberry	Yk	17370	D11	2955
GRANDVIEW DR., Newberry	Yk	17370	E1	3060
GRANDVIEW DR., Newberry	Yk	17370	A3	3061
GRANDVIEW DR., York Twp	Yk	17403	E3	3375
GRANDVIEW PARK DR., West Manchester	Yk	17404	B3	3270
GRANDVIEW RD., Jackson	Yk	17362	D8	3373
GRANDVIEW RD., Jackson	Yk	17404	D8	3373
GRANDVIEW RD., Penn	Yk	17331	F7	3579
GRANDVIEW RD., Penn	Yk	17331	G3	3579
GRANDVIEW RD., Spring Garden	Yk	17403	G9	3271
GRANDVIEW RD., Windsor Twp	Yk	17356	A5	3377
GRANGER ST., Penn	Yk	17331	B5	3579
GRANITE QUARRY RD., Fairview	Yk	17070	G10	2849
GRANITE SCHOOLHOUSE RD., Cumberland	Ad	17325	C2	3575
GRANITE STATION RD., Mount Pleasant	Ad	17325	F8	3472
GRANITE STATION RD., Straban	Ad	17325	D11	3368
GRANITE STATION RD., Straban	Ad	17325	D1	3472
GRANT COVE, Reading	Ad	17316	D5	3266
GRANT DR., Hanover	Yk	17331	D11	3475
GRANT DR., Jackson	Yk	17404	E3	3373
GRANT DR., Mount Pleasant	Ad	17325	B11	3472
GRANT DR., Mount Pleasant	Ad	17325	B1	3576
GRANT DR., Springettsbury	Yk	17402	F10	3166
GRANT LA., Hellam	Yk	17406	B9	3168
GRANT RD. N., Jackson	Yk	17364	A2	3373
GRANT RD. S., Jackson	Yk	17364	B3	3373
GRANT RD., Springfield	Yk	17360	A1	3479
GRANT ST., York City	Yk	17401	B7	3271
GRANT ST., York City	Yk	17404	B7	3271
GRANTHAM RD. N., Monaghan	Yk	17019	A7	2952
GRANTHAM RD. N., Monaghan	Yk	17019	C7	2952
GRANTHAM RD. S., Monaghan	Yk	17019	C9	2952
GRANTLEY CT., Spring Garden	Yk	17403	B11	3271
GRANTLEY RD., Spring Garden	Yk	17403	C11	3271
GRANTLEY RD., Spring Garden	Yk	17403	D1	3375
GRANTLEY RD., York Twp	Yk	17403	D1	3375
GRANTLEY ST., York City	Yk	17404	B9	3271
GRANVIEW DR., Fairview	Yk	17339	E4	2954
GRASSHOPPER LA., Hamiltonban	Ad	17320	A7	3573
GRAVE RUN RD., Manheim	Yk	17327	A3	3686
GRAVEL HILL RD., East Manchester	Yk	17347	G10	3061
GRAVEL HILL RD., East Manchester	Yk	17347	A11	3062
GRAVEL HILL RD., East Manchester	Yk	17347	A1	3167
GRAVEL LA., Warrington	Yk	17315	E2	3163
GRAYBILL RD., West Manchester	Yk	17404	H6	3373
GRAYBILL RD., West Manchester	Yk	17404	B4	3374
GRAYDON RD., Springfield	Yk	17327	A6	3480
GRAYDON RD., Springfield	Yk	17360	A6	3480
GREEN BRANCH RD., Chanceford	Yk	17356	E11	3275
GREEN BRANCH RD., Chanceford	Yk	17356	C1	3379
GREEN BRANCH RD., Chanceford	Yk	17356	E1	3379
GREEN LANE DR., Fairview	Yk	17011	E6	2848
GREEN LANE DR., Penn	Yk	17331	A7	3579
GREEN MEADOWS DR., York Twp	Yk	17313	H8	3376
GREEN RD., Peach Bottom	Yk	17314	A5	3694
GREEN RIDGE LA., Codorus	Yk	17329	F7	3581
GREEN RIDGE RD., Franklin	Ad	17353	F10	3364
GREEN RIDGE RD., Franklin	Ad	17353	D5	3468
GREEN RIDGE RD., Hamilton	Ad	17350	D3	3370
GREEN RIDGE RD., Reading	Ad	17316	D2	3370
GREEN SPRING DR., Springettsbury	Yk	17402	A8	3272
GREEN SPRING RD., Conewago	Yk	17402	D6	3060
GREEN SPRING RD., Conewago	Yk	17404	D6	3060
GREEN SPRING RD., York Twp	Yk	17403	G1	3375
GREEN SPRINGS RD., Berwick	Ad	17331	H6	3474
GREEN SPRINGS RD., Berwick	Ad	17331	A4	3475
GREEN ST., Wellsville	Yk	17365	H2	3162
GREEN ST., York City	Yk	17404	B8	3271
GREEN TR., Carroll Valley	Ad	17320	A5	3677
GREEN VALLEY CT., Hopewell	Yk	17363	F6	3585
GREEN VALLEY RD., Codorus	Yk	17362	F10	3477
GREEN VALLEY RD., North Codorus	Yk	17360	F8	3477
GREEN VALLEY RD., North Codorus	Yk	17360	C5	3478
GREEN VALLEY RD., York Twp	Yk	17403	A7	3376
GREEN VALLEY RD., York Twp	Yk	17403	H8	3375
GREENAMYER LA., Straban	Ad	17325	D3	3472
GREENAWALT RD., Franklin	Ad	17222	H8	3363
GREENAWALT RD., Franklin	Ad	17222	A8	3364
GREENBRIAR DR., Jacobus	Yk	17407	E9	3375
GREENBRIAR LA., Cumberland	Ad	17325	F9	3470
GREENBRIAR LA., Dillsburg	Yk	17019	D2	3056
GREENBRIAR RD., Conewago	Yk	17404	A8	3165
GREENBRIAR RD., Huntington	Ad	17372	C3	3265
GREENBRIAR RD., Manchester Twp	Yk	17404	D10	3165
GREENBRIAR RD., Manchester Twp	Yk	17404	E1	3270
GREENBRIAR RD., Manchester Twp	Yk	17404	F1	3270
GREENDALE RD., Spring Garden	Yk	17403	F11	3271
GREENDALE RD., Spring Garden	Yk	17403	G10	3271
GREENDALE RD., Spring Garden	Yk	17403	E1	3375
GREENFIELD DR., Dover Twp	Yk	17315	B4	3269
GREENFIELD ST., East Manchester	Yk	17345	C4	3166
GREENHILL RD., Spring Garden	Yk	17403	H9	3271
GREENHOUSE RD., Franklin	Yk	17019	H4	3055
GREENHOUSE RD., Franklin	Yk	17019	A4	3056
GREENLEAF RD., Manchester Twp	Yk	17402	C1	3271
GREENMEADOW DR., West Manchester	Yk	17404	B1	3270
GREENMOUNT AV., Shrewsbury Boro	Yk	17361	A10	3584
GREENMOUNT CHURCH RD., Codorus	Yk	17327	A1	3582
GREENMOUNT CHURCH RD., Codorus	Yk	17362	A1	3582
GREENRIDGE LA., Springettsbury	Yk	17402	G9	3166
GREENSPRING DR., Conewago	Yk	17404	E1	3165
GREENTREE LA., Dover Twp	Yk	17315	G2	3269
GREENVIEW DR., Shrewsbury Boro	Yk	17361	B6	3584
GREENWAY DR., Springettsbury	Yk	17402	B9	3272
GREENWAY DR., York Twp	Yk	17356	A9	3377
GREENWICH RD., Peach Bottom	Yk	17314	B10	3589
GREENWOOD DR., Dover Twp	Yk	17404	A2	3270
GREENWOOD DR., Fairview	Yk	17070	D1	2954
GREENWOOD DR., Jackson	Yk	17362	B8	3373
GREENWOOD RD., West Manchester	Yk	17404	C7	3270
GREENWOOD RD., West Manchester	Yk	17404	D11	3270
GREESEY CT., Manchester Twp	Yk	17404	H2	3270
GREGG AV., Mount Pleasant	Ad	17325	B8	3472
GREGG LA., Mount Pleasant	Ad	17325	C11	3472
GREGORY RD., Heidelberg	Yk	17362	E10	3476
GRENWAY DR., Dover Twp	Yk	17315	G4	3269
GREY FOX CIR., Dover Twp	Yk	17315	G3	3269
GREYSTONE RD., Springettsbury	Yk	17402	D5	3272
GREYWOOD DR., Springettsbury	Yk	17402	H4	3272
GRIFFIN CT., New Freedom	Yk	17349	H5	3687
GRIFFITH LA., East Manchester	Yk	17345	C8	3061
GRIFFITH RD., Peach Bottom	Yk	17314	E5	3693
GRIFFITH ST., Stewartstown	Yk	17363	D11	3585
GRIM HOLLOW RD., Windsor Twp	Yk	17356	D11	3377
GRIM HOLLOW RD., Windsor Twp	Yk	17356	D1	3481
GRIM LA., Manchester Twp	Yk	17402	D10	3166
GRIM RD., North Hopewell	Yk	17322	D5	3481
GRIM RD., North Hopewell	Yk	17356	D5	3481
GRIST VALLEY RD., Hellam	Yk	17406	B8	3169
GROFT DR., Oxford	Ad	17350	H6	3473
GROFT DR., Oxford	Ad	17350	A6	3474
GROSS AV., Dover Twp	Yk	17315	C10	3164
GROSS CT., Manchester Twp	Yk	17404	H2	3270
GROSS RD., Fawn	Yk	17321	D4	3692
GROSS RD., Peach Bottom	Yk	17321	D4	3692
GROTHEY RD., North Codorus	Yk	17360	E2	3478
GROTON LA., Dover Twp	Yk	17315	G3	3269
GROUND OAK CHURCH RD., Huntington	Ad	17324	B11	3159
GROUND OAK CHURCH RD., Huntington	Ad	17324	A2	3264
GROUND OAK CHURCH RD., Huntington	Ad	17372	B11	3159
GROUP MILL RD., Reading	Ad	17350	F5	3369
GROUP MILL RD., Reading	Ad	17350	F7	3369
GROUSE RD., Dillsburg	Yk	17019	E4	3056
GROUSE TR., Carroll Valley	Ad	17320	G7	3572
GROVE LA., Lower Windsor	Yk	17368	G10	3274
GROVE MILL RD., East Hopewell	Yk	17363	F9	3586
GROVE MILL RD., Fawn	Yk	17363	F9	3586
GROVE MILL RD., Hopewell	Yk	17363	D10	3586
GROVE RD., Fawn	Yk	17363	F11	3586
GROVE RD., Fawn	Yk	17363	F1	3690
GROVE RD., Peach Bottom	Yk	17314	D8	3590
GROVE RD., Warrington	Yk	17315	F5	3163
GROVE RD., Windsor Twp	Yk	17356	D11	3377
GROVE RD., Windsor Twp	Yk	17356	E1	3481
GRUMBACHER RD., Manchester Twp	Yk	17402	A6	3166
GUERNSEY RD., Butler	Ad	17304	C10	3263
GUERNSEY RD., Butler	Ad	17307	C10	3263
GUERNSEY RD., Butler	Ad	17307	C1	3367
GUILDFORD AV., Manchester Twp	Yk	17404	C10	3164
GUINEVERE CT., Springettsbury	Yk	17402	G2	3271
GUINSTON FORGE RD., Chanceford	Yk	17302	A9	3483
GUINSTON RD., Chanceford	Yk	17302	B8	3483
GULTON RD., West Manchester	Yk	17404	C11	3270
GUM SPRINGS RD., Hamiltonban	Ad	17320	E11	3571
GUM TREE RD., Chanceford	Yk	17309	H11	3379
GUM TREE RD., Chanceford	Yk	17309	A9	3380
GUM TREE RD., Chanceford	Yk	17309	E2	3483
GUN CLUB RD., East Hopewell	Yk	17322	F3	3586
GUN CLUB RD., East Hopewell	Yk	17352	F5	3586
GUN CLUB RD., East Hopewell	Yk	17363	F5	3586
GUN CLUB RD., Franklin	Ad	17353	A10	3261
GUN CLUB RD., Hamilton	Ad	17350	A11	3370
GUN CLUB RD., Huntington	Ad	17372	A8	3265
GUN CLUB RD., Lower Windsor	Yk	17402	E8	3273
GUN CLUB RD., Lower Windsor	Yk	17406	E8	3273
GUN CLUB RD., Lower Windsor	Yk	17406	A8	3274
GUN CLUB RD., Menallen	Ad	17307	A10	3261
GUN CLUB RD., Menallen	Ad	17353	A10	3261
GUN CLUB RD., Tyrone	Ad	17372	H9	3264
GUN CLUB RD., Windsor Twp	Yk	17402	E8	3273
GUNNISON ST., York City	Yk	17404	A5	3271
GURTNER RD., Fairview	Yk	17070	C11	2849
GUT RD., East Manchester	Yk	17347	H7	3061
GUY ST., Hallam	Yk	17406	C11	3168
GUYRAY DR., Windsor Twp	Yk	17356	B2	3377
GWEN DR., Manchester Twp	Yk	17404	A2	3271

H

Street	Co.	ZIP	Grid	Page
H ST. N., York Spring	Ad	17372	B10	3160
H ST. S., York Spring	Ad	17372	A10	3160
HAAR RD., North Codorus	Yk	17362	G5	3476
HAAR RD., North Codorus	Yk	17362	A6	3477
HABELSTON RD., Shrewsbury Boro	Yk	17361	B10	3584
HACKBERRY DR., East Manchester	Yk	17347	G7	3166
HACKBERRY LA., Manchester Twp	Yk	17404	F8	3165
HACKNEY LA., Shrewsbury Boro	Yk	17327	H8	3583
HADLEIGH DR., West Manchester	Yk	17404	G3	3373
HADLEY DR., West Manchester	Yk	17404	F7	3269
HAILEAH CT., Dover Twp	Yk	17404	A3	3270
HAIN RD., Fairview	Yk	17070	B10	2849
HAIN RD., North Hopewell	Yk	17349	E3	3584
HAIN RD., Shrewsbury Twp	Yk	17349	C2	3584
HAINES LA., Red Lion	Yk	17356	B9	3377
HAINES RD., Springettsbury	Yk	17402	A7	3272
HAINES RD., Springettsbury	Yk	17402	A8	3272
HAKE RD., Chanceford	Yk	17322	D6	3379
HAKE RD., Conewago	Yk	17315	H6	3059
HAKE ST., Hallam	Yk	17406	C11	3168
HAKES HOLLOW RD., Lower Windsor	Yk	17368	F11	3274
HALE IRWIN DR., Newberry	Yk	17319	E6	2955
HALF DR., New Freedom	Yk	17349	G1	3687
HALL DR., East Manchester	Yk	17347	H2	3166
HALL DR., Monaghan	Yk	17019	C8	2952
HALL DR., Penn	Yk	17331	F4	3579
HALL LA., Hellam	Yk	17406	C8	3168
HALL ST., Stewartstown	Yk	17363	E10	3585
HALLECK DR., Reading	Ad	17316	B5	3266
HALLS RD., Chanceford	Yk	17356	E9	3378
HAMBILTONIAN WAY, Manchester Twp	Yk	17404	D11	3165
HAMBILTONIAN WAY, Manchester Twp	Yk	17404	D1	3270
HAMETOWN RD., Shrewsbury Twp	Yk	17327	E1	3583
HAMETOWN RD., Shrewsbury Twp	Yk	17327	E3	3583
HAMETOWN RD., Shrewsbury Twp	Yk	17327	G3	3583
HAMETOWN RD., Shrewsbury Twp	Yk	17349	A2	3584
HAMILTON AV., York City	Yk	17404	B7	3271
HAMILTON DR., Hamilton	Ad	17301	A7	3371
HAMILTON ST., Hanover	Yk	17331	A1	3579
HAMILTON ST., Springettsbury	Yk	17402	F3	3271
HAMLET DR. W., Spring Grove	Yk	17362	B9	3373
HAMME RD., Codorus	Yk	17362	H4	3581
HAMME RD., Codorus	Yk	17362	A4	3582
HAMME RD., Manheim	Yk	17329	B11	3581
HAMME RD., Manheim	Yk	17329	C11	3581
HAMMOND AV., Penn	Yk	17331	C4	3579
HAMMOND RD., Springettsbury	Yk	17402	F10	3166
HAMPSHIRE DR., Oxford	Ad	17350	B1	3474
HAMPSTEAD CT., York Twp	Yk	17403	C6	3376
HAMPTON CT., Windsor Twp	Yk	17356	G3	3376
HAMPTON DR., Reading	Ad	17316	B1	3370
HAMPTON LA., Mount Pleasant	Ad	17325	C10	3472
HAMPTON ST., West Manchester	Yk	17404	D4	3270
HANCOCK AV., Cumberland	Ad	17325	B1	3575
HANCOCK CT., New Freedom	Yk	17349	G3	3687
HANCOCK DR., Mount Joy	Ad	17325	A1	3576
HANCOCK DR., Mount Pleasant	Ad	17325	A1	3576
HANCOCK DR., Reading	Ad	17316	D1	3266
HANOVER PIKE, Conewago	Ad	17331	F8	3578
HANOVER PIKE, Union	Ad	17331	A11	3578
HANOVER PIKE, Union	Ad	17340	G11	3577
HANOVER PIKE, Union	Ad	17340	A11	3578
HANOVER RD., Bonneauville	Ad	17325	H1	3576
HANOVER RD., Conewago	Ad	17331	A3	3578
HANOVER RD., Gettysburg	Ad	17325	D8	3471
HANOVER RD., Jackson	Yk	17404	D6	3373
HANOVER RD., Mount Pleasant	Ad	17325	A1	3577
HANOVER RD., Mount Pleasant	Ad	17331	E2	3577
HANOVER RD., Mount Pleasant	Ad	17331	A3	3578
HANOVER RD., Straban	Ad	17325	D8	3471
HANOVER RD., Union	Ad	17331	E2	3577
HANOVER RD., Union	Ad	17331	A3	3578
HANOVER RD., West Manchester	Yk	17404	F4	3373
HANOVER ST. E., Biglerville	Ad	17307	A2	3367
HANOVER ST. W., Biglerville	Ad	17307	H2	3366
HANOVER ST. W., Biglerville	Ad	17307	A3	3367
HANOVER ST., Bonneauville	Ad	17325	B10	3472
HANOVER ST., Codorus	Yk	17362	C1	3581
HANOVER ST., Dillsburg	Yk	17019	D4	3056
HANOVER ST., Glen Rock	Yk	17327	B4	3583
HANOVER ST., Hanover	Yk	17331	D2	3579
HANOVER ST., Jefferson	Yk	17362	D11	3477
HANOVER ST., Mount Pleasant	Ad	17325	B10	3472
HANOVER ST., New Oxford	Ad	17350	B3	3474
HANOVER ST., Oxford	Ad	17331	G7	3474
HANOVER ST., Oxford	Ad	17350	B3	3474
HANOVER ST., Oxford	Ad	17350	D5	3474
HANOVER ST., Spring Grove	Yk	17362	A11	3373
HANOVER ST., Straban	Ad	17325	B10	3472
HAPPY HOLLOW LA., Lower Windsor	Yk	17368	A1	3275
HARBAUGH VALLEY RD., Liberty	Ad	17320	A5	3676
HARBOLD ATLAND RD., Washington	Yk	17365	C3	3162
HARBOR CT., Manheim	Yk	17331	F6	3580
HARBOR LA., Lower Windsor	Yk	17368	A6	3275
HARBORTOWN WAY, East Manchester	Yk	17347	F9	3061
HARDING CT., Yoe	Yk	17313	G6	3376
HARDING CT., York City	Yk	17403	D8	3271
HARDING ST., Manchester Boro	Yk	17345	D1	3166
HARGARMAN DR., West Manchester	Yk	17404	E7	3270
HARGET DR., West Manheim	Yk	17331	H2	3683
HARLACHER RD., Reading	Ad	17316	G2	3266
HARLAN ST., Springettsbury	Yk	17402	A5	3272
HARMANS WAY, Manheim	Yk	17329	B7	3581
HARMONY DR., Oxford	Ad	17350	D3	3474
HARMONY GROVE RD., Dover Twp	Yk	17315	A8	3163
HARMONY GROVE RD., Dover Twp	Yk	17315	A10	3164
HARMONY GROVE RD., Warrington	Yk	17315	A8	3163
HARMONY GROVE RD., Warrington	Yk	17365	F3	3162
HARMONY GROVE RD., Warrington	Yk	17365	G5	3162
HARMONY ROSE CT., Dover Twp	Yk	17315	C3	3269
HARNESS LA., Newberry	Yk	17319	F9	2955
HARNEY RD., Germany	Ad	17340	F4	3680
HARNEY RD., Germany	Ad	17340	A4	3681
HARNEY RD., Mount Joy	Ad	17340	G5	3679
HARNEY RD., Mount Joy	Ad	17340	A4	3680
HAROLD RD., North Codorus	Yk	17362	A4	3478
HAROLD ST., Hallam	Yk	17406	D10	3168
HARRISBURG PIKE, Carroll	Yk	17019	G9	2951
HARRISBURG PIKE, Carroll	Yk	17019	D2	3056
HARRISBURG PIKE, Dillsburg	Yk	17019	D2	3056
HARRISBURG ST. W., Dillsburg	Yk	17019	C3	3056
HARRISBURG ST., Dillsburg	Yk	17019	F3	3056
HARRISBURG ST., East Berlin	Ad	17316	C11	3267
HARRISBURG ST., Latimore	Ad	17372	B10	3160
HARRISBURG-BALTIMORE EXP., Fairview	Yk	17070	H7	2848
HARRISBURG-BALTIMORE EXP., Manchester Twp	Yk	17402	A5	3166
HARRISBURG-BALTIMORE EXP., Manchester Twp	Yk	17404	A5	3166
HARRISON DR., Mount Pleasant	Ad	17325	A1	3576
HARRISON RD., Shrewsbury Twp	Yk	17349	B1	3688
HARRISON ST. N., York City	Yk	17403	F5	3271
HARRISON ST. S., Spring Garden	Yk	17403	G6	3271
HARRISON ST. S., York City	Yk	17403	G6	3271
HARRISON ST., Springettsbury	Yk	17402	F3	3271

HARRISON ST., Springettsbury	Yk	17402	G2	3271
HARROWGATE RD., Springettsbury	Yk	17402	D6	3272
HARRY CT., Shrewsbury Twp	Yk	17349	B3	3584
HARTFORD RD., Springettsbury	Yk	17402	B8	3272
HARTLEY ST. N., York City	Yk	17404	A7	3271
HARTLEY ST. S., York City	Yk	17404	B8	3271
HARTLEY ST., York Twp	Yk	17404	H6	3270
HARTMAN AV., Hanover	Yk	17331	B4	3579
HARTMAN AV., Penn	Yk	17331	A5	3579
HARTMAN ST. N., York City	Yk	17403	F5	3271
HARTMAN ST. S., York City	Yk	17403	F6	3271
HARTMAN ST., Manchester Boro	Yk	17345	E11	3061
HARTMAN ST., Manchester Boro	Yk	17345	E1	3166
HARVARD ST., Manchester Twp	Yk	17404	B3	3271
HARVEST DR., Manchester Twp	Yk	17404	H1	3270
HARVEST DR., Manchester Twp	Yk	17404	A1	3271
HARVEST DR., Mount Pleasant	Ad	17325	E1	3576
HARVEST DR., Newberry	Yk	17319	E8	2955
HARVEST DR., York Twp	Yk	17313	E5	3376
HARVEST VIEW CT., Hopewell	Yk	17349	C6	3584
HARWICK PL., York City	Yk	17404	A3	3271
HARWICK RD., Dover Twp	Yk	17315	C4	3269
HASTINGS BLVD., Windsor Twp	Yk	17402	F9	3272
HATCHERY RD., Hellam	Yk	17406	E8	3168
HATHAWAY GARTH, Windsor Twp	Yk	17356	C3	3377
HAUER TER., Spring Grove	Yk	17362	B9	3373
HAUGH RD., East Hopewell	Yk	17363	C9	3586
HAUGH RD., Hellam	Yk	17368	D11	3169
HAUGH RD., Hopewell	Yk	17363	C9	3586
HAUGH RD., Lower Windsor	Yk	17368	D11	3169
HAUSER SCHOOL RD., Hellam	Yk	17406	G6	3168
HAVENWOOD RD., Carroll	Yk	17019	G6	3056
HAVERFORD CIR., Manchester Boro	Yk	17345	D11	3061
HAVERFORD CT., Manchester Boro	Yk	17345	E11	3061
HAVILAND RD., West Manchester	Yk	17404	E6	3270
HAWTHORN LA., Red Lion	Yk	17356	B9	3377
HAWTHORNE RD., Springettsbury	Yk	17402	H2	3271
HAWTHORNE ST. N., York City	Yk	17404	A8	3271
HAWTHORNE ST. N., York Twp	Yk	17404	H7	3270
HAWTHORNE ST. S., York City	Yk	17404	A9	3271
HAY ST. S., Gettysburg	Ad	17325	A9	3471
HAY ST., Gettysburg	Ad	17325	A8	3471
HAY ST., York City	Yk	17403	C6	3271
HAY ST., York City	Yk	17403	E5	3271
HAYBROOK DR., Manchester Twp	Yk	17402	C11	3166
HAYDEN HEIGHTS RD., West Manchester	Yk	17404	D6	3270
HAYES CT., Springfield	Yk	17360	A11	3375
HAYES CT., Springfield	Yk	17360	A1	3479
HAYFIELD CT., Shrewsbury Twp	Yk	17349	F5	3688
HAYLEY DR., Manchester Twp	Yk	17404	H11	3165
HAYLEY DR., Manchester Twp	Yk	17404	G1	3270
HAYMARKET CT., Manchester Twp	Yk	17402	C10	3166
HAYMEADOW DR., Manchester Twp	Yk	17402	C10	3166
HAYRICK RD., Heidelberg	Yk	17362	F7	3476
HAYRICK RD., North Codorus	Yk	17362	F7	3476
HAYSHIRE DR., Manchester Twp	Yk	17402	C1	3166
HAYWARD HEIGHTS, Glen Rock	Yk	17327	C3	3583
HAYWOOD DR., West Manchester	Yk	17404	C6	3270
HAZEL LA., Mount Pleasant	Ad	17350	F6	3473
HAZEL ST. E., Red Lion	Yk	17356	C6	3377
HAZEL ST. W., Red Lion	Yk	17356	B7	3377
HAZEL WAY, Menallen	Ad	17307	H6	3260
HAZEL WAY, Menallen	Ad	17307	A6	3261
HEARTHRIDGE LA., Manchester Twp	Yk	17404	H1	3270
HEARTHSTONE CT., Springettsbury	Yk	17402	F2	3272
HEATH LA., Manchester Twp	Yk	17404	H2	3270
HEATHER DR., North Codorus	Yk	17403	E5	3374
HEATHER DR., Stewartstown	Yk	17363	E11	3585
HEATHER DR., York Twp	Yk	17402	D1	3376
HEATHER GLEN DR., York Twp	Yk	17356	G4	3376
HEATHER RD., West Manchester	Yk	17404	C5	3270
HEATHER WAY, Chanceford	Yk	17322	A1	3482
HEATHER WAY, Conewago	Yk	17404	D2	3165
HEATHERFIELD WAY E., Windsor Twp	Yk	17356	B2	3377
HEATHERFIELD WAY W., Windsor Twp	Yk	17356	B2	3377
HEATHERWOOD DR., Carroll	Yk	17019	E9	2951
HEAVENLIGHT CIR., York Twp	Yk	17402	C9	3272
HEBEL RD., Shrewsbury Twp	Yk	17363	H4	3688
HEBEL RD., Shrewsbury Twp	Yk	17363	A4	3689
HECK HILL RD., Fairview	Yk	17339	B6	2954
HECK HILL RD., Lewisberry	Yk	17339	B6	2954
HECK HILL RD., Newberry	Yk	17339	B6	2954
HECKENLUBER RD., Menallen	Ad	17307	B11	3262
HECKENLUBER RD., Menallen	Ad	17307	B1	3366
HEDGE ROW, Straban	Ad	17325	E6	3471
HEDGEROW CT., Hanover	Yk	17331	C10	3475
HEDGEWICK LA., East Prospect	Yk	17317	F5	3274
HEDGEWICK LA., East Prospect	Yk	17368	F5	3274
HEEFNER RD., Menallen	Ad	17307	G4	3260
HEFFNER RD. E., Lower Chanceford	Yk	17309	D1	3484
HEFFNER RD. W., Chanceford	Yk	17309	B2	3484
HEFFNER RD. W., Lower Chanceford	Yk	17309	B2	3484
HEFFNER RD., Lower Windsor	Yk	17356	E6	3378
HEIDELBERG AV., Manchester Twp	Yk	17404	B3	3271
HEIDI RD., Peach Bottom	Yk	17314	B10	3589
HEIDLERSBURG RD., Butler	Ad	17304	F11	3263
HEIDLERSBURG RD., Butler	Ad	17307	C11	3263
HEIDLERSBURG RD., Butler	Ad	17307	B1	3367
HEIDLERSBURG RD., Tyrone	Ad	17304	A10	3264
HEIDLERSBURG RD., Tyrone	Ad	17325	D10	3264
HEIGHTS AV., Penn	Yk	17331	D4	3579
HEIGHTS CT., Abbottstown	Ad	17301	C10	3371
HEINDEL AV., Windsor Boro	Yk	17366	F4	3377
HEINDEL RD., Codorus	Yk	17360	C7	3478
HEINDEL RD., North Codorus	Yk	17360	F5	3374
HEINDEL RD., North Codorus	Yk	17403	F5	3374
HEINDEL RD., Springettsbury	Yk	17402	E2	3272
HEISTAND RD., Springettsbury	Yk	17402	F1	3272
HELB ST., Railroad	Yk	17355	G11	3583
HELEN AV., Cumberland	Ad	17325	C4	3471
HELEN TR., Carroll Valley	Ad	17320	F10	3572
HELLAM ST., Wrightsville	Yk	17368	C7	3169
HELLER LA., Hellam	Yk	17406	A6	3168
HEMLER DR., West Manheim	Yk	17331	H11	3579
HEMLOCK CT., Hanover	Yk	17331	D11	3475
HEMLOCK CT., Manchester Boro	Yk	17345	E2	3166
HEMLOCK DR., Dover Twp	Yk	17404	A2	3270
HEMLOCK DR., Fairview	Yk	17070	H9	2848
HEMLOCK DR., Fairview	Yk	17070	A9	2849
HEMLOCK DR., Tyrone	Ad	17325	D10	3264
HEMLOCK HILL RD., Peach Bottom	Yk	17302	B8	3589
HEMLOCK HOLLOW RD., Peach Bottom	Yk	17302	H9	3588
HEMLOCK LA., Lower Chanceford	Yk	17314	H2	3589
HEMLOCK LA., Newberry	Yk	17319	B6	2955
HEMLOCK LA., Red Lion	Yk	17356	B9	3377
HEMLOCK RD., Conewago	Yk	17345	F5	3060
HEMLOCK RD., Newberry	Yk	17319	C6	2955
HEMLOCK ST., Stewartstown	Yk	17363	D11	3585
HEMLOCK TR., Carroll Valley	Ad	17320	H10	3572
HEMLOCK TR., Carroll Valley	Ad	17320	A11	3573
HEMLOCK TR., Franklin	Ad	17353	F9	3260
HEMPFIELD DR., West Manchester	Yk	17404	A7	3270
HENDLE RD., Railroad	Yk	17355	H9	3583
HENGST CT., Hallam	Yk	17406	B1	3273
HENRIETTA ST., Red Lion	Yk	17356	C7	3377
HENRY LA., Windsor Twp	Yk	17402	D7	3272
HENRY ST., Penn	Yk	17331	A8	3579
HEPPLEWHITE DR., Manchester Twp	Yk	17404	E11	3165
HERBST RD., North Hopewell	Yk	17356	B2	3481
HERBST RD., North Hopewell	Yk	17356	D3	3481
HERBST RD., Windsor Twp	Yk	17356	B2	3481
HERITAGE CT., Oxford	Ad	17350	B2	3474
HERITAGE DR., Mount Joy	Ad	17325	G11	3471
HERITAGE DR., Mount Joy	Ad	17325	G3	3575
HERITAGE DR., Mount Joy	Ad	17325	H3	3575
HERITAGE DR., Mount Joy	Ad	17325	A2	3576
HERITAGE DR., Mount Pleasant	Ad	17325	A11	3472
HERITAGE DR., Springettsbury	Yk	17402	E5	3272
HERITAGE DR., Straban	Ad	17325	A11	3472
HERITAGE FARM DR., Shrewsbury Twp	Yk	17349	F5	3688
HERITAGE HILLS CIR., York Twp	Yk	17402	B10	3272
HERITAGE HILLS DR., York Twp	Yk	17402	B10	3272
HERITAGE VIEW DR., Springettsbury	Yk	17402	B8	3272
HERMAN AV., West Manchester	Yk	17404	H9	3270
HERMAN CT., Springettsbury	Yk	17402	G2	3271
HERMAN DR., West Manchester	Yk	17404	B3	3270
HERMAN DR., West Manchester	Yk	17404	C4	3270
HERMAN RD., Straban	Ad	17325	H5	3367
HERMAN RD., Straban	Ad	17325	A5	3368
HERRLYN CT., York Twp	Yk	17313	D6	3376
HERRLYN CT., York Twp	Yk	17313	D7	3376
HERR'S RIDGE RD., Cumberland	Ad	17325	A11	3367
HERR'S RIDGE RD., Cumberland	Ad	17325	E9	3470
HERR'S RIDGE RD., Cumberland	Ad	17325	G6	3470
HERR'S RIDGE RD., Cumberland	Ad	17325	A1	3471
HERSH RD., Washington	Yk	17019	E3	3161
HERSHEY CIR., Hopewell	Yk	17363	C10	3585
HERSHEY CT., Manchester Twp	Yk	17404	H2	3270
HERSHEY HEIGHTS RD., Berwick	Ad	17331	G8	3474
HERSHEY HEIGHTS RD., Berwick	Ad	17331	A8	3475
HERSHEY HEIGHTS RD., Penn	Yk	17331	B7	3475
HERSHEY RD., Jackson	Yk	17362	C10	3373
HERSHEY RD., North Codorus	Yk	17362	C11	3373
HERSHEY RD., North Codorus	Yk	17362	D1	3477
HESS FARM DR., York Twp	Yk	17313	D1	3480
HESS FARM RD., Springfield	Yk	17403	F9	3375
HESS FARM RD., York Twp	Yk	17313	D11	3376
HESS FARM RD., York Twp	Yk	17313	C10	3376
HESS FARM RD., York Twp	Yk	17403	A10	3376
HESS LA., Red Lion	Yk	17356	A7	3377
HESS RD., Hopewell	Yk	17363	A4	3585
HESS RD., Hopewell	Yk	17363	C3	3585
HESS RD., North Hopewell	Yk	17363	C3	3585
HESS RD., North York	Yk	17404	C5	3271
HESS RD., West Manchester	Yk	17404	E7	3270
HETH ST., Cumberland	Ad	17325	F6	3470
HICKORY AV., Bonneauville	Ad	17325	H1	3576
HICKORY BRIDGE RD., Franklin	Ad	17353	A5	3469
HICKORY BRIDGE RD., Hamiltonban	Ad	17353	A5	3469
HICKORY CT., Bonneauville	Ad	17340	H2	3576
HICKORY CT., Dover Twp	Yk	17315	F7	3164
HICKORY CT., Newberry	Yk	17315	D4	3059
HICKORY CT., West Manheim	Yk	17331	H1	3683
HICKORY DR., East Manchester	Yk	17345	C5	3166
HICKORY DR., Menallen	Ad	17304	E2	3262
HICKORY DR., Tyrone	Ad	17325	E10	3264
HICKORY HILL LA., Springettsbury	Yk	17402	C7	3272
HICKORY LA. N., Reading	Ad	17350	H6	3369
HICKORY LA. S., Reading	Ad	17350	H7	3369
HICKORY LA., Jackson	Yk	17364	B5	3373
HICKORY LA., Manchester Twp	Yk	17404	F10	3165
HICKORY LA., Penn	Yk	17331	D7	3475
HICKORY LA., Red Lion	Yk	17356	B9	3377
HICKORY LA., Union	Ad	17340	F10	3577
HICKORY NUT RD., Shrewsbury Twp	Yk	17361	C10	3584
HICKORY PL., Fairview	Yk	17011	F6	2848
HICKORY RD., Bonneauville	Ad	17325	G2	3576
HICKORY RD., Bonneauville	Ad	17340	G2	3576
HICKORY RD., East Hopewell	Yk	17322	E3	3586
HICKORY RD., East Hopewell	Yk	17363	H6	3585
HICKORY RD., East Hopewell	Yk	17363	A6	3586
HICKORY RD., East Hopewell	Yk	17363	B4	3586
HICKORY RD., Franklin	Yk	17019	H8	3055
HICKORY RD., Hopewell	Yk	17363	E8	3585
HICKORY RD., Mount Joy	Ad	17340	E7	3576
HICKORY RD., Mount Pleasant	Ad	17340	G4	3576
HICKORY RD., Stewartstown	Yk	17363	D11	3585
HICKORY ST., Newberry	Yk	17370	G1	3060
HICKORY TR., Carroll Valley	Ad	17320	G5	3676
HICKORY TREE PL., Carroll	Yk	17019	B2	3056
HICKORY VIEW DR., North Codorus	Yk	17362	E2	3477
HIDDEN ACRES DR., Oxford	Ad	17350	A4	3474
HIDDEN CREEK RD., Franklin	Yk	17019	B4	3161
HIDDEN FARM LA., Lower Windsor	Yk	17406	H3	3273
HIDDEN HILL FARM LA., Jacobus	Yk	17407	F11	3375
HIDDEN HILL FARM LA., Jacobus	Yk	17407	F1	3479
HIDDEN HILL FARM LA., Springfield	Yk	17407	F1	3479
HIDDEN LA., Jackson	Yk	17364	D1	3373
HIDDEN SPRINGS RD., Carroll	Yk	17019	H11	2951
HIDDEN VALLEY RD., Fairview	Yk	17070	C1	2954
HIDDEN VALLEY RD., Springfield	Yk	17360	C6	3479
HIDEAWAY LA., Lower Windsor	Yk	17368	B10	3275
HIDEAWAY TR., Carroll Valley	Ad	17320	H4	3676
HIGH DR., Fairview	Yk	17070	B10	2849
HIGH POINT RD., North Hopewell	Yk	17322	C9	3481
HIGH RD., Menallen	Ad	17324	A8	3158
HIGH RD., Tyrone	Ad	17324	A8	3158
HIGH RIDGE RD., Peach Bottom	Yk	17314	C10	3589
HIGH ROCK LA., Springettsbury	Yk	17402	D11	3167
HIGH ROCK RD. N., Heidelberg	Yk	17331	F4	3475
HIGH ROCK RD. W., Heidelberg	Yk	17331	G3	3475
HIGH ROCK RD., Berwick	Ad	17331	D3	3475
HIGH ROCK RD., East Hopewell	Yk	17302	C11	3483
HIGH ROCK RD., East Hopewell	Yk	17302	G2	3586
HIGH ROCK RD., East Hopewell	Yk	17302	A2	3587
HIGH ROCK RD., East Hopewell	Yk	17352	G2	3586
HIGH ROCK RD., Hamiltonban	Ad	17222	H10	3467
HIGH ROCK RD., Hamiltonban	Ad	17222	F3	3571
HIGH ROCK RD., Lower Chanceford	Yk	17302	C11	3483
HIGH ROCK RD., Paradise	Yk	17301	D3	3475
HIGH ROCK RD., Penn	Yk	17331	F7	3475
HIGH ST. E., Gettysburg	Ad	17325	C9	3471
HIGH ST. E., New Freedom	Yk	17349	G3	3687
HIGH ST. E., New Oxford	Ad	17350	B2	3474
HIGH ST. E., Red Lion	Yk	17356	C7	3377
HIGH ST. E., Windsor Boro	Yk	17366	F4	3377
HIGH ST. E., Yoe	Yk	17313	G5	3376
HIGH ST. N., Dallastown	Yk	17313	H7	3376
HIGH ST. S., Arendtsville	Ad	17307	B3	3366
HIGH ST. W., Gettysburg	Ad	17325	B9	3471
HIGH ST. W., New Freedom	Yk	17349	F3	3687
HIGH ST. W., New Oxford	Ad	17350	A3	3474
HIGH ST. W., Red Lion	Yk	17356	B7	3377
HIGH ST. W., Windsor Boro	Yk	17366	E4	3377
HIGH ST. W., Yoe	Yk	17313	G5	3376
HIGH ST., Abbottstown	Ad	17301	B9	3371
HIGH ST., Biglerville	Ad	17307	H2	3366
HIGH ST., Conewago	Ad	17331	H9	3474
HIGH ST., Dover Twp	Yk	17404	H4	3269
HIGH ST., Dover Twp	Yk	17404	A4	3270
HIGH ST., Felton	Yk	17322	H3	3481
HIGH ST., Franklin	Ad	17353	C9	3365
HIGH ST., Glen Rock	Yk	17327	C3	3583
HIGH ST., Hanover	Yk	17331	A11	3475
HIGH ST., Hanover	Yk	17331	A2	3579
HIGH ST., Hanover	Yk	17331	A1	3579
HIGH ST., Hopewell	Yk	17363	C9	3585
HIGH ST., Manchester Boro	Yk	17345	D11	3061
HIGH ST., Manchester Boro	Yk	17345	D1	3166
HIGH ST., Manchester Twp	Yk	17402	C8	3166
HIGH ST., Newberry	Yk	17319	C10	2955
HIGH ST., Penn	Yk	17331	A11	3475
HIGH ST., Penn	Yk	17331	C4	3579
HIGH ST., Spring Grove	Yk	17362	A11	3373
HIGH ST., Stewartstown	Yk	17363	D9	3585
HIGH ST., West Manchester	Yk	17404	C5	3270
HIGH ST., Windsor Twp	Yk	17322	H3	3481
HIGH ST., York Spring	Ad	17372	B10	3160
HIGH TR., Carroll Valley	Ad	17320	F11	3572
HIGH TR., Carroll Valley	Ad	17320	F1	3676
HIGHFIELD RD., Peach Bottom	Yk	17302	B9	3589
HIGHLAND AV. N., West York	Yk	17404	G8	3270
HIGHLAND AV. S., West Manchester	Yk	17404	G9	3270
HIGHLAND AV., Dover Twp	Yk	17315	H2	3269
HIGHLAND AV., Gettysburg	Ad	17325	B11	3471
HIGHLAND AV., Hamilton	Ad	17301	A8	3371
HIGHLAND AV., Hanover	Yk	17331	B1	3579
HIGHLAND AV., Mount Joy	Ad	17325	G11	3471
HIGHLAND AV., Newberry	Yk	17345	D8	3061
HIGHLAND AV., Newberry	Yk	17345	E7	3061
HIGHLAND AV., Spring Grove	Yk	17362	A11	3373
HIGHLAND AV., Straban	Ad	17325	G11	3471
HIGHLAND CIR., Newberry	Yk	17319	B6	2955
HIGHLAND DR. N., Shrewsbury Boro	Yk	17361	B7	3584
HIGHLAND DR. N., Shrewsbury Boro	Yk	17361	B8	3584
HIGHLAND DR., Fairview	Yk	17055	C6	2953
HIGHLAND DR., Red Lion	Yk	17356	B9	3377
HIGHLAND DR., Union	Ad	17331	F2	3682
HIGHLAND LA., Chanceford	Yk	17309	E7	3380
HIGHLAND MANOR DR., Stewartstown	Yk	17363	D10	3585
HIGHLAND MEADOW CT., New Freedom	Yk	17349	G5	3687
HIGHLAND RD., Codorus	Yk	17360	F11	3477
HIGHLAND RD., Jefferson	Yk	17311	F11	3477
HIGHLAND RD., Loganville	Yk	17360	E3	3479
HIGHLAND RD., Mount Joy	Ad	17325	G2	3575
HIGHLAND RD., Spring Garden	Yk	17403	E10	3271
HIGHLAND TER., Spring Garden	Yk	17403	C11	3271
HIGHLANDS PATH, York Twp	Yk	17402	D11	3272
HIGHVIEW DR., West Manheim	Yk	17331	H10	3579
HIGHVIEW RD., Peach Bottom	Yk	17302	H7	3588
HIKEY ST., Dover Twp	Yk	17315	C2	3269
HILDEBRAND DR., Manchester Twp	Yk	17402	D2	3271
HILDEBRAND RD., Codorus	Yk	17327	F4	3686
HILDERBRAND RD., Codorus	Yk	17327	H11	3582
HILL & DALE RD., Codorus	Yk	17327	B4	3582
HILL AV., Glen Rock	Yk	17327	B4	3583
HILL AV., Newberry	Yk	17370	E1	3060
HILL CLIMB RD., Codorus	Yk	17362	C3	3581
HILL DR., Newberry	Yk	17370	D1	3060
HILL DR., Reading	Ad	17316	C4	3266
HILL POINT DR., Goldsboro	Yk	17319	H5	2955
HILL RD. S., Springettsbury	Yk	17402	G10	3166
HILL RD., Lower Chanceford	Yk	17314	D8	3589
HILL RD., Mount Pleasant	Ad	17331	H11	3473
HILL RD., Mount Pleasant	Ad	17331	A10	3474
HILL RD., Peach Bottom	Yk	17314	H4	3693
HILL RD., Shrewsbury Twp	Yk	17349	B4	3688
HILL RD., Springfield	Yk	17313	A3	3480
HILL RD., Springfield	Yk	17403	H2	3479
HILL ST. E., Winterstown	Yk	17322	B7	3481
HILL ST. N., Dallastown	Yk	17313	H7	3376
HILL ST. W., Winterstown	Yk	17322	H7	3480
HILL ST. W., Winterstown	Yk	17322	A7	3481
HILL ST., Chanceford	Yk	17322	E2	3379
HILL ST., East Manchester	Yk	17345	D9	3061
HILL ST., North Hopewell	Yk	17356	C5	3481
HILL ST., Penn	Yk	17331	C5	3579
HILL ST., Railroad	Yk	17355	G10	3583
HILL ST., Shrewsbury Boro	Yk	17361	A8	3584
HILL ST., Spring Garden	Yk	17403	G6	3271
HILL ST., Spring Garden	Yk	17403	G8	3271
HILL ST., Spring Garden	Yk	17403	G8	3271
HILL ST., Stewartstown	Yk	17363	D10	3585
HILL ST., Stewartstown	Yk	17363	D11	3585
HILL TOP RD., Latimore	Ad	17372	H3	3159
HILL TOP TR., Carroll Valley	Ad	17320	G11	3572
HILL VIEW RD., Hellam	Yk	17406	E10	3168
HILL VIEW RD., Hellam	Yk	17406	E1	3273
HILL VIEW RD., Menallen	Ad	17324	H10	3157
HILL VIEW RD., Menallen	Ad	17324	A10	3158
HILLCREST AV., Shrewsbury Boro	Yk	17349	C7	3584
HILLCREST AV., York Twp	Yk	17356	A8	3377
HILLCREST CIR., Newberry	Yk	17319	B6	2955
HILLCREST DR., Biglerville	Ad	17307	H2	3366
HILLCREST DR., Butler	Ad	17307	H2	3366
HILLCREST DR., Dillsburg	Yk	17019	D2	3056
HILLCREST DR., Fairview	Yk	17070	C1	2954
HILLCREST DR., Paradise	Yk	17301	F10	3371
HILLCREST DR., West Manheim	Yk	17331	F1	3683
HILLCREST LA., Codorus	Yk	17362	F11	3477
HILLCREST LA., Jefferson	Yk	17362	F11	3477
HILLCREST PL., Gettysburg	Ad	17325	C9	3471
HILLCREST RD., Franklin	Ad	17222	H9	3363
HILLCREST RD., Franklin	Ad	17222	A9	3364
HILLCREST RD., Jackson	Yk	17362	F11	3372
HILLCREST RD., Jackson	Yk	17362	F1	3476
HILLCREST RD., Spring Garden	Yk	17403	F11	3271
HILLCREST RD., Spring Garden	Yk	17403	G10	3271
HILLCREST RD., Spring Garden	Yk	17403	G11	3271
HILLCREST RD., York Twp	Yk	17403	F11	3271
HILLCREST RD., York Twp	Yk	17403	F1	3375
HILLCROFT AV., Spring Garden	Yk	17403	G9	3271
HILLCROFT LA., Spring Garden	Yk	17403	F10	3271
HILLDALE RD., Newberry	Yk	17319	F8	2954
HILLERY CT., Springettsbury	Yk	17402	A8	3272
HILL-N-DALE CT., York Twp	Yk	17403	H1	3375
HILL-N-DALE DR. N., York Twp	Yk	17403	G1	3375
HILL-N-DALE DR. S., York Twp	Yk	17403	G1	3375
HILL-N-DALE RD., Conewago	Yk	17345	F5	3060
HILL-N-DALE RD., Peach Bottom	Yk	17314	H3	3694
HILLOCK LA., Spring Garden	Yk	17403	F10	3271
HILL'S DR., Cumberland	Ad	17325	A9	3471
HILLSIDE AV., Fairview	Yk	17070	D1	2954
HILLSIDE CT., Springettsbury	Yk	17402	F3	3271
HILLSIDE DR. S., Butler	Ad	17307	G1	3366
HILLSIDE DR., Butler	Ad	17307	G1	3366
HILLSIDE DR., East Berlin	Ad	17316	C1	3371
HILLSIDE DR., Franklin	Ad	17353	G1	3468
HILLSIDE DR., Jacobus	Yk	17407	C10	3375
HILLSIDE DR., Red Lion	Yk	17356	B9	3377
HILLSIDE DR., Spring Garden	Yk	17403	D10	3271
HILLSIDE LA., Newberry	Yk	17319	B9	2955
HILLSIDE LA., North Codorus	Yk	17362	H3	3476
HILLSIDE LA., Spring Garden	Yk	17403	F10	3271
HILLSIDE RD., North Codorus	Yk	17362	B2	3477
HILLSIDE RD., Paradise	Yk	17301	H10	3371
HILLSIDE RD., Paradise	Yk	17362	H10	3371
HILLSIDE RD., Paradise	Yk	17362	A10	3372
HILLSIDE RD., Penn	Yk	17331	E7	3579
HILLSIDE TER., Glen Rock	Yk	17327	C4	3583
HILLSIDE TER., West Manchester	Yk	17404	D8	3270
HILLSIDE TR., Franklin	Ad	17353	F8	3260
HILLSTREAM RD., Windsor Twp	Yk	17356	G2	3376
HILLTOP CT., Shrewsbury Twp	Yk	17349	C5	3688
HILLTOP DR. E., Heidelberg	Yk	17362	E7	3476
HILLTOP DR. S., Heidelberg	Yk	17362	E6	3476
HILLTOP DR., Dover Twp	Yk	17404	A3	3270
HILLTOP DR., Newberry	Yk	17319	D11	2955
HILLTOP DR., Springettsbury	Yk	17402	G11	3166
HILLTOP LA., Jackson	Yk	17362	D6	3372
HILLTOP PL., Jacobus	Yk	17407	F1	3479
HILLTOP PL., Spring Garden	Yk	17403	C1	3375
HILLTOP PL., Springfield	Yk	17407	F1	3479
HILLTOP RD., Chanceford	Yk	17309	E7	3379
HILLTOP RD., North Codorus	Yk	17404	C5	3374
HILLTOP RD., Peach Bottom	Yk	17314	B10	3589
HILLTOWN RD., Franklin	Ad	17307	G8	3364
HILLTOWN RD., Franklin	Ad	17307	A8	3365
HILLTOWN RD., Franklin	Ad	17325	A10	3366
HILLVIEW CT., Dover Twp	Yk	17315	C4	3269
HILLVIEW CT., Fairfield	Ad	17320	B5	3573
HILLVIEW DR., East Manchester	Yk	17347	A3	3167
HILLVIEW RD., Peach Bottom	Yk	17302	G7	3588
HILTON AV., Conewago	Yk	17404	A11	3165
HILTON AV., Dover Twp	Yk	17315	H3	3269
HILTON AV., Dover Twp	Yk	17315	A1	3270
HILTON AV., Dover Twp	Yk	17404	A11	3165
HILTS RD., Lower Windsor	Yk	17368	F11	3169
HINES DR., Latimore	Ad	17316	B2	3266
HIRSCHMANN RD., Menallen	Ad	17307	H4	3260
HIRTLAND AV., Penn	Yk	17331	F2	3579
HITCHING POST CIR., Jackson	Yk	17364	A2	3373
HIVELY RD., Chanceford	Yk	17309	C11	3380
HIVELY RD., Chanceford	Yk	17309	A3	3484

HOBART RD., West Manheim	Yk	17331	C4	3684
HOBART RD., West Manheim	Yk	17331	E1	3684
HOBROOK AV., Manchester Twp	Yk	17404	H5	3165
HOFF RD., Heidelberg	Yk	17362	G11	3476
HOFF RD., Heidelberg	Yk	17362	E2	3580
HOFF RD., North Codorus	Yk	17360	H5	3477
HOFF RD., North Codorus	Yk	17360	A6	3478
HOFF RD., Penn	Yk	17331	A3	3580
HOFFACKER RD., Manheim	Yk	17329	F1	3684
HOFFACKER RD., Manheim	Yk	17329	A5	3685
HOFFACKER RD., Mount Pleasant	Ad	17340	E4	3577
HOFFACKER RD., Union	Ad	17340	E4	3577
HOFFHEINS DR., New Freedom	Yk	17349	H3	3687
HOFFMAN CT., Washington	Yk	17316	D9	3267
HOFFMAN HOME RD., Mount Joy	Ad	17325	C11	3576
HOFFMAN HOME RD., Mount Joy	Ad	17340	A4	3680
HOFFMAN RD., Latimore	Ad	17372	E5	3160
HOFFMAN RD., Lower Windsor	Yk	17366	D8	3274
HOFFMAN RD., Spring Garden	Yk	17403	G10	3271
HOFFMAN RD., Straban	Ad	17325	A9	3472
HOFFMAN RD., Washington	Yk	17316	D3	3267
HOFFMAN ST., Hanover	Yk	17331	B3	3579
HOGANS COVE, Manchester Twp	Yk	17404	E1	3270
HOKE DR., Straban	Ad	17325	E5	3471
HOKE RD., North Codorus	Yk	17360	B2	3478
HOKE ST., Spring Grove	Yk	17362	A11	3373
HOKE ST., West Manchester	Yk	17404	H9	3270
HOKE ST., West York	Yk	17404	H9	3270
HOKES MILL RD., Spring Garden	Yk	17403	G1	3374
HOKES MILL RD., West Manchester	Yk	17403	G1	3374
HOKES MILL RD., West Manchester	Yk	17404	F9	3270
HOKES MILL RD., West Manchester	Yk	17404	G1	3374
HOKES RD., Manheim	Yk	17327	E3	3685
HOLBROOK AV., Springettsbury	Yk	17402	F1	3272
HOLIDAY DR., Shrewsbury Boro	Yk	17361	A6	3584
HOLIDAY TR., Carroll Valley	Ad	17320	F10	3572
HOLLOW CREEK RD., Newberry	Yk	17315	E4	3059
HOLLOW CREEK RD., Springfield	Yk	17403	D2	3479
HOLLOW RD., East Hopewell	Yk	17322	B6	3482
HOLLOW RD., Fawn	Yk	17352	G1	3690
HOLLOW RD., Franklin	Ad	17222	F7	3363
HOLLOW RD., Hopewell	Yk	17363	F10	3585
HOLLOW RD., Latimore	Ad	17372	A1	3160
HOLLOW RD., North Hopewell	Yk	17322	A5	3482
HOLLOW RD., Peach Bottom	Yk	17314	F5	3692
HOLLOW RD., Peach Bottom	Yk	17314	A2	3693
HOLLY CT., Bonneauville	Ad	17340	H2	3576
HOLLY CT., East Manchester	Yk	17345	D3	3166
HOLLY CT., Fairview	Yk	17339	F5	2954
HOLLY CT., Hanover	Yk	17331	B11	3475
HOLLY CT., Hellam	Yk	17406	A11	3169
HOLLY CT., North Codorus	Yk	17360	E9	3374
HOLLY DR., East Manchester	Yk	17347	H2	3166
HOLLY DR., Fairview	Yk	17070	G8	2848
HOLLY DR., Red Lion	Yk	17356	B6	3377
HOLLY HILL DR., York Twp	Yk	17313	H7	3376
HOLLY LA. E., Newberry	Yk	17319	F7	2955
HOLLY LA. W., Newberry	Yk	17319	F7	2955
HOLLY LA., Glen Rock	Yk	17327	B3	3583
HOLLY LA., Mount Joy	Ad	17325	H4	3575
HOLLY LA., Mount Joy	Ad	17325	A4	3576
HOLLY LA., Red Lion	Yk	17356	D8	3377
HOLLY LA., West Manchester	Yk	17404	F7	3270
HOLLY RD., Dover Twp	Yk	17315	F3	3269
HOLLY RD., Shrewsbury Twp	Yk	17327	B9	3583
HOLLY TR., Peach Bottom	Yk	17314	A9	3589
HOLLY TREE CT., Cross Roads	Yk	17322	G11	3481
HOLLYWOOD AV., Hanover	Yk	17331	D10	3475
HOLLYWOOD AV., New Oxford	Ad	17350	A3	3474
HOLLYWOOD DR., Spring Garden	Yk	17403	G9	3271
HOLLYWOOD DR., York Twp	Yk	17403	G9	3271
HOLLYWOOD PKWY., Spring Garden	Yk	17403	H9	3271
HOLLYWOOD TER., Spring Garden	Yk	17403	H9	3271
HOLMGREN LA., Lower Windsor	Yk	17366	D2	3378
HOLTSCHWAM RD., Jackson	Yk	17364	D11	3268
HOLTSCHWAM RD., Paradise	Yk	17364	D11	3268
HOLTWOOD RD., Lower Chanceford	Yk	17302	C3	3589
HOLTWOOD RD., Lower Chanceford	Yk	17314	C3	3589
HOLTZAPPLE RD., Windsor Twp	Yk	17356	G3	3376
HOLTZAPPLE RD., Windsor Twp	Yk	17356	G1	3376
HOLYOKE DR., York Twp	Yk	17402	A6	3376
HOLYOKE DR., York Twp	Yk	17402	H7	3375
HOME RD., Hamilton	Ad	17301	C6	3371
HOME RD., Paradise	Yk	17301	C6	3371
HOMEDALE RD., York Twp	Yk	17403	F3	3375
HOMELAND RD., York Twp	Yk	17403	E3	3375
HOMESTEAD CT., York Twp	Yk	17403	E5	3375
HOMESTEAD DR., Hopewell	Yk	17363	E9	3585
HOMESTEAD DR., Mount Pleasant	Ad	17325	F2	3576
HOMESTEAD DR., Paradise	Yk	17301	F9	3371
HOMESTEAD LA., Fairview	Yk	17011	F6	2848
HOMESTEAD LA., Hamilton	Ad	17316	H5	3370
HOMESTEAD LA., Hamilton	Ad	17316	A4	3371
HOMESTEAD RD., York Twp	Yk	17402	A3	3376
HOMEWOOD DR., York Twp	Yk	17403	E4	3375
HOMEWOOD RD., Windsor Twp	Yk	17402	A7	3273
HOMEWOOD ST, Carroll	Yk	17019	C3	3056
HONDA RD., Mount Pleasant	Ad	17331	G11	3473
HONDA RD., Mount Pleasant	Ad	17331	F2	3577
HONDA RD., Mount Pleasant	Ad	17340	E4	3577
HONDA RD., Mount Pleasant	Ad	17340	C5	3577
HONEY LA., Paradise	Yk	17316	H11	3267
HONEY LA., Paradise	Yk	17316	H1	3371
HONEY RD., Paradise	Yk	17364	H2	3371
HONEY RD., Warrington	Yk	17019	H8	3057
HONEY RUN DR., West Manchester	Yk	17404	F6	3269
HONEY VALLEY RD., York Twp	Yk	17313	C6	3376
HONEY VALLEY RD., York Twp	Yk	17313	B10	3376
HONEYMOON LA., Peach Bottom	Yk	17302	B9	3589
HONEYSUCKLE CT., Hanover	Yk	17331	C10	3475
HOOD COVE, Reading	Ad	17316	C5	3266
HOOD DR., Straban	Ad	17325	H11	3471
HOOKER COVE, Reading	Ad	17316	D3	3266
HOOKER DR., Mount Pleasant	Ad	17325	A11	3472
HOOKER DR., Reading	Ad	17316	D3	3266
HOOVER RD., Union	Ad	17331	F6	3577
HOOVER RD., Union	Ad	17340	F6	3577
HOOVER'S SCHOOL RD., Reading	Ad	17316	B8	3266
HOOVER'S SCHOOL RD., Reading	Ad	17316	D1	3370
HOPE AV. E., York City	Yk	17403	D8	3271
HOPE AV. W., York City	Yk	17403	C8	3271
HOPE AV. W., York City	Yk	17404	B8	3271
HOPE DR., Windsor Twp	Yk	17356	C3	3377
HOPE LA., Menallen	Ad	17304	E3	3262
HOPE LA., Oxford	Ad	17350	E2	3474
HOPE WAY, Heidelberg	Yk	17331	C1	3580
HOPEWELL CENTER RD., East Hopewell	Yk	17352	H3	3586
HOPEWELL CT., Hopewell	Yk	17363	E9	3585
HOPEWELL RD., Fawn	Yk	17352	C3	3690
HOPEWELL RD., Hopewell	Yk	17352	C3	3690
HORACE MANN AV., Red Lion	Yk	17356	C8	3377
HORN FARM RD., Hellam	Yk	17406	B9	3168
HORN FARM RD., Hellam	Yk	17406	C10	3168
HORN RD., Hellam	Yk	17406	B9	3168
HORN RD., York Twp	Yk	17356	H11	3376
HORN RD., York Twp	Yk	17356	H1	3480
HORNER RD., Cumberland	Ad	17325	H4	3678
HORNER RD., Cumberland	Ad	17325	A5	3679
HORSESHOE AV., Newberry	Yk	17345	E7	3061
HOSIERY AL., Spring Grove	Yk	17362	B11	3373
HOSIERY AL., Spring Grove	Yk	17362	B1	3477
HOSPITAL RD. EXT., Cumberland	Ad	17325	E5	3575
HOSPITAL RD., Cumberland	Ad	17325	E3	3575
HOSTETTER RD., Conewago	Ad	17331	B5	3578
HOSTETTER RD., Union	Ad	17331	H4	3577
HOSTETTER RD., Union	Ad	17331	A5	3578
HOUGHTON LA., Lower Windsor	Yk	17402	E5	3273
HOUNDS RUN, Straban	Ad	17325	E6	3471
HOUSE RD., Hellam	Yk	17406	G1	3272
HOUSEHOLDER AV., Red Lion	Yk	17356	B9	3377
HOUSTON LA., Hellam	Yk	17406	G6	3167
HOVER AL., New Oxford	Ad	17350	C1	3474
HOWARD AV. N., Gettysburg	Ad	17325	B8	3471
HOWARD AV. N., North York	Yk	17404	C4	3271
HOWARD AV. S., Gettysburg	Ad	17325	B9	3471
HOWARD AV., Cumberland	Ad	17325	C6	3471
HOWARD AV., Gettysburg	Ad	17325	C6	3471
HOWARD DR., Latimore	Ad	17316	B2	3266
HOWARD END, York Twp	Yk	17403	G2	3375
HOWARD ST. S., Dallastown	Yk	17313	F8	3376
HOWARD ST. S., York City	Yk	17403	D8	3271
HOWARD ST. S., York Twp	Yk	17313	F8	3376
HOWARD ST. W., Dallastown	Yk	17313	F7	3376
HOWARD ST. W., Red Lion	Yk	17356	B6	3377
HOWARD ST., York City	Yk	17403	C6	3271
HOWE AV., Cumberland	Ad	17325	C6	3575
HREBIK RD., Hopewell	Yk	17363	B4	3689
HREBIK RD., Shrewsbury Twp	Yk	17363	B4	3689
HUB CT., Dover Twp	Yk	17315	C3	3269
HUBER LA., Hellam	Yk	17368	D5	3169
HUDSON RD., York Twp	Yk	17402	B2	3376
HUDSON ST., Spring Garden	Yk	17403	E5	3271
HUFF RD., Berwick	Ad	17331	H5	3474
HUFFMANVILLE RD., Codorus	Yk	17327	F5	3686
HUFNAGEL DR., Penn	Yk	17331	F3	3579
HUGHES DR., Abbottstown	Ad	17301	A10	3371
HUGHLYN DR., Newberry	Yk	17315	F4	3059
HULL AV., Dover Twp	Yk	17315	H1	3269
HULL DR., Washington	Yk	17316	C11	3162
HULL DR., West Manchester	Yk	17404	D10	3270
HULL TR., Liberty	Ad	17320	E7	3573
HUNT AV., Cumberland	Ad	17325	C11	3471
HUNT CLUB DR., York Twp	Yk	17402	C11	3272
HUNT CLUB RD., Fawn	Yk	17321	D4	3691
HUNTER CIR., Hamilton	Ad	17301	A7	3371
HUNTER DR., Dover Twp	Yk	17315	G1	3269
HUNTER MILL RD., Lower Chanceford	Yk	17302	E11	3484
HUNTER MILL RD., Lower Chanceford	Yk	17302	E1	3588
HUNTER ST., Conewago	Ad	17331	D11	3474
HUNTERS CHASE, Newberry	Yk	17319	G4	2955
HUNTERS CREST DR., York Twp	Yk	17402	C11	3272
HUNTER'S LA., Cumberland	Ad	17325	G7	3470
HUNTERS LA., Fairview	Yk	17339	B3	2954
HUNTER'S WAY, Straban	Ad	17325	H8	3367
HUNTER'S WAY, Straban	Ad	17325	A8	3368
HUNTERSTOWN RD., Straban	Ad	17325	C11	3368
HUNTERSTOWN RD., Straban	Ad	17325	E6	3471
HUNTERSTOWN RD., Straban	Ad	17325	A2	3472
HUNTERSTOWN-HAMPTON RD., Reading	Ad	17350	F5	3369
HUNTERSTOWN-HAMPTON RD., Reading	Ad	17350	A3	3370
HUNTERSTOWN-HAMPTON RD., Straban	Ad	17325	D10	3368
HUNTERSTOWN-HAMPTON RD., Straban	Ad	17350	D10	3368
HUNTERSTOWN-HAMPTON RD., Straban	Ad	17350	A8	3369
HUNTFIELD DR., Manchester Twp	Yk	17404	D10	3165
HUNTING PARK CT., Springettsbury	Yk	17402	B6	3272
HUNTING PARK LA., Springettsbury	Yk	17402	B6	3272
HUNTINGTON RD., Dover Twp	Yk	17315	F3	3269
HUNTLY CT., West Manchester	Yk	17404	B7	3270
HUNTSMAN CT., Hanover	Yk	17331	C10	3475
HUSHON RD., Peach Bottom	Yk	17314	G2	3692
HUSK LA., Fairview	Yk	17319	A3	2955
HUSON RD., North Hopewell	Yk	17356	E4	3481
HUSSON RD., Windsor Twp	Yk	17322	E3	3481
HUTTON RD., Fairview	Yk	17070	B7	2849
HYKES MILL RD., Conewago	Yk	17345	F6	3060
HYSON LA., Red Lion	Yk	17356	B7	3377
HYSON MILL RD., East Hopewell	Yk	17363	H4	3585
HYSON MILL RD., East Hopewell	Yk	17363	A4	3586
HYSON SCHOOL RD., East Hopewell	Yk	17363	E2	3585

I

ICE HOUSE DR., Stewartstown	Yk	17363	E1	3689
IDAVILLE-YORK SPRINGS RD., Huntington	Ad	17324	B9	3159
IDAVILLE-YORK SPRINGS RD., Huntington	Ad	17372	B9	3159
IDAVILLE-YORK SPRINGS RD., York Spring	Ad	17372	A9	3160
IDYLWYLD RD., Springettsbury	Yk	17402	H3	3271
IDYLWYLD RD., Springettsbury	Yk	17402	A2	3272
IMPALA DR., Dillsburg	Yk	17019	D2	3056
IMPERIAL DR., Dover Twp	Yk	17315	A1	3270
IMPERIAL DR., York Twp	Yk	17403	B4	3375
IMPOUNDING DAM RD., West Manheim	Yk	17331	B10	3579
IMPOUNDING DAM RD., West Manheim	Yk	17331	F4	3683
IMPOUNDING DAM RD., West Manheim	Yk	17331	A5	3684
INDEPENDENCE AV., Jefferson	Yk	17362	E10	3477
INDEPENDENCE DR., Littlestown	Ad	17340	E3	3681
INDEPENDENCE DR., New Freedom	Yk	17349	G11	3583
INDEPENDENCE DR., New Freedom	Yk	17349	G1	3687
INDIAN LA., Chanceford	Yk	17322	C6	3379
INDIAN ROCK DAM RD., North Codorus	Yk	17403	D6	3374
INDIAN ROCK DAM RD., North Codorus	Yk	17403	E6	3374
INDIAN ROCK DAM RD., North Codorus	Yk	17404	D6	3374
INDIAN ROCK DAM RD., Spring Garden	Yk	17403	H11	3270
INDIAN ROCK DAM RD., Spring Garden	Yk	17403	A11	3271
INDIAN ROCK DAM RD., Spring Garden	Yk	17403	A2	3375
INDIAN ROCK DAM RD., West Manchester	Yk	17403	G3	3374
INDIAN ROCK DAM RD., York Twp	Yk	17403	B4	3375
INDIAN SPRINGS DR., York Twp	Yk	17402	D10	3272
INDIAN STEPS RD., Lower Chanceford	Yk	17302	G4	3484
INDIAN STEPS RD., Lower Chanceford	Yk	17302	A3	3485
INDUSTRIAL DR., Fairview	Yk	17339	E4	2954
INDUSTRIAL DR., Newberry	Yk	17345	E6	3061
INDUSTRIAL HWY., Springettsbury	Yk	17402	H4	3271
INDUSTRIAL HWY., Springettsbury	Yk	17402	A4	3272
INDUSTRIAL HWY., Springettsbury	Yk	17402	D4	3272
INDUSTRIAL RD., Conewago	Yk	17345	F7	3060
INDUSTRIAL RD., Springfield	Yk	17327	H11	3479
INDUSTRIAL RD., Springfield	Yk	17327	A10	3480
INGA CT., Berwick	Ad	17331	B4	3475
INGHAM RD., Shrewsbury Twp	Yk	17327	B10	3583
INGHAM RD., Shrewsbury Twp	Yk	17349	A3	3687
INGHAM RD., Shrewsbury Twp	Yk	17349	B1	3687
INNERST RD., North Hopewell	Yk	17356	E2	3480
INTERCHANGE PL., Manchester Twp	Yk	17402	B8	3166
INTERMEDIATE AV., Dover Twp	Yk	17315	C1	3269
INTERSECTION RD., Manheim	Yk	17327	D4	3685
IRENE LA., Freedom	Ad	17325	B7	3574
IRIS CT., Penn	Yk	17331	G3	3579
IRIS DR, Franklin	Yk	17019	A1	3161
IRIS LA., Reading	Ad	17316	B9	3266
IRISHTOWN RD., Liberty	Ad	17320	F5	3677
IRISHTOWN RD., Mount Pleasant	Ad	17331	A11	3474
IRISHTOWN RD., Oxford	Ad	17350	B6	3474
IRISHTOWN RD., Oxford	Ad	17350	A9	3474
IRON BRIDGE RD., Hopewell	Yk	17363	A10	3585
IRON RIDGE RD., Heidelberg	Yk	17331	C3	3476
IRON RIDGE RD., Heidelberg	Yk	17362	C6	3476
IRON RIDGE RD., Jackson	Yk	17331	C3	3476
IRON SPRINGS RD., Hamiltonban	Ad	17320	G11	3571
IRON SPRINGS RD., Hamiltonban	Ad	17320	B8	3572
IRON SPRINGS RD., Hamiltonban	Ad	17320	F1	3675
IRON STONE HILL RD., Springfield	Yk	17313	A1	3480
IRON STONE HILL RD., York Twp	Yk	17313	A1	3480
IRONSTONE DR., Manchester Twp	Yk	17402	C1	3271
IRONSTONE HILL RD., York Twp	Yk	17403	B6	3376
IRONSTONE RD., Fairview	Yk	17070	H1	2953
IRONSTONE RD., Latimore	Ad	17372	H2	3265
IRONWOOD WAY, Manchester Twp	Yk	17404	F8	3165
IROQUOIS TR., Newberry	Yk	17370	A9	2956
IRVING AV., Spring Garden	Yk	17403	G9	3271
IRVING RD., York City	Yk	17403	E10	3271
IRWIN CT., York City	Yk	17404	A6	3271
IRWIN RD., Lower Chanceford	Yk	17314	A3	3590
ISAAC CT., York Twp	Yk	17313	C6	3376
IVAN RD., West Manchester	Yk	17404	G4	3270
IVORY RD., Springettsbury	Yk	17402	C6	3272
IVY CIR., Penn	Yk	17331	G5	3579
IVY DR., East Manchester	Yk	17345	C5	3166
IVY DR., Red Lion	Yk	17356	B5	3377
IVY HILL LA., Peach Bottom	Yk	17314	A9	3589
IVY LA., Springettsbury	Yk	17402	A5	3272
IVY PUMP LA., West Manchester	Yk	17404	B7	3270
IVY ST., York Twp	Yk	17402	A4	3376
IVY TR., Carroll Valley	Ad	17320	D1	3676
IVYSIDE DR., Windsor Twp	Yk	17402	A8	3273

J

J H KANE AV., Fairfield	Ad	17320	A5	3573
J. F. K. DR., Menallen	Ad	17307	D3	3260
JACK IN THE PULPIT LA., Hamilton	Ad	17316	C4	3371
JACK NICKLAUS LA., Newberry	Yk	17319	D7	2955
JACK RD., Franklin	Ad	17353	F7	3468
JACK RD., Franklin	Ad	17353	A6	3469
JACK'S MOUNTAIN RD., Carroll Valley	Ad	17320	E11	3572
JACK'S MOUNTAIN RD., Carroll Valley	Ad	17320	D1	3676
JACK'S MOUNTAIN RD., Hamiltonban	Ad	17320	E11	3572
JACK'S MOUNTAIN RD., Hamiltonban	Ad	17320	D1	3676
JACK'S MOUNTAIN RD., Liberty	Ad	17320	D1	3676
JACKSON DR., Reading	Ad	17316	D2	3266
JACKSON DR., Springfield	Yk	17360	A11	3375
JACKSON RD., Mount Joy	Ad	17325	G2	3575
JACKSON SQUARE RD., Jackson	Yk	17362	B8	3372
JACKSON SQUARE RD., Jackson	Yk	17364	D6	3372
JACKSON ST. E., Spring Garden	Yk	17403	G8	3271
JACKSON ST. E., York City	Yk	17403	D9	3271
JACKSON ST. W., Spring Garden	Yk	17403	C9	3271
JACKSON ST. W., York City	Yk	17403	C9	3271
JACKSON ST., Abbottstown	Ad	17301	A10	3371
JACKSON ST., Conewago	Ad	17331	H1	3578
JACKSON ST., Hanover	Yk	17331	B2	3579
JACKSON ST., Spring Grove	Yk	17362	A11	3373
JACOBS AL. N., Abbottstown	Ad	17301	B10	3371
JACOBS AL. S., Abbottstown	Ad	17301	B10	3371
JACOBS AL., Straban	Ad	17350	D6	3369
JACOB'S MILL RD., Hamilton	Ad	17301	C5	3371
JACOBS MILL RD., Heidelberg	Yk	17331	A7	3476
JACOB'S MILL RD., Paradise	Yk	17316	E3	3371
JACOBS RD., Chanceford	Yk	17309	H11	3378
JACOB'S RD., Conewago	Yk	17331	H8	3474
JACOBS ST., East Berlin	Ad	17316	C1	3371
JACOBS TR., Carroll Valley	Ad	17320	F10	3572
JACQUELINE DR., Mount Pleasant	Ad	17350	F6	3473
JAMES AV., Littlestown	Ad	17340	E1	3681
JAMES DR., Manchester Twp	Yk	17404	G10	3165
JAMES LA., Fairview	Yk	17055	C7	2953
JAMES TR., Highland	Ad	17320	F5	3573
JAMES TR., Liberty	Ad	17320	F5	3573
JAMES WAY, Lower Windsor	Yk	17406	G4	3273
JAMIE CT., Chanceford	Yk	17322	G8	3482
JAMISON RD., Lower Windsor	Yk	17366	F1	3378
JANES WAY, East Hopewell	Yk	17322	E3	3586
JANET ST., Penn	Yk	17331	E6	3579
JANET TR., Carroll Valley	Ad	17320	F11	3572
JANET TR., Carroll Valley	Ad	17320	E1	3676
JASMINE DR., Penn	Yk	17331	F4	3579
JASMINE LA., Stewartstown	Yk	17363	F11	3585
JASMINE RD., Peach Bottom	Yk	17314	B10	3589
JASPER AV., Manchester Twp	Yk	17404	B3	3271
JAY ST., Newberry	Yk	17315	D3	3059
JAY ST., Newberry	Yk	17315	D4	3059
JAYME DR., Springettsbury	Yk	17402	B8	3272
JEAN LO WAY, Springettsbury	Yk	17402	B1	3272
JEFFERSON AV., Jefferson	Yk	17362	E10	3477
JEFFERSON AV., York City	Yk	17404	B6	3271
JEFFERSON CT., New Freedom	Yk	17349	H3	3687
JEFFERSON DR., Hamilton	Ad	17301	A7	3371
JEFFERSON LA., Windsor Twp	Yk	17356	E7	3377
JEFFERSON RD., North Codorus	Yk	17362	B6	3477
JEFFERSON ST., Conewago	Ad	17331	G3	3578
JEFFERSON ST., Conewago	Ad	17331	H1	3578
JEFFERY LA., York Twp	Yk	17402	D4	3376
JENNA LA., Oxford	Ad	17350	B4	3474
JENNIFER DR., Fairview	Yk	17070	C2	2954
JENNIFER DR., Mount Pleasant	Ad	17350	F6	3473
JENNIFER LA., Carroll	Yk	17019	H7	2951
JENNIFER LA., Hellam	Yk	17406	E3	3167
JENNY LA., Hopewell	Yk	17363	F8	3585
JERUSALEM SCHOOL RD., East Manchester	Yk	17347	H5	3166
JERUSALEM SCHOOL RD., East Manchester	Yk	17347	A5	3167
JESSAMINE WAY, Manchester Twp	Yk	17404	B2	3270
JESSE LA., Manchester Twp	Yk	17404	G1	3270
JESSICA DR., Bonneauville	Ad	17325	G1	3576
JESSICA DR., Dover Twp	Yk	17315	F4	3269
JESSICA DR., Dover Twp	Yk	17315	G4	3269
JESSICA LA., Monaghan	Yk	17019	A7	2952
JESSOP PL., York City	Yk	17403	C9	3271
JILLIAN DR., Dover Twp	Yk	17315	E5	3269
JIMS RD., Hopewell	Yk	17363	C8	3585
JO TR., Carroll Valley	Ad	17320	E11	3572
JOAN DR., Conewago	Yk	17404	D2	3165
JOAN DR., Newberry	Yk	17370	H9	2955
JOAN DR., Newberry	Yk	17370	H10	2955
JOAN ST., Penn	Yk	17331	E6	3579
JODI LA., Dover Twp	Yk	17315	F4	3269
JOEL LA., Cumberland	Ad	17325	F9	3470
JOHN AL., New Freedom	Yk	17349	G3	3687
JOHN DR., Oxford	Ad	17350	B4	3474
JOHN EDWARD DR., Union	Ad	17340	B2	3682
JOHN RANDOLPH DR., New Freedom	Yk	17349	G5	3687
JOHN ST., Penn	Yk	17331	D3	3579
JOHNAMAC N., Littlestown	Ad	17340	C11	3577
JOHNAMAC N., Littlestown	Ad	17340	C1	3681
JOHNAMAC S., Littlestown	Ad	17340	C1	3681
JOHNATHAN DR., Conewago	Yk	17344	E1	3578
JOHNNY DR., East Hopewell	Yk	17363	F3	3585
JOHNS AV., Gettysburg	Ad	17325	B11	3471
JOHNS DR., Windsor Twp	Yk	17402	A8	3273
JOHNSON DR., Mount Joy	Ad	17325	A3	3576
JOHNSON DR., Reading	Ad	17316	B5	3266
JOHNSON DR., Straban	Ad	17325	D5	3471
JOHNSON RD., Hopewell	Yk	17363	D3	3689
JOHNSON RD., Lower Chanceford	Yk	17314	F3	3589
JOHNSON RD., Lower Chanceford	Yk	17314	H4	3589
JOHNSON RD., Lower Chanceford	Yk	17314	A4	3590
JOHNSTON CIR., Penn	Yk	17331	G7	3579
JOLO WAY, York Twp	Yk	17403	E4	3375
JONATHAN LA., Bonneauville	Ad	17325	H1	3576
JONATHAN WAY N., York Twp	Yk	17356	G4	3376
JONATHAN WAY, York Twp	Yk	17356	H5	3376
JONATHON RD., Manchester Twp	Yk	17404	D10	3165
JONES AV., Straban	Ad	17325	E5	3471
JONES RD., Fawn	Yk	17321	A9	3588
JONQUIL RD., Peach Bottom	Yk	17314	A10	3589
JONQUIL RD., York Twp	Yk	17403	F3	3375
JOPPA RD., York Twp	Yk	17403	E4	3375
JORDAN CT., Dover Twp	Yk	17315	C3	3269
JORETTA CT., Hopewell	Yk	17349	C6	3584
JOSEPH RD., North Codorus	Yk	17404	A9	3374
JOSEPH RD., West Manchester	Yk	17404	B5	3374
JOY RD., Hopewell	Yk	17363	F8	3584
JUANITA CT., Oxford	Ad	17350	E2	3474
JUD RD., Conewago	Yk	17315	A2	3165
JUD RD., Conewago	Yk	17404	A4	3165

JU-DAN CT., Latimore	Ad	17372	A11	3055
JUDITH CT., Dover Twp	Yk	17404	F8	3269
JUDY WAY, Bonneauville	Ad	17325	G1	3576
JUG RD., Conewago	Yk	17315	H3	3164
JULES LA., Dover Twp	Yk	17315	E11	3164
JULI DR., Hopewell	Yk	17349	C6	3584
JULIE CT., Fairview	Yk	17055	D8	2953
JULIUS LA., Washington	Yk	17315	H4	3267
JULIUS LA., Washington	Yk	17315	A3	3268
JUNCTION AL., Wrightsville	Yk	17368	E8	3169
JUNCTION RD., Carroll	Yk	17019	D9	2951
JUNCTION RD., Hopewell	Yk	17349	C5	3584
JUNCTION RD., North Codorus	Yk	17360	D5	3478
JUNE ST., York City	Yk	17404	A5	3271
JUNIOR ST., Glen Rock	Yk	17327	C4	3583
JUNIPER CT., East Manchester	Yk	17345	D2	3166
JUNIPER DR., Newberry	Yk	17319	D5	2955
JUNIPER DR., Union	Ad	17340	B3	3682
JUNIPER LA., Hanover	Yk	17331	A3	3579
JUNIPER LA., Washington	Yk	17316	B6	3267
JUNIPER RD., Peach Bottom	Yk	17314	A10	3589
JUPITER RD., East Manchester	Yk	17347	H4	3166
JUSTABEE LA., Carroll	Yk	17019	C11	2951

K

K ST. S., York Spring	Ad	17372	A10	3160
KAIN RD., West Manchester	Yk	17404	D5	3270
KAISER RD., Chanceford	Yk	17322	E2	3379
KALREDA RD., Springettsbury	Yk	17402	F1	3271
KAREN LA., Penn	Yk	17331	F11	3475
KARENS WAY, Windsor Twp	Yk	17402	A10	3273
KARYL LA., Manchester Twp	Yk	17404	G2	3270
KATIE CT., Stewartstown	Yk	17363	D1	3689
KATONAH DR., York Twp	Yk	17356	G4	3376
KAUFFMAN LA., Hellam	Yk	17406	D7	3168
KAUFFMAN RD., Chanceford	Yk	17368	B11	3275
KAUFFMAN RD., Chanceford	Yk	17368	C1	3379
KAYLA BLVD., Conewago	Yk	17315	H11	3165
KBS RD., Jackson	Yk	17362	A7	3373
KBS RD., Jackson	Yk	17364	C5	3373
KBS RD., Jackson	Yk	17404	D4	3373
KEEFER LA., Hamiltonban	Ad	17353	F9	3468
KEENER AV., Red Lion	Yk	17356	A7	3377
KEENER DR., Fairfield	Ad	17320	B5	3573
KEENER LA., Red Lion	Yk	17356	A7	3377
KEENEY DR., York Twp	Yk	17403	D5	3375
KEENEY RD., North Codorus	Yk	17362	A11	3374
KEENEY SUNSET DR., Shrewsbury Twp	Yk	17361	C10	3584
KEENY CT., North Codorus	Yk	17362	B1	3478
KEENY DR. E., North Codorus	Yk	17362	A1	3478
KEENY DR. W., North Codorus	Yk	17362	A1	3478
KEENY DR., Hellam	Yk	17406	H8	3168
KEENY LA., Shrewsbury Twp	Yk	17349	D9	3584
KEENY MILL RD., Shrewsbury Twp	Yk	17349	D5	3687
KEENY RD., North Codorus	Yk	17362	A1	3478
KEESEY CT., East Hopewell	Yk	17363	G3	3585
KEESEY RD., New Freedom	Yk	17349	H3	3687
KEESEY ST., Springettsbury	Yk	17402	H5	3271
KEITH DR., Hanover	Yk	17331	A11	3475
KELLER AV., Hellam	Yk	17406	F10	3168
KELLER DR., York Twp	Yk	17356	F1	3376
KELLER RD., Lower Windsor	Yk	17406	B3	3274
KELLER RD., Shrewsbury Twp	Yk	17349	B5	3688
KELLER RD., Straban	Ad	17325	G9	3367
KELLINGER RD., Fairview	Yk	17339	E5	2954
KELLY AV., Heidelberg	Yk	17362	F10	3476
KELLY AV., Shrewsbury Boro	Yk	17361	B7	3584
KELLY DR., Conewago	Yk	17404	G2	3165
KELLY DR., East Manchester	Yk	17347	A2	3167
KELLY DR., York City	Yk	17404	A5	3271
KELLY DR., York Twp	Yk	17404	H5	3270
KELLY RD., Berwick	Ad	17301	G11	3370
KELLY RD., Berwick	Ad	17301	F1	3474
KELLY TR., Liberty	Ad	17320	G6	3573
KEMP TR., Liberty	Ad	17320	F6	3573
KEN LIN DR., Franklin	Yk	17019	B9	3055
KEN RD., Shrewsbury Twp	Yk	17349	B5	3584
KENDALE RD., Windsor Twp	Yk	17356	G10	3272
KENDALE RD., Windsor Twp	Yk	17356	H11	3272
KENDALE RD., Windsor Twp	Yk	17356	H1	3376
KENDALE RD., Windsor Twp	Yk	17356	C3	3377
KENDALE RD., Windsor Twp	Yk	17356	A1	3377
KENDALE RD., Windsor Twp	Yk	17356	B3	3377
KENDALL LA., Dover Twp	Yk	17315	F5	3269
KENLEE CIR., West Manheim	Yk	17331	H2	3683
KENMAR DR., Fairview	Yk	17070	A8	2849
KENNARD DALE AV. S., Stewartstown	Yk	17363	F11	3585
KENNARD DALE AV. S., Stewartstown	Yk	17363	F1	3689
KENNEDY CT., Hanover	Yk	17331	B10	3475
KENNEDY DR., Oxford	Ad	17350	A6	3474
KENNEDY DR., West Manheim	Yk	17331	E1	3683
KENNEDY LA., Newberry	Yk	17319	D8	2955
KENNEDY RD., Lower Chanceford	Yk	17302	G1	3587
KENNEDY RD., Lower Chanceford	Yk	17302	A1	3588
KENNETH RD., West Manchester	Yk	17404	D3	3270
KENNETH WAY, Hellam	Yk	17368	C8	3169
KENNICK DR., Lower Windsor	Yk	17366	A9	3274
KENRAY DR., Dover Boro	Yk	17315	C11	3164
KENSINGTON CT., York Twp	Yk	17402	C8	3272
KENSINGTON DR., Germany	Ad	17340	C11	3577
KENT DR., York Twp	Yk	17313	D8	3376
KENT RD., Springettsbury	Yk	17402	A5	3272
KENTWOOD LA., Spring Garden	Yk	17403	C1	3375
KENWAY, York Twp	Yk	17402	G6	3375
KENWOOD RD., Windsor Twp	Yk	17402	C6	3273
KENYON DR., Windsor Twp	Yk	17356	C10	3377
KERMISS CT., Conewago	Yk	17315	G7	3164
KERN RD., Conewago	Yk	17402	F8	3060
KERN TR., Carroll Valley	Ad	17320	B11	3573
KERNEL LA., Fairview	Yk	17319	B3	2955
KERSHAW ST., Springettsbury	Yk	17402	A5	3272
KESTREL LA., Lower Windsor	Yk	17402	E4	3273
KEVIN DR., Jackson	Yk	17404	E5	3373
KEVIN DR., Oxford	Ad	17350	A1	3474
KEVIN DR., West Manheim	Yk	17331	F9	3579
KEYMAR DR., York Twp	Yk	17402	B4	3376
KEYSTONE DR., Manchester Twp	Yk	17402	B11	3166
KEYSTONE ST., Fairview	Yk	17070	A8	2849
KEYSTONE ST., Littlestown	Ad	17340	F1	3681
KIDD LA., Penn	Yk	17331	E7	3475
KIERSTEN DR., Dover Twp	Yk	17315	F5	3269
KILDORE CT., Manchester Twp	Yk	17404	E10	3165
KILGORE RD., Hopewell	Yk	17363	C10	3586
KILGORE RD., Hopewell	Yk	17363	C1	3690
KILGORE RD., Lower Chanceford	Yk	17302	F7	3484
KILGORE RD., Peach Bottom	Yk	17314	B2	3693
KILLINGER RD., Newberry	Yk	17319	B6	2955
KILPATRICK AV., Hanover	Yk	17331	B4	3579
KILPATRICK RD., Mount Pleasant	Ad	17325	A7	3473
KILPATRICK RD., Mount Pleasant	Ad	17350	A7	3473
KIMBERLY ANN LA., Oxford	Ad	17350	A1	3474
KIMBERLY CT., Reading	Ad	17350	B2	3370
KIMBERLY DR., West Manheim	Yk	17331	E9	3579
KIMBERLY LA., Dover Twp	Yk	17315	E5	3269
KIMBERLY LA., Reading	Ad	17350	B2	3370
KIME AV., Bendersville	Ad	17304	H3	3262
KIME HATCHERY RD., Tyrone	Ad	17324	G11	3158
KIME HATCHERY RD., Tyrone	Ad	17324	G1	3263
KIMES RD., York Twp	Yk	17402	H5	3375
KINARD, Lower Windsor	Yk	17368	A1	3275
KINDIG LA., Conewago	Ad	17331	G1	3578
KINDIG LA., Conewago	Ad	17344	G1	3578
KINDIG LA., Hanover	Yk	17331	A1	3579
KINDIG RD., Germany	Ad	17340	G2	3681
KINDIG RD., Germany	Ad	17340	A3	3682
KINEMAN RD., Berwick	Ad	17301	A11	3371
KINEMAN RD., Berwick	Ad	17301	A1	3475
KING AL., Manchester Boro	Yk	17345	E1	3166
KING RD., Mount Joy	Ad	17325	H9	3575
KING RD., Mount Joy	Ad	17325	A9	3576
KING ST. E., Abbottstown	Ad	17301	C9	3371
KING ST. E., Littlestown	Ad	17340	F1	3681
KING ST. E., Spring Garden	Yk	17403	G6	3271
KING ST. E., York City	Yk	17401	E7	3271
KING ST. E., York City	Yk	17403	E7	3271
KING ST. W., Abbottstown	Ad	17301	A10	3371
KING ST. W., Littlestown	Ad	17340	D2	3681
KING ST. W., York City	Yk	17401	B8	3271
KING ST. W., York City	Yk	17404	B8	3271
KING ST., Dallastown	Yk	17313	F6	3376
KING ST., East Berlin	Ad	17316	B11	3267
KING ST., East Berlin	Ad	17316	D1	3371
KING ST., East Manchester	Yk	17347	C11	3062
KING ST., Fairview	Yk	17339	F4	2953
KING ST., Gettysburg	Ad	17325	B10	3471
KING ST., York Twp	Yk	17313	F6	3376
KINGS ARMS LA., Springettsbury	Yk	17402	F1	3272
KINGS MILL RD., Spring Garden	Yk	17403	B10	3271
KINGS MILL RD., York City	Yk	17403	B10	3271
KINGS WAY, Stewartstown	Yk	17363	E1	3689
KINGSDALE RD., Germany	Ad	17340	H4	3680
KINGSDALE RD., Germany	Ad	17340	A5	3681
KINGSGATE CT., Cumberland	Ad	17325	F8	3470
KINGSTON CT., Springettsbury	Yk	17402	B6	3272
KINGSTON RD., Springettsbury	Yk	17402	B6	3272
KINGSWOOD DR., York Twp	Yk	17403	H11	3271
KINROSS AV., York Twp	Yk	17356	E10	3272
KINSEY DR., Cumberland	Ad	17325	D5	3470
KIPLING LA., Hellam	Yk	17406	G11	3167
KIRCH RD., York Twp	Yk	17402	G4	3375
KIRCHNER RD., Shrewsbury Twp	Yk	17349	H11	3583
KIRCHNER RD., Shrewsbury Twp	Yk	17349	H1	3687
KIRKLAND DR., Windsor Twp	Yk	17356	G3	3376
KISE MILL RD., Newberry	Yk	17370	G3	3059
KISE MILL RD., Newberry	Yk	17370	A2	3060
KISTER ST., Goldsboro	Yk	17319	H7	2955
KITZMILLER RD., Manheim	Yk	17362	B4	3581
KLINE AV., Newberry	Yk	17345	E7	3061
KLINE HILL RD., Shrewsbury Twp	Yk	17349	D10	3480
KLINE RD., Chanceford	Yk	17309	D11	3380
KLINE YOUNG RD., East Hopewell	Yk	17363	C4	3586
KLINES RUN RD., Lower Windsor	Yk	17368	H2	3274
KLINES RUN RD., Lower Windsor	Yk	17368	G3	3274
KLINES RUN RD., Lower Windsor	Yk	17368	A2	3275
KNIGHT RD., Cumberland	Ad	17325	H7	3574
KNIGHT RD., Cumberland	Ad	17325	A7	3575
KNIGHTS VIEW RD., Hellam	Yk	17368	D11	3169
KNIGHTS VIEW RD., Lower Windsor	Yk	17368	D11	3169
KNISELY DR., Conewago	Ad	17331	H3	3578
KNISLEY LA., Red Lion	Yk	17356	C7	3377
KNOB CREEK LA., Windsor Twp	Yk	17402	D7	3272
KNOBB HILL RD., Peach Bottom	Yk	17314	D11	3589
KNOBHILL RD., York Twp	Yk	17403	G1	3375
KNOLL DR., Hopewell	Yk	17349	C6	3584
KNOLL LA., Manchester Twp	Yk	17402	B11	3166
KNOLLWOOD LA., West Manheim	Yk	17331	C9	3580
KNOPP RD., Jackson	Yk	17362	D2	3476
KNORR RD., Freedom	Ad	17325	B2	3574
KNORR RD., Highland	Ad	17325	A11	3470
KNORR RD., Highland	Ad	17325	A1	3574
KNOX RD., Hamiltonban	Ad	17353	C9	3469
KNOX RD., Highland	Ad	17325	C9	3469
KNOXLYN RD., Cumberland	Ad	17325	C6	3470
KNOXLYN RD., Highland	Ad	17325	H8	3469
KNOXLYN RD., Highland	Ad	17325	A7	3470
KNOXLYN-ORRTANNA RD., Highland	Ad	17325	G8	3469
KNOXLYN-ORRTANNA RD., Highland	Ad	17325	A9	3470
KNOXLYN-ORRTANNA RD., Highland	Ad	17353	D7	3469
KOALA DR., Penn	Yk	17331	A5	3580
KOCHENDOUR LA., Dover Twp	Yk	17315	A6	3164
KOCHENOUR LA., Manchester Twp	Yk	17404	F9	3165
KOHLER CT., Windsor Twp	Yk	17356	G11	3272
KOHLER LA., Newberry	Yk	17319	C6	2955
KOHLER MILL RD., New Oxford	Ad	17350	H3	3473
KOHLER MILL RD., Oxford	Ad	17350	H5	3473
KOHLER MILL RD., Oxford	Ad	17350	A6	3474
KOHLER RD, Chanceford	Yk	17322	A5	3380
KOHLER SCHOOL RD., Mount Pleasant	Ad	17350	E7	3473
KOHLER SCHOOL RD., Mount Pleasant	Ad	17350	F5	3473
KOONTZ LA., West Manchester	Yk	17404	B6	3270
KOPP RD., Jackson	Yk	17362	E11	3372
KOPPS RD., Manheim	Yk	17329	F11	3580
KORMIT DR., Windsor Twp	Yk	17356	C11	3273
KORMIT DR., Windsor Twp	Yk	17356	B1	3377
KORTNI DR., Dover Twp	Yk	17315	F7	3269
KOTUR AV., West Manchester	Yk	17404	D7	3270
KRAFT MILL RD., North Codorus	Yk	17362	B11	3477
KRALLTOWN RD., Warrington	Yk	17019	H11	3056
KRALLTOWN RD., Washington	Yk	17019	H11	3056
KRALLTOWN RD., Washington	Yk	17316	E9	3162
KRALLTOWN RD., Washington	Yk	17316	E1	3267
KRALLTOWN RD., Washington	Yk	17365	H1	3161
KRALLTOWN RD., Washington	Yk	17365	A1	3162
KRALLTOWN RD., Washington	Yk	17365	E9	3162
KRATZ RD., Shrewsbury Boro	Yk	17327	H8	3583
KRATZ RD., Shrewsbury Twp	Yk	17327	G7	3583
KRAUS FARM LA., Lower Windsor	Yk	17368	H8	3274
KREBS RD., Codorus	Yk	17327	F4	3582
KREBS RD., Codorus	Yk	17329	B6	3582
KREIDLER AV., York Twp	Yk	17402	A3	3376
KREIDLER RD., Springfield	Yk	17403	G11	3375
KRENTLER DR., Penn	Yk	17331	B8	3579
KRESTA DR., York Twp	Yk	17403	D6	3375
KREUTZ CREEK AV., Hellam	Yk	17406	B11	3168
KREUTZ CREEK RD., Hellam	Yk	17406	H7	3167
KREUTZ CREEK RD., Hellam	Yk	17406	A8	3168
KREUTZ CREEK RD., Hellam	Yk	17406	A10	3168
KRICK RD., Peach Bottom	Yk	17314	D2	3694
KRIDLER SCHOOLHOUSE RD., West Manheim	Yk	17331	G4	3683
KRIEDLER RD., Springfield	Yk	17403	G1	3479
KRISTA LA., Dallastown	Yk	17313	G8	3376
KRISTA LA., York Twp	Yk	17313	G8	3376
KRISTI LA., Biglerville	Ad	17307	B2	3367
KRISTINE CIR., West Manheim	Yk	17331	E9	3579
KRISTY DR., West Manheim	Yk	17331	D10	3580
KRONE RD., Warrington	Yk	17339	B3	3059
KRUG AV., Hanover	Yk	17331	A1	3579
KRUG RD., Mount Joy	Ad	17340	D1	3680
KUHN DR., East Berlin	Ad	17316	B1	3371
KUHN DR., Hanover	Yk	17331	A11	3475
KUHN FORDING RD., Hamilton	Ad	17316	A3	3371
KUHN FORDING RD., Reading	Ad	17316	B11	3267
KUHN FORDING RD., Reading	Ad	17316	B2	3371
KUHN RD., Mount Pleasant	Ad	17331	E3	3577
KUHN RD., Mount Pleasant	Ad	17340	E3	3577
KUNKLE MILL RD., Dover Twp	Yk	17315	B11	3059
KUNKLE RD., Fawn	Yk	17321	E11	3587
KUNKLE RD., Fawn	Yk	17321	D2	3691
KURTZ AV., York City	Yk	17403	C9	3271
KURTZ SCHOOL RD., Hopewell	Yk	17363	F8	3585
KYLE RD., Manchester Twp	Yk	17404	H1	3270
KYLEMORE WAY, York Twp	Yk	17356	E10	3272

L

LABOR CAMP RD., Huntington	Ad	17324	A6	3159
LABOTT RD., Jackson	Yk	17364	G4	3372
LACEY LA., Jackson	Yk	17362	B9	3372
LAFAYETTE DR., Fairview	Yk	17070	E11	2849
LAFAYETTE DR., Fairview	Yk	17070	E1	2954
LAFAYETTE DR., Littlestown	Ad	17340	E2	3681
LAFAYETTE ST., West Manchester	Yk	17404	H10	3270
LAFAYETTE ST., West Manchester	Yk	17404	A10	3271
LAFAYETTE ST., York City	Yk	17403	C8	3271
LAKE DR., East Manchester	Yk	17347	H2	3166
LAKE DR., East Manchester	Yk	17347	A2	3167
LAKE LA., Mount Pleasant	Ad	17350	E2	3473
LAKE LEA DR., Franklin	Yk	17019	G11	3055
LAKE LEA DR., Franklin	Yk	17019	G1	3160
LAKE MEADE DR., Latimore	Ad	17316	B3	3266
LAKE MEADE DR., Reading	Ad	17316	D2	3266
LAKE MEADE RD., Latimore	Ad	17316	A2	3266
LAKE MEADE RD., Latimore	Ad	17372	G6	3265
LAKE MEADE RD., Latimore	Ad	17372	A2	3266
LAKE MEADE RD., Latimore	Ad	17316	F11	3161
LAKE MEADE RD., Reading	Ad	17372	G6	3265
LAKE MEADE RD., Reading	Ad	17372	E9	3265
LAKE RD., Jackson	Yk	17362	D7	3372
LAKE RD., Paradise	Yk	17316	F1	3371
LAKE RD., Paradise	Yk	17364	A3	3372
LAKE RD., Paradise	Yk	17364	C4	3372
LAKE RD., Peach Bottom	Yk	17314	G10	3588
LAKE RD., Springfield	Yk	17403	H10	3375
LAKE RD., Springfield	Yk	17403	H1	3479
LAKE RD., York City	Yk	17403	C9	3271
LAKE VIEW DR., Cumberland	Ad	17325	G9	3470
LAKE VIEW RD., Peach Bottom	Yk	17314	D9	3590
LAKE WOOD CT., Penn	Yk	17331	A6	3580
LAKEFIELD RD., Windsor Twp	Yk	17402	F8	3272
LAKESIDE DR., Shrewsbury Twp	Yk	17349	C2	3688
LAKESIDE TR., Carroll Valley	Ad	17320	G10	3572
LAKEVIEW CIR., Littlestown	Ad	17340	F2	3681
LAKEVIEW CIR., West Manheim	Yk	17331	A7	3580
LAKEVIEW CT., Warrington	Yk	17365	E10	3058
LAKEVIEW DR. E., Littlestown	Ad	17340	F2	3681
LAKEVIEW DR., Jackson	Yk	17362	H9	3372
LAKEVIEW DR., Jefferson	Yk	17362	E11	3477
LAKEVIEW DR., Manheim	Yk	17362	H7	3580
LAKEVIEW DR., Manheim	Yk	17362	A6	3581
LAKEVIEW DR., North Codorus	Yk	17362	B2	3477
LAKEVIEW DR., York Twp	Yk	17403	H2	3375
LAKEVIEW TER., West Manheim	Yk	17331	A7	3580
LAKEVIEW TR., Carroll Valley	Ad	17320	G10	3572
LAKEWOOD DR., Jackson	Yk	17362	E10	3372
LAKVIEW DR., York Twp	Yk	17403	A1	3376
LAMBETH WALK, Spring Garden	Yk	17403	F10	3271
LAMONT ST., Fairview	Yk	17070	A7	2849
LAMOUR ST., York City	Yk	17403	E7	3271
LAMP POST LA., Fairview	Yk	17319	A2	2955
LAMPLITE DR., Dover Twp	Yk	17315	E7	3164
LANCASTER AV., Spring Garden	Yk	17403	G9	3271
LANCASTER AV., Spring Garden	Yk	17403	G10	3271
LANCASTER AV., York Twp	Yk	17403	G10	3271
LANCASTER ST. E., Red Lion	Yk	17356	D7	3377
LANCASTER ST. E., Red Lion	Yk	17356	E8	3377
LANCASTER ST. W., Red Lion	Yk	17356	E8	3377
LANCELOT CT., Cumberland	Ad	17325	F8	3470
LANCELOT LA., Springettsbury	Yk	17402	G3	3271
LANCER LA., York Twp	Yk	17404	H4	3270
LANDAU CT., Fairview	Yk	17011	F8	2848
LANDFILL RD., Chanceford	Yk	17322	C6	3379
LANDIS DR. E., Fairfield	Ad	17320	A5	3573
LANDIS DR. W., Fairfield	Ad	17320	A5	3573
LANDIS RD., Manheim	Yk	17331	D7	3580
LANDOLA AV., East Manchester	Yk	17347	H2	3166
LANDON DR., Paradise	Yk	17364	G6	3371
LANDON LA., York Twp	Yk	17403	E3	3375
LANDVALE ST., York Haven	Yk	17370	D3	3061
LANE AV., Cumberland	Ad	17325	E6	3470
LANE RD., Paradise	Yk	17316	F11	3267
LANGSHIRE DR., Manchester Twp	Yk	17404	D9	3165
LANIE CT., York Twp	Yk	17402	H6	3375
LANIUS RD., Hopewell	Yk	17363	B10	3586
LANTERN RD., Hopewell	Yk	17363	F10	3585
LARCH DR., Penn	Yk	17331	G5	3579
LARCHMOUNT DR., Manchester Twp	Yk	17404	D9	3165
LARK AV., Penn	Yk	17331	E7	3579
LARK LA., Dover Twp	Yk	17315	C6	3269
LARKIN DR., Windsor Twp	Yk	17356	B2	3377
LARKSPUR LA. N., York Twp	Yk	17403	F3	3375
LARKSPUR LA. S., York Twp	Yk	17403	F3	3375
LARTRY DR., Windsor Twp	Yk	17356	C11	3273
LARTRY DR., Windsor Twp	Yk	17356	C1	3377
LARUE RD., Codorus	Yk	17327	G10	3478
LARUE RD., Springfield	Yk	17360	G10	3478
LARUE RD., Springfield	Yk	17360	C9	3479
LATIMER AV., Straban	Ad	17325	E9	3471
LATIMER ST., North York	Yk	17404	C5	3271
LATIMORE CREEK RD., Latimore	Ad	17372	D2	3160
LATIMORE RD., Latimore	Ad	17372	F5	3159
LATIMORE RD., Latimore	Ad	17372	A4	3160
LATIMORE VALLEY RD., Latimore	Ad	17372	A1	3266
LATIMORE VALLEY RD., Latimore	Ad	17372	G8	3160
LATIMORE VALLEY RD., Latimore	Ad	17372	A10	3161
LAU RD., North Codorus	Yk	17360	E4	3478
LAUER LA., Dover Twp	Yk	17315	D5	3269
LAURA CT., Fairview	Yk	17339	F4	2954
LAURA LA., York Twp	Yk	17402	C11	3272
LAUREL CIR., Franklin	Ad	17353	D7	3364
LAUREL DR., East Manchester	Yk	17347	G8	3166
LAUREL DR., Heidelberg	Yk	17331	G4	3475
LAUREL DR., Hellam	Yk	17406	H11	3168
LAUREL DR., Hellam	Yk	17406	A11	3169
LAUREL DR., Hellam	Yk	17406	A10	3169
LAUREL DR., Hellam	Yk	17406	A1	3274
LAUREL DR., Hopewell	Yk	17363	C11	3585
LAUREL DR., Manchester Twp	Yk	17404	E2	3270
LAUREL DR., Newberry	Yk	17319	G8	2954
LAUREL DR., Peach Bottom	Yk	17302	H9	3588
LAUREL DR., Penn	Yk	17331	H4	3579
LAUREL DR., Stewartstown	Yk	17363	C11	3585
LAUREL HILL RD., North Hopewell	Yk	17322	D10	3481
LAUREL LA., Bendersville	Ad	17304	G3	3262
LAUREL LA., Bendersville	Ad	17304	A3	3263
LAUREL LA., Franklin	Ad	17353	F9	3260
LAUREL LA., Newberry	Yk	17315	D3	3059
LAUREL LA., Windsor Twp	Yk	17402	G6	3272
LAUREL OAK LA., Spring Garden	Yk	17403	A11	3271
LAUREL OAK LA., Spring Garden	Yk	17403	A1	3375
LAUREL RD., Chanceford	Yk	17309	G11	3378
LAUREL RD., Chanceford	Yk	17309	G3	3482
LAUREL RD., Chanceford	Yk	17322	G6	3482
LAUREL RD., East Hopewell	Yk	17322	F10	3482
LAUREL RD., East Hopewell	Yk	17322	E1	3586
LAUREL RD., Fairview	Yk	17070	E1	2954
LAUREL RD., Menallen	Ad	17304	G9	3157
LAUREL RUN RD., Franklin	Yk	17019	G4	3055
LAUREL ST., Cross Roads	Yk	17322	G9	3481
LAUREL ST., East Hopewell	Yk	17322	G9	3481
LAUREL ST., North York	Yk	17404	C4	3271
LAUREL SUMMIT DR., Heidelberg	Yk	17331	F4	3475
LAUREL TER., Hellam	Yk	17406	H11	3168
LAUREL TR., Carroll Valley	Ad	17320	F5	3676
LAUREL WOODS DR., Heidelberg	Yk	17331	G4	3475
LAWNCREST DR., Springettsbury	Yk	17402	F2	3272
LAWNDALE DR., Dover Twp	Yk	17315	E3	3269
LAWRENCE PL., New Oxford	Ad	17350	H3	3473
LAWRENCE RD., West Manheim	Yk	17331	E2	3683
LAWSON AV., Dallastown	Yk	17313	F7	3376
LAY RD., Peach Bottom	Yk	17314	B11	3590
LAY RD., Peach Bottom	Yk	17314	G2	3693
LAY RD., Peach Bottom	Yk	17314	A1	3694
LEADER DR., Springfield	Yk	17407	E11	3375
LEADER ST., Spring Garden	Yk	17403	F11	3271
LEADERS HEIGHTS RD., York Twp	Yk	17402	A5	3376
LEADERS HEIGHTS RD., York Twp	Yk	17403	E5	3375
LEADERTON DR., York Twp	Yk	17313	E7	3376
LEAF ST., Manchester Twp	Yk	17404	H2	3270

LEAFYDALE DR., Spring Garden	Yk	17403	A10	3272
LEAH ST., Carroll	Yk	17019	A3	3057
LEAMAN LA., Hallam	Yk	17406	B1	3273
LEANN DR., Codorus	Yk	17327	H8	3582
LEATHERY RD., Latimore	Ad	17316	E9	3161
LEBANON CHURCH RD., North Hopewell	Yk	17322	E9	3481
LEBANON CHURCH RD., North Hopewell	Yk	17322	F5	3481
LECRONE LA., North York	Yk	17404	B5	3271
LEDGE LA., Hamiltonban	Ad	17320	E11	3572
LEE ANN CT., West Manheim	Yk	17331	H2	3683
LEE COVE, Reading	Ad	17316	D3	3266
LEE CT., Springettsbury	Yk	17402	F10	3166
LEE DR., Mount Pleasant	Ad	17325	A11	3472
LEE DR., Mount Pleasant	Ad	17325	A1	3576
LEE RD., Manheim	Yk	17329	G8	3580
LEE ST. N., Hallam	Yk	17406	B11	3168
LEE ST. S., Hallam	Yk	17406	B11	3168
LEE ST., Hanover	Yk	17331	C11	3475
LEE ST., Hanover	Yk	17331	C1	3579
LEE ST., Hopewell	Yk	17363	D10	3585
LEE ST., York City	Yk	17403	E6	3271
LEE TR., Carroll Valley	Ad	17320	F1	3676
LEEDS RD., Spring Garden	Yk	17403	E10	3271
LEEDY RD., Jackson	Yk	17362	C9	3372
LEEDY RD., Straban	Ad	17325	H6	3367
LEEDY RD., Straban	Ad	17325	A7	3368
LEEVER RD., Dover Twp	Yk	17364	G10	3268
LEEWARD CT., Spring Garden	Yk	17403	C2	3375
LEEWOOD LA., Hellam	Yk	17406	D6	3168
LEFEVER RD., Jackson	Yk	17364	G10	3268
LEFEVER RD., Jackson	Yk	17364	A11	3269
LEFEVER ST., Gettysburg	Ad	17325	C9	3471
LEGACY LA., Menallen	Ad	17304	E4	3263
LEGION DR., Biglerville	Ad	17307	B2	3367
LEHIGH RD., Springettsbury	Yk	17402	C7	3272
LEHMAN DR., York Twp	Yk	17403	E4	3375
LEHMAN RD., North Codorus	Yk	17362	F11	3373
LEHMAN RD., North Codorus	Yk	17362	B2	3477
LEHMAN RD., Springfield	Yk	17313	A4	3480
LEHMAN ST. N., York City	Yk	17403	F5	3271
LEHMAN ST. S., York City	Yk	17403	F6	3271
LEHRS DR., Manchester Twp	Yk	17404	G8	3165
LEIB RD., Fawn	Yk	17352	A7	3587
LEIB SCHOOL RD., Hopewell	Yk	17363	G11	3585
LEIB SCHOOL RD., Hopewell	Yk	17363	F2	3689
LEIGH DR., Manchester Twp	Yk	17402	B5	3166
LEIPHART LA., Hellam	Yk	17368	B11	3169
LEIPHART RD., Chanceford	Yk	17309	G2	3483
LEMON AL., East Prospect	Yk	17317	F6	3274
LEMON AL., East Prospect	Yk	17368	F6	3274
LEMON AV., East Prospect	Yk	17317	F6	3274
LEMON AV., East Prospect	Yk	17368	F6	3274
LEMON AV., Red Lion	Yk	17356	D8	3377
LEMON ST., West Manchester	Yk	17404	F10	3270
LEMON ST., West Manchester	Yk	17404	C1	3374
LEMON ST., Wrightsville	Yk	17368	E8	3169
LENA DR., Jackson	Yk	17404	E4	3373
LENNON LA., Shrewsbury Twp	Yk	17349	B1	3688
LENOX PL., Dover Twp	Yk	17404	D7	3269
LENTZ RD., East Hopewell	Yk	17322	H11	3481
LENTZ RD., East Hopewell	Yk	17322	B11	3482
LENTZLYN DR., York Twp	Yk	17403	C7	3375
LEO CT., Fairview	Yk	17339	E5	2954
LEONARD ST., West Manchester	Yk	17404	E8	3270
LEPPO MILL RD., West Manheim	Yk	17331	C2	3683
LESCHEYS CHURCH RD., North Codorus	Yk	17362	H4	3476
LESCHEYS CHURCH RD., North Codorus	Yk	17362	A4	3477
LESLYNN RD., Spring Garden	Yk	17403	A9	3272
LESTER AV., Jackson	Yk	17404	E6	3373
LEWES RD., Spring Garden	Yk	17403	B1	3375
LEWIS AL., Conewago	Ad	17331	D10	3474
LEWIS DR., Glen Rock	Yk	17327	C3	3583
LEWIS LA., Chanceford	Yk	17322	E2	3482
LEWIS RD., Lower Windsor	Yk	17366	C3	3378
LEWIS RD., Windsor Twp	Yk	17366	C3	3378
LEWIS ST., Lewisberry	Yk	17339	B10	2954
LEWIS ST., Newberry	Yk	17339	B10	2954
LEWISBERRY RD. N., Monaghan	Yk	17019	D5	2952
LEWISBERRY RD. N., Monaghan	Yk	17055	D5	2952
LEWISBERRY RD. S., Monaghan	Yk	17055	G7	2952
LEWISBERRY RD., Conewago	Yk	17315	G7	3059
LEWISBERRY RD., Conewago	Yk	17315	A10	3060
LEWISBERRY RD., Conewago	Yk	17315	A1	3165
LEWISBERRY RD., Conewago	Yk	17404	D4	3165
LEWISBERRY RD., Fairview	Yk	17070	G9	2848
LEWISBERRY RD., Fairview	Yk	17070	A8	2849
LEWISBERRY RD., Fairview	Yk	17070	G1	2953
LEWISBERRY RD., Fairview	Yk	17339	F3	2953
LEWISBERRY RD., Fairview	Yk	17339	A9	2954
LEWISBERRY RD., Lewisberry	Yk	17339	A9	2954
LEWISBERRY RD., Manchester Twp	Yk	17404	F5	3165
LEWISBERRY RD., Monaghan	Yk	17055	A8	2953
LEWISBERRY RD., Monaghan	Yk	17339	A8	2953
LEWISBERRY RD., Newberry	Yk	17319	A9	2954
LEWISBERRY RD., Newberry	Yk	17319	A10	2955
LEWISBERRY RD., Newberry	Yk	17370	A9	2954
LEWISBERRY RD., Newberry	Yk	17370	A10	2955
LEXINGTON RD., York Twp	Yk	17402	H3	3375
LEXINGTON AV., Dover Twp	Yk	17315	H1	3269
LEXINGTON AV., Dover Twp	Yk	17315	B2	3270
LEXINGTON DR., Penn	Yk	17331	F5	3579
LEXINGTON DR., Shrewsbury Boro	Yk	17361	B11	3584
LEXINGTON DR., Shrewsbury Boro	Yk	17361	B1	3688
LEXINGTON PL., Fairview	Yk	17339	G6	2953
LEXINGTON ST., York City	Yk	17403	F7	3271
LEXINGTON WAY, Littlestown	Ad	17340	D3	3681
LEXTON DR., Manchester Twp	Yk	17404	A1	3271
LEXUS DR., Heidelberg	Yk	17362	F11	3476
LIBERTY AV., New Freedom	Yk	17349	H3	3687
LIBERTY CT., York City	Yk	17403	E7	3271
LIBERTY DR., East Manchester	Yk	17347	H2	3166
LIBERTY DR., Oxford	Ad	17350	B1	3474
LIBERTY HALL RD., Liberty	Ad	17320	E9	3573
LIBERTY LA., Bendersville	Ad	17304	A4	3263
LIBERTY RD. W., Hopewell	Yk	17363	F4	3689
LIBERTY RD., Heidelberg	Yk	17362	C9	3476
LIBERTY ST., Gettysburg	Ad	17325	C8	3471
LIBERTY ST., York City	Yk	17403	D8	3271
LIBHART MILL RD., Hellam	Yk	17406	C3	3273
LIBRARY PL., Hanover	Yk	17331	B2	3579
LIGHTNER RD., Manchester Twp	Yk	17404	B2	3271
LIGHTNING TR., Hamiltonban	Ad	17320	H11	3571
LIGHTNING TR., Hamiltonban	Ad	17320	A11	3572
LILAC CT., Penn	Yk	17331	C4	3579
LILAC DR., Franklin	Yk	17019	A1	3161
LILAC LA., Hamiltonban	Ad	17320	G2	3675
LILAC LA., York City	Yk	17403	D9	3271
LILAC RD., West Manchester	Yk	17404	C4	3270
LILY PAD LA., Hamilton	Ad	17301	B4	3371
LILY SPRINGS RD., Manheim	Yk	17329	G2	3684
LILY SPRINGS RD., West Manheim	Yk	17329	F4	3684
LIME ROCK MILL RD., Huntington	Ad	17324	C3	3264
LIME ROCK MILL RD., Tyrone	Ad	17324	C3	3264
LIMEKILN AV., Wrightsville	Yk	17368	D7	3169
LIMEKILN RD., Fairview	Yk	17070	C9	2848
LIMEKILN RD., Fairview	Yk	17070	G8	2848
LIMEKILN RD., Fairview	Yk	17070	A7	2849
LINCOLN AV. E., Gettysburg	Ad	17325	C7	3471
LINCOLN AV. W., Gettysburg	Ad	17325	B7	3471
LINCOLN COVE, Latimore	Ad	17316	B3	3266
LINCOLN DR., Conewago	Ad	17331	H2	3578
LINCOLN DR., Fairview	Yk	17070	A8	2849
LINCOLN DR., Latimore	Ad	17316	B3	3266
LINCOLN HWY., Abbottstown	Ad	17301	A10	3371
LINCOLN HWY., Hellam	Yk	17406	F9	3168
LINCOLN HWY., Hellam	Yk	17368	A8	3169
LINCOLN HWY., Hellam	Yk	17402	H1	3272
LINCOLN HWY., Hellam	Yk	17406	A8	3169
LINCOLN HWY., Hellam	Yk	17406	H1	3272
LINCOLN HWY., Jackson	Yk	17364	A3	3373
LINCOLN HWY., Jackson	Yk	17404	E2	3373
LINCOLN HWY., Jackson	Yk	17364	F3	3372
LINCOLN HWY., Paradise	Yk	17301	F8	3371
LINCOLN HWY., Paradise	Yk	17364	F8	3371
LINCOLN HWY., Paradise	Yk	17364	A5	3372
LINCOLN HWY., West Manchester	Yk	17404	C11	3270
LINCOLN HWY., West Manchester	Yk	17404	E2	3373
LINCOLN HWY., West Manchester	Yk	17404	A1	3374
LINCOLN HWY., Wrightsville	Yk	17368	A8	3169
LINCOLN PL., East Manchester	Yk	17345	C4	3166
LINCOLN SQ., Gettysburg	Ad	17325	D7	3471
LINCOLN ST., Conewago	Ad	17331	G1	3578
LINCOLN ST., Oxford	Ad	17350	C2	3474
LINCOLN ST., York City	Yk	17404	A8	3271
LINCOLN ST., York City	Yk	17404	B6	3271
LINCOLN VIEW DR., Franklin	Ad	17307	G1	3469
LINCOLN VIEW RD., Paradise	Yk	17301	E8	3371
LINCOLN WAY, Cumberland	Ad	17325	D4	3470
LINCOLNWAY CT., West Manchester	Yk	17404	F2	3373
LINCOLNWAY DR., Jackson	Yk	17404	E3	3373
LINCOLNWAY DR., West Manchester	Yk	17404	E3	3373
LINCOLNWAY E., New Oxford	Ad	17350	B2	3474
LINCOLNWAY E., Oxford	Ad	17350	B2	3474
LINCOLNWAY W., New Oxford	Ad	17350	A3	3474
LINCOLNWOOD DR., Jackson	Yk	17404	E3	3373
LINDA AV., West Manheim	Yk	17331	F9	3579
LINDA DR., Mount Pleasant	Ad	17350	F6	3473
LINDA LA., Newberry	Yk	17370	H9	2955
LINDA TR., Carroll Valley	Ad	17320	F11	3572
LINDBERG AV., York City	Yk	17403	C8	3271
LINDEN AV., Conewago	Ad	17331	H2	3578
LINDEN AV., Conewago	Ad	17344	G1	3578
LINDEN AV., Hanover	Yk	17331	A1	3579
LINDEN AV., Red Lion	Yk	17356	B8	3377
LINDEN AV., Shrewsbury Boro	Yk	17349	C7	3584
LINDEN AV., West Manchester	Yk	17404	C5	3270
LINDEN AV., York City	Yk	17404	A7	3271
LINDENBERGH AV., Windsor Twp	Yk	17356	D7	3377
LINDSAY LA., West Manheim	Yk	17331	A8	3580
LINDSAY TR., Liberty	Ad	17320	G5	3573
LINDY AV., York Spring	Ad	17372	B10	3160
LINDY RD., Springfield	Yk	17360	F7	3479
LINE AV., Dallastown	Yk	17313	G6	3376
LINE AV., York Twp	Yk	17313	G6	3376
LINE RD., Germany	Ad	17340	C5	3682
LINE RD., North Hopewell	Yk	17327	F8	3480
LINE RD., North Hopewell	Yk	17349	E11	3480
LINE RD., North Hopewell	Yk	17349	F10	3480
LINE RD., North Hopewell	Yk	17349	C3	3584
LINE RD., North Hopewell	Yk	17349	E1	3584
LINE RD., Peach Bottom	Yk	17314	H6	3692
LINE RD., Peach Bottom	Yk	17314	D6	3693
LINE RD., Shrewsbury Twp	Yk	17349	E1	3584
LINE RD., Springfield	Yk	17327	E6	3480
LINE RD., Union	Ad	17331	C5	3682
LINE RD., Union	Ad	17340	C5	3682
LINEBORO RD., Codorus	Yk	17327	A2	3686
LINEBORO RD., Manheim	Yk	17327	E5	3685
LINEBORO RD., Manheim	Yk	17327	B5	3685
LINGG RD., Oxford	Ad	17350	B5	3474
LINGG RD., Oxford	Ad	17350	A4	3474
LINTON TER., North Codorus	Yk	17404	D9	3374
LION ARCHER RD., Germany	Ad	17340	D5	3680
LION CT., Dover Twp	Yk	17315	C3	3269
LION DR., Penn	Yk	17331	C5	3579
LION TR., Carroll Valley	Ad	17320	A11	3573
LION TR., Carroll Valley	Ad	17320	H1	3676
LIONERS CREEK RD., York Twp	Yk	17313	B8	3376
LIONS DR., York Twp	Yk	17313	D9	3376
LISA CIR., Lower Windsor	Yk	17406	G4	3273
LISA LA., Springettsbury	Yk	17402	A9	3272
LISA TR., Carroll Valley	Ad	17320	F11	3572
LISA WOOD CT., West Manheim	Yk	17331	E2	3683
LISBURN AV., Shrewsbury Boro	Yk	17361	A10	3584
LISBURN HEIGHTS DR., Fairview	Yk	17339	D3	2953
LISBURN RD., Warrington	Yk	17365	B8	3058
LISBURN RD., Warrington	Yk	17365	A2	3163
LISMORE BLVD., York Twp	Yk	17402	E10	3272
LIST RD., North Hopewell	Yk	17356	D3	3480
LIST RD., North Hopewell	Yk	17356	H3	3480
LIST RD., North Hopewell	Yk	17356	A3	3481
LITTLE AV., Berwick	Ad	17301	E2	3474
LITTLE BRIDGE RD., Penn	Yk	17331	A6	3579
LITTLE CREEK RD., Jackson	Yk	17362	A8	3373
LITTLE CREEK RD., West Manchester	Yk	17404	B1	3270
LITTLE JOHN CT., Penn	Yk	17331	F6	3579
LITTLE JOHN DR., Franklin	Yk	17019	H7	3055
LITTLE JOHN DR., New Salem	Yk	17371	C5	3374
LITTLE JOHN DR., North Codorus	Yk	17404	C5	3374
LITTLE KNOLL DR., Penn	Yk	17331	D6	3579
LITTLE RD., Hopewell	Yk	17363	A11	3586
LITTLE RD., Hopewell	Yk	17363	H4	3689
LITTLE RD., Hopewell	Yk	17363	A1	3690
LITTLE TR., Carroll Valley	Ad	17320	G4	3676
LITTLESTOWN RD., Union	Ad	17331	F5	3577
LITTLESTOWN RD., Union	Ad	17340	F5	3577
LITTLESTOWN RD., Union	Ad	17340	E8	3577
LITTLETON DR., Penn	Yk	17331	G2	3579
LITTONIAN RD., Germany	Ad	17340	C3	3681
LIVERPOOL ST., Manchester Boro	Yk	17345	D1	3166
LIVINGSTONE DR., Springettsbury	Yk	17402	H4	3272
LIVINGSTONE DR., Springettsbury	Yk	17402	A3	3273
LIVINGSTONE RD., York City	Yk	17404	A4	3271
LLOYD'S LA., Lower Windsor	Yk	17368	A3	3275
LOBAUGH RD., Tyrone	Ad	17304	G3	3263
LOBAUGH RD., Tyrone	Ad	17304	A2	3264
LOBELL RD., Berwick	Ad	17301	H11	3370
LOBELL RD., Berwick	Ad	17301	A11	3371
LOBELL RD., Berwick	Ad	17301	H1	3474
LOCK LA., York City	Yk	17403	C6	3271
LOCKPORT RD., Chanceford	Yk	17309	C7	3380
LOCUST AL., New Freedom	Yk	17349	F3	3687
LOCUST AV., Bonneauville	Ad	17325	G1	3576
LOCUST AV., Newberry	Yk	17345	E7	3061
LOCUST AV., Shrewsbury Boro	Yk	17361	A7	3584
LOCUST CIR., Newberry	Yk	17319	C6	2955
LOCUST CT., East Manchester	Yk	17345	C5	3166
LOCUST DR., Conewago	Ad	17331	D10	3474
LOCUST DR., Germany	Ad	17340	D11	3577
LOCUST DR., Tyrone	Ad	17325	E10	3264
LOCUST GROVE RD., Franklin	Yk	17019	B3	3161
LOCUST GROVE RD., Springettsbury	Yk	17402	F4	3272
LOCUST GROVE RD., Windsor Twp	Yk	17402	G6	3272
LOCUST HILL RD., York Twp	Yk	17313	C5	3376
LOCUST HONEY CIR., Dover Twp	Yk	17315	F5	3269
LOCUST LA., Carroll	Yk	17019	G10	2951
LOCUST LA., Dover Boro	Yk	17315	C11	3164
LOCUST LA., Germany	Ad	17340	B7	3577
LOCUST LA., Hamilton	Ad	17301	A5	3371
LOCUST LA., Lower Windsor	Yk	17366	A9	3274
LOCUST LA., Manchester Twp	Yk	17402	A10	3166
LOCUST LA., Manchester Twp	Yk	17402	C10	3166
LOCUST LA., Manchester Twp	Yk	17404	A10	3166
LOCUST LA., Monaghan	Yk	17019	D10	2952
LOCUST LA., Mount Pleasant	Ad	17340	B4	3577
LOCUST LA., Oxford	Ad	17350	B4	3474
LOCUST LA., Oxford	Ad	17350	B3	3474
LOCUST LA., Paradise	Yk	17364	E4	3372
LOCUST LA., Red Lion	Yk	17356	B7	3377
LOCUST LA., West Manchester	Yk	17404	C5	3270
LOCUST POINT CT., Dover Twp	Yk	17315	C4	3269
LOCUST POINT RD. S., Carroll	Yk	17019	B1	2951
LOCUST POINT RD., Conewago	Yk	17345	G8	3060
LOCUST POINT RD., Conewago	Yk	17402	G8	3060
LOCUST POINT RD., Conewago	Yk	17402	G8	3060
LOCUST POINT RD., Conewago	Yk	17402	A11	3061
LOCUST POINT RD., East Manchester	Yk	17402	A11	3061
LOCUST POINT RD., Manchester Boro	Yk	17345	A1	3166
LOCUST RD., Dover Twp	Yk	17315	F4	3269
LOCUST RD., Fairview	Yk	17070	E1	2954
LOCUST RD., Heidelberg	Yk	17362	D11	3476
LOCUST RD., Heidelberg	Yk	17362	D1	3580
LOCUST RD., Loganville	Yk	17360	F4	3479
LOCUST RD., Manchester Twp	Yk	17404	H10	3165
LOCUST RD., York Haven	Yk	17370	E3	3061
LOCUST RD., York Haven	Yk	17370	E3	3061
LOCUST RD., York Twp	Yk	17403	G11	3271
LOCUST RD., York Twp	Yk	17403	G1	3375
LOCUST SPRING RD., Chanceford	Yk	17309	D11	3379
LOCUST SPRING RD., Chanceford	Yk	17309	D1	3483
LOCUST ST. E., York City	Yk	17403	D7	3271
LOCUST ST. W., York City	Yk	17404	A9	3271
LOCUST ST., Dallastown	Yk	17313	G7	3376
LOCUST ST., East Berlin	Ad	17316	B11	3267
LOCUST ST., East Berlin	Ad	17316	C1	3371
LOCUST ST., East Manchester	Yk	17347	B11	3062
LOCUST ST., Fairview	Yk	17070	D1	2954
LOCUST ST., Hanover	Yk	17331	C3	3579
LOCUST ST., Hopewell	Yk	17363	C11	3585
LOCUST ST., Littlestown	Ad	17340	E2	3681
LOCUST ST., McSherrystown	Ad	17344	E2	3578
LOCUST ST., Newberry	Yk	17370	G1	3060
LOCUST ST., Penn	Yk	17331	C3	3579
LOCUST ST., Stewartstown	Yk	17363	C11	3585
LOCUST ST., Wrightsville	Yk	17368	C7	3169
LOCUST ST., York Haven	Yk	17370	E3	3061
LOCUST ST., York Twp	Yk	17313	G7	3376
LOCUST TR., Carroll Valley	Ad	17320	G4	3676
LODGE LA., East Berlin	Ad	17316	D2	3371
LODI LA., Littlestown	Ad	17340	D1	3681
LOG CABIN RD., West Manchester	Yk	17404	H5	3269
LOG CABIN RD., West Manchester	Yk	17404	A4	3270
LOG RD., Springfield	Yk	17403	H1	3479
LOG RD., Springfield	Yk	17403	A1	3480
LOGAN CIR., Germany	Ad	17340	A4	3682
LOGAN GREENS DR., Springfield	Yk	17403	E1	3479
LOGAN HEIGHTS RD., Loganville	Yk	17403	G3	3479
LOGAN LA., Penn	Yk	17331	A5	3579
LOGAN RD., Carroll	Yk	17019	F11	2951
LOGAN RD., Carroll	Yk	17019	E1	3056
LOGAN RD., Cross Roads	Yk	17322	E11	3481
LOGAN RD., East Hopewell	Yk	17322	D1	3585
LOGAN RD., North Hopewell	Yk	17322	D1	3585
LOGAN RD., West Manchester	Yk	17404	D7	3270
LOIS LA., Shrewsbury Twp	Yk	17361	C10	3584
LOLA TR., Carroll Valley	Ad	17320	E1	3676
LOMAN AV., West Manchester	Yk	17404	H7	3269
LOMAN AV., West Manchester	Yk	17404	A7	3270
LOMBARD LA., Red Lion	Yk	17356	A7	3377
LOMBARD RD., Windsor Twp	Yk	17356	G5	3376
LOMBARD RD., Windsor Twp	Yk	17356	A4	3377
LOMBARD RD., York Twp	Yk	17356	G5	3376
LOMBARD ST., Dallastown	Yk	17313	G7	3376
LOMBARD ST., York Twp	Yk	17313	G9	3376
LONG AL., Franklintown	Yk	17323	E9	3056
LONG DR., Springettsbury	Yk	17402	C1	3272
LONG LA., Gettysburg	Ad	17325	B10	3471
LONG LA., Huntington	Ad	17372	B1	3265
LONG LA., Newberry	Yk	17370	F11	2955
LONG LA., Newberry	Yk	17370	F1	3060
LONG LEVEL RD., Hellam	Yk	17368	F9	3169
LONG LEVEL RD., Lower Windsor	Yk	17368	F9	3169
LONG LEVEL RD., Lower Windsor	Yk	17368	G1	3274
LONG LEVEL RD., Lower Windsor	Yk	17368	A4	3275
LONG MEADOW DR., Dover Twp	Yk	17315	H11	3164
LONG POINT DR., Springettsbury	Yk	17402	E7	3272
LONG QUARTER RD., Shrewsbury Twp	Yk	17349	G5	3688
LONG RD., East Manchester	Yk	17347	H1	3166
LONG RD., East Manchester	Yk	17347	A1	3167
LONG RD., Mount Joy	Ad	17325	B10	3576
LONG VIEW CT., Shrewsbury Twp	Yk	17349	G4	3688
LONGHORN LA., Fairfield	Ad	17320	B5	3573
LONGSTOWN RD., Springettsbury	Yk	17402	D4	3272
LONGSTREET DR., Mount Joy	Ad	17325	H11	3471
LONGSTREET DR., Mount Joy	Ad	17325	H1	3575
LONGSTREET DR., Reading	Ad	17316	C5	3266
LONGSTREET DR., Straban	Ad	17325	H11	3471
LONGSTREET DR., Straban	Ad	17325	A11	3472
LONGVIEW AV., Fairview	Yk	17070	C1	2954
LONGVIEW BLVD., Cumberland	Ad	17325	A1	3471
LONGVIEW DR., Cumberland	Ad	17325	A1	3471
LONGVIEW DR., Heidelberg	Yk	17362	B8	3476
LONGVIEW DR., Jackson	Yk	17362	H8	3372
LONGVIEW DR., North Codorus	Yk	17362	H11	3373
LONGVIEW DR., North Codorus	Yk	17362	H1	3477
LONGVIEW DR., West Manheim	Yk	17331	G11	3579
LONGVIEW RD., Loganville	Yk	17360	E3	3479
LONGVIEW RD., Manchester Twp	Yk	17402	B10	3166
LONGWOOD CT., Dover Twp	Yk	17315	F3	3269
LOOP DR., Penn	Yk	17331	F8	3579
LOOP RD., Menallen	Ad	17307	H6	3260
LOOP RD., Newberry	Yk	17370	E11	2954
LOOP RD., Springfield	Yk	17360	H7	3479
LOOT AV., Conewago	Ad	17331	H2	3578
LOPICCOLO HEIGHTS RD., Shrewsbury Twp	Yk	17327	E9	3583
LORI DR., Manchester Twp	Yk	17404	D10	3165
LORING CT., Fairview	Yk	17070	F2	2954
LORRAINE AV., Manchester Twp	Yk	17404	H6	3165
LOS ALAMITOS CIR., Conewago	Ad	17331	B4	3578
LOST AV., Mount Joy	Ad	17325	E1	3575
LOST HOLLOW RD., Franklin	Yk	17019	A4	3161
LOST HOLLW RD., Franklin	Yk	17019	H4	3160
LOST LIME LA., Hamiltonban	Ad	17320	B2	3572
LOUCKS MILL RD., Spring Garden	Yk	17403	D5	3271
LOUCKS MILL RD., Springettsbury	Yk	17402	D5	3271
LOUCKS MILL RD., York City	Yk	17403	D6	3271
LOUCKS MILL RD., York City	Yk	17404	A3	3271
LOUCKS PL., York Twp	Yk	17404	H5	3270
LOUCKS RD., Manchester Twp	Yk	17402	A3	3271
LOUCKS RD., Manchester Twp	Yk	17404	A3	3271
LOUCKS RD., West Manchester	Yk	17404	D7	3270
LOUCKS RD., West Manchester	Yk	17404	G4	3270
LOUCKS ST., East Manchester	Yk	17345	D3	3166
LOUCKS ST., Loganville	Yk	17403	G3	3479
LOUCKS ST., Springfield	Yk	17403	G4	3479
LOUGH ST., New Oxford	Ad	17350	A2	3474
LOUISE AV., York Twp	Yk	17403	H1	3375
LOUISE TR., Carroll Valley	Ad	17320	F11	3572
LOUISE TR., Carroll Valley	Ad	17320	F1	3676
LOVE AV., York Twp	Yk	17356	G4	3376
LOVE LAND DR., Menallen	Ad	17304	F3	3262
LOVEGREN CT., Manchester Twp	Yk	17404	H2	3270
LOVELY CT., Oxford	Ad	17350	E3	3474
LOVELY LA., Oxford	Ad	17350	E2	3474
LOVER'S DR., Conewago	Ad	17331	F8	3578
LOW DUTCH RD., Mount Joy	Ad	17325	A4	3576
LOW DUTCH RD., Mount Pleasant	Ad	17325	D10	3472
LOW DUTCH RD., Mount Pleasant	Ad	17325	C11	3472
LOW DUTCH RD., Mount Pleasant	Ad	17325	A4	3576
LOW DUTCH RD., Straban	Ad	17325	E7	3472
LOWE RD., East Hopewell	Yk	17363	F4	3585
LOWE RD., Fawn	Yk	17321	C1	3691
LOWE RD., Fawn	Yk	17352	B11	3587
LOWE RD., Hopewell	Yk	17363	E7	3585
LOWER GLADES RD., Springettsbury	Yk	17402	H9	3166
LOWER GLADES RD., Springettsbury	Yk	17402	A9	3167
LOWER GUM SPRINGS RD., Hamiltonban	Ad	17320	H8	3571
LOWER GUM SPRINGS RD., Hamiltonban	Ad	17320	A8	3572
LOWER RIVER RD., Chanceford	Yk	17309	F8	3380
LOWER TR., Carroll Valley	Ad	17320	H5	3676
LOWER TR., Carroll Valley	Ad	17320	A5	3677
LOWTHER RD., Fairview	Yk	17339	F4	2954
LUCABAUGH RD., Codorus	Yk	17327	D4	3686

LUCAS DR., Germany	Ad	17340	H3	3681
LUCAS DR., Germany	Ad	17340	A3	3682
LUCKY RD., Chanceford	Yk	17309	E8	3379
LUCKY RD., Chanceford	Yk	17309	B1	3483
LUCKY RD., Chanceford	Yk	17322	H6	3379
LUCKY RD., Chanceford	Yk	17322	A6	3380
LUCY LA., Manchester Twp	Yk	17404	E2	3270
LUDLOW AV., Spring Garden	Yk	17403	B10	3271
LUMBER ST., Littlestown	Ad	17340	F2	3681
LURE TR., Carroll Valley	Ad	17320	H8	3572
LUTHER DR. E., Shrewsbury Boro	Yk	17361	A11	3584
LUTHER DR. E., Shrewsbury Twp	Yk	17361	A1	3688
LUTHER DR. W., Shrewsbury Boro	Yk	17361	A11	3584
LUTHER DR. W., Shrewsbury Twp	Yk	17361	A1	3688
LUTHER RD., Shrewsbury Boro	Yk	17361	A11	3584
LUTZ RD., East Hopewell	Yk	17363	C6	3586
LYCAN DR., West Manchester	Yk	17404	B6	3270
LYDON LA., Hellam	Yk	17406	F2	3273
LYLE CIR., York Twp	Yk	17403	G1	3375
LYN CIR., York Twp	Yk	17403	G1	3375
LYNBROOK DR., Springettsbury	Yk	17402	F4	3272
LYNCH WAY, York City	Yk	17403	E7	3271
LYNES RD., Carroll	Yk	17019	C10	2951
LYNHURST RD., Springettsbury	Yk	17402	D5	3272
LYNLEE DR., Lower Windsor	Yk	17366	H11	3273
LYNLEE DR., Lower Windsor	Yk	17366	A11	3274
LYNN DR. E., East Berlin	Ad	17316	D11	3267
LYNN DR., East Manchester	Yk	17347	E9	3061
LYNN TR., Carroll Valley	Ad	17320	F1	3676
LYNWOOD DR., North Codorus	Yk	17362	A1	3478
LYNWOOD DR., York Twp	Yk	17402	H5	3375
LYNWOOD LA., Springettsbury	Yk	17402	D7	3272
LYNX DR., Conewago	Ad	17331	F3	3578

M

M ST., Littlestown	Ad	17340	E2	3681
MACADAM DR., Codorus	Yk	17327	B2	3686
MacDONALD CT., Shrewsbury Twp	Yk	17327	C5	3583
MACE RD., North Codorus	Yk	17362	A3	3478
MACK WAY, York City	Yk	17404	B7	3271
MACKS RD., East Hopewell	Yk	17363	E6	3585
MACKS RD., Hopewell	Yk	17363	E6	3585
MADARA DR., Penn	Yk	17331	E8	3475
MADDOX RD., Hopewell	Yk	17363	H6	3584
MADDOX RD., Hopewell	Yk	17363	A7	3585
MADISON AV., York City	Yk	17404	A7	3271
MADISON ST., Conewago	Ad	17331	H2	3578
MADISON ST., Conewago	Ad	17331	H1	3578
MAE TR., Carroll Valley	Ad	17320	E1	3676
MAGGIE CIR., York Twp	Yk	17402	B10	3272
MAGGIE LYNN CT., New Oxford	Ad	17350	C1	3474
MAGNOLIA AV., York Twp	Yk	17356	B8	3377
MAGNOLIA CIR., Shrewsbury Twp	Yk	17361	C11	3584
MAGNOLIA DR., Shrewsbury Twp	Yk	17349	C2	3688
MAGNOLIA LA., Penn	Yk	17331	G5	3579
MAGNOLIA TR., Peach Bottom	Yk	17314	H10	3588
MAHOPAC DR., York Twp	Yk	17356	G5	3376
MAIDSTONE AV., Chanceford	Yk	17322	C2	3482
MAIN ST. N., Dover Boro	Yk	17315	C11	3164
MAIN ST. E., Dallastown	Yk	17313	G7	3376
MAIN ST. E., Fairfield	Ad	17320	A5	3573
MAIN ST. E., Fawn Grove	Yk	17321	G4	3691
MAIN ST. E., Felton	Yk	17322	H4	3481
MAIN ST. E., Felton	Yk	17322	A4	3482
MAIN ST. E., New Freedom	Yk	17349	G3	3687
MAIN ST. E., New Freedom	Yk	17349	H3	3687
MAIN ST. E., Railroad	Yk	17355	G10	3583
MAIN ST. E., Windsor Boro	Yk	17366	G4	3377
MAIN ST. N., Biglerville	Ad	17307	A1	3367
MAIN ST. N., East Prospect	Yk	17317	E5	3274
MAIN ST. N., East Prospect	Yk	17368	E5	3274
MAIN ST. N., Jacobus	Yk	17407	F9	3375
MAIN ST. N., Loganville	Yk	17403	F3	3479
MAIN ST. N., Railroad	Yk	17355	G9	3583
MAIN ST. N., Red Lion	Yk	17356	B6	3377
MAIN ST. N., Shrewsbury Boro	Yk	17361	A7	3584
MAIN ST. N., Shrewsbury Twp	Yk	17327	B1	3583
MAIN ST. N., Spring Grove	Yk	17362	B11	3373
MAIN ST. N., Springfield	Yk	17327	C11	3479
MAIN ST. N., Springfield	Yk	17327	B1	3583
MAIN ST. N., Stewartstown	Yk	17363	E10	3585
MAIN ST. N., Windsor Twp	Yk	17356	B6	3377
MAIN ST. N., York Twp	Yk	17356	B6	3377
MAIN ST. S., Biglerville	Ad	17307	A2	3367
MAIN ST. S., East Prospect	Yk	17317	F6	3274
MAIN ST. S., East Prospect	Yk	17368	F6	3274
MAIN ST. S., Jacobus	Yk	17407	F11	3375
MAIN ST. S., Loganville	Yk	17360	E5	3479
MAIN ST. S., Railroad	Yk	17355	G10	3583
MAIN ST. S., Railroad	Yk	17355	G11	3583
MAIN ST. S., Red Lion	Yk	17356	D8	3377
MAIN ST. S., Shrewsbury Boro	Yk	17361	B10	3584
MAIN ST. S., Stewartstown	Yk	17363	E11	3585
MAIN ST. S., Stewartstown	Yk	17363	E1	3689
MAIN ST. W., Dallastown	Yk	17313	F7	3376
MAIN ST. W., Fairfield	Ad	17320	A5	3573
MAIN ST. W., Fawn Grove	Yk	17321	F4	3691
MAIN ST. W., Felton	Yk	17322	H4	3481
MAIN ST. W., New Freedom	Yk	17349	F2	3687
MAIN ST. W., Windsor Boro	Yk	17366	E5	3377
MAIN ST. W., Windsor Twp	Yk	17366	E5	3377
MAIN ST., Arendtsville	Ad	17307	B3	3366
MAIN ST., Bendersville	Ad	17304	H3	3262
MAIN ST., Bendersville	Ad	17304	A4	3263
MAIN ST., Cross Roads	Yk	17322	A8	3482
MAIN ST., Cross Roads	Yk	17363	E2	3585
MAIN ST., East Hopewell	Yk	17363	E2	3585
MAIN ST., Fawn	Yk	17321	A1	3691
MAIN ST., Fawn	Yk	17352	C4	3691
MAIN ST., Glen Rock	Yk	17327	B3	3583
MAIN ST., Jackson	Yk	17362	C7	3373
MAIN ST., Manchester Boro	Yk	17345	D2	3166
MAIN ST., McSherrystown	Ad	17344	E2	3578
MAIN ST., Mount Wolf	Yk	17347	F11	3061
MAIN ST., Mount Wolf	Yk	17347	E1	3166
MAIN ST., New Salem	Yk	17371	C6	3374
MAIN ST., North Codorus	Yk	17362	B1	3477
MAIN ST., Peach Bottom	Yk	17314	F5	3693
MAIN ST., Seven Valleys	Yk	17360	F4	3478
MAIN ST., Shrewsbury Twp	Yk	17327	B3	3583
MAIN ST., Wellsville	Yk	17365	G2	3162
MAIN ST., Yoe	Yk	17313	G6	3376
MAIN ST., York Spring	Ad	17372	A9	3160
MAIN ST., Yorkana	Yk	17402	E5	3273
MAIN TR., Carroll Valley	Ad	17320	G7	3572
MAJESTIC CIR., York Twp	Yk	17313	C6	3376
MAJOR BELL LA., Straban	Ad	17325	D3	3472
MALL RD., Newberry	Yk	17319	H6	2954
MALLARD DR., Fairview	Yk	17319	G3	2954
MALLARD LA., Codorus	Yk	17327	C10	3582
MALLET CT., Hopewell	Yk	17363	E10	3585
MALVERN DR. N., Manchester Boro	Yk	17345	E11	3061
MALVERN DR., Manchester Boro	Yk	17345	E10	3061
MANCHESTER ST., East Manchester	Yk	17345	C10	3061
MANCHESTER ST., Glen Rock	Yk	17327	A6	3583
MANCHESTER ST., Manchester Boro	Yk	17345	C10	3061
MANCHESTER ST., Shrewsbury Twp	Yk	17327	A6	3583
MANCHESTER ST., West Manchester	Yk	17404	D9	3270
MANCHESTER ST., York City	Yk	17404	A7	3271
MANDY LA., Carroll	Yk	17019	G5	3056
MANDY LA., Tyrone	Ad	17325	E8	3264
MANHAVEN DR., East Manchester	Yk	17345	C10	3061
MANHEIM RD., Manheim	Yk	17329	C10	3581
MANHEIM RD., Manheim	Yk	17329	D1	3685
MANHEIM ST., Springettsbury	Yk	17402	H5	3271
MANIFOLD SCHOOL RD., East Hopewell	Yk	17352	G4	3586
MANIFOLD SCHOOL RD., East Hopewell	Yk	17352	E5	3586
MANOR CIR., Union	Ad	17340	G11	3577
MANOR CT., Codorus	Yk	17362	D1	3581
MANOR CT., West Manchester	Yk	17404	B5	3270
MANOR DR., Monaghan	Yk	17019	E9	2952
MANOR DR., Mount Pleasant	Ad	17350	E3	3473
MANOR FURNACE RD., Chanceford	Yk	17322	E5	3482
MANOR LA., Hellam	Yk	17368	A5	3169
MANOR RD., Heidelberg	Yk	17331	A7	3476
MANOR RD., Lower Windsor	Yk	17366	G10	3273
MANOR RD., Lower Windsor	Yk	17366	A8	3274
MANOR RD., Lower Windsor	Yk	17406	A8	3274
MANOR RD., Manchester Twp	Yk	17404	B5	3270
MANOR RD., West Manchester	Yk	17404	A5	3270
MANOR RD., West Manchester	Yk	17404	B4	3270
MANOR RD., Windsor Twp	Yk	17356	D4	3377
MANOR RD., Windsor Twp	Yk	17366	G10	3273
MANOR RD., Windsor Twp	Yk	17366	D4	3377
MANOR ST., Penn	Yk	17331	C4	3579
MANOR ST., York City	Yk	17403	C9	3271
MANSBERGER AV., Goldsboro	Yk	17319	H7	2955
MANSBERGER AV., Goldsboro	Yk	17319	A7	2956
MANSBERGER AV., Newberry	Yk	17319	A7	2956
MANSBERGER AV., Newberry	Yk	17370	A7	2956
MANTLE LA., Springettsbury	Yk	17402	G11	3166
MANUM RD., Conewago	Yk	17345	G6	3060
MAPHELIAH RD., Lower Windsor	Yk	17402	F5	3273
MAPHELIAH RD., Yorkana	Yk	17402	F5	3273
MAPLE AL., New Freedom	Yk	17349	G2	3687
MAPLE AV., Biglerville	Ad	17307	H2	3366
MAPLE AV., Biglerville	Ad	17307	A3	3367
MAPLE AV., Conewago	Ad	17331	H1	3578
MAPLE AV., Cumberland	Ad	17325	C5	3471
MAPLE AV., Hanover	Yk	17331	A1	3579
MAPLE AV., Littlestown	Ad	17340	E1	3681
MAPLE AV., Shrewsbury Boro	Yk	17361	A8	3584
MAPLE AV., West Manchester	Yk	17404	B5	3270
MAPLE DR., Carroll	Yk	17019	E2	3056
MAPLE DR., Conewago	Ad	17331	E10	3474
MAPLE DR., Dillsburg	Yk	17019	E2	3056
MAPLE DR., Fairview	Yk	17319	G5	2954
MAPLE DR., Newberry	Yk	17319	G8	2954
MAPLE DR., Tyrone	Ad	17325	E10	3264
MAPLE DR., Windsor Twp	Yk	17356	G11	3272
MAPLE DR., Windsor Twp	Yk	17356	G1	3376
MAPLE GROVE RD., Berwick	Ad	17331	C2	3475
MAPLE GROVE RD., Paradise	Yk	17301	F11	3371
MAPLE GROVE RD., Paradise	Yk	17362	H10	3371
MAPLE GROVE RD., Paradise	Yk	17362	A8	3372
MAPLE HILL CT., Newberry	Yk	17319	B9	2955
MAPLE HILL DR., Newberry	Yk	17319	B9	2955
MAPLE LA., Franklin	Ad	17353	G8	3260
MAPLE LA., Penn	Yk	17331	D6	3579
MAPLE LA., Red Lion	Yk	17356	C7	3377
MAPLE LAWN RD. E., Fawn	Yk	17352	E6	3587
MAPLE LAWN RD. W., Fawn	Yk	17352	D7	3587
MAPLE RD., Dover Twp	Yk	17315	F5	3269
MAPLE RD., York Twp	Yk	17403	G2	3375
MAPLE ST. E., Dallastown	Yk	17313	G7	3376
MAPLE ST. E., East Prospect	Yk	17317	F5	3274
MAPLE ST. E., East Prospect	Yk	17368	F5	3274
MAPLE ST. E., York City	Yk	17403	D8	3271
MAPLE ST. E., York City	Yk	17403	E8	3271
MAPLE ST. W., Dallastown	Yk	17313	E6	3376
MAPLE ST. W., York City	Yk	17403	C9	3271
MAPLE ST. W., York City	Yk	17403	D8	3271
MAPLE ST., Bonneauville	Ad	17325	G1	3576
MAPLE ST., Bonneauville	Ad	17340	G1	3576
MAPLE ST., Jacobus	Yk	17407	E11	3375
MAPLE ST., Manchester Boro	Yk	17345	E1	3166
MAPLE ST., Mount Wolf	Yk	17345	E11	3061
MAPLE ST., Mount Wolf	Yk	17347	F1	3166
MAPLE ST., Newberry	Yk	17370	G11	2955
MAPLE ST., Newberry	Yk	17370	G1	3060
MAPLE ST., North Codorus	Yk	17360	E5	3478
MAPLE ST., Red Lion	Yk	17356	A7	3377
MAPLE ST., Seven Valleys	Yk	17360	E5	3478
MAPLE ST., Spring Garden	Yk	17403	G7	3271
MAPLE ST., Stewartstown	Yk	17363	D11	3585
MAPLE ST., Wrightsville	Yk	17368	D8	3169
MAPLE ST., Yoe	Yk	17313	G5	3376
MAPLE TR., Carroll Valley	Ad	17320	H3	3676
MAPLEWOOD DR., Dover Boro	Yk	17315	E10	3164
MAPLEWOOD DR., Newberry	Yk	17319	H10	2954
MAPLEWOOD DR., Newberry	Yk	17319	A9	2955
MAPLEWOOD DR., York Twp	Yk	17403	H11	3271
MARAL ST., Jackson	Yk	17364	A2	3373
MARBROOK LA., York Twp	Yk	17404	G5	3270
MARBROOK LA., York Twp	Yk	17404	H4	3270
MARBURG RD., Heidelberg	Yk	17362	F11	3476
MARBURG RD., Heidelberg	Yk	17362	F10	3476
MARBURG RD., Heidelberg	Yk	17362	F1	3580
MARDALE DR., York Twp	Yk	17403	D4	3375
MARFIELD CIR., West Manheim	Yk	17331	B3	3684
MARGARET ST., West Manchester	Yk	17404	D7	3270
MARGARETTA ST., Fairview	Yk	17070	C6	2849
MARGATE RD., West Manchester	Yk	17404	F3	3373
MARGHERITA CT., Windsor Twp	Yk	17356	A10	3273
MARIA DR., McSherrystown	Ad	17344	E3	3578
MARIANNE DR., Manchester Twp	Yk	17402	B5	3166
MARIE AV., Fairview	Yk	17339	A9	2954
MARIE DR., Penn	Yk	17331	F7	3579
MARIE LA., Biglerville	Ad	17307	H2	3366
MARIETTA AV., Penn	Yk	17331	F3	3579
MARIGOLD RD., West Manchester	Yk	17404	C4	3270
MARINA RD., Manheim	Yk	17331	E5	3580
MARINE CORPS LEAGUE MEMORIAL HWY, Cumberland	Ad	17325	A8	3575
MARINE CORPS LEAGUE MEMORIAL HWY, Mount Joy	Ad	17325	A8	3575
MARINE CORPS LEAGUE MEMORIAL HWY., Cumberland	Ad	17325	F11	3574
MARINE CORPS LEAGUE MEMORIAL HWY., Mount Joy	Ad	17325	G11	3471
MARINE CORPS LEAGUE MEMORIAL HWY., Straban	Ad	17325	G11	3471
MARION RD., Springettsbury	Yk	17402	F1	3271
MARION ST., West Manchester	Yk	17404	D7	3270
MARK AV., Arendtsville	Ad	17307	B2	3366
MARKEL RD., Shrewsbury Twp	Yk	17327	E2	3583
MARKET AV. E., Dallastown	Yk	17313	G7	3376
MARKET AV. E., Dallastown	Yk	17313	F7	3376
MARKET ST. E., Hallam	Yk	17406	C11	3168
MARKET ST. E., Spring Garden	Yk	17403	G5	3271
MARKET ST. E., Springettsbury	Yk	17402	G5	3271
MARKET ST. E., Springettsbury	Yk	17402	B5	3272
MARKET ST. E., York City	Yk	17401	D7	3271
MARKET ST. E., York City	Yk	17403	D7	3271
MARKET ST. N., Fawn Grove	Yk	17321	G4	3691
MARKET ST. S., Fawn Grove	Yk	17321	G5	3691
MARKET ST. W., Hallam	Yk	17406	C11	3168
MARKET ST. W., West York	Yk	17404	G9	3270
MARKET ST. W., York City	Yk	17401	B8	3271
MARKET ST. W., York City	Yk	17404	B8	3271
MARKET ST., East Manchester	Yk	17347	B11	3062
MARKET ST., Fairview	Yk	17070	C5	2849
MARKET ST., Lewisberry	Yk	17339	B11	2954
MARKET ST., Newberry	Yk	17339	B11	2954
MARKHAM CT., Fairview	Yk	17339	G9	2953
MARKLE RD., Chanceford	Yk	17309	H7	3379
MARKLE RD., Chanceford	Yk	17309	A8	3380
MARKLE RD., North Codorus	Yk	17403	F5	3374
MARKLE RD., West Manchester	Yk	17403	G2	3374
MARKLE RD., West Manchester	Yk	17404	F11	3270
MARKLE RUN RD., Reading	Ad	17316	G11	3266
MARKLE RUN RD., Reading	Ad	17316	F3	3370
MARKLE ST., West Manchester	Yk	17404	E2	3374
MARKLEY DR., Newberry	Yk	17370	H2	3060
MARKLEY DR., Newberry	Yk	17370	A2	3061
MARLBOROUGH DR., York Twp	Yk	17403	E3	3375
MARLBOROUGH RD., Dover Twp	Yk	17315	C4	3269
MARLENE TR., Carroll Valley	Ad	17320	G11	3572
MARLENE TR., Carroll Valley	Ad	17320	G1	3676
MARLETTE DR., East Manchester	Yk	17347	H2	3166
MARLOW DR., Springettsbury	Yk	17402	D7	3272
MARLOWE GARTH, Windsor Twp	Yk	17356	C3	3377
MARSH CREEK HEIGHTS RD., Freedom	Ad	17325	E10	3574
MARSH CREEK RD., Cumberland	Ad	17325	E10	3574
MARSH CREEK RD., Cumberland	Ad	17325	F1	3678
MARSH RUN RD., Fairview	Yk	17070	H9	2849
MARSH RUN RD., Fairview	Yk	17070	E9	2849
MARSH RUN RD., Fairview	Yk	17070	A9	2850
MARSHALL AV., York Twp	Yk	17403	A1	3376
MARSHALL CT., Springettsbury	Yk	17402	H6	3271
MARSHALL ST., Red Lion	Yk	17356	D8	3377
MARSHALL ST., Springettsbury	Yk	17402	H5	3271
MARSHALL ST., Windsor Twp	Yk	17356	D8	3377
MARSTELLER RD., Fawn	Yk	17352	D5	3690
MARSTELLER RD., Hopewell	Yk	17352	D5	3690
MARTEL CIR., Carroll	Yk	17019	F9	2951
MARTEN TR., Carroll Valley	Ad	17320	G2	3676
MARTIN DR., Fairview	Yk	17055	C7	2953
MARTIN DR., New Salem	Yk	17371	C6	3374
MARTIN DR., Newberry	Yk	17319	H8	2954
MARTIN DR., Penn	Yk	17331	G4	3579
MARTIN LA., Fairview	Yk	17011	G7	2848
MARTIN LA., Red Lion	Yk	17356	C8	3377
MARTIN RD., Codorus	Yk	17360	D9	3478
MARTIN RD., Jackson	Yk	17362	C7	3373
MARTIN RD., Jackson	Yk	17362	E9	3373
MARTIN RD., North Codorus	Yk	17362	E9	3373
MARTIN RD., North Codorus	Yk	17404	G8	3373
MARTIN RD., Straban	Ad	17325	A10	3368
MARTIN RD., Straban	Ad	17325	A1	3472
MARTINGALE DR., Fairview	Yk	17011	F7	2848
MARTINGALE DR., Manchester Twp	Yk	17404	D1	3270
MARVELL DR., Windsor Twp	Yk	17402	F6	3272
MARVIN ST., Littlestown	Ad	17340	D1	3681
MARY DR., Franklin	Yk	17019	A6	3056
MARY SMITH LA., York City	Yk	17403	F5	3271
MARY ST., Paradise	Yk	17301	D9	3371
MARY-ANN TR., Carroll Valley	Ad	17320	D1	3676
MARYLAND AV., Littlestown	Ad	17340	D2	3681
MARYLAND AV., Menallen	Ad	17304	E3	3262
MARYLAND AV., York City	Yk	17404	A7	3271
MARYLAND AV., York Twp	Yk	17404	H7	3270
MARYLAND LINE RD., Mount Joy	Ad	17340	A6	3680
MARY'S CIR., East Hopewell	Yk	17363	H4	3585
MASIMOER RD., New Freedom	Yk	17349	H5	3687
MASON AV. E., York City	Yk	17401	D7	3271
MASON AV. E., York City	Yk	17403	D7	3271
MASON AV. E., York City	Yk	17403	F6	3271
MASON AV. N., Dallastown	Yk	17313	E7	3376
MASON AV. S., Dallastown	Yk	17313	E7	3376
MASON AV. W., York City	Yk	17401	C7	3271
MASON AV. W., York City	Yk	17404	A8	3271
MASON AV., Seven Valleys	Yk	17360	F4	3478
MASON AV., Yoe	Yk	17313	G6	3376
MASON DIXON DR., Littlestown	Ad	17340	E3	3681
MASON DIXON TR., Carroll Valley	Ad	17320	A6	3677
MASON RD., Mount Pleasant	Ad	17325	H5	3472
MASON-DIXON RD., Cumberland	Ad	17325	F5	3678
MASON-DIXON RD., Cumberland	Ad	17325	A4	3679
MASON-DIXON RD., Freedom	Ad	17325	F5	3678
MASON-DIXON RD., Mount Joy	Ad	17325	A4	3679
MASONIC DR., Manchester Twp	Yk	17402	C1	3271
MASSA DR., Lower Windsor	Yk	17366	D1	3378
MATHEWS RD., Lower Chanceford	Yk	17314	B7	3589
MATHIAS RD., Germany	Ad	17340	H6	3681
MATHIAS RD., Germany	Ad	17340	A6	3682
MATHIAS RD., Union	Ad	17340	A4	3682
MATTHEW CT., Germany	Ad	17340	C10	3577
MATTHEW DR., Conewago	Yk	17404	E2	3165
MATTHEW DR., Oxford	Ad	17350	A11	3370
MATTHEW DR., Oxford	Ad	17350	A1	3474
MATTHEWS CT., New Freedom	Yk	17349	H3	3687
MAURICE ST., Manchester Twp	Yk	17404	G10	3165
MAUSS RD., Butler	Ad	17307	B3	3368
MAXINE TR., Carroll Valley	Ad	17320	E1	3676
MAY APPLE DR., York Twp	Yk	17402	A3	3376
MAY DR., Franklin	Yk	17019	A6	3056
MAY RD., Lower Windsor	Yk	17402	E4	3273
MAY RD., Manchester Twp	Yk	17402	A6	3166
MAY ST., York City	Yk	17404	A6	3271
MAYAPPLE CIR., Newberry	Yk	17319	F7	2955
MAYERS BLVD., Germany	Ad	17340	G4	3681
MAYFAIR LA., Manchester Twp	Yk	17404	C1	3270
MAYFAIR ST., Dover Boro	Yk	17315	C11	3164
MAYFIELD DR., Dover Twp	Yk	17315	H5	3269
MAYFIELD ST., Manchester Twp	Yk	17402	C1	3271
MAYLYN AV., Dallastown	Yk	17313	G8	3376
MAYWOOD RD., Jackson	Yk	17364	G2	3372
MAYWOOD RD., Springettsbury	Yk	17402	C5	3272
McALLISTER MILL BLVD., Cumberland	Ad	17325	E1	3575
McALLISTER MILL BLVD., Mount Joy	Ad	17325	E1	3575
McALLISTER ST., Hanover	Yk	17331	C3	3579
McCALL RD., Peach Bottom	Yk	17314	C11	3589
McCALL RD., Peach Bottom	Yk	17314	C1	3693
McCALLS FERRY RD., Lower Chanceford	Yk	17302	G10	3484
McCALLS FERRY RD., Lower Chanceford	Yk	17302	A10	3485
McCANDLESS DR., Latimore	Ad	17316	A4	3266
McCARTNEY RD., Shrewsbury Twp	Yk	17349	B2	3688
McCLEAF LA., Carroll Valley	Ad	17320	G9	3572
McCLEARY CT., Shrewsbury Boro	Yk	17361	B6	3584
McCLEARY RD., East Hopewell	Yk	17363	A4	3586
McCLELLAN DR., Mount Joy	Ad	17325	A1	3576
McCLELLAN DR., Reading	Ad	17316	D2	3266
McCLELLAN LA., Penn	Yk	17331	G7	3579
McCOSH ST., Hanover	Yk	17331	B11	3475
McCOSH ST., Hanover	Yk	17331	B1	3579
McCOY LA., Hellam	Yk	17406	F10	3167
McCULLOUGH DR., Shrewsbury Twp	Yk	17327	B5	3583
McCURLEY DR., New Freedom	Yk	17349	H4	3687
McDERMOTT RD. N., Fawn	Yk	17321	A4	3692
McDONALD LA., York City	Yk	17403	D8	3271
McDOWELL DR., York Twp	Yk	17313	D5	3376
McELWAIN HEIGHTS LA., Hopewell	Yk	17363	D8	3585
McGINLEY DR., Fairfield	Ad	17320	A6	3573
McGLAUGHLIN RD., Freedom	Ad	17325	F7	3573
McGLAUGHLIN RD., Freedom	Ad	17325	A5	3574
McGLAUGHLIN RD., Liberty	Ad	17320	F7	3573
McINTOSH DR., Littlestown	Ad	17340	C1	3681
McKENZIE ST., York City	Yk	17403	D8	3271
McKINLEY AV., Hanover	Yk	17331	B11	3475
McKINLEY AV., Hanover	Yk	17331	C1	3579
McKINLEY DR., York Twp	Yk	17403	G6	3375
McKINLEY RD. E., Lower Chanceford	Yk	17314	E7	3589
McKINLEY RD. W., Lower Chanceford	Yk	17314	D8	3589
McKINLEY RD., Chanceford	Yk	17309	A10	3380
McMANNIS RD., Fairview	Yk	17339	E2	2954
McMILLAN ST., Gettysburg	Ad	17325	B9	3471
McSHERRY WOODS DR., Littlestown	Ad	17340	E2	3681
MEADE AV., Hanover	Yk	17331	B3	3579
MEADE AV., Penn	Yk	17331	C5	3579
MEADE COVE, Latimore	Ad	17316	B3	3266
MEADE DR., Mount Joy	Ad	17325	H1	3575
MEADE ST., North York	Yk	17404	C5	3271
MEADHILL RD., East Hopewell	Yk	17322	F11	3482
MEADOW BROOK LA., Highland	Ad	17325	H8	3469
MEADOW BROOK LA., Highland	Ad	17325	G5	3469
MEADOW BROOK LA., Paradise	Yk	17301	F10	3371
MEADOW CIR., Oxford	Ad	17350	E3	3474
MEADOW CT., Dover Twp	Yk	17315	C1	3269
MEADOW DR., Cumberland	Ad	17325	A2	3471
MEADOW DR., Fairview	Yk	17011	F7	2848

MEADOW DR., Monaghan	Yk	17019	E9	2952
MEADOW GLEN, York Twp	Yk	17402	D11	3272
MEADOW HILL DR., Springettsbury	Yk	17402	D7	3272
MEADOW HILL DR., Windsor Twp	Yk	17402	E8	3272
MEADOW HILL DR., Windsor Twp	Yk	17402	D7	3272
MEADOW LA., Cumberland	Ad	17325	B2	3471
MEADOW LA., Hellam	Yk	17368	D8	3169
MEADOW LA., Paradise	Yk	17301	F8	3371
MEADOW LA., Penn	Yk	17331	E8	3579
MEADOW LA., Springettsbury	Yk	17402	E4	3272
MEADOW LA., Windsor Twp	Yk	17402	C10	3273
MEADOW LA., Windsor Twp	Yk	17402	D6	3273
MEADOW LARK TR., Carroll Valley	Ad	17320	G1	3676
MEADOW RD., Dover Boro	Yk	17315	D10	3164
MEADOW ST., Jacobus	Yk	17407	F10	3375
MEADOW ST., New Freedom	Yk	17349	H3	3687
MEADOW ST., New Freedom	Yk	17349	A4	3688
MEADOW TR., Carroll Valley	Ad	17320	G9	3572
MEADOW TR., Monaghan	Yk	17019	E9	2952
MEADOW TR., Peach Bottom	Yk	17314	H11	3588
MEADOW TR., Peach Bottom	Yk	17314	H1	3692
MEADOW VIEW RD., Huntington	Ad	17372	G6	3159
MEADOW VIEW RD., Latimore	Ad	17372	G6	3159
MEADOWBROOK AV., Hellam	Yk	17406	B11	3168
MEADOWBROOK BLVD., Manchester Twp	Yk	17402	B10	3166
MEADOWBROOK RD., Fairview	Yk	17070	B6	2849
MEADOWBROOK RD., Springettsbury	Yk	17402	G4	3272
MEADOWLARK LA., Newberry	Yk	17319	F7	2954
MEADOWSWEET LA., Glen Rock	Yk	17327	D4	3583
MEADOWVIEW CT., Union	Ad	17340	H10	3577
MEADOWVIEW DR., Dover Twp	Yk	17315	E5	3269
MEADOWVIEW DR., Franklin	Yk	17019	A2	3161
MEADOWVIEW DR., Penn	Yk	17331	F3	3579
MEADOWVIEW DR., Union	Ad	17340	H10	3577
MEADOWVIEW DR., York Twp	Yk	17356	H11	3376
MEADOWVIEW DR., York Twp	Yk	17356	A11	3377
MEADOWVIEW DR., York Twp	Yk	17402	B5	3376
MEADOWVIEW RD., Carroll	Yk	17019	H4	3056
MEADOWVIEW RD., Franklin	Yk	17019	H2	3160
MEADTOWN RD., East Hopewell	Yk	17322	E10	3482
MEALS RD., Huntington	Ad	17324	B3	3159
MEALS RD., Latimore	Ad	17324	B3	3159
MECKLEY RD., Codorus	Yk	17327	E8	3582
MEDIA DR., Cumberland	Ad	17325	F10	3470
MEETING HOUSE RD., East Manchester	Yk	17345	D10	3061
MEETING HOUSE RD., North Codorus	Yk	17362	G3	3477
MEETING HOUSE RD., North Codorus	Yk	17362	A1	3478
MEETING HOUSE RD., Paradise	Yk	17315	C8	3268
MEETING HOUSE RD., Paradise	Yk	17364	C8	3268
MEGAN WAY, Fairview	Yk	17339	F5	2954
MEGGON RD., Windsor Twp	Yk	17356	F1	3376
MEHRING RD., Union	Ad	17340	A11	3578
MEHRING RD., Union	Ad	17340	A1	3682
MEILER RD., Springfield	Yk	17327	C9	3480
MEISENHELDER RD., East Prospect	Yk	17317	E7	3274
MEISENHELDER RD., Lower Windsor	Yk	17368	E7	3274
MEISENHELDER RD., Lower Windsor	Yk	17406	E7	3274
MELENA CIR., West Manheim	Yk	17331	F8	3579
MELINDA DR., Jackson	Yk	17404	D5	3373
MELLINGER DR, York Twp	Yk	17313	G9	3376
MELLINGER RD., Lower Windsor	Yk	17368	H6	3274
MELODIE LA., Penn	Yk	17331	F7	3579
MELRIE DR., York Twp	Yk	17403	A6	3376
MELROSE LA., Springettsbury	Yk	17402	C7	3272
MELROSE ST., Dover Twp	Yk	17315	A2	3270
MELVALE RD., York Twp	Yk	17313	E9	3376
MELVIN LA., Codorus	Yk	17327	A1	3582
MEMORY LA., Hopewell	Yk	17363	G7	3585
MEMORY LA., Shrewsbury Boro	Yk	17361	A7	3584
MEMORY LA., Springettsbury	Yk	17402	A3	3272
MEMORY LA., Springettsbury	Yk	17402	A2	3272
MEMORY LA., Springettsbury	Yk	17402	A3	3272
MEMORY LA., Stewartstown	Yk	17363	D10	3585
MEMORY LA., Warrington	Yk	17315	D6	3163
MEMORY LA., Windsor Twp	Yk	17356	D8	3377
MEMORY LA., York Twp	Yk	17402	A4	3376
MEMORY LANE RD., Menallen	Ad	17304	C11	3157
MEMORY LANE RD., Menallen	Ad	17304	C1	3262
MENEGES MILL RD., Heidelberg	Yk	17362	E4	3476
MENEGES MILL RD., Heidelberg	Yk	17362	E6	3476
MENGUS MILL RD., Germany	Ad	17340	D5	3681
MEREDITH AV., Cumberland	Ad	17325	H8	3470
MERIDIAN LA., Springettsbury	Yk	17402	B6	3272
MERINO DR., East Manchester	Yk	17345	C4	3166
MERION RD., York City	Yk	17403	D9	3271
MERRILL RD., York Twp	Yk	17403	D3	3375
MERRIN RD., York Twp	Yk	17402	H5	3375
MESSERSMITH RD., Codorus	Yk	17327	D2	3582
MESSERSMITH RD., North Codorus	Yk	17360	D10	3374
MESSERSMITH RD., North Codorus	Yk	17404	F8	3374
MESSMAN LA., Hellam	Yk	17402	C6	3167
METROPOLITAN LA., Penn	Yk	17331	F10	3475
METZ LA., Hamiltonban	Ad	17320	B2	3572
MIABRAE CT., Manchester Twp	Yk	17402	C6	3166
MICHAEL DR., Dover Twp	Yk	17315	G11	3173
MICHAEL LA., Hellam	Yk	17406	A9	3169
MICHAEL LA., Manchester Twp	Yk	17404	D10	3165
MICHAEL ST., Conewago	Ad	17331	C2	3578
MICHELLE DR., McSherrystown	Ad	17344	E2	3578
MICHELLE DR., West Manchester	Yk	17404	A7	3270
MICHELLE WAY, West Manheim	Yk	17331	G1	3683
MICKEY LA., Hamiltonban	Ad	17320	E2	3572
MIDDLE AL., East Prospect	Yk	17317	F6	3274
MIDDLE AL., East Prospect	Yk	17368	F6	3274
MIDDLE AL., Straban	Ad	17350	D6	3369
MIDDLE CREEK RD., Freedom	Ad	17320	H11	3573
MIDDLE CREEK RD., Freedom	Ad	17320	H1	3677
MIDDLE CREEK RD., Freedom	Ad	17320	A1	3678
MIDDLE RD., Menallen	Ad	17304	D11	3157
MIDDLE RD., Menallen	Ad	17304	A2	3262
MIDDLE RIVER RD., Chanceford	Yk	17309	F8	3380
MIDDLE ST. E., Gettysburg	Ad	17325	D8	3471
MIDDLE ST. E., Hanover	Yk	17331	C2	3579
MIDDLE ST. W., Gettysburg	Ad	17325	B8	3471
MIDDLE ST. W., Hanover	Yk	17331	B4	3579
MIDDLE ST. W., Penn	Yk	17331	A4	3579
MIDDLE ST., West Manchester	Yk	17404	B4	3270
MIDDLE ST., York Spring	Ad	17372	B10	3160
MIDDLEBORO RD., Dover Twp	Yk	17315	E3	3269
MIDDLEVIEW DR., York Twp	Yk	17402	A5	3376
MIDHILL RD., North Codorus	Yk	17362	H3	3476
MIDLAND AV., Spring Garden	Yk	17403	G9	3271
MIDPINE DR., Manchester Twp	Yk	17404	D11	3165
MIDVALE RD. E., Peach Bottom	Yk	17302	A8	3589
MIDVALE RD. W., Peach Bottom	Yk	17302	H7	3588
MIDVALE RD. W., Peach Bottom	Yk	17302	A8	3589
MIDWAY AL., Wrightsville	Yk	17368	E8	3169
MIDWAY DR., Carroll	Yk	17019	A4	3056
MIDWAY RD., Newberry	Yk	17370	E11	2955
MIDWAY RD., Newberry	Yk	17370	F10	2955
MIFFLIN AV., Fairview	Yk	17070	G9	2849
MILE TR., Carroll Valley	Ad	17320	G4	3676
MILE TR., Carroll Valley	Ad	17320	A4	3677
MILESBURN RD., Franklin	Ad	17222	F9	3259
MILESBURN RD., Franklin	Ad	17222	F2	3363
MILFORD GREEN RD., Washington	Yk	17316	H8	3161
MILFORD GREEN RD., Washington	Yk	17365	A8	3162
MILFORD LA., Springettsbury	Yk	17402	C8	3272
MILKY WAY, Dover Twp	Yk	17315	F6	3269
MILL CREEK RD., Conewago	Yk	17315	G6	3164
MILL CREEK RD., Conewago	Yk	17315	A7	3165
MILL CREEK RD., Manchester Twp	Yk	17404	D8	3165
MILL DR., Franklin	Yk	17019	A11	3056
MILL LA., York City	Yk	17403	E8	3271
MILL RACE RD., Manchester Twp	Yk	17404	C9	3165
MILL RD., Butler	Ad	17307	C2	3366
MILL RD., Chanceford	Yk	17309	D8	3380
MILL RD., Fawn Grove	Yk	17321	G3	3691
MILL RD., Heidelberg	Yk	17362	E4	3476
MILL RD., Lower Chanceford	Yk	17314	H2	3589
MILL RD., Springfield	Yk	17360	C4	3479
MILL ST. N., Red Lion	Yk	17356	A8	3377
MILL ST. S., Red Lion	Yk	17356	A8	3377
MILL ST., Hopewell	Yk	17363	C1	3689
MILL ST., Loganville	Yk	17360	E5	3479
MILL ST., Stewartstown	Yk	17363	D11	3585
MILL ST., Stewartstown	Yk	17363	C1	3689
MILL TR., Carroll Valley	Ad	17320	B1	3677
MILLAR RD., Tyrone	Ad	17325	F2	3368
MILLDAM AL., Wrightsville	Yk	17368	E8	3169
MILLER AV., Windsor Twp	Yk	17356	D9	3377
MILLER BOTTOM RD., Conewago	Ad	17331	B5	3578
MILLER BOTTOM RD., Union	Ad	17340	B5	3578
MILLER LA., Lower Windsor	Yk	17366	D2	3378
MILLER LA., Windsor Twp	Yk	17402	F8	3272
MILLER RD., Codorus	Yk	17329	G8	3581
MILLER RD., Codorus	Yk	17329	A7	3582
MILLER RD., Cumberland	Ad	17325	D2	3471
MILLER RD., Fairfield	Ad	17320	H4	3572
MILLER RD., Hamiltonban	Ad	17320	H4	3572
MILLER RD., Mount Joy	Ad	17340	H11	3576
MILLER RD., Newberry	Yk	17370	G11	2954
MILLER RD., Newberry	Yk	17370	H1	3059
MILLER RD., Newberry	Yk	17370	A1	3060
MILLER RD., Peach Bottom	Yk	17302	E8	3588
MILLER RD., Peach Bottom	Yk	17314	E8	3588
MILLER RD., Peach Bottom	Yk	17314	F1	3692
MILLER RD., Reading	Ad	17350	G11	3265
MILLER RD., Reading	Ad	17350	F1	3369
MILLER SCHOOL RD., North Hopewell	Yk	17322	G9	3480
MILLER ST. N., Fairfield	Ad	17320	A5	3573
MILLER ST. S., Fairfield	Ad	17320	A5	3573
MILLER ST., Franklin	Yk	17019	B7	3056
MILLERS SCHOOL RD., North Hopewell	Yk	17322	A9	3481
MILLERS SPRING RD., Lower Windsor	Yk	17406	B2	3274
MILLERSTOWN RD., Cumberland	Ad	17325	G3	3574
MILLHIMES RD., Straban	Ad	17325	G10	3368
MILLHIMES RD., Straban	Ad	17350	G10	3368
MILLRACE RD., Berwick	Ad	17301	B2	3475
MILLS ST., Springettsbury	Yk	17402	C5	3272
MILLSTONE RD., Hellam	Yk	17406	C6	3168
MILLSTONE RD., Hellam	Yk	17406	D5	3168
MILNER DR., Windsor Twp	Yk	17356	C11	3273
MILNER DR., Windsor Twp	Yk	17356	C1	3377
MILTON DR., Windsor Twp	Yk	17402	D8	3272
MILTONBERGER RD., Franklin	Ad	17353	E8	3260
MILTONBERGER RD., Franklin	Ad	17353	F1	3364
MIMOSA DR., Hellam	Yk	17402	H2	3272
MIMOSA DR., Penn	Yk	17331	G5	3579
MINDY TR., Carroll Valley	Ad	17320	F11	3572
MINE BANK RD., Warrington	Yk	17365	C7	3162
MINE BANK RD., Washington	Yk	17365	C7	3162
MINUTEMAN CT., New Freedom	Yk	17349	G1	3687
MIRAMAR ST., Fairview	Yk	17070	B5	2849
MIRLYN DR., Lower Windsor	Yk	17406	G6	3273
MISERY RD., Oxford	Ad	17350	C6	3474
MISTY CT., West Manheim	Yk	17331	H2	3683
MISTY DR., West Manchester	Yk	17404	B7	3270
MISTY HILL LA., York Twp	Yk	17313	E6	3376
MISTY LA., Franklin	Ad	17307	E10	3365
MITCHELL RD., Fawn	Yk	17302	C11	3588
MITCHELL RD., Fawn	Yk	17302	C1	3692
MOCKING BIRD RD., Warrington	Yk	17365	D1	3163
MOCKINGBIRD DR., York Twp	Yk	17313	G9	3376
MOCKINGBIRD LA., Springfield	Yk	17403	D11	3375
MOFFETT LA., Spring Garden	Yk	17403	G9	3271
MOHAWK AV., Dover Twp	Yk	17315	F2	3269
MOHAWK CT., Newberry	Yk	17370	A9	2956
MOHAWK DR., Windsor Twp	Yk	17356	B4	3377
MONAGHAN ST., Warrington	Yk	17365	A2	3163
MONARCH ST., Littlestown	Ad	17340	F2	3681
MONOCACY RD., Manchester Twp	Yk	17404	H3	3270
MONOCACY TR., Spring Grove	Yk	17362	B10	3373
MONROE ST., Hanover	Yk	17331	A1	3579
MONROE ST., West Manchester	Yk	17404	E9	3270
MONROE ST., West York	Yk	17404	G9	3270
MONT RD., North Hopewell	Yk	17322	G11	3480
MONT RD., North Hopewell	Yk	17363	G1	3584
MONTADALE DR., Carroll	Yk	17019	E2	3056
MONTAQUE DR., Carroll	Yk	17019	F2	3056
MONTASERE CT., Carroll	Yk	17019	F3	3056
MONTASERE DR., Carroll	Yk	17019	E3	3056
MONTCLAIR RD., Straban	Ad	17325	H10	3471
MONTEGO CT., Carroll	Yk	17019	H4	3056
MONTEREY CT., Dover Twp	Yk	17315	A1	3270
MONTEVIEW DR., Manchester Twp	Yk	17404	D10	3165
MONTICELLO AV., Jefferson	Yk	17362	E10	3477
MONTICELLO PL., West Manchester	Yk	17404	F7	3269
MONUMENT RD., York Twp	Yk	17403	D4	3375
MONYA CT., Manchester Twp	Yk	17404	G11	3165
MOONLIGHT DR., York Twp	Yk	17402	D8	3272
MOORE DR., Fairfield	Ad	17320	B5	3573
MOORE DR., Penn	Yk	17331	F4	3579
MOORE'S MT. RD., Fairview	Yk	17055	D8	2953
MOORE'S MT. RD., Fairview	Yk	17339	D8	2953
MOORE'S MT. RD., Fairview	Yk	17339	E1	3058
MOORE'S MT. RD., Warrington	Yk	17339	E4	3058
MOOSE RD., Straban	Ad	17325	C4	3472
MORARI DR., Carroll	Yk	17019	A3	3056
MORELAND LA., Mount Pleasant	Ad	17325	C11	3472
MORGAN DR., Latimore	Ad	17316	B4	3266
MORGAN DR., Mount Joy	Ad	17325	A3	3576
MORGAN DR., Shrewsbury Boro	Yk	17327	G8	3583
MORGAN LA., Manchester Twp	Yk	17402	C6	3166
MORGAN TR., Liberty	Ad	17320	F6	3573
MORITZ RD., Hamiltonban	Ad	17353	D9	3468
MORN MIST LA., West Manheim	Yk	17331	D9	3580
MORNINGSIDE DR., Windsor Twp	Yk	17356	C8	3378
MORNINGSTAR CT., Penn	Yk	17331	F4	3579
MORNINGSTAR RD., Manheim	Yk	17329	H7	3580
MORNINGSTAR RD., Manheim	Yk	17329	A7	3581
MORRIS AV., Fawn Grove	Yk	17321	G4	3691
MORRIS LA., Lower Windsor	Yk	17368	A6	3275
MORRIS RD., Fawn	Yk	17321	G11	3587
MORRIS RD., Fawn	Yk	17321	F1	3691
MOUL AV., Felton	Yk	17322	H4	3481
MOUL AV., Hanover	Yk	17331	D11	3475
MOUL AV., Hanover	Yk	17331	D1	3579
MOUL RD., Jackson	Yk	17364	E2	3372
MOUL RD., Paradise	Yk	17364	D3	3372
MOULSTOWN RD. E., Hanover	Yk	17331	D9	3475
MOULSTOWN RD. E., Heidelberg	Yk	17331	G8	3475
MOULSTOWN RD. E., Heidelberg	Yk	17331	A7	3476
MOULSTOWN RD. E., Penn	Yk	17331	E9	3475
MOULSTOWN RD. N., Heidelberg	Yk	17331	G2	3475
MOULSTOWN RD. N., Heidelberg	Yk	17331	A4	3476
MOULSTOWN RD. N., Heidelberg	Yk	17331	A6	3476
MOULSTOWN RD. N., Paradise	Yk	17301	G2	3475
MOULSTOWN RD., Paradise	Yk	17301	E8	3371
MOUNTAIN ASH DR., Penn	Yk	17331	G5	3579
MOUNTAIN CREST WAY, Carroll	Yk	17019	B3	3056
MOUNTAIN CT., Heidelberg	Yk	17331	G5	3475
MOUNTAIN DR, Franklin	Ad	17353	F8	3260
MOUNTAIN DR., Heidelberg	Yk	17331	G5	3475
MOUNTAIN LA., Hamiltonban	Ad	17320	A11	3468
MOUNTAIN LA., Hamiltonban	Ad	17320	A2	3572
MOUNTAIN LAUREL LA., Hellam	Yk	17406	C7	3168
MOUNTAIN RD., Carroll	Yk	17019	A5	3056
MOUNTAIN RD., Cross Roads	Yk	17322	F7	3481
MOUNTAIN RD., Dover Twp	Yk	17315	H4	3163
MOUNTAIN RD., Dover Twp	Yk	17315	A5	3164
MOUNTAIN RD., East Hopewell	Yk	17322	F7	3481
MOUNTAIN RD., Franklin	Ad	17353	G9	3260
MOUNTAIN RD., Franklin	Ad	17353	A10	3261
MOUNTAIN RD., Franklin	Ad	17353	E2	3364
MOUNTAIN RD., Franklin	Yk	17019	A5	3056
MOUNTAIN RD., Latimore	Ad	17372	B2	3160
MOUNTAIN RD., Monaghan	Yk	17339	A9	2953
MOUNTAIN RD., Monaghan	Yk	17339	A1	3058
MOUNTAIN RD., North Hopewell	Yk	17322	F7	3481
MOUNTAIN RD., Windsor Twp	Yk	17402	H6	3272
MOUNTAIN RD., Windsor Twp	Yk	17402	A8	3273
MOUNTAIN SIDE RD., Carroll	Yk	17019	C11	2951
MOUNTAIN TOP DR. W., Franklin	Ad	17353	A8	3364
MOUNTAIN TOP DR., Franklin	Ad	17353	B8	3364
MOUNTAIN VIEW AV., Menallen	Ad	17307	E2	3260
MOUNTAIN VIEW CT., Warrington	Yk	17365	E9	3058
MOUNTAIN VIEW DR., Dover Twp	Yk	17315	D2	3269
MOUNTAIN VIEW DR., Fairview	Yk	17319	D1	2955
MOUNTAIN VIEW DR., Manchester Twp	Yk	17404	F6	3165
MOUNTAIN VIEW TR., Carroll Valley	Ad	17320	G10	3572
MOUNTAIN VISTA CT., Windsor Twp	Yk	17402	H6	3272
MOURNING DOVE LA., Lower Windsor	Yk	17402	E6	3273
MT. AIRY RD., Monaghan	Yk	17019	F10	2952
MT. AIRY RD., Monaghan	Yk	17339	A1	3058
MT. AIRY RD. E., Monaghan	Yk	17019	G10	2952
MT. AIRY RD. E., Monaghan	Yk	17019	A1	3058
MT. AIRY RD. W., Monaghan	Yk	17019	E9	2952
MT. AIRY RD., Fairview	Yk	17339	E2	3058
MT. AIRY RD., Shrewsbury Boro	Yk	17349	C7	3584
MT. AIRY RD., Warrington	Yk	17339	E5	3058
MT. CARMEL DR., Littlestown	Ad	17340	E2	3681
MT. CARMEL RD., Franklin	Ad	17353	E5	3468
MT. CARMEL RD., Franklin	Ad	17353	A4	3469
MT. CARMEL RD., Hamiltonban	Ad	17353	C8	3468
MT. HEBRON RD., East Manchester	Yk	17347	A2	3167
MT. HERMAN BLVD., Springettsbury	Yk	17402	F2	3271
MT. HOPE RD., Hamiltonban	Ad	17320	H8	3571
MT. HOPE RD., Hamiltonban	Ad	17320	A6	3572
MT. HOPE RD., Hamiltonban	Ad	17320	D2	3572
MT. HOPE RD., Hamiltonban	Ad	17320	A2	3573
MT. JOY RD., Straban	Ad	17325	G10	3471
MT. LAUREL CT., Newberry	Yk	17315	F3	3059
MT. MISERY RD., Oxford	Ad	17331	C6	3474
MT. OLIVET CHURCH RD., Fawn	Yk	17302	B11	3588
MT. OLIVET CHURCH RD., Fawn	Yk	17321	C1	3692
MT. OLIVET CHURCH RD., Peach Bottom	Yk	17321	C1	3692
MT. OLIVET RD., Hopewell	Yk	17363	G5	3584
MT. OLIVET RD., North Hopewell	Yk	17322	H11	3480
MT. OLIVET RD., North Hopewell	Yk	17363	H11	3480
MT. OLIVET RD., North Hopewell	Yk	17363	H2	3584
MT. OLIVET RD., Winterstown	Yk	17322	H11	3480
MT. OLIVET RD., Winterstown	Yk	17322	A8	3481
MT. PISGAH RD., Hellam	Yk	17368	A2	3274
MT. PISGAH RD., Hellam	Yk	17406	G4	3273
MT. PISGAH RD., Hellam	Yk	17406	A2	3274
MT. PISGAH RD., Lower Windsor	Yk	17368	A2	3274
MT. PISGAH RD., Lower Windsor	Yk	17402	D10	3273
MT. PISGAH RD., Lower Windsor	Yk	17406	G4	3273
MT. PISGAH RD., Lower Windsor	Yk	17406	A2	3274
MT. PISGAH RD., Windsor Twp	Yk	17402	D10	3273
MT. PLEASANT RD., Conewago	Ad	17331	F3	3578
MT. ROSE AV., Spring Garden	Yk	17403	F7	3271
MT. ROSE AV., Springettsbury	Yk	17402	A8	3272
MT. ROSE AV., York Twp	Yk	17402	A8	3272
MT. ROYAL AV., Hanover	Yk	17331	C4	3579
MT. TABOR RD., Menallen	Ad	17304	G10	3157
MT. TABOR RD., Menallen	Ad	17304	H1	3262
MT. TABOR RD., Menallen	Ad	17324	G10	3157
MT. TABOR RD., Menallen	Ad	17324	A9	3158
MT. TABOR RD., Menallen	Ad	17324	H1	3262
MT. TOP RD., Washington	Yk	17019	F3	3161
MT. TOP RD., Washington	Yk	17365	A2	3162
MT. VERNON ST., Hanover	Yk	17331	C3	3579
MT. ZION RD., Shrewsbury Twp	Yk	17327	B11	3480
MT. ZION RD., Shrewsbury Twp	Yk	17327	A1	3584
MT. ZION RD., Springettsbury	Yk	17402	H9	3166
MT. ZION RD., Springettsbury	Yk	17402	A10	3167
MT. ZION RD., Springettsbury	Yk	17402	B1	3272
MT. ZION RD., Springfield	Yk	17327	C9	3480
MT. ZION RD., Warrington	Yk	17019	H8	3056
MT. ZION RD., Warrington	Yk	17019	A8	3057
MT. ZION RD., Warrington	Yk	17019	B9	3057
MUD COLLEGE RD., Mount Joy	Ad	17340	F11	3576
MUD COLLEGE RD., Mount Joy	Ad	17340	E2	3680
MUD RUN RD. W., Reading	Ad	17372	F7	3265
MUD RUN RD., Huntington	Ad	17372	C6	3265
MUD RUN RD., Latimore	Ad	17372	A4	3266
MUD RUN RD., Reading	Ad	17372	H5	3265
MUDDY CREEK FORKS RD., Chanceford	Yk	17302	B7	3483
MUDDY CREEK FORKS RD., Chanceford	Yk	17309	B6	3483
MUDDY CREEK FORKS RD., East Hopewell	Yk	17302	H4	3586
MUDDY CREEK FORKS RD., East Hopewell	Yk	17302	A3	3587
MUDDY CREEK FORKS RD., East Hopewell	Yk	17322	E1	3586
MUDDY CREEK FORKS RD., East Hopewell	Yk	17352	G2	3586
MUDDY CREEK FORKS RD., Lower Chanceford	Yk	17302	D10	3483
MUDDY CREEK FORKS RD., Lower Chanceford	Yk	17302	D1	3587
MUDDY CREEK RD., East Hopewell	Yk	17302	C4	3587
MUDDY CREEK RD., East Hopewell	Yk	17352	A4	3587
MUDDY CREEK RD., Fawn	Yk	17302	C4	3587
MUDDY CREEK RD., Fawn	Yk	17352	A4	3587
MUIRFIELD RD., Dover Twp	Yk	17315	B3	3269
MULBERRY CT., Dover Boro	Yk	17315	C11	3164
MULBERRY LA., Dover Twp	Yk	17315	E1	3269
MULBERRY LA., New Freedom	Yk	17349	G4	3687
MULBERRY LA., Peach Bottom	Yk	17314	A11	3589
MULBERRY RD., Springfield	Yk	17360	H3	3478
MULBERRY ST., Spring Garden	Yk	17403	E5	3271
MULBERRY ST., Wrightsville	Yk	17368	E8	3169
MULBERRY ST., York City	Yk	17403	E5	3271
MULLIGAN DR., Newberry	Yk	17319	D6	2955
MUMMASBURG RD., Cumberland	Ad	17325	F2	3470
MUMMASBURG RD., Cumberland	Ad	17325	A5	3471
MUMMASBURG RD., Franklin	Ad	17307	C5	3366
MUMMASBURG RD., Franklin	Ad	17325	D10	3366
MUMMASBURG RD., Franklin	Ad	17325	F2	3470
MUMMASBURG RD., Gettysburg	Ad	17325	A5	3471
MUMMASBURG ST., Gettysburg	Ad	17325	D7	3471
MUMMERT AV., West Manheim	Yk	17331	C10	3580
MUMMERT DR., Springfield	Yk	17327	G10	3479
MUMMERT RD., Codorus	Yk	17327	G8	3582
MUMMERT'S CHURCH RD., Hamilton	Ad	17301	B5	3371
MUMMERT'S DR., Union	Ad	17340	H11	3577
MUMPER LA., Carroll	Yk	17019	E3	3056
MUMPER LA., Carroll	Yk	17019	A3	3057
MUMPER LA., Dillsburg	Yk	17019	E3	3056
MUNDIE LA., Manchester Twp	Yk	17402	D8	3166
MUNDIS MILL RD., Manchester Twp	Yk	17402	E10	3166
MUNDIS MILL RD., Springettsbury	Yk	17402	E10	3166
MUNDIS RACE RD., East Manchester	Yk	17402	E9	3166
MUNDIS RACE RD., Manchester Twp	Yk	17402	E9	3166
MUNICIPAL RD., Berwick	Ad	17331	G5	3474
MUNICIPAL RD., Dover Twp	Yk	17315	C2	3269
MURIFIELD DR., Manchester Twp	Yk	17404	D8	3165
MURPHY RD., Peach Bottom	Yk	17302	F8	3588
MURRAY PL., York City	Yk	17403	F5	3271
MURTAUGH RD., Peach Bottom	Yk	17314	D9	3590
MUSKET CT., Fairview	Yk	17339	C3	2954
MUSKET CT., North Codorus	Yk	17404	C10	3374
MUSKET RIDGE RD., Hamilton	Ad	17301	C4	3371
MUSKET RIDGE RD., Hamilton	Ad	17316	C4	3371
MUSSELMAN AV., Biglerville	Ad	17307	A2	3367
MUSSELMAN RD., West Manheim	Yk	17331	C11	3580
MUSSER ST., Manchester Boro	Yk	17345	D2	3166
MUSSETTA ST., Penn	Yk	17331	D3	3579
MUSSLEMAN RD., West Manheim	Yk	17331	B3	3684
MUTTON RD., East Hopewell	Yk	17352	A5	3587
MYERS AV., Red Lion	Yk	17356	C7	3377

MYERS AV., West Manchester	Yk	17404	A1	3374
MYERS LA., Fairview	Yk	17070	D9	2848
MYERS LA., Springfield	Yk	17403	H1	3479
MYERS LA., Springfield	Yk	17403	H2	3479
MYERS LA., Springfield	Yk	17403	A2	3480
MYERS RD., Carroll	Yk	17019	B3	3057
MYERS RD., Chanceford	Yk	17356	G5	3378
MYERS RD., Codorus	Yk	17327	B11	3582
MYERS RD., Codorus	Yk	17327	E9	3582
MYERS RD., Felton	Yk	17322	B3	3482
MYERS RD., Jackson	Yk	17404	E5	3373
MYERS RD., Latimore	Ad	17372	B2	3160
MYERS RD., North Codorus	Yk	17360	F7	3477
MYERS RD., North Codorus	Yk	17362	D3	3477
MYERS RD., Peach Bottom	Yk	17314	D11	3589
MYERS RD., Washington	Yk	17315	E10	3162
MYERS RD., Washington	Yk	17316	E10	3162
MYERS SCHOOLHOUSE RD., North Hopewell	Yk	17356	E3	3480
MYERSTOWN RD., Huntington	Ad	17324	B6	3159
MYRTLE LA., Red Lion	Yk	17356	D7	3377
MYRTLE ST. E., Littlestown	Ad	17340	E1	3681
MYRTLE ST. W., Littlestown	Ad	17340	D1	3681

N

NACE DR., West Manheim	Yk	17331	F11	3579
NACE MILL LA., Manheim	Yk	17329	B5	3581
NACE RD., Fawn	Yk	17302	D9	3588
NACE RD., Fawn	Yk	17321	B8	3588
NACE RD., Peach Bottom	Yk	17302	D9	3588
NAFE SAWMILL RD., Codorus	Yk	17327	B8	3582
NAFE SAWMILL RD., Codorus	Yk	17329	B8	3582
NAILOR RD., Washington	Yk	17019	F6	3161
NANCY AV., York Twp	Yk	17402	G4	3375
NANCY LOPEZ LA., Newberry	Yk	17319	E7	2955
NANCY LOU LA., East Hopewell	Yk	17363	G2	3585
NANCY ST., Penn	Yk	17331	F6	3579
NAPOLEAN DR., Springettsbury	Yk	17402	E11	3167
NAPOLEAN DR., Springettsbury	Yk	17402	F1	3272
NARNIA CT., Manchester Twp	Yk	17404	E2	3270
NARNIA DR., Manchester Twp	Yk	17404	E2	3270
NARROW DR., Conewago	Ad	17331	H7	3578
NARROW GAUGE RD., Codorus	Yk	17327	H6	3582
NARROW GAUGE RD., Codorus	Yk	17327	A5	3583
NARROW RD., Penn	Yk	17331	E6	3579
NARROWS RD., Franklin	Ad	17307	B2	3366
NARROWS RD., Menallen	Ad	17307	E10	3261
NARROWS RD., Menallen	Ad	17307	G1	3365
NASHVILLE BLVD., Jackson	Yk	17362	B6	3373
NATALIE DR., York Twp	Yk	17402	H6	3375
NATALIE LA., Dover Twp	Yk	17315	E5	3269
NATURAL DAM RD., Cumberland	Ad	17325	G3	3678
NATURAL DAM RD., Freedom	Ad	17325	E3	3678
NATURAL SPRINGS RD., Straban	Ad	17325	F7	3471
NAUGLE LA., Hamiltonban	Ad	17222	F5	3467
NAUGLES HOLLOW LA., Hamiltonban	Ad	17222	G7	3467
NAUVOO RD., Fairview	Yk	17339	E4	2953
NAVAJO DR., Windsor Twp	Yk	17356	A3	3377
NAWAKWA RD., Menallen	Ad	17307	E8	3261
NAYLOR DR., Dover Twp	Yk	17315	B6	3164
NEATER ST., York City	Yk	17404	B8	3271
NEBINGER ST., Lewisberry	Yk	17339	B10	2954
NEBINGER ST., Newberry	Yk	17339	B10	2954
NEEDHAM CIR. E., Manchester Twp	Yk	17404	C11	3165
NEEDHAM CIR. W, Manchester Twp	Yk	17404	C11	3165
NEFF RD., Windsor Twp	Yk	17356	B11	3377
NEFF RD., Windsor Twp	Yk	17356	C1	3481
NEFF ST., Red Lion	Yk	17356	B7	3377
NEHRT LA., Carroll	Yk	17019	H6	3056
NEIGHBORS LA., Lower Windsor	Yk	17406	E4	3273
NEILL RUN RD., Peach Bottom	Yk	17302	H9	3588
NEILL RUN RD., Peach Bottom	Yk	17314	H9	3588
NELL RD., Reading	Ad	17316	E2	3266
NELSON RD., Dover Boro	Yk	17315	C11	3164
NENA DR., West Manchester	Yk	17404	C7	3270
NEONLIGHT DR., York Twp	Yk	17402	C9	3272
NESS CT., Loganville	Yk	17360	E5	3479
NESS RD., Windsor Twp	Yk	17356	A11	3273
NESS RD., Windsor Twp	Yk	17402	A11	3273
NEU RD., York City	Yk	17404	A3	3271
NEW BRIDGEVILLE RD., Chanceford	Yk	17322	F10	3378
NEW BRIDGEVILLE RD., Chanceford	Yk	17356	F10	3378
NEW BRIDGEVILLE RD., Chanceford	Yk	17356	A7	3379
NEW BRIDGEVILLE RD., Chanceford	Yk	17368	A10	3275
NEW BRIDGEVILLE RD., Chanceford	Yk	17368	B3	3379
NEW BRIDGEVILLE RD., Lower Windsor	Yk	17368	G10	3274
NEW BRIDGEVILLE RD., Lower Windsor	Yk	17368	A10	3275
NEW CHESTER RD., Straban	Ad	17325	A3	3473
NEW CHESTER RD., Straban	Ad	17350	B11	3369
NEW CHESTER RD., Straban	Ad	17350	A3	3473
NEW CUT RD., Lower Chanceford	Yk	17302	G5	3484
NEW FAIRVIEW CHURCH RD., York Twp	Yk	17403	F3	3375
NEW FREEDOM RD., New Freedom	Yk	17349	H3	3687
NEW FREEDOM RD., Shrewsbury Boro	Yk	17361	A11	3584
NEW FREEDOM RD., Shrewsbury Twp	Yk	17349	A11	3584
NEW FREEDOM RD., Shrewsbury Twp	Yk	17349	F5	3687
NEW FREEDOM RD., Shrewsbury Twp	Yk	17349	A2	3688
NEW KUNKLES MILL RD., Warrington	Yk	17339	A8	3059
NEW PARK RD., Fawn	Yk	17321	C11	3587
NEW PARK RD., Fawn	Yk	17321	A2	3691
NEW PARK RD., Fawn	Yk	17352	C11	3587
NEW PARK RD., Fawn	Yk	17352	D2	3587
NEW PARK RD., Fawn	Yk	17352	G3	3690
NEW PARK RD., Fawn	Yk	17352	A2	3691
NEW RD., Franklin	Ad	17353	F3	3364
NEW RD., Franklin	Ad	17353	A6	3365
NEW SCHOOL LA., York Twp	Yk	17313	C9	3376
NEW ST., Glen Rock	Yk	17327	C3	3583
NEW YORK RD., Warrington	Yk	17315	A7	3163
NEWARK ST., Littlestown	Ad	17340	E1	3681
NEWBERRY ST. N., York City	Yk	17401	B7	3271
NEWBERRY ST. N., York City	Yk	17404	B7	3271
NEWBERRY ST. S., York City	Yk	17401	C8	3271
NEWBERRY ST., Penn	Yk	17331	E2	3579
NEWBERRY ST., York City	Yk	17403	C9	3271
NEWBERRY ST., York City	Yk	17404	C8	3271
NEWCOMER RD., Lower Windsor	Yk	17366	C3	3378
NEWCOMER RD., Windsor Twp	Yk	17366	C3	3378
NEWLIN RD., York City	Yk	17403	E10	3271
NEWMAN RD., Franklin	Ad	17222	A11	3364
NEWMAN RD., Franklin	Ad	17222	A2	3468
NEWMAN RD., Hamiltonban	Ad	17222	F5	3467
NEWMAN RD., Hamiltonban	Ad	17222	A2	3468
NEWPORT RD., Dover Twp	Yk	17315	E4	3268
NEWTON AL., Abbottstown	Ad	17301	B10	3371
NEWTON AV. E., York City	Yk	17403	D7	3271
NEWTON AV. S., Dallastown	Yk	17313	F8	3376
NEWTON AV. W., York City	Yk	17404	C8	3271
NEWTON LA., Red Lion	Yk	17356	D7	3377
NEWTON LA., Red Lion	Yk	17356	C7	3377
NIAGRA LA., West Manchester	Yk	17404	D4	3270
NIBLICK CT., Carroll	Yk	17019	B4	3056
NICOLE CT., Dover Twp	Yk	17315	F4	3269
NIGHT-IN-GALE CIR., Dover Twp	Yk	17315	D7	3269
NIGHTLIGHT DR., York Twp	Yk	17402	C9	3272
NILES LA., Spring Garden	Yk	17403	F10	3271
NILES RD., Spring Garden	Yk	17403	G10	3271
NINA DR., Windsor Twp	Yk	17402	A7	3273
NISSEL LA., Fairview	Yk	17070	G11	2848
NISSEL LA., Fairview	Yk	17070	G1	2953
NITTANY CT., New Freedom	Yk	17349	H2	3687
NITTANY LA., Berwick	Ad	17301	C11	3371
NIXON DR., Shrewsbury Twp	Yk	17361	C10	3584
NOAH'S PASS, Manchester Twp	Yk	17404	G10	3165
NOLLYN DR., York Twp	Yk	17313	D7	3376
NOONAN RD., York City	Yk	17404	A6	3271
NORA LA., Hellam	Yk	17406	A9	3169
NORHT GABRIEL CT., West Manchester	Yk	17404	C7	3270
NORHURST RD., Springettsbury	Yk	17402	G1	3272
NORMAN RD., Manchester Twp	Yk	17402	D11	3166
NORMANDIE DR., West Manchester	Yk	17404	D4	3270
NORMANDY DR., Fairview	Yk	17070	C8	2849
NORRIS RD., Delta	Yk	17314	G4	3693
NORRIS RD., Lower Chanceford	Yk	17314	A5	3589
NORRIS RD., Lower Chanceford	Yk	17302	G5	3588
NORRIS RD., Menallen	Ad	17307	G4	3260
NORTH A ST., York Spring	Ad	17372	B11	3160
NORTH ABBOTT ST., Abbottstown	Ad	17301	A10	3371
NORTH ADAM ST. , West York	Yk	17404	G8	3270
NORTH AL., Wellsville	Yk	17365	H2	3162
NORTH ALBEMARLE ST., York City	Yk	17403	F5	3271
NORTH ALLWOOD DR., Conewago	Ad	17331	B4	3578
NORTH ALWINE AV., West Manchester	Yk	17404	H1	3373
NORTH AV. E., York City	Yk	17403	C6	3271
NORTH AV., Cumberland	Ad	17325	B2	3471
NORTH AV., Delta	Yk	17314	G4	3693
NORTH AV., East Berlin	Ad	17316	B11	3267
NORTH AV., East Berlin	Ad	17316	D1	3371
NORTH AV., Goldsboro	Yk	17319	H6	2955
NORTH AV., Goldsboro	Yk	17319	A6	2956
NORTH AV., Loganville	Yk	17403	G2	3479
NORTH AV., Windsor Boro	Yk	17366	E4	3377
NORTH BALDER ST., Fairfield	Ad	17320	A5	3573
NORTH BALTIMORE ST., Dillsburg	Yk	17019	D2	3056
NORTH BARRENS RD., Hopewell	Yk	17363	D4	3585
NORTH BEAVER ST., York City	Yk	17401	C7	3271
NORTH BEAVER ST., York City	Yk	17404	C6	3271
NORTH BEAVER ST., York City	Yk	17404	C7	3271
NORTH BELVIDERE AV., York City	Yk	17404	A7	3271
NORTH BELVIDERE ST., York Twp	Yk	17404	H7	3270
NORTH BERLIN AV., New Oxford	Ad	17350	B2	3474
NORTH BIESECKER RD., Jackson	Yk	17364	C1	3373
NORTH BOLTON ST., New Oxford	Ad	17350	A3	3474
NORTH BROAD ST., Spring Garden	Yk	17403	D5	3271
NORTH BROOKWOOD DR., York Twp	Yk	17403	F2	3375
NORTH BROWN'S DAM DR., Reading	Ad	17350	C3	3370
NORTH CAMP ST., Windsor Boro	Yk	17366	E4	3377
NORTH CAMP ST., Windsor Twp	Yk	17366	E4	3377
NORTH CEDAR ST., Dallastown	Yk	17313	E6	3376
NORTH CESSNA TR., Liberty	Ad	17320	C10	3573
NORTH CHARLES ST., Dallastown	Yk	17313	F7	3376
NORTH CHARLES ST., Red Lion	Yk	17356	B7	3377
NORTH CHESTNUT ST., Dillsburg	Yk	17019	D3	3056
NORTH CHURCH AV., Dallastown	Yk	17313	G7	3376
NORTH CHURCH ST., New Oxford	Ad	17350	B2	3474
NORTH CIRCLE BLVD., Manchester Twp	Yk	17402	B10	3166
NORTH CLINTON AL., Abbottstown	Ad	17301	B9	3371
NORTH CLINTON ST., West York	Yk	17404	F8	3270
NORTH COLLEGE ST., New Oxford	Ad	17350	B2	3474
NORTH CONFEDERATE AV., Cumberland	Ad	17325	A5	3471
NORTH CONSTITUTION AV., New Freedom	Yk	17349	G2	3687
NORTH CONWAY AV., Dallastown	Yk	17313	E6	3376
NORTH COURT ST., York City	Yk	17401	C6	3271
NORTH COURT ST., York City	Yk	17403	C6	3271
NORTH D ST., York Spring	Ad	17372	B10	3160
NORTH DIAMOND ST., West Manchester	Yk	17404	F8	3270
NORTH DR., West Manchester	Yk	17404	C6	3270
NORTH DUELLA CT., Manchester Twp	Yk	17404	F2	3270
NORTH DUKE ST., Dallastown	Yk	17313	H7	3376
NORTH DUKE ST., North York	Yk	17404	C4	3271
NORTH DUKE ST., York City	Yk	17401	C6	3271
NORTH DUKE ST., York City	Yk	17403	C7	3271
NORTH EAST ST., Spring Grove	Yk	17362	B11	3373
NORTH EXETER DR. , York Twp	Yk	17403	C7	3376
NORTH FERN AV., Dallastown	Yk	17313	G7	3376
NORTH FILEYS RD., Monaghan	Yk	17019	B7	2952
NORTH FORNEY AV., Hanover	Yk	17331	B3	3579
NORTH FORREST ST., West Manchester	Yk	17404	E8	3270
NORTH FRANKLIN ST., Red Lion	Yk	17356	B7	3377
NORTH FROG POND HOLLOW, Hamilton	Ad	17301	B3	3371
NORTH FROG POND HOLLOW, Hamilton	Ad	17316	B3	3371
NORTH FRONT ST., Wrightsville	Yk	17368	E6	3169
NORTH GALA, Littlestown	Ad	17340	C1	3681
NORTH GARY DR., York Twp	Yk	17313	D8	3376
NORTH GEORGE ST., East Manchester	Yk	17345	D4	3166
NORTH GEORGE ST., Manchester Twp	Yk	17402	C9	3166
NORTH GEORGE ST., Manchester Twp	Yk	17402	B2	3271
NORTH GEORGE ST., Manchester Twp	Yk	17404	B2	3271
NORTH GEORGE ST., North York	Yk	17404	C4	3271
NORTH GEORGE ST., York City	Yk	17401	C6	3271
NORTH GEORGE ST., York City	Yk	17403	C6	3271
NORTH GEORGE ST., York City	Yk	17404	C6	3271
NORTH GLEN AV., Dallastown	Yk	17313	G7	3376
NORTH GOHN LA., Red Lion	Yk	17356	B7	3377
NORTH GORA RD., Manchester Twp	Yk	17404	G11	3165
NORTH GOTWALT ST., West Manchester	Yk	17404	E9	3270
NORTH GRANT RD., Jackson	Yk	17364	A2	3373
NORTH GRANTHAM RD., Monaghan	Yk	17019	A7	2952
NORTH GRANTHAM RD., Monaghan	Yk	17019	C7	2952
NORTH H ST., York Spring	Ad	17372	B10	3160
NORTH HARRISON ST., York City	Yk	17403	F5	3271
NORTH HARTLEY ST., York City	Yk	17404	A7	3271
NORTH HARTMAN ST., York City	Yk	17403	F5	3271
NORTH HAWTHORNE ST., York City	Yk	17404	A8	3271
NORTH HAWTHORNE ST., York Twp	Yk	17404	H7	3270
NORTH HICKORY LA., Reading	Ad	17350	H6	3369
NORTH HIGH ROCK RD., Heidelberg	Yk	17331	F4	3475
NORTH HIGH ST., Arendtsville	Ad	17307	B2	3366
NORTH HIGH ST., Dallastown	Yk	17313	H7	3376
NORTH HIGHLAND AV., West York	Yk	17404	G8	3270
NORTH HIGHLAND DR., Shrewsbury Boro	Yk	17361	B7	3584
NORTH HIGHLAND DR., Shrewsbury Boro	Yk	17361	B8	3584
NORTH HILL ST., Dallastown	Yk	17313	H7	3376
NORTH HILL-N-DALE, York Twp	Yk	17403	G1	3375
NORTH HILLS RD., Springettsbury	Yk	17402	H3	3271
NORTH HOWARD AV., Gettysburg	Ad	17325	B8	3471
NORTH HOWARD AV., North York	Yk	17404	C4	3271
NORTH JACOBS AL., Abbottstown	Ad	17301	B10	3371
NORTH JOHNAMAC, Littlestown	Ad	17340	C11	3577
NORTH JOHNAMAC, Littlestown	Ad	17340	C1	3681
NORTH JONATHAN WAY , York Twp	Yk	17356	G4	3376
NORTH LARKSPUR LA., York Twp	Yk	17403	F3	3375
NORTH LEE ST., Hallam	Yk	17406	B11	3168
NORTH LEHMAN ST., York City	Yk	17403	F5	3271
NORTH LEWISBERRY RD., Monaghan	Yk	17019	D5	2952
NORTH LEWISBERRY RD., Monaghan	Yk	17055	D5	2952
NORTH MAIN ST., Biglerville	Ad	17307	A1	3367
NORTH MAIN ST., Dover Boro	Yk	17315	C11	3164
NORTH MAIN ST., East Prospect	Yk	17317	E5	3274
NORTH MAIN ST., East Prospect	Yk	17368	E5	3274
NORTH MAIN ST., Jacobus	Yk	17407	F9	3375
NORTH MAIN ST., Loganville	Yk	17403	F3	3479
NORTH MAIN ST., Manchester Boro	Yk	17345	D11	3061
NORTH MAIN ST., Railroad	Yk	17355	G9	3583
NORTH MAIN ST., Red Lion	Yk	17356	B6	3377
NORTH MAIN ST., Shrewsbury Boro	Yk	17361	A7	3584
NORTH MAIN ST., Shrewsbury Twp	Yk	17327	B1	3583
NORTH MAIN ST., Spring Grove	Yk	17362	B11	3373
NORTH MAIN ST., Springfield	Yk	17327	C11	3479
NORTH MAIN ST., Springfield	Yk	17327	B1	3583
NORTH MAIN ST., Stewartstown	Yk	17363	E10	3585
NORTH MAIN ST., Windsor Twp	Yk	17356	B6	3377
NORTH MAIN ST., York Twp	Yk	17356	B6	3377
NORTH MALVERN DR., Manchester Boro	Yk	17345	E11	3061
NORTH MARKET ST., Fawn Grove	Yk	17321	G4	3691
NORTH MASON AV., Dallastown	Yk	17313	E7	3376
NORTH McDERMOTT RD., Fawn	Yk	17321	A4	3692
NORTH MILL ST., Red Lion	Yk	17356	A8	3377
NORTH MILLER ST., Fairfield	Ad	17320	A5	3573
NORTH MOULSTOWN RD., Heidelberg	Yk	17331	G2	3475
NORTH MOULSTOWN RD., Heidelberg	Yk	17331	A6	3476
NORTH MOULSTOWN RD., Heidelberg	Yk	17331	A4	3476
NORTH MOULSTOWN RD., Paradise	Yk	17301	G2	3475
NORTH NEWBERRY ST., York City	Yk	17401	B7	3271
NORTH NEWBERRY ST., York City	Yk	17404	B7	3271
NORTH OAK HEIGHTS TR., Peach Bottom	Yk	17314	H10	3588
NORTH OAKWOOD CT., York Twp	Yk	17356	E2	3376
NORTH ORCHARD VIEW DR., Berwick	Ad	17331	C4	3475
NORTH OXFORD ST., West Manchester	Yk	17404	F8	3270
NORTH PARK LA., Red Lion	Yk	17356	B7	3377
NORTH PARK ST., Dallastown	Yk	17313	G7	3376
NORTH PARK ST., Red Lion	Yk	17356	B7	3377
NORTH PARTRIDGE CIR., Dover Twp	Yk	17315	D7	3269
NORTH PENN ST., Windsor Boro	Yk	17366	F4	3377
NORTH PENN ST., York City	Yk	17401	B7	3271
NORTH PENN ST., York City	Yk	17404	B7	3271
NORTH PERSHING AV., York City	Yk	17401	C7	3271
NORTH PERSHING ST., York City	Yk	17404	B6	3271
NORTH PERSHING ST., York City	Yk	17404	C7	3271
NORTH PETER ST., New Oxford	Ad	17350	A2	3474
NORTH PHEASANT WAY, Hamilton	Ad	17301	H8	3370
NORTH PHEASANT WAY, Hamilton	Ad	17301	A8	3371
NORTH PINE AV., Spring Grove	Yk	17362	B11	3373
NORTH PINE ST , North York	Yk	17404	C5	3271
NORTH PINE ST., Bonneauville	Ad	17325	G11	3472
NORTH PINE ST., York City	Yk	17403	D6	3271
NORTH PLEASANT AV., Dallastown	Yk	17313	G7	3376
NORTH POINT DR., Manchester Twp	Yk	17402	C2	3271
NORTH POINT DR., Shrewsbury Boro	Yk	17361	B7	3584
NORTH POPLAR ST., Dallastown	Yk	17313	E6	3376
NORTH PREAKNESS ST., Conewago	Ad	17331	B5	3578
NORTH PRIMROSE LA., Manchester Twp	Yk	17404	D10	3165
NORTH PROSPECT ST., Hallam	Yk	17406	C10	3168
NORTH PROSPECT ST., Hellam	Yk	17406	C10	3168
NORTH QUEEN ST., Littlestown	Ad	17340	E1	3681
NORTH QUEEN ST., Manchester Twp	Yk	17404	C4	3271
NORTH QUEEN ST., North York	Yk	17404	C4	3271
NORTH QUEEN ST., York City	Yk	17403	D6	3271
NORTH RAILROAD LA., Red Lion	Yk	17356	B6	3377
NORTH RD., Springfield	Yk	17403	G2	3479
NORTH SALEM CHURCH RD., Dover Twp	Yk	17315	A1	3269
NORTH SCHOOL PL., Dallastown	Yk	17313	F7	3376
NORTH SCOTT ST., West Manchester	Yk	17404	E8	3270
NORTH SEASONS DR., Monaghan	Yk	17019	A9	2952
NORTH SEWARD ST., West York	Yk	17404	G8	3270
NORTH SHERMAN ST., East Manchester	Yk	17347	H2	3166
NORTH SHERMAN ST., Spring Garden	Yk	17403	E5	3271
NORTH SHERMAN ST., Springettsbury	Yk	17402	G10	3166
NORTH SHERMAN ST., York City	Yk	17403	E5	3271
NORTH SPRING ST., Fairfield	Ad	17320	A5	3573
NORTH ST. JAMES ST., Abbottstown	Ad	17301	B9	3371
NORTH ST. W., York City	Yk	17403	C6	3271
NORTH ST. W., York City	Yk	17404	B7	3271
NORTH ST., Conewago	Ad	17331	G1	3578
NORTH ST., Conewago	Ad	17344	G1	3578
NORTH ST., Hanover	Yk	17331	B2	3579
NORTH ST., Lewisberry	Yk	17339	B9	2954
NORTH ST., Littlestown	Ad	17340	G1	3681
NORTH ST., McSherrystown	Ad	17344	E2	3578
NORTH STAR AV., Dallastown	Yk	17313	E7	3376
NORTH STEEPLE CHASE, Straban	Ad	17325	E6	3471
NORTH STRATHCONA DR., Spring Garden	Yk	17403	E10	3271
NORTH STRATTON ST., Gettysburg	Ad	17325	C8	3471
NORTH SUMMER ST., West York	Yk	17404	G8	3270
NORTH SUMMIT CIR., Spring Garden	Yk	17403	B1	3375
NORTH SUNSET DR., Shrewsbury Boro	Yk	17361	A8	3584
NORTH SYCAMORE LA., Stewartstown	Yk	17363	F11	3585
NORTH TERRACE DR., Monaghan	Yk	17019	B10	2952
NORTH TR., Carroll Valley	Ad	17320	A4	3677
NORTH TREMONT ST., York City	Yk	17403	E5	3271
NORTH VERDAN DR., Spring Garden	Yk	17403	E11	3271
NORTH WALNUT ST., Dallastown	Yk	17313	F7	3376
NORTH WALNUT ST., Spring Grove	Yk	17362	A11	3373
NORTH WASHINGTON ST., Gettysburg	Ad	17325	C8	3471
NORTH WATER ST., New Oxford	Ad	17350	A3	3474
NORTH WAY, Loganville	Yk	17360	E4	3479
NORTH WEBSTER DR., Hellam	Yk	17402	A3	3273
NORTH WEST ST., York City	Yk	17404	A7	3271
NORTH WHITE PINE TR., Peach Bottom	Yk	17314	H10	3588
NORTH WILLIAM ST., West Manchester	Yk	17404	E8	3270
NORTH WILLOW SPRINGS CIR., Manchester Twp	Yk	17402	A4	3166
NORTH WILSON LA., Hallam	Yk	17406	D10	3168
NORTH WILSON LA., Hellam	Yk	17406	D10	3168
NORTH WINDING RD., Warrington	Yk	17365	G6	3162
NORTH WYNDHAM DR., Spring Garden	Yk	17403	B11	3271
NORTH WYNDHAM DR., Spring Garden	Yk	17403	B1	3375
NORTH WYNTRE BROOK DR., York Twp	Yk	17403	E2	3375
NORTH YORK RD., Monaghan	Yk	17019	D5	2952
NORTH YORK RD., Monaghan	Yk	17055	D5	2952
NORTH ZARFOSS DR., West Manchester	Yk	17404	C11	3270
NORTHBRIAR DR., York Twp	Yk	17404	H5	3270
NORTHBROOK CIR., York Twp	Yk	17403	F1	3375
NORTHBROOK LA., Manchester Twp	Yk	17402	A7	3166
NORTHBROOK LA., Shrewsbury Boro	Yk	17349	B6	3584
NORTHCREST DR., Newberry	Yk	17370	E1	3060
NORTHERN DANCER DR., Carroll	Yk	17019	F1	3056
NORTHERN PIKE TR., Carroll Valley	Ad	17320	H7	3572
NORTHERN PIKE TR., Carroll Valley	Ad	17320	A7	3573
NORTHERN WAY, Springettsbury	Yk	17402	B4	3272
NORTHGATE DR., West Manchester	Yk	17404	E3	3270
NORTHLAND AV., Manchester Twp	Yk	17402	C11	3166
NORTHLAND AV., Manchester Twp	Yk	17402	B1	3271
NORTHRIDGE DR., West Manheim	Yk	17331	A4	3684
NORTHRIDGE LA., Hellam	Yk	17406	D6	3168
NORTHVIEW DR., Penn	Yk	17331	G3	3579
NORTHVIEW RD., Fairview	Yk	17070	G10	2848
NORTHVIEW RD., Springettsbury	Yk	17402	G11	3166
NORTHVIEW RD., Springettsbury	Yk	17402	G1	3271
NORTHVUE LA., West Manchester	Yk	17404	H5	3269
NORWAY ST., York City	Yk	17403	F7	3271
NORWOOD AV., Penn	Yk	17331	B4	3579
NORWOOD AV., Penn	Yk	17331	C5	3579
NORWOOD PL., West Manchester	Yk	17404	F7	3269
NORWOOD RD., Springettsbury	Yk	17402	B1	3272
NOSS RD., North Codorus	Yk	17404	B10	3374
NOSS RD., North Codorus	Yk	17404	C1	3478
NOTTINGHAM WAY, Windsor Twp	Yk	17356	B3	3377
NOVA LIGHT DR., York Twp	Yk	17402	D9	3272
NOVARA ST., Fairview	Yk	17070	C5	2849
NOVICE RUN TR., Carroll Valley	Ad	17320	A8	3573
NPS RD., Cumberland	Ad	17325	C6	3471
NPS RD., Gettysburg	Ad	17325	C6	3471
NULL RD., Fairview	Yk	17070	G10	2848
NURSERY RD., Carroll	Yk	17019	A3	3057
NURSERY RD., Dover Twp	Yk	17315	A6	3164
NURSERY RD., Lower Windsor	Yk	17368	D4	3274
NURSERY RD., Menallen	Ad	17304	E6	3263
NURSERY RD., Warrington	Yk	17365	B4	3163

O

OAK AL., Spring Grove	Yk	17362	A1	3477
OAK AV., Dillsburg	Yk	17019	D4	3056
OAK AV., Windsor Twp	Yk	17356	E10	3377
OAK CIR., Hanover	Yk	17331	B1	3579
OAK CROSSING, York Twp	Yk	17313	B4	3376
OAK DR. , Franklin	Ad	17353	D7	3364
OAK DR., Conewago	Ad	17331	D10	3474
OAK DR., East Manchester	Yk	17347	B11	3062
OAK DR., East Manchester	Yk	17347	G6	3166
OAK DR., Fairview	Yk	17011	E6	2848
OAK DR., Fairview	Yk	17070	B10	2849
OAK DR., Newberry	Yk	17315	F8	3059
OAK DR., Oxford	Ad	17350	C1	3474
OAK DR., Peach Bottom	Yk	17314	H9	3588

Street	County	ZIP	Grid	Map
OAK DR., Tyrone	Ad	17325	E10	3264
OAK DR., Windsor Twp	Yk	17356	D10	3377
OAK FOREST DR., Warrington	Yk	17339	B5	3059
OAK FOREST RD., Peach Bottom	Yk	17314	H9	3588
OAK GROVE DR., Liberty	Ad	17320	C10	3573
OAK GROVE RD., Tyrone	Ad	17350	B5	3369
OAK HEIGHTS TR. N., Peach Bottom	Yk	17314	H10	3588
OAK HEIGHTS TR. S., Peach Bottom	Yk	17314	A11	3589
OAK HILL CIR., Penn	Yk	17331	D5	3475
OAK HILL CT., Lower Windsor	Yk	17368	C3	3274
OAK HILL DR., Berwick	Ad	17331	C5	3475
OAK HILL DR., Newberry	Yk	17319	D10	2955
OAK HILL DR., Penn	Yk	17331	C5	3475
OAK HILL LA., Dover Twp	Yk	17315	E4	3269
OAK HILL RD., Butler	Ad	17307	G4	3367
OAK HILL RD., Butler	Ad	17307	A4	3368
OAK HILL RD., Fairview	Yk	17339	D3	2953
OAK HILL RD., Huntington	Ad	17372	G10	3159
OAK HILLS DR., West Manheim	Yk	17331	E9	3579
OAK HOLLOW RD., Chanceford	Yk	17356	E5	3378
OAK HOLLOW RD., Lower Windsor	Yk	17356	E5	3378
OAK KNOLL LA., York Twp	Yk	17403	D6	3375
OAK KNOLL RD., Fairview	Yk	17070	B10	2849
OAK LA., Dover Twp	Yk	17315	E11	3164
OAK LA., Franklin	Ad	17353	G8	3260
OAK LA., Stewartstown	Yk	17363	E10	3585
OAK LA., Straban	Ad	17325	E5	3471
OAK LA., York City	Yk	17403	C8	3271
OAK MANOR DR., York Twp	Yk	17402	B4	3376
OAK RD., Newberry	Yk	17370	F2	3060
OAK RD., York Twp	Yk	17313	B4	3376
OAK RIDGE AV., Winterstown	Yk	17322	H6	3480
OAK RIDGE AV., Winterstown	Yk	17356	H6	3480
OAK RIDGE AV., Winterstown	Yk	17356	A6	3481
OAK RIDGE DR., North Codorus	Yk	17362	B1	3478
OAK RIDGE DR., York Twp	Yk	17402	H3	3375
OAK RIDGE LA., York Twp	Yk	17313	B4	3376
OAK RIDGE RD., Springfield	Yk	17327	H9	3479
OAK RIDGE TR., Carroll Valley	Ad	17320	G5	3676
OAK ST., Hanover	Yk	17331	B1	3579
OAK ST., Newberry	Yk	17370	G1	3060
OAK ST., York Twp	Yk	17402	A4	3376
OAK TR., Carroll Valley	Ad	17320	G2	3676
OAK TREE LA., Franklin	Ad	17307	D11	3365
OAK TREE LA., Manheim	Yk	17362	H3	3580
OAKBROOK CIR., Chanceford	Yk	17322	B2	3482
OAKBROOK DR., Chanceford	Yk	17322	A2	3482
OAKCREST DR., Conewago	Ad	17331	B3	3578
OAKDALE DR., Spring Garden	Yk	17403	C2	3375
OAKES AV., Manchester Twp	Yk	17404	H2	3270
OAKHAM DR., Springettsbury	Yk	17402	E5	3272
OAKLAND DR., Dover Twp	Yk	17315	F5	3269
OAKLAND RD., Dover Twp	Yk	17315	G3	3269
OAKLEAF CIR., Shrewsbury Twp	Yk	17361	C11	3584
OAKLEIGH DR., Springettsbury	Yk	17402	F2	3272
OAKLEY DR., Dover Twp	Yk	17315	A2	3270
OAKLEY DR., Dover Twp	Yk	17404	A2	3270
OAKLY DR., Dover Twp	Yk	17404	H3	3269
OAKLYN CIR., Shrewsbury Boro	Yk	17361	B5	3584
OAKLYN DR., Newberry	Yk	17370	D2	3060
OAKMONT CIR., Shrewsbury Twp	Yk	17349	C3	3688
OAKVIEW LA., Hellam	Yk	17406	A6	3168
OAKVIEW LA., Spring Garden	Yk	17403	A1	3375
OAKWOOD AV., Heidelberg	Yk	17362	E7	3476
OAKWOOD CT. N., York Twp	Yk	17356	E2	3376
OAKWOOD CT. S., York Twp	Yk	17356	F1	3376
OAKWOOD CT., Springfield	Yk	17407	E11	3375
OAKWOOD DR., Dover Boro	Yk	17315	E10	3164
OAKWOOD DR., Jackson	Yk	17362	E10	3372
OAKWOOD DR., Lower Chanceford	Yk	17314	H3	3589
OAKWOOD DR., Newberry	Yk	17319	H10	2954
OAKWOOD DR., Springfield	Yk	17360	G8	3479
OAKWOOD DR., West Manheim	Yk	17331	H8	3579
OAKWOOD DR., West Manheim	Yk	17331	A9	3580
OAKWOOD DR., Windsor Twp	Yk	17356	C10	3377
OAKWOOD DR., York Twp	Yk	17356	E2	3376
OAKWOOD HEIGHTS DR., Hopewell	Yk	17363	G7	3584
OAKWOOD LA., Spring Garden	Yk	17403	A11	3271
OAKWOOD RD., Shrewsbury Twp	Yk	17349	B3	3688
OATFIELD CT., West Manchester	Yk	17404	C3	3270
OATMAN ST., York City	Yk	17404	A5	3271
OBERDORFF RD., Windsor Twp	Yk	17366	H3	3377
OBERDORFF RD., Windsor Twp	Yk	17366	A3	3378
OBERG DR., Peach Bottom	Yk	17314	B10	3589
OBERLIN DR., Manchester Twp	Yk	17404	F10	3165
OBOLD AV., Hanover	Yk	17331	D1	3579
O'BRIEN LA., Conewago	Ad	17331	E2	3578
O'BRIEN LA., Conewago	Ad	17344	E2	3578
OBSERVATORY DR., Fairview	Yk	17339	E8	2953
OCELOT DR., Conewago	Ad	17331	G3	3578
OCKER AV., Littlestown	Ad	17340	F1	3681
OGONTZ ST., Spring Garden	Yk	17403	G5	3271
OGONTZ ST., Spring Garden	Yk	17403	G7	3271
OGONTZ ST., Spring Garden	Yk	17403	G9	3271
OLD BALTIMORE PIKE, York Twp	Yk	17403	E2	3375
OLD BRIDGEVILLE RD., Chanceford	Yk	17322	E4	3379
OLD CARLISLE RD., Butler	Ad	17304	D11	3263
OLD CARLISLE RD., Butler	Ad	17307	D3	3367
OLD CARLISLE RD., Dover Twp	Yk	17315	A6	3164
OLD CARLISLE RD., Dover Twp	Yk	17365	F4	3163
OLD CARLISLE RD., Tyrone	Ad	17304	E8	3263
OLD CARLISLE RD., Tyrone	Ad	17324	F11	3158
OLD COLONY RD., York Twp	Yk	17402	A2	3376
OLD COMMONS RD., Lower Windsor	Yk	17366	H11	3273
OLD COMMONS RD., Lower Windsor	Yk	17366	B11	3274
OLD COMMONS RD., Lower Windsor	Yk	17366	H1	3377
OLD COMMONS RD., Lower Windsor	Yk	17366	A1	3378
OLD DEPOT RD., Fairview	Yk	17070	C7	2849
OLD DOMINION RD., Warrington	Yk	17365	G5	3162
OLD DUTCH LA., York Twp	Yk	17402	D10	3272
OLD FARM LA., Lower Windsor	Yk	17406	G6	3273
OLD FARM LA., New Freedom	Yk	17349	H5	3687
OLD FARM LA., Shrewsbury Boro	Yk	17361	B11	3584
OLD FARM LA., Spring Garden	Yk	17403	F10	3271
OLD FORD DR., Fairview	Yk	17011	E5	2848
OLD FORGE RD., Chanceford	Yk	17309	G9	3482
OLD FORGE RD., Chanceford	Yk	17309	A7	3483
OLD FORGE RD., Chanceford	Yk	17322	G9	3482
OLD FORGE RD., Fairview	Yk	17070	E11	2848
OLD FORGE RD., Fairview	Yk	17070	C2	2953
OLD FORGE RD., Fairview	Yk	17339	C2	2953
OLD FRONTIER LA., Lower Windsor	Yk	17406	G5	3273
OLD GARDEN LA., Spring Garden	Yk	17403	F10	3271
OLD GARDNERS STATION RD., Tyrone	Ad	17324	E11	3158
OLD GETTYSBURG PK., Carroll	Yk	17019	F9	2951
OLD GETTYSBURG PK., Carroll	Yk	17019	F9	2951
OLD HANOVER RD., Conewago	Ad	17331	E9	3578
OLD HANOVER RD., Heidelberg	Yk	17331	A6	3476
OLD HANOVER RD., Heidelberg	Yk	17362	D5	3476
OLD HANOVER RD., Jackson	Yk	17362	H11	3372
OLD HANOVER RD., Jackson	Yk	17362	F2	3476
OLD HANOVER RD., Union	Ad	17331	E9	3578
OLD HARRISBURG RD., Butler	Ad	17325	C4	3368
OLD HARRISBURG RD., Cumberland	Ad	17325	D6	3471
OLD HARRISBURG RD., Huntington	Ad	17372	B11	3160
OLD HARRISBURG RD., Huntington	Ad	17372	G7	3264
OLD HARRISBURG RD., Huntington	Ad	17372	A3	3265
OLD HARRISBURG RD., Straban	Ad	17325	G11	3367
OLD HARRISBURG RD., Straban	Ad	17325	C4	3368
OLD HARRISBURG RD., Straban	Ad	17325	D6	3471
OLD HARRISBURG RD., Tyrone	Ad	17325	E11	3264
OLD HARRISBURG RD., Tyrone	Ad	17325	C4	3368
OLD HARRISBURG RD., York Spring	Ad	17372	B11	3160
OLD HICKORY RD., East Manchester	Yk	17347	G7	3166
OLD LOG HOUSE LA., Reading	Ad	17316	D6	3266
OLD MILL INN RD., Manchester Twp	Yk	17404	G3	3165
OLD MILL RD., Carroll	Yk	17019	B2	3056
OLD MILL RD., Cumberland	Ad	17325	E7	3470
OLD MILL RD., Dillsburg	Yk	17019	B2	3056
OLD MILL RD., Reading	Ad	17350	E5	3370
OLD MOUNTAIN RD., Warrington	Yk	17019	B11	3057
OLD MOUNTAIN RD., Warrington	Yk	17365	B11	3057
OLD MOUNTAIN RD., Washington	Yk	17365	B1	3162
OLD NOSS RD., North Codorus	Yk	17404	C10	3374
OLD ORCHARD LA., Spring Garden	Yk	17403	F10	3271
OLD ORCHARD RD., Hellam	Yk	17402	A4	3273
OLD ORCHARD RD., Loganville	Yk	17403	G3	3479
OLD ORCHARD RD., Springettsbury	Yk	17402	A4	3273
OLD ORCHARD RD., Warrington	Yk	17370	C6	3057
OLD PINETOWN RD., Fairview	Yk	17339	G11	2953
OLD PINETOWN RD., Fairview	Yk	17339	E1	3058
OLD QUAKER RD., Fairview	Yk	17339	H6	2953
OLD QUAKER RD., Fairview	Yk	17339	A6	2954
OLD QUAKER RD., Newberry	Yk	17319	A6	2954
OLD QUAKER RD., Newberry	Yk	17319	A10	2955
OLD QUAKER RD., Newberry	Yk	17339	A6	2954
OLD RAILROAD RD., Menallen	Ad	17307	G11	3156
OLD RAILROAD RD., Menallen	Ad	17307	E3	3261
OLD ROHRBAUGH RD., North Codorus	Yk	17360	E3	3478
OLD ROUTE 30, Franklin	Ad	17307	F1	3469
OLD ROUTE 30, Franklin	Ad	17353	A7	3364
OLD ROUTE 30, Franklin	Ad	17353	A9	3365
OLD SALEM RD., West Manchester	Yk	17404	F11	3270
OLD SALEM RD., West Manchester	Yk	17404	H10	3270
OLD SCHOOL LA., East Manchester	Yk	17345	D9	3061
OLD STAGE RD., Fairview	Yk	17339	E1	2953
OLD STATE RD., Chanceford	Yk	17356	B2	3379
OLD STATE RD., Chanceford	Yk	17368	B2	3379
OLD TAXVILLE RD., West Manchester	Yk	17404	E8	3270
OLD TRAIL CT., Fairview	Yk	17319	G5	2954
OLD TRAIL RD., Fairview	Yk	17319	G4	2954
OLD TRAIL RD., Newberry	Yk	17319	G4	2954
OLD TRAIL RD., Newberry	Yk	17319	A9	2955
OLD TRAIL RD., Newberry	Yk	17370	A9	2955
OLD TRAIL RD., Newberry	Yk	17370	D1	3060
OLD TROLLEY LA., Dover Twp	Yk	17315	G11	3164
OLD TROLLEY RD., Dover Twp	Yk	17315	G1	3269
OLD US ROUTE 15, Latimore	Ad	17372	C10	3160
OLD WAYNESBORO RD., Carroll Valley	Ad	17320	C2	3676
OLD WAYNESBORO RD., Hamiltonban	Ad	17320	G2	3675
OLD WAYNESBORO RD., Hamiltonban	Ad	17320	A2	3676
OLD WAYNESBORO RD., Hamiltonban	Ad	17320	C2	3676
OLD WAYNESBORO RD., Liberty	Ad	17320	C2	3676
OLD WESTMINSTER RD., Union	Ad	17331	H11	3578
OLD WESTMINSTER RD., Union	Ad	17331	H4	3682
OLD WESTMINSTER RD., West Manheim	Yk	17331	A10	3579
OLD WESTMINSTER RD., West Manheim	Yk	17331	A1	3683
OLD YORK RD., Carroll	Yk	17019	F4	3056
OLD YORK RD., Carroll	Yk	17019	A5	3057
OLD YORK RD., Dover Twp	Yk	17315	F11	3164
OLD YORK RD., Fairview	Yk	17070	C7	2849
OLD YORK RD., Fairview	Yk	17070	F1	2954
OLD YORK RD., Fairview	Yk	17319	F1	2954
OLD YORK RD., Warrington	Yk	17019	A5	3057
OLD YORK RD., Warrington	Yk	17019	A8	3058
OLD YORK RD., Warrington	Yk	17365	A8	3058
OLD ZIEGLER MILL RD., Huntington	Ad	17324	D4	3264
OLDE FIELD DR., West Manchester	Yk	17404	A7	3270
OLDE GLOUCESTER RD., York Twp	Yk	17313	F7	3376
OLDE OAK LA., York Twp	Yk	17402	D3	3376
OLIVE ST., Spring Garden	Yk	17403	E5	3271
OLMSTEAD WAY, Manchester Twp	Yk	17404	G11	3165
OLNEY RD., York Twp	Yk	17313	B6	3376
OLSON ST., West Manchester	Yk	17404	A9	3271
OLYMPIA AV., North York	Yk	17404	B4	3271
OMAHA AV., Dover Twp	Yk	17315	F1	3269
ONEILL AV., Penn	Yk	17331	D4	3579
ONION BLVD., Shrewsbury Boro	Yk	17361	B10	3584
ONYX RD., West Manchester	Yk	17404	C7	3270
OPAL RD., West Manchester	Yk	17404	C7	3270
OPOSSUM HILL RD., Menallen	Ad	17304	B2	3263
OPPORTUNITY LA., Hellam	Yk	17406	H1	3272
ORANGE ST. S., New Oxford	Ad	17350	C1	3474
ORANGE ST. S., Oxford	Ad	17350	A3	3474
ORANGE ST., Jefferson	Yk	17362	D11	3477
ORANGE ST., West Manchester	Yk	17404	F8	3270
ORANGE ST., West York	Yk	17404	F8	3270
ORANGE ST., Wrightsville	Yk	17368	D8	3169
ORCHARD AV., Newberry	Yk	17370	E1	3060
ORCHARD BLVD., Fairview	Yk	17070	F2	2954
ORCHARD CT., Menallen	Ad	17307	C8	3262
ORCHARD CT., York Twp	Yk	17356	G5	3376
ORCHARD DR., Berwick	Ad	17331	B4	3475
ORCHARD DR., Dillsburg	Yk	17019	D2	3056
ORCHARD DR., Lower Windsor	Yk	17406	G3	3273
ORCHARD DR., Monaghan	Yk	17019	F11	2952
ORCHARD LA., Butler	Ad	17307	A7	3263
ORCHARD LA., Menallen	Ad	17304	A7	3263
ORCHARD RD., Fairview	Yk	17070	B10	2849
ORCHARD RD., Fawn	Yk	17352	C4	3587
ORCHARD RD., Fawn	Yk	17352	D7	3587
ORCHARD RD., Franklin	Ad	17353	G11	3364
ORCHARD RD., Franklin	Ad	17353	A11	3365
ORCHARD RD., Franklin	Ad	17353	G1	3468
ORCHARD RD., Hopewell	Yk	17363	D3	3689
ORCHARD RD., Jackson	Yk	17362	C10	3372
ORCHARD RD., Jackson	Yk	17362	D1	3476
ORCHARD RD., Liberty	Ad	17320	C5	3677
ORCHARD RD., North Codorus	Yk	17362	B2	3477
ORCHARD RD., Paradise	Yk	17362	B8	3372
ORCHARD RD., Paradise	Yk	17364	B6	3372
ORCHARD RD., Peach Bottom	Yk	17314	E4	3694
ORCHARD RD., Springettsbury	Yk	17402	F4	3272
ORCHARD ST., Hanover	Yk	17331	C3	3579
ORCHARD ST., Yoe	Yk	17313	F5	3376
ORCHARD ST., York Twp	Yk	17313	F5	3376
ORCHARD VIEW DR. N., Berwick	Ad	17331	C4	3475
ORCHARD VIEW DR. S., Berwick	Ad	17331	C4	3475
ORCHARD VIEW DR., Bendersville	Ad	17304	H2	3262
ORCHARD VIEW DR., East Manchester	Yk	17345	C4	3166
ORCHARD VIEW DR., Manheim	Yk	17329	A5	3685
ORCHARD VIEW LA., Menallen	Ad	17304	F2	3262
ORCHARD VIEW RD., Huntington	Ad	17324	B5	3159
ORE BANK RD., Carroll	Yk	17019	F1	3056
ORE BANK RD., Hellam	Yk	17406	H9	3167
ORE BANK RD., Hellam	Yk	17406	F10	3167
ORE BANK RD., Hellam	Yk	17406	A8	3168
ORE LA., Hellam	Yk	17406	G9	3167
ORE ST. E., Loganville	Yk	17403	F4	3479
ORE ST. W., Loganville	Yk	17360	E4	3479
OREFIELD RD., Heidelberg	Yk	17362	B9	3476
ORIN CT., Penn	Yk	17331	E8	3579
ORIOLE DR., Chanceford	Yk	17322	B2	3482
ORIOLE DR., York Twp	Yk	17403	H7	3375
ORIOLE LA., Dover Twp	Yk	17315	F6	3163
ORIOLE TR., Peach Bottom	Yk	17314	F11	3588
ORPHANAGE RD., Mount Joy	Ad	17325	G11	3575
ORPHANAGE RD., Mount Joy	Ad	17340	G11	3575
ORPHANAGE RD., Mount Joy	Ad	17340	A11	3576
ORPHANAGE RD., Mount Joy	Ad	17340	B1	3680
ORRTANNA RD., Franklin	Ad	17353	B11	3365
ORRTANNA RD., Franklin	Ad	17353	C3	3469
ORRTANNA RD., Hamiltonban	Ad	17353	C3	3469
ORRTANNA RD., Highland	Ad	17353	C3	3469
ORSON HOLLOW RD., Lower Chanceford	Yk	17302	F4	3588
ORWIG KRALL RD., Washington	Yk	17316	F5	3267
ORWIG RD., Hopewell	Yk	17363	H8	3584
ORWIG RD., Hopewell	Yk	17363	A8	3585
ORWIG RD., New Freedom	Yk	17349	G5	3687
ORWIG RD., Shrewsbury Twp	Yk	17349	B6	3688
OSAN LA., Red Lion	Yk	17356	C7	3377
OSAN LA., Red Lion	Yk	17356	D8	3377
OSAN LA., Windsor Twp	Yk	17356	D8	3377
OSCARS RD., Chanceford	Yk	17309	C3	3483
OSPREY CIR., Berwick	Ad	17331	A4	3475
OTIS CT., New Freedom	Yk	17349	G3	3687
OTTAR LA., York City	Yk	17404	A4	3271
OTTER TR., Carroll Valley	Ad	17320	F2	3676
OUTBACK DR., Penn	Yk	17331	H6	3579
OVELTON AV., Stewartstown	Yk	17363	D10	3585
OVERBROOK CIR., Spring Garden	Yk	17403	B2	3375
OVERBROOK DR., West Manchester	Yk	17404	H10	3270
OVERLAND WAY, Fairview	Yk	17070	B1	2954
OVERLOOK CT., Hopewell	Yk	17349	F6	3584
OVERLOOK DR., Goldsboro	Yk	17319	H5	2955
OVERLOOK DR., Lower Windsor	Yk	17368	G4	3274
OVERLOOK DR., Penn	Yk	17331	F4	3579
OVERLOOK LA., Hellam	Yk	17368	C11	3169
OVERLOOK ST., York Twp	Yk	17403	B6	3375
OVERLOOK TR., Carroll Valley	Ad	17320	H10	3572
OVERLOOK TR., Carroll Valley	Ad	17320	A11	3573
OVERVIEW CIR. E., Windsor Twp	Yk	17356	C11	3273
OVERVIEW CIR. W., Windsor Twp	Yk	17356	B11	3273
OVERVIEW CIR. W., Windsor Twp	Yk	17356	B1	3377
OVERVIEW DR., Springettsbury	Yk	17402	B1	3272
OVERVIEW LA., Hopewell	Yk	17363	H7	3585
OWEN RD., York Twp	Yk	17403	A11	3272
OWEN RD., York Twp	Yk	17403	H11	3271
OWL VALLEY RD., Hellam	Yk	17406	C3	3273
OXFORD AV., Conewago	Ad	17331	F11	3474
OXFORD AV., Conewago	Ad	17331	F1	3578
OXFORD AV., Conewago	Ad	17344	F1	3578
OXFORD AV., McSherrystown	Ad	17344	F1	3578
OXFORD CT., Codorus	Yk	17362	F3	3581
OXFORD CT., New Freedom	Yk	17349	H4	3687
OXFORD CT., New Oxford	Ad	17350	A3	3474
OXFORD DR., Oxford	Ad	17350	C1	3474
OXFORD RD., Conewago	Ad	17331	D9	3474
OXFORD RD., Huntington	Ad	17324	C6	3159
OXFORD RD., Huntington	Ad	17324	D1	3264
OXFORD RD., Huntington	Ad	17372	C6	3159
OXFORD RD., Huntington	Ad	17372	E5	3264
OXFORD RD., Mount Pleasant	Ad	17350	E8	3369
OXFORD RD., Oxford	Ad	17350	H1	3473
OXFORD RD., Oxford	Ad	17350	A1	3474
OXFORD RD., Straban	Ad	17350	E8	3369
OXFORD RD., Tyrone	Ad	17325	G11	3264
OXFORD RD., Tyrone	Ad	17325	G1	3368
OXFORD RD., Tyrone	Ad	17350	G1	3368
OXFORD ST. N., West Manchester	Yk	17404	F8	3270
OXFORD ST., New Oxford	Ad	17350	A3	3474
OXFORD ST., Springettsbury	Yk	17402	H5	3271
OXWOOD CIR., New Oxford	Ad	17350	A3	3474

P

Street	County	ZIP	Grid	Map
P&Q RD., Menallen	Ad	17307	C9	3262
PA STATE RD., Straban	Ad	17325	B9	3368
PACIFIC AV., York City	Yk	17404	A6	3271
PACKING HOUSE RD., Heidelberg	Yk	17331	B4	3476
PACKING HOUSE RD., Jackson	Yk	17331	B4	3476
PADDLETOWN RD., Newberry	Yk	17319	C10	2955
PADDLETOWN RD., Newberry	Yk	17319	E9	2955
PADDOCK CIR., Newberry	Yk	17319	F9	2955
PADDOCK CT., Newberry	Yk	17319	G4	2955
PAHAGACO RD., Jackson	Yk	17362	G9	3372
PAHAGACO RD., Jackson	Yk	17362	A8	3373
PAINE BLVD., North Codorus	Yk	17404	B10	3374
PAINTER AL., New Freedom	Yk	17349	G3	3687
PALACE DR., Cumberland	Ad	17325	B3	3471
PALMER AV., North Codorus	Yk	17404	B8	3374
PALMER DR., Newberry	Yk	17319	D6	2955
PALOMINO DR., Windsor Twp	Yk	17402	C10	3273
PALOMINO PKWY., Carroll	Yk	17019	B4	3057
PALOMINO RD., Dover Twp	Yk	17315	F11	3164
PALOMINO RD., Dover Twp	Yk	17315	E1	3269
PALOMINO TR., Carroll Valley	Ad	17320	A4	3677
PAMADEVA DR., Heidelberg	Yk	17362	C11	3476
PAMADEVA RD., Heidelberg	Yk	17331	B2	3580
PAMPAS DR., Manchester Twp	Yk	17404	H11	3165
PANARAMA CT., Codorus	Yk	17362	G3	3581
PANORAMA LA., West Manheim	Yk	17331	H10	3579
PANSY LA., Hellam	Yk	17406	H11	3168
PANSY LA., Hellam	Yk	17406	A11	3169
PANTHER DR., Conewago	Ad	17331	F3	3578
PANTHER HILL RD., Codorus	Yk	17360	B9	3478
PANTHER HILL RD., North Codorus	Yk	17360	B5	3478
PANTOWN RD., Conewago	Yk	17345	F6	3060
PAPER MILL RD., Lower Chanceford	Yk	17314	F7	3589
PAPER MILL RD., Peach Bottom	Yk	17314	F7	3589
PAPER MILL RD., Peach Bottom	Yk	17314	A8	3590
PAPER ST., Penn	Yk	17331	E5	3579
PARADISE CT., Dover Twp	Yk	17315	C5	3268
PARADISE CT., New Oxford	Ad	17350	H3	3473
PARADISE CT., Penn	Yk	17331	D6	3579
PARADISE HEIGHTS RD., Paradise	Yk	17301	G11	3371
PARADISE HEIGHTS RD., Paradise	Yk	17301	G1	3475
PARADISE RD., Dover Twp	Yk	17315	H7	3267
PARADISE RD., Dover Twp	Yk	17315	A6	3268
PARADISE RD., Paradise	Yk	17315	H7	3267
PARADISE RD., Springettsbury	Yk	17402	E2	3271
PARISH RD., Paradise	Yk	17316	A1	3372
PARISH TR., Liberty	Ad	17320	E6	3573
PARK AV., Cumberland	Ad	17325	G9	3470
PARK AV., East Berlin	Ad	17316	C1	3371
PARK AV., Glen Rock	Yk	17327	C3	3583
PARK AV., Hanover	Yk	17331	B2	3579
PARK AV., Littlestown	Ad	17340	E1	3681
PARK AV., Newberry	Yk	17345	D7	3061
PARK DR., Dillsburg	Yk	17019	E2	3056
PARK DR., Fairview	Yk	17339	C1	2953
PARK DR., Newberry	Yk	17315	E7	3059
PARK HEIGHTS BLVD., Penn	Yk	17331	B4	3579
PARK LA. E., Dallastown	Yk	17313	G7	3376
PARK LA. N., Red Lion	Yk	17356	B7	3377
PARK LA. S., Red Lion	Yk	17356	C7	3377
PARK LA. W., Dallastown	Yk	17313	E6	3376
PARK LA., Hellam	Yk	17406	D3	3273
PARK LA., Mount Pleasant	Ad	17350	F3	3473
PARK LA., York Twp	Yk	17403	E4	3375
PARK PL., York City	Yk	17404	B7	3271
PARK RD., East Berlin	Ad	17316	B4	3371
PARK RD., Fairview	Yk	17070	D11	2849
PARK RD., Manheim	Yk	17362	H2	3580
PARK RD., Manheim	Yk	17362	A1	3581
PARK RD., North Codorus	Yk	17362	A11	3477
PARK RD., Shrewsbury Twp	Yk	17327	C10	3480
PARK RD., Springfield	Yk	17327	D8	3480
PARK RIDGE CT., Lower Windsor	Yk	17368	C2	3274
PARK ST. N., Dallastown	Yk	17313	G7	3376
PARK ST. N., Red Lion	Yk	17356	B7	3377
PARK ST. S., Dallastown	Yk	17313	G8	3376
PARK ST. S., North Hopewell	Yk	17356	A1	3481
PARK ST. S., Red Lion	Yk	17356	B7	3377
PARK ST. S., York Twp	Yk	17313	H10	3376
PARK ST. S., York Twp	Yk	17356	H11	3376
PARK ST. S., York Twp	Yk	17356	A11	3377
PARK ST. S., York Twp	Yk	17356	A1	3481
PARK ST., Bendersville	Ad	17304	A3	3263
PARK ST., Delta	Yk	17314	E5	3693
PARK ST., Dover Twp	Yk	17315	E11	3164
PARK ST., Dover Twp	Yk	17315	D1	3269
PARK ST., Dover Twp	Yk	17404	A4	3270
PARK ST., East Manchester	Yk	17345	D8	3061
PARK ST., East Manchester	Yk	17345	D9	3061
PARK ST., Gettysburg	Ad	17325	B10	3471
PARK ST., Hopewell	Yk	17363	E10	3585
PARK ST., Jacobus	Yk	17407	E10	3375
PARK ST., Loganville	Yk	17360	E4	3479
PARK ST., Peach Bottom	Yk	17314	F5	3693
PARK ST., Penn	Yk	17331	E3	3579
PARK ST., Red Lion	Yk	17356	C8	3377

PARK ST., Seven Valleys	Yk	17360	F4	3478
PARK ST., York City	Yk	17404	A7	3271
PARK VIEW DR., North Hopewell	Yk	17322	F5	3480
PARKLYN DR., Manchester Twp	Yk	17402	C2	3271
PARKS RD., Newberry	Yk	17339	B1	3059
PARKSIDE AV., Manchester Twp	Yk	17402	H6	3165
PARKTON LA., West Manchester	Yk	17404	C4	3270
PARKVIEW DR., Loganville	Yk	17360	E4	3479
PARKVIEW DR., Windsor Twp	Yk	17356	B4	3377
PARKVIEW RD., Manchester Boro	Yk	17345	D11	3061
PARKVIEW RD., Springettsbury	Yk	17402	G11	3166
PARKWAY BLVD., York City	Yk	17404	A6	3271
PARKWAY BLVD., York Twp	Yk	17404	H6	3270
PARKWAY DR., Littlestown	Ad	17340	F11	3577
PARKWAY DR., Littlestown	Ad	17340	F1	3681
PARKWAY DR., Union	Ad	17340	F11	3577
PARKWOOD DR., East Manchester	Yk	17347	H2	3166
PARKWOOD DR., Manchester Twp	Yk	17404	G11	3165
PARLETT RD., Lower Chanceford	Yk	17302	A5	3589
PARLETT RD., Lower Chanceford	Yk	17302	H3	3588
PARRISH RD., Codorus	Yk	17329	B4	3582
PARRISH RD., Shrewsbury Twp	Yk	17349	D3	3687
PARROT LA., Conewago	Yk	17345	G8	3060
PARSONAGE LA., Lewisberry	Yk	17339	C9	2954
PARSONAGE LA., Newberry	Yk	17339	C9	2954
PARSONS TR., Liberty	Ad	17320	E6	3573
PARTHERMORE CIR., Fairview	Yk	17339	C2	2953
PARTRIDGE CIR. N., Dover Twp	Yk	17315	D7	3269
PARTRIDGE CIR., Dover Twp	Yk	17315	D7	3269
PARTRIDGE CT., Penn	Yk	17331	G7	3579
PARTRIDGE DR., Dover Twp	Yk	17315	E7	3269
PARTRIDGE TR., Carroll Valley	Ad	17320	H3	3676
PATRICK AV., Littlestown	Ad	17340	E1	3681
PATRICK DR., North Codorus	Yk	17404	B7	3374
PATRIOT ST., North Codorus	Yk	17404	C10	3374
PATTERSON RD., Mount Joy	Ad	17325	H8	3575
PATTERSON RD., Mount Joy	Ad	17325	A8	3576
PATTI LA., Penn	Yk	17331	B9	3579
PATTISON ST., York City	Yk	17403	E7	3271
PATTON LA., Chanceford	Yk	17309	G7	3380
PATTON LA., Lower Windsor	Yk	17366	G10	3273
PATWIL PL., West Manheim	Yk	17331	H2	3683
PAUL ST., Hanover	Yk	17331	C11	3475
PAUL ST., Hanover	Yk	17331	C1	3579
PAUL ST., Manchester Twp	Yk	17402	C11	3166
PAUL ST., West Manchester	Yk	17404	B4	3270
PAULA DR., York Twp	Yk	17402	A3	3376
PAULES CT., Windsor Twp	Yk	17356	B9	3378
PAULINE AV., Jackson	Yk	17404	E4	3373
PAULINE DR., Windsor Twp	Yk	17356	B2	3377
PAULINE DR., York Twp	Yk	17402	A1	3376
PAULOWNIA LA., Manchester Twp	Yk	17404	F8	3165
PAULSON DR., Springettsbury	Yk	17402	F11	3166
PAWNEE AV., Dover Twp	Yk	17315	F1	3269
PAWNEE DR., Lower Windsor	Yk	17366	B9	3274
PAYNE DR., East Manchester	Yk	17347	F9	3061
PEACE CIR., Oxford	Ad	17350	E3	3474
PEACE CIR., Oxford	Ad	17350	E2	3474
PEACE CT., Oxford	Ad	17350	E2	3474
PEACH AL., Warrington	Yk	17365	A2	3163
PEACH AL., Wellsville	Yk	17365	H2	3162
PEACH BLOSSOM LA., Hopewell	Yk	17363	E2	3689
PEACH GLEN-IDAVILLE RD., Huntington	Ad	17324	D8	3158
PEACH LA., Bendersville	Ad	17304	H3	3262
PEACH RD., Fawn	Yk	17352	C7	3587
PEACH TREE RD., Franklin	Ad	17353	A1	3469
PEACH TREE TR., Carroll Valley	Ad	17320	G4	3676
PEAK VIEW RD., Latimore	Ad	17372	A11	3055
PEAK VIEW RD., Latimore	Ad	17372	H1	3159
PEANUT DR., Conewago	Ad	17331	D10	3474
PEAR AV., Newberry	Yk	17345	D7	3061
PEARL DR., Penn	Yk	17331	D6	3579
PEARL ST., Arendtsville	Ad	17307	B3	3366
PEARSON DR., West Manchester	Yk	17404	A6	3270
PEBBLE BEACH DR., East Manchester	Yk	17347	F10	3061
PEBBLE LA., Menallen	Ad	17307	B8	3261
PEBBLE RIDGE DR., Springettsbury	Yk	17402	D6	3272
PECAN TR., Carroll Valley	Ad	17320	G4	3676
PECAN WAY, Penn	Yk	17331	D8	3475
PECHER RD., Carroll Valley	Ad	17320	C10	3573
PECHER RD., Liberty	Ad	17320	C10	3573
PECHER RD., Liberty	Ad	17320	B2	3677
PEDANT DR., York Twp	Yk	17402	G5	3375
PEEPYTOWN RD., Reading	Ad	17316	D1	3370
PEGRAM ST., Cumberland	Ad	17325	E6	3470
PEIFFER RD., Washington	Yk	17365	E8	3162
PELHAM DR., Springettsbury	Yk	17402	H3	3271
PELICAN LA., Lower Windsor	Yk	17368	A3	3275
PEMBERTON DR., Reading	Ad	17316	D4	3266
PEMBERTON PL., West Manchester	Yk	17404	B5	3270
PEMBROOK CIR., Springettsbury	Yk	17402	F5	3272
PEN MAR CT., Shrewsbury Twp	Yk	17349	D5	3687
PEN ST. W., New Freedom	Yk	17349	G2	3687
PENN AV., Windsor Twp	Yk	17356	E10	3377
PENN BLVD., York Twp	Yk	17402	C2	3376
PENN CIR., Penn	Yk	17331	H7	3579
PENN ST. N., Windsor Boro	Yk	17366	F4	3377
PENN ST. N., York City	Yk	17401	B7	3271
PENN ST. N., York City	Yk	17404	B7	3271
PENN ST. S., Windsor Boro	Yk	17366	F5	3377
PENN ST. S., Windsor Twp	Yk	17366	F5	3377
PENN ST. S., York City	Yk	17403	C9	3271
PENN ST. S., York City	Yk	17404	B8	3271
PENN ST., Biglerville	Ad	17307	A2	3367
PENN ST., Hanover	Yk	17331	C11	3475
PENN ST., Hanover	Yk	17331	C1	3579
PENN ST., Lewisberry	Yk	17339	C10	2954
PENN ST., Newberry	Yk	17339	C10	2954
PENN STATE DR., Manchester Twp	Yk	17404	G11	3165
PENNSYLVANIA AV. , York Twp	Yk	17404	H8	3270
PENNSYLVANIA AV. E., Stewartstown	Yk	17363	E11	3585

PENNSYLVANIA AV. E., Yoe	Yk	17313	G6	3376
PENNSYLVANIA AV. W., Stewartstown	Yk	17363	D11	3585
PENNSYLVANIA AV. W., Yoe	Yk	17313	G5	3376
PENNSYLVANIA AV., Goldsboro	Yk	17319	G7	2955
PENNSYLVANIA AV., Goldsboro	Yk	17319	A6	2956
PENNSYLVANIA AV., Hanover	Yk	17331	A3	3579
PENNSYLVANIA AV., Littlestown	Ad	17340	D2	3681
PENNSYLVANIA AV., Manchester Twp	Yk	17404	A2	3271
PENNSYLVANIA AV., York City	Yk	17404	A2	3271
PENNSYLVANIA AV., York City	Yk	17404	A7	3271
PENNSYLVANIA AV., York Haven	Yk	17370	D3	3061
PENNY LA., Shrewsbury Twp	Yk	17349	B2	3688
PENNY LA., Windsor Twp	Yk	17402	E8	3272
PENTLAND RD., Codorus	Yk	17362	C4	3581
PENTZ RD., Reading	Ad	17316	D2	3370
PENWOOD RD., Manchester Twp	Yk	17402	C1	3271
PENZA CT., Carroll	Ad	17019	C5	3057
PEPPERMILL LA., Manchester Twp	Yk	17404	H1	3270
PERCHRON DR., Windsor Twp	Yk	17402	C9	3273
PERRIN AV., Cumberland	Ad	17325	E6	3470
PERRING DR., York Twp	Yk	17313	D7	3376
PERRY AV., Jackson	Yk	17404	E5	3373
PERRY AV., York City	Yk	17403	C6	3271
PERRY DR., Windsor Twp	Yk	17356	C1	3377
PERRY LA., Spring Garden	Yk	17403	G9	3271
PERRY RD., Windsor Twp	Yk	17356	D2	3377
PERRY SQ., Oxford	Ad	17350	E2	3474
PERSHING AV. N., York City	Yk	17401	C7	3271
PERSHING AV. S., York City	Yk	17401	C8	3271
PERSHING AV., Windsor Twp	Yk	17356	E7	3377
PERSHING ST. N., York City	Yk	17404	B6	3271
PERSHING ST. N., York City	Yk	17404	C7	3271
PERSHING ST. S., York City	Yk	17403	C8	3271
PERSIAN LILAC DR., Newberry	Yk	17319	G5	2954
PERSIAN LILAC DR., Newberry	Yk	17319	A6	2955
PERSIMMON DR., Manchester Twp	Yk	17404	D8	3165
PERSIMMON TR., Carroll Valley	Ad	17320	H6	3676
PETER ST. N., New Oxford	Ad	17350	A2	3474
PETER ST. S., New Oxford	Ad	17350	B3	3474
PETER ST., Penn	Yk	17331	D3	3579
PETERS LA., Hamiltonban	Ad	17320	H9	3571
PETERS LA., Hamiltonban	Ad	17320	A9	3572
PETTIGREW AV., Cumberland	Ad	17325	F5	3470
PEYTON RD., Spring Garden	Yk	17403	E10	3271
PEYTON RD., York City	Yk	17403	E10	3271
PFEIFFER LA., New Oxford	Ad	17350	B2	3474
PHEASANT CIR. , Dover Twp	Yk	17315	D7	3269
PHEASANT CIR. E., Dover Twp	Yk	17315	D7	3269
PHEASANT DR., Dover Twp	Yk	17315	D7	3269
PHEASANT DR., Dover Twp	Yk	17315	D8	3269
PHEASANT RIDGE RD., Dillsburg	Yk	17019	D4	3056
PHEASANT RIDGE RD., West Manheim	Yk	17331	G11	3579
PHEASANT RUN , Newberry	Yk	17370	A2	3061
PHEASANT RUN LA., Penn	Yk	17331	G7	3579
PHEASANT RUN RD., Hellam	Yk	17406	G11	3168
PHEASANT RUN RD., West Manheim	Yk	17331	G1	3683
PHEASANT TR., Carroll Valley	Ad	17320	G7	3572
PHEASANT TR., Franklin	Ad	17353	G8	3260
PHEASANT VIEW DR., Carroll	Yk	17019	G8	3056
PHEASANT WAY N., Hamilton	Ad	17301	H8	3370
PHEASANT WAY N., Hamilton	Ad	17301	A8	3371
PHEASANT WAY S., Hamilton	Ad	17301	A8	3371
PHILADELPHIA ST. E., Yoe	Yk	17313	G6	3376
PHILADELPHIA ST. E., York City	Yk	17401	D6	3271
PHILADELPHIA ST. E., York City	Yk	17403	D6	3271
PHILADELPHIA ST. W., Yoe	Yk	17313	G6	3376
PHILADELPHIA ST. W., York City	Yk	17401	B7	3271
PHILADELPHIA ST. W., York City	Yk	17404	B7	3271
PHILADELPHIA ST., Hanover	Yk	17331	C1	3579
PHILADELPHIA ST., Spring Garden	Yk	17403	G5	3271
PHILADELPHIA ST., Springettsbury	Yk	17402	H5	3271
PHILADELPHIA ST., West Manchester	Yk	17404	E9	3270
PHILLIP CT., Manchester Twp	Yk	17404	F2	3270
PICKETT COVE , Reading	Ad	17316	C4	3266
PICKETT DR., Straban	Ad	17325	H11	3471
PICKETT RD., Washington	Yk	17315	B11	3163
PICKETT RD., Washington	Yk	17315	G2	3267
PICKETT RD., Washington	Yk	17315	A1	3268
PICKING RD., Hellam	Yk	17406	E2	3273
PICKLE RD., Chanceford	Yk	17309	A8	3380
PICKLE RD., Chanceford	Yk	17322	A5	3380
PICKS WAY, York City	Yk	17403	D7	3271
PICNIC LA., Railroad	Yk	17355	H10	3583
PICTURESQUE DR., Lower Windsor	Yk	17368	C1	3274
PIEDMONT CIR., York City	Yk	17404	A3	3271
PIEDMONT DR., Manchester Twp	Yk	17404	A3	3271
PIEDMONT DR., York City	Yk	17404	A3	3271
PIEDMONT RD., Hopewell	Yk	17363	H9	3585
PIERCEVILLE RD., Codorus	Yk	17327	E11	3582
PIERCEVILLE RD., Codorus	Yk	17327	C2	3686
PIGEON HILL PARK RD., Penn	Yk	17331	D5	3475
PIGEON HILL RD., Jackson	Yk	17331	B2	3476
PIGEON HILL RD., Jackson	Yk	17362	C9	3372
PIGEON HILL RD., Jackson	Yk	17362	E2	3476
PIGEON TR., Carroll Valley	Ad	17320	H2	3676
PIGEON TR., Carroll Valley	Ad	17320	A3	3677
PIKES PEAK RD., Peach Bottom	Yk	17314	G10	3589
PIKES PEAK RD., Peach Bottom	Yk	17314	H1	3693
PIKES PEAK RD., Peach Bottom	Yk	17314	A2	3694
PILGRIM RD., Springettsbury	Yk	17402	G10	3166
PIN OAK DR., Bonneauville	Ad	17325	H1	3576
PIN OAK DR., Fairview	Yk	17011	E8	2848
PIN OAK DR., Manchester Twp	Yk	17402	C2	3271
PIN OAK DR., Mount Pleasant	Ad	17325	H1	3576
PIN OAK DR., North Codorus	Yk	17362	A1	3478
PIN OAK DR., York Twp	Yk	17402	G5	3375
PIN OAK LA., Cumberland	Ad	17325	C4	3471
PIN OAK LA., Cumberland	Ad	17325	B3	3471
PIN OAK PL., McSherrystown	Ad	17344	E2	3578
PIN OAK TR., Peach Bottom	Yk	17314	H11	3588
PINCHTOWN RD., Dover Twp	Yk	17315	C3	3268

PINE AL., Manchester Boro	Yk	17345	D1	3166
PINE AL., New Freedom	Yk	17349	F3	3687
PINE AV. N., Spring Grove	Yk	17362	B11	3373
PINE CREEK LA., Manchester Twp	Yk	17402	F3	3165
PINE CT., Berwick	Ad	17301	C1	3475
PINE CT., Windsor Twp	Yk	17356	B9	3378
PINE DR., Heidelberg	Yk	17331	B5	3476
PINE DR., Hellam	Yk	17402	D8	3167
PINE DR., Mount Pleasant	Ad	17350	E3	3473
PINE DR., Straban	Ad	17325	C9	3368
PINE GROVE FURNACE RD., Menallen	Ad	17304	E9	3157
PINE GROVE FURNACE RD., Menallen	Ad	17304	F1	3262
PINE GROVE RD., Franklin	Ad	17222	E4	3363
PINE GROVE RD., Franklin	Ad	17222	A1	3364
PINE GROVE RD., Franklin	Ad	17353	B10	3260
PINE GROVE RD., Lower Chanceford	Yk	17302	B2	3589
PINE GROVE RD., Menallen	Ad	17307	C11	3156
PINE GROVE RD., Menallen	Ad	17307	G4	3260
PINE GROVE RD., Menallen	Ad	17307	A2	3261
PINE GROVE RD., Union	Ad	17331	D10	3578
PINE GROVE RD., Union	Ad	17331	F1	3682
PINE GROVE RD., York Twp	Yk	17403	F3	3375
PINE HAVEN DR., Franklin	Ad	17353	E7	3364
PINE HILL LA., Hellam	Yk	17406	E5	3168
PINE HILL LA., Peach Bottom	Yk	17314	A11	3589
PINE HILL LA., Spring Garden	Yk	17403	F10	3271
PINE HILL RD., Dover Twp	Yk	17315	G7	3267
PINE HILL RD., Dover Twp	Yk	17315	A5	3268
PINE HILL TR., Carroll Valley	Ad	17320	F10	3572
PINE HILL TR., Hamiltonban	Ad	17320	F10	3572
PINE HOLLOW DR., Jackson	Yk	17404	E6	3373
PINE HOLLOW RD., Lower Windsor	Yk	17366	D9	3274
PINE HOLLOW RD., Lower Windsor	Yk	17368	D9	3274
PINE HOLLOW RD., Lower Windsor	Yk	17368	D9	3274
PINE KNOLL RD., Dover Twp	Yk	17364	G8	3268
PINE LA., North Codorus	Yk	17362	F10	3373
PINE LA., Oxford	Ad	17350	B3	3474
PINE LA., Red Lion	Yk	17356	D7	3377
PINE RD., Jackson	Yk	17364	F2	3372
PINE RD., Jackson	Yk	17364	A1	3373
PINE RD., Paradise	Yk	17301	E10	3371
PINE RD., York Twp	Yk	17403	E5	3375
PINE RIDGE CIR., Fairview	Yk	17339	D2	2954
PINE RIDGE LA., Franklin	Ad	17222	A8	3364
PINE RIDGE RD., Menallen	Ad	17304	E2	3262
PINE RIDGE RD., Washington	Yk	17316	D11	3162
PINE RIDGE RD., Washington	Yk	17316	C1	3267
PINE RUN RD., Hamilton	Ad	17301	A5	3371
PINE RUN RD., Hamilton	Ad	17350	E9	3370
PINE SPRINGS BLVD., Jackson	Yk	17404	E5	3373
PINE ST, York Haven	Yk	17370	E4	3061
PINE ST. N., Bonneauville	Ad	17325	G11	3472
PINE ST. N., North York	Yk	17404	C5	3271
PINE ST. N., York City	Yk	17403	D6	3271
PINE ST. S., Red Lion	Yk	17356	C7	3377
PINE ST. S., York City	Yk	17403	E8	3271
PINE ST., Carroll	Yk	17019	H3	3055
PINE ST., Carroll	Yk	17019	A3	3056
PINE ST., Dover Twp	Yk	17404	A4	3270
PINE ST., Gettysburg	Ad	17325	C8	3471
PINE ST., Glen Rock	Yk	17327	B5	3583
PINE ST., Hanover	Yk	17331	A3	3579
PINE ST., Jacobus	Yk	17407	E10	3375
PINE ST., Loganville	Yk	17360	F4	3479
PINE ST., Manchester Twp	Yk	17404	C4	3271
PINE ST., Shrewsbury Boro	Yk	17361	A8	3584
PINE ST., Shrewsbury Twp	Yk	17327	B5	3583
PINE ST., Spring Grove	Yk	17362	B1	3477
PINE ST., Stewartstown	Yk	17363	D11	3585
PINE ST., Winterstown	Yk	17322	C7	3481
PINE ST., York Twp	Yk	17403	H1	3375
PINE SWAMP RD., Huntington	Ad	17372	C9	3159
PINE TOWN RD., Union	Ad	17331	G3	3682
PINE TR., Peach Bottom	Yk	17314	H11	3588
PINE TR., Peach Bottom	Yk	17314	A11	3589
PINE TREE DR., Fairview	Yk	17070	G8	2848
PINE TREE LA., Hamilton	Ad	17316	C4	3371
PINE TREE LA., Jackson	Yk	17362	D7	3372
PINE TREE RD., Conewago	Yk	17345	E5	3060
PINE TREE RD., Franklin	Ad	17353	G11	3260
PINE TREE RD., Franklin	Ad	17353	G1	3364
PINE TREE RD., Manheim	Yk	17362	G5	3580
PINE TREE RD., Straban	Ad	17350	E8	3368
PINE TREE TR., Franklin	Ad	17353	G8	3260
PINE VALLEY CT., Codorus	Yk	17327	B5	3686
PINE VALLEY DR., Chanceford	Yk	17322	B1	3482
PINE VALLEY RD., Franklin	Ad	17307	G11	3365
PINE VALLEY RD., Franklin	Ad	17307	F1	3469
PINE VIEW DR., Codorus	Yk	17327	B5	3686
PINE VIEW LA., York Twp	Yk	17403	D7	3375
PINE WOOD DR., Codorus	Yk	17327	C5	3686
PINE WOODS DR., Washington	Yk	17365	E8	3162
PINEHURST PL., West Manchester	Yk	17404	G9	3269
PINEHURST RD., Springettsbury	Yk	17402	C5	3272
PINEHURST TR., Carroll Valley	Ad	17320	B11	3573
PINEHURST TR., Carroll Valley	Ad	17320	B1	3677
PINES RD., Goldsboro	Yk	17319	H7	2955
PINES RD., Newberry	Yk	17319	C8	2955
PINETOWN RD., Fairview	Yk	17339	C10	2953
PINETOWN RD., Fairview	Yk	17339	E1	3058
PINETOWN RD., Fairview	Yk	17339	A1	3059
PINETOWN RD., Warrington	Yk	17339	D6	3058
PINETOWN RD., Warrington	Yk	17365	D6	3058
PINEVIEW DR., Dover Twp	Yk	17315	F3	3269
PINEVIEW DR., Dover Twp	Yk	17404	H3	3269
PINEVIEW DR., Dover Twp	Yk	17404	A3	3270
PINEWOOD CIR., Penn	Yk	17331	G6	3579
PINEWOOD LA., Hellam	Yk	17402	A4	3273
PINEY HILL RD., Lower Chanceford	Yk	17302	H1	3587
PINEY HILL RD., Lower Chanceford	Yk	17302	A2	3588
PINEY HOLLOW RD., Dover Twp	Yk	17315	D9	3163

PINEY MOUNTAIN RIDGE RD., Franklin	Ad	17222	E6	3363
PINEY MOUNTAIN RIDGE RD., Franklin	Ad	17222	D6	3363
PINEY MOUNTAIN RIDGE RD., Franklin	Ad	17222	A3	3364
PINEY MOUNTAIN RIDGE RD., Franklin	Ad	17353	E9	3260
PINEY MOUNTAIN RIDGE RD., Menallen	Ad	17307	F11	3156
PINEY MOUNTAIN RIDGE RD., Menallen	Ad	17307	A10	3157
PINEY MOUNTAIN RIDGE RD., Menallen	Ad	17307	H6	3260
PINEY MOUNTAIN RIDGE RD., Menallen	Ad	17307	A5	3261
PINTALL DR., Fairview	Yk	17319	G4	2954
PINTO TR., Carroll Valley	Ad	17320	B5	3677
PINY AL., York Haven	Yk	17370	E4	3061
PIONEER LA., Mount Pleasant	Ad	17325	F2	3576
PIPER DR., Oxford	Ad	17350	H1	3473
PIPER DR., Oxford	Ad	17350	A1	3474
PIPER TR., Liberty	Ad	17320	C9	3573
PISTON CT., Hopewell	Yk	17363	E10	3585
PLAIN VIEW TR., Carroll Valley	Ad	17320	A11	3573
PLAINVIEW RD., Butler	Ad	17325	C2	3368
PLAINVIEW RD., North Codorus	Yk	17362	C7	3477
PLANK RD., Cumberland	Ad	17325	D11	3470
PLANK RD., Cumberland	Ad	17325	D1	3574
PLANK RD., Hopewell	Yk	17349	E5	3584
PLANK RD., Hopewell	Yk	17363	G6	3584
PLANK RD., Hopewell	Yk	17363	B6	3585
PLANK RD., Latimore	Ad	17372	D9	3160
PLANK RD., Latimore	Ad	17372	D10	3160
PLANK RD., Shrewsbury Boro	Yk	17361	B6	3584
PLANK RD., Shrewsbury Twp	Yk	17349	B6	3584
PLANT AL., New Freedom	Yk	17349	F3	3687
PLANT DR., Lower Windsor	Yk	17406	G4	3273
PLANTATION LA., Hellam	Yk	17406	C3	3273
PLANTATION RD., Franklin	Ad	17353	G9	3260
PLANTATION RD., Menallen	Ad	17307	A7	3261
PLAYGROUND AL., New Freedom	Yk	17349	G3	3687
PLAYGROUND AV., Shrewsbury Boro	Yk	17349	C7	3584
PLAYGROUND PL., Littlestown	Ad	17340	E1	3681
PLEASANT ACRES RD., Springettsbury	Yk	17402	E1	3272
PLEASANT AV. N., Dallastown	Yk	17313	G7	3376
PLEASANT AV. S., York Twp	Yk	17313	B11	3376
PLEASANT AV., Jacobus	Yk	17407	E10	3375
PLEASANT AV., New Freedom	Yk	17349	G1	3687
PLEASANT CORNER CT., Windsor Twp	Yk	17356	C7	3378
PLEASANT DALE RD., Menallen	Ad	17307	B9	3262
PLEASANT DR., Newberry	Yk	17315	E1	3059
PLEASANT DR., Newberry	Yk	17339	C11	2954
PLEASANT DR., Newberry	Yk	17370	E1	3059
PLEASANT GROVE RD., Chanceford	Yk	17356	E8	3378
PLEASANT GROVE RD., Newberry	Yk	17370	A1	3061
PLEASANT GROVE RD., Newberry	Yk	17370	B2	3061
PLEASANT GROVE RD., Windsor Twp	Yk	17356	A8	3378
PLEASANT HILL CT., Carroll	Yk	17019	B5	3057
PLEASANT HILL RD., Lower Windsor	Yk	17368	B9	3275
PLEASANT HILL RD., Newberry	Yk	17339	C2	3059
PLEASANT HILL RD., West Manheim	Yk	17331	A11	3580
PLEASANT HILL RD., West Manheim	Yk	17331	A2	3684
PLEASANT LA., Red Lion	Yk	17356	B8	3377
PLEASANT PLAINS CT., Hopewell	Yk	17349	D5	3584
PLEASANT PLAINS CT., North Hopewell	Yk	17349	D5	3584
PLEASANT ST., Abbottstown	Ad	17301	B9	3371
PLEASANT ST., Hanover	Yk	17331	D2	3579
PLEASANT ST., New Oxford	Ad	17350	A3	3474
PLEASANT VALLEY RD., Chanceford	Yk	17322	B1	3482
PLEASANT VALLEY RD., East Hopewell	Yk	17322	C5	3586
PLEASANT VALLEY RD., East Hopewell	Yk	17352	C5	3586
PLEASANT VALLEY RD., East Hopewell	Yk	17363	C5	3586
PLEASANT VALLEY RD., Franklin	Ad	17307	H6	3365
PLEASANT VALLEY RD., Franklin	Ad	17307	A8	3366
PLEASANT VALLEY RD., Hellam	Yk	17402	F11	3167
PLEASANT VALLEY RD., Hellam	Yk	17406	F11	3167
PLEASANT VALLEY RD., Hellam	Yk	17406	A10	3168
PLEASANT VALLEY RD., Hopewell	Yk	17363	G11	3585
PLEASANT VALLEY RD., Hopewell	Yk	17363	B9	3586
PLEASANT VALLEY RD., Hopewell	Yk	17363	A10	3586
PLEASANT VALLEY RD., Shrewsbury Twp	Yk	17327	D7	3583
PLEASANT VALLEY RD., Springettsbury	Yk	17402	F11	3167
PLEASANT VALLEY RD., Springettsbury	Yk	17402	E1	3272
PLEASANT VALLEY RD., Springettsbury	Yk	17402	B2	3272
PLEASANT VIEW CT., East Berlin	Ad	17316	C1	3371
PLEASANT VIEW DR., Conewago	Ad	17331	H6	3578
PLEASANT VIEW DR., Lower Windsor	Yk	17406	F4	3273
PLEASANT VIEW DR., Newberry	Yk	17319	H8	2954
PLEASANT VIEW DR., Newberry	Yk	17319	A7	2955
PLEASANT VIEW DR., Paradise	Yk	17364	C3	3372
PLEASANT VIEW DR., Springettsbury	Yk	17402	F1	3271
PLEASANT VIEW DR., Windsor Twp	Yk	17356	D7	3378
PLEASANT VIEW RD., Fairview	Yk	17339	D1	2954
PLEASANT VIEW RD., North Hopewell	Yk	17356	B2	3481
PLEASANT VIEW ST., Red Lion	Yk	17356	D7	3377
PLEASANTON AV., Cumberland	Ad	17325	B1	3575
PLEASANTON DR., Mount Pleasant	Ad	17325	B11	3472
PLEASANTON DR., Reading	Ad	17316	B5	3266
PLEASANTVIEW RD., Fairview	Yk	17070	B10	2849
PLEASANTVIEW RD., Fairview	Yk	17070	D1	2954
PLEASANTVIEW RD., Fairview	Yk	17339	D5	2954
PLEASANTVIEW TER., Fairview	Yk	17070	B8	2849
PLUM RUN RD., Tyrone	Ad	17350	D5	3369
PLUM ST., Spring Garden	Yk	17403	E4	3271
PLUNKERT RD., Mount Joy	Ad	17340	H9	3576
PLUNKERT RD., Mount Joy	Ad	17340	A8	3577
PLUNKERT RD., Mount Pleasant	Ad	17340	A8	3577
PLYMOUTH RD., Springettsbury	Yk	17402	C7	3272
POCONO DR., York Twp	Yk	17402	A6	3376
POFF RD., Lower Windsor	Yk	17406	A2	3274
POINT CIR., Manchester Twp	Yk	17402	C2	3271
POINT DR. E., Shrewsbury Twp	Yk	17349	C1	3688
POINT DR. N., Manchester Twp	Yk	17402	C2	3271
POINT DR. N., Shrewsbury Boro	Yk	17361	B7	3584
POINT RIDGE DR., Springettsbury	Yk	17402	A9	3272
POLARIS DR., East Manchester	Yk	17347	G4	3166
POLLY DR., Fairfield	Ad	17320	B5	3573
POLLY TR., Carroll Valley	Ad	17320	E1	3676

POMO CT., Franklin	Yk	17019	B11	3055
POMRANING RD., Chanceford	Yk	17309	F11	3379
POMRANING RD., Chanceford	Yk	17309	F1	3483
POND BANK RD., Straban	Ad	17325	D3	3368
POND DR., Shrewsbury Twp	Yk	17327	A1	3584
POND DR., Springettsbury	Yk	17402	F7	3272
POND DR., Windsor Twp	Yk	17402	F7	3272
POND LA., Lower Windsor	Yk	17368	D2	3274
POND RD., Chanceford	Yk	17322	B2	3482
POND RD., Menallen	Ad	17324	E1	3263
POND RD., Peach Bottom	Yk	17314	B11	3589
POND RIDGE LA., Penn	Yk	17331	A7	3579
POND VIEW DR., Lower Chanceford	Yk	17314	D8	3589
PONDTOWN RD., Latimore	Ad	17372	A10	3161
PONDTOWN RD., Washington	Yk	17019	D8	3161
PONO FARM LA., North Codorus	Yk	17362	E7	3477
PONTIAC PL., Conewago	Ad	17331	D3	3578
POOR HOUSE RUN, York City	Yk	17403	D6	3271
POPLAR AL., New Freedom	Yk	17349	G3	3687
POPLAR CT., Manchester Boro	Yk	17345	D2	3166
POPLAR DR., Peach Bottom	Yk	17314	F2	3693
POPLAR DR., Tyrone	Ad	17325	E10	3264
POPLAR HILL RD., Huntington	Ad	17324	D11	3159
POPLAR HILL RD., Huntington	Ad	17324	D1	3264
POPLAR HILL RD., Huntington	Ad	17372	D11	3159
POPLAR LA., East Manchester	Yk	17347	H3	3166
POPLAR RD., Dover Twp	Yk	17315	E11	3164
POPLAR RD., Fairview	Yk	17070	A7	2849
POPLAR RD., Newberry	Yk	17315	E4	3059
POPLAR RD., Oxford	Ad	17350	H6	3473
POPLAR RD., Oxford	Ad	17350	A5	3474
POPLAR RD., Oxford	Ad	17350	A4	3474
POPLAR RD., Warrington	Yk	17019	F8	3057
POPLAR RIDGE RD., Peach Bottom	Yk	17302	H8	3588
POPLAR SPRING RD., Franklin	Ad	17353	E4	3468
POPLAR SPRING RD., Franklin	Ad	17353	A3	3469
POPLAR SPRINGS BLVD., Stewartstown	Yk	17363	E11	3585
POPLAR ST. E., York City	Yk	17403	D7	3271
POPLAR ST. E., York City	Yk	17403	F6	3271
POPLAR ST. N., Dallastown	Yk	17313	E6	3376
POPLAR ST. W., West York	Yk	17404	H9	32710
POPLAR ST., Conewago	Ad	17331	G3	3578
POPLAR ST., Conewago	Ad	17331	H2	3578
POPLAR ST., East Manchester	Yk	17345	D2	3166
POPLAR ST., Hanover	Yk	17331	A3	3579
POPLAR ST., Manchester Boro	Yk	17345	D2	3166
POPLAR ST., Yoe	Yk	17313	G5	3376
POPLAR ST., York City	Yk	17404	A9	3271
POPLAR TER., Peach Bottom	Yk	17314	F2	3693
POPLAR TER., West York	Yk	17404	G10	3270
POPLAR TER., West York	Yk	17404	G10	3270
POPLAR VIEW RD., Peach Bottom	Yk	17314	F2	3693
POPLARS RD., Dover Twp	Yk	17404	H3	3269
POPLARS RD., West Manchester	Yk	17404	A2	3270
POPPS FORD RD., Newberry	Yk	17370	H4	3059
POPPY HILLS LA., East Manchester	Yk	17347	F10	3061
PORTERS RD., Heidelberg	Yk	17362	F10	3476
PORTERS RD., Heidelberg	Yk	17362	D7	3476
PORTERS RD., North Codorus	Yk	17362	F8	3476
PORTERS RD., North Codorus	Yk	17362	G8	3476
PORTERS RD., North Codorus	Yk	17362	A7	3477
POSEY RD. E., Lower Chanceford	Yk	17302	F6	3484
POSEY RD. E., Lower Chanceford	Yk	17302	A6	3485
POSEY RD. W., Lower Chanceford	Yk	17302	B7	3484
POSSUM HOLLOW RD., Reading	Ad	17316	G11	3266
POSSUM HOLLOW RD., Reading	Ad	17316	A9	3267
POSSUM TR., Carroll Valley	Ad	17320	F2	3676
POTATO RD., Menallen	Ad	17304	F5	3262
POTATO RD., Menallen	Ad	17307	A9	3262
POTOMAC AV., Hanover	Yk	17331	B1	3579
POTOMAC AV., West Manchester	Yk	17404	C6	3270
POTOMAC ST., Littlestown	Ad	17340	E3	3681
POTOSI RD., Shrewsbury Twp	Yk	17349	D10	3480
POTOSI RD., Springfield	Yk	17327	A9	3480
POTOSI RD., Springfield	Yk	17349	D10	3480
POTTER CT., Heidelberg	Yk	17362	D9	3476
POTTER DR., Lower Chanceford	Yk	17314	D8	3589
POTTS HILL RD., Fairview	Yk	17339	C9	2954
POTTS HILL RD., Newberry	Yk	17319	E7	2954
POTTS HILL RD., Newberry	Yk	17339	C9	2954
POTTS MILL RD., Newberry	Yk	17319	C9	2954
POWDER MILL RD., York Twp	Yk	17403	F2	3375
POWER LINE RD., Peach Bottom	Yk	17314	G9	3588
POWER ST., York City	Yk	17404	B6	3271
PRAIL LA., Hopewell	Yk	17363	G5	3584
PRAYER MISSION RD., Lower Windsor	Yk	17366	D7	3274
PRAYER MISSION RD., Lower Windsor	Yk	17406	D7	3274
PREAKNESS ST. S., Conewago	Ad	17331	C5	3578
PREAKNESS ST. S., Conewago	Ad	17331	B5	3578
PRENKLE CT., Manchester Twp	Yk	17404	H2	3270
PRESCOTT RD., Spring Garden	Yk	17403	F11	3271
PRESERVE DR., Union	Ad	17340	F10	3577
PRESTON RD., Shrewsbury Twp	Yk	17349	E5	3688
PRIMROSE LA. N., Manchester Twp	Yk	17404	D10	3165
PRIMROSE LA., Hanover	Yk	17331	B10	3475
PRIMROSE LA., Manchester Twp	Yk	17404	D10	3165
PRIMROSE LA., Windsor Twp	Yk	17402	A9	3273
PRIMROSE LA., York Twp	Yk	17402	C11	3272
PRIMROSE LA., York Twp	Yk	17402	D1	3376
PRINCE ST., Littlestown	Ad	17340	D11	3577
PRINCE ST., Littlestown	Ad	17340	E1	3681
PRINCESS ST. E., York City	Yk	17403	E7	3271
PRINCESS ST. W., West York	Yk	17404	H9	3270
PRINCESS ST. W., York City	Yk	17404	B8	3271
PRINCESS ST., Gettysburg	Ad	17325	A9	3471
PRINCESS ST., Hanover	Yk	17331	A2	3579
PRINCETON RD., Springettsbury	Yk	17402	A7	3272
PRIORITY RD., York City	Yk	17404	A5	3271
PRIVATE LA., Chanceford	Yk	17322	D3	3379
PRIVATE RUN WAY, Springettsbury	Yk	17402	B8	3167
PRIVET DR., Newberry	Yk	17319	H6	2954
PROGRESS AV., Penn	Yk	17331	E9	3475
PROLINE PL., Straban	Ad	17325	H6	3471
PROLINE PL., Straban	Ad	17325	H7	3471
PROLINE PL., Straban	Ad	17325	A6	3472
PROSPECT AV., Dover Twp	Yk	17404	H4	3269
PROSPECT AV., Dover Twp	Yk	17404	A4	3270
PROSPECT HILL RD., North Codorus	Yk	17362	B10	3477
PROSPECT RD. E., Lower Windsor	Yk	17402	F6	3273
PROSPECT RD. E., Lower Windsor	Yk	17406	F6	3273
PROSPECT RD. E., Windsor Twp	Yk	17402	G8	3272
PROSPECT RD. E., Windsor Twp	Yk	17402	B7	3273
PROSPECT RD., Peach Bottom	Yk	17314	B5	3694
PROSPECT ST. E., Red Lion	Yk	17356	B6	3377
PROSPECT ST. E., Windsor Twp	Yk	17356	B6	3377
PROSPECT ST. N., Hallam	Yk	17406	C10	3168
PROSPECT ST. N., Hellam	Yk	17406	C10	3168
PROSPECT ST. W., Red Lion	Yk	17356	B6	3377
PROSPECT ST., Hallam	Yk	17406	C11	3168
PROSPECT ST., Menallen	Ad	17304	D4	3263
PROSPECT ST., Penn	Yk	17331	B5	3579
PROSPECT ST., Spring Garden	Yk	17403	F7	3271
PROSPECT ST., York City	Yk	17403	E7	3271
PROSPECT ST., York City	Yk	17403	F7	3271
PROTECTORY RD., Hamilton	Ad	17301	C7	3371
PROTECTORY RD., Paradise	Yk	17301	C7	3371
PROVIDENCE DR., Conewago	Ad	17344	F1	3578
PROWELL LA., Fairview	Yk	17070	G10	2848
PULASKI PL., York Twp	Yk	17313	E7	3376
PUMA DR., Conewago	Ad	17331	E3	3578
PUMP ST., North York	Yk	17404	B5	3271
PUMPING STATION RD., Cumberland	Ad	17325	E3	3574
PUMPING STATION RD., Freedom	Ad	17320	G10	3573
PUMPING STATION RD., Freedom	Ad	17325	A7	3574
PUMPING STATION RD., Liberty	Ad	17320	F10	3573
PUMPING STATION RD., West Manheim	Yk	17331	G8	3579
PUNCH RD., Butler	Ad	17307	D4	3366
PUTTERS CIR., Carroll	Yk	17019	A5	3056
PUTTERS COVE, West Manchester	Yk	17404	H9	3269

Q

QUAIL CIR., Newberry	Yk	17370	A3	3061
QUAIL CT., Dillsburg	Yk	17019	E4	3056
QUAIL CT., Germany	Ad	17340	G2	3680
QUAIL LA., West Manchester	Yk	17404	H7	3269
QUAIL RIDGE RD., Penn	Yk	17331	G7	3579
QUAIL RUN RD., Springettsbury	Yk	17402	B10	3167
QUAKER CHURCH RD., Latimore	Ad	17372	E2	3265
QUAKER CHURCH RD., Latimore	Ad	17372	A11	3161
QUAKER DR., Springettsbury	Yk	17402	C6	3272
QUAKER MEETING RD., Warrington	Yk	17365	G6	3162
QUAKER MEETING RD., Warrington	Yk	17365	A5	3163
QUAKER RUN RD., Butler	Ad	17307	B6	3263
QUAKER RUN RD., Menallen	Ad	17304	B6	3263
QUAKER VALLEY RD., Menallen	Ad	17304	F8	3262
QUAKER VALLEY RD., Menallen	Ad	17307	C9	3262
QUARRY RD., Bendersville	Ad	17304	H3	3262
QUARRY RD., Peach Bottom	Yk	17314	G5	3693
QUARRY RD., Peach Bottom	Yk	17314	H4	3693
QUARRY RD., Warrington	Yk	17019	H11	3057
QUARRY RD., Warrington	Yk	17365	H11	3057
QUARRY RD., Warrington	Yk	17365	G1	3162
QUEEN ST., Dover Boro	Yk	17315	D11	3164
QUEEN AL., Manchester Boro	Yk	17345	D1	3166
QUEEN ST. E., Dallastown	Yk	17313	F7	3376
QUEEN ST. N., Littlestown	Ad	17340	E1	3681
QUEEN ST. N., Manchester Twp	Yk	17404	C4	3271
QUEEN ST. N., North York	Yk	17404	C4	3271
QUEEN ST. N., York City	Yk	17403	D6	3271
QUEEN ST. S., Littlestown	Ad	17340	E2	3681
QUEEN ST. S., Spring Garden	Yk	17403	F11	3271
QUEEN ST. S., York City	Yk	17403	E9	3271
QUEEN ST. S., York Twp	Yk	17313	C6	3376
QUEEN ST. S., York Twp	Yk	17402	A3	3376
QUEEN ST. S., York Twp	Yk	17403	A3	3376
QUEEN ST. S., York Twp	Yk	17402	H1	3375
QUEEN ST. S., York Twp	Yk	17403	F11	3271
QUEEN ST. S., York Twp	Yk	17403	H1	3375
QUEEN ST., Abbottstown	Ad	17301	B9	3371
QUEEN ST., Arendtsville	Ad	17307	B2	3366
QUEEN ST., Gettysburg	Ad	17325	B10	3471
QUEEN ST., Hanover	Yk	17331	A2	3579
QUEENS CREST, York Twp	Yk	17403	G11	3271
QUEENSDALE DR., York Twp	Yk	17403	H11	3271
QUEENSWOOD DR., York Twp	Yk	17403	H11	3271
QUESENBERRY LA., Hopewell	Yk	17363	B7	3585
QUICKEL RD., Conewago	Yk	17315	A6	3165
QUIET STREAM LA., Peach Bottom	Yk	17302	C10	3589

R

RABBIT SLIDE RD., Newberry	Yk	17319	D10	2955
RABBIT TR., Carroll Valley	Ad	17320	A5	3677
RABER RD., Jefferson	Yk	17362	E11	3477
RABER RD., Straban	Ad	17350	E7	3369
RABORN LA., Hellam	Yk	17406	F7	3167
RACE HORSE AL., Gettysburg	Ad	17325	B8	3471
RACE HORSE RD., Conewago	Ad	17331	C4	3578
RACE TRACK RD., Berwick	Ad	17301	F3	3474
RACE TRACK RD., Berwick	Ad	17301	A2	3475
RACE TRACK RD., Berwick	Ad	17331	F3	3474
RACETRACK RD., Windsor Twp	Yk	17356	D4	3377
RACHEL DR., Conewago	Yk	17404	D2	3165
RACHEL RD., Dover Boro	Yk	17315	C11	3164
RADESKY ST., Fairview	Yk	17070	C6	2849
RADIANTLIGHT DR., York Twp	Yk	17402	C9	3272
RADIO RD., Conewago	Ad	17331	H10	3474
RADIO RD., Hanover	Yk	17331	A10	3475
RADIO RD., Penn	Yk	17331	A10	3475
RADIO RD., Springettsbury	Yk	17402	G1	3271
RADNOR RD., York Twp	Yk	17402	G5	3375
RAGGED EDGE RD., Franklin	Ad	17353	G4	3468
RAILROAD AV. W., Railroad	Yk	17355	H9	3583
RAILROAD AV. W., Railroad	Yk	17355	A9	3584
RAILROAD AV. W., Shrewsbury Boro	Yk	17361	A9	3584
RAILROAD AV., Red Lion	Yk	17356	A7	3377
RAILROAD AV., Shrewsbury Boro	Yk	17361	A8	3584
RAILROAD AV., Windsor Twp	Yk	17356	E9	3377
RAILROAD LA. N., Red Lion	Yk	17356	B6	3377
RAILROAD LA. S., Red Lion	Yk	17356	C7	3377
RAILROAD LA., Franklin	Ad	17353	D4	3469
RAILROAD LA., Highland	Ad	17353	E5	3469
RAILROAD ST. E., Gettysburg	Ad	17325	D8	3471
RAILROAD ST., Gettysburg	Ad	17325	C8	3471
RAILROAD ST., Goldsboro	Yk	17319	A7	2956
RAILROAD ST., Hanover	Yk	17331	C3	3579
RAILROAD ST., Spring Grove	Yk	17362	B1	3477
RAILWAY DR., Hellam	Yk	17402	H2	3272
RAILWAY DR., Hellam	Yk	17402	A2	3273
RAIN DOVE DR., Windsor Twp	Yk	17356	A2	3377
RAINBOW CIR., West Manchester	Yk	17404	B7	3270
RAINBOW TRAIL, Warrington	Yk	17365	H10	3058
RAINIER CT., York Twp	Yk	17402	A7	3376
RAINTREE LA., Hamiltonban	Ad	17320	B1	3676
RAINTREE RD., Manchester Twp	Yk	17404	E8	3165
RAKE FACTORY RD., Butler	Ad	17307	A5	3367
RALEIGH CT., Codorus	Yk	17362	F3	3581
RALEIGH DR., Springettsbury	Yk	17402	A7	3272
RAM DR., Conewago	Ad	17331	G4	3578
RAMBLER RD., Jackson	Yk	17364	E3	3372
RAMBLEWOOD DR., Newberry	Yk	17319	G7	2954
RAMBLEWOOD RD., West Manchester	Yk	17404	A5	3270
RAMBLING LA., Hellam	Yk	17406	D7	3168
RAMBO HILL RD., East Hopewell	Yk	17322	D10	3482
RAMBO HILL RD., East Hopewell	Yk	17322	E1	3586
RAMBO RD., East Hopewell	Yk	17322	B9	3482
RAMBO RD., York Twp	Yk	17356	H5	3376
RAMER LA., Hellam	Yk	17406	F7	3167
RAMPIKE HILL RD., Bendersville	Ad	17304	A3	3263
RAMPIKE HILL RD., Menallen	Ad	17304	A3	3263
RAMPIKE RD., Bendersville	Ad	17304	A3	3263
RAMSAY CIR., East Hopewell	Yk	17363	A6	3586
RAMSGATE CT., West Manchester	Yk	17404	D8	3270
RANCH RD., Jackson	Yk	17362	B9	3372
RANCH RD., Springfield	Yk	17360	H11	3374
RANCH RD., Springfield	Yk	17360	A11	3375
RANCH TR. E., Carroll Valley	Ad	17320	A3	3677
RANCH TR., Carroll Valley	Ad	17320	A5	3677
RANCH TR., Liberty	Ad	17320	A5	3677
RANDOLPH CT., Hanover	Yk	17331	A11	3475
RANDOLPH DR., Spring Garden	Yk	17403	F11	3271
RANDOLPH ST., Hanover	Yk	17331	A11	3475
RANDOLPH ST., Hanover	Yk	17331	A1	3579
RANDOLPH ST., Penn	Yk	17331	A10	3475
RANDOW RD., Spring Garden	Yk	17403	A9	3272
RANGE END MANOR RD., Carroll	Yk	17019	B4	3056
RANGE END RD., Carroll	Yk	17019	A10	3056
RANGE END RD., Franklin	Yk	17019	A10	3056
RANGE RD., Hellam	Yk	17402	E8	3167
RANGE RD., Hellam	Yk	17402	D5	3167
RAPHIEL CT. E., West Manheim	Yk	17331	E11	3579
RAPHIEL CT. W., West Manheim	Yk	17331	D11	3579
RAPHIEL DR., West Manheim	Yk	17331	D11	3579
RATHTON RD., Spring Garden	Yk	17403	F10	3271
RATHTON RD., York City	Yk	17403	D10	3271
RAUB RD., Chanceford	Yk	17322	C1	3482
RAUBENSTINE RD., Union	Ad	17331	H3	3682
RAUBENSTINE RD., West Manheim	Yk	17331	A3	3683
RAVEN TR., Carroll Valley	Ad	17320	G2	3676
RAVENWOOD TR., Carroll Valley	Ad	17320	B3	3677
RAVER LA., Shrewsbury Twp	Yk	17327	F1	3583
RAVER LA., Springfield	Yk	17327	F11	3479
RAVER RD., Lower Windsor	Ad	17366	C2	3378
RAY CT., Reading	Ad	17350	B1	3370
RAYCOM RD., Dover Twp	Yk	17315	D10	3164
RAYLIGHT DR., York Twp	Yk	17402	D9	3272
RAYPAULA DR., Shrewsbury Boro	Yk	17361	B7	3584
RAYS HILL LA., Hamiltonban	Ad	17320	F5	3572
READE AV., Spring Garden	Yk	17403	B10	3271
REBA DR., Oxford	Ad	17350	H7	3473
REBECCA DR., Newberry	Yk	17370	H10	2955
REBECCA LA., Penn	Yk	17331	B9	3579
REBECCA LA., York Twp	Yk	17403	G2	3375
REBECCA TR., Carroll Valley	Ad	17320	E11	3572
REBEL VIEW, Cumberland	Ad	17325	D5	3470
RED BANK RD., Newberry	Yk	17315	E4	3059
RED BARBERRY DR., Newberry	Yk	17319	G5	2954
RED BARBERRY DR., Newberry	Yk	17319	A6	2955
RED BRIDGE RD., Straban	Ad	17325	E6	3368
RED BRIDGE RD., Tyrone	Ad	17350	F4	3368
RED FOX CT., Fairview	Yk	17339	A5	2954
RED FRONT RD., Lower Windsor	Yk	17402	E6	3273
RED HILL RD., Oxford	Ad	17350	B8	3474
RED HILL RD., Oxford	Ad	17350	E5	3474
RED LION AV., Felton	Yk	17322	H4	3481
RED LION AV., North Hopewell	Yk	17322	H4	3481
RED MAPLE CIR., Newberry	Yk	17319	E8	2955
RED MILL RD., Newberry	Yk	17319	H5	2954
RED MILL RD., Newberry	Yk	17319	A5	2955
RED MOUNT RD., Washington	Yk	17316	G11	3161
RED OAK LA., Cumberland	Ad	17325	E9	3470
RED OAK TR., Peach Bottom	Yk	17314	H10	3588
RED PATCH RD., Gettysburg	Ad	17325	A9	3471
RED ROCK AV., Warrington	Yk	17315	B9	3163
RED ROCK RD., Conewago	Yk	17402	F8	3060
RED ROCK RD., Cumberland	Ad	17325	E5	3574
RED ROCK RD., Freedom	Ad	17325	C6	3574
RED RUN CHURCH, Washington	Yk	17316	D5	3267
RED SPIRE LA., Stewartstown	Yk	17363	F1	3689
RED WING LA., Conewago	Yk	17315	A11	3165
REDBUD CT., Manchester Twp	Yk	17404	F8	3165
REDBUD TR., Carroll Valley	Ad	17320	A4	3677
REDCOAT CT., Hanover	Yk	17331	C10	3475
REDDING AV., Cumberland	Ad	17325	H9	3470
REDDING LA., Cumberland	Ad	17325	H10	3470
REDHAVEN RD., Fairview	Yk	17070	F2	2954
REDSTONE DR., Newberry	Yk	17370	E11	2954
REDSTONE DR., Newberry	Yk	17370	D1	3059
REDWOOD LA., Hanover	Yk	17331	A1	3579
REDWOOD PL., Fairview	Yk	17011	F6	2848
REDWOOD RD., Dover Twp	Yk	17315	F3	3269
REDWOOD RD., West Manchester	Yk	17404	A5	3270
REED RD., Lower Chanceford	Yk	17302	G9	3483
REED RD., Lower Chanceford	Yk	17302	A10	3484
REEDS RD., Chanceford	Yk	17322	C9	3379
REEHLING RD., New Freedom	Yk	17349	H2	3687
REESE RD., New Freedom	Yk	17349	H2	3687
REESER DR., Newberry	Yk	17370	E11	2955
REESER DR., Newberry	Yk	17370	E1	3060
REESERS MILL RD., Newberry	Yk	17370	A1	3061
REGAL DR., Penn	Yk	17331	F4	3579
REGAN DR., Shrewsbury Twp	Yk	17361	C9	3584
REGENCY CIR., Straban	Ad	17325	G10	3471
REGENCY LA., Springettsbury	Yk	17402	E5	3272
REGENTS GLEN BLVD., Spring Garden	Yk	17403	H11	3270
REGENTS GLEN BLVD., Spring Garden	Yk	17403	A11	3271
REHMEYER HOLLOWS RD., North Hopewell	Yk	17349	E2	3584
REINECKE PL., York City	Yk	17403	D7	3271
REINECKE RD., Lower Chanceford	Yk	17302	F1	3588
REISINGER AV., Lower Windsor	Yk	17368	G10	3274
REMINGTON DR., Fairview	Yk	17319	G4	2954
RENAISSANCE DR., Hopewell	Yk	17349	D8	3584
RENNER ST., Littlestown	Ad	17340	F1	3681
RENNOLL RD., Shrewsbury Twp	Yk	17327	E6	3583
RENTZEL RD., Butler	Ad	17307	E1	3367
RENTZEL RD., Straban	Ad	17325	H6	3367
RENTZEL RD., Straban	Ad	17325	A5	3368
REPUBLIC CLARK AL., New Freedom	Yk	17349	G3	3687
RESERVOIR AV., Shrewsbury Boro	Yk	17361	B9	3584
RESERVOIR AV., Shrewsbury Twp	Yk	17361	B9	3584
RESERVOIR RD., Codorus	Yk	17362	F1	3581
RESERVOIR RD., Shrewsbury Twp	Yk	17327	G2	3583
RESERVOIR RD., Shrewsbury Twp	Yk	17327	A3	3584
RESERVOIR RD., Tyrone	Ad	17324	C9	3158
RESSLER RD., Codorus	Yk	17327	C9	3582
RETRIEVER TR., Liberty	Ad	17320	E9	3573
REVERE CIR., Fairview	Yk	17339	G6	2953
REVERE CT., Littlestown	Ad	17340	D3	3681
REVERE DR., New Freedom	Yk	17349	G1	3687
REVERE RD., York Twp	Yk	17402	A3	3376
REVERE RD., York Twp	Yk	17402	G5	3375
REXROTH RD., Chanceford	Yk	17302	B6	3483
REXROTH RD., Chanceford	Yk	17309	B6	3483
REXWOOD DR., Glen Rock	Yk	17327	B4	3583
REXWOOD DR., Shrewsbury Twp	Yk	17327	B5	3583
REYNOLD ST., Gettysburg	Ad	17325	B8	3471
REYNOLDS AV., Cumberland	Ad	17325	H8	3470
REYNOLDS AV., Cumberland	Ad	17325	A7	3471
REYNOLDS DR., Reading	Ad	17316	D4	3266
REYNOLDS MILL RD., Springfield	Yk	17360	A8	3375
REYNOLDS MILL RD., Springfield	Yk	17360	C3	3479
REYNOLDS MILL RD., Springfield	Yk	17360	C1	3479
REYNOLDS MILL RD., York Twp	Yk	17403	B7	3375
REYNOLDS RD. W., Tyrone	Ad	17350	A3	3369
REYNOLDS RD., Tyrone	Ad	17350	C2	3369
REYNOLDS RD., Washington	Yk	17316	D8	3267
REYNOLDS WAY, North York	Yk	17404	C4	3271
RHODODENDRON DR., Franklin	Ad	17353	A8	3364
RHODODENDRON TR., Franklin	Ad	17353	F9	3260
RHONDA DR., West Manchester	Yk	17404	F3	3373
RIALE OAK RD., Springettsbury	Yk	17402	F2	3271
RICE AV., Biglerville	Ad	17307	H1	3366
RICE AV., Biglerville	Ad	17307	A3	3367
RICE CT., Penn	Yk	17331	B8	3579
RICE LA., Bendersville	Ad	17304	G3	3262
RICE RD., Codorus	Yk	17360	C9	3478
RICHARD ST., West Manchester	Yk	17404	D7	3270
RICHARDS CT., Hopewell	Yk	17349	D6	3584
RICHARDSON RD., Fawn	Yk	17302	B10	3588
RICHARDSON RD., Lower Chanceford	Yk	17302	F10	3484
RICHARSON RD., West Manchester	Yk	17404	D9	3270
RICHCREEK LA., North York	Yk	17404	C4	3271
RICHLAND AV. S., West Manchester	Yk	17404	A9	3271
RICHLAND AV. S., York City	Yk	17404	A9	3271
RICHLAND AV., Spring Garden	Yk	17403	A10	3271
RICHMOND RD., Chanceford	Yk	17356	H3	3378
RICHMOND RD., Chanceford	Yk	17356	A4	3379
RICHMOND RD., Chanceford	Yk	17366	H2	3378
RICHMOND RD., Chanceford	Yk	17368	H11	3274
RICHMOND RD., Chanceford	Yk	17368	H2	3378
RICHMOND RD., Lower Windsor	Yk	17368	H10	3274
RICHWILL DR., York Twp	Yk	17404	H4	3270
RICHWILL LA., York Twp	Yk	17404	G5	3270
RICKEY DR., West Manheim	Yk	17331	H1	3683
RIDDLE RD., Windsor Twp	Yk	17402	D8	3273
RIDGE AL., McSherrystown	Ad	17344	F1	3578
RIDGE AV., Biglerville	Ad	17307	H2	3366
RIDGE AV., Gettysburg	Ad	17325	A9	3471
RIDGE AV., Glen Rock	Yk	17327	B5	3583
RIDGE AV., Hanover	Yk	17331	D1	3579
RIDGE AV., McSherrystown	Ad	17344	F2	3578
RIDGE AV., Penn	Yk	17331	E1	3579
RIDGE AV., Spring Garden	Yk	17403	E5	3271
RIDGE AV., Springettsbury	Yk	17402	E1	3271
RIDGE AV., York City	Yk	17403	E6	3271
RIDGE DR., Franklin	Yk	17019	A6	3161
RIDGE LA., Hellam	Yk	17368	A5	3169
RIDGE MEADOW RD., Hopewell	Yk	17363	A10	3585
RIDGE MEADOW RD., Hopewell	Yk	17363	C2	3689

RIDGE MEADOW RD., Hopewell	Yk	17363	B1	3689
RIDGE RD. E., Monaghan	Yk	17019	H11	2952
RIDGE RD. S., Huntington	Ad	17372	A4	3265
RIDGE RD. W., Monaghan	Yk	17019	D3	3057
RIDGE RD., Carroll	Yk	17019	B5	3057
RIDGE RD., Codorus	Yk	17327	G11	3582
RIDGE RD., Codorus	Yk	17327	A9	3583
RIDGE RD., Codorus	Yk	17327	F1	3686
RIDGE RD., Conewago	Ad	17344	G1	3578
RIDGE RD., Cumberland	Ad	17325	H6	3574
RIDGE RD., Cumberland	Ad	17325	H9	3574
RIDGE RD., Cumberland	Ad	17325	G3	3678
RIDGE RD., Delta	Yk	17314	E5	3693
RIDGE RD., Fairview	Yk	17070	A3	2954
RIDGE RD., Fairview	Yk	17339	A3	2954
RIDGE RD., Fawn	Yk	17321	A6	3588
RIDGE RD., Franklin	Yk	17019	H7	3160
RIDGE RD., Hopewell	Yk	17363	H10	3584
RIDGE RD., Jackson	Yk	17362	A11	3372
RIDGE RD., Latimore	Ad	17372	C11	3160
RIDGE RD., Latimore	Ad	17372	A8	3161
RIDGE RD., Manheim	Yk	17329	F11	3580
RIDGE RD., Menallen	Ad	17304	E3	3262
RIDGE RD., Monaghan	Yk	17019	A10	2953
RIDGE RD., Monaghan	Yk	17019	F2	3057
RIDGE RD., Newberry	Yk	17319	E8	2954
RIDGE RD., North Hopewell	Yk	17363	G2	3584
RIDGE RD., Paradise	Yk	17364	F6	3371
RIDGE RD., Peach Bottom	Yk	17302	H8	3588
RIDGE RD., Peach Bottom	Yk	17314	A5	3694
RIDGE RD., Warrington	Yk	17019	E11	3057
RIDGE RD., Warrington	Yk	17019	F10	3057
RIDGE RD., Warrington	Yk	17019	A9	3058
RIDGE RD., Warrington	Yk	17019	E2	3162
RIDGE RD., Warrington	Yk	17365	E2	3162
RIDGE RD., Washington	Yk	17316	G7	3161
RIDGE RD., Washington	Yk	17365	A6	3162
RIDGE RD., York Twp	Yk	17402	B2	3376
RIDGE TR., Carroll Valley	Ad	17320	F10	3572
RIDGEFIELD DR., York Twp	Yk	17403	D4	3375
RIDGEFORD RD., York Twp	Yk	17313	E7	3376
RIDGELR RD., Springfield	Yk	17327	E1	3583
RIDGELYN DR., York Twp	Yk	17313	F9	3376
RIDGEVIEW DR., Carroll	Yk	17019	E2	3056
RIDGEVIEW DR., Dillsburg	Yk	17019	E2	3056
RIDGEVIEW DR., Newberry	Yk	17319	E10	2955
RIDGEVIEW DR., York Twp	Yk	17402	A5	3376
RIDGEVIEW LA., Hellam	Yk	17406	H8	3167
RIDGEVIEW RD., Fairview	Yk	17070	B10	2849
RIDGEVIEW RD., Springfield	Yk	17313	C3	3480
RIDGEVIEW RD., Springfield	Yk	17360	G8	3479
RIDGEVIEW RD., Springfield	Yk	17360	A5	3480
RIDGEWAY AV., McSherrystown	Ad	17344	F2	3578
RIDGEWAY DR., Hellam	Yk	17368	D8	3169
RIDGEWAY DR., North Hopewell	Yk	17322	F7	3480
RIDGEWAY DR., West Manchester	Yk	17404	E8	3270
RIDGEWAY DR., Winterstown	Yk	17322	F7	3480
RIDGEWOOD AV., Chanceford	Yk	17322	B2	3482
RIDGEWOOD CIR., Cumberland	Ad	17325	A4	3471
RIDGEWOOD DR., Cumberland	Ad	17325	A3	3471
RIDGEWOOD DR., Cumberland	Ad	17325	A5	3471
RIDGEWOOD DR., West Manheim	Yk	17331	B4	3684
RIDGEWOOD LA., Cumberland	Ad	17325	A3	3471
RIDGEWOOD RD., Shrewsbury Twp	Yk	17327	C5	3583
RIDGEWOOD RD., Spring Garden	Yk	17403	F1	3375
RIDGEWOOD RD., Springettsbury	Yk	17402	D11	3167
RIDGEWOOD RD., Springettsbury	Yk	17402	G2	3271
RIDGEWOOD RD., Springettsbury	Yk	17402	A2	3272
RIDGEWOOD RD., York Twp	Yk	17403	F1	3375
RIDGEWOOD TR., Cumberland	Ad	17325	A4	3471
RIDGEWOOD WAY, Cumberland	Ad	17325	A3	3471
RIDGEWWOD CT., Cumberland	Ad	17325	A4	3471
RIDING CLUB RD., Manchester Twp	Yk	17404	F7	3165
RIDING SILKS LA., Manchester Twp	Yk	17404	E1	3270
RIDING WAY, West Manchester	Yk	17404	G6	3269
RIDINGER LA., Hellam	Yk	17406	G7	3167
RIDINGS WAY, West Manchester	Yk	17404	A7	3270
RIDLEY DR., York Twp	Yk	17402	G5	3375
RIFE RD., Reading	Ad	17316	B7	3267
RIGHT OF WAY, Windsor Twp	Yk	17402	B8	3273
RILEY RD., Straban	Ad	17325	A4	3472
RILLIAN LA., Manchester Twp	Yk	17404	E2	3270
RIMROCK RD., Springettsbury	Yk	17402	E6	3272
RINELY RD., Hopewell	Yk	17363	H6	3584
RINELY RD., Hopewell	Yk	17363	A5	3585
RINGNECK CIR., Hamilton	Ad	17301	H8	3370
RINGNECK TR., Carroll Valley	Ad	17320	G2	3676
RINGNECK TR., Carroll Valley	Ad	17320	A3	3677
RIPPLING RUN RD., Felton	Yk	17322	F4	3481
RIPPLING RUN RD., North Hopewell	Yk	17322	C5	3481
RIPPLING RUN RD., North Hopewell	Yk	17356	C5	3481
RIPPLING RUN RD., Winterstown	Yk	17356	A6	3481
RISHEL RD., Springfield	Yk	17327	D10	3479
RISLYN CT., North Codorus	Yk	17362	E6	3477
RIST TR., Liberty	Ad	17320	F6	3573
RITA MARIE AV. S., Littlestown	Ad	17340	E2	3681
RITA MARIE AV., Littlestown	Ad	17340	D1	3681
RITA RD., Springettsbury	Yk	17402	F1	3272
RIVER DR. E., Hellam	Yk	17368	D5	3169
RIVER DR. E., Hellam	Yk	17368	D4	3169
RIVER DR. E., Hellam	Yk	17406	B3	3169
RIVER DR., Hellam	Yk	17406	B2	3168
RIVER DR., Hellam	Yk	17406	F3	3168
RIVER DRIVE RD., Newberry	Yk	17370	C2	3061
RIVER FARM RD., Hellam	Yk	17347	E3	3167
RIVER FARM RD., Hellam	Yk	17347	A3	3168
RIVER FARM RD., Hellam	Yk	17406	H3	3167
RIVER FARM RD., Hellam	Yk	17406	G3	3167
RIVER FARM RD., Hellam	Yk	17406	A3	3168
RIVER FARMS RD., Lower Windsor	Yk	17368	A7	3275
RIVER RD., Hellam	Yk	17406	G5	3168
RIVER RD., Hellam	Yk	17406	E5	3168
RIVER RD., Lower Chanceford	Yk	17314	F3	3589
RIVER RD., Lower Chanceford	Yk	17314	G1	3589
RIVER RD., Lower Chanceford	Yk	17314	A2	3590
RIVER RD., Newberry	Yk	17370	H11	2955
RIVER RD., Newberry	Yk	17370	F3	3060
RIVERBANK LA., Hellam	Yk	17368	D4	3169
RIVERHAVEN LA., Hellam	Yk	17368	D3	3169
RIVERSTONE LA., Lower Windsor	Yk	17368	B7	3275
RIVERVIEW CT., Hellam	Yk	17406	C8	3168
RIVERVIEW CT., Windsor Twp	Yk	17356	B5	3377
RIVERVIEW DR., East Prospect	Yk	17317	F6	3274
RIVERVIEW DR., East Prospect	Yk	17368	F6	3274
RIVERVIEW DR., Goldsboro	Yk	17319	H5	2955
RIVERVIEW DR., Lower Windsor	Yk	17368	G8	3274
RIVERVIEW DR., Lower Windsor	Yk	17368	H10	3274
RIVERVIEW DR., Lower Windsor	Yk	17368	A10	3275
RIVERVIEW RD. E., Lower Chanceford	Yk	17314	H2	3589
RIVERVIEW RD. W., Lower Chanceford	Yk	17314	G2	3589
RIVERVIEW RD., East Manchester	Yk	17347	D1	3167
RIVERVIEW RD., East Manchester	Yk	17347	E2	3167
RIVERVIEW RD., Lower Chanceford	Yk	17314	H2	3589
RIVIERA CT., East Manchester	Yk	17347	F10	3061
ROAD A, York Twp	Yk	17402	B10	3272
ROAD B, York Twp	Yk	17402	B10	3272
ROADSIDE TR., Carroll Valley	Ad	17320	H10	3572
ROAN LA., Hellam	Yk	17368	B5	3169
ROBBINS LA., Franklin	Ad	17307	A8	3365
ROBERT PAUL DR., Newberry	Yk	17319	C9	2955
ROBERTA JEAN AV., Littlestown	Ad	17340	D2	3681
ROBERTA WAY, Cumberland	Ad	17325	F3	3574
ROBERTS RD., Mount Joy	Ad	17340	A8	3577
ROBESOW RD., Warrington	Yk	17019	D9	3057
ROBIN ANN CT., Hallam	Yk	17406	D11	3168
ROBIN CIR., Mount Joy	Ad	17325	G5	3575
ROBIN CIR., Newberry	Yk	17319	G8	2954
ROBIN CIR., West Manchester	Yk	17404	E10	3270
ROBIN DR., Windsor Twp	Yk	17356	A1	3377
ROBIN HILL CIR., Manchester Twp	Yk	17404	H1	3270
ROBIN HILL CIR., Manchester Twp	Yk	17404	A1	3271
ROBIN HOOD RD., Franklin	Yk	17019	H7	3055
ROBIN NEST TR., Carroll Valley	Ad	17320	H1	3676
ROBIN RD., Dover Twp	Yk	17315	B6	3268
ROBIN RD., West Manchester	Yk	17404	D10	3270
ROBIN TR., Carroll Valley	Ad	17320	G1	3676
ROBIN TR., Peach Bottom	Yk	17314	F10	3588
ROBINHOOD DR., New Salem	Yk	17371	C6	3374
ROBINHOOD DR., Newberry	Yk	17319	G5	2954
ROBINSON DR., Oxford	Ad	17350	A4	3474
ROBINWOOD RD., Springettsbury	Yk	17402	G4	3272
ROCK CREEK DR., Dover Twp	Yk	17315	E4	3269
ROCK CREEK FORD RD., Mount Joy	Ad	17325	E10	3575
ROCK JIM RD., East Hopewell	Yk	17322	A3	3586
ROCK JIM RD., East Hopewell	Yk	17363	G5	3585
ROCK JIM RD., East Hopewell	Yk	17363	A4	3586
ROCK LA., Red Lion	Yk	17356	C7	3377
ROCK RIDGE RD., Warrington	Yk	17339	C4	3059
ROCK TOP, Menallen	Ad	17304	C6	3262
ROCK VALLEY RD., Tyrone	Ad	17304	C7	3264
ROCKBURN ST., Springettsbury	Yk	17402	H5	3271
ROCKDALE AV., York City	Yk	17403	D9	3271
ROCKDALE DR., Loganville	Yk	17360	E4	3479
ROCKERY RD., North Codorus	Yk	17362	D11	3373
ROCKERY RD., North Codorus	Yk	17362	B1	3477
ROCKHILL LA., Hellam	Yk	17406	G10	3167
ROCKVILLE RD., Codorus	Yk	17327	B9	3582
ROCKVILLE RD., Codorus	Yk	17327	G6	3582
ROCKVILLE RD., Codorus	Yk	17327	A4	3583
ROCKVILLE RD., Jackson	Yk	17362	F7	3372
ROCKVILLE RD., North Codorus	Yk	17362	D6	3477
ROCKVILLE RD., Shrewsbury Twp	Yk	17327	A4	3583
ROCKWOOD AV., Manchester Twp	Yk	17402	C11	3166
ROCKY GROVE RD., Straban	Ad	17325	G9	3471
ROCKY RD., Chanceford	Yk	17322	F9	3378
ROCKY RD., Chanceford	Yk	17356	F9	3378
ROCKY RD., Dover Twp	Yk	17315	E11	3164
ROCKY RD., Lower Windsor	Yk	17356	E6	3378
ROCKY RD., Manheim	Yk	17329	D1	3685
ROCKY RD., Menallen	Ad	17307	B8	3261
ROCKY RD., Windsor Twp	Yk	17356	E6	3378
ROCKY RIDGE CT., Springettsbury	Yk	17402	B10	3167
ROCKY RIDGE RD., Franklin	Yk	17019	A7	3056
ROCKY RIDGE RD., Paradise	Yk	17362	A10	3372
ROCKY RIDGE RD., Washington	Yk	17315	H1	3267
ROCKY WOOD LA., Warrington	Yk	17339	D4	3058
RODES AV., Straban	Ad	17325	D5	3471
RODKO CT., North Codorus	Yk	17362	H11	3373
RODNEY LEE DR., Franklin	Ad	17353	H2	3468
RODNEY RD., West Manchester	Yk	17404	F5	3270
ROELKER RD., Latimore	Ad	17372	F2	3265
ROGERS RD., Berwick	Ad	17331	A3	3475
ROHLERS CHURCH RD., Dover Twp	Yk	17315	C11	3059
ROHLERS CHURCH RD., Dover Twp	Yk	17315	H3	3163
ROHLERS CHURCH RD., Dover Twp	Yk	17315	A2	3164
ROHRBAUGH RD., Codorus	Yk	17360	E8	3478
ROHRBAUGH RD., Freedom	Ad	17320	H2	3677
ROHRBAUGH RD., Freedom	Ad	17320	A1	3678
ROHRBAUGH RD., Liberty	Ad	17320	H2	3677
ROHRBAUGH RD., North Codorus	Yk	17360	E3	3478
ROLAND RD., Reading	Ad	17316	A5	3267
ROLAND RD., Washington	Yk	17316	B4	3267
ROLLER CIR., Conewago	Ad	17331	H1	3578
ROLLING GREEN DR., Manchester Twp	Yk	17404	E10	3165
ROLLING LA., Hamilton	Ad	17301	H9	3370
ROLLING LA., Hamilton	Ad	17301	A9	3371
ROLLING RD., Huntington	Ad	17372	F4	3264
ROLLING RD., Peach Bottom	Yk	17314	H9	3588
ROLLING RIDGE RD., Peach Bottom	Yk	17314	B10	3589
ROMAN CT., Manchester Twp	Yk	17404	H11	3165
ROMAN LA., West Manheim	Yk	17331	D9	3580
ROMANIC LA., Hamiltonban	Ad	17222	F3	3467
ROOSEVELT AV., Manchester Boro	Yk	17345	D2	3166
ROOSEVELT AV., Manchester Twp	Yk	17404	D3	3270
ROOSEVELT AV., West Manchester	Yk	17404	D3	3270
ROOSEVELT AV., York City	Yk	17404	A7	3271
ROOSEVELT AV., York Twp	Yk	17404	G5	3270
ROOSEVELT CT., Hanover	Yk	17331	B10	3475
ROOSEVELT EXT., York Twp	Yk	17404	H5	3270
ROOSEVELT LA., Shrewsbury Twp	Yk	17361	C9	3584
ROOSTER LA., Conewago	Yk	17345	A8	3061
ROSALIA CIR., Windsor Twp	Yk	17402	A8	3273
ROSE AV. E., Dallastown	Yk	17313	G7	3376
ROSE AV. E., Dallastown	Yk	17313	E6	3376
ROSE CT., Manchester Twp	Yk	17402	A7	3166
ROSE DR., Franklin	Yk	17019	A1	3161
ROSE FARM RD., Washington	Yk	17019	G3	3161
ROSE HILL DR., Fairview	Yk	17070	E9	2848
ROSE LA., Butler	Ad	17325	G5	3366
ROSE LA., Oxford	Ad	17350	B5	3474
ROSE LA., Springfield	Yk	17403	F1	3479
ROSE LA., Windsor Twp	Yk	17366	E3	3377
ROSE OF SHARON DR., Newberry	Yk	17319	G5	2954
ROSE OF SHARON DR., Newberry	Yk	17319	A6	2955
ROSE POINTE WAY, Heidelberg	Yk	17362	E1	3580
ROSEBAY CT., Manchester Twp	Yk	17404	B2	3270
ROSEBAY DR., Manchester Twp	Yk	17404	B2	3270
ROSECROFT ST., Conewago	Ad	17331	B4	3578
ROSEDALE DR., East Manchester	Yk	17345	C3	3166
ROSELYN DR., Springettsbury	Yk	17402	G4	3272
ROSEMILL CT., York Twp	Yk	17403	D2	3375
ROSEMONT RD., Dover Twp	Yk	17315	G4	3269
ROSEPOINTE DR., Manchester Twp	Yk	17404	D11	3165
ROSER RD., Codorus	Yk	17327	G3	3582
ROSER RD., Codorus	Yk	17327	A3	3583
ROSEWOOD CIR., Penn	Yk	17331	G5	3579
ROSEWOOD CIR., Shrewsbury Twp	Yk	17361	C11	3584
ROSEWOOD DR., Hopewell	Yk	17363	C2	3689
ROSEWOOD LA., Spring Garden	Yk	17403	C2	3375
ROSS AV., Fairview	Yk	17070	C5	2849
ROSS RD., West Manheim	Yk	17331	C3	3684
ROSSLARE RD., York Twp	Yk	17356	E10	3272
ROSSTOWN RD., Newberry	Yk	17339	B2	3059
ROSSTOWN RD., Warrington	Yk	17339	C11	3058
ROSSTOWN RD., Warrington	Yk	17339	A5	3059
ROSSTOWN RD., Warrington	Yk	17365	C11	3058
ROSSVILLE RD., Fairview	Yk	17319	E6	2954
ROSSVILLE RD., Fairview	Yk	17339	E6	2954
ROSSVILLE RD., Fairview	Yk	17339	A2	3059
ROSSVILLE RD., Newberry	Yk	17339	E6	2954
ROST LA., Red Lion	Yk	17356	A7	3377
ROTH CHURCH RD., Jackson	Yk	17362	A7	3373
ROTH CHURCH RD., Spring Grove	Yk	17362	A9	3373
ROTHS CHURCH RD., Jackson	Yk	17362	G5	3372
ROTHS CHURCH RD., Jackson	Yk	17364	F4	3372
ROUND HILL CHURCH RD., East Hopewell	Yk	17322	H11	3481
ROUND HILL CHURCH RD., East Hopewell	Yk	17363	H11	3481
ROUND HILL CHURCH RD., East Hopewell	Yk	17363	G4	3585
ROUND HILL RD., Reading	Ad	17316	H8	3265
ROUND HILL RD., Reading	Ad	17316	A7	3266
ROUND HILL RD., Reading	Ad	17372	F10	3265
ROUND HILL RD., Springettsbury	Yk	17402	D7	3272
ROUND TOP LA., Cumberland	Ad	17325	A6	3575
ROUNDTOP LA., Hellam	Yk	17368	B4	3169
ROUNDTOP RD., Warrington	Yk	17339	B3	3058
ROXBERRY RD., Newberry	Yk	17370	A11	2955
ROXBERRY RD., Newberry	Yk	17370	A1	3060
ROXBORO RD., York Twp	Yk	17402	G3	3375
ROYAL ST., Dover Twp	Yk	17404	A4	3270
ROYAL ST., Springettsbury	Yk	17402	A5	3272
ROYAL ST., York City	Yk	17404	A8	3271
ROYCROFT LA., Peach Bottom	Yk	17314	E1	3693
RUBY DR., Dover Twp	Yk	17315	C2	3269
RUBY LA., East Prospect	Yk	17317	E6	3274
RUBY LA., Lower Windsor	Yk	17368	E6	3274
RUDDYTOWN RD., Fairview	Yk	17070	E11	2848
RUDY RD., Hellam	Yk	17406	E7	3168
RUEL AV., Penn	Yk	17331	F3	3579
RUFFED GROUSE DR., Dover Twp	Yk	17315	F7	3269
RUFFIAN CIR., Carroll	Yk	17019	G11	2951
RUFFIAN LA., Lower Windsor	Yk	17366	H11	3273
RUFFIAN LA., Lower Windsor	Yk	17366	A11	3274
RUHL RD., Shrewsbury Twp	Yk	17349	C5	3687
RUM TR., Hamiltonban	Ad	17320	H11	3571
RUN WAY, Hellam	Yk	17406	H11	3167
RUNAWAY RD., Hamilton	Ad	17301	B3	3371
RUNAWAY RD., Hamilton	Ad	17316	B3	3371
RUNKLE RD., Chanceford	Yk	17322	A3	3482
RUNKLE RD., Felton	Yk	17322	A4	3482
RUNKLES LA., Hamiltonban	Ad	17320	A4	3572
RUNNINGBOARD RD., Hopewell	Yk	17363	E9	3585
RUPP RD., Tyrone	Ad	17325	E8	3264
RUPPERT RD., Dover Twp	Yk	17404	D10	3269
RUPPERT RD., Jackson	Yk	17404	D10	3269
RUPPERT RD., Reading	Ad	17316	C9	3267
RUPPERT RD., Washington	Yk	17316	C8	3267
RUPPERT RD., Windsor Twp	Yk	17356	F10	3272
RUSHMORE DR., York Twp	Yk	17402	A6	3376
RUSSEL ST., Springettsbury	Yk	17402	A5	3272
RUSSELL TAVERN RD., Butler	Ad	17325	G7	3366
RUSSELL TAVERN RD., Butler	Ad	17325	G2	3470
RUSSELL TAVERN RD., Cumberland	Ad	17325	G2	3470
RUSSIAN OLIVE DR., Newberry	Yk	17319	A6	2955
RUSSLYN DR., Shrewsbury Boro	Yk	17361	A6	3584
RUSTIC RD., Carroll	Yk	17019	C5	3057
RUTH AV., Hanover	Yk	17331	C3	3579
RUTH AV., Spring Grove	Yk	17362	A11	3373
RUTH DR., York Twp	Yk	17403	H1	3375
RUTH FARM LA., Paradise	Yk	17364	F3	3371
RUTH ST., West Manchester	Yk	17404	D7	3270
RUTLAND AV., Manchester Twp	Yk	17402	C11	3166
RUTLEDGE RD., New Freedom	Yk	17349	G4	3687
RUXTON RD., Spring Garden	Yk	17403	H10	3271
RUXTON RD., Spring Garden	Yk	17403	A10	3272
RYANS RUN, Manchester Twp	Yk	17404	H11	3165
RYDELL DR., York Twp	Yk	17313	G9	3376
RYE ST. E., Dallastown	Yk	17313	F8	3376
RYE TR., Hamiltonban	Ad	17320	H11	3571

S

SACH'S RD., Cumberland	Ad	17325	D4	3575
SACRAMENTO CT., Conewago	Ad	17331	C4	3578
SADDLE CIR., Windsor Twp	Yk	17366	F2	3377
SADDLE HILL RD., Jackson	Yk	17362	F10	3372
SADDLE VIEW LA., Hamiltonban	Ad	17320	A5	3572
SADDLEBACK RD., West Manchester	Yk	17404	C7	3270
SADDLEBROOK WAY, Newberry	Yk	17319	F9	2955
SADDLERS CHURCH RD., Hopewell	Yk	17349	E9	3584
SADDLERS CHURCH RD., Hopewell	Yk	17363	E9	3584
SAGAMORE DR., Springettsbury	Yk	17402	H3	3271
SAGE AV., York City	Yk	17403	D7	3271
SAGE DR., Hellam	Yk	17402	H2	3272
SAGINAW RD., East Manchester	Yk	17347	A2	3167
SALEM AV., Dover Twp	Yk	17315	H2	3269
SALEM AV., York City	Yk	17404	A9	3271
SALEM CHURCH RD. N., Dover Twp	Yk	17315	A1	3269
SALEM CHURCH RD., Chanceford	Yk	17366	F2	3378
SALEM CHURCH RD., Dover Twp	Yk	17315	G11	3163
SALEM CHURCH RD., Dover Twp	Yk	17315	H1	3268
SALEM CHURCH RD., Lower Windsor	Yk	17366	F2	3378
SALEM CHURCH RD., Mount Pleasant	Ad	17325	G5	3472
SALEM CHURCH RD., Mount Pleasant	Ad	17325	A6	3473
SALEM CT., Springfield	Yk	17407	E11	3375
SALEM RD., Fairview	Yk	17319	G4	2954
SALEM RD., North Codorus	Yk	17362	H9	3373
SALEM RD., North Codorus	Yk	17362	A8	3374
SALEM RD., North Codorus	Yk	17404	A8	3374
SALEM RUN RD., Dover Twp	Yk	17315	H5	3267
SALEM RUN RD., Dover Twp	Yk	17315	A6	3268
SALEM SPRINGS DR., North Codorus	Yk	17404	E9	3374
SALISBURY RD., Lower Chanceford	Yk	17302	F11	3484
SALISBURY RD., Lower Chanceford	Yk	17302	G1	3588
SALISBURY ST., West Manchester	Yk	17404	C3	3270
SALLY ANNE CT., East Hopewell	Yk	17363	G3	3585
SALLY ANNE RD., East Hopewell	Yk	17363	G2	3585
SALMON RUN RD., Dover Twp	Yk	17315	F4	3268
SALT LAKE CIR., Fawn	Yk	17321	B4	3691
SALT LAKE RD., Fawn	Yk	17321	B5	3691
SAM HILL RD., Manheim	Yk	17329	G11	3580
SAM SNEAD CIR., Newberry	Yk	17319	C6	2955
SAM SNEAD CIR., Newberry	Yk	17319	C7	2955
SAMANTHA DR., Dover Twp	Yk	17315	F4	3269
SAMPSON WAY, North York	Yk	17404	C5	3271
SAM'S LA., Highland	Ad	17325	B7	3470
SAMS RD., Chanceford	Yk	17322	F7	3378
SAN CARLOS ST., Manchester Twp	Yk	17402	C3	3271
SAN GABRIEL DR., Springettsbury	Yk	17402	H3	3271
SAN REMO PL., Fairview	Yk	17339	H3	2953
SAND BANK RD., Springettsbury	Yk	17402	D2	3271
SAND HILL AL., McSherrystown	Ad	17344	G1	3578
SAND SPUR DR., Fairview	Yk	17319	G3	2954
SANDALWOOD CT., Manchester Twp	Yk	17404	A2	3271
SANDERS LA., Hamiltonban	Ad	17320	A6	3573
SANDER'S RD., Carroll Valley	Ad	17320	H9	3572
SANDER'S RD., Carroll Valley	Ad	17320	G8	3572
SANDER'S RD., Carroll Valley	Ad	17320	A9	3573
SANDER'S RD., Liberty	Ad	17320	A9	3573
SANDER'S RD., Straban	Ad	17325	H10	3367
SANDERSON DR. (PVT), Warrington	Yk	17365	D7	3058
SANDHURST DR., Manchester Twp	Yk	17402	C7	3166
SANDHURST DR., Manchester Twp	Yk	17404	C8	3166
SANDOE RD., Straban	Ad	17325	A9	3368
SANDPATCH LA., Hopewell	Yk	17363	E9	3585
SANDRA AV., York Twp	Yk	17356	F11	3272
SANDRA DR., Springettsbury	Yk	17402	F1	3272
SANDY CIR., Manchester Boro	Yk	17345	D10	3061
SANDY CT., Conewago	Ad	17331	D3	3578
SANFORD AV., Penn	Yk	17331	E2	3579
SANGER LA., Newberry	Yk	17370	H10	2954
SANGER LA., Newberry	Yk	17370	A10	2955
SAPPHIRE RD., West Manchester	Yk	17404	C7	3270
SARA LA., West Manheim	Yk	17331	G8	3579
SARAH CT., Fairview	Yk	17339	E5	2954
SARAH DR., Newberry	Yk	17315	E6	3059
SARAH WOODS DR., Windsor Twp	Yk	17356	B4	3377
SARATOGA CT., Conewago	Ad	17331	C5	3578
SARATOGA RD., York Twp	Yk	17402	G3	3375
SARAZEN WAY, Manchester Twp	Yk	17404	E2	3270
SARVER RD., Windsor Twp	Yk	17402	C6	3273
SASSAFRAS LA., Fairview	Yk	17055	C7	2953
SATELLITE DR., York Twp	Yk	17402	D8	3272
SAVOIR DR., Conewago	Ad	17331	C4	3578
SAVOY DR., Hanover	Yk	17331	A11	3475
SAW MILL RD., Fairview	Yk	17055	B7	2953
SAW MILL RD., Fairview	Yk	17339	E2	3058
SAW MILL RD., Monaghan	Yk	17019	C11	2952
SAW MILL RD., Warrington	Yk	17339	E2	3058
SAWANNA CT., Shrewsbury Twp	Yk	17327	B8	3583
SAWGRASS AV., Chanceford	Yk	17322	B2	3482
SAWMILL RD., Hopewell	Yk	17363	G9	3584
SAWMILL RD., Latimore	Ad	17372	B10	3160
SAWMILL RD., Lower Chanceford	Yk	17309	E1	3484
SAWMILL RD., Shrewsbury Twp	Yk	17327	C11	3480
SCARBORO DR., Spring Garden	Yk	17403	E11	3271
SCARBOROUGH FARE, Hopewell	Yk	17363	D9	3585
SCARBOROUGH FARE, Hopewell	Yk	17363	E9	3585
SCARLET OAK DR., Newberry	Yk	17319	E7	2955
SCARLET OAK TR., Peach Bottom	Yk	17314	H11	3588

SCARLET WAY, Menallen	Ad	17307	H6	3260
SCARLET WAY, Menallen	Ad	17307	A6	3261
SCENIC CIR., Fairview	Yk	17070	G10	2848
SCENIC DR., Lower Windsor	Yk	17368	G8	3274
SCENIC DR., Penn	Yk	17331	F4	3579
SCENIC LA., Hellam	Yk	17406	D3	3273
SCHELL LA., North Hopewell	Yk	17356	E3	3480
SCHIBERT, Union	Ad	17331	F10	3578
SCHIMMEL LA., Hellam	Yk	17368	A6	3169
SCHMUCK RD., Lower Windsor	Yk	17406	H3	3273
SCHMUCK RD., Lower Windsor	Yk	17406	A4	3274
SCHOLFIELD DR., Reading	Ad	17316	D5	3266
SCHOOL AL., New Freedom	Yk	17349	G3	3687
SCHOOL AV., East Prospect	Yk	17317	E5	3274
SCHOOL AV., East Prospect	Yk	17368	E5	3274
SCHOOL CT., Red Lion	Yk	17356	C8	3377
SCHOOL DR., Peach Bottom	Yk	17314	H4	3693
SCHOOL HIUSE RD., Paradise	Yk	17364	H4	3371
SCHOOL HOUSE HILL RD., Franklin	Ad	17222	H9	3363
SCHOOL HOUSE HILL RD., Franklin	Ad	17222	A7	3364
SCHOOL HOUSE LA., Fairview	Yk	17339	F7	2953
SCHOOL HOUSE LA., Hamiltonban	Ad	17320	E7	3572
SCHOOL HOUSE RD., Mount Pleasant	Ad	17340	C5	3577
SCHOOL HOUSE RD., Paradise	Yk	17364	A2	3372
SCHOOL HOUSE RD., Paradise	Yk	17364	A7	3372
SCHOOL HOUSE RD., Tyrone	Ad	17304	B6	3264
SCHOOL LA., Bendersville	Ad	17304	H3	3262
SCHOOL PL. N., Dallastown	Yk	17313	F7	3376
SCHOOL PL. S., Dallastown	Yk	17313	E7	3376
SCHOOL PL., York City	Yk	17404	A9	3271
SCHOOL RD., Springfield	Yk	17407	E11	3375
SCHOOL ST., Glen Rock	Yk	17327	C4	3583
SCHOOL ST., Manheim	Yk	17329	C9	3581
SCHOOL ST., New Oxford	Ad	17350	C1	3474
SCHOOL ST., West Manchester	Yk	17404	B5	3270
SCHOOL ST., York Twp	Yk	17402	B2	3376
SCHOOL ST., York Twp	Yk	17402	A4	3376
SCHOOLHOUSE LA., Hallam	Yk	17406	C11	3168
SCHOOLHOUSE LA., Springettsbury	Yk	17402	A7	3272
SCHOOLHOUSE LA., Windsor Boro	Yk	17366	F4	3377
SCHOOLHOUSE LA., Windsor Twp	Yk	17366	E3	3377
SCHOOLHOUSE RD., Dover Twp	Yk	17315	F11	3163
SCHOOLHOUSE RD., Dover Twp	Yk	17315	C2	3268
SCHOOLHOUSE RD., Dover Twp	Yk	17315	D2	3268
SCHOTTIE RD., Mount Joy	Ad	17340	B4	3680
SCHRIVER RD., Freedom	Ad	17325	C8	3574
SCHRIVER SCHOOL RD., Conewago	Ad	17331	E8	3578
SCHRIVER SCHOOL RD., Union	Ad	17331	E8	3578
SCHUMAN RD., Codorus	Yk	17327	D3	3582
SCHUMAN RD., Codorus	Yk	17327	G6	3582
SCHWARTZ RD., Mount Joy	Ad	17325	E11	3575
SCHWARTZ RD., Mount Joy	Ad	17325	D1	3679
SCIORTINO LA., Windsor Twp	Yk	17356	B2	3377
SCOTCH PINE RD., Franklin	Ad	17019	F3	3160
SCOTCH ST., Manchester Twp	Yk	17404	G3	3270
SCOTCH TR., Hamiltonban	Ad	17320	G11	3571
SCOTCH TR., Hamiltonban	Ad	17320	H1	3675
SCOTT COVE, Latimore	Ad	17316	B4	3266
SCOTT PLAZA, Lower Chanceford	Yk	17314	H3	3589
SCOTT RD., Freedom	Ad	17325	C1	3574
SCOTT RD., York Twp	Yk	17403	E6	3375
SCOTT RIDGE LA., Hellam	Yk	17406	F10	3167
SCOTT SCHOOL RD., Franklin	Ad	17353	A4	3469
SCOTT ST. N., West Manchester	Yk	17404	E8	3270
SCOTT ST., Penn	Yk	17331	B5	3579
SCOUT CAMP RD., Chanceford	Yk	17322	E3	3379
SCOUT RD., North Hopewell	Yk	17322	G6	3481
SEAKS RUN RD., North Hopewell	Yk	17322	E5	3480
SEAKS RUN RD., North Hopewell	Yk	17322	C7	3480
SEAKS RUN RD., Springfield	Yk	17327	G9	3479
SEAKS RUN RD., Springfield	Yk	17327	A9	3480
SEAKS RUN RD., Springfield	Yk	17327	C7	3480
SEASE DR., Conewago	Ad	17331	D10	3578
SEASONS DR. N., Monaghan	Yk	17019	A9	2952
SEASONS DR. S., Monaghan	Yk	17019	A10	2952
SECHRIST FLAT RD., Chanceford	Yk	17322	B2	3482
SECHRIST RD., Chanceford	Yk	17309	C6	3483
SECRETARIAT DR., Carroll	Yk	17019	F1	3056
SECURITY DR., York Twp	Yk	17402	G5	3375
SEDGEWICK AV., Dover Twp	Yk	17315	H5	3269
SEDGWICK AV., Cumberland	Ad	17325	B3	3575
SEDGWICK DR., Mount Joy	Ad	17325	A2	3576
SEDGWICK DR., Reading	Ad	17316	B5	3266
SEGOVIA CT., Berwick	Ad	17331	B5	3475
SEILING RD., Shrewsbury Twp	Yk	17349	C3	3687
SEITZ DR., Fairview	Yk	17339	F8	2953
SEITZ RD., Felton	Yk	17322	F5	3481
SEITZ RD., North Hopewell	Yk	17322	F5	3481
SEITZLAND RD., Shrewsbury Twp	Yk	17327	B6	3583
SEITZLAND RD., Shrewsbury Twp	Yk	17327	D6	3583
SEITZVILLE RD., Codorus	Yk	17360	H8	3478
SEITZVILLE RD., Springfield	Yk	17360	H8	3478
SELL'S STATION RD., Union	Ad	17340	F6	3577
SELL'S STATION RD., Union	Ad	17340	A7	3578
SEMINARY AV., Cumberland	Ad	17325	A8	3471
SEMINARY AV., Gettysburg	Ad	17325	A8	3471
SEMINARY ST., Gettysburg	Ad	17325	A8	3471
SEMINOLE CT., Windsor Twp	Yk	17356	B4	3377
SEMINOLE DR., Springfield	Yk	17407	F1	3479
SENECA AV., Dover Twp	Yk	17315	F1	3269
SENECA DR., Conewago	Ad	17331	D3	3578
SENECA DR., West Manchester	Yk	17404	C6	3270
SENECA RIDGE DR., Springfield	Yk	17403	F1	3479
SENECA RIDGE DR., Springfield	Yk	17407	F1	3479
SENECA WAY, Spring Grove	Yk	17362	B9	3373
SENFT RD., North Codorus	Yk	17362	G6	3476
SENFT ST., Jefferson	Yk	17362	D11	3477
SENTZ RD., Cumberland	Ad	17325	H1	3678
SENTZ RD., Cumberland	Ad	17325	A1	3679
SEQUOIA ST., Manchester Twp	Yk	17404	F8	3165
SEQUOYA CT., Latimore	Ad	17372	A11	3055
SEQUOYA CT., Latimore	Ad	17372	B1	3160
SERENITY LA., Chanceford	Yk	17309	F9	3379
SETTER RUN CT., West Manchester	Yk	17404	C7	3270
SETTER TR., Liberty	Ad	17320	E9	3573
SETTING SUN LA., Hopewell	Yk	17363	D8	3586
SEVEN STARS RD., Franklin	Ad	17325	A5	3470
SEVEN VALLEYS RD., North Codorus	Yk	17360	D1	3478
SEVEN VALLEYS RD., North Codorus	Yk	17404	D8	3374
SEVEN VALLEYS RD., North Codorus	Yk	17404	D1	3478
SEVILLE DR., Windsor Twp	Yk	17356	D4	3377
SEWARD ST. N., West York	Yk	17404	G8	3270
SEWARD ST. S., West York	Yk	17404	G9	3270
SEWARD ST., West Manchester	Yk	17404	G7	3270
SEWEL DR., Conewago	Yk	17404	D2	3165
SEWERED RD., Fairview	Yk	17070	B7	2849
SEYMORE RD., Mount Pleasant	Ad	17325	B7	3473
SEYMORE RD., Mount Pleasant	Ad	17350	B7	3473
SHADY CREEK LA., Manheim	Yk	17329	A2	3685
SHADY DELL RD., Jackson	Yk	17364	E9	3268
SHADY DELL RD., Jackson	Yk	17364	G1	3372
SHADY DELL RD., Paradise	Yk	17315	B8	3268
SHADY DELL RD., Spring Garden	Yk	17403	D1	3375
SHADY KNOLL CIR., Newberry	Yk	17315	G4	3059
SHADY LA., Manchester Twp	Yk	17402	B5	3166
SHADY LA., Manchester Twp	Yk	17402	B5	3166
SHADY LA., Menallen	Ad	17304	F3	3262
SHADY LA., Newberry	Yk	17370	E2	3060
SHADY LA., West Manheim	Yk	17331	C8	3580
SHADY WOODS LA., Hopewell	Yk	17349	G11	3584
SHAFFER CHURCH RD., Codorus	Yk	17327	B3	3582
SHAFFER CHURCH RD., Codorus	Yk	17329	A5	3582
SHAFFER CHURCH RD., Codorus	Yk	17360	D8	3478
SHAFFER CIR., West Manheim	Yk	17331	B5	3684
SHAFFER DR., Fairview	Yk	17070	E9	2848
SHAFFER DR., Hanover	Yk	17331	A11	3475
SHAFFER DR., New Freedom	Yk	17349	G5	3687
SHAFFER DR., New Freedom	Yk	17349	H3	3687
SHAFFER LA., Hamiltonban	Ad	17320	F1	3572
SHAFFER LA., Lower Windsor	Yk	17368	G6	3274
SHAFFER RD., Codorus	Yk	17360	H11	3477
SHAFFER RD., Codorus	Yk	17360	A10	3478
SHAFFERS CHURCH RD., Codorus	Yk	17327	C10	3478
SHAGBARK CT., Manchester Twp	Yk	17402	C1	3271
SHALARD RUN RD., Lower Windsor	Yk	17366	B8	3274
SHALOM DR., Oxford	Ad	17350	E2	3474
SHAMROCK LA., Newberry	Yk	17319	C5	2955
SHANGRI-LA RD., North Hopewell	Yk	17363	H2	3584
SHANGRI-LA RD., North Hopewell	Yk	17363	A1	3585
SHANK RD., Oxford	Ad	17331	F5	3474
SHANNON LA., Hellam	Yk	17406	H9	3168
SHARODEN DR., North Codorus	Yk	17404	C8	3374
SHARON AV., York Twp	Yk	17356	F11	3272
SHARON AV., York Twp	Yk	17356	F1	3376
SHARON DR., Fairview	Yk	17070	C1	2954
SHARON DR., Spring Garden	Yk	17403	E10	3271
SHARP WAY, North York	Yk	17404	C4	3271
SHARPSHIN LA., Lower Windsor	Yk	17402	E5	3273
SHARRER MILL RD., Straban	Ad	17350	D6	3369
SHASTA DR., York Twp	Yk	17402	H6	3375
SHAUB RD., Railroad	Yk	17355	H10	3583
SHAUFFNERTOWN RD., Fairview	Yk	17070	E10	2848
SHAULLS RD., Chanceford	Yk	17309	A11	3379
SHAULLS RD., Chanceford	Yk	17322	H9	3378
SHAW RD., Hopewell	Yk	17363	C9	3585
SHAW RD., Windsor Twp	Yk	17366	F3	3377
SHAWAN LA., Springettsbury	Yk	17402	D1	3272
SHAWNA AV., York Twp	Yk	17402	C10	3272
SHAWNEE AV., Dover Twp	Yk	17315	F1	3269
SHAWNEE DR., Stewartstown	Yk	17363	D11	3585
SHAWNEE TR., Newberry	Yk	17370	A8	2956
SHAWS SCHOOL RD., Chanceford	Yk	17309	F7	3379
SHEALER RD., Straban	Ad	17325	F5	3471
SHEARER DR., Carroll	Yk	17019	G8	3056
SHEARER DR., Warrington	Yk	17019	G8	3056
SHEEPBRIDGE RD., Conewago	Yk	17370	B2	3060
SHEEPBRIDGE RD., Newberry	Yk	17370	B2	3060
SHEEPFORD RD., Fairview	Yk	17070	D1	2953
SHEETWOOD DR., Carroll	Yk	17019	G7	3056
SHEFFER AV., Shrewsbury Boro	Yk	17361	B11	3584
SHEFFIELD DR., Carroll	Yk	17019	E9	2951
SHEFFIELD DR., York Twp	Yk	17313	B5	3376
SHEFFIELD LA., West Manchester	Yk	17404	F3	3373
SHEILA LA., Hopewell	Yk	17363	H7	3585
SHELBOURNE DR., Spring Garden	Yk	17403	E11	3271
SHELDON DR., Latimore	Ad	17372	B10	3160
SHELDON DR., Windsor Twp	Yk	17356	F1	3376
SHELLBORNE LA., Heidelberg	Yk	17362	C10	3476
SHELLEY DR., Newberry	Yk	17370	F1	3060
SHELLEY'S LA., Goldsboro	Yk	17319	H6	2955
SHELLY DR., Newberry	Yk	17370	E11	2955
SHELLYS AV., Goldsboro	Yk	17319	H6	2955
SHENANDOAH CT., Littlestown	Ad	17340	E3	3681
SHENANDOAH DR., York Twp	Yk	17403	D6	3375
SHENANDOAH LA., Manchester Twp	Yk	17404	F10	3165
SHENBERGER LA., Springfield	Yk	17313	B5	3480
SHENBERGER LA., Springfield	Yk	17327	B5	3480
SHENK RD., Chanceford	Yk	17322	A4	3482
SHENK RD., Cross Roads	Yk	17322	A10	3482
SHENK RD., East Hopewell	Yk	17322	A10	3482
SHENK RD., Felton	Yk	17322	A4	3482
SHENKS FERRY RD., Chanceford	Yk	17309	E7	3380
SHEPPARD RD., Union	Ad	17331	D10	3578
SHEPPARD RD., Union	Ad	17340	D10	3578
SHERATON DR., Fairview	Yk	17070	H7	2848
SHERECK LA., Hellam	Yk	17406	F2	3273
SHERIDAN DR., Penn	Yk	17331	G7	3579
SHERIDAN RD., Springettsbury	Yk	17402	F10	3166
SHERIDAN ST., York City	Yk	17404	A9	3271
SHERIDAN TR., Liberty	Ad	17320	E7	3573
SHERMAN DR., Mount Joy	Ad	17325	A2	3576
SHERMAN DR., Mount Pleasant	Ad	17325	A2	3576
SHERMAN DR., Reading	Ad	17316	D1	3266
SHERMAN ST. N., East Manchester	Yk	17347	H2	3166
SHERMAN ST. N., Spring Garden	Yk	17403	E5	3271
SHERMAN ST. N., Springettsbury	Yk	17402	G10	3166
SHERMAN ST. N., York City	Yk	17403	E5	3271
SHERMAN ST. S., York City	Yk	17403	F7	3271
SHERMAN ST., Penn	Yk	17331	B5	3579
SHERMAN ST., Springettsbury	Yk	17403	F3	3271
SHERRILL DR., Mount Pleasant	Ad	17350	F6	3473
SHERRY DAWN DR., York Twp	Yk	17313	G9	3376
SHERRY DR., Conewago	Ad	17344	E1	3578
SHERRY DR., Manchester Twp	Yk	17404	E11	3165
SHERWIN CT., New Freedom	Yk	17349	H2	3687
SHERWOOD DR., Dover Twp	Yk	17315	B3	3269
SHERWOOD DR., New Salem	Yk	17371	C6	3374
SHERWOOD DR., North Codorus	Yk	17404	B10	3374
SHERWOOD DR., Windsor Twp	Yk	17402	B6	3273
SHERWOOD DR., York Twp	Yk	17403	H11	3271
SHERWOOD ST., Hanover	Yk	17331	B11	3475
SHETLAND DR., Shrewsbury Boro	Yk	17327	H8	3583
SHETLAND LA., Windsor Twp	Yk	17402	C9	3273
SHILOH DR., West Manchester	Yk	17404	D4	3270
SHINDEL DR., Fairview	Yk	17070	D10	2849
SHINDLER CT., North York	Yk	17404	B5	3271
SHIPPENSBURG RD., Menallen	Ad	17307	E3	3260
SHIPPENSBURG RD., Menallen	Ad	17307	A7	3261
SHIPPENSBURG RD., Washington	Yk	17316	G10	3161
SHIPPENSBURG RD., Washington	Yk	17316	A11	3162
SHIPPENSBURG RD., Washington	Yk	17316	C1	3267
SHIRLEY LA., Germany	Ad	17340	C2	3681
SHIRLEY TR., Carroll Valley	Ad	17320	E11	3572
SHIRLEY TR., Carroll Valley	Ad	17320	E2	3676
SHIRLEY TR., Liberty	Ad	17320	E2	3676
SHOE HOUSE RD., Hellam	Yk	17406	G10	3167
SHOE RD., Hellam	Yk	17406	G1	3272
SHOFF RD. E., Chanceford	Yk	17356	B2	3379
SHOFF RD. W., Chanceford	Yk	17368	H1	3378
SHOFF RD. W., Chanceford	Yk	17368	A2	3379
SHORBS HILL RD., West Manheim	Yk	17331	D1	3683
SHORB'S MILL RD., Freedom	Ad	17320	C3	3678
SHORE LA., Hellam	Yk	17368	D4	3169
SHORE RD., Shrewsbury Twp	Yk	17327	E6	3583
SHORT CT., Shrewsbury Twp	Yk	17327	F4	3583
SHORT CUT RD., Chanceford	Yk	17322	H8	3378
SHORT CUT RD., Chanceford	Yk	17322	A9	3379
SHORT CUT RD., Codorus	Yk	17327	F9	3582
SHORT CUT RD., Franklin	Ad	17307	B8	3365
SHORT CUT RD., Hamilton	Ad	17301	B8	3371
SHORT CUT RD., Huntington	Ad	17324	H10	3158
SHORT LA., Fairview	Yk	17011	F6	2848
SHORT LA., Hamilton	Ad	17350	E8	3370
SHORT LA., Hamiltonban	Ad	17320	E2	3572
SHORT RD., East Hopewell	Yk	17363	H1	3585
SHORT RD., East Hopewell	Yk	17363	A1	3586
SHORT RD., North Codorus	Yk	17362	G1	3477
SHORT RD., Paradise	Yk	17316	F10	3267
SHORT TR., Carroll Valley	Ad	17320	G8	3572
SHOSHONE DR., Conewago	Ad	17331	D3	3578
SHOTGUN LA., Dover Twp	Yk	17315	B11	3163
SHRIVER'S CORNER RD., Butler	Ad	17325	D5	3367
SHRIVER'S CORNER RD., Straban	Ad	17325	D5	3367
SHRIVER'S CORNER RD., Straban	Ad	17325	A9	3368
SHUE LA., Manheim	Yk	17329	B9	3581
SHUEY RD., Fairview	Yk	17070	B1	2954
SHUEY ST., Fairview	Yk	17070	B11	2849
SHUFF DR., Windsor Twp	Yk	17356	B5	3377
SHULER RD., Fairview	Yk	17319	G4	2954
SHULTON DR., Springettsbury	Yk	17402	D11	3167
SHULTON DR., Springettsbury	Yk	17402	D1	3272
SHUTT RD., Heidelberg	Yk	17362	D9	3476
SI RODE LA., Newberry	Yk	17370	H1	3060
SI RODE LA., Newberry	Yk	17370	A1	3061
SIBERT RD., Straban	Ad	17325	H10	3368
SIBERT RD., Straban	Ad	17325	A11	3369
SIBERT RD., Straban	Ad	17325	H1	3472
SIBERT RD., Straban	Ad	17350	H10	3368
SICKLES AV., Cumberland	Ad	17325	A3	3575
SICKLES DR., Reading	Ad	17316	D4	3266
SIDDONSBURG RD. E., Monaghan	Yk	17019	E8	2952
SIDDONSBURG RD. E., Monaghan	Yk	17055	G7	2952
SIDDONSBURG RD. E., Monaghan	Yk	17055	A6	2953
SIDDONSBURG RD. W., Carroll	Yk	17019	G11	2951
SIDDONSBURG RD. W., Monaghan	Yk	17019	A10	2952
SIDDONSBURG RD. W., Monaghan	Yk	17019	B9	2952
SIDDONSBURG RD., Fairview	Yk	17055	C9	2953
SIDDONSBURG RD., Fairview	Yk	17339	C9	2953
SIDDONSBURG RD., Fairview	Yk	17339	A9	2954
SIDE TRACK TR., Carroll Valley	Ad	17320	H11	3572
SIDE TRACK TR., Carroll Valley	Ad	17320	H1	3676
SIELING RD., Hopewell	Yk	17349	E7	3584
SIERRA DR., York Twp	Yk	17402	H7	3375
SIGSBEE AV., North York	Yk	17404	B4	3271
SILEO RD., Carroll	Yk	17019	C5	3057
SILO RD., Franklin	Ad	17353	E5	3469
SILO RD., Highland	Ad	17353	E5	3469
SILVER LAKE RD., Fairview	Yk	17339	G10	2953
SILVER LAKE RD., Fairview	Yk	17339	A10	2954
SILVER MAPLE CT., Cross Roads	Yk	17347	G7	3166
SILVER MAPLE CT., East Manchester	Yk	17347	G6	3166
SILVER SPUR DR., Springettsbury	Yk	17402	G1	3272
SILVER SPUR DR., Springettsbury	Yk	17402	F1	3272
SILVERWOOD DR., Springettsbury	Yk	17402	E6	3272
SIMPSON RD., Manheim	Yk	17327	D4	3685
SIMPSON ST., York City	Yk	17403	F7	3271
SINCLAIR CIR., Hellam	Yk	17368	D8	3169
SINCLAIR RD., Lower Chanceford	Yk	17314	F4	3589
SINCLAIR RD., North Hopewell	Yk	17356	B1	3481
SINCLAIR RD., Windsor Twp	Yk	17356	B1	3481
SINGER RD., New Freedom	Yk	17349	G4	3687
SINKING SPRINGS LA., Manchester Twp	Yk	17402	A9	3166
SINKING SPRINGS LA., Manchester Twp	Yk	17402	C9	3166
SINKING SPRINGS LA., Manchester Twp	Yk	17404	G8	3165
SINSHEIM RD., Codorus	Yk	17362	B2	3581
SINSHEIM RD., Manheim	Yk	17362	A2	3581
SINSHEIM SCHOOL RD., Codorus	Yk	17362	D2	3581
SINSHEM RD., Manheim	Yk	17362	G3	3580
SIPE RD., Newberry	Yk	17370	B11	2955
SIPE RD., Newberry	Yk	17370	C1	3060
SITLER LA., Windsor Twp	Yk	17402	A6	3273
SIX LA., Hamiltonban	Ad	17222	F3	3467
SKI RUN TR., Carroll Valley	Ad	17320	H8	3572
SKI RUN TR., Carroll Valley	Ad	17320	A8	3573
SKUNK HOLLOW LA., Lower Windsor	Yk	17406	H4	3273
SKUNK HOLLOW LA., Lower Windsor	Yk	17406	A4	3274
SKY TOP TR., Dover Twp	Yk	17315	D10	3163
SKYLARK TR., Carroll Valley	Ad	17320	E11	3572
SKYLARK TR., Carroll Valley	Ad	17320	F1	3676
SKYLIGHT DR. E., York Twp	Yk	17402	D9	3272
SKYLIGHT DR. W., York Twp	Yk	17402	D9	3272
SKYLIGHT DR., York Twp	Yk	17402	E9	3272
SKYLINE CT., Cumberland	Ad	17325	F8	3470
SKYLINE DR., Fairview	Yk	17070	C9	2849
SKYLINE DR., Manchester Twp	Yk	17404	F6	3165
SKYLINE DR., Springettsbury	Yk	17402	F1	3271
SKYLINE TR., Carroll Valley	Ad	17320	A1	3677
SKYLITE DR., West Manheim	Yk	17331	F1	3683
SKYVIEW DR., Manchester Twp	Yk	17402	C1	3271
SKYVIEW DR., Manheim	Yk	17329	C8	3581
SKYVIEW DR., Shrewsbury Boro	Yk	17361	B7	3584
SKYVIEW LA., Hellam	Yk	17406	F11	3168
SKYVIEW RD., Peach Bottom	Yk	17314	D11	3589
SLAB RD., Lower Chanceford	Yk	17302	B3	3589
SLAB RD., Lower Chanceford	Yk	17302	F1	3589
SLAB RD., Lower Chanceford	Yk	17314	C3	3589
SLAB RD., Lower Chanceford	Yk	17314	F2	3589
SLAGEL RD., North Codorus	Yk	17362	H10	3373
SLAGEL RD., North Codorus	Yk	17362	H1	3477
SLAGEL RD., North Codorus	Yk	17362	A1	3478
SLASEMANS DR., Fairview	Yk	17070	D10	2849
SLATE RIDGE RD., Jackson	Yk	17404	E5	3373
SLATE ROCK RD., Franklin	Ad	17307	H7	3364
SLATE ROCK RD., Franklin	Ad	17307	A7	3365
SLATE SPRING RD., Peach Bottom	Yk	17314	H5	3693
SLATEHILL RD., West Manchester	Yk	17404	H5	3269
SLATER HILL LA., Manchester Twp	Yk	17402	C2	3271
SLATERSVILLE RD., Menallen	Ad	17307	G3	3261
SLATEVILLE RD., Peach Bottom	Yk	17314	H3	3693
SLATEVILLE RD., Peach Bottom	Yk	17314	C3	3694
SLATEVILLE RD., Peach Bottom	Yk	17314	A4	3694
SLAYBAUGH TOWN RD., Huntington	Ad	17372	C7	3159
SLEEPY HOLLOW RD., Spring Garden	Yk	17403	E10	3271
SLOCUM AV., Cumberland	Ad	17325	D10	3471
SLOE GIN TR., Hamiltonban	Ad	17320	H1	3571
SMALL ST., West Manchester	Yk	17404	F7	3270
SMALLBROOK LA., Spring Garden	Yk	17403	C11	3271
SMEACH DR., West Manheim	Yk	17331	G10	3579
SMELTZER RD., Springfield	Yk	17360	C7	3479
SMELTZER ST., Loganville	Yk	17360	E6	3479
SMILE WAY, York Twp	Yk	17404	H3	3270
SMITH RD., Peach Bottom	Yk	17314	D9	3590
SMITH HILL RD., New Salem	Yk	17371	C5	3374
SMITH HILL RD., North Codorus	Yk	17404	C5	3374
SMITH HOLLOW RD., Chanceford	Yk	17309	G11	3379
SMITH LA., Glen Rock	Yk	17327	B4	3583
SMITH MILL RD., New Freedom	Yk	17349	G5	3687
SMITH MILL RD., Shrewsbury Twp	Yk	17349	E6	3687
SMITH RD., Codorus	Yk	17327	D9	3582
SMITH RD., Conewago	Yk	17402	F11	3060
SMITH RD., Conewago	Yk	17402	F1	3165
SMITH RD., Dover Twp	Yk	17315	E11	3164
SMITH RD., Huntington	Ad	17372	F9	3264
SMITH RD., Straban	Ad	17325	G4	3471
SMITH RD., Straban	Ad	17325	H5	3471
SMITH RD., Tyrone	Ad	17372	F9	3264
SMITH RD., Washington	Yk	17315	G10	3162
SMITH RD., Washington	Yk	17315	A11	3163
SMITH RD., West Manchester	Yk	17404	G6	3373
SMITH RD., Windsor Twp	Yk	17356	F8	3377
SMITH ST., Carroll	Yk	17019	B3	3056
SMITH ST., Jacobus	Yk	17407	E10	3375
SMITH ST., York City	Yk	17404	B6	3271
SMITH ST., York Haven	Yk	17370	E3	3061
SMITH STATION RD., Heidelberg	Yk	17331	B1	3580
SMITH STATION RD., Heidelberg	Yk	17362	A9	3476
SMOKEBOX CIR., Hopewell	Yk	17363	F10	3585
SMOKEHOUSE CT., Littlestown	Ad	17340	D1	3681
SMOKETOWN RD., Manheim	Yk	17329	A6	3581
SMOKETOWN RD., Manheim	Yk	17362	H5	3580
SMOKETOWN RD., Manheim	Yk	17362	A6	3581
SMOKETOWN RD., Mount Pleasant	Ad	17331	G11	3473
SMOKETOWN RD., Mount Pleasant	Ad	17331	G1	3577
SMOKETOWN RD., Mount Pleasant	Ad	17331	H1	3577
SMYSER RD., Lower Windsor	Yk	17366	F9	3273
SMYSER RD., North Codorus	Yk	17403	F4	3374
SMYSER ST., York City	Yk	17404	B7	3271
SNAFFLE LA., Manchester Twp	Yk	17404	E1	3270
SNODGRASS RD., Lower Chanceford	Yk	17314	A5	3589
SNOW BIRD TR., Carroll Valley	Ad	17320	A8	3573
SNOW PLOW TR., Carroll Valley	Ad	17320	A8	3573
SNOW TR., Carroll Valley	Ad	17320	A7	3573
SNYDER CORNER RD., Chanceford	Yk	17356	C10	3378
SNYDER CORNER RD., Lower Windsor	Yk	17356	D5	3378
SNYDER CORNER RD., Lower Windsor	Yk	17366	E11	3274
SNYDER CORNER RD., Lower Windsor	Yk	17366	E3	3378
SNYDER CORNER RD., Windsor Twp	Yk	17356	D7	3378
SNYDER LA., Hellam	Yk	17406	B6	3168
SNYDER MILL RD., Codorus	Yk	17362	E5	3581
SNYDER PL., York City	Yk	17403	D8	3271
SNYDER RD., Chanceford	Yk	17356	E10	3378
SNYDER RD., Codorus	Yk	17327	C3	3582
SNYDER RD., Codorus	Yk	17327	E2	3582
SNYDER RD., Huntington	Ad	17372	C5	3159

SNYDER RD., Lower Chanceford	Yk	17314	D7	3589
SNYDER SQ., Oxford	Ad	17350	E1	3474
SNYDERS HOLLOW LA., Hamiltonban	Ad	17320	F9	3571
SOLAR DR., Dover Twp	Yk	17315	F6	3269
SOLARLIGHT DR., York Twp	Yk	17402	C9	3272
SOLOMON RD., Cumberland	Ad	17325	D7	3575
SOLOMON RD., Cumberland	Ad	17325	D7	3575
SOLOMON RD., Mount Joy	Ad	17325	D7	3575
SOMERSET LA., Spring Garden	Yk	17403	B11	3271
SOMERSET RD., Dover Twp	Yk	17315	E11	3164
SOMERSET RD., Dover Twp	Yk	17315	E1	3269
SONNY ST., Penn	Yk	17331	F6	3579
SORREL RIDGE LA., New Freedom	Yk	17349	G5	3687
SORREL RIDGE LA., Springettsbury	Yk	17402	E1	3272
SORREL ST., Manchester Twp	Yk	17404	F8	3165
SOUR MASH RD., Hamiltonban	Ad	17320	H1	3675
SOUR MASH TR., Hamiltonban	Ad	17320	H11	3571
SOUR MASH TR., Hamiltonban	Ad	17320	A11	3572
SOUTH A ST., York Spring	Ad	17372	B11	3160
SOUTH ABBOT ST., Abbottstown	Ad	17301	A10	3371
SOUTH ADAMS ST., West York	Yk	17404	G9	3270
SOUTH AL., Wellsville	Yk	17365	H2	3162
SOUTH AL., Wrightsville	Yk	17368	D7	3169
SOUTH ALBEMARLE ST., York City	Yk	17403	F6	3271
SOUTH ALLWOOD DR., Conewago	Ad	17331	C5	3578
SOUTH ALWINE AV., West Manchester	Yk	17404	H2	3373
SOUTH AV., Cumberland	Ad	17325	B3	3471
SOUTH AV., Delta	Yk	17314	H4	3693
SOUTH AV., East Berlin	Ad	17316	B11	3267
SOUTH AV., East Berlin	Ad	17316	C1	3371
SOUTH AV., Windsor Boro	Yk	17366	E4	3377
SOUTH B ST., York Spring	Ad	17372	B11	3160
SOUTH BALDER ST., Fairfield	Ad	17320	A5	3573
SOUTH BALTIMORE ST., Carroll	Yk	17019	D4	3056
SOUTH BALTIMORE ST., Dillsburg	Yk	17019	D4	3056
SOUTH BALTIMORE ST., Franklin	Yk	17019	D4	3056
SOUTH BALTIMORE ST., Franklintown	Yk	17323	D4	3056
SOUTH BARRENS RD., Hopewell	Yk	17363	E2	3689
SOUTH BARRENS RD., Hopewell	Yk	17363	A5	3690
SOUTH BEAVER ST., York City	Yk	17403	C8	3271
SOUTH BEAVER ST., York City	Yk	17403	D9	3271
SOUTH BELMONT ST., Spring Garden	Yk	17403	H8	3271
SOUTH BELVIDERE AV., York City	Yk	17404	A8	3271
SOUTH BERLIN AV., New Oxford	Ad	17350	B3	3474
SOUTH BIESECKER RD., Jackson	Yk	17364	C3	3373
SOUTH BIESECKER RD., Jackson	Yk	17404	C3	3373
SOUTH BOLTON ST. , New Oxford	Ad	17350	A3	3474
SOUTH BONNIEFIELD DR., Bonneauville	Ad	17325	H2	3576
SOUTH BROAD ST., Hallam	Yk	17406	C11	3168
SOUTH BROAD ST., New Freedom	Yk	17349	F3	3687
SOUTH BROOKWOOD DR., York Twp	Yk	17403	F2	3375
SOUTH BROWN'S DAM DR., Reading	Ad	17350	C4	3370
SOUTH CAMP ST., Windsor Boro	Yk	17366	E6	3377
SOUTH CAMP ST., Windsor Twp	Yk	17356	E6	3377
SOUTH CAMP ST., Windsor Twp	Yk	17366	E6	3377
SOUTH CENTER ST., Penn	Yk	17331	E4	3579
SOUTH CESSINA TR., Liberty	Ad	17320	C10	3573
SOUTH CHARLES ST., Dallastown	Yk	17313	F8	3376
SOUTH CHARLES ST., New Freedom	Yk	17349	G3	3687
SOUTH CHARLES ST., Red Lion	Yk	17356	C7	3377
SOUTH CHESTNUT ST., Carroll	Yk	17019	E4	3056
SOUTH CHESTNUT ST., Dillsburg	Yk	17019	E4	3056
SOUTH CHURCH RD., Shrewsbury Boro	Yk	17361	B9	3584
SOUTH CHURCH ST. , East Hopewell	Yk	17322	H11	3481
SOUTH CHURCH ST., East Hopewell	Yk	17322	A11	3482
SOUTH CHURCH ST., New Oxford	Ad	17350	B3	3474
SOUTH CHURCH ST., Shrewsbury Twp	Yk	17361	B9	3584
SOUTH CLINTON ST., Abbottstown	Ad	17301	B10	3371
SOUTH CLINTON ST., West York	Yk	17404	F9	3270
SOUTH COLLEGE ST., New Oxford	Ad	17350	B3	3474
SOUTH COLLEGE ST., Oxford	Ad	17350	B3	3474
SOUTH COLUMBUS AV., Littlestown	Ad	17340	D3	3681
SOUTH CONFEDERATE AV., Cumberland	Ad	17325	H5	3574
SOUTH CONFEDERATE AV., Cumberland	Ad	17325	A5	3575
SOUTH CONSTITUTION AV., New Freedom	Yk	17349	G3	3687
SOUTH CONWAY AV., Dallastown	Yk	17313	E7	3376
SOUTH COURT ST., York City	Yk	17403	D8	3271
SOUTH CT., Newberry	Yk	17370	F11	2955
SOUTH CT., Newberry	Yk	17370	F1	3060
SOUTH CYPRESS RD., Dover Twp	Yk	17315	F4	3269
SOUTH D ST., York Spring	Ad	17372	B10	3160
SOUTH DR., West Manchester	Yk	17404	C6	3270
SOUTH DUKE ST., Dallastown	Yk	17313	H8	3376
SOUTH DUKE ST., North York	Yk	17404	C5	3271
SOUTH DUKE ST., Spring Garden	Yk	17403	E11	3271
SOUTH DUKE ST., Spring Garden	Yk	17403	E1	3375
SOUTH DUKE ST., York City	Yk	17403	D8	3271
SOUTH DUKE ST., York Twp	Yk	17313	H8	3376
SOUTH DUKE ST., York Twp	Yk	17313	A11	3377
SOUTH DUKE ST., York Twp	Yk	17356	A11	3377
SOUTH EAST ST., Spring Grove	Yk	17362	B1	3477
SOUTH EMERALD RD., West Manchester	Yk	17404	C7	3270
SOUTH EXETER DR., York Twp	Yk	17403	C7	3376
SOUTH F ST., York Spring	Ad	17372	B10	3160
SOUTH FERN AV., Dallastown	Yk	17313	F8	3376
SOUTH FILEYS RD., Monaghan	Yk	17019	B9	2952
SOUTH FORNEY AV., Hanover	Yk	17331	B4	3579
SOUTH FORREST ST., West Manchester	Yk	17404	E9	3270
SOUTH FRANKLIN ST., Dallastown	Yk	17313	D7	3376
SOUTH FRANKLIN ST., Hanover	Yk	17331	C4	3579
SOUTH FRANKLIN ST., Penn	Yk	17331	C4	3579
SOUTH FRANKLIN ST., Red Lion	Yk	17356	B8	3377
SOUTH FRANKLIN ST., York Twp	Yk	17313	D7	3376
SOUTH FRANKLIN ST., York Twp	Yk	17356	H10	3376
SOUTH FRANKLIN ST., York Twp	Yk	17356	A10	3377
SOUTH FROG POND HOLLOW, Hamilton	Ad	17301	B3	3371
SOUTH FRONT ST., Wrightsville	Yk	17368	E7	3169
SOUTH G ST., York Spring	Ad	17372	B10	3160
SOUTH GALA, Littlestown	Ad	17340	C1	3681
SOUTH GEORGE ST., Spring Garden	Yk	17403	E11	3271
SOUTH GEORGE ST., Spring Garden	Yk	17403	E2	3375
SOUTH GEORGE ST., York City	Yk	17401	D8	3271
SOUTH GEORGE ST., York City	Yk	17403	D8	3271
SOUTH GEORGE ST., York Twp	Yk	17403	E2	3375
SOUTH GOHN LA., Red Lion	Yk	17356	B8	3377
SOUTH GORA RD., Manchester Twp	Yk	17404	G11	3165
SOUTH GRAND AV., Dallastown	Yk	17313	G7	3376
SOUTH GRANT RD., Jackson	Yk	17364	B3	3373
SOUTH GRANTHAM RD., Monaghan	Yk	17019	C9	2952
SOUTH H ST., York Spring	Ad	17372	A10	3160
SOUTH HARRISON ST., Spring Garden	Yk	17403	G6	3271
SOUTH HARRISON ST., York City	Yk	17403	G6	3271
SOUTH HARTLEY ST., York City	Yk	17404	B8	3271
SOUTH HARTMAN ST., York City	Yk	17403	F6	3271
SOUTH HAWTHORNE ST., York City	Yk	17404	A9	3271
SOUTH HAY ST., Gettysburg	Ad	17325	A9	3471
SOUTH HICKORY LA., Reading	Ad	17350	H7	3369
SOUTH HIGH ST., Arendtsville	Ad	17307	B3	3366
SOUTH HIGHLAND AV., West Manchester	Yk	17404	G9	3270
SOUTH HIGHLAND AV., West York	Yk	17404	G9	3270
SOUTH HILL RD., Springettsbury	Yk	17402	G10	3166
SOUTH HILL-N-DALE, York Twp	Yk	17403	G1	3375
SOUTH HILLSIDE DR., Butler	Ad	17307	G1	3366
SOUTH HILLTOP DR., Heidelberg	Yk	17362	E6	3476
SOUTH HOWARD AV., Gettysburg	Ad	17325	B9	3471
SOUTH HOWARD ST., Dallastown	Yk	17313	F8	3376
SOUTH HOWARD ST., York City	Yk	17403	D8	3271
SOUTH HOWARD ST., York Twp	Yk	17313	F8	3376
SOUTH JACOBS AL., Abbottstown	Ad	17301	B10	3371
SOUTH JOHNAMAC, Littlestown	Ad	17340	C1	3681
SOUTH K ST., York Spring	Ad	17372	A10	3160
SOUTH KENNARD DALE AV., Stewartstown	Yk	17363	F11	3585
SOUTH KENNARD DALE AV., Stewartstown	Yk	17363	F1	3689
SOUTH LARKSPUR LA., York Twp	Yk	17403	F3	3375
SOUTH LEE ST., Hallam	Yk	17406	B11	3168
SOUTH LEHMAN ST., York City	Yk	17403	F6	3271
SOUTH LEWISBERRY RD., Monaghan	Yk	17055	G7	2952
SOUTH LOCUST POINT RD., Carroll	Yk	17019	B1	2951
SOUTH MAIN ST., Biglerville	Ad	17307	A2	3367
SOUTH MAIN ST., East Prospect	Yk	17317	F6	3274
SOUTH MAIN ST., East Prospect	Yk	17368	F6	3274
SOUTH MAIN ST., Jacobus	Yk	17407	F11	3375
SOUTH MAIN ST., Loganville	Yk	17360	E5	3479
SOUTH MAIN ST., Railroad	Yk	17355	G10	3583
SOUTH MAIN ST., Railroad	Yk	17355	G11	3583
SOUTH MAIN ST., Red Lion	Yk	17356	D8	3377
SOUTH MAIN ST., Shrewsbury Boro	Yk	17361	B10	3584
SOUTH MAIN ST., Springfield	Yk	17407	F11	3375
SOUTH MAIN ST., Stewartstown	Yk	17363	E11	3585
SOUTH MAIN ST., Stewartstown	Yk	17363	E1	3689
SOUTH MARKET ST., Fawn Grove	Yk	17321	G5	3691
SOUTH MASON AV., Dallastown	Yk	17313	E7	3376
SOUTH MAURICE ST., Manchester Twp	Yk	17404	G10	3165
SOUTH McDERMOTT RD., Fawn	Yk	17321	A6	3692
SOUTH MILL ST., Red Lion	Yk	17356	A8	3377
SOUTH MILLER ST., Fairfield	Ad	17320	A5	3573
SOUTH MOUNTAIN RD., Franklin	Yk	17019	B11	3055
SOUTH MOUNTAIN RD., Franklin	Yk	17019	F9	3055
SOUTH NEWBERRY ST., York City	Yk	17404	C8	3271
SOUTH NEWTON AV., Dallastown	Yk	17313	F8	3376
SOUTH OAK HEIGHTS TR., Peach Bottom	Yk	17314	A11	3589
SOUTH OAKWOOD CT., York Twp	Yk	17356	F1	3376
SOUTH ORANGE ST., New Oxford	Ad	17350	C1	3474
SOUTH ORANGE ST., Oxford	Ad	17350	A3	3474
SOUTH ORCHARD VIEW DR., Berwick	Ad	17331	C4	3475
SOUTH PARK LA., Red Lion	Yk	17356	C7	3377
SOUTH PARK ST., Dallastown	Yk	17313	G8	3376
SOUTH PARK ST., North Hopewell	Yk	17356	A1	3481
SOUTH PARK ST., Red Lion	Yk	17356	B7	3377
SOUTH PARK ST., York Twp	Yk	17313	H10	3376
SOUTH PARK ST., York Twp	Yk	17356	H11	3376
SOUTH PARK ST., York Twp	Yk	17356	A11	3377
SOUTH PARK ST., York Twp	Yk	17356	A1	3481
SOUTH PENN ST., Windsor Boro	Yk	17366	F5	3377
SOUTH PENN ST., Windsor Twp	Yk	17366	F5	3377
SOUTH PENN ST., York City	Yk	17403	C9	3271
SOUTH PENN ST., York City	Yk	17404	B8	3271
SOUTH PERSHING AV., York City	Yk	17401	C8	3271
SOUTH PERSHING AV., York City	Yk	17403	C8	3271
SOUTH PETER ST., New Oxford	Ad	17350	B3	3474
SOUTH PHEASANT WAY, Hamilton	Ad	17301	A8	3371
SOUTH PINE ST., Red Lion	Yk	17356	C7	3377
SOUTH PINE ST., York City	Yk	17403	E8	3271
SOUTH PLEASANT AV., Dallastown	Yk	17313	E9	3376
SOUTH PLEASANT AV., York Twp	Yk	17313	D11	3376
SOUTH PLEASANT AV., York Twp	Yk	17313	B11	3376
SOUTH PREAKNESS ST., Conewago	Ad	17331	C5	3578
SOUTH QUEEN ST., Littlestown	Ad	17340	E2	3681
SOUTH QUEEN ST., Spring Garden	Yk	17403	F11	3271
SOUTH QUEEN ST., York City	Yk	17403	E9	3271
SOUTH QUEEN ST., York Twp	Yk	17313	C6	3376
SOUTH QUEEN ST., York Twp	Yk	17402	A3	3376
SOUTH QUEEN ST., York Twp	Yk	17403	A3	3376
SOUTH QUEEN ST., York Twp	Yk	17402	H1	3375
SOUTH QUEEN ST., York Twp	Yk	17403	F11	3271
SOUTH QUEEN ST., York Twp	Yk	17403	H1	3375
SOUTH RAILROAD LA., Red Lion	Yk	17356	C7	3377
SOUTH RD., Seven Valleys	Yk	17360	F5	3478
SOUTH RD., Springfield	Yk	17360	G6	3478
SOUTH RD., Springfield	Yk	17360	H10	3478
SOUTH RD., Springfield	Yk	17360	A8	3479
SOUTH RICHLAND AV., West Manchester	Yk	17404	A9	3271
SOUTH RICHLAND AV., York City	Yk	17404	A9	3271
SOUTH RIDGE RD., Huntington	Ad	17372	A4	3265
SOUTH RITA MARIE AV., Littlestown	Ad	17340	E2	3681
SOUTH SCHOOL PL., Dallastown	Yk	17313	E7	3376
SOUTH SEASONS DR., Monaghan	Yk	17019	A10	2952
SOUTH SEWARD ST., West York	Yk	17404	G9	3270
SOUTH SHERMAN ST., York City	Yk	17403	F7	3271
SOUTH SPRING ST., Fairfield	Ad	17320	A5	3573
SOUTH ST. E., York City	Yk	17403	D8	3271
SOUTH ST. E., York City	Yk	17403	E8	3271
SOUTH ST. JAMES ST., Abbottstown	Ad	17301	B9	3371
SOUTH ST. W., York City	Yk	17403	D8	3271
SOUTH ST., Conewago	Ad	17331	H2	3578
SOUTH ST., Franklintown	Yk	17323	E9	3056
SOUTH ST., Gettysburg	Ad	17325	C9	3471
SOUTH ST., Hanover	Yk	17331	A2	3579
SOUTH ST., Lewisberry	Yk	17339	B10	2954
SOUTH ST., Littlestown	Ad	17340	G1	3681
SOUTH ST., Manchester Boro	Yk	17345	E1	3166
SOUTH ST., McSherrystown	Ad	17344	F3	3578
SOUTH ST., Spring Garden	Yk	17403	G7	3271
SOUTH STAR AV., Dallastown	Yk	17313	E7	3376
SOUTH STEEPLE CHASE , Straban	Ad	17325	E6	3471
SOUTH STRATHCONA DR., Spring Garden	Yk	17403	E10	3271
SOUTH SUMMER ST., West York	Yk	17404	G10	3270
SOUTH SUMMIT CIR., Spring Garden	Yk	17403	B2	3375
SOUTH SUNSET DR., Shrewsbury Boro	Yk	17361	A9	3584
SOUTH SUSQUEHANNA TRAIL, Springfield	Yk	17403	F1	3479
SOUTH SUSQUEHANNA TRAIL, Springfield	Yk	17407	F1	3479
SOUTH SYCAMORE LA., Stewartstown	Yk	17363	F11	3585
SOUTH TERRACE DR., Monaghan	Yk	17019	B10	2952
SOUTH TR., Carroll Valley	Ad	17320	A5	3677
SOUTH TREMONT ST., York City	Yk	17403	F6	3271
SOUTH VAIL DR., Penn	Yk	17331	C6	3579
SOUTH VERDAN DR., Spring Garden	Yk	17403	F11	3271
SOUTH VIEW DR., Butler	Ad	17307	G1	3366
SOUTH WALNUT ST., Dallastown	Yk	17313	F7	3376
SOUTH WALNUT ST., Spring Grove	Yk	17362	A1	3477
SOUTH WASHINGTON ST., Gettysburg	Ad	17325	C9	3471
SOUTH WATER ST., New Oxford	Ad	17350	A3	3474
SOUTH WATER ST., Oxford	Ad	17350	A3	3474
SOUTH WATER ST., Spring Grove	Yk	17362	A1	3477
SOUTH WEST ST., York City	Yk	17404	A8	3271
SOUTH WHITE PINE TR., Peach Bottom	Yk	17314	H10	3588
SOUTH WILLIAM ST., West Manchester	Yk	17404	E9	3270
SOUTH WILLOW LA., Red Lion	Yk	17356	B8	3377
SOUTH WILLOW SPRINGS CIR., Manchester Twp	Yk	17402	A3	3166
SOUTH WILSON LA., Hallam	Yk	17406	D11	3168
SOUTH WILSON LA., Hellam	Yk	17406	D11	3168
SOUTH WINDING RD., Warrington	Yk	17315	H6	3162
SOUTH WINNERS CIRCLE DR., York Twp	Yk	17356	A6	3377
SOUTH WYNDHAM DR., Spring Garden	Yk	17403	C2	3375
SOUTH WYNTRE BROOK, York Twp	Yk	17403	E2	3375
SOUTH YORK RD., Monaghan	Yk	17019	E8	2952
SOUTHBROOK DR., York Twp	Yk	17403	G2	3375
SOUTHCREST RD., Newberry	Yk	17370	E1	3060
SOUTHERN RD., Spring Garden	Yk	17403	G10	3271
SOUTHERN RD., Spring Garden	Yk	17403	A10	3272
SOUTHGATE DR., West Manchester	Yk	17404	F3	3270
SOUTHRIDGE DR., Fairview	Yk	17055	E7	2953
SOUTHRIDGE LA., Hellam	Yk	17368	B10	3169
SOUTHVIEW DR., North Codorus	Yk	17404	C8	3374
SOUTHVIEW DR., Windsor Twp	Yk	17402	A6	3273
SOUTHVIEW DR., York Twp	Yk	17402	H6	3375
SOUTHWOOD DR., Shrewsbury Twp	Yk	17349	C4	3688
SOUTHWYND CT., York Twp	Yk	17403	C3	3375
SOWERS RD., Reading	Ad	17316	G3	3266
SPAHN AV., Spring Garden	Yk	17403	G7	3271
SPAHR AV., East Berlin	Ad	17316	C11	3267
SPAHR SEILING RD., Washington	Yk	17019	F2	3161
SPANGLER AV., Dover Twp	Yk	17315	H2	3269
SPANGLER AV., Dover Twp	Yk	17315	A2	3270
SPANGLER AV., East Berlin	Ad	17316	C11	3267
SPANGLER CIR., Springettsbury	Yk	17402	A11	3167
SPANGLER LA., Hellam	Yk	17406	D9	3168
SPANGLER LA., York City	Yk	17403	E8	3271
SPANGLER RD., Mount Pleasant	Ad	17350	E11	3369
SPANGLER RD., Mount Pleasant	Ad	17350	E1	3473
SPANGLER SCHOOL RD., Mount Joy	Ad	17325	F5	3679
SPANGLER SCHOOL RD., Mount Joy	Ad	17340	F5	3679
SPANGLERS MILL RD., Fairview	Yk	17011	D7	2848
SPANGLERS MILL RD., Fairview	Yk	17070	E10	2848
SPANGLERS RD., North Codorus	Yk	17360	A8	3478
SPANGLERS RD., Warrington	Yk	17339	A8	3059
SPARKLIN' SPRINGS LA., East Hopewell	Yk	17302	B11	3483
SPARKLIN' SPRINGS LA., East Hopewell	Yk	17302	A1	3587
SPARROW DR., West Manchester	Yk	17404	H7	3269
SPARROW DR., West Manchester	Yk	17404	A7	3270
SPARROW LA., Chanceford	Yk	17322	B3	3482
SPARTAN AV., Littlestown	Ad	17340	D1	3681
SPARTON RD., York Twp	Yk	17403	A8	3376
SPARTON RD., York Twp	Yk	17403	H10	3375
SPECTRUM RD., Dover Twp	Yk	17315	F6	3269
SPECTRUM RD., Dover Twp	Yk	17315	F6	3269
SPEEDWAY LA., Union	Ad	17331	H6	3577
SPEELMAN-KLINGER RD., Mount Joy	Ad	17325	D9	3576
SPENCER CT., Dover Twp	Yk	17404	H3	3269
SPENCER RD., Lower Chanceford	Yk	17302	B3	3588
SPEND A BUCK DR., Carroll	Yk	17019	F1	3056
SPICER DR., Abbottstown	Ad	17301	C10	3371
SPICER RD., Tyrone	Ad	17325	F10	3264
SPIGOT VALLEY RD., Franklin	Ad	17307	G8	3364
SPINELLI LA., Dover Twp	Yk	17315	D10	3163
SPIRIT LA., Codorus	Yk	17329	F6	3581
SPONDIN DR., Windsor Twp	Yk	17402	D8	3272
SPOOK LA., Mount Pleasant	Ad	17325	A9	3473
SPORTS TR., Carroll Valley	Ad	17320	A10	3573
SPORTSMAN CLUB RD., Codorus	Yk	17362	H3	3581
SPORTSMAN CLUB RD., Codorus	Yk	17362	A2	3582
SPORTSMANS CLUB RD., North Codorus	Yk	17362	B4	3477
SPRENKLE CT., West Manchester	Yk	17404	D6	3270
SPRENKLE DR., Manchester Twp	Yk	17404	A2	3271
SPRENKLE RD., Jackson	Yk	17362	C9	3373
SPRING AV., Hanover	Yk	17331	D3	3579
SPRING AV., Penn	Yk	17331	D2	3579
SPRING CREEK CIR., Mount Joy	Ad	17325	G3	3575
SPRING CREEK DR., Shrewsbury Boro	Yk	17361	B5	3584
SPRING CT., Abbottstown	Ad	17301	B10	3371
SPRING DR., Bonneauville	Ad	17325	G1	3576
SPRING DR., Menallen	Ad	17304	C4	3262
SPRING DR., Monaghan	Yk	17019	A9	2952
SPRING DRIVE RD., Franklin	Yk	17019	E2	3160
SPRING FORGE DR., Spring Grove	Yk	17362	B10	3373
SPRING GARDEN AV., Penn	Yk	17331	E3	3579
SPRING HOLLOW , Spring Grove	Yk	17362	A10	3373
SPRING HOLLOW RD., Lower Windsor	Yk	17366	C2	3378
SPRING LA., Mount Pleasant	Ad	17340	A5	3577
SPRING LA., Spring Garden	Yk	17403	B11	3271
SPRING LAKE TER., Springettsbury	Yk	17402	H2	3271
SPRING LANE RD., Carroll	Yk	17019	D10	2951
SPRING RD., Carroll	Yk	17019	G10	2951
SPRING RD., Hellam	Yk	17406	H7	3167
SPRING RD., Hellam	Yk	17406	A6	3168
SPRING RD., North Hopewell	Yk	17356	E4	3481
SPRING RD., Paradise	Yk	17331	A2	3476
SPRING RD., Peach Bottom	Yk	17314	A11	3589
SPRING RD., Springfield	Yk	17360	A2	3479
SPRING RIDGE DR., Jackson	Yk	17404	E6	3373
SPRING RUN CT., Fairview	Yk	17319	A3	2955
SPRING RUN LA., Hamiltonban	Ad	17320	F9	3571
SPRING ST. N., Fairfield	Ad	17320	A5	3573
SPRING ST. S., Fairfield	Ad	17320	A5	3573
SPRING ST., Franklintown	Yk	17323	D9	3056
SPRING ST., Heidelberg	Yk	17362	B8	3476
SPRING ST., Red Lion	Yk	17356	D9	3377
SPRING ST., Spring Grove	Yk	17362	A11	3373
SPRING ST., West Manchester	Yk	17404	C4	3270
SPRING ST., West Manchester	Yk	17404	D5	3270
SPRING ST., Windsor Twp	Yk	17356	D9	3377
SPRING TR., Carroll Valley	Ad	17320	G11	3572
SPRING VALLEY RD., Hopewell	Yk	17363	A3	3690
SPRING VALLEY RD., Warrington	Yk	17365	C1	3162
SPRING VIEW CIR., Franklin	Yk	17019	A6	3056
SPRING WOOD TR., Carroll Valley	Ad	17320	H6	3676
SPRING WOOD TR., Carroll Valley	Ad	17320	A6	3677
SPRINGDALE AV., Spring Garden	Yk	17403	G8	3271
SPRINGDALE AV., York City	Yk	17403	E9	3271
SPRINGDALE RD., York City	Yk	17403	D10	3271
SPRINGERS LA., Fairview	Yk	17070	B7	2849
SPRINGETTS DR., Springettsbury	Yk	17402	D1	3272
SPRINGETTSBURY AV. E., Spring Garden	Yk	17403	G8	3271
SPRINGETTSBURY AV. E., York City	Yk	17403	D9	3271
SPRINGETTSBURY AV. W., Spring Garden	Yk	17403	C9	3271
SPRINGETTSBURY AV. W., York City	Yk	17403	C9	3271
SPRINGFIELD DR., Jackson	Yk	17404	E3	3373
SPRINGFIELD DR., West Manchester	Yk	17404	E3	3373
SPRINGFIELD RD. E., Springfield	Yk	17360	F7	3479
SPRINGFIELD RD. E., Springfield	Yk	17360	H4	3479
SPRINGFIELD RD. W., Springfield	Yk	17327	H10	3478
SPRINGFIELD RD. W., Springfield	Yk	17327	B11	3479
SPRINGFIELD RD. W., Springfield	Yk	17360	D9	3479
SPRINGFIELD RD., Codorus	Yk	17327	H11	3478
SPRINGFIELD RD., Springfield	Yk	17327	H11	3478
SPRINGFIELD RD., Springfield	Yk	17360	E8	3479
SPRINGHOUSE CIR., Hellam	Yk	17368	C8	3169
SPRINGHOUSE CIR., Newberry	Yk	17319	E10	2955
SPRINGHOUSE LA., Hellam	Yk	17368	C8	3169
SPRINGHOUSE LA., Jackson	Yk	17362	E9	3372
SPRINGS AV., Cumberland	Ad	17325	A8	3471
SPRINGS AV., Gettysburg	Ad	17325	A8	3471
SPRINGVALE RD., Windsor Twp	Yk	17356	E9	3377
SPRINGWOOD AV., Stewartstown	Yk	17363	D9	3585
SPRINGWOOD RD., Red Lion	Yk	17356	A7	3377
SPRINGWOOD RD., York Twp	Yk	17313	F3	3376
SPRINGWOOD RD., York Twp	Yk	17356	E2	3376
SPRINGWOOD RD., York Twp	Yk	17356	H6	3376
SPRINGWOOD RD., York Twp	Yk	17356	A7	3377
SPRINGWOOD RD., York Twp	Yk	17402	B1	3376
SPRINGWOOD RD., York Twp	Yk	17403	A11	3272
SPRINGWOOD RD., York Twp	Yk	17403	H11	3271
SPRINT WAY, Fairview	Yk	17011	E8	2848
SPRUCE CT., East Manchester	Yk	17345	D2	3166
SPRUCE DR., Cumberland	Ad	17325	G9	3470
SPRUCE DR., Hanover	Yk	17331	D11	3475
SPRUCE DR., Tyrone	Ad	17325	E11	3264
SPRUCE LA., Lewisberry	Yk	17339	B10	2954
SPRUCE LA., Manchester Boro	Yk	17345	E2	3166
SPRUCE LA., Oxford	Ad	17350	B4	3474
SPRUCE RD., Fairview	Yk	17070	E1	2954
SPRUCE RD., North Hopewell	Yk	17322	C6	3481
SPRUCE RD., Railroad	Yk	17355	G11	3583
SPRUCE ST., Red Lion	Yk	17356	C8	3377
SPUR TR., Carroll Valley	Ad	17320	A7	3573
SPYKER LA., Lower Windsor	Yk	17406	A6	3274
SQUIRE AV., Conewago	Ad	17331	H2	3578
SQUIRE CIR., McSherrystown	Ad	17344	E2	3578
SQUIRE GRATZ RD., Warrington	Yk	17365	C10	3058
SQUIRE WAY, Penn	Yk	17331	F7	3579
ST. ANDREWS CT., Springettsbury	Yk	17402	B8	3272
ST. ANDREWS CT., West Manchester	Yk	17404	G9	3269
ST. ANDREWS WAY, Manchester Twp	Yk	17404	D10	3165
ST. ANDREWS WAY, Newberry	Yk	17319	D6	2955
ST. BARTHOLOMEW RD., West Manheim	Yk	17331	D5	3683
ST. CHARLES WAY, York Twp	Yk	17402	H2	3375
ST. GEORGE DR., Franklin	Yk	17019	H6	3055
ST. GEORGIA DR., West Manheim	Yk	17331	E11	3579
ST. GEORGIA DR., West Manheim	Yk	17331	E1	3683
ST. JAMES ST. N., Abbottstown	Ad	17301	B9	3371
ST. JAMES ST. S., Abbottstown	Ad	17301	B9	3371
ST. JOHNS CHURCH RD., Manheim	Yk	17329	A11	3581
ST. JOHNS CHURCH RD., Manheim	Yk	17329	B1	3685
ST. JOHNS CT., Shrewsbury Twp	Yk	17349	A1	3687
ST. JOHNS CT., Springettsbury	Yk	17402	A11	3167

ST. JOHNS PL., York Twp	Yk	17313	C6	3376
ST. JOHNS RD., Germany	Ad	17340	B11	3577
ST. JOHNS RD., Germany	Ad	17340	A1	3681
ST. JOHNS RD., Germany	Ad	17340	B1	3681
ST. JOSEPH DR., McSherrystown	Ad	17344	E3	3578
ST. LUKE'S RD., Mount Pleasant	Ad	17340	H4	3576
ST. LUKE'S RD., Mount Pleasant	Ad	17340	A3	3577
ST. MARKS ST., Manchester Twp	Yk	17402	C9	3166
ST. MARY'S RD., Hamilton	Ad	17301	C5	3371
ST. MARY'S RD., Paradise	Yk	17301	D6	3371
ST. MATTHEWS LA., Shrewsbury Twp	Yk	17361	A1	3688
ST. PAUL ST., York City	Yk	17404	B7	3271
ST. RENE LA., West Manheim	Yk	17331	E11	3579
ST. THOMAS WAY, West Manheim	Yk	17331	E11	3579
ST. VINCENTS AL., Hanover	Yk	17331	A2	3579
STABLEY LA., Windsor Twp	Yk	17356	E6	3377
STAFFORD DR., Conewago	Ad	17331	E3	3578
STALEY LA., Hamiltonban	Ad	17222	E5	3467
STAMBACH ST., McSherrystown	Ad	17344	F1	3578
STAMBAUGH RD., North Codorus	Yk	17362	B8	3477
STAMBAUGH RD., North Codorus	Yk	17362	C7	3477
STAMPER RD., Chanceford	Yk	17309	H1	3482
STAMPER RD., Chanceford	Yk	17309	A3	3483
STANFORD DR., Springettsbury	Yk	17402	B7	3272
STANLEY DR., Berwick	Ad	17301	F1	3474
STANLEY PL., York City	Yk	17403	E7	3271
STANTON ST., West Manchester	Yk	17404	E9	3270
STANTON ST., West York	Yk	17404	F8	3270
STANYON RD., York Twp	Yk	17403	G2	3375
STAR AV. N., Dallastown	Yk	17313	E7	3376
STAR AV. S., Dallastown	Yk	17313	E7	3376
STARCROSS RD., Spring Garden	Yk	17403	D11	3271
STARCROSS RD., Spring Garden	Yk	17403	E1	3375
STARE WAY, Carroll	Yk	17019	B2	3056
STARFIRE DR., York Twp	Yk	17403	C7	3376
STARLIGHT DR., Windsor Twp	Yk	17402	D8	3272
STARLIGHT DR., York Twp	Yk	17402	C8	3272
STARLIGHT DR., York Twp	Yk	17402	D9	3272
STARLING LA., Hellam	Yk	17406	A2	3274
STARLITE DR., Jefferson	Yk	17362	E11	3477
STARLITE DR., Littlestown	Ad	17340	F2	3681
STARNER STATION RD., Huntington	Ad	17324	D6	3158
STARR LA., Hamiltonban	Ad	17320	C2	3572
STARVIEW BLVD., East Manchester	Yk	17347	H2	3166
STARVIEW DR., Glen Rock	Yk	17327	D3	3583
STARVIEW DR., Shrewsbury Twp	Yk	17327	D3	3583
STARVIEW DR., Springettsbury	Yk	17402	E7	3272
STARVIEW DR., Windsor Twp	Yk	17402	E7	3272
STARVIEW RD., East Manchester	Yk	17347	E6	3166
STARVIEW RD., Manchester Twp	Yk	17402	E6	3166
STATE GAME LAND RD., Washington	Yk	17019	E2	3161
STATE ST., Huntington	Ad	17372	B11	3160
STATE ST., Manchester Twp	Yk	17404	B3	3271
STATE ST., Spring Garden	Yk	17403	D5	3271
STATE ST., York City	Yk	17403	D6	3271
STATE ST., York Spring	Ad	17372	B11	3160
STAUB RD., Reading	Ad	17350	B5	3370
STAUFFER LA., Spring Garden	Yk	17403	H7	3271
STAUFFER RD., North Codorus	Yk	17362	G7	3477
STAUNTON AV., Dover Twp	Yk	17315	H1	3269
STAUNTON AV., Dover Twp	Yk	17315	A2	3270
STAYMAN WAY, Littlestown	Ad	17340	D1	3681
STEELMAN MARKER RD., Carroll Valley	Ad	17320	B4	3677
STEELMAN MARKER RD., Liberty	Ad	17320	B4	3677
STEELMAN ST., Fairfield	Ad	17320	A6	3573
STEEPLE AV., York Twp	Yk	17356	G4	3376
STEEPLE CHASE DR., Dover Twp	Yk	17315	G1	3269
STEEPLE CHASE DR., York Twp	Yk	17402	C11	3272
STEEPLE CHASE N., Straban	Ad	17325	E6	3471
STEEPLE CHASE S., Straban	Ad	17325	E6	3471
STEEPLECHASE CT., Hanover	Yk	17331	C10	3475
STEFFIE DR., East Manchester	Yk	17347	E10	3061
STEIGERWALT HOLLOW RD., Fairview	Yk	17070	H9	2848
STEIGERWALT HOLLOW RD., Fairview	Yk	17070	A11	2849
STEINFELT RD., Windsor Twp	Yk	17356	G11	3272
STEINFELT RD., Windsor Twp	Yk	17356	F1	3376
STEINHOUR RD., Newberry	Yk	17370	H3	3059
STEINHOUR RD., Newberry	Yk	17370	A3	3060
STEINWEHR AV., Cumberland	Ad	17325	B11	3471
STEINWEHR AV., Gettysburg	Ad	17325	B11	3471
STELLA AV., Manchester Twp	Yk	17402	H6	3156
STELLER RD., Fairview	Yk	17070	F9	2848
STELTZ RD., Codorus	Yk	17327	H5	3686
STELTZ RD., Shrewsbury Twp	Yk	17349	H5	3686
STELTZ RD., Shrewsbury Twp	Yk	17349	A4	3687
STELTZ RD., Shrewsbury Twp	Yk	17349	E4	3687
STEPHANIE DR., Franklin	Yk	17019	H6	3055
STEPHEN AV., North Codorus	Yk	17404	B11	3374
STEPHEN PL., Hanover	Yk	17331	C11	3475
STEPHEN ST., Carroll	Yk	17019	H6	3056
STERLING DR., Conewago	Ad	17331	F3	3578
STERLING DR., Manchester Twp	Yk	17404	D2	3270
STERLING DR., Windsor Twp	Yk	17356	B1	3377
STERLING RD., Hopewell	Yk	17363	C1	3689
STERNER DR., Heidelberg	Yk	17362	E11	3476
STERNER RD., Codorus	Yk	17327	G9	3478
STEUBEN RD., Fairview	Yk	17070	G2	2954
STEVEN DR., Hallam	Yk	17406	D10	3168
STEVEN PL., Hanover	Yk	17331	C1	3579
STEVENS AV., York City	Yk	17404	B7	3271
STEVENS RD., Newberry	Yk	17370	C11	2955
STEVENS RD., Newberry	Yk	17370	D2	3060
STEVENS RD., North Codorus	Yk	17362	G5	3476
STEVENS ST. E., Gettysburg	Ad	17325	C7	3471
STEVENS ST. W., Gettysburg	Ad	17325	C7	3471
STEVENS ST., Conewago	Ad	17331	D2	3578
STEVENS ST., Fairfield	Ad	17320	B6	3573
STEVENSON CT., Springettsbury	Yk	17402	B8	3272
STEVENSON DR., Manchester Twp	Yk	17404	D11	3165
STEWARD ST., West Manchester	Yk	17404	D8	3270
STEWART LA., Springettsbury	Yk	17402	F4	3271
STEWART RD., Lower Chanceford	Yk	17302	G10	3483
STEWART RD., Lower Chanceford	Yk	17302	G1	3587
STEWARTSTOWN RD., Hopewell	Yk	17363	B1	3689
STEWARTSTOWN RD., Hopewell	Yk	17363	A2	3689
STEWARTSTOWN RD., Shrewsbury Twp	Yk	17349	E5	3688
STEWARTSTOWN RD., Shrewsbury Twp	Yk	17363	A2	3689
STICKS RD., Codorus	Yk	17327	G8	3582
STICKS SCHOOL RD., Codorus	Yk	17327	C11	3582
STICKS SCHOOL RD., Codorus	Yk	17327	B1	3686
STILL CREEK LA., Hellam	Yk	17406	A9	3168
STILL HOUSE RD., Huntington	Ad	17372	D6	3159
STILL HOUSE RD., Latimore	Ad	17372	D6	3159
STILL POND CT., Shrewsbury Twp	Yk	17349	F5	3688
STILL POND DR., Shrewsbury Twp	Yk	17349	F4	3688
STILL WATER CIR., Carroll	Yk	17019	E3	3056
STILLHOUSE RD., Newberry	Yk	17319	E5	2955
STILLHOUSE RD., Newberry	Yk	17319	G3	2955
STILLMEADOW LA., Manchester Twp	Yk	17404	F9	3165
STINE HILL RD., North Hopewell	Yk	17356	G1	3480
STINE HILL RD., York Twp	Yk	17313	D11	3376
STINE HILL RD., York Twp	Yk	17356	G1	3480
STINE TR., Carroll Valley	Ad	17320	H1	3676
STIRLING DR., Springettsbury	Yk	17402	F5	3272
STITT DR., Jackson	Yk	17404	E5	3373
STOCK ST., Hanover	Yk	17331	B2	3579
STOKER CT., Hopewell	Yk	17363	F9	3585
STONE ARCH RD., Shrewsbury Twp	Yk	17349	A11	3584
STONE AV., Cumberland	Ad	17325	H8	3470
STONE AV., York City	Yk	17404	C9	3271
STONE BRIDGE RD., Mount Pleasant	Ad	17325	C8	3473
STONE BRIDGE RD., Mount Pleasant	Ad	17350	C8	3473
STONE CHURCH RD., Codorus	Yk	17329	G8	3581
STONE CHURCH RD., Codorus	Yk	17329	A8	3582
STONE EDGE RD., Menallen	Ad	17304	F4	3262
STONE HEAD DR., Franklin	Yk	17019	A6	3056
STONE HEAD RD., Franklin	Yk	17019	A11	3055
STONE HEDGE DR., Manchester Twp	Yk	17404	D11	3165
STONE HEDGE DR., Manchester Twp	Yk	17404	D1	3270
STONE JUG RD., Butler	Ad	17304	G11	3263
STONE JUG RD., Butler	Ad	17307	G1	3367
STONE JUG RD., Butler	Ad	17307	A3	3368
STONE JUG RD., Warrington	Yk	17339	E6	3058
STONE LA., Jackson	Yk	17364	B2	3373
STONE RD., Peach Bottom	Yk	17314	A1	3694
STONE RD., Springettsbury	Yk	17402	H4	3272
STONE RIDGE DR., New Freedom	Yk	17349	G4	3687
STONE ROW LA., Fairview	Yk	17070	D10	2849
STONEGATE RD., West Manchester	Yk	17404	D4	3270
STONEHEATH LA., East Prospect	Yk	17317	F5	3274
STONEHEATH LA., East Prospect	Yk	17368	F5	3274
STONEHEDGE LA., Hellam	Yk	17402	E8	3167
STONEHEDGE LA., Springettsbury	Yk	17402	E8	3167
STONEHURST RD., Springettsbury	Yk	17402	F4	3272
STONER AV., Hanover	Yk	17331	B3	3579
STONERIDGE RD., Springettsbury	Yk	17402	D5	3272
STONESIFER DR., Littlestown	Ad	17340	F2	3681
STONEWALL LA., Hellam	Yk	17406	A8	3169
STONEWOOD DR., Jacobus	Yk	17407	D10	3375
STONEWOOD RD., Springettsbury	Yk	17402	G3	3272
STONEWOOD RD., Springettsbury	Yk	17402	H5	3272
STONEWOOD RD., Windsor Twp	Yk	17402	H5	3272
STONEWOOD RD., Windsor Twp	Yk	17402	A6	3273
STONEWYCK HILL RD., East Prospect	Yk	17317	F4	3274
STONEWYCK HILL RD., Lower Windsor	Yk	17368	F4	3274
STONEY BROOK RD., North Hopewell	Yk	17349	C4	3584
STONEY LA., Fawn	Yk	17352	E9	3587
STONEY POINT RD., Reading	Ad	17316	E2	3266
STONEY POINT RD., Reading	Ad	17316	A2	3370
STONEY POINT RD., Reading	Ad	17350	A2	3370
STONEY RUN RD., Carroll	Yk	17019	E8	3056
STONEY RUN RD., Franklin	Yk	17019	E8	3056
STONY BROOK DR., Springettsbury	Yk	17402	F3	3272
STONY LA., Dover Boro	Yk	17315	C11	3164
STONY LA., Manheim	Yk	17329	G3	3684
STONY RD., Monaghan	Yk	17339	B9	2953
STONY RUN RD., Monaghan	Yk	17019	A8	2952
STONYBROOK LA., Fairview	Yk	17339	H10	2953
STONYBROOK RD., Springettsbury	Yk	17402	F3	3272
STOOPS RD., Highland	Ad	17320	E5	3573
STOOPS RD., Highland	Ad	17325	G4	3573
STOOPS RD., Liberty	Ad	17320	E5	3573
STOOPS RD., Liberty	Ad	17320	H4	3676
STORMS STORE RD., Mount Pleasant	Ad	17325	D11	3473
STORMS STORE RD., Mount Pleasant	Ad	17325	B3	3577
STORMS STORE RD., Mount Pleasant	Ad	17340	B3	3577
STORMS STORE RD., Mount Pleasant	Ad	17350	D11	3473
STORMS STORE RD., Oxford	Ad	17350	G7	3473
STORMS STORE RD., Oxford	Ad	17350	A7	3474
STORMY HILL RD., North Codorus	Yk	17362	H7	3476
STORMY HILL RD., North Codorus	Yk	17362	A7	3477
STOVERSTOWN RD., Jackson	Yk	17404	E5	3373
STOVERSTOWN RD., North Codorus	Yk	17362	G11	3373
STOVERSTOWN RD., North Codorus	Yk	17362	C6	3477
STOVERSTOWN RD., West Manchester	Yk	17404	F6	3373
STOVERSTOWN RD., West Manchester	Yk	17404	H7	3373
STRAIGHT HILL RD., Warrington	Yk	17315	E3	3163
STRALEY'S RD., Mount Joy	Ad	17340	D5	3576
STRATFORD RD., Spring Garden	Yk	17403	E10	3271
STRATHCONA DR. N., Spring Garden	Yk	17403	E10	3271
STRATHCONA DR. S., Spring Garden	Yk	17403	E10	3271
STRATON DR., Springfield	Yk	17360	G8	3479
STRATTON ST. N., Gettysburg	Ad	17325	C8	3471
STRATTON ST., Gettysburg	Ad	17325	C9	3471
STRAUSBAUGH TR., Liberty	Ad	17320	F5	3573
STRAW ACRES RD., Heidelberg	Yk	17362	D8	3476
STRAW CT., Union	Ad	17340	G11	3577
STRAWBERRY LA., Manchester Twp	Yk	17404	G1	3270
STRAWBERRY ST., Shrewsbury Twp	Yk	17349	A1	3688
STRAWBRIDGE RD., Fawn	Yk	17352	C7	3587
STRAYER DR., Carroll	Yk	17019	F9	2951
STRAYER DR., Windsor Twp	Yk	17356	D6	3377
STRAYER DR., Windsor Twp	Yk	17366	D6	3377
STRAYER RD., Latimore	Ad	17372	H4	3159
STRAYER RD., Latimore	Ad	17372	A5	3160
STRICKHOUSER RD., Codorus	Yk	17360	A7	3478
STRICKHOUSER RD., North Codorus	Yk	17360	A7	3478
STRICKLER DR., Newberry	Yk	17370	D11	2954
STRICKLER DR., Newberry	Yk	17370	D1	3059
STRICKLERS LA., Hellam	Yk	17406	A8	3169
STRICKLERS SCHOOL RD., Hellam	Yk	17368	B10	3169
STRICKLERS SCHOOL RD., Hellam	Yk	17406	H8	3168
STRICKLERS SCHOOL RD., Hellam	Yk	17406	A9	3169
STUART AV., Penn	Yk	17331	B4	3579
STUART CIR., Penn	Yk	17331	B4	3579
STUART DR., Reading	Ad	17316	B5	3266
STUART DR., Springettsbury	Yk	17402	F3	3272
STUART LA., Mount Pleasant	Ad	17325	C10	3472
STUART RD., Mount Joy	Ad	17325	H1	3575
STUDEBAKER LA., Tyrone	Ad	17350	G4	3368
STUDEBAKER LA., Tyrone	Ad	17350	A4	3369
STUDY RD., Mount Joy	Ad	17340	A5	3680
STULTZ RD., Liberty	Ad	17320	G3	3677
STULTZ TR., Liberty	Ad	17320	F5	3573
STUMP LA., North Codorus	Yk	17362	H3	3477
STUMP LA., North Codorus	Yk	17362	A3	3478
SUBURBAN RD., York Twp	Yk	17403	G11	3271
SUGAR MAPLE DR., Newberry	Yk	17319	C5	2955
SUGARBOOT LA., West Manheim	Yk	17331	G10	3579
SULTZBACK LA., Hellam	Yk	17406	B11	3168
SUMAC DR., Penn	Yk	17331	D8	3475
SUMMER DR., Bonneauville	Ad	17325	F1	3576
SUMMER DR., Monaghan	Yk	17019	B9	2952
SUMMER HOUSE LA., West Manchester	Yk	17404	B7	3270
SUMMER ST. N., West York	Yk	17404	G8	3270
SUMMER ST. S., West York	Yk	17404	G10	3270
SUMMER ST., West Manchester	Yk	17404	F7	3270
SUMMER TR., Carroll Valley	Ad	17320	F2	3676
SUMMERS LA., New Freedom	Yk	17349	G4	3687
SUMMIT AL., New Freedom	Yk	17349	F2	3687
SUMMIT AV., East Berlin	Ad	17316	C11	3267
SUMMIT AV., Fairview	Yk	17070	B9	2849
SUMMIT CIR. N., Spring Garden	Yk	17403	B1	3375
SUMMIT CT., Berwick	Ad	17331	B4	3475
SUMMIT DR. E., Germany	Ad	17340	G3	3681
SUMMIT DR. W., Germany	Ad	17340	G3	3681
SUMMIT DR., Monaghan	Yk	17019	A7	2952
SUMMIT DR., Red Lion	Yk	17356	B5	3377
SUMMIT DR., Spring Garden	Yk	17403	D11	3271
SUMMIT DR., Springfield	Yk	17360	G6	3479
SUMMIT DR., York Twp	Yk	17313	G9	3376
SUMMIT LA., Red Lion	Yk	17356	A8	3377
SUMMIT RD., Fairview	Yk	17070	B9	2849
SUMMIT RD., Manheim	Yk	17327	F1	3685
SUMMIT RD., York Twp	Yk	17403	G2	3375
SUMMIT TER., Spring Garden	Yk	17403	C11	3271
SUN AV. E., Dallastown	Yk	17313	G7	3376
SUNCREST LA., Hamiltonban	Ad	17320	H11	3468
SUNCREST LA., Hamiltonban	Ad	17320	H1	3572
SUNDALE DR., Springettsbury	Yk	17402	B7	3272
SUNDANCE LA., Shrewsbury Boro	Yk	17361	A6	3584
SUNDAY DR., Conewago	Ad	17331	C3	3578
SUNDIAL RD., Dover Twp	Yk	17315	E6	3269
SUNFISH TR., Carroll Valley	Ad	17320	A7	3573
SUNLIGHT DR., Conewago	Ad	17331	C1	3578
SUNLIGHT DR., North Hopewell	Yk	17322	F8	3480
SUNLIGHT DR., Winterstown	Yk	17322	H8	3480
SUNLIGHT DR., York Twp	Yk	17402	D8	3272
SUNNY LA., Carroll	Yk	17019	B3	3057
SUNNY MOUNTAIN DR., Menallen	Ad	17307	G2	3261
SUNNY SLOPE RD., Codorus	Yk	17327	F10	3582
SUNNYSIDE CEMETERY RD., Latimore	Ad	17372	A8	3160
SUNNYSIDE DR., West Manheim	Yk	17331	F1	3683
SUNNYSIDE LA., Manheim	Yk	17362	H4	3580
SUNNYSIDE LA., Manheim	Yk	17362	A4	3581
SUNNYSIDE RD., Jackson	Yk	17404	F7	3373
SUNNYSIDE RD., North Codorus	Yk	17362	G9	3373
SUNNYSIDE RD., North Codorus	Yk	17404	F7	3373
SUNNYSIDE RD., West Manchester	Yk	17404	F7	3373
SUNNYSIDE RD., West Manchester	Yk	17404	F6	3373
SUNRISE AV., Fairview	Yk	17070	C1	2954
SUNRISE AV., Warrington	Yk	17365	H10	3058
SUNRISE DR., Abbottstown	Ad	17301	B10	3371
SUNRISE DR., Newberry	Yk	17315	E8	3059
SUNRISE LA., Hellam	Yk	17368	C11	3169
SUNRISE LA., Lower Windsor	Yk	17368	F6	3274
SUNRISE TR., Carroll Valley	Ad	17320	A11	3573
SUNSET AV., Gettysburg	Ad	17325	B10	3471
SUNSET AV., Hanover	Yk	17331	B11	3475
SUNSET AV., Hanover	Yk	17331	B1	3579
SUNSET AV., New Oxford	Ad	17350	B3	3474
SUNSET CIR., Manheim	Yk	17329	F11	3580
SUNSET CIR., Windsor Twp	Yk	17356	B4	3377
SUNSET CT., Carroll	Yk	17019	A2	3056
SUNSET DR. N., Shrewsbury Boro	Yk	17361	A8	3584
SUNSET DR. S., Shrewsbury Boro	Yk	17361	A9	3584
SUNSET DR., Berwick	Ad	17301	B10	3371
SUNSET DR., Bonneauville	Ad	17325	F11	3472
SUNSET DR., Bonneauville	Ad	17325	F1	3576
SUNSET DR., Dillsburg	Yk	17019	D2	3056
SUNSET DR., East Manchester	Yk	17345	D3	3166
SUNSET DR., Fairview	Yk	17070	D11	2849
SUNSET DR., Fairview	Yk	17070	D1	2954
SUNSET DR., Hellam	Yk	17368	D8	3169
SUNSET DR., Manchester Boro	Yk	17345	D2	3166
SUNSET DR., West Manheim	Yk	17331	C11	3579
SUNSET DR., York Twp	Yk	17313	C6	3376
SUNSET LA., Huntington	Ad	17372	A2	3265
SUNSET LA., Lower Windsor	Yk	17406	G3	3273
SUNSET LA., Paradise	Yk	17301	G10	3371
SUNSET LA., West Manchester	Yk	17404	H7	3269
SUNSET LA., West Manchester	Yk	17404	A6	3270
SUNSET RD., Franklin	Ad	17353	D2	3469
SUNSET RD., Jackson	Yk	17364	E1	3372
SUNSET RD., Springettsbury	Yk	17402	F1	3271
SUNSET VIEW DR., Fairview	Yk	17070	F10	2848
SUNSET VIEW ST., Jefferson	Yk	17362	D11	3477
SUNSHINE AV., Cumberland	Ad	17325	F10	3470
SUNSHINE DR., Dover Twp	Yk	17315	H11	3164
SUNSHINE TR., Carroll Valley	Ad	17320	G7	3572
SUNSPOT TR., Carroll Valley	Ad	17320	A7	3573
SURREY CT., Fairview	Yk	17011	F8	2848
SURREY DR., Lower Windsor	Yk	17368	G8	3274
SURREY DR., Springettsbury	Yk	17402	D1	3272
SURREY LA., Windsor Twp	Yk	17402	A8	3273
SURREY RUN CT., West Manchester	Yk	17404	B7	3270
SUSAN DR., Chanceford	Yk	17309	E1	3483
SUSAN DR., Dallastown	Yk	17313	F6	3376
SUSAN DR., York Twp	Yk	17313	F6	3376
SUSAN LA., Reading	Ad	17350	B2	3370
SUSAN TR., Carroll Valley	Ad	17320	F11	3572
SUSQUEHANNA AV., East Prospect	Yk	17317	F5	3274
SUSQUEHANNA AV., East Prospect	Yk	17368	F5	3274
SUSQUEHANNA AV., York City	Yk	17403	D8	3271
SUSQUEHANNA AV., York Haven	Yk	17370	E4	3061
SUSQUEHANNA DR., Newberry	Yk	17370	A10	2956
SUSQUEHANNA PLAZA DR., Hellam	Yk	17406	H8	3168
SUSQUEHANNA RD., Peach Bottom	Yk	17314	H9	3588
SUSQUEHANNA TR. S., Springfield	Yk	17403	F1	3479
SUSQUEHANNA TR. S., Springfield	Yk	17407	F1	3479
SUSQUEHANNA TR., Conewago	Yk	17345	G5	3060
SUSQUEHANNA TR., Conewago	Yk	17402	F11	3060
SUSQUEHANNA TR., Conewago	Yk	17402	F2	3165
SUSQUEHANNA TR., Manchester Twp	Yk	17402	A8	3166
SUSQUEHANNA TR., Manchester Twp	Yk	17404	A8	3166
SUSQUEHANNA TR., Manchester Twp	Yk	17404	A1	3271
SUSQUEHANNA TR., Newberry	Yk	17370	C11	2955
SUSQUEHANNA TR., Shrewsbury Twp	Yk	17327	A11	3480
SUSQUEHANNA TR., Shrewsbury Twp	Yk	17327	A2	3584
SUSQUEHANNA TR., Shrewsbury Twp	Yk	17349	A2	3584
SUSQUEHANNA TR., Shrewsbury Boro	Yk	17361	B1	3688
SUSQUEHANNA TR., Shrewsbury Twp	Yk	17349	C4	3688
SUSQUEHANNA TR., Springfield	Yk	17327	F7	3479
SUSQUEHANNA TR., Springfield	Yk	17360	F7	3479
SUSQUEHANNOCK DR., Newberry	Yk	17370	A9	2956
SUSQUEVIEW LA., Lower Windsor	Yk	17368	H9	3274
SUSSET LA., Codorus	Yk	17362	F10	3477
SUSSEX CIR., West Manchester	Yk	17404	A6	3270
SUTTON CT., Germany	Ad	17340	C11	3577
SUTTON RD., Abbottstown	Ad	17301	A11	3371
SUTTON RD., York Twp	Yk	17403	E3	3375
SWALLOW TR., Carroll Valley	Ad	17320	H1	3676
SWALLOW TR., Carroll Valley	Ad	17320	A2	3677
SWAMP CREEK LA., Hamiltonban	Ad	17320	D2	3572
SWAMP CREEK LA., Hamiltonban	Ad	17353	D11	3468
SWAMP HOLLOW LA., Springfield	Yk	17313	D2	3480
SWAMP RD., North Hopewell	Yk	17313	D2	3480
SWAMP RD., North Hopewell	Yk	17322	DF	3480
SWAMP RD., North Hopewell	Yk	17322	E5	3480
SWAMP RD., North Hopewell	Yk	17356	D4	3480
SWEENY CT., Shrewsbury Twp	Yk	17349	C4	3688
SWEET GUM DR., Manchester Twp	Yk	17402	C1	3271
SWEET GUM LA., Hallam	Yk	17406	C10	3168
SWEETGUM CT., East Manchester	Yk	17347	H7	3166
SWEITZER CT., East Manchester	Yk	17345	C8	3061
SWEITZER DR., Springfield	Yk	17407	E1	3479
SWEITZER RD., Hopewell	Yk	17349	D5	3584
SWETLAND RD., Cumberland	Ad	17325	C3	3679
SWIFT RUN RD., Mount Pleasant	Ad	17350	A10	3473
SWIFT RUN RD., Straban	Ad	17325	F11	3368
SWIFT RUN RD., Straban	Ad	17325	H1	3472
SWIFT RUN RD., Straban	Ad	17325	A10	3473
SWIFT RUN RD., Straban	Ad	17350	A10	3473
SWIMMING POOL RD., West Manheim	Yk	17331	C7	3580
SWITCHPOINT DR., Hopewell	Yk	17363	F9	3585
SWITH CT., Manchester Twp	Yk	17404	H11	3165
SYCAMORE CIR., Newberry	Yk	17319	D5	2955
SYCAMORE DR., Heidelberg	Yk	17362	D6	3476
SYCAMORE LA. N., Stewartstown	Yk	17363	F11	3585
SYCAMORE LA. S., Stewartstown	Yk	17363	F11	3585
SYCAMORE LA., Codorus	Yk	17327	H4	3582
SYCAMORE LA., Conewago	Ad	17331	H3	3578
SYCAMORE LA., Hanover	Yk	17331	A3	3579
SYCAMORE LA., Manchester Twp	Yk	17402	B11	3166
SYCAMORE LA., North Hopewell	Yk	17356	H5	3480
SYCAMORE LA., Winterstown	Yk	17356	H5	3480
SYCAMORE LA., Winterstown	Yk	17356	A5	3481
SYCAMORE RD., Dover Twp	Yk	17315	F3	3269
SYCAMORE RD., West Manchester	Yk	17404	A5	3270
SYCAMORE TR., Peach Bottom	Yk	17314	H11	3588
SYCAMORE TR., Peach Bottom	Yk	17314	A11	3589
SYDNEY CT., Penn	Yk	17331	A5	3580
SYDNEY DR., Penn	Yk	17331	H6	3579
SYDNEY DR., Penn	Yk	17331	A5	3580
SYKES AV., Cumberland	Ad	17325	B4	3575
SYLVAN DR., Springettsbury	Yk	17402	E2	3272
SYNDOR TR., Highland	Ad	17320	F5	3573
SYNDOR TR., Liberty	Ad	17320	F5	3573

T

TABLE ROCK RD., Butler	Ad	17307	B3	3367
TABLE ROCK RD., Butler	Ad	17325	C7	3367
TABLE ROCK RD., Cumberland	Ad	17325	C11	3367
TABLE ROCK RD., Cumberland	Ad	17325	C5	3471
TAFT AV., Manchester Twp	Yk	17404	B3	3271
TALBOT ST., Littlestown	Ad	17340	F1	3681
TALISMAN CT., York City	Yk	17404	A6	3271
TALL FIR DR., Dover Twp	Yk	17315	H6	3163
TALL OAK DR., Fairview	Yk	17070	G9	2848
TALL OAK LA., Manheim	Yk	17329	G4	3684
TALL OAKS DR., Straban	Ad	17325	C9	3368

TALL OAKS LA., Springettsbury	Yk	17402	C10	3167
TALL OAKS LA., York Twp	Yk	17403	D2	3375
TALL OAKS RD., Mount Pleasant	Ad	17325	G7	3472
TALL OAKS RD., Mount Pleasant	Ad	17325	A8	3473
TALL TREE DR., Fairview	Yk	17011	F6	2848
TALL TREE DR., Fairview	Yk	17070	G8	2848
TALL TREE LA., Hopewell	Yk	17363	G9	3584
TALLAHASSEE BLVD., Berwick	Ad	17301	B10	3371
TALTON DR., Peach Bottom	Yk	17314	E5	3694
TAMARIND DR., Heidelberg	Yk	17362	E1	3580
TAMELA AV., Dover Twp	Yk	17315	C2	3269
TAMMY CT., West Manheim	Yk	17331	G11	3579
TAMMY DR., Huntington	Ad	17372	B1	3265
TAMMY RD., Huntington	Ad	17372	B11	3160
TANEYTOWN RD., Cumberland	Ad	17325	C10	3471
TANEYTOWN RD., Cumberland	Ad	17325	C2	3575
TANEYTOWN RD., Gettysburg	Ad	17325	C10	3471
TANEYTOWN RD., Mount Joy	Ad	17325	C8	3575
TANEYTOWN RD., Mount Joy	Ad	17325	D2	3679
TANGLEWOOD LA., Springettsbury	Yk	17402	G10	3166
TANK AL., New Freedom	Yk	17349	F2	3687
TANNERBAUM CIR., Monaghan	Yk	17019	C11	2952
TANNERY RD., Carroll	Yk	17019	G7	3056
TANNERY RD., Codorus	Yk	17329	E6	3581
TANNERY RD., Codorus	Yk	17362	E6	3581
TAPE WORM RD., Tyrone	Ad	17350	C11	3265
TAPE WORM RD., Tyrone	Ad	17350	C3	3369
TARA LA., Manchester Twp	Yk	17404	H11	3165
TARA LA., West Manchester	Yk	17404	G6	3269
TARALEE DR., Springettsbury	Yk	17402	D11	3167
TARPLEY DR., Springettsbury	Yk	17402	F1	3272
TASSLE LA., Fairview	Yk	17319	A3	2955
TATE TR., Liberty	Ad	17320	G6	3573
TAUNTON RD., Springettsbury	Yk	17402	E5	3272
TAXVILLE RD., Dover Twp	Yk	17404	F8	3269
TAXVILLE RD., West Manchester	Yk	17404	F8	3269
TAXVILLE RD., West Manchester	Yk	17404	A8	3270
TAXVILLE RD., West Manchester	Yk	17404	D7	3270
TAYLOR AV., Dallastown	Yk	17313	F7	3376
TAYLOR CT., Dover Twp	Yk	17315	B8	3164
TAYLOR DR., Penn	Yk	17331	D8	3475
TAYLOR HILL RD., Shrewsbury Twp	Yk	17327	E10	3583
TAYLOR LA., Hamiltonban	Ad	17320	D1	3676
TAYLOR RD., Conewago	Yk	17404	D1	3165
TAYLOR RD., Lower Chanceford	Yk	17302	A9	3484
TAYLOR RD., Lower Windsor	Yk	17366	A9	3274
TAYLOR RD., Newberry	Yk	17319	H9	2954
TAYLOR RD., Windsor Twp	Yk	17402	C9	3273
TAYLOR ST., Red Lion	Yk	17356	C7	3377
TEABERRY RD., Franklin	Ad	17222	A5	3468
TEABERRY RD., Hamiltonban	Ad	17222	H8	3467
TEABERRY RD., Hamiltonban	Ad	17222	A5	3468
TEAL DR., Fairview	Yk	17319	G3	2954
TED WALLACE RD., Chanceford	Yk	17302	D9	3483
TED WALLACE RD., Chanceford	Yk	17309	D6	3483
TEETER RD., Germany	Ad	17340	G3	3680
TEETER RD., Germany	Ad	17340	A3	3681
TEILA DR., York Twp	Yk	17313	E7	3376
TELEGRAPH RD., Lower Chanceford	Yk	17302	A2	3589
TELEGRAPH RD., Lower Chanceford	Yk	17302	G4	3588
TEMPLE CT., Dover Twp	Yk	17315	C8	3164
TEMPLE SCHOOL RD., Dover Twp	Yk	17315	B8	3164
TENBY CT., York Twp	Yk	17402	E10	3272
TENNYSON GARTH, Windsor Twp	Yk	17356	C3	3377
TERESA DR., Reading	Ad	17350	B2	3370
TERRACE AV., Hanover	Yk	17331	C2	3579
TERRACE DR. N., Monaghan	Yk	17019	B10	2952
TERRACE DR. S., Monaghan	Yk	17019	B10	2952
TERRACE HEIGHTS, Glen Rock	Yk	17327	C4	3583
TERRACE PL., Fairview	Yk	17070	C7	2849
TERRACE RD., York City	Yk	17404	A4	3271
TESLIN RD., Manchester Twp	Yk	17404	A2	3271
TEST RD., Conewago	Yk	17404	D1	3165
TEST RD., Penn	Yk	17331	E8	3475
TEXAS AV., York Twp	Yk	17404	H7	3270
THAMES AV., West Manchester	Yk	17404	D3	3270
THE SPANGLER RD., Hamilton	Ad	17350	A8	3370
THELON DR., West Manchester	Yk	17404	B6	3270
THOMAN DR., Heidelberg	Yk	17362	C11	3476
THOMAN DR., Heidelberg	Yk	17362	E9	3476
THOMAS ARMOR DR., Windsor Twp	Yk	17356	E6	3377
THOMAS AV., York Twp	Yk	17313	D9	3376
THOMAS CIR., Arendtsville	Ad	17307	B2	3366
THOMAS CIR., New Freedom	Yk	17349	G4	3687
THOMAS DR., Conewago	Ad	17344	F1	3578
THOMAS DR., Mount Joy	Ad	17325	H11	3471
THOMAS DR., Reading	Ad	17316	C5	3266
THOMAS DR., Straban	Ad	17325	H11	3471
THOMAS LA., Penn	Yk	17331	E8	3475
THOMAS ST., Conewago	Yk	17404	D1	3165
THOMAS ST., York City	Yk	17404	B6	3271
THOMPSON HOLLOW RD., Southampton	Ad	17257	H1	3259
THOMPSON LA., Highland	Ad	17325	H10	3469
THOMPSON LA., Red Lion	Yk	17356	E8	3377
THOMPSON RD., East Hopewell	Yk	17363	D4	3585
THOMPSON RD., Fawn	Yk	17321	C2	3691
THOMPSON RD., Fawn Grove	Yk	17321	E2	3691
THOMPSON RD., Hopewell	Yk	17363	D4	3585
THOMPSON RD., Lower Chanceford	Yk	17314	C6	3589
THOMPSON RD., Shrewsbury Twp	Yk	17349	A10	3584
THORELY RD., Fairview	Yk	17070	H10	2849
THORNBRIDGE RD., West Manchester	Yk	17404	H5	3269
THORNBRIDGE RD., West Manchester	Yk	17404	A5	3270
THORNHILL DR., Penn	Yk	17331	E7	3475
THOROUGHBRED CT., West Manchester	Yk	17404	C6	3270
THREE HILL RD., Jackson	Yk	17362	D11	3372
THREE PONDS LA., Manheim	Yk	17329	G4	3684
THREE SPRINGS RD., Franklin	Ad	17222	A5	3468
THREE SPRINGS RD., Hamiltonban	Ad	17222	H6	3467
THREE SPRINGS RD., Hamiltonban	Ad	17222	A5	3468
THREE SPRINGS RD., Straban	Ad	17325	G3	3471
THRONE AV., Springettsbury	Yk	17402	F2	3272
THRONE RD., Fawn	Yk	17321	E5	3587
THROTTLE CT., Hopewell	Yk	17363	E8	3585
THRUSH TR., Carroll Valley	Ad	17320	F1	3676
THUNDER GUST MILL RD., Warrington	Yk	17365	B8	3058
THUNDER TR., Hamiltonban	Ad	17320	H11	3571
THUNDERBIRD AV., Dover Twp	Yk	17315	F1	3269
THUNDERHILL RD., Springettsbury	Yk	17402	E6	3272
TIFFANY CT., Conewago	Ad	17331	D10	3578
TIFFANY DR., Dover Twp	Yk	17315	E4	3269
TIFFANY LA., Cumberland	Ad	17325	G8	3470
TIGER TR., Carroll Valley	Ad	17320	B3	3677
TIGER TR., Liberty	Ad	17320	B3	3677
TILLIE TOWN RD., Franklin	Ad	17307	G2	3469
TILLIE TOWN RD., Franklin	Ad	17325	G2	3469
TILLIE TOWN RD., Highland	Ad	17325	G2	3469
TIMBER AL., Franklintown	Yk	17323	E10	3056
TIMBER CT., North Codorus	Yk	17360	E9	3374
TIMBER LA. W., Penn	Yk	17331	G5	3579
TIMBER LA., Fairview	Yk	17070	G8	2848
TIMBER LA., Menallen	Ad	17304	C5	3262
TIMBER LA., Penn	Yk	17331	H5	3579
TIMBER RD., Fairview	Yk	17070	H1	2954
TIMBERLANE DR., Manchester Twp	Yk	17404	E10	3165
TIMBERLYN DR., Dover Twp	Yk	17315	D9	3163
TIOGA ST., York Twp	Yk	17404	H5	3270
TIOGA ST., York Twp	Yk	17404	H6	3270
TOAD RD., Menallen	Ad	17304	F3	3262
TOAD VALLEY RD., Shrewsbury Boro	Yk	17361	A5	3584
TOAD VALLEY RD., Shrewsbury Twp	Yk	17327	G5	3583
TOAD VALLEY RD., Shrewsbury Twp	Yk	17327	A5	3584
TOANN RD., Spring Garden	Yk	17403	H9	3271
TOANN RD., Spring Garden	Yk	17403	A9	3272
TODD CT., Fairview	Yk	17339	E2	2954
TOLLGATE RD., Spring Garden	Yk	17403	F10	3271
TOLLGATE RD., West Manheim	Yk	17331	H3	3683
TOLNA LA. E., Shrewsbury Boro	Yk	17361	B10	3584
TOLNA LA. E., Shrewsbury Twp	Yk	17349	D10	3584
TOLNA LA. E., Shrewsbury Twp	Yk	17361	B10	3584
TOM SWIFT WALK, Menallen	Ad	17304	F3	3262
TOME FARMS LA., Lower Windsor	Yk	17406	H3	3273
TOME RD., Codorus	Yk	17327	C2	3582
TOMLINSON RD., Lower Chanceford	Yk	17302	H7	3483
TOMLINSON RD., Lower Chanceford	Yk	17302	A7	3484
TOMMYS RD., Chanceford	Yk	17309	A6	3483
TOMS CREEK TR., Carroll Valley	Ad	17320	H6	3676
TOMS CREEK TR., Carroll Valley	Ad	17320	A5	3677
TONDEN DR., York Twp	Yk	17402	B4	3376
TONY WAY, Dover Twp	Yk	17315	F6	3269
TOPAZ RD., West Manchester	Yk	17404	C7	3270
TOPPER RD., Liberty	Ad	17320	C3	3677
TOPPER ST., Springettsbury	Yk	17402	F3	3271
TORBERT RD., Fawn	Yk	17321	A1	3692
TORONITA ST., Manchester Twp	Yk	17402	C3	3271
TORRY PINES DR., East Manchester	Yk	17347	F10	3061
TORWAY RD., Huntington	Ad	17324	H9	3158
TORWAY RD., Huntington	Ad	17324	A7	3159
TOWER DR., Dover Twp	Yk	17315	E3	3269
TOWER RD., Hellam	Yk	17406	H6	3167
TOWER RD., Hellam	Yk	17406	A5	3168
TOWER ST., West Manchester	Yk	17404	D3	3270
TOWN CIR., Abbottstown	Ad	17301	C10	3371
TOWN HILL RD., Latimore	Ad	17372	A11	3055
TOWN HILL RD., Latimore	Ad	17372	A9	3160
TOWNSEND CT., York Twp	Yk	17402	G3	3375
TOWNSHIP LINE RD., Huntington	Ad	17372	E2	3265
TRACK LA., Hellam	Yk	17406	E1	3273
TRACT RD., Hamiltonban	Ad	17320	A7	3573
TRACT RD., Liberty	Ad	17320	F10	3573
TRACT RD., Liberty	Ad	17320	C8	3573
TRACT RD., Liberty	Ad	17320	E5	3677
TRACY AV., New Oxford	Ad	17350	H2	3473
TRACY AV., Oxford	Ad	17350	H2	3473
TRACY DR., Huntington	Ad	17372	B1	3265
TRACY RD., Huntington	Ad	17372	B11	3160
TRACY RD., West Manheim	Yk	17331	C5	3684
TRACY RD., West Manheim	Yk	17331	D3	3684
TRACY SCHOOL RD., Hellam	Yk	17406	B9	3168
TRACY SCHOOL RD., Hellam	Yk	17406	C9	3168
TRAIL VIEW DR., New Freedom	Yk	17349	G5	3687
TRAILS RD. E., Peach Bottom	Yk	17302	A8	3589
TRAILS RD. W., Peach Bottom	Yk	17302	H7	3588
TRAILS RD. W., Peach Bottom	Yk	17302	A8	3589
TRANSMITTER LA., Hellam	Yk	17406	A6	3168
TRAVER DR., Fairview	Yk	17339	A2	3059
TRAVIS CIR., Hellam	Yk	17368	C8	3169
TRAVIS CT., York Twp	Yk	17403	C7	3376
TRAYMORE VILLAGE, York Twp	Yk	17402	E9	3272
TREE FARM LA., Hamiltonban	Ad	17320	A7	3572
TREE LA., Butler	Ad	17304	F5	3263
TREE LA., Menallen	Ad	17304	F5	3263
TREE TOP TR., Carroll Valley	Ad	17320	F7	3572
TREETOP LA., Jackson	Yk	17362	C9	3372
TREMONT ST. N., York City	Yk	17403	E5	3271
TREMONT ST. S., York City	Yk	17403	F6	3271
TRENT LA., Windsor Twp	Yk	17356	C1	3377
TRENTON CT., Littlestown	Ad	17340	D2	3681
TREVOR RD., Conewago	Yk	17404	E1	3165
TRIDENT ST., West Manchester	Yk	17404	G1	3373
TRI-HILL DR., Spring Garden	Yk	17403	F11	3271
TRI-HILL RD., Spring Garden	Yk	17403	E11	3271
TRIMMER DR., Fairview	Yk	17055	D5	2953
TRINITY ACRES LA., Hamiltonban	Ad	17222	F5	3467
TRINITY CHURCH RD., Lower Windsor	Yk	17368	F1	3274
TRINITY NORTH RD., Lower Windsor	Yk	17368	F1	3274
TRINITY RD., Chanceford	Yk	17322	C11	3378
TRINITY RD., Chanceford	Yk	17322	C11	3378
TRINITY RD., Chanceford	Yk	17322	C1	3482
TRINITY RD., Chanceford	Yk	17322	D6	3482
TRINITY RD., Chanceford	Yk	17356	C11	3378
TRINITY RD., North Codorus	Yk	17404	A2	3374
TRINITY RD., West Manchester	Yk	17404	A2	3374
TRIPLECROWN LA., Lower Windsor	Yk	17368	F1	3274
TRIPLETT CT., Carroll	Yk	17019	C2	3056
TRISTAN DR., Carroll	Yk	17019	F10	2951
TROLLEY DR., Dallastown	Yk	17313	H8	3376
TROLLEY DR., York Twp	Yk	17313	H8	3376
TROLLEY RD., Heidelberg	Yk	17331	H8	3475
TROLLEY RD., Heidelberg	Yk	17331	A8	3476
TROLLEY RD., Huntington	Ad	17372	H11	3159
TROLLEY RD., Huntington	Ad	17372	F11	3159
TROLLEY RD., Huntington	Ad	17372	A10	3160
TROLLEY RD., Lower Windsor	Yk	17366	A3	3378
TROLLEY RD., West Manchester	Yk	17404	B4	3270
TROLLEY RD., West Manchester	Yk	17404	D4	3270
TROLLEY RD., Windsor Twp	Yk	17366	A3	3378
TRONE RD., Manheim	Yk	17329	C7	3581
TROON CIR., Newberry	Yk	17319	D5	2955
TROTTER RIDGE CT., West Manchester	Yk	17404	B6	3270
TROUT RD., Hopewell	Yk	17363	A8	3586
TROUT RUN RD., Hellam	Yk	17402	D5	3167
TROUT RUN RD., Hellam	Yk	17406	D5	3167
TROUT RUN RD., Springettsbury	Yk	17402	A10	3167
TROUT RUN TR., Carroll Valley	Ad	17320	A8	3573
TROUT RUN, Shrewsbury Twp	Yk	17327	E5	3583
TROUT SCHOOL RD., East Hopewell	Yk	17322	C8	3482
TROUT SCHOOL RD., East Hopewell	Yk	17322	D10	3482
TROUT SCHOOL RD., East Hopewell	Yk	17322	E1	3586
TROUTS LA., Stewartstown	Yk	17363	D2	3689
TROWBRIDGE RD., Springettsbury	Yk	17402	H4	3272
TROY RD., York Twp	Yk	17313	E8	3376
TRUDY CT., Hanover	Yk	17331	C11	3475
TRUDY TR., Carroll Valley	Ad	17320	D2	3676
TRUMP RD., Codorus	Yk	17329	H9	3581
TRUMPETER WAY, Oxford	Ad	17350	H2	3473
TUCKAHOE RD., Franklin	Yk	17019	E4	3055
TUDOR CT., Union	Ad	17340	G11	3577
TULIP LA., Hellam	Yk	17406	E7	3168
TULIP TREE LA., Springettsbury	Yk	17402	H2	3271
TULSA RD., Springettsbury	Yk	17402	H3	3271
TUNNEL HILL RD., North Codorus	Yk	17360	G7	3374
TUNNEL HILL RD., North Codorus	Yk	17360	E9	3374
TUNNEL HILL RD., North Codorus	Yk	17404	D9	3374
TUNNEL HILL RD., York Twp	Yk	17403	G7	3374
TUNNEL LA., Hamiltonban	Ad	17320	H2	3675
TURKEY LA., Hamiltonban	Ad	17320	G6	3571
TURKEY PIT SCHOOL RD., Reading	Ad	17350	F2	3369
TURKEY PIT SCHOOL RD., Reading	Ad	17350	G4	3369
TURKEY PIT SCHOOL RD., Reading	Ad	17350	A5	3370
TURKEY RD., McSherrystown	Ad	17331	G2	3578
TURNBERRY CT., Manchester Twp	Yk	17404	E10	3165
TURNBERRY CT., Spring Garden	Yk	17403	A11	3271
TURNBERRY DR., Newberry	Yk	17319	D5	2955
TURNBERRY LA., Spring Garden	Yk	17403	A11	3271
TUSCARORA DR., York Twp	Yk	17403	G6	3375
TWIG TER., East Berlin	Ad	17316	D2	3371
TWIGDEN CT., York Twp	Yk	17403	F2	3375
TWILIGHT DR., York Twp	Yk	17402	D9	3272
TWILIGHT LA., Hellam	Yk	17406	D8	3168
TWIN ARCH RD., North Codorus	Yk	17360	H6	3374
TWIN ARCH RD., North Codorus	Yk	17360	A6	3375
TWIN BRIDGE CT., Washington	Yk	17316	F6	3267
TWIN BRIDGE RD., Tyrone	Ad	17325	B10	3264
TWIN BRIDGE RD., Tyrone	Ad	17325	C1	3368
TWIN BROOK DR., West Manchester	Yk	17404	A5	3270
TWIN DR., Straban	Ad	17325	H6	3471
TWIN DR., Straban	Ad	17325	A6	3472
TWIN HILLS RD., Franklin	Yk	17019	A5	3056
TWIN LA., York Twp	Yk	17402	D3	3376
TWIN LAKES DR., Cumberland	Ad	17325	G9	3470
TWIN LAKES RD., Warrington	Yk	17339	B4	3059
TWIN OAK DR., Menallen	Ad	17304	E2	3262
TWIN PINE LA., Dover Twp	Yk	17315	F3	3269
TWIN RUN RD., Franklin	Ad	17307	H8	3364
TWO CHURCHES RD., Latimore	Ad	17316	C1	3266
TWO CHURCHES RD., Latimore	Ad	17372	B11	3161
TWO RING RD., Menallen	Ad	17304	E3	3262
TWO TAVERNS RD., Mount Joy	Ad	17325	C6	3576
TWO TAVERNS RD., Mount Joy	Ad	17340	C6	3576
TWO TAVERNS RD., Mount Pleasant	Ad	17325	D3	3576
TYLER RUN RD., York Twp	Yk	17403	F1	3375
TYSON RD., Fawn	Yk	17321	G5	3587

U

ULRICKTOWN RD., Germany	Ad	17340	B4	3681
ULTRA TR., Carroll Valley	Ad	17320	A11	3573
UMBERTO ST., Fairview	Yk	17070	C5	2849
UNION AL., Wrightsville	Yk	17368	D7	3169
UNION AV., Dallastown	Yk	17313	G7	3376
UNION CHURCH RD., East Hopewell	Yk	17322	B3	3586
UNION CHURCH RD., Franklin	Yk	17019	E11	3055
UNION CHURCH RD., Springfield	Yk	17360	H3	3478
UNION CHURCH RD., Springfield	Yk	17360	A3	3479
UNION LA., Red Lion	Yk	17356	A7	3377
UNION ST., Manchester Boro	Yk	17345	E1	3166
UNION ST., Union	Ad	17340	G10	3577
UNITED AV., Jacobus	Yk	17407	E11	3375
UNITED STATES AV., Cumberland	Ad	17325	A2	3575
UNIVERSITY DR. E., Butler	Ad	17307	H1	3366
UNIVERSITY DR. E., Menallen	Ad	17307	H11	3262
UNIVERSITY DR., Biglerville	Ad	17307	G1	3367
UNIVERSITY DR., Butler	Ad	17307	G1	3366
UPDYKE RD., Germany	Ad	17340	A10	3577
UPDYKE RD., Mount Joy	Ad	17340	G11	3576
UPLAND DR., East Berlin	Ad	17316	D1	3371
UPLAND RD., Spring Garden	Yk	17403	B1	3375
UPPER AL., Abbottstown	Ad	17301	B9	3371
UPPER BERMUDIAN RD., Huntington	Ad	17324	F10	3158
UPPER BERMUDIAN RD., Huntington	Ad	17324	H10	3158
UPPER BERMUDIAN RD., Huntington	Ad	17324	H1	3263
UPPER BERMUDIAN RD., Huntington	Ad	17324	A2	3264
UPPER BERMUDIAN RD., Tyrone	Ad	17324	F10	3158
UPPER BERMUDIAN RD., Tyrone	Ad	17324	C3	3264
UPPER TEMPLE RD., Menallen	Ad	17307	G8	3261
UPPER TR., Carroll Valley	Ad	17320	G4	3676
UPPERIDGE LA., Spring Garden	Yk	17403	F10	3271
URIEL CT., West Manheim	Yk	17331	E11	3579
URIEL CT., West Manheim	Yk	17331	E1	3683
UTZ DR., West Manheim	Yk	17331	H2	3683

V

VAIL DR. S., Penn	Yk	17331	C6	3579
VALLEY ACRES RD., Hellam	Yk	17406	B2	3273
VALLEY DR., Conewago	Ad	17331	H3	3578
VALLEY DR., York Twp	Yk	17313	G10	3376
VALLEY GREEN RD., Newberry	Yk	17319	C4	2955
VALLEY LA., Peach Bottom	Yk	17314	A11	3589
VALLEY PARK TR., Liberty	Ad	17320	E6	3573
VALLEY RD. E., Shrewsbury Twp	Yk	17327	H2	3583
VALLEY RD., Fairview	Yk	17319	G3	2954
VALLEY RD., Fairview	Yk	17319	A3	2955
VALLEY RD., Glen Rock	Yk	17327	D3	3583
VALLEY RD., Goldsboro	Yk	17319	G4	2955
VALLEY RD., Hopewell	Yk	17363	C11	3585
VALLEY RD., Hopewell	Yk	17363	B1	3689
VALLEY RD., Jacobus	Yk	17407	D11	3375
VALLEY RD., Manchester Twp	Yk	17404	H10	3165
VALLEY RD., Newberry	Yk	17319	G4	2955
VALLEY RD., Paradise	Yk	17364	G5	3371
VALLEY RD., Shrewsbury Twp	Yk	17327	F2	3583
VALLEY RD., Springfield	Yk	17360	H2	3478
VALLEY RD., Springfield	Yk	17360	A2	3479
VALLEY RD., Springfield	Yk	17360	C1	3479
VALLEY RD., Springfield	Yk	17403	C11	3375
VALLEY RD., Springfield	Yk	17403	D11	3375
VALLEY RD., Windsor Twp	Yk	17366	E6	3377
VALLEY RD., York Twp	Yk	17403	G2	3375
VALLEY RUN CIR., Penn	Yk	17331	D6	3579
VALLEY ST., Glen Rock	Yk	17327	C4	3583
VALLEY TR., Carroll Valley	Ad	17320	G3	3676
VALLEY TR., Liberty	Ad	17320	G3	3676
VALLEY VIEW , Menallen	Ad	17304	F3	3262
VALLEY VIEW CIR., Fairview	Yk	17070	B1	2954
VALLEY VIEW DR., Spring Garden	Yk	17403	G10	3271
VALLEY VIEW DR., Union	Ad	17340	A3	3682
VALLEY VIEW LA., Manheim	Yk	17329	C3	3685
VALLEY VIEW RD., Codorus	Yk	17362	D1	3581
VALLEY VIEW RD., Loganville	Yk	17403	G3	3479
VALLEY VIEW RD., Lower Windsor	Yk	17402	E4	3273
VALLEY VIEW RD., Peach Bottom	Yk	17314	B11	3589
VALLEY VIEW RD., Penn	Yk	17331	F6	3579
VALLEY VIEW RD., Spring Garden	Yk	17403	H10	3271
VALLEY VIEW RD., Spring Garden	Yk	17403	A10	3272
VALLEY VIEW RD., West Manheim	Yk	17331	A8	3580
VALLEY VIEW RD., Windsor Twp	Yk	17366	F2	3377
VALLEY VIEW RD., Yorkana	Yk	17402	E5	3273
VALLEY VIEW TR., Carroll Valley	Ad	17320	G10	3572
VALLEY VISTA DR., Springettsbury	Yk	17402	H9	3166
VALLEY VISTA DR., Springettsbury	Yk	17402	A10	3167
VALLEYBROOK DR., Springettsbury	Yk	17402	G2	3272
VAN CLEVE RD., Tyrone	Ad	17350	D10	3265
VAN SCOYOIC RD., Latimore	Ad	17372	B9	3160
VAN ZANDT WAY, Windsor Twp	Yk	17366	E6	3377
VANDER AV., York City	Yk	17403	E7	3271
VEACH RD., East Hopewell	Yk	17302	A2	3587
VELTMAN DR., Reading	Ad	17316	D3	3266
VERDAN CT., Spring Garden	Yk	17403	E11	3271
VERDAN DR. N., Spring Garden	Yk	17403	E11	3271
VERDAN DR. S., Spring Garden	Yk	17403	F11	3271
VERNON ST., Springettsbury	Yk	17402	A5	3272
VERONICA TR., Carroll Valley	Ad	17320	F1	3676
VICKI CIR., Mount Joy	Ad	17325	H4	3575
VICKI DR., Spring Garden	Yk	17403	A10	3272
VICKILEE DR., East Prospect	Yk	17317	E6	3274
VICKILEE DR., East Prospect	Yk	17368	E6	3274
VICTOR DR., Arendtsville	Ad	17307	C3	3366
VICTOR ST., Gettysburg	Ad	17325	C7	3471
VICTORIA DR., Windsor Twp	Yk	17356	C1	3377
VICTORIA RD., York Twp	Yk	17403	A11	3272
VIDA LA., Conewago	Yk	17315	F4	3164
VIEW TR., Carroll Valley	Ad	17320	H5	3676
VIEW TR., Carroll Valley	Ad	17320	A5	3677
VILLA TER., Spring Garden	Yk	17403	C10	3271
VILLA VISTA DR., Berwick	Ad	17331	B5	3475
VILLAGE CIR. E., Manchester Twp	Yk	17404	A1	3271
VILLAGE CIR. W., Manchester Twp	Yk	17404	A2	3271
VILLAGE DR., Gettysburg	Ad	17325	B9	3471
VILLAGE DR., Oxford	Ad	17350	E1	3474
VILLAGE RD., Dover Twp	Yk	17315	E3	3269
VILLAGE RD., Newberry	Yk	17319	H9	2954
VILLAGE RD., Newberry	Yk	17319	A9	2955
VILLAGE RD., York City	Yk	17404	A6	3271
VILLAGE SQUARE DR., Dover Twp	Yk	17315	E6	3269
VILLAGE WAY, Manchester Twp	Yk	17404	A1	3271
VILLAGE WAY, Windsor Twp	Yk	17402	G8	3272
VINCENT DR., Conewago	Ad	17331	F11	3474
VINCENT DR., Conewago	Ad	17344	E1	3578
VINE ST., Red Lion	Yk	17356	D7	3377
VINE ST., Wrightsville	Yk	17368	D7	3169
VINEYARD AV., York City	Yk	17404	B7	3271
VINLYN DR., Jackson	Yk	17362	H8	3372
VINLYN DR., Newberry	Yk	17370	E1	3060
VINMAR DR., York Twp	Yk	17402	G4	3375
VINTON DR., Windsor Twp	Yk	17402	B6	3273
VIOLET CT., Penn	Yk	17331	G4	3579
VIOLET DR., Newberry	Yk	17319	D11	2955
VIOLET TR., Carroll Valley	Ad	17320	G7	3572

VIREO RD. WEST SPRINGFIELD RD.

VIREO RD., York Twp	Yk	17403	H6	3375
VIRGINIA AV., Dover Twp	Yk	17315	H2	3269
VIRGINIA AV., Shrewsbury Boro	Yk	17361	B11	3584
VIRGINIA AV., Shrewsbury Boro	Yk	17361	B1	3688
VIRGINIA AV., Spring Garden	Yk	17403	C10	3271
VISTA CIR., Newberry	Yk	17319	A6	2955
VISTA DR., Fairview	Yk	17070	H9	2848
VISTA DR., Windsor Twp	Yk	17356	H5	3376
VISTA DR., Windsor Twp	Yk	17356	A5	3377
VISTA LA., Hellam	Yk	17368	C11	3169
VISTA LARGA DR., Cumberland	Ad	17325	A2	3471
VISTA TR., Carroll Valley	Ad	17320	A11	3573
VOGELSONG RD., York City	Yk	17404	A3	3271
VOGELSONG RD., York Twp	Yk	17404	G4	3270
VOWERY RD., Monaghan	Yk	17019	D5	2952
VULCAN LA., Red Lion	Yk	17356	A7	3377

W

WADE ST., Gettysburg	Ad	17325	C9	3471
WADELYN DR., Windsor Twp	Yk	17356	B9	3378
WADSWORTH AV., Cumberland	Ad	17325	H6	3470
WADSWORTH AV., Cumberland	Ad	17325	A6	3471
WADSWORTH DR., Reading	Ad	17316	D4	3266
WAGNER RD., Franklin	Ad	17222	H8	3363
WAGNER RD., Franklin	Ad	17222	A8	3364
WAGNER ST., East Berlin	Ad	17316	C11	3267
WAGNER ST., Penn	Yk	17331	E4	3579
WAGO RD., East Manchester	Yk	17345	F4	3061
WAGO RD., East Manchester	Yk	17347	G10	3061
WAINWRIGHT AV., Cumberland	Ad	17325	C9	3471
WAINWRIGHT AV., Gettysburg	Ad	17325	C9	3471
WALDEN CT., Manchester Twp	Yk	17404	C9	3165
WALDHEIM RD., Hamilton	Ad	17350	A6	3370
WALDORF DR., Conewago	Yk	17404	A9	3165
WALKER AV., Cumberland	Ad	17325	E6	3470
WALKER AV., Dover Twp	Yk	17315	H1	3269
WALKER DR., Oxford	Ad	17350	C1	3474
WALKER PL., Manchester Twp	Yk	17404	A2	3271
WALKER RD., Chanceford	Yk	17302	H5	3483
WALKER RD., Hopewell	Yk	17363	B4	3690
WALKER RD., Lower Chanceford	Yk	17302	H5	3483
WALKER RD., Shrewsbury Twp	Yk	17327	D6	3583
WALL ST., Gettysburg	Ad	17325	C9	3471
WALLACE ST., Springettsbury	Yk	17402	H5	3271
WALLACE ST., Springettsbury	Yk	17402	A5	3272
WALLACE ST., York City	Yk	17403	D6	3271
WALLACE ST., York City	Yk	17403	F5	3271
WALLER RD., Manchester Twp	Yk	17404	E10	3165
WALLICK LA. W., Red Lion	Yk	17356	B8	3377
WALLICKS RD., Hellam	Yk	17406	G7	3168
WALLOBY LA., Penn	Yk	17331	H6	3579
WALLOBY LA., Penn	Yk	17331	A5	3580
WAL-MAR DR., Franklin	Yk	17019	A1	3161
WALNUT AV., Shrewsbury Boro	Yk	17361	A8	3584
WALNUT BOTTOM RD., West Manchester	Yk	17404	H6	3269
WALNUT DR., Newberry	Yk	17370	E2	3060
WALNUT DR., Tyrone	Ad	17325	E10	3264
WALNUT DR., Warrington	Yk	17365	D3	3162
WALNUT GROVE RD. E., Fawn	Yk	17321	F11	3587
WALNUT GROVE RD. W., Fawn	Yk	17352	D11	3587
WALNUT LA., Lewisberry	Yk	17339	B10	2954
WALNUT LA., Oxford	Ad	17350	B4	3474
WALNUT LA., Spring Garden	Yk	17403	F10	3271
WALNUT LA., Springfield	Yk	17360	B11	3375
WALNUT LEVEL RD., Fairview	Yk	17070	B9	2849
WALNUT RD., East Hopewell	Yk	17352	H6	3586
WALNUT RD., East Hopewell	Yk	17352	A6	3587
WALNUT RIDGE, Dallastown	Yk	17313	F6	3376
WALNUT SPRINGS RD., Hellam	Yk	17406	F9	3168
WALNUT ST. E., Hanover	Yk	17331	D10	3475
WALNUT ST. E., Hanover	Yk	17331	C1	3579
WALNUT ST. E., Red Lion	Yk	17356	D8	3377
WALNUT ST. E., Windsor Twp	Yk	17356	D8	3377
WALNUT ST. N., Dallastown	Yk	17313	F7	3376
WALNUT ST. N., Spring Grove	Yk	17362	A11	3373
WALNUT ST. S., Dallastown	Yk	17313	F7	3376
WALNUT ST. S., Spring Grove	Yk	17362	A1	3477
WALNUT ST. W., Hanover	Yk	17331	B3	3579
WALNUT ST. W., Red Lion	Yk	17356	D9	3377
WALNUT ST. W., York Twp	Yk	17356	D9	3377
WALNUT ST., East Berlin	Ad	17316	C1	3371
WALNUT ST., Glen Rock	Yk	17327	C3	3583
WALNUT ST., Jefferson	Yk	17362	E10	3477
WALNUT ST., Littlestown	Ad	17340	F1	3681
WALNUT ST., McSherrystown	Ad	17344	F2	3578
WALNUT ST., Mount Wolf	Yk	17347	F1	3166
WALNUT ST., Spring Grove	Yk	17362	A11	3373
WALNUT ST., Wrightsville	Yk	17368	D7	3169
WALNUT ST., Yoe	Yk	17313	F5	3376
WALNUT ST., York City	Yk	17403	D6	3271
WALNUT ST., York City	Yk	17403	F5	3271
WALNUT ST., York Twp	Yk	17313	F6	3376
WALNUT TR., Carroll Valley	Ad	17320	H4	3676
WALNUT TR., Carroll Valley	Ad	17320	A4	3677
WALNUT VALLEY CT., Lower Windsor	Yk	17368	F11	3274
WALNUT VALLEY CT., Lower Windsor	Yk	17368	F1	3378
WALNUT WAY, Hopewell	Yk	17363	B1	3689
WALTEMYER SCHOOL RD., Hopewell	Yk	17349	G11	3584
WALTER DR., Manchester Twp	Yk	17404	B8	3166
WALTER RD., York Twp	Yk	17402	G4	3375
WALTERS HATCHERY RD., North Codorus	Yk	17360	B2	3478
WALTERS HATCHERY RD., North Codorus	Yk	17362	G5	3477
WALTERS HATCHERY RD., North Codorus	Yk	17362	A3	3478
WALTERS HATCHERY RD., North Codorus	Yk	17404	B2	3478
WALTER'S HATCHERY RD., North Codorus	Yk	17404	C11	3374
WALTERSDORF RD., North Codorus	Yk	17362	G8	3476
WALTERSDORF RD., North Codorus	Yk	17362	A9	3477
WALTERSDORF RD., North Codorus	Yk	17362	D7	3477
WALTIMYER RD., Shrewsbury Twp	Yk	17349	A4	3688
WALTON ST., York Haven	Yk	17370	E4	3061
WANDA DR., West Manheim	Yk	17331	F8	3579
WANETA ST., New Freedom	Yk	17349	G2	3687
WANETTE AV., Latimore	Ad	17372	B10	3160
WANTZ LA., Hellam	Yk	17406	H4	3168
WANTZ LA., Hellam	Yk	17406	A5	3169
WAPPLER DR., Conewago	Ad	17331	D11	3474
WAREHOUSE RD., Shrewsbury Twp	Yk	17349	D10	3584
WARM BREEZE CT., Conewago	Ad	17331	C4	3578
WARNER RD., Chanceford	Yk	17309	B3	3483
WARNER RD., Codorus	Yk	17327	C6	3582
WARNER RD., West Manheim	Yk	17331	B5	3684
WARREN AV., Cumberland	Ad	17325	B4	3575
WARREN RD., Manchester Twp	Yk	17404	H6	3165
WARREN ST., York City	Yk	17403	F7	3271
WARREN TR., Carroll Valley	Ad	17320	E11	3572
WARRINGTON RD., Carroll	Yk	17019	H5	3056
WARRINGTON RD., Warrington	Yk	17019	H5	3056
WARRINGTON ST., Warrington	Yk	17365	G3	3162
WARRINGTON ST., Wellsville	Yk	17365	G3	3162
WARRINGTON WAY, Warrington	Yk	17365	G2	3162
WARWICK RD., West Manchester	Yk	17404	C6	3270
WASHINGTON AV., Hanover	Yk	17331	D11	3475
WASHINGTON CT., Springettsbury	Yk	17402	F5	3272
WASHINGTON RD., New Freedom	Yk	17349	G11	3583
WASHINGTON RD., New Freedom	Yk	17349	G1	3687
WASHINGTON RD., Springettsbury	Yk	17402	A8	3272
WASHINGTON ST. N., Gettysburg	Ad	17325	C8	3471
WASHINGTON ST. S., Gettysburg	Ad	17325	C9	3471
WASHINGTON ST., Conewago	Ad	17331	G1	3578
WASHINGTON ST., York City	Yk	17403	C6	3271
WATER DR., Conewago	Ad	17331	B3	3578
WATER RD., Washington	Yk	17019	F2	3161
WATER ST. E., Abbottstown	Ad	17301	C9	3371
WATER ST. E., Gettysburg	Ad	17325	C8	3471
WATER ST. N., New Oxford	Ad	17350	A3	3474
WATER ST. S., New Oxford	Ad	17350	A3	3474
WATER ST. S., Oxford	Ad	17350	A3	3474
WATER ST. S., Spring Grove	Yk	17362	A1	3477
WATER ST. W., Gettysburg	Ad	17325	C8	3471
WATER ST., Abbottstown	Ad	17301	C9	3371
WATER ST., East Berlin	Ad	17316	C11	3267
WATER ST., Fairfield	Ad	17320	B5	3573
WATER ST., Fairview	Yk	17070	C5	2849
WATER ST., Felton	Yk	17322	H4	3481
WATER ST., Franklin	Yk	17019	F9	3055
WATER ST., Franklintown	Yk	17323	E9	3056
WATER ST., Glen Rock	Yk	17327	C4	3583
WATER ST., Hamiltonban	Ad	17320	B6	3573
WATER ST., Jacobus	Yk	17407	E10	3375
WATER ST., Liberty	Ad	17320	D6	3573
WATER ST., Loganville	Yk	17403	F3	3479
WATER ST., Lower Windsor	Yk	17368	E4	3274
WATER ST., McSherrystown	Ad	17344	E3	3578
WATER ST., New Salem	Yk	17371	C7	3374
WATER ST., Windsor Boro	Yk	17366	F4	3377
WATER ST., Wrightsville	Yk	17368	E8	3169
WATER ST., Yoe	Yk	17313	G5	3376
WATER ST., York Twp	Yk	17403	B8	3375
WATER TANK RD., Codorus	Yk	17329	G6	3581
WATER WORKS RD., Cumberland	Ad	17325	E3	3574
WATERFRONT DR., Penn	Yk	17331	H7	3579
WATERS RD., York Twp	Yk	17403	G11	3271
WATERS RD., York Twp	Yk	17403	F1	3375
WATERSHED CT., Hellam	Yk	17406	H7	3167
WATERVIEW RD., West Manheim	Yk	17331	E3	3683
WATSON RD., Peach Bottom	Yk	17314	E3	3693
WATTERS RD., Fawn	Yk	17352	H5	3690
WATTERS RD., Fawn	Yk	17352	A5	3691
WAUGHTEL RD., Chanceford	Yk	17322	E11	3378
WAUGHTEL RD., Chanceford	Yk	17322	E1	3482
WAVERLY CT., Springettsbury	Yk	17402	G2	3272
WAVERLY DR., Dover Twp	Yk	17315	C4	3269
WAYNE AV., Penn	Yk	17331	D4	3579
WAYNE AV., Spring Garden	Yk	17403	G5	3271
WAYNE AV., York City	Yk	17403	E6	3271
WAYNESBORO PIKE, Carroll Valley	Ad	17320	B2	3676
WAYNESBORO PIKE, Carroll Valley	Ad	17320	A3	3677
WAYNESBORO PIKE, Hamiltonban	Ad	17320	F3	3675
WAYNESBORO PIKE, Hamiltonban	Ad	17320	B2	3676
WAYNESBORO PIKE, Liberty	Ad	17320	F3	3675
WAYNESBORO PIKE, Liberty	Ad	17320	B2	3676
WAYNESBORO PIKE, Liberty	Ad	17320	G3	3676
WAYNESBORO PIKE, Liberty	Ad	17320	A3	3677
WAYSIDE CT., Dillsburg	Yk	17019	E2	3056
WEANER RD., Straban	Ad	17325	F2	3471
WEATHER CT., Windsor Twp	Yk	17356	B9	3378
WEAVER LA., Red Lion	Yk	17356	C6	3377
WEAVER LA., Red Lion	Yk	17356	B7	3377
WEAVER RD., Tyrone	Ad	17325	F1	3368
WEBB LA., Fawn Grove	Yk	17321	E5	3691
WEBB RD., Hopewell	Yk	17363	H7	3585
WEBB RD., Hopewell	Yk	17363	A8	3586
WEBSTER AV., Manchester Twp	Yk	17404	B3	3271
WEBSTER DR. E., Hellam	Yk	17402	A4	3273
WEBSTER DR. E., Springettsbury	Yk	17402	A4	3273
WEBSTER DR. N., Hellam	Yk	17402	A3	3273
WEBSTER DR., Springettsbury	Yk	17402	H4	3272
WEBSTER DR., Springettsbury	Yk	17402	A4	3273
WEDGEWOOD CIR., Newberry	Yk	17319	D6	2955
WEDGEWOOD WAY, West Manchester	Yk	17404	G9	3269
WEEPING WILLOW LA., Conewago	Yk	17315	A11	3165
WEEPING WILLOW LA., Dover Twp	Yk	17315	H11	3164
WEHLER ST., New Oxford	Ad	17350	B2	3474
WEIGLE LA., Carroll	Yk	17019	G10	2951
WEIKERT RD., Highland	Ad	17325	F4	3573
WEIRE RD., Conewago	Yk	17404	F2	3165
WEISGERBER WAY, Manchester Twp	Yk	17404	H2	3270
WEISHAAR TR., Liberty	Ad	17320	E7	3573
WELDON CT., West Manchester	Yk	17404	D8	3270
WELDON DR., West Manchester	Yk	17404	D8	3270
WELDON DR., West Manchester	Yk	17404	E9	3270
WELL DR., Shrewsbury Twp	Yk	17349	C2	3688
WELLINGTON DR., Springettsbury	Yk	17402	G5	3272
WELLINGTON DR., West Manchester	Yk	17404	B7	3270
WELLINGTON ST., York City	Yk	17403	F6	3271
WELLSLEY CT., Springettsbury	Yk	17402	G5	3272
WELLSPRINGS RD., Hopewell	Yk	17349	D7	3584
WELLSVILLE RD., Warrington	Yk	17365	G4	3162
WELLSVILLE RD., Washington	Yk	17365	D8	3162
WELLYN DR., Windsor Boro	Yk	17366	F4	3377
WELTY AV., Dillsburg	Yk	17019	D3	3056
WENCHOFF RD., Freedom	Ad	17320	F1	3677
WENCHOFF RD., Liberty	Ad	17320	F1	3677
WENDY AV., Latimore	Ad	17372	B10	3160
WENDY DR., Huntington	Ad	17372	B11	3160
WENKSVILLE RD., Menallen	Ad	17304	A2	3262
WENKSVILLE RD., Menallen	Ad	17307	B6	3261
WENKSVILLE RD., Menallen	Ad	17307	A2	3262
WENTWORTH RD., North Codorus	Yk	17403	G4	3374
WENZEL RD., Peach Bottom	Yk	17302	H9	3588
WENZEL RD., Peach Bottom	Yk	17302	A9	3589
WERTZ AV., Newberry	Yk	17345	E7	3061
WEST ABINGTON CIR., Hopewell	Yk	17363	F4	3584
WEST ABINGTON CIR., North Hopewell	Yk	17363	F4	3584
WEST ALVIN ST., Penn	Yk	17331	E3	3579
WEST AV., East Manchester	Yk	17345	C8	3061
WEST AV., Hanover	Yk	17331	B11	3475
WEST AV., Red Lion	Yk	17356	A9	3377
WEST AV., York Twp	Yk	17356	A9	3377
WEST BEAVER ST., New Oxford	Ad	17350	C1	3474
WEST BERLIN ST., New Oxford	Ad	17350	C1	3474
WEST BONNIEFIELD DR., Bonneauville	Ad	17325	G1	3576
WEST BOUNDARY AV., Dallastown	Yk	17313	F8	3376
WEST BOUNDARY AV., York City	Yk	17403	B9	3271
WEST BOUNDARY AV., York Twp	Yk	17313	F8	3376
WEST BROAD ST., Dallastown	Yk	17313	E6	3376
WEST BROADWAY, Gettysburg	Ad	17325	C7	3471
WEST BROADWAY ST., Goldsboro	Yk	17319	G7	2955
WEST BROADWAY ST., Red Lion	Yk	17356	A8	3377
WEST BROOK CIR., York Twp	Yk	17403	F1	3375
WEST BRUCE RD., Fawn	Yk	17302	F5	3587
WEST BRUCE RD., Fawn	Yk	17321	F5	3587
WEST CANAL DR., Dover Twp	Yk	17315	A4	3269
WEST CANAL RD., Dover Twp	Yk	17315	D6	3268
WEST CANAL RD., Paradise	Yk	17315	A8	3268
WEST CARBRIDGE RD., North Hopewell	Yk	17363	G4	3584
WEST CENTER ST., Glen Rock	Yk	17327	C3	3583
WEST CHARLES LA., York City	Yk	17403	D8	3271
WEST CHARLES ST., Littlestown	Ad	17340	E2	3681
WEST CHERRY LA., Dallastown	Yk	17313	F7	3376
WEST CHERRYWINE DR., Manchester Twp	Yk	17404	F1	3270
WEST CHESTNUT AV., Penn	Yk	17331	A4	3579
WEST CHESTNUT HILL RD., Butler	Ad	17304	G9	3263
WEST CHESTNUT ST., Dallastown	Yk	17313	F6	3376
WEST CHESTNUT ST., Hanover	Yk	17331	B3	3579
WEST CHESTNUT ST., Red Lion	Yk	17356	C8	3377
WEST CHESTNUT ST., York Twp	Yk	17313	F6	3376
WEST CHESTNUT ST., York Twp	Yk	17356	C8	3377
WEST CHURCH AV., Shrewsbury Boro	Yk	17361	A9	3584
WEST CHURCH ST., Dillsburg	Yk	17019	F3	3056
WEST CLARK AV., York City	Yk	17401	A8	3271
WEST CLARK AV., York City	Yk	17404	A8	3271
WEST CLEARVIEW DR., Shrewsbury Boro	Yk	17361	A7	3584
WEST CLEARVIEW RD., Hanover	Yk	17331	A11	3475
WEST CLEARVIEW RD., Shrewsbury Twp	Yk	17327	G5	3583
WEST CLOVERDALE AV., Shrewsbury Boro	Yk	17361	A10	3584
WEST COLLEGE AV., North Codorus	Yk	17404	D4	3374
WEST COLLEGE AV., West Manchester	Yk	17404	G10	3270
WEST COLLEGE AV., West Manchester	Yk	17404	E2	3374
WEST COLLEGE AV., York City	Yk	17403	B9	3271
WEST COLLEGE AV., York City	Yk	17404	A9	3271
WEST COLLEGE AV., York City	Yk	17404	B9	3271
WEST CONFEDERATE AV., Cumberland	Ad	17325	H11	3470
WEST CONFEDERATE AV., Cumberland	Ad	17325	A9	3471
WEST CONFEDERATE AV., Cumberland	Ad	17325	H3	3574
WEST CONFEDERATE AV., Gettysburg	Ad	17325	A9	3471
WEST COTTAGE PL., York City	Yk	17403	C9	3271
WEST CRANBERRY LA., Windsor Twp	Yk	17402	A9	3273
WEST ELM AV., Hanover	Yk	17331	A1	3579
WEST ELM ST., Red Lion	Yk	17356	C7	3377
WEST FISHING CREEK RD., Newberry	Yk	17319	A6	2955
WEST FLOUR MILL RD., Manchester Twp	Yk	17402	E11	3166
WEST FOREST AV., Shrewsbury Boro	Yk	17327	G7	3583
WEST FOREST AV., Shrewsbury Twp	Yk	17327	G7	3583
WEST FORREST AV., Shrewsbury Boro	Yk	17361	A8	3584
WEST FRANKLIN ST., New Freedom	Yk	17349	F2	3687
WEST GARY DR., York Twp	Yk	17313	D8	3376
WEST GAS AV., York City	Yk	17401	C7	3271
WEST GAS ST., York City	Yk	17404	B7	3271
WEST GATEHOUSE LA., Springettsbury	Yk	17402	D6	3272
WEST GAY AV., York City	Yk	17401	C7	3271
WEST GAY AV., York City	Yk	17404	B7	3271
WEST GAY AV., York City	Yk	17404	B7	3271
WEST GAY ST., Red Lion	Yk	17356	B7	3377
WEST GAY ST., Windsor Boro	Yk	17366	E5	3377
WEST GAY ST., York City	Yk	17401	C7	3271
WEST GEORGE ST., New Oxford	Ad	17350	A3	3474
WEST GEORGE ST., New Salem	Yk	17371	C7	3374
WEST GOLDEN LA., New Oxford	Ad	17350	A2	3474
WEST GUERNSEY RD., Butler	Ad	17307	A9	3263
WEST HAMLET DR., Spring Grove	Yk	17362	B9	3373
WEST HANOVER ST., Biglerville	Ad	17307	H2	3366
WEST HANOVER ST., Biglerville	Ad	17307	A3	3367
WEST HARRISBURG ST., Dillsburg	Yk	17019	C3	3056
WEST HAZEL ST., Red Lion	Yk	17356	B7	3377
WEST HEATHERFIELD WAY, Windsor Twp	Yk	17356	B2	3377
WEST HEFFNER RD., Chanceford	Yk	17309	B2	3484
WEST HEFFNER RD., Lower Chanceford	Yk	17309	B2	3484
WEST HIGH ROCK RD., Heidelberg	Yk	17331	G3	3475
WEST HIGH ST., New Freedom	Yk	17349	F3	3687
WEST HIGH ST., Gettysburg	Ad	17325	B9	3471
WEST HIGH ST., New Oxford	Ad	17350	A3	3474
WEST HIGH ST., Red Lion	Yk	17356	B7	3377
WEST HIGH ST., Windsor Boro	Yk	17366	E4	3377
WEST HIGH ST., Yoe	Yk	17313	G5	3376
WEST HILL ST., Wintersown	Yk	17322	H7	3480
WEST HILL ST., Winterstown	Yk	17322	A7	3481
WEST HOLLY LA., Newberry	Yk	17319	F8	2955
WEST HOPE AV., York City	Yk	17403	C8	3271
WEST HOPE AV., York City	Yk	17404	B8	3271
WEST HOWARD ST., Dallastown	Yk	17313	F7	3376
WEST HOWARD ST., Red Lion	Yk	17356	B6	3377
WEST JACKSON ST., Spring Garden	Yk	17403	C9	3271
WEST JACKSON ST., York City	Yk	17403	C9	3271
WEST KEENY DR., North Codorus	Yk	17362	A1	3478
WEST KING ST., Abbottstown	Ad	17301	A10	3371
WEST KING ST., Littlestown	Ad	17340	D2	3681
WEST KING ST., West York	Yk	17404	G10	3270
WEST KING ST., York City	Yk	17401	B8	3271
WEST KING ST., York City	Yk	17404	B8	3271
WEST LANCASTER ST., Red Lion	Yk	17356	E8	3377
WEST LANDIS DR., Fairfield	Ad	17320	A5	3573
WEST LIBERTY RD., Hopewell	Yk	17363	F4	3689
WEST LINCOLN AV., Gettysburg	Ad	17325	B7	3471
WEST LINCOLNWAY, New Oxford	Ad	17350	A3	3474
WEST LOCUST ST., York City	Yk	17404	A9	3271
WEST LUTHER DR., Shrewsbury Boro	Yk	17361	A11	3584
WEST LUTHER DR., Shrewsbury Twp	Yk	17361	A1	3688
WEST MAIN ST., Dallastown	Yk	17313	F7	3376
WEST MAIN ST., Fairfield	Ad	17320	A5	3573
WEST MAIN ST., Fawn Grove	Yk	17321	F4	3691
WEST MAIN ST., Felton	Yk	17322	H4	3481
WEST MAIN ST., New Freedom	Yk	17349	F2	3687
WEST MAIN ST., Windsor Boro	Yk	17366	E5	3377
WEST MAIN ST., Windsor Twp	Yk	17366	E5	3377
WEST MAPLE LAWN RD., Fawn	Yk	17352	D7	3587
WEST MAPLE ST., Dallastown	Yk	17313	E6	3376
WEST MAPLE ST., East Prospect	Yk	17317	E6	3274
WEST MAPLE ST., East Prospect	Yk	17317	E6	3274
WEST MAPLE ST., East Prospect	Yk	17368	E6	3274
WEST MAPLE ST., East Prospect	Yk	17368	E6	3274
WEST MAPLE ST., York City	Yk	17403	C9	3271
WEST MAPLE ST., York City	Yk	17403	D8	3271
WEST MARKET ST., Hallam	Yk	17406	C11	3168
WEST MARKET ST., West York	Yk	17404	G9	3270
WEST MARKET ST., York City	Yk	17401	B8	3271
WEST MARKET ST., York City	Yk	17404	B8	3271
WEST MASON AV., York City	Yk	17401	C7	3271
WEST MASON AV., York City	Yk	17404	A8	3271
WEST McKINLEY RD., Lower Chanceford	Yk	17314	D8	3589
WEST MIDDLE ST., Gettysburg	Ad	17325	B8	3471
WEST MIDDLE ST., Hanover	Yk	17331	B4	3579
WEST MIDDLE ST., Penn	Yk	17331	A4	3579
WEST MIDVALE RD., Peach Bottom	Yk	17302	H7	3588
WEST MIDVALE RD., Peach Bottom	Yk	17302	A8	3589
WEST MOUNTAIN TOP DR., Franklin	Ad	17353	A8	3364
WEST MT. AIRY RD., Monaghan	Yk	17019	E9	2952
WEST MUD RUN RD., Reading	Ad	17372	F7	3265
WEST MYRTLE ST., Littlestown	Ad	17340	D1	3681
WEST NEEDHAM CIR., Manchester Twp	Yk	17404	C11	3165
WEST NEWTON AV., York City	Yk	17404	C8	3271
WEST NORTH ST., York City	Yk	17403	C6	3271
WEST NORTH ST., York City	Yk	17404	B7	3271
WEST ORE ST., Loganville	Yk	17360	E4	3479
WEST OVERVIEW CIR., Windsor Twp	Yk	17356	B11	3273
WEST OVERVIEW CIR., Windsor Twp	Yk	17356	B1	3377
WEST PARK LA., Dallastown	Yk	17313	E6	3376
WEST PENN ST., New Freedom	Yk	17349	G2	3687
WEST PENNSYLVANIA AV., Stewartstown	Yk	17363	D11	3585
WEST PENNSYLVANIA AV., Yoe	Yk	17313	G5	3376
WEST PHILADELPHIA ST., Yoe	Yk	17313	G6	3376
WEST PHILADELPHIA ST., York City	Yk	17401	B7	3271
WEST PHILADELPHIA ST., York City	Yk	17404	B7	3271
WEST POINT RD., Menallen	Ad	17304	D11	3157
WEST POPLAR ST., West York	Yk	17404	H9	3270
WEST POSEY RD., Lower Chanceford	Yk	17302	B7	3484
WEST PRINCESS ST., West York	Yk	17404	H9	3270
WEST PRINCESS ST., York City	Yk	17404	B8	3271
WEST PROSPECT ST., Red Lion	Yk	17356	B6	3377
WEST RAILROAD AV., Railroad	Yk	17355	H9	3583
WEST RAILROAD AV., Railroad	Yk	17355	A9	3584
WEST RAILROAD AV., Shrewsbury Boro	Yk	17361	A9	3584
WEST RAPHIEL CT., West Manheim	Yk	17331	D11	3579
WEST RD., Springfield	Yk	17403	H2	3479
WEST REYNOLDS RD., Tyrone	Ad	17350	A3	3369
WEST RIDGE AV., East Prospect	Yk	17317	F6	3274
WEST RIDGE AV., East Prospect	Yk	17368	F6	3274
WEST RIDGE RD., Monaghan	Yk	17019	D3	3057
WEST RIVERVIEW RD., Lower Chanceford	Yk	17314	G2	3589
WEST ROSE AV., Dallastown	Yk	17313	E6	3376
WEST SHOFF RD., Chanceford	Yk	17368	H1	3378
WEST SHOFF RD., Chanceford	Yk	17368	A2	3379
WEST SIDDONSBURG RD., Carroll	Yk	17019	G11	2951
WEST SIDDONSBURG RD., Monaghan	Yk	17019	A10	2952
WEST SIDDONSBURG RD., Monaghan	Yk	17019	B9	2952
WEST SKYLIGHT DR., York Twp	Yk	17402	D9	3272
WEST SOUTH ST., York City	Yk	17403	D8	3271
WEST SPRINGETTSBURY ST., Spring Garden	Yk	17403	C9	3271
WEST SPRINGETTSBURY ST., York City	Yk	17403	C9	3271
WEST SPRINGFIELD RD., Springfield	Yk	17327	H10	3478
WEST SPRINGFIELD RD., Springfield	Yk	17327	B11	3479

WEST SPRINGFIELD RD., Springfield	Yk	17360	D9	3479
WEST ST, Fairview	Yk	17339	A9	2954
WEST ST. N., York City	Yk	17404	A7	3271
WEST ST. S., York City	Yk	17404	A8	3271
WEST ST., Gettysburg	Ad	17325	B9	3471
WEST ST., Glen Rock	Yk	17327	C3	3583
WEST ST., Littlestown	Yk	17340	G1	3681
WEST STEVENS ST., Gettysburg	Ad	17325	C7	3471
WEST SUMMIT DR., Germany	Ad	17340	G3	3681
WEST TIMBER LA., Penn	Yk	17331	G5	3579
WEST TRAILS RD., Peach Bottom	Yk	17302	H7	3588
WEST TRAILS RD., Peach Bottom	Yk	17302	A8	3589
WEST VILLAGE CIR., Manchester Twp	Yk	17404	A2	3271
WEST WALLICK LA., Red Lion	Yk	17356	B8	3377
WEST WALNUT GROVE RD., Fawn	Yk	17352	D11	3587
WEST WALNUT ST., Hanover	Yk	17331	B3	3579
WEST WALNUT ST., Red Lion	Yk	17356	D9	3377
WEST WALNUT ST., York Twp	Yk	17356	D9	3377
WEST WATER ST., Gettysburg	Ad	17325	C8	3471
WEST WILLOW AV., Dallastown	Yk	17313	E6	3376
WEST WINNERS CIRCLE DR., York Twp	Yk	17356	B6	3377
WEST YORK ST., Biglerville	Ad	17307	H2	3366
WEST YORK ST., Biglerville	Ad	17307	A3	3367
WEST YORK ST., Dillsburg	Yk	17019	F3	3056
WESTBROOK CIR., Shrewsbury Twp	Yk	17361	B11	3584
WESTER AV., Warrington	Yk	17365	A2	3163
WESTER LAU DR., Carroll	Yk	17019	E7	3056
WESTER LAU DR., Franklin	Yk	17019	E7	3056
WESTERLY DR., Germany	Ad	17340	E5	3680
WESTERN AV., Red Lion	Yk	17356	B7	3377
WESTERN AV., York Twp	Yk	17356	B7	3377
WESTERN RD., Franklin	Yk	17019	B10	3055
WESTGATE DR., West Manchester	Yk	17404	E4	3270
WESTLY DR., Dover Twp	Yk	17315	G5	3269
WESTMINSTER DR., West Manchester	Yk	17404	A6	3270
WESTMINSTER AV., Penn	Yk	17331	A8	3579
WESTMINSTER CT., East Manchester	Yk	17347	E2	3167
WESTMINSTER RD., West Manheim	Yk	17331	A10	3579
WESTOVER LA., Spring Garden	Yk	17403	C2	3375
WESTRIDGE DR., Loganville	Yk	17360	E3	3479
WESTVIEW DR., McSherrystown	Ad	17344	E2	3578
WESTVIEW DR., North Hopewell	Yk	17363	B2	3585
WESTVIEW DR., Shrewsbury Boro	Yk	17361	B8	3584
WESTWIND LA., Manchester Twp	Yk	17404	C9	3165
WESTWOOD CT., Springettsbury	Yk	17402	G5	3272
WESTWOOD DR., Conewago	Yk	17404	A9	3165
WESTWOOD DR., West Manheim	Yk	17331	B4	3684
WESTWOOD RD., Spring Garden	Yk	17403	E11	3271
WESTWOOD RD., Spring Garden	Yk	17403	E1	3375
WESTWOOD VILLAGE CIR., Conewago	Yk	17404	A9	3165
WETHERBURN CT., Manchester Twp	Yk	17404	E9	3165
WETHERBURN DR., Manchester Twp	Yk	17404	E10	3165
WETTON MILL DR., Springettsbury	Yk	17402	F6	3272
WETZEL DR., Conewago	Ad	17331	H9	3474
WETZEL DR., Penn	Yk	17331	A9	3475
WEXFORD LA., Manchester Twp	Yk	17404	F10	3165
WEYMOUTH CT., West Manchester	Yk	17404	E8	3270
WHARF RD., Monaghan	Yk	17055	H5	2952
WHARF RD., Monaghan	Yk	17055	A5	2953
WHARTON RD., Springettsbury	Yk	17402	A7	3272
WHEAT RD., East Hopewell	Yk	17352	F6	3586
WHEATFIELD RD., Cumberland	Ad	17325	A3	3575
WHEATFIELD ST., West Manchester	Yk	17404	B1	3270
WHEATFIELD ST., York City	Yk	17403	F7	3271
WHEATFIELD TR., Carroll Valley	Ad	17320	A5	3677
WHEATLAND DR., Dover Twp	Yk	17315	E5	3269
WHEATLAND DR., Mount Pleasant	Ad	17325	E11	3472
WHEATLAND DR., Mount Pleasant	Ad	17325	E1	3576
WHEATLAND RD., Fairview	Yk	17339	B1	2953
WHEATLYN DR., Spring Garden	Yk	17403	F8	3271
WHEATLYN RD., Windsor Twp	Yk	17402	E8	3272
WHEATON DR., Littlestown	Ad	17340	F11	3577
WHEATON DR., Union	Ad	17340	F11	3577
WHEATON ST., Spring Garden	Yk	17403	H6	3271
WHIPPOORWILL LA., Hamiltonban	Ad	17353	B9	3468
WHISKEY SPRINGS RD., Franklin	Yk	17019	A9	3055
WHISLER RD., Newberry	Yk	17319	E11	2955
WHISPERING PINES RD., York Twp	Yk	17403	D6	3375
WHISPERING SPRINGS DR., North Codorus	Yk	17404	D9	3374
WHISTLER RD., Mount Pleasant	Ad	17325	F7	3472
WHITCRAFT LA., Shrewsbury Boro	Yk	17361	A8	3584
WHITCRAFT RD., Shrewsbury Boro	Yk	17355	H8	3583
WHITE BIRCH DR., Bonneauville	Ad	17340	H2	3576
WHITE BIRCH LA., Newberry	Yk	17319	D4	2955
WHITE CHURCH RD., Huntington	Ad	17372	H9	3264
WHITE CHURCH RD., Huntington	Ad	17372	A6	3265
WHITE CHURCH RD., Mount Joy	Ad	17325	H5	3575
WHITE CHURCH RD., Springfield	Yk	17360	B6	3479
WHITE CHURCH RD., Tyrone	Ad	17372	H9	3264
WHITE DOGWOOD DR., Newberry	Yk	17319	H6	2954
WHITE DOGWOOD DR., Newberry	Yk	17319	A6	2955
WHITE DR., North Codorus	Yk	17404	E8	3374
WHITE OAK DR., Manchester Twp	Yk	17402	C1	3271
WHITE OAK DR., Newberry	Yk	17319	F7	2955
WHITE OAK DR., Newberry	Yk	17370	D1	3060
WHITE OAK LA., Newberry	Yk	17319	C5	2955
WHITE OAK LP., Newberry	Yk	17370	D1	3060
WHITE OAK RD., Chanceford	Yk	17322	A7	3379
WHITE OAK RD., Chanceford	Yk	17356	A7	3379
WHITE OAK RD., Shrewsbury Twp	Yk	17349	D11	3480
WHITE OAK RD., Shrewsbury Twp	Yk	17349	C2	3584
WHITE OAK RD., Windsor Twp	Yk	17356	D11	3273
WHITE OAK RD., Windsor Twp	Yk	17366	E1	3377
WHITE OAK TR., Carroll Valley	Ad	17320	G7	3572
WHITE OAK TR., Cumberland	Ad	17325	A10	3367
WHITE OAK TREE RD., Huntington	Ad	17372	E11	3159
WHITE OAK TREE RD., Huntington	Ad	17372	E2	3264
WHITE PINE DR., Franklin	Ad	17353	A8	3364
WHITE PINE LA., Newberry	Yk	17315	E3	3059
WHITE PINE TR. N., Peach Bottom	Yk	17314	H10	3588
WHITE PINE TR. S., Peach Bottom	Yk	17314	H10	3588
WHITE PINES LA., Hamiltonban	Ad	17222	F3	3467
WHITE PUMP LA., West Manchester	Yk	17404	B7	3270
WHITE RD., Mount Joy	Ad	17325	G3	3575
WHITE RD., Peach Bottom	Yk	17302	H8	3588
WHITE ROSE LA., Windsor Twp	Yk	17402	D7	3272
WHITE ROSE LA., York City	Yk	17404	A4	3271
WHITE RUN LA., Mount Joy	Ad	17325	G5	3575
WHITE RUN RD., Mount Pleasant	Ad	17325	C1	3576
WHITE ST., West Manchester	Yk	17404	E7	3270
WHITE ST., West Manchester	Yk	17404	F8	3270
WHITE TAIL DR., Fairview	Yk	17339	C3	2954
WHITE TAIL TER., Warrington	Yk	17019	H8	3057
WHITECRAFT RD., Shrewsbury Twp	Yk	17349	D1	3688
WHITEFIELD LA., Windsor Twp	Yk	17356	A9	3378
WHITEFORD DR., Fairview	Yk	17339	A2	3059
WHITEFORD RD., Peach Bottom	Yk	17314	A4	3693
WHITEFORD RD., Springettsbury	Yk	17402	F4	3271
WHITEFORD RD., Springettsbury	Yk	17402	H3	3271
WHITEFORD RD., Springettsbury	Yk	17402	C3	3272
WHITEFORD RD., Springettsbury	Yk	17402	A3	3272
WHITEHALL RD., Germany	Ad	17340	D7	3577
WHITEHALL RD., Mount Pleasant	Ad	17340	A2	3577
WHITEHALL RD., Union	Ad	17340	D7	3577
WHITEHURST CT., Manchester Twp	Yk	17404	E8	3165
WHITETAIL LA., Hellam	Yk	17406	E5	3168
WHITNEY DR., York Twp	Yk	17402	A6	3376
WICKLOW DR., Manchester Twp	Yk	17404	C11	3165
WICKLOW DR., Manchester Twp	Yk	17404	C1	3270
WIERMAN'S MILL RD., Huntington	Ad	17372	A4	3265
WIERMAN'S MILL RD., Huntington	Ad	17372	B7	3265
WILCOX DR., Fairview	Yk	17070	C1	2954
WILD GAME LA., Chanceford	Yk	17322	H3	3379
WILDASIN DR., Jacobus	Yk	17407	D10	3375
WILDASIN RD., North Codorus	Yk	17362	G2	3477
WILDCAT LA., Hellam	Yk	17406	B2	3168
WILDE LA., Hellam	Yk	17406	C8	3168
WILDERNESS LA., Hamiltonban	Ad	17320	A1	3572
WILDFLOWER CT., Glen Rock	Yk	17327	D4	3583
WILDON DR., York Twp	Yk	17403	E5	3375
WILEY LA., Hellam	Yk	17368	C10	3169
WILEY MILL RD., Fawn	Yk	17352	H11	3586
WILEY MILL RD., Fawn	Yk	17352	A11	3587
WILEY RD., Lower Chanceford	Yk	17314	E7	3589
WILEY RD., Peach Bottom	Yk	17314	H2	3693
WILEY RD., Peach Bottom	Yk	17314	A1	3694
WILLAPA DR., Dover Twp	Yk	17315	G5	3269
WILLETA CT., York Twp	Yk	17402	B2	3376
WILLIAM ST. N., West Manchester	Yk	17404	E8	3270
WILLIAM ST. S., West Manchester	Yk	17404	E9	3270
WILLIAM ST., Penn	Yk	17331	A8	3579
WILLIAMS GROVE RD., Carroll	Yk	17019	C9	2951
WILLIAMS LA., Hamiltonban	Ad	17320	E4	3572
WILLIAMS PL., Glen Rock	Yk	17327	C4	3583
WILLIAMS RD., Springettsbury	Yk	17402	C1	3272
WILLIAMSBURG CT., Littlestown	Ad	17340	F3	3681
WILLIAMSBURG DR., Springettsbury	Yk	17402	G5	3272
WILLIAMSTOWN CIR., Manchester Twp	Yk	17404	A1	3271
WILLIS LA., York City	Yk	17404	B6	3271
WILLIS RD., Fairview	Yk	17319	B2	2955
WILLIS RD., Manchester Twp	Yk	17404	B5	3271
WILLIS RD., York City	Yk	17404	B5	3271
WILLOMETTE CT., Springettsbury	Yk	17402	G4	3272
WILLOUGHBY RUN RD., Cumberland	Ad	17325	F11	3470
WILLOUGHBY RUN RD., Cumberland	Ad	17325	F1	3574
WILLOW AV. E., Dallastown	Yk	17313	G7	3376
WILLOW AV. W., Dallastown	Yk	17313	E6	3376
WILLOW CREEK RD., Lower Windsor	Yk	17368	D7	3274
WILLOW CREEK RD., Lower Windsor	Yk	17406	D7	3274
WILLOW CT., Penn	Yk	17331	E7	3579
WILLOW CT., York Twp	Yk	17402	D1	3376
WILLOW GLEN RD., Franklin	Yk	17019	B11	3056
WILLOW GLEN RD., Franklin	Yk	17019	C1	3161
WILLOW LA. S., Red Lion	Yk	17356	B8	3377
WILLOW LA., Huntington	Ad	17372	E4	3264
WILLOW RD., Dover Twp	Yk	17315	F3	3269
WILLOW RD., Hellam	Yk	17406	G7	3168
WILLOW RD., Mount Pleasant	Ad	17325	C2	3576
WILLOW RD., Springettsbury	Yk	17402	F11	3166
WILLOW RD., Warrington	Yk	17365	D11	3057
WILLOW RD., Warrington	Yk	17365	D1	3162
WILLOW RD., West Manchester	Yk	17404	B5	3270
WILLOW RIDGE DR., Manchester Twp	Yk	17404	E2	3270
WILLOW RIDGE DR., Manchester Twp	Yk	17404	F2	3270
WILLOW RUN RD., Dover Boro	Yk	17315	D11	3164
WILLOW SPRINGS CIR S., Manchester Twp	Yk	17402	A3	3166
WILLOW SPRINGS CIR. N., Manchester Twp	Yk	17402	A4	3166
WILLOW SPRINGS LA., East Manchester	Yk	17402	A3	3166
WILLOW SPRINGS LA., Manchester Twp	Yk	17402	A3	3166
WILLOW ST. E., Codorus	Yk	17362	F11	3477
WILLOW ST., Hanover	Yk	17331	C1	3579
WILLOW ST., Hopewell	Yk	17363	C2	3689
WILLOW ST., McSherrystown	Ad	17344	E2	3578
WILLOW ST., Wrightsville	Yk	17368	E8	3169
WILLOW ST., York Spring	Ad	17372	B11	3160
WILLOW TR., Carroll Valley	Ad	17320	G8	3572
WILLOW TREE LA., Dover Twp	Yk	17315	F5	3269
WILLOWBROOK WAY, Spring Garden	Yk	17403	C11	3271
WILLWERT RD., Hopewell	Yk	17363	A6	3585
WILLYN DR., Lower Windsor	Yk	17368	C1	3274
WILMAR AV., Penn	Yk	17331	D4	3579
WILMAR RD., Dover Twp	Yk	17315	F4	3269
WILMER LA., Washington	Yk	17316	B4	3267
WILMINGTON AV., York Twp	Yk	17404	H7	3270
WILSHIRE DR., Springettsbury	Yk	17402	G5	3272
WILSON AV., Hanover	Yk	17331	D10	3475
WILSON AV., Manchester Twp	Yk	17404	B3	3271
WILSON AV., New Freedom	Yk	17349	H4	3687
WILSON AV., Penn	Yk	17331	D10	3475
WILSON AV., Penn	Yk	17331	F1	3579
WILSON AV., York Twp	Yk	17313	G8	3376
WILSON CT., Red Lion	Yk	17356	E7	3377
WILSON CT., Yoe	Yk	17313	G6	3376
WILSON CT., York City	Yk	17403	D8	3271
WILSON LA. N., Hallam	Yk	17406	D10	3168
WILSON LA. N., Hellam	Yk	17406	D10	3168
WILSON LA. S., Hallam	Yk	17406	D11	3168
WILSON LA. S., Hellam	Yk	17406	D11	3168
WILSON RD., Newberry	Yk	17370	D2	3060
WILSON SPRINGS RD., West Manheim	Yk	17331	D4	3683
WILT DR., Paradise	Yk	17315	G9	3267
WILT DR., West Manchester	Yk	17404	D6	3270
WILTSHIRE RD., Spring Garden	Yk	17403	B11	3271
WIMBLETON WAY, Windsor Twp	Yk	17356	D3	3377
WINBRIAR LA., Cumberland	Ad	17325	H10	3470
WINCHESTER RD., Dover Twp	Yk	17315	B3	3269
WINCHESTER RD., Shrewsbury Twp	Yk	17361	B11	3584
WIND CREST RD., West Manchester	Yk	17404	A4	3270
WIND IN THE WILLOWS LA., Hamilton	Ad	17301	C4	3371
WIND IN THE WILLOWS LA., Hamilton	Ad	17316	C4	3371
WIND RUSH DR., York Twp	Yk	17313	H9	3376
WINDASIN DR., Heidelberg	Yk	17362	E9	3476
WINDERMERE CT., Springettsbury	Yk	17402	G5	3272
WINDING BROOK RD., Butler	Ad	17307	G3	3366
WINDING BROOK RD., Butler	Ad	17307	A5	3367
WINDING HILL DR., Newberry	Yk	17319	E10	2955
WINDING LA., Codorus	Yk	17329	G5	3581
WINDING LA., Hamilton	Ad	17316	A3	3371
WINDING OAK DR., Spring Garden	Yk	17403	A1	3375
WINDING RD. N., Warrington	Yk	17365	G6	3162
WINDING RD. S., Warrington	Yk	17315	H6	3162
WINDING RD., Franklin	Ad	17307	H1	3365
WINDING RD., Franklin	Ad	17307	A3	3366
WINDING RD., Newberry	Yk	17315	E3	3059
WINDING RD., Newberry	Yk	17315	E4	3059
WINDING RD., Paradise	Yk	17316	E2	3371
WINDING RD., Warrington	Yk	17315	H8	3162
WINDING RD., Warrington	Yk	17315	A7	3163
WINDING RD., Washington	Yk	17315	G9	3162
WINDING RD., West Manchester	Yk	17404	D5	3270
WINDING WAY, Menallen	Ad	17304	D4	3262
WINDSOR CT., Germany	Ad	17340	C11	3577
WINDSOR CT., Penn	Yk	17331	E8	3579
WINDSOR LA., Red Lion	Yk	17356	C7	3377
WINDSOR RD., Manchester Twp	Yk	17402	H6	3165
WINDSOR RD., Windsor Boro	Yk	17366	E3	3377
WINDSOR RD., Windsor Twp	Yk	17356	E9	3272
WINDSOR RD., Windsor Twp	Yk	17356	A11	3273
WINDSOR RD., Windsor Twp	Yk	17356	B1	3377
WINDSOR RD., Windsor Twp	Yk	17356	F6	3377
WINDSOR RD., Windsor Twp	Yk	17356	C2	3377
WINDSOR RD., Windsor Twp	Yk	17366	E3	3377
WINDSOR RD., Windsor Twp	Yk	17366	F6	3377
WINDSOR RD., Windsor Twp	Yk	17402	E9	3272
WINDSOR ST., Littlestown	Ad	17340	E1	3681
WINDSOR ST., Spring Garden	Yk	17403	D5	3271
WINDVIEW CT., Hopewell	Yk	17349	C6	3584
WINDY CT., West Manheim	Yk	17331	F1	3683
WINDY HILL RD., Shrewsbury Twp	Yk	17349	D11	3584
WINDY HILL RD., Shrewsbury Twp	Yk	17349	B2	3688
WINEBARY CIR., Fairview	Yk	17339	A4	2954
WINEBERRY DR., Shrewsbury Boro	Yk	17361	B6	3584
WINEBRENNER WOOD DR., Penn	Yk	17331	A7	3579
WINEMILLER LA., West Manchester	Yk	17404	A5	3270
WINESAP DR., Littlestown	Ad	17340	D1	3681
WINGFIELD DR., Springettsbury	Yk	17402	E1	3272
WINNERS CIRCLE DR. S., York Twp	Yk	17356	A6	3377
WINNERS CIRCLE DR. W., York Twp	Yk	17356	B6	3377
WINNERS CIRCLE DR., York Twp	Yk	17356	A6	3377
WINSFORD LA., Manchester Twp	Yk	17404	C10	3165
WINSHIP RD., Manchester Twp	Yk	17402	A5	3166
WINSTON DR., West Manchester	Yk	17404	C3	3270
WINTER AV., Glen Rock	Yk	17327	B4	3583
WINTER DR., Bonneauville	Ad	17325	F1	3576
WINTER DR., Monaghan	Yk	17019	A10	2952
WINTER LA., Red Lion	Yk	17356	E8	3377
WINTER TR., Carroll Valley	Ad	17320	G2	3676
WINTERBERRY CT., Manchester Twp	Yk	17404	B2	3270
WINTERBERRY DR., Manchester Twp	Yk	17402	C1	3271
WINTERBERRY LA., Newberry	Yk	17319	E7	2955
WINTERS AV., Stewartstown	Yk	17363	E1	3689
WINTERS RD., Lower Windsor	Yk	17366	H1	3377
WINTERS RD., Lower Windsor	Yk	17366	A1	3378
WINTERSTOWN RD., North Hopewell	Yk	17322	B10	3481
WINTERSTOWN RD., North Hopewell	Yk	17356	A2	3481
WINTERSTOWN RD., North Hopewell	Yk	17363	D1	3585
WINTERSTOWN RD., Windsor Twp	Yk	17356	B11	3377
WINTERSTOWN RD., Windsor Twp	Yk	17356	A2	3481
WINTERSTOWN RD., Winterstown	Yk	17322	A8	3481
WINTERSTOWN RD., Winterstown	Yk	17356	A3	3481
WINTERSTOWN RD., York Twp	Yk	17356	B11	3377
WINTERSTOWN RD., York Twp	Yk	17356	A2	3481
WINWOOD RD., Glen Rock	Yk	17327	D4	3583
WIRE RD., York Twp	Yk	17402	B2	3376
WIRT AV., Penn	Yk	17331	D4	3579
WISE AV., Red Lion	Yk	17356	D8	3377
WISE AV., Windsor Twp	Yk	17356	E9	3377
WISE RD., Chanceford	Yk	17309	H4	3482
WISE RD., Peach Bottom	Yk	17314	B4	3693
WISE RD., Peach Bottom	Yk	17314	C2	3693
WISE RD., York Twp	Yk	17403	D5	3375
WISHING WELL CT., North Codorus	Yk	17404	D9	3374
WISPERING WINDS LA., Hamilton	Ad	17301	C4	3371
WITMER RD., Conewago	Ad	17331	B4	3578
WITMER RD., Conewago	Yk	17404	D10	3060
WITMER RD., North York	Yk	17404	C4	3271
WITMER RD., Springettsbury	Yk	17402	H4	3272
WITMER RD., Springettsbury	Yk	17402	A5	3273
WITMER RD., Windsor Twp	Yk	17402	B6	3273
WITMER ST., Hanover	Yk	17331	D10	3475
WITNESS RD., Spring Garden	Yk	17403	C2	3375
WOGAN RD., York City	Yk	17404	A4	3271
WOLF RD., Chanceford	Yk	17322	H7	3482
WOLF RD., Reading	Ad	17316	D6	3266
WOLF RUN RD., Warrington	Yk	17019	E10	3057
WOLF ST., Glen Rock	Yk	17327	C3	3583
WOLFE RD., Hopewell	Yk	17349	D6	3584
WOLFE RD., Springfield	Yk	17360	A6	3480
WOLFGANG RD., Codorus	Yk	17329	G4	3581
WOLFGANG SCHOOL RD., Manheim	Yk	17327	H11	3581
WOLFGANG SCHOOL RD., Manheim	Yk	17327	F3	3685
WOLFS CHURCH RD., West Manchester	Yk	17404	G3	3373
WOLFS CHURCH RD., West Manchester	Yk	17404	A2	3374
WOLSEY AV., York Twp	Yk	17313	E9	3376
WOOD DR., Dover Twp	Yk	17315	D7	3269
WOOD DUCK LA., Lower Windsor	Yk	17368	A3	3275
WOOD ST., Carroll	Yk	17019	B3	3056
WOOD ST., York City	Yk	17404	A6	3271
WOOD ST., York Twp	Yk	17404	H6	3270
WOODBERRY RD., Spring Garden	Yk	17403	G10	3271
WOODBERRY RD., West Manchester	Yk	17404	A1	3374
WOODBERRY RD., West Manchester	Yk	17404	E2	3374
WOODBINE RD., Fawn	Yk	17302	B9	3588
WOODBINE RD., Fawn	Yk	17302	C7	3588
WOODBINE RD., Fawn	Yk	17321	B9	3588
WOODBINE RD., Fawn	Yk	17321	G2	3691
WOODBINE RD., Fawn	Yk	17321	A1	3692
WOODBINE RD., Lower Chanceford	Yk	17302	C10	3484
WOODBINE RD., Lower Chanceford	Yk	17302	D1	3588
WOODBINE RD., Peach Bottom	Yk	17302	C7	3588
WOODBINE RD., Peach Bottom	Yk	17302	F7	3588
WOODBINE RD., Peach Bottom	Yk	17302	A8	3589
WOODBINE RD., Peach Bottom	Yk	17314	C11	3589
WOODBRIDGE CT., Manchester Twp	Yk	17402	H7	3165
WOODBRIDGE DR., Fairview	Yk	17319	H2	2954
WOODBRIDGE DR., Fairview	Yk	17319	A2	2955
WOODBRIDGE RD., Springettsbury	Yk	17402	D7	3272
WOODBURNE RD., Fairview	Yk	17339	B5	2954
WOODCLIFF CIR., North Codorus	Yk	17360	D11	3374
WOODCREST CIR., Union	Ad	17340	B3	3682
WOODCREST DR., Cumberland	Ad	17325	H10	3470
WOODCREST DR., Cumberland	Ad	17325	A9	3471
WOODCREST DR., York Twp	Yk	17402	B3	3376
WOODED RUN DR., Carroll	Yk	17019	E3	3056
WOODLAKE CT., Shrewsbury Boro	Yk	17361	B7	3584
WOODLAND AV., Manchester Twp	Yk	17404	B2	3271
WOODLAND AV., Newberry	Yk	17345	E8	3061
WOODLAND AV., York Twp	Yk	17313	H8	3376
WOODLAND AV., York Twp	Yk	17356	A8	3377
WOODLAND CT., Spring Garden	Yk	17403	C1	3375
WOODLAND DELL RD., Peach Bottom	Yk	17314	C7	3590
WOODLAND DR., Carroll	Yk	17019	E2	3056
WOODLAND DR., East Manchester	Yk	17347	B11	3062
WOODLAND DR., Heidelberg	Yk	17331	H4	3475
WOODLAND DR., Jacobus	Yk	17407	D10	3375
WOODLAND DR., Shrewsbury Boro	Yk	17361	B5	3584
WOODLAND DR., Spring Garden	Yk	17403	D11	3271
WOODLAND DR., York Twp	Yk	17403	F1	3375
WOODLAND LA., Hellam	Yk	17368	C10	3169
WOODLAND PATH, Manheim	Yk	17329	D7	3581
WOODLAND RD., Heidelberg	Yk	17331	A3	3476
WOODLAND RD., Jackson	Yk	17331	H2	3476
WOODLAND RD., Jackson	Yk	17362	C11	3372
WOODLAND RD., Jackson	Yk	17362	A2	3476
WOODLAND RD., Paradise	Yk	17331	A2	3476
WOODLAND RD., Spring Garden	Yk	17403	C11	3271
WOODLAND RD., Spring Garden	Yk	17403	C1	3375
WOODLAND RD., Springfield	Yk	17327	B9	3480
WOODLAND RD., York Twp	Yk	17403	D6	3375
WOODLAND TR., Carroll Valley	Ad	17320	F2	3676
WOODLAND VIEW DR., Manchester Twp	Yk	17402	C11	3166
WOODLAND VIEW DR., Manchester Twp	Yk	17402	B1	3271
WOODLAWN AV., Fairview	Yk	17339	E6	2954
WOODLAWN AV., West Manchester	Yk	17404	D7	3270
WOODLAWN DR., North Hopewell	Yk	17322	C9	3481
WOODLAWN DR., Winterstown	Yk	17322	C9	3481
WOODLOT CIR., Windsor Twp	Yk	17366	G2	3377
WOODLYN TER., Springettsbury	Yk	17402	H4	3272
WOODMONT DR., Manchester Twp	Yk	17404	H1	3270
WOODMONT DR., Manchester Twp	Yk	17404	A1	3271
WOODMYERS RD. (PVT), York Twp	Yk	17403	D6	3375
WOODRIDGE DR., Berwick	Ad	17331	E5	3475
WOODRIDGE DR., Penn	Ad	17331	E5	3475
WOODRIDGE RD., Windsor Twp	Yk	17356	A5	3377
WOODS DR., Windsor Twp	Yk	17402	F6	3272
WOODS LA., York Twp	Yk	17403	G11	3271
WOODS RD., Berwick	Ad	17301	A10	3371
WOODS RD., East Hopewell	Yk	17363	F2	3585
WOODS RD., Hamilton	Ad	17301	G9	3370
WOODS RD., Hamilton	Ad	17301	A10	3371
WOODSDALE DR., Windsor Twp	Yk	17356	B9	3378
WOODSHEAD TER., Hellam	Yk	17406	B10	3169
WOODSHEAD TER., York Twp	Yk	17403	C7	3376
WOODSIDE AV., Penn	Yk	17331	E5	3579
WOODSIDE DR., York Twp	Yk	17402	H5	3375
WOODSIDE RD., Springettsbury	Yk	17402	F10	3166
WOODSIDE RD., Straban	Ad	17325	D5	3368
WOODSPRING DR., York Twp	Yk	17402	C11	3272
WOODSPRING LA., Windsor Twp	Yk	17402	F8	3272
WOODSTONE CT., Springettsbury	Yk	17402	H4	3272
WOODSTREAM DR., Springettsbury	Yk	17402	H2	3271
WOODSVIEW DR., Windsor Twp	Yk	17356	A8	3378
WOODSVIEW LA., Hellam	Yk	17406	G1	3273
WOODTHRUSH LA., York Twp	Yk	17403	G8	3375
WOODVALE RD., Peach Bottom	Yk	17302	H8	3588
WOODVIEW DR., Fawn	Yk	17321	B8	3588
WOODVIEW RD., Menallen	Ad	17307	H7	3260
WOODWARD DR., Fairview	Yk	17319	G5	2954
WOODWARD DR., Manchester Twp	Yk	17402	B1	3271
WOOL MILL RD., Manheim	Yk	17329	E10	3581
WOOL MILL RD., Manheim	Yk	17329	C1	3685

WOOLEN MILL RD. INTERSTATE RT. 83

WOOLEN MILL RD., Hopewell	Yk	17363	B3	3586
WOOLEN MILL RD., Hopewell	Yk	17363	D1	3690
WOOSTER DR., Dover Twp	Yk	17315	F4	3269
WORKINGER RD., Chanceford	Yk	17309	D3	3483
WORTH ST., West Manchester	Yk	17404	E8	3270
WORTH ST., West York	Yk	17404	E8	3270
WORTZ DR., Fairfield	Ad	17320	A5	3573
WREN DR., Shrewsbury Twp	Yk	17327	B5	3583
WREN RD., Dover Twp	Yk	17364	F9	3268
WREN RD., Jackson	Yk	17364	F9	3268
WREN TER., York Twp	Yk	17403	E5	3375
WREN TR., Carroll Valley	Ad	17320	H2	3676
WRIGHT AV., Cumberland	Ad	17325	B5	3575
WRIGHT RD., Latimore	Ad	17372	H7	3160
WRIGHT RD., Lower Chanceford	Yk	17314	A7	3589
WYATT CIR., Dover Twp	Yk	17315	E11	3164
WYATT CIR., Dover Twp	Yk	17315	E1	3269
WYATT LA., Windsor Twp	Yk	17356	B3	3377
WYE TR., Liberty	Ad	17320	E5	3573
WYNDAMERE RD., Fairview	Yk	17339	F5	2954
WYNDFIELD DR., West Manheim	Yk	17331	B4	3684
WYNDHAM DR. N., Spring Garden	Yk	17403	B11	3271
WYNDHAM DR. N., Spring Garden	Yk	17403	B1	3375
WYNDHAM DR. S., Spring Garden	Yk	17403	C2	3375
WYNDHAM DR., Spring Garden	Yk	17403	B11	3271
WYNDHAM LA., Glen Rock	Yk	17327	A4	3583
WYNDHURST CT., West Manchester	Yk	17404	C6	3270
WYNDSONG DR., Spring Garden	Yk	17403	C3	3375
WYNDSONG DR., York Twp	Yk	17403	C3	3375
WYNDWARD CT., Spring Garden	Yk	17403	C3	3375
WYNGATE DR., York Twp	Yk	17403	B7	3376
WYNGATE RD., Dover Twp	Yk	17315	E4	3269
WYNNEFIELD DR., Dover Twp	Yk	17315	B3	3269
WYNSHIRE LA., Windsor Twp	Yk	17356	H10	3272
WYNTER BROOKE DR., York Twp	Yk	17403	E2	3375
WYNTRE BROOKE DR. N., York Twp	Yk	17403	E2	3375
WYNTRE BROOKE DR. S., York Twp	Yk	17403	E2	3375
WYNTRE BROOKE DR. S.E., York Twp	Yk	17403	E2	3375
WYNWOOD CT., Springettsbury	Yk	17402	D6	3272
WYNWOOD RD., Springettsbury	Yk	17402	D5	3272

Y

YALE ST., Spring Garden	Yk	17403	G5	3271
YALE ST., Spring Garden	Yk	17403	G7	3271
YANKEE LA., Hamiltonban	Ad	17320	E2	3572
YANKEE MOUNTAIN LA., Hamiltonban	Ad	17320	C8	3572
YARSHIRE RD., Manchester Twp	Yk	17404	G9	3165
YATES FORD RD., Fairview	Yk	17319	A2	2955
YEAGER RD., Warrington	Yk	17019	H11	3057
YEAGER RD., Warrington	Yk	17365	H11	3057
YEAGER RD., Warrington	Yk	17365	A11	3058
YELLOW BREECHES DR., Fairview	Yk	17011	F5	2848
YELLOW CHURCH RD., Springfield	Yk	17360	G4	3478
YELLOW CHURCH RD., Springfield	Yk	17360	B7	3479
YELLOW HILL RD., Butler	Ad	17307	F11	3262
YELLOW HILL RD., Butler	Ad	17307	F1	3366
YELLOW HILL RD., Menallen	Ad	17307	B10	3262
YELLOWBIRD TR., Carroll Valley	Ad	17320	B4	3677
YELLOWSTONE LA., Hopewell	Yk	17363	F9	3585
YINGLING DR., Heidelberg	Yk	17362	B11	3476
YINGLING RD., Mount Joy	Ad	17325	F3	3679
YINGLING RD., Mount Joy	Ad	17340	F11	3575
YINGLING RD., Mount Joy	Ad	17340	F3	3679
YMCA DR., Fairview	Yk	17070	H9	2848
YMCA DR., Fairview	Yk	17070	A9	2849
YOCUMTOWN RD., Newberry	Yk	17319	H7	2954
YOCUMTOWN RD., Newberry	Yk	17319	A6	2955
YOE DR., Yoe	Yk	17356	F4	3376
YOE DR., York Twp	Yk	17356	F4	3376
YORK AV., Spring Grove	Yk	17362	B11	3373
YORK CROSSING DR., West Manchester	Yk	17404	E6	3270
YORK DR., Oxford	Ad	17350	E2	3474
YORK HAVEN RD., Newberry	Yk	17319	D11	2955
YORK HAVEN RD., Newberry	Yk	17345	E5	3061
YORK HAVEN RD., Newberry	Yk	17370	D11	2955
YORK HAVEN RD., Newberry	Yk	17370	B2	3061
YORK HILL RD., Newberry	Yk	17319	H7	2954
YORK RD. N., Monaghan	Yk	17019	D5	2952
YORK RD. N., Monaghan	Yk	17055	D5	2952
YORK RD. S., Monaghan	Yk	17019	E8	2952
YORK RD., Berwick	Ad	17350	C2	3474
YORK RD., Carroll	Yk	17019	A9	2951
YORK RD., Carroll	Yk	17019	D1	3056
YORK RD., Fairview	Yk	17070	B7	2849
YORK RD., Gettysburg	Ad	17325	C8	3471
YORK RD., Hamilton	Ad	17301	G11	3370
YORK RD., Hamilton	Ad	17350	C2	3474
YORK RD., Heidelberg	Yk	17331	H11	3475
YORK RD., Heidelberg	Yk	17331	A9	3476
YORK RD., Heidelberg	Yk	17362	D7	3476
YORK RD., Jacobus	Yk	17407	F10	3375
YORK RD., Jefferson	Yk	17362	E10	3477
YORK RD., Monaghan	Yk	17019	F1	3057
YORK RD., Mount Pleasant	Ad	17350	B3	3473
YORK RD., New Oxford	Ad	17350	B3	3473
YORK RD., Newberry	Yk	17315	F4	3059
YORK RD., Newberry	Yk	17370	G11	2954
YORK RD., Newberry	Yk	17370	F4	3059
YORK RD., North Codorus	Yk	17362	F4	3476
YORK RD., North Codorus	Yk	17362	A2	3477
YORK RD., Oxford	Ad	17350	B3	3473
YORK RD., Oxford	Ad	17350	C2	3474
YORK RD., Straban	Ad	17325	D8	3471
YORK RD., Straban	Ad	17325	B3	3473
YORK RD., Straban	Ad	17350	B3	3473
YORK RD., Warrington	Yk	17019	F1	3057
YORK ST. E., Biglerville	Ad	17307	A2	3367
YORK ST. E., Dillsburg	Yk	17019	F3	3056
YORK ST. W., Biglerville	Ad	17307	H2	3366
YORK ST. W., Biglerville	Ad	17307	A3	3367
YORK ST. W., Dillsburg	Yk	17019	F3	3056
YORK ST., East Manchester	Yk	17345	C7	3061
YORK ST., East Manchester	Yk	17345	D2	3166
YORK ST., East Manchester	Yk	17347	B11	3062
YORK ST., Glen Rock	Yk	17327	C3	3583
YORK ST., Goldsboro	Yk	17319	H6	2955
YORK ST., Goldsboro	Yk	17319	A7	2956
YORK ST., Hanover	Yk	17331	C3	3579
YORK ST., Manchester Boro	Yk	17345	D2	3166
YORK ST., Penn	Yk	17331	F3	3579
YORK ST., Straban	Ad	17325	A5	3472
YORK ST., Straban	Ad	17325	E4	3472
YORK ST., Wellsville	Yk	17365	H3	3162
YORK ST., Wellsville	Yk	17365	A2	3163
YORK ST., West Manchester	Yk	17404	C4	3270
YORK ST., York City	Yk	17403	D6	3271
YORK ST., York City	Yk	17403	E6	3271
YORKANA RD., Hellam	Yk	17406	C1	3273
YORKANA RD., Lower Windsor	Yk	17406	E3	3273
YORKLYN GATE, Springettsbury	Yk	17402	F2	3272
YORKSHIRE TER., Spring Garden	Yk	17403	C11	3271
YORKTOWNE CT., Littlestown	Ad	17340	E3	3681
YORKTOWNE DR., West Manchester	Yk	17404	E4	3270
YOUNG AL., New Freedom	Yk	17349	G3	3687
YOUNG CIR., Hanover	Yk	17331	A2	3579
YOUNG RD., Codorus	Yk	17327	G11	3582
YOUNGS RD., Penn	Yk	17331	D6	3475
YVONNE TR., Carroll Valley	Ad	17320	E1	3676

Z

ZACHARY DR., West Manheim	Yk	17331	G8	3579
ZARFOSS DR. N., West Manchester	Yk	17404	C11	3270
ZEIGLER CHURCH RD., North Codorus	Yk	17360	A5	3478
ZEIGLER CHURCH RD., North Codorus	Yk	17362	F6	3477
ZEIGLER CHURCH RD., North Codorus	Yk	17362	C4	3478
ZEIGLER MILL RD., Butler	Ad	17307	D5	3366
ZEIGLER MILL RD., Butler	Ad	17325	G6	3366
ZEIGLER MILL RD., Butler	Ad	17325	A5	3367
ZEIGLER RD., Codorus	Yk	17327	D3	3686
ZEIGLER RD., Warrington	Yk	17315	C4	3163
ZEIGLER RD., Warrington	Yk	17365	H3	3162
ZEIGLER RD., Warrington	Yk	17365	A3	3163
ZEIGLER SCHOOL RD., Hopewell	Yk	17363	B10	3585
ZEIGLER ST., Goldsboro	Yk	17319	G7	2955
ZEIGLER ST., Goldsboro	Yk	17319	A6	2956
ZEIGLER ST., York Haven	Yk	17370	E3	3061
ZEPP RD., Straban	Ad	17325	C8	3368
ZIMMERMAN DR., West Manchester	Yk	17404	H2	3373
ZIMMERMAN RD., Windsor Twp	Yk	17356	A11	3378
ZIMMY'S DR., Conewago	Yk	17402	F9	3060
ZINN DR., Newberry	Yk	17339	B10	2954
ZINNS QUARRY RD., West Manchester	Yk	17404	H10	3270
ZINNS QUARRY RD., West Manchester	Yk	17404	A10	3271
ZION CHURCH RD., Windsor Twp	Yk	17356	F9	3377
ZION CHURCH RD., Windsor Twp	Yk	17356	D11	3377
ZION CHURCH RD., Windsor Twp	Yk	17356	D1	3481
ZIONS VIEW RD., East Manchester	Yk	17345	A1	3166
ZOAR AV., Manchester Twp	Yk	17404	B3	3271
ZOO RD., Hamiltonban	Ad	17320	F7	3572
ZUMBRUM RD., Manheim	Yk	17329	G10	3580

NUMBERED STREETS

1ST AV., Fairfield	Ad	17320	B5	3573
1ST AV., Goldsboro	Yk	17319	A6	2956
1ST AV., Newberry	Yk	17345	E7	3061
1ST AV., Red Lion	Yk	17356	B7	3377
1ST AV., Spring Garden	Yk	17403	G6	3271
1ST AV., Spring Grove	Yk	17362	B11	3373
1ST AV., Springettsbury	Yk	17402	D5	3272
1ST AV., Winterstown	Yk	17322	A9	3481
1ST AV. E., Windsor Boro	Yk	17366	G5	3377
1ST AV. W., Windsor Boro	Yk	17366	E5	3377
1ST ST., Fairview	Yk	17070	D5	2849
1ST ST., Hamiltonban	Ad	17353	C5	3469
1ST ST., Jackson	Yk	17364	C1	3373
1ST ST., Menallen	Ad	17304	D4	3263
1ST ST., Windsor Twp	Yk	17366	E3	3377
2ND AV., Fairfield	Ad	17320	A4	3573
2ND AV., Goldsboro	Yk	17319	H7	2955
2ND AV., Hanover	Yk	17331	B3	3579
2ND AV., Newberry	Yk	17345	D7	3061
2ND AV., North York	Yk	17404	C6	3271
2ND AV., Spring Garden	Yk	17403	G6	3271
2ND AV., Spring Grove	Yk	17362	B11	3373
2ND AV., Springettsbury	Yk	17402	H6	3271
2ND AV., Springettsbury	Yk	17402	A6	3272
2ND ST., East Manchester	Yk	17347	B10	3062
2ND ST., Fairview	Yk	17070	C5	2849
2ND ST., Hamiltonban	Ad	17353	B6	3469
2ND ST., Jackson	Yk	17364	C1	3373
2ND ST., Lewisberry	Yk	17339	B10	2954
2ND ST., Mount Wolf	Yk	17347	F11	3061
2ND ST., Mount Wolf	Yk	17347	F1	3166
2ND ST., Windsor Twp	Yk	17366	E3	3377
2ND ST., York Haven	Yk	17370	E3	3061
2ND ST., York Spring	Ad	17372	A10	3160
2ND ST., York Spring	Ad	17372	B11	3160
2ND ST. N., Dillsburg	Yk	17019	D2	3056
2ND ST. N., McSherrystown	Ad	17344	E2	3578
2ND ST. N., New Freedom	Yk	17349	G11	3583
2ND ST. N., New Freedom	Yk	17349	G2	3687
2ND ST. N., Wrightsville	Yk	17368	D6	3169
2ND ST. S., Dillsburg	Yk	17019	D3	3056
2ND ST. S., McSherrystown	Ad	17344	F2	3578
2ND ST. S., Wrightsville	Yk	17368	E7	3169
3RD AV., Goldsboro	Yk	17319	H7	2955
3RD AV., Newberry	Yk	17345	D7	3061
3RD AV., North York	Yk	17404	C5	3271
3RD AV., Spring Garden	Yk	17403	G6	3271
3RD AV., Spring Grove	Yk	17362	B11	3373
3RD AV., Springettsbury	Yk	17402	H6	3271
3RD AV., Springettsbury	Yk	17402	A6	3272
3RD AV., Springettsbury	Yk	17402	C5	3272
3RD AV. N., Fairfield	Ad	17320	B5	3573
3RD AV. S., Fairfield	Ad	17320	B5	3573
3RD ST, East Berlin	Ad	17316	C1	3371
3RD ST., Biglerville	Ad	17307	A2	3367
3RD ST., Conewago	Ad	17331	H2	3578
3RD ST., Conewago	Ad	17344	E1	3578
3RD ST., East Berlin	Ad	17316	C11	3267
3RD ST., East Manchester	Yk	17347	C11	3062
3RD ST., Gettysburg	Ad	17325	D8	3471
3RD ST., Hamiltonban	Ad	17353	B6	3469
3RD ST., Hanover	Yk	17331	A2	3579
3RD ST., Jackson	Yk	17364	C11	3269
3RD ST., Jackson	Yk	17364	C1	3373
3RD ST., Lewisberry	Yk	17339	B9	2954
3RD ST., Mount Wolf	Yk	17347	F11	3061
3RD ST., Mount Wolf	Yk	17347	F1	3166
3RD ST., Windsor Twp	Yk	17366	E3	3377
3RD ST., York Haven	Yk	17370	E3	3061
3RD ST. E., Yoe	Yk	17313	G6	3376
3RD ST. N., McSherrystown	Ad	17344	F2	3578
3RD ST. N., New Freedom	Yk	17349	G2	3687
3RD ST. N., Wrightsville	Yk	17368	D6	3169
3RD ST. S., McSherrystown	Ad	17344	F2	3578
3RD ST. S., New Freedom	Yk	17349	F3	3687
3RD ST. S., Wrightsville	Yk	17368	D7	3169
4TH AV., East Berlin	Ad	17316	B11	3267
4TH AV., Newberry	Yk	17345	D7	3061
4TH AV., North York	Yk	17404	C5	3271
4TH AV., Spring Garden	Yk	17403	G6	3271
4TH AV. N., Fairfield	Ad	17320	A5	3573
4TH ST., Biglerville	Ad	17307	B2	3367
4TH ST., East Berlin	Ad	17316	C11	3267
4TH ST., East Manchester	Yk	17347	B11	3062
4TH ST., Gettysburg	Ad	17325	D8	3471
4TH ST., Hanover	Yk	17331	A2	3579
4TH ST., Jackson	Yk	17364	C11	3269
4TH ST., Jackson	Yk	17364	C1	3373
4TH ST., Lewisberry	Yk	17339	B9	2954
4TH ST., Mount Wolf	Yk	17347	F11	3061
4TH ST., Mount Wolf	Yk	17347	F1	3166
4TH ST., New Freedom	Yk	17349	F3	3687
4TH ST. E., Dallastown	Yk	17313	G6	3376
4TH ST. E., Yoe	Yk	17313	G6	3376
4TH ST. N., McSherrystown	Ad	17344	F2	3578
4TH ST. N., Wrightsville	Yk	17368	D7	3169
4TH ST. S., McSherrystown	Ad	17344	F2	3578
4TH ST. S., McSherrystown	Ad	17331	F2	3578
4TH ST. S., Wrightsville	Yk	17368	D7	3169
4TH ST. W., Dallastown	Yk	17313	G6	3376
4TH ST. W., Yoe	Yk	17313	F6	3376
4TH ST. W., York	Yk	17313	F6	3376
5TH AV., East Berlin	Ad	17316	B11	3267
5TH AV., North York	Yk	17404	C5	3271
5TH AV., Spring Garden	Yk	17403	G6	3271
5TH AV., Springettsbury	Yk	17402	H6	3271
5TH AV., Springettsbury	Yk	17402	A6	3272
5TH AV., Springettsbury	Yk	17402	C5	3272
5TH AV. N., Fairfield	Ad	17320	A5	3573
5TH ST., Biglerville	Ad	17307	B2	3367
5TH ST., East Berlin	Ad	17316	B11	3267
5TH ST., East Manchester	Yk	17347	B11	3062
5TH ST., Gettysburg	Ad	17325	D8	3471
5TH ST., Hanover	Yk	17331	A1	3579
5TH ST., Jackson	Yk	17364	C1	3373
5TH ST., Lewisberry	Yk	17339	C9	2954
5TH ST., Mount Wolf	Yk	17347	G11	3061
5TH ST., Mount Wolf	Yk	17347	F1	3166
5TH ST., Newberry	Yk	17339	C9	2954
5TH ST. N., McSherrystown	Ad	17344	F1	3578
5TH ST. N., Wrightsville	Yk	17368	D7	3169
5TH ST. S., McSherrystown	Ad	17344	G2	3578
5TH ST. S., McSherrystown	Ad	17331	G2	3578
6TH AV., East Berlin	Ad	17316	B11	3267
6TH AV., Spring Garden	Yk	17403	G7	3271
6TH AV. E., North York	Yk	17404	C4	3271
6TH AV. N., Fairfield	Ad	17320	A5	3573
6TH AV. W., North York	Yk	17404	B5	3271
6TH ST., East Berlin	Ad	17316	B11	3267
6TH ST., Gettysburg	Ad	17325	D8	3471
6TH ST., Jackson	Yk	17364	C1	3373
6TH ST., Mount Wolf	Yk	17347	G11	3061
6TH ST., Mount Wolf	Yk	17347	F1	3166
6TH ST. N., McSherrystown	Ad	17344	G1	3578
6TH ST. N., Wrightsville	Yk	17368	D7	3169
6TH ST. S., Hellam	Yk	17368	D8	3169
6TH ST. S., McSherrystown	Ad	17331	G2	3578
6TH ST. S., McSherrystown	Ad	17344	G2	3578
6TH ST. S., Wrightsville	Yk	17368	D8	3169
7TH AV., Fairfield	Ad	17320	B6	3573
7TH AV., Spring Garden	Yk	17403	H7	3271
7TH AV., Springettsbury	Yk	17402	A7	3272
7TH AV. E., North York	Yk	17404	C4	3271
7TH AV. W., North York	Yk	17404	B4	3271
7TH ST., Jackson	Yk	17364	C1	3373
7TH ST., Mount Wolf	Yk	17347	F1	3166
7TH ST., Wrightsville	Yk	17368	C7	3169
8TH AV. E., North York	Yk	17404	C4	3271
8TH AV. N., Fairfield	Ad	17320	A5	3573
8TH AV. W., North York	Yk	17404	B4	3271
8TH ST., Mount Wolf	Yk	17347	G1	3166
8TH ST., Wrightsville	Yk	17368	C7	3169
9TH AV., Manchester	Yk	17404	B4	3271
9TH AV., Springettsbury	Yk	17402	A7	3272
9TH AV. E., North York	Yk	17404	C4	3271
9TH AV. W., North York	Yk	17404	B4	3271
9TH ST., Wrightsville	Yk	17368	C7	3169
10TH AV., Manchester	Yk	17402	C3	3271
10TH AV., Springettsbury	Yk	17402	F4	3271
10TH AV. E., North York	Yk	17404	C4	3271
10TH AV. W., North York	Yk	17404	B4	3271
11TH AV., Manchester	Yk	17404	B3	3271
11TH AV., North York	Yk	17404	C3	3271
11TH AV., Springettsbury	Yk	17402	F4	3271
12TH PL., Felton	Yk	17322	H4	3481
700 RD., Hamilton	Ad	17019	A9	3370
700 RD., Oxford	Ad	17350	A11	3370
700 RD., Oxford	Ad	17350	H1	3473
EAST 1ST AV., Windsor Boro	Yk	17366	G5	3377
EAST 4TH ST., Dallastown	Yk	17313	G6	3376
EAST 4TH ST., Yoe	Yk	17313	G6	3376
EAST 6TH AV., North York	Yk	17404	C4	3271
EAST 7TH AV., North York	Yk	17404	C4	3271
EAST 8TH AV., North York	Yk	17404	C4	3271
EAST 9TH AV., North York	Yk	17404	C4	3271
EAST 10TH AV., North York	Yk	17404	C4	3271
NORTH 2ND ST., Dillsburg	Yk	17019	D2	3056
NORTH 2ND ST., McSherrystown	Ad	17344	E2	3578
NORTH 2ND ST., New Freedom	Yk	17349	G11	3583
NORTH 2ND ST., New Freedom	Yk	17349	G2	3687
NORTH 2ND ST., Wrightsville	Yk	17368	D6	3169
NORTH 3RD AV., Fairfield	Ad	17320	B5	3573
NORTH 3RD ST., New Freedom	Yk	17349	G2	3687
NORTH 3RD ST., Wrightsville	Yk	17368	D6	3169
NORTH 3RD. ST., McSherrystown	Ad	17344	F2	3578
NORTH 4TH AV., Fairfield	Ad	17320	A5	3573
NORTH 4TH ST., McSherrystown	Ad	17344	F2	3578
NORTH 4TH ST., Wrightsville	Yk	17368	D7	3169
NORTH 5TH AV., Fairfield	Ad	17320	A5	3573
NORTH 5TH ST., McSherrystown	Ad	17344	F1	3578
NORTH 5TH ST., Wrightsville	Yk	17368	D7	3169
NORTH 6TH AV., Fairfield	Ad	17320	A5	3573
NORTH 6TH ST., McSherrystown	Ad	17344	G1	3578
NORTH 6TH ST., Wrightsville	Yk	17368	D7	3169
NORTH 8TH AV., Fairfield	Ad	17320	A5	3573
SOUTH 2ND ST., Dillsburg	Yk	17019	D3	3056
SOUTH 2ND ST., McSherrystown	Ad	17344	F2	3578
SOUTH 2ND ST., Wrightsville	Yk	17368	E7	3169
SOUTH 3RD AV., Fairfield	Ad	17320	B5	3573
SOUTH 3RD ST., McSherrystown	Ad	17344	F2	3578
SOUTH 3RD ST., New Freedom	Yk	17349	F3	3687
SOUTH 3RD ST., Wrightsville	Yk	17368	D7	3169
SOUTH 4TH ST., McSherrystown	Ad	17344	F2	3578
SOUTH 4TH ST., McSherrystown	Ad	17331	F2	3578
SOUTH 4TH ST., Wrightsville	Yk	17368	D7	3169
SOUTH 5TH ST., McSherrystown	Ad	17344	G2	3578
SOUTH 5TH ST., McSherrystown	Ad	17331	G2	3578
SOUTH 6TH ST., Hellam	Yk	17368	D8	3169
SOUTH 6TH ST., McSherrystown	Ad	17331	G2	3578
SOUTH 6TH ST., McSherrystown	Ad	17344	G2	3578
SOUTH 6TH ST., Wrightsville	Yk	17368	D8	3169
WEST 1ST AV., Windsor Boro	Yk	17366	E5	3377
WEST 3RD ST., Yoe	Yk	17313	G6	3376
WEST 4TH ST., Dallastown	Yk	17313	G6	3376
WEST 4TH ST., Yoe	Yk	17313	F6	3376
WEST 4TH ST., York	Yk	17313	F6	3376
WEST 6TH AV., North York	Yk	17404	B5	3271
WEST 7TH AV., North York	Yk	17404	B4	3271
WEST 8TH AV., North York	Yk	17404	B4	3271
WEST 9TH AV., North York	Yk	17404	B4	3271
WEST 10TH AV., North York	Yk	17404	B4	3271

INTERSTATES

INTERSTATE RT. 30, Jackson	Yk	17364	B2	3373
INTERSTATE RT. 30, Jackson	Yk	17404	E2	3373
INTERSTATE RT. 30, West Manchester	Yk	17404	H2	3373
INTERSTATE RT. 30, West Manchester	Yk	17404	B1	3374
INTERSTATE RT. 76, Fairview	Yk	17070	G8	2848
INTERSTATE RT. 76, Fairview	Yk	17070	E9	2849
INTERSTATE RT. 76, Fairview	Yk	17070	A10	2850
INTERSTATE RT. 76, Fairview	Yk	17070	A10	2850
INTERSTATE RT. 83, Conewago	Yk	17345	D3	3060
INTERSTATE RT. 83, Conewago	Yk	17402	D3	3060
INTERSTATE RT. 83, East Manchester	Yk	17402	H1	3165
INTERSTATE RT. 83, Fairview	Yk	17070	C10	2849
INTERSTATE RT. 83, Fairview	Yk	17070	E2	2954
INTERSTATE RT. 83, Fairview	Yk	17339	E2	2954
INTERSTATE RT. 83, Manchester Twp	Yk	17402	A6	3166
INTERSTATE RT. 83, Manchester Twp	Yk	17404	B11	3166
INTERSTATE RT. 83, Manchester Twp	Yk	17402	B1	3271
INTERSTATE RT. 83, Manchester Twp	Yk	17402	B1	3271
INTERSTATE RT. 83, Manchester Twp	Yk	17404	B1	3271
INTERSTATE RT. 83, Manchester Twp	Yk	17404	B1	3271
INTERSTATE RT. 83, Newberry	Yk	17319	E2	2954
INTERSTATE RT. 83, Newberry	Yk	17319	B10	2955
INTERSTATE RT. 83, Newberry	Yk	17370	D3	3060
INTERSTATE RT. 83, North York	Yk	17402	B1	3271
INTERSTATE RT. 83, North York	Yk	17402	B1	3271
INTERSTATE RT. 83, North York	Yk	17404	B1	3271
INTERSTATE RT. 83, North York	Yk	17404	B1	3271
INTERSTATE RT. 83, Shrewsbury Boro	Yk	17361	C9	3584
INTERSTATE RT. 83, Shrewsbury Twp	Yk	17327	A10	3480
INTERSTATE RT. 83, Shrewsbury Twp	Yk	17327	B2	3584
INTERSTATE RT. 83, Shrewsbury Twp	Yk	17349	B2	3584
INTERSTATE RT. 83, Shrewsbury Twp	Yk	17349	C9	3584
INTERSTATE RT. 83, Shrewsbury Twp	Yk	17361	C9	3584
INTERSTATE RT. 83, Spring Garden	Yk	17402	G4	3271
INTERSTATE RT. 83, Spring Garden	Yk	17403	G4	3271
INTERSTATE RT. 83, Spring Garden	Yk	17403	B10	3272
INTERSTATE RT. 83, Springettsbury	Yk	17402	G4	3271
INTERSTATE RT. 83, Springettsbury	Yk	17402	G4	3271

INTERSTATE RT. 83, Springettsbury	Yk	17402	B10	3272
INTERSTATE RT. 83, Springfield	Yk	17403	G8	3375
INTERSTATE RT. 83, Springfield	Yk	17360	H5	3479
INTERSTATE RT. 83, Springfield	Yk	17403	G1	3479
INTERSTATE RT. 83, Springfield	Yk	17327	A8	3480
INTERSTATE RT. 83, York Twp	Yk	17402	B10	3272
INTERSTATE RT. 83, York Twp	Yk	17403	B10	3272
INTERSTATE RT. 83, York Twp	Yk	17403	A1	3376
INTERSTATE RT. 83, York Twp	Yk	17402	H2	3375
INTERSTATE RT. 83, York Twp	Yk	17403	G8	3375
INTERSTATE RT. 83 BUS RT., Manchester Twp	Yk	17404	B4	3271
INTERSTATE RT. 83 BUS RT., North York	Yk	17404	B4	3271
INTERSTATE RT. 83 BUS RT., Spring Garden	Yk	17403	E11	3271
INTERSTATE RT. 83 BUS RT., Spring Garden	Yk	17403	F2	3375
INTERSTATE RT. 83 BUS RT., York City	Yk	17401	C6	3271
INTERSTATE RT. 83 BUS RT., York City	Yk	17403	C6	3271
INTERSTATE RT. 83 BUS RT., York City	Yk	17404	C6	3271
INTERSTATE RT. 83 BUS RT., York Twp	Yk	17403	F2	3375

STATE ROUTES

PA STATE RT. 16, Carroll Valley	Ad	17320	G3	3676
PA STATE RT. 16, Carroll Valley	Ad	17320	A3	3677
PA STATE RT. 16, Hamiltonban	Ad	17320	G3	3675
PA STATE RT. 16, Hamiltonban	Ad	17320	B2	3676
PA STATE RT. 16, Liberty	Ad	17320	G3	3675
PA STATE RT. 16, Liberty	Ad	17320	G3	3676
PA STATE RT. 16, Liberty	Ad	17320	C5	3677
PA STATE RT. 24, East Manchester	Yk	17347	G5	3166
PA STATE RT. 24, Hopewell	Yk	17363	E8	3585
PA STATE RT. 24, Hopewell	Yk	17363	G4	3689
PA STATE RT. 24, Hopewell	Yk	17363	A5	3690
PA STATE RT. 24, Mount Wolf	Yk	17347	F11	3061
PA STATE RT. 24, Mount Wolf	Yk	17347	G1	3166
PA STATE RT. 24, North Hopewell	Yk	17322	B9	3481
PA STATE RT. 24, North Hopewell	Yk	17356	A3	3481
PA STATE RT. 24, North Hopewell	Yk	17363	D2	3585
PA STATE RT. 24, Red Lion	Yk	17356	D8	3377
PA STATE RT. 24, Springettsbury	Yk	17402	H9	3166
PA STATE RT. 24, Springettsbury	Yk	17402	A10	3167
PA STATE RT. 24, Springettsbury	Yk	17402	B1	3272
PA STATE RT. 24, Stewartstown	Yk	17363	E8	3585
PA STATE RT. 24, Stewartstown	Yk	17363	E1	3689
PA STATE RT. 24, Windsor Twp	Yk	17356	F11	3272
PA STATE RT. 24, Windsor Twp	Yk	17402	D7	3272
PA STATE RT. 24, Windsor Twp	Yk	17356	H5	3376
PA STATE RT. 24, Windsor Twp	Yk	17356	A5	3377
PA STATE RT. 24, Windsor Twp	Yk	17356	C10	3377
PA STATE RT. 24, Winterstown	Yk	17356	A3	3481
PA STATE RT. 24, York Twp	Yk	17356	F11	3272
PA STATE RT. 24, York Twp	Yk	17402	D7	3272
PA STATE RT. 24, York Twp	Yk	17356	F2	3376
PA STATE RT. 24, York Twp	Yk	17356	A5	3377
PA STATE RT. 24, York Twp	Yk	17356	C10	3377
PA STATE RT. 24, York Twp	Yk	17356	A3	3481
PA STATE RT. 34, Biglerville	Ad	17307	A1	3367
PA STATE RT. 34, Butler	Ad	17307	A11	3263
PA STATE RT. 34, Butler	Ad	17325	A5	3367
PA STATE RT. 34, Cumberland	Ad	17325	A10	3367
PA STATE RT. 34, Cumberland	Ad	17325	B4	3471
PA STATE RT. 34, Gettysburg	Ad	17325	B4	3471
PA STATE RT. 34, Huntington	Ad	17324	F10	3158
PA STATE RT. 34, Menallen	Ad	17324	D1	3263
PA STATE RT. 34, Menallen	Ad	17304	C3	3263
PA STATE RT. 34, Tyrone	Ad	17324	F10	3158
PA STATE RT. 74, Carroll	Yk	17019	A8	2951
PA STATE RT. 74, Carroll	Yk	17019	D1	3056
PA STATE RT. 74, Carroll	Yk	17019	G8	3056
PA STATE RT. 74, Chanceford	Yk	17322	G11	3378
PA STATE RT. 74, Chanceford	Yk	17322	H1	3482
PA STATE RT. 74, Chanceford	Yk	17302	G4	3483
PA STATE RT. 74, Chanceford	Yk	17309	B1	3483
PA STATE RT. 74, Chanceford	Yk	17322	B1	3483
PA STATE RT. 74, Dallastown	Yk	17313	H7	3376
PA STATE RT. 74, Dillsburg	Yk	17019	D4	3056
PA STATE RT. 74, Dover	Yk	17315	F4	3163
PA STATE RT. 74, Dover	Yk	17315	A8	3164
PA STATE RT. 74, Dover	Yk	17315	E2	3269
PA STATE RT. 74, Dover	Yk	17404	A4	3270
PA STATE RT. 74, Lower Chanceford	Yk	17302	A2	3589
PA STATE RT. 74, Lower Chanceford	Yk	17314	D7	3589
PA STATE RT. 74, Lower Chanceford	Yk	17309	B5	3484
PA STATE RT. 74, Lower Chanceford	Yk	17302	F10	3486
PA STATE RT. 74, Lower Chanceford	Yk	17302	H1	3588
PA STATE RT. 74, Peach Bottom	Yk	17314	F11	3589
PA STATE RT. 74, Peach Bottom	Yk	17314	F2	3693
PA STATE RT. 74, Red Lion	Yk	17356	A8	3377
PA STATE RT. 74, Spring Garden	Yk	17403	E10	3271
PA STATE RT. 74, Warrington	Yk	17019	D4	3056
PA STATE RT. 74, Warrington	Yk	17019	A11	3057
PA STATE RT. 74, Warrington	Yk	17365	F2	3162
PA STATE RT. 74, Warrington	Yk	17365	B1	3163
PA STATE RT. 74, Washington	Yk	17365	B2	3162
PA STATE RT. 74, West Manchester	Yk	17404	D5	3270
PA STATE RT. 74, Windsor Twp	Yk	17356	G7	3377
PA STATE RT. 74, Windsor Twp	Yk	17356	B9	3378
PA STATE RT. 74, York City	Yk	17401	A8	3271
PA STATE RT. 74, York City	Yk	17404	A8	3271
PA STATE RT. 74, York Twp	Yk	17404	H8	3270
PA STATE RT. 74, York Twp	Yk	17313	D6	3376
PA STATE RT. 74, York Twp	Yk	17402	A3	3376
PA STATE RT. 74, York Twp	Yk	17403	A3	3376
PA STATE RT. 74, York Twp	Yk	17313	A8	3377
PA STATE RT. 74, York Twp	Yk	17403	E10	3271
PA STATE RT. 74, York Twp	Yk	17402	H1	3375
PA STATE RT. 74, York Twp	Yk	17403	H1	3375
PA STATE RT. 94, Berwick	Ad	17350	F3	3474
PA STATE RT. 94, Berwick	Ad	17331	H7	3474
PA STATE RT. 94, Conewago	Ad	17331	H7	3474
PA STATE RT. 94, Hamilton	Ad	17350	D9	3370
PA STATE RT. 94, Hamilton	Ad	17350	F3	3474
PA STATE RT. 94, Hanover	Yk	17331	A9	3475
PA STATE RT. 94, Hanover	Yk	17331	B2	3579
PA STATE RT. 94, Huntington	Ad	17372	H7	3159
PA STATE RT. 94, Huntington	Ad	17372	E3	3265
PA STATE RT. 94, Latimore	Ad	17372	E2	3159
PA STATE RT. 94, Latimore	Ad	17324	E2	3159
PA STATE RT. 94, Oxford	Ad	17350	F3	3474
PA STATE RT. 94, Oxford	Ad	17331	H7	3474
PA STATE RT. 94, Penn	Yk	17331	D4	3579
PA STATE RT. 94, Reading	Ad	17316	G8	3265
PA STATE RT. 94, Reading	Ad	17350	A3	3370
PA STATE RT. 94, West Manheim	Yk	17331	F10	3579
PA STATE RT. 94, West Manheim	Yk	17331	G2	3683
PA STATE RT. 94, West Manheim	Yk	17331	C5	3684
PA STATE RT. 97, Germany	Ad	17340	B10	3577
PA STATE RT. 97, Germany	Ad	17340	E1	3681
PA STATE RT. 97, Littlestown	Ad	17340	B10	3577
PA STATE RT. 97, Littlestown	Ad	17340	E1	3681
PA STATE RT. 97, Mount Joy	Ad	17325	H4	3575
PA STATE RT. 97, Mount Joy	Ad	17325	B6	3576
PA STATE RT. 97, Mount Joy	Ad	17340	G9	3576
PA STATE RT. 97, Union	Ad	17340	B10	3577
PA STATE RT. 114, Fairview	Yk	17070	H9	2848
PA STATE RT. 114, Fairview	Yk	17070	B7	2849
PA STATE RT. 114, Fairview	Yk	17070	G1	2953
PA STATE RT. 114, Fairview	Yk	17339	G1	2953
PA STATE RT. 116, Bonneauville	Ad	17325	F11	3472
PA STATE RT. 116, Bonneauville	Ad	17325	G1	3576
PA STATE RT. 116, Carroll Valley	Ad	17320	H8	3572
PA STATE RT. 116, Carroll Valley	Ad	17320	H1	3676
PA STATE RT. 116, Carroll Valley	Ad	17320	A2	3677
PA STATE RT. 116, Conewago	Ad	17331	B3	3578
PA STATE RT. 116, Cumberland	Ad	17325	G9	3470
PA STATE RT. 116, Cumberland	Ad	17325	B8	3471
PA STATE RT. 116, Fairfield	Ad	17320	B4	3573
PA STATE RT. 116, Gettysburg	Ad	17325	B8	3471
PA STATE RT. 116, Hamiltonban	Ad	17320	H8	3572
PA STATE RT. 116, Hamiltonban	Ad	17320	B4	3573
PA STATE RT. 116, Hanover	Yk	17331	A2	3579
PA STATE RT. 116, Heidelberg	Yk	17331	H10	3475
PA STATE RT. 116, Heidelberg	Yk	17331	A9	3476
PA STATE RT. 116, Heidelberg	Yk	17362	A9	3476
PA STATE RT. 116, Highland	Ad	17325	A11	3470
PA STATE RT. 116, Highland	Ad	17325	F1	3573
PA STATE RT. 116, Jackson	Yk	17362	B10	3373
PA STATE RT. 116, Jackson	Yk	17362	C8	3373
PA STATE RT. 116, Jackson	Yk	17404	F4	3373
PA STATE RT. 116, McSherrystown	Ad	17344	G2	3578
PA STATE RT. 116, Mount Pleasant	Ad	17325	F11	3472
PA STATE RT. 116, Mount Pleasant	Ad	17325	B1	3577
PA STATE RT. 116, Mount Pleasant	Ad	17331	G3	3577
PA STATE RT. 116, Mount Pleasant	Ad	17331	B3	3578
PA STATE RT. 116, North Codorus	Yk	17362	F5	3476
PA STATE RT. 116, North Codorus	Yk	17362	A2	3477
PA STATE RT. 116, Penn	Yk	17331	G2	3579
PA STATE RT. 116, Spring Grove	Yk	17362	B10	3373
PA STATE RT. 116, Spring Grove	Yk	17362	B1	3477
PA STATE RT. 116, Straban	Ad	17325	F9	3471
PA STATE RT. 116, Straban	Ad	17325	A10	3472
PA STATE RT. 116, Union	Ad	17331	G3	3577
PA STATE RT. 116, Union	Ad	17331	B3	3578
PA STATE RT. 116, West Manchester	Yk	17404	F4	3373
PA STATE RT. 124, East Prospect	Yk	17317	G6	3274
PA STATE RT. 124, Lower Windsor	Yk	17402	F6	3273
PA STATE RT. 124, Lower Windsor	Yk	17406	F6	3273
PA STATE RT. 124, Lower Windsor	Yk	17368	G9	3274
PA STATE RT. 124, Lower Windsor	Yk	17406	B6	3274
PA STATE RT. 124, Spring Garden	Yk	17403	H8	3271
PA STATE RT. 124, Windsor Twp	Yk	17402	A7	3273
PA STATE RT. 124, York City	Yk	17403	D7	3271
PA STATE RT. 124 , Springettsbury	Yk	17402	C8	3272
PA STATE RT. 124 , Windsor Twp	Yk	17402	G7	3272
PA STATE RT. 124 , York Twp	Yk	17402	C8	3272
PA STATE RT. 134, Cumberland	Ad	17325	C11	3471
PA STATE RT. 134, Cumberland	Ad	17325	C1	3575
PA STATE RT. 134, Gettysburg	Ad	17325	C11	3471
PA STATE RT. 134, Mount Joy	Ad	17325	C10	3575
PA STATE RT. 134, MountJoy	Ad	17325	D2	3679
PA STATE RT. 177, Fairview	Yk	17319	C8	2954
PA STATE RT. 177, Fairview	Yk	17339	C8	2954
PA STATE RT. 177, Fairview	Yk	17339	A2	3059
PA STATE RT. 177, Newberry	Yk	17319	C8	2954
PA STATE RT. 177, Newberry	Yk	17339	C8	2954
PA STATE RT. 177, Warrington	Yk	17365	D11	3058
PA STATE RT. 177, Warrington	Yk	17339	A2	3059
PA STATE RT. 178, Warrington	Yk	17339	D11	3058
PA STATE RT. 181, East Manchester	Yk	17345	D9	3061
PA STATE RT. 181, East Manchester	Yk	17345	D3	3166
PA STATE RT. 181, Manchester Boro	Yk	17345	D9	3061
PA STATE RT. 181, Manchester Twp	Yk	17402	C10	3166
PA STATE RT. 181, Newberry	Yk	17345	E5	3061
PA STATE RT. 181, York Haven	Yk	17345	E5	3061
PA STATE RT. 182, Spring Garden	Yk	17403	G1	3374
PA STATE RT. 182, Spring Garden	Yk	17403	A4	3375
PA STATE RT. 182, West Manchester	Yk	17404	F9	3270
PA STATE RT. 182, West Manchester	Yk	17403	G1	3374
PA STATE RT. 182, West Manchester	Yk	17404	G1	3374
PA STATE RT. 182, York Twp	Yk	17402	A5	3376
PA STATE RT. 182, York Twp	Yk	17402	G5	3375
PA STATE RT. 182, York Twp	Yk	17403	A4	3375
PA STATE RT. 194, Berwick	Ad	17301	B3	3475
PA STATE RT. 194, Berwick	Ad	17331	B3	3475
PA STATE RT. 194, Carroll	Yk	17019	E7	3056
PA STATE RT. 194, Conewago	Ad	17331	H6	3578
PA STATE RT. 194, Franklin	Yk	17019	E7	3056
PA STATE RT. 194, Franklintown	Yk	17323	E7	3056
PA STATE RT. 194, Germany	Ad	17340	A5	3681
PA STATE RT. 194, Hamilton	Ad	17316	C2	3371
PA STATE RT. 194, Hanover	Yk	17331	D7	3475
PA STATE RT. 194, Hanover	Yk	17331	C1	3579
PA STATE RT. 194, Littlestown	Ad	17340	F1	3681
PA STATE RT. 194, Penn	Yk	17331	D7	3475
PA STATE RT. 194, Penn	Yk	17331	A4	3579
PA STATE RT. 194, Union	Ad	17340	B11	3578
PA STATE RT. 194, Union	Ad	17331	B11	3578
PA STATE RT. 194, Union	Ad	17340	F1	3681
PA STATE RT. 194, Washington	Yk	17316	H1	3266
PA STATE RT. 194, Washington	Yk	17316	C3	3267
PA STATE RT. 214, Dallastown	Yk	17313	F8	3376
PA STATE RT. 214, Loganville	Yk	17360	C3	3479
PA STATE RT. 214, Loganville	Yk	17403	F4	3479
PA STATE RT. 214, Seven Valleys	Yk	17360	G3	3478
PA STATE RT. 214, Springfield	Yk	17360	G3	3478
PA STATE RT. 214, Springfield	Yk	17360	C3	3479
PA STATE RT. 214, Springfield	Yk	17403	F4	3479
PA STATE RT. 214, Springfield	Yk	17313	A3	3480
PA STATE RT. 214, York Twp	Yk	17313	D11	3376
PA STATE RT. 214, York Twp	Yk	17313	C2	3480
PA STATE RT. 216, Codorus	Yk	17329	F8	3581
PA STATE RT. 216, Codorus	Yk	17327	A11	3582
PA STATE RT. 216, Codorus	Yk	17327	H8	3582
PA STATE RT. 216, Codorus	Yk	17327	B1	3686
PA STATE RT. 216, Glen Rock	Yk	17327	A6	3583
PA STATE RT. 216, Manheim	Yk	17329	H6	3580
PA STATE RT. 216, Manheim	Yk	17362	H6	3580
PA STATE RT. 216, Manheim	Yk	17329	B9	3581
PA STATE RT. 216, North Hopewell	Yk	17322	E5	3480
PA STATE RT. 216, Penn	Yk	17331	G3	3579
PA STATE RT. 216, Penn	Yk	17331	C4	3580
PA STATE RT. 216, Shrewsbury Twp	Yk	17327	A6	3583
PA STATE RT. 216, Springfield	Yk	17327	G9	3479
PA STATE RT. 216, Springfield	Yk	17327	B9	3480
PA STATE RT. 216, Springfield	Yk	17327	C1	3583
PA STATE RT. 216, Winterstown	Yk	17322	H7	3480
PA STATE RT. 216, Winterstown	Yk	17322	A7	3481
PA STATE RT. 233, Franklin	Ad	17222	G3	3363
PA STATE RT. 233, Menallen	Ad	17307	D10	3156
PA STATE RT. 233, Menallen	Ad	17307	A1	3261
PA STATE RT. 234, Biglerville	Ad	17307	A2	3367
PA STATE RT. 234, Butler	Ad	17307	D11	3263
PA STATE RT. 234, Butler	Ad	17304	H10	3263
PA STATE RT. 234, Butler	Ad	17037	E2	3366
PA STATE RT. 234, East Berlin	Ad	17316	D1	3371
PA STATE RT. 234, Franklin	Ad	17353	B10	3261
PA STATE RT. 234, Franklin	Ad	17353	B6	3364
PA STATE RT. 234, Franklin	Ad	17037	B2	3366
PA STATE RT. 234, Jackson	Yk	17364	B11	3269
PA STATE RT. 234, Menallen	Ad	17307	F10	3261
PA STATE RT. 234, Paradise	Yk	17316	H1	3371
PA STATE RT. 234, Reading	Ad	17350	G11	3265
PA STATE RT. 234, Reading	Ad	17316	H11	3266
PA STATE RT. 234, Reading	Ad	17316	A11	3267
PA STATE RT. 234, Reading	Ad	17316	C1	3370
PA STATE RT. 234, Tyrone	Ad	17304	B10	3264
PA STATE RT. 234, Tyrone	Ad	17325	G9	3264
PA STATE RT. 234, Tyrone	Ad	17350	B9	3265
PA STATE RT. 234, West Manchester	Yk	17404	G10	3269
PA STATE RT. 234, West Manchester	Yk	17404	B10	3270
PA STATE RT. 238, Manchester Twp	Yk	17404	F11	3165
PA STATE RT. 238, Manchester Twp	Yk	17402	A9	3166
PA STATE RT. 238, Manchester Twp	Yk	17402	B8	3166
PA STATE RT. 238, Manchester Twp	Yk	17404	E1	3270
PA STATE RT. 238, West Manchester	Yk	17404	C3	3270
PA STATE RT. 262, Fairview	Yk	17070	H2	2953
PA STATE RT. 262, Fairview	Yk	17070	A2	2954
PA STATE RT. 262, Fairview	Yk	17319	A2	2954
PA STATE RT. 262, Fairview	Yk	17339	A2	2954
PA STATE RT. 262, Fairview	Yk	17319	A3	2955
PA STATE RT. 262, Goldsboro	Yk	17319	G5	2955
PA STATE RT. 262, Goldsboro	Yk	17319	A7	2956
PA STATE RT. 262, Newberry	Yk	17319	G5	2955
PA STATE RT. 262, Newberry	Yk	17370	H9	2955
PA STATE RT. 262, Newberry	Yk	17319	A7	2956
PA STATE RT. 262, Newberry	Yk	17370	A10	2956
PA STATE RT. 262, Newberry	Yk	17370	B1	3061
PA STATE RT. 291, Conewago	Yk	17315	B7	3165
PA STATE RT. 295, Conewago	Yk	17345	F10	3060
PA STATE RT. 295, Conewago	Yk	17402	F10	3060
PA STATE RT. 295, Conewago	Yk	17404	F1	3165
PA STATE RT. 295, Newberry	Yk	17370	H3	3060
PA STATE RT. 295, Newberry	Yk	17370	A2	3061
PA STATE RT. 333, Franklin	Ad	17222	C9	3260
PA STATE RT. 333, Menallen	Ad	17073	G4	3260
PA STATE RT. 372, Lower Chanceford	Yk	17302	E1	3589
PA STATE RT. 372, Lower Chanceford	Yk	17314	B4	3589
PA STATE RT. 372, Lower Chanceford	Yk	17302	H10	3485
PA STATE RT. 382, Fairview	Yk	17339	G4	2953
PA STATE RT. 382, Fairview	Yk	17339	A8	2954
PA STATE RT. 382, Lewisberry	Yk	17339	A8	2954
PA STATE RT. 382, Newberry	Yk	17319	A8	2954
PA STATE RT. 382, Newberry	Yk	17370	A8	2954
PA STATE RT. 382, Newberry	Yk	17319	A10	2955
PA STATE RT. 382, Newberry	Yk	17370	H1	3060
PA STATE RT. 382, Newberry	Yk	17370	A1	3061
PA STATE RT. 382, York Haven	Yk	17370	A1	3061
PA STATE RT. 392, Newberry	Yk	17319	F7	2954
PA STATE RT. 392, Newberry	Yk	17319	B5	2955
PA STATE RT. 394, Biglerville	Ad	17037	H2	3366
PA STATE RT. 394, Biglerville	Ad	17307	A2	3367
PA STATE RT. 394, Butler	Ad	17307	D5	3367
PA STATE RT. 394, Reading	Ad	17350	C8	3369
PA STATE RT. 394, Reading	Ad	17316	B1	3370
PA STATE RT. 394, Straban	Ad	17325	G8	3367
PA STATE RT. 394, Straban	Ad	17350	G4	3369
PA STATE RT. 425, Chanceford	Yk	17368	B11	3275
PA STATE RT. 425, Chanceford	Yk	17322	F4	3379
PA STATE RT. 425, Chanceford	Yk	17356	B5	3379
PA STATE RT. 425, Chanceford	Yk	17368	B1	3379
PA STATE RT. 425, Chanceford	Yk	17309	C7	3380
PA STATE RT. 425, Chanceford	Yk	17322	C7	3380
PA STATE RT. 425, Fawn	Yk	17302	B7	3588
PA STATE RT. 425, Fawn	Yk	17321	B7	3588
PA STATE RT. 425, Fawn	Yk	17321	H1	3691
PA STATE RT. 425, Fawn	Yk	17321	A1	3692
PA STATE RT. 425, Fawn Grove	Yk	17321	G3	3691
PA STATE RT. 425, Lower Chanceford	Yk	17309	G10	3380
PA STATE RT. 425, Lower Chanceford	Yk	17302	C9	3486
PA STATE RT. 425, Lower Chanceford	Yk	17302	D2	3588
PA STATE RT. 425, Lower Windsor	Yk	17368	H10	3274
PA STATE RT. 425, Lower Windsor	Yk	17368	B11	3275
PA STATE RT. 462, Hallam	Yk	17406	A11	3168
PA STATE RT. 462, Hellam	Yk	17406	G9	3168
PA STATE RT. 462, Hellam	Yk	17368	B8	3169
PA STATE RT. 462, Hellam	Yk	17406	B8	3169
PA STATE RT. 462, Hellam	Yk	17402	G2	3272
PA STATE RT. 462, Hellam	Yk	17406	G2	3272
PA STATE RT. 462, Hellam	Yk	17406	A11	3273
PA STATE RT. 462, Spring Garden	Yk	17403	G5	3271
PA STATE RT. 462, Springettsbury	Yk	17402	G5	3271
PA STATE RT. 462, Springettsbury	Yk	17402	B5	3272
PA STATE RT. 462, West Manchester	Yk	17404	D11	3270
PA STATE RT. 462, Wrightsville	Yk	17368	B8	3169
PA STATE RT. 462, York City	Yk	17401	B8	3271
PA STATE RT. 462, York City	Yk	17403	G5	3271
PA STATE RT. 462, York City	Yk	17404	B8	3271
PA STATE RT. 462, York Twp	Yk	17404	H9	3270
PA STATE RT. 516, Codorus	Yk	17329	G3	3581
PA STATE RT. 516, Codorus	Yk	17362	E1	3581
PA STATE RT. 516, Codorus	Yk	17327	B10	3582
PA STATE RT. 516, Codorus	Yk	17329	A6	3582
PA STATE RT. 516, Codorus	Yk	17327	A1	3686
PA STATE RT. 516, Jefferson	Yk	17362	C8	3477
PA STATE RT. 516, Manheim	Yk	17327	F4	3685
PA STATE RT. 516, North Codorus	Yk	17362	A4	3477
PA STATE RT. 616, Codorus	Yk	17327	F9	3478
PA STATE RT. 616, Codorus	Yk	17360	F9	3478
PA STATE RT. 616, Codorus	Yk	17327	H1	3582
PA STATE RT. 616, Codorus	Yk	17327	A2	3583
PA STATE RT. 616, Glen Rock	Yk	17327	A2	3583
PA STATE RT. 616, New Salem	Yk	17371	C6	3374
PA STATE RT. 616, North Codorus	Yk	17404	D10	3374
PA STATE RT. 616, North Codorus	Yk	17360	E4	3478
PA STATE RT. 616, North Codorus	Yk	17404	D1	3478
PA STATE RT. 616, Railroad	Yk	17355	E8	3583
PA STATE RT. 616, Shrewsbury Twp	Yk	17327	E8	3583
PA STATE RT. 616, West Manchester	Yk	17404	B3	3374
PA STATE RT. 624, Hellam	Yk	17368	F10	3169
PA STATE RT. 624, Lower Windsor	Yk	17368	F10	3169
PA STATE RT. 624, Lower Windsor	Yk	17366	E11	3274
PA STATE RT. 624, Lower Windsor	Yk	17368	H9	3274
PA STATE RT. 624, Lower Windsor	Yk	17368	A4	3275
PA STATE RT. 624, Lower Windsor	Yk	17368	B8	3275
PA STATE RT. 624, Red Lion	Yk	17356	D6	3377
PA STATE RT. 624, Windsor Boro	Yk	17366	H4	3377
PA STATE RT. 624, Windsor Twp	Yk	17356	D6	3377
PA STATE RT. 624, Windsor Twp	Yk	17366	H4	3377
PA STATE RT. 624, Wrightsville	Yk	17368	E7	3169
PA STATE RT. 624 , Lower Windsor	Yk	17366	D1	3378
PA STATE RT. 624 , Windsor Twp	Yk	17366	A4	3378
PA STATE RT. 851, Codorus	Yk	17327	D2	3686
PA STATE RT. 851, Fawn	Yk	17352	H3	3690
PA STATE RT. 851, Fawn	Yk	17352	B4	3691
PA STATE RT. 851, Fawn	Yk	17321	D4	3692
PA STATE RT. 851, Fawn Grove	Yk	17321	H5	3691
PA STATE RT. 851, Hopewell	Yk	17349	G10	3584
PA STATE RT. 851, Hopewell	Yk	17363	G10	3584
PA STATE RT. 851, Hopewell	Yk	17363	B10	3585
PA STATE RT. 851, Hopewell	Yk	17363	B10	3586
PA STATE RT. 851, Hopewell	Yk	17363	D1	3690
PA STATE RT. 851, New Freedom	Yk	17349	G10	3583
PA STATE RT. 851, New Freedom	Yk	17349	G1	3687
PA STATE RT. 851, Peach Bottom	Yk	17314	E11	3589
PA STATE RT. 851, Peach Bottom	Yk	17314	H1	3692
PA STATE RT. 851, Peach Bottom	Yk	17314	B1	3693
PA STATE RT. 851, Peach Bottom	Yk	17314	F1	3693
PA STATE RT. 851, Railroad	Yk	17355	G10	3583
PA STATE RT. 851, Shrewsbury Boro	Yk	17361	C8	3584
PA STATE RT. 851, Shrewsbury Twp	Yk	17349	C8	3584
PA STATE RT. 851, Shrewsbury Twp	Yk	17349	H5	3686
PA STATE RT. 851, Shrewsbury Twp	Yk	17349	E4	3687
PA STATE RT. 851, Stewartstown	Yk	17363	G11	3585
PA STATE RT. 921, Dover	Yk	17315	F10	3164
PA STATE RT. 921, East Manchester	Yk	17345	B1	3166
PA STATE RT. 921, East Manchester	Yk	17402	A2	3166
PA STATE RT. 921, Manchester Boro	Yk	17345	E1	3166
PA STATE RT. 921, Mount Wolf	Yk	17347	F11	3061

PENNSYLVANIA TURNPIKE

PENNSYLVANIA TPK., Fairview	Yk	17070	C10	2848
PENNSYLVANIA TPK., Fairview	Yk	17070	B8	2849
PENNSYLVANIA TPK., Fairview	Yk	17070	A9	2850

UNITED STATES ROUTES

US RT. 15, Carroll	Yk	17019	F10	2951
US RT. 15, Carroll	Yk	17019	B9	3056
US RT. 15, Cumberland	Ad	17325	B7	3575
US RT. 15, Cumberland	Ad	17325	E1	3678
US RT. 15, Dillsburg	Yk	17019	B9	3056
US RT. 15, Franklin	Yk	17019	H11	3055
US RT. 15, Franklin	Yk	17019	B9	3056
US RT. 15, Franklin	Yk	17019	H2	3160
US RT. 15, Freedom	Ad	17325	E1	3678
US RT. 15, Freedom	Ad	17320	A5	3678

US RT. 15, Hungtinton	Ad	17372	H5	3264
US RT. 15, Huntington	Ad	17372	B2	3265
US RT. 15, Mount Joy	Ad	17325	G9	3471
US RT. 15, Mount Joy	Ad	17325	G2	3575
US RT. 15, Straban	Ad	17325	H11	3367
US RT. 15, Straban	Ad	17325	H1	3471
US RT. 15, Straban	Ad	17325	C5	3368
US RT. 15, Tyrone	Ad	17325	G11	3264
US RT. 15 , Cumberland	Ad	17325	G9	3574
US RT. 15 BUS, Cumberland	Ad	17325	B11	3471
US RT. 15 BUS, Cumberland	Ad	17325	E10	3574
US RT. 15 BUS, Cumberland	Ad	17325	H4	3574
US RT. 15 BUS, Cumberland	Ad	17325	A2	3575
US RT. 15 BUS, Freedom	Ad	17325	E10	3574
US RT. 15 BUS, Freedom	Ad	17325	D1	3678
US RT. 15 BUS, Freedom	Ad	17320	D1	3678
US RT. 15 BUS, Gettysburg	Ad	17325	B11	3471
US RT. 15 BUS, Straban	Ad	17325	H9	3367
US RT. 15 BUS, Straban	Ad	17325	E4	3471
US RT. 30, Abbottsown	Ad	17301	A10	3371
US RT. 30, Berwick	Ad	17350	D2	3474
US RT. 30, Cumberland	Ad	17325	F6	3470
US RT. 30, Cumberland	Ad	17325	A7	3471
US RT. 30, Franklin	Ad	17325	H2	3469
US RT. 30, Franklin	Ad	17307	H2	3469
US RT. 30, Franklin	Ad	17222	G7	3363
US RT. 30, Franklin	Ad	17253	C7	3364
US RT. 30, Franklin	Ad	17307	G8	3364
US RT. 30, Franklin	Ad	17307	B8	3365
US RT. 30, Franklin	Ad	17325	B3	3470
US RT. 30, Gettysburg	Ad	17325	A7	3471
US RT. 30, Hamilton	Ad	17350	D2	3474
US RT. 30, Hellam	Yk	17406	H11	3167
US RT. 30, Hellam	Yk	17406	A11	3168
US RT. 30, Hellam	Yk	17406	G8	3168
US RT. 30, Hellam	Yk	17368	D6	3169
US RT. 30, Hellam	Yk	17406	D6	3169
US RT. 30, Hellam	Yk	17402	G1	3272
US RT. 30, Hellam	Yk	17406	G1	3272
US RT. 30, Manchester Twp	Yk	17402	A4	3271
US RT. 30, Manchester Twp	Yk	17404	A4	3271
US RT. 30, Mount Pleasant	Ad	17350	B3	3473
US RT. 30, New Oxford	Ad	17350	G3	3473
US RT. 30, New Oxford	Ad	17350	D2	3474
US RT. 30, Oxford	Ad	17350	G3	3473
US RT. 30, Oxford	Ad	17350	D2	3474
US RT. 30, Paradise	Yk	17364	G7	3371
US RT. 30, Paradise	Yk	17301	A10	3371
US RT. 30, Paradise	Yk	17364	B5	3372
US RT. 30, Springettsbury	Yk	17402	H4	3271
US RT. 30, Springettsbury	Yk	17402	B3	3272
US RT. 30, Straban	Ad	17325	F7	3471
US RT. 30, Straban	Ad	17325	B5	3472
US RT. 30, Straban	Ad	17325	H3	3472
US RT. 30, Straban	Ad	17325	B3	3473
US RT. 30, Straban	Ad	17350	B3	3473
US RT. 30, West Manchester	Yk	17404	G4	3270
US RT. 30, York City	Yk	17404	A4	3271
US RT. 30, York Twp	Yk	17404	G4	3270

INTERCHANGES

Interstate Rt. 76

Exit 242 (Interstate Rt. 76)	Yk	A7	2849

Interstate Rt. 83

Exit 4 (Interstate Rt. 83)	Yk	C8	3584
Exit 8 (Interstate Rt. 83)	Yk	A9	3480
Exit 10 (Interstate Rt. 83)	Yk	G2	3479
Exit 14 (Interstate Rt. 83)	Yk	G5	3375
Exit 15 (Interstate Rt. 83)	Yk	F4	3375
Exit 16A (Interstate Rt. 83)	Yk	H2	3375
Exit 16B (Interstate Rt. 83)	Yk	H2	3375
Exit 18 (Interstate Rt. 83)	Yk	A8	3272
Exit 19 (Interstate Rt. 83)	Yk	H5	3271
Exit 19A (Interstate Rt. 83)	Yk	H5	3271
Exit 19B (Interstate Rt. 83)	Yk	G5	3271
Exit 21A (Interstate Rt. 83)	Yk	C3	3271
Exit 21B (Interstate Rt. 83)	Yk	C3	3271
Exit 22 (Interstate Rt. 83)	Yk	C2	3271
Exit 24 (Interstate Rt. 83)	Yk	A8	3166
Exit 28 (Interstate Rt. 83)	Yk	F8	3060
Exit 32 (Interstate Rt. 83)	Yk	B10	2955
Exit 33 (Interstate Rt. 83)	Yk	H8	2954
Exit 34 (Interstate Rt. 83)	Yk	H7	2954
Exit 35 (Interstate Rt. 83)	Yk	F4	2954
Exit 36 (Interstate Rt. 83)	Yk	F2	2954
Exit 38 (Interstate Rt. 83)	Yk	B10	2849
Exit 39A (Interstate Rt. 83)	Yk	A8	2849
Exit 39B (Interstate Rt. 83)	Yk	H8	2848
Exit 40A (Interstate Rt. 83)	Yk	H7	2848

169

West Branch Codorus Creek	Yk	C3	3684
White Run	Ad	E9	3472
White Run	Ad	G5	3575
White Run	Ad	A3	3576
Wildcat Run	Yk	C3	3168
Willis Run	Yk	B6	3271
Willoughby Run	Ad	A10	3367
Willoughby Run	Ad	G4	3470
Willoughby Run	Ad	G11	3470
Willoughby Run	Ad	F2	3574
Wilson Run	Yk	C6	3380
Wolf Run	Yk	B4	3162
Yellow Breeches Creek	Yk	E8	2951
Yellow Breeches Creek	Yk	B6	2952
Yellow Breeches Creek	Yk	A5	2953
York Sulphur Springs	Ad	E1	3265

BRIDGES, DAMS & TUNNELS

Bowmansdale Covered Bridge	Yk	A6	2952
Hanover Dam	Yk	F3	3683
Harlacher Bridge	Yk	A3	3268
Indian Rock Dam	Yk	H3	3374
Jacks Mountain Bridge	Ad	G9	3572
Jacks Mountain Tunnel	Ad	H1	3675
P.H. Glatfelter Paper Co Dam	Yk	H1	3580
Sauks Covered Bridge	Ad	E3	3574
Waynesboro Dam	Ad	F11	3467

CAMPS & CAMPGROUNDS

Cabin Area (Gifford Pinchot State Park)	Yk	G8	3058
Camp Conewago	Ad	G8	3369
Camp Echo Trails (Girl Scouts)	Yk	G2	3379
Camp Echo Trails (Girl Scouts)	Yk	A2	3380
Camp El-Wa-Ho Girl Scouts	Ad	F8	3363
Camp Tuckahoe	Yk	E5	3055
Campground (Huntington Twp)	Ad	C1	3265
Camping Area (Gifford Pinchot State Park)	Yk	F11	3058
Cann-edi-on Camp	Yk	C3	3060
Codorus State Park Tenting Area	Yk	E7	3580
Conewago Campground	Ad	E9	3261
Drummer Boy Camping Area	Ad	H9	3471
Fellowship Camp Grove	Yk	A2	3580
Gettysburg Campground	Ad	D11	3470
Gettysburg KOA Campground	Ad	F9	3469
Granite Hill Campground	Ad	F2	3573
Happy Valley Camp	Ad	E6	3573
Hosack Camp Area	Ad	D4	3363
Indian Rock Campground	Yk	A3	3375
Lower Camp Nawakwa	Ad	G7	3261
McMillan Woods Campground	Ad	H10	3470
Mt. Olive Camp Meeting Grounds	Yk	C11	2951
New Dawn Camp	Ad	H4	3573
Otter Creek Campground	Yk	G11	3380
Park Away Campground	Yk	H7	2954
Park Away Campground	Yk	A7	2955
Rocky Spring Camp	Yk	C3	3057
Round Top Campground	Ad	B7	3575
Summit Grove Camp	Yk	F3	3687
Upper Camp Nawakwa	Ad	G6	3261
West Shore YMCA Camp	Yk	A9	2849
Youth Group Campground	Ad	A10	3471

CEMETERIES

Altland Cem	Yk	C9	3268
Barts Cem	Ad	E2	3682
Beidler Cem	Yk	H10	3168
Benders Lutheran Cem	Ad	E2	3367
Bethel Cem	Yk	A7	2953
Bethel Cem	Yk	D7	3380
Bethlehem Cem	Ad	F7	3263
Bethlehem Cem	Yk	G8	3377
Bethlehem Cem	Yk	G5	3686
Black Cem	Ad	F3	3470
Black Rock Cem	Yk	A5	3685
Blymire Cem	Yk	F9	3376
Book Chapel Cem	Yk	C3	3688
Bowser Cem	Yk	E2	3687
Bryansville Cem	Yk	C1	3693
Bucher Cem	Yk	A8	3475
Burg Cem	Yk	H7	3168
Canadochly Cem	Yk	H5	3273
Canadochly Cem	Yk	A5	3274
Cassels Cem	Yk	D5	3061
Catholic Cem	Ad	B9	3471
Catholic Cem	Yk	D11	3271
Catholic Cem	Yk	D1	3375
Centre Presbyterian Cem	Yk	F5	3690
Chanceford Cem	Yk	A8	3484
Chanceford Cem	Yk	D1	3588
Chestnut Grove United Methodist Cem	Yk	A2	3057
Chestnut Grove United Methodist Cem	Yk	F2	3581
Chestnut Hill Cem	Yk	A4	3583
Christ Cem	Yk	B8	3584
Christ Lutheran Cem	Yk	G6	3372
Codorus Meeting House Cem	Yk	H7	3373
Conewago Chapel Cem	Ad	D10	3474
Cross Roads Cem	Yk	G10	3481
Crossroad Cem	Yk	C2	2954
Deitz Cem	Yk	F11	3168
Dillsburg Cem	Yk	C3	3056
Dover Bethany Cem	Yk	F6	3164
Druck Cem	Yk	H6	3167
Dubs Cem	Yk	E5	3580
East End Cem	Yk	D7	3378
Ebenezer UMC Cem	Yk	B8	3275
Emanuel Cem	Yk	A1	3059
Emanuel Reformed Cem	Yk	C2	3377
Evergreen Cem	Ad	C11	3471
Fairview Bethel Cem	Yk	D1	2953
Fairview Cem	Ad	B4	3366
Fairview Cem	Yk	D8	3169
Fawn United Methodist Cem	Yk	G5	3691
Fetrow Cem	Yk	C5	2955
Fileys Cem	Yk	B9	2952
Fisher Cem	Yk	D3	2955
Flohrs Lutheran Cem	Ad	E1	3469
Flohrs Lutheran Cem	Ad	D11	3365
Forry Cem	Yk	F7	3168
Friedensaals Evangelical Lutheran Cem	Yk	B6	3479
Friend Grove Cem	Ad	G10	3263
Gerber Cem	Yk	G11	3168
Glen Rock Cem	Yk	C2	3583
Grace Bible Cem	Ad	D2	3264
Grace Luthern Cem	Ad	C7	3576
Great Conewago Presbyterian Cem	Ad	C9	3368
Greenmount Cem	Ad	A4	3366
Greenmount Cem	Ad	B1	3582
Greenmount Cem	Yk	G7	3270
Guinston Cem	Yk	A8	3483
Heindels Cem	Yk	G5	3374
Helland View Cem	Yk	G3	3376
Hershey Cem	Yk	H6	3268
Hershey Cem	Yk	E10	3373
Highmount Cem	Yk	E6	3168
Holy Saviour Cem	Yk	A6	3166
Holy Saviour Cem	Yk	H6	3165
Hopewell Cem	Yk	B1	3586
Hopewell Cem	Yk	F3	3689
Houston Cem	Yk	H6	3167
Huber Cem	Yk	E1	3273
Huntington Friends Cem	Ad	F1	3265
Jefferson Cem	Yk	A3	3581
King James Bible Cem	Yk	E4	3272
Kreutz Creek Cem	Yk	A10	3168
Latimore Cem	Ad	G6	3160
Lebanon Cem	Yk	B4	3271
Lebanon Cem	Yk	F5	3481
Leibs Creek	Yk	C11	3586
Libhart Cem	Yk	C3	3273
Lincoln Cem	Ad	B9	3471
Low Dutch Cem	Ad	A1	3473
Lower Bermudian Cem	Ad	B1	3266
Lower Bermudian Cem	Ad	G2	3267
Lower Marsh Creek Cem	Ad	B8	3470
Machpelah Cem	Yk	G4	3273
Manchester Cem	Yk	E10	3061
Marsh Creek Cem	Ad	C7	3470
Mauls Cemetery	Yk	A4	3476
McClelland Cem	Ad	D10	3470
McKendree Cem	Yk	F10	3484
Menallen Cem	Ad	A7	3263
Miller Cem	Yk	F4	2955
Moores Cem	Yk	D9	2953
Mt. Airy Cem	Yk	D5	3058
Mt. Carmel Cem	Ad	F5	3468
Mt. Carmel Cem	Ad	E2	3681
Mt. Hope UMC Cem	Ad	B2	3572
Mt. Joy Cem	Ad	D1	3679
Mt. Nebo Cem	Yk	C2	3694
Mt. Olive Cem	Yk	D5	3579
Mt. Olive Cem	Ad	C10	3371
Mt. Olivet Cem	Yk	C7	2849
Mt. Olivet Cem	Yk	B7	3163
Mt. Olivet UMC Cem	Yk	G6	3584
Mt. Rose Cem	Yk	H8	3271
Mt. Tabor Cem	Ad	A8	3158
Mt. Zion Cem	Yk	C10	3057
Mt. Zion Cem	Yk	C10	3480
Mt. Zion Cem	Yk	H2	3693
Mt. Zion Cem	Yk	A2	3694
Mt. Zion Luth Cem	Yk	A11	3167
Mumma Cem	Yk	E3	3579
Myers Cem	Yk	B1	3058
National Cem	Ad	C10	3471
Ness Cem	Yk	B1	3480
New Oxford Cem	Ad	G3	3473
Oak Lawn Memorial Gardens Park	Ad	E5	3470
Old Roundhill Cem	Yk	G7	3481
Old Wildasin Burial Grounds	Yk	E7	3580
Oliwiler Cem	Yk	G9	3274
Otterbein United Methodist Cem	Yk	A4	3376
Paddletown Cem	Yk	D10	2955
Parkville Cem	Yk	F4	3059
Penn Memorial Garden	Yk	G4	3579
Pet Cem (Codorus)	Yk	E3	3478
Pine Bank Cem	Ad	F7	3575
Pine Grove United Evangelist Cem	Yk	F4	3375
Pine Swamp Cem	Yk	E6	3168
Pleasant Hill Cem	Yk	C10	3372
Pleasant Hill Cem	Yk	A2	3481
Pleasant View Grove UM Cem	Yk	A2	3061
Pleasureville EUB Cem	Yk	F10	3166
Porters Cem	Yk	F10	3476
Prospect Cem	Yk	D8	3587
Prospect Hill Cem	Yk	B5	3271
Red Lion Cem	Yk	C6	3377
Red Run Cem	Yk	F2	3267
Redland Friends Meetinghouse	Yk	G10	2954
Reformed Cem	Yk	A5	3583
Rest Haver Cem	Yk	B5	3579
Riverview Cem	Yk	E5	3274
Rohler's Assembly of God Cem	Yk	C11	3059
Roth Cem	Yk	A5	3169
Roth Cem	Yk	G7	3372
Round Hill Cem	Ad	F9	3265
Round Hill Cem	Yk	H11	3481
Rudy Cem	Yk	E10	3168
Salem Cem	Ad	F5	3472
Salem Cem	Yk	G3	2954
Salem Cem	Yk	F2	3378
Salem Cem	Yk	E7	3589
Seitz Cem	Yk	B7	3583
Shaffer Cem	Yk	A3	3481
Shenbergers Cem	Yk	B3	3379
Shiloh Lutheran Cem	Yk	A4	3270
Slate Ridge Cem	Yk	E5	3693
Slateville Cem	Yk	B4	3694
South Hill Hebrew Cem	Yk	E1	3375
Springville Cem	Yk	A9	3275
St. Aloysius Cem	Ad	F3	3681
St. Ignatius-Loyola Cem	Ad	F4	3364
St. Jacobs Stone Cem	Yk	H8	3581
St. James Cem	Ad	D3	3680
St. John Cem	Yk	B9	2954
St. John the Baptist Cem	Yk	H1	3687
St. Johns Cem	Ad	E6	3369
St. Johns Cem	Ad	G2	3469
St. Johns Cem	Ad	C2	3681
St. Johns Cem	Yk	C2	3685
St. Johns Luth Cem	Yk	B8	3272
St. Luke Cem	Yk	D4	3379
St. Marks Cem	Ad	G4	3575
St. Mary Cem	Ad	H7	3572
St. Mary Cem	Yk	D8	3169
St. Marys Cem	Ad	F1	3578
St. Marys Cem	Yk	F6	3371
St. Michaels Cem	Yk	C11	3058
St. Paul Lutheran Cem of Hametown	Yk	A2	3584
St. Paul Zeiglers Cem	Yk	D3	3478
St. Pauls Cem	Ad	B8	3369
St. Pauls Lutheran Cem	Yk	D2	3585
St. Pauls UMC Cem	Yk	G9	3274
St. Pauls Union Cem	Yk	H11	3373
St. Peters Cem	Yk	B7	3479
St. Vincents DePaul Cem	Ad	G3	3578
Stoner Cem	Yk	H8	3168
Strayers Cem	Yk	B2	3269
Strickler Cem	Yk	A8	3169
Strinestown Cem	Yk	G6	3060
Stump Cem	Yk	F3	3375
Suburban Memorial Gardens	Yk	H8	3164
Sunny Side Cem	Ad	B8	3160
Susquehanna Memorial Gardens	Yk	E4	3376
Trinity Cem	Yk	C3	3482
Union Cem	Yk	D1	3166
Union Cem	Yk	E6	3376
Union Chapel Cem	Yk	C3	3589
United Church of Christ Cem	Yk	E11	3477
United Methodist Cem	Ad	C7	3365
Unnamed (Bonneauville)	Ad	G1	3576
Unnamed (Carroll)	Yk	A5	3057
Unnamed (Chanceford)	Yk	D4	3379
Unnamed (Chanceford)	Yk	C6	3483
Unnamed (Codorus)	Yk	A8	3582
Unnamed (Conewago)	Ad	G11	3474
Unnamed (Conewago)	Yk	G2	3165
Unnamed (Conewago)	Yk	F3	3165
Unnamed (Cumberland)	Ad	C6	3471
Unnamed (Dallastown)	Yk	G7	3376
Unnamed (Dallastown)	Yk	F7	3376
Unnamed (Dover)	Yk	C10	3059
Unnamed (Dover)	Yk	B2	3269
Unnamed (Dover)	Yk	C6	3269
Unnamed (East Berlin)	Ad	C11	3267
Unnamed (East Manchester)	Yk	F7	3061
Unnamed (East Manchester)	Yk	C11	3062
Unnamed (East Manchester)	Yk	H3	3166
Unnamed (East Manchester)	Yk	A3	3167
Unnamed (East Manchester)	Yk	C2	3167
Unnamed (Fairview)	Yk	A8	2849
Unnamed (Fairview)	Yk	F3	2953
Unnamed (Fairview)	Yk	D4	2954
Unnamed (Fawn)	Yk	C9	3587
Unnamed (Fawn)	Yk	G3	3690
Unnamed (Franklin)	Yk	A11	3056
Unnamed (Franklintown)	Yk	D9	3056
Unnamed (Hamilton)	Ad	B4	3371
Unnamed (Hamiltonban)	Ad	F6	3467
Unnamed (Hamiltonban)	Ad	F7	3571
Unnamed (Heidelberg)	Yk	A6	3476
Unnamed (Heidelberg)	Yk	F4	3476
Unnamed (Hopewell)	Yk	G7	3584
Unnamed (Hopewell)	Yk	C10	3586
Unnamed (Huntington)	Ad	G8	3158
Unnamed (Lewisberry)	Yk	B10	2954
Unnamed (Loganville)	Yk	F3	3479
Unnamed (Lower Chanceford)	Yk	D8	3484
Unnamed (Lower Chanceford)	Yk	A2	3589
Unnamed (Lower Chanceford)	Yk	G2	3589
Unnamed (Lower Windsor)	Yk	C2	3274
Unnamed (Manchester Boro)	Yk	D2	3166
Unnamed (Manchester)	Yk	H5	3165
Unnamed (Mount Joy)	Ad	C6	3576
Unnamed (Mount Pleasant)	Ad	B2	3576
Unnamed (Mount Pleasant)	Ad	A3	3577
Unnamed (New Oxford)	Ad	C2	3474
Unnamed (New Salem)	Yk	D6	3374
Unnamed (Newberry)	Yk	B9	2954
Unnamed (Newberry)	Yk	G11	2954
Unnamed (Newberry)	Yk	B5	2955
Unnamed (Newberry)	Yk	G3	2955
Unnamed (North Codorus)	Yk	H4	3376
Unnamed (North Codorus)	Yk	D3	3478
Unnamed (North Hopewell)	Yk	E1	3480
Unnamed (North Hopewell)	Yk	F5	3481
Unnamed (Peach Bottom)	Yk	A4	3695
Unnamed (Seven Valleys)	Yk	G4	3478
Unnamed (Shrewsbury Boro)	Yk	A8	3584
Unnamed (Shrewsbury Twp)	Yk	B8	3583
Unnamed (Spring Grove)	Yk	A1	3477
Unnamed (Springfield)	Yk	C2	3479
Unnamed (Stewartstown)	Yk	D11	3585
Unnamed (Union)	Ad	A6	3578
Unnamed (Union)	Ad	B10	3578
Unnamed (Warrington)	Yk	A6	3059
Unnamed (Warrington)	Yk	B2	3163
Unnamed (Warrington)	Yk	E2	3163
Unnamed (Washington)	Yk	H11	3056
Unnamed (West Manchester)	Yk	G3	3373
Unnamed (Windsor)	Yk	H7	3272
Unnamed (Wrightsville)	Yk	D7	3169
Unnamed (York)	Yk	G5	3376
Upper Bermudian Lutheran Cem	Ad	B1	3264
Wesley Chapel Cem	Ad	A3	3676
White Church Cem	Ad	H8	3264
Wildasin Meeting House Cem	Yk	B5	3580
Williams Cem	Yk	D1	3480
Windsor Cem	Yk	F1	3377
Windsor Cem	Yk	F3	3377
Winters Cem	Yk	F9	3479
Wolf Cem	Yk	G11	3269
Wolf Cem	Yk	E5	3270
York Road Cem	Yk	H11	3475
Zion Cem	Yk	F10	3377
Zion Shaffers Cem	Yk	B9	3478

COLLEGES & UNIVERSITIES

Bradley Academy	Yk	C2	3272
Gettysburg College	Ad	B8	3471
Lutheran Theological Seminary	Ad	A8	3471
Penn State University (York Campus)	Yk	F9	3271
York College of Pennsylvania	Yk	C10	3271
York Technical Institute	Yk	D2	3272

FIRE STATIONS

Airville Volunteer Fire Co	Yk	C8	3484
Alert Fire Co No 1	Yk	B9	3166
Alert Fire Co No 2	Yk	H8	3165
Alpha Fire Co	Ad	E1	3681
Barlow Fire Sta No 22	Ad	B10	3575
Bendersville Community Fire Co	Ad	A4	3263
Biglerville Fire Co	Ad	A2	3367
Buchanan Fire Co	Ad	E3	3364
Canadochly Valley Ambulance Club	Yk	G6	3274
Cashtown Community Fire Co	Ad	C10	3365
Centennial Fire Co	Ad	A10	3474
Clearview Fire Station	Yk	C11	3475
Commonwealth Fire Co	Yk	F2	3271
Community Fire Co	Ad	A2	3474
Conewago Twp Fire Co	Ad	E11	3474
Craley Fire Station	Yk	G10	3274
Dallastown Fire Co	Yk	E7	3376

Dillsburg Fire Co	Yk	D3	3056
Dover Fire Co No 1	Yk	D11	3164
Dover Twp Fire Department	Yk	E5	3269
East Berlin Fire Co	Ad	D1	3371
East Prospect Vol Fire Co	Yk	F6	3274
Eureka Fire Co	Yk	D9	3585
Fairfield Fire Co	Ad	A5	3573
Fairview Twp Station No 1	Yk	A8	2849
Fairview Twp Station No 2	Yk	F2	2954
Felton Union Fire Co	Yk	H4	3481
Fire Station (Reading Twp)	Ad	A2	3370
Fire Station No 1	Ad	C8	3471
Fountainville Fire Co	Ad	F2	3675
Franklintown Community Fire Co	Yk	D10	3056
Friendship Fire Co	Yk	C10	3168
Glen Rock Hose & Ladder Fire Co	Yk	C4	3583
Goldsboro Fire Co No 1	Yk	A6	2956
Goodwill Fire Co	Yk	F11	3375
Goodwill Fire Co	Yk	H3	3375
Goodwill Station No 5	Yk	E6	3271
Grantley Fire Co	Yk	B10	3271
Greenmount Fire Station 23	Ad	D11	3574
Irishtown Fire Co	Ad	B8	3474
Lake Clarke Rescue	Yk	A6	3275
Lake Meade Fire Co	Ad	D5	3266
Laurel Fire Co	Yk	F4	3377
Leo Fire Co No 1	Yk	B7	3377
Lewisberry Community Fire Co	Yk	A9	2954
Loganville Volunteer Fire Co	Yk	F5	3479
McSherrystown Fire Co	Ad	E2	3578
Nashville Volunteer Fire Co	Yk	C7	3373
Newberry Fire Station No 31	Yk	D10	2955
North Codorus Twp Fire Department	Yk	A9	3374
Parkville Fire Company	Yk	E6	3579
Penn Twp Ambulance Club	Yk	D5	3579
Rex/Laurel Station No 1	Yk	D7	3271
Rose Fire Co	Yk	G3	3687
Shiloh Fire Co	Yk	B5	3270
Shrewsbury Fire Co	Yk	A8	3584
Springetts Fire Co	Yk	C4	3272
Strinestown Community Fire Co	Yk	G7	3060
Union Vol Fire Co (Felton Fire Co)	Yk	H4	3481
Vigilant Station 2	Yk	B7	3271
Wellsville Fire Co	Yk	H2	3162
Winterstown Volunteer Fire Co	Yk	A7	3481
Wirt Park Station	Yk	B2	3579
Yoe Fire Co	Yk	G6	3376
York New Salem Fire Co	Yk	D7	3374
York Springs Fire Department	Ad	B10	3160
Yorkana Community Volunteer Fire Co	Yk	E5	3273

GOLF COURSES & COUNTRY CLUBS

Bon Air CC	Yk	D9	3583
Briar GC	Yk	F1	3373
Briar GC	Yk	F11	3269
Bridges GC	Ad	H11	3370
Bridges GC	Ad	A11	3371
Bridges GC	Ad	H1	3474
Bridges GC	Ad	A1	3475
Carroll Valley GC	Ad	H10	3572
Carroll Valley GC	Ad	F1	3676
Cedar Ridge GC	Ad	H8	3575
Cedar Ridge GC	Ad	A9	3576
Cool Creek CC	Yk	B9	3169
Country Club of York	Yk	A2	3375
Flatbush GC	Ad	E5	3577
Gettysburg CC	Ad	G8	3470
Grandview GC	Yk	A3	3270
Hanover GC	Yk	C8	3371
Hawk Hill GC	Yk	F4	3270
Heritage Hills GC	Yk	B9	3272
Hickory Heights GC	Yk	G11	3373
Hickory Heights GC	Yk	F1	3477
Honey Run Golf & CC	Yk	G8	3269
Meadow Brook GC	Yk	G6	3575
Mountain View GC	Ad	C3	3573
Outdoor CC	Yk	E9	3165
Piney Apple GC	Ad	H2	3261
Pleasant Valley GC	Yk	A6	3586
Quail Valley GC	Ad	G2	3680
Range End GC	Yk	C4	3056
Red Lion CC	Yk	C9	3377
Regents Glen CC	Yk	A1	3375
Regents Glen CC	Yk	H1	3374
Regents Glen CC	Yk	H10	3270
Regents Glen CC	Yk	A11	3271
Rolling Acres GC	Yk	G9	3272
South Hills GC	Ad	H8	3578
South Hills GC	Yk	A8	3579
Springwood GC	Yk	B11	3272
Springwood GC	Yk	B1	3376
The Links at Gettysburg	Ad	D4	3679
Valley Green GC	Yk	E6	2955

GOVERNMENT FACILITIES

Adams County Courthouse	Ad	C8	3471
Adams County Prison	Ad	C6	3471
Adams County Prison	Ad	D4	3472
Army Reserve	Yk	E3	3271
Defense Distribution Region East	Yk	D7	2849
Department of Transportation	Yk	A3	3271
District Justice (Dillsburg)	Yk	C3	3056
Green Acres Home (County Home for the Aged)	Ad	C7	3471
Market Way (City Offices)	Yk	C7	3271
PennDot	Yk	C9	3587
State Police (Loganville)	Yk	G3	3479
United States Coast Guard	Yk	A6	3275
US Naval Reserve	Yk	D2	3271
York County Courthouse	Yk	C7	3271
York County Department Building	Yk	E3	3272
York County Detention House	Yk	D3	3272
York County Prison	Yk	D3	3272

HOSPITALS & MEDICAL FACILITIES

Apple Hill Medical Center	Yk	D3	3375
Fairfield Medical Center	Ad	H6	3572
Gettysburg Hosp	Ad	B9	3471
Hanover General Hosp	Yk	C1	3579
Memorial Hosp	Yk	H6	3271
Pleasant Acres (York County Hosp & Home)	Yk	E2	3272
York Hospital	Yk	D10	3271

INDUSTRIAL PARKS & BUSINESS CENTERS

183 Ind Park	Yk	A5	3166
Adams Commercial Center Bus Park	Ad	A6	3472
Adams Commercial Center Bus Park	Ad	H7	3471
Brunner Island Steam Electric Company	Yk	G5	3061
Caterpillar Incorporated	Yk	H4	3271
Caterpillar Incorporated	Yk	B3	3272
Church Road Industrial Center	Yk	B8	3166
Conewgao Ind Park	Ad	G3	3578
East Manchester Ind Park	Yk	D3	3166
Exit Two Ind Park	Yk	H10	3479
Exit Two Ind Park	Yk	A11	3480
Fairview Ind Park	Yk	E3	2954
Farmbrook Ind Park	Yk	H7	3165
Fleming Companies Incorporated	Yk	E4	3271
Funkhouser Quarry	Yk	B3	3694
Hanover Business Center	Ad	H4	3578
Hanover Business Center	Yk	A3	3579
Harley-Davidson Plant	Yk	E3	3271
Heather Ind Park	Yk	B5	3166
Industrial Museum of York	Yk	C8	3271
Interstate Industrial Plaza	Yk	B4	3166
L. Allen Water Pollution Control Plant	Yk	H6	2848
Modern Landfill	Yk	D7	3273
Morgan Ind Park	Yk	C6	3166
Orchard Bus Park	Yk	A2	3166
Peach Bottom Atomic Power Station	Yk	F10	3590
Reliante Energy Power	Ad	C1	3472
Snyder's of Hanover	Yk	F1	3579
Stonebridge Bus Park	Yk	C7	3584
Tarmac Quarry	Ad	E7	3474
Tarmac Quarry	Ad	G6	3474
Thomasville Stone & Lime Company	Yk	C3	3373
United Defense	Yk	H6	3373
United Defense	Yk	A4	3374
West Manchester Bus Park	Yk	G1	3373
Willow Spring Ind Park	Yk	A4	3166
Willow Spring Ind Park	Yk	H3	3165
York Building Company Incorporated	Yk	B4	3373
York County Ind Park	Yk	D8	3166
York Silica Sand Incorporated	Yk	D1	3271
York Water Company	Yk	E7	3375

LIBRARIES

Adams County Lib (Main)	Ad	C9	3471
Annie E. Sterling Lib	Yk	B9	2954
Collinsville Mini Lib	Yk	E3	3483
Dillsburg Lib	Yk	D3	3056
Dover Area Community Lib	Yk	E4	3269
East Berlin Community Lib	Ad	C1	3371
Glatfelter Memorial Lib	Yk	B9	3373
Glen Rock Lib	Yk	C4	3583
Hanover Lib	Yk	B2	3579
Kreutz Creek Valley Lib	Yk	F9	3168
Littlestown Lib	Ad	E1	3681
Martin Lib	Yk	D7	3271
Mason-Dixon Public Lib	Yk	D10	3585
New Oxford Area Lib	Ad	A2	3474
Red Land Community Lib	Yk	G5	2954
Shrewsbury Borough Public Lib	Yk	B8	3584
The Village Lib	Yk	F10	3375
York Haven Lib	Yk	E3	3061

MUNICIPAL BUILDINGS

*** Includes Police Station**

Abbottstown	Ad	B9	3371
Berwick	Ad	G5	3474
Biglerville	Ad	A2	3367
Bonneauville	Ad	G1	3576
Butler	Ad	D5	3367
Carroll Valley	Ad	H10	3572
Carroll*	Yk	B3	3057
Chanceford	Yk	B2	3483
Codorus	Yk	A5	3582
Conewago*	Ad	F10	3474
Cumberland*	Ad	G10	3470
Dallastown	Yk	F7	3376
Delta	Yk	G5	3693
Dillsburg	Yk	D3	3056
East Berlin*	Ad	C11	3267
East Hopewell	Yk	D3	3586
East Manchester*	Yk	G1	3166
East Prospect	Yk	F6	3274
Fairfield*	Ad	A5	3573
Fairview*	Yk	F11	2848
Fawn	Yk	C9	3587
Fawn Grove	Yk	H5	3691
Felton (meets in Fire hall)	Yk	H4	3481
Franklin	Ad	B1	3469
Franklin	Yk	A9	3056
Franklintown	Yk	E10	3056
Freedom	Ad	H10	3573
Germany	Ad	C5	3681
Gettysburg*	Ad	C9	3471
Glen Rock	Yk	C4	3583
Hamilton*	Ad	B5	3371
Hamiltonban*	Ad	B3	3573
Hanover*	Yk	B3	3579
Heidelberg*	Yk	D7	3476
Hellam*	Yk	F9	3168
Highland	Ad	D2	3573
Hopewell	Yk	A10	3585
Huntington	Ad	A10	3160
Jacobus*	Yk	E10	3375
Jefferson	Yk	E11	3477
Latimore*	Ad	D9	3160
Lewisberry	Yk	B10	2954
Liberty*	Ad	B3	3677
Littlestown*	Ad	E1	3681
Lower Chanceford	Yk	H1	3588
Lower Windsor*	Yk	F11	3274
Manchester	Yk	D2	3166
Manheim*	Yk	D11	3581
McSherrystown*	Ad	F2	3578
Menallen	Ad	B1	3262
Monaghan	Yk	E10	2952
Mount Joy	Ad	C11	3576
Mount Pleasant	Ad	B8	3473
Mount Wolf	Yk	G11	3061
New Freedom*	Yk	G3	3687
New Oxford*	Ad	A2	3474
Newberry	Yk	A10	2955
North Codorus*	Yk	H10	3373
North Hopewell*	Yk	D9	3481
North York	Yk	C5	3271
Oxford*	Ad	C5	3474
Peach Bottom	Yk	G3	3693
Penn*	Yk	D4	3579
Reading	Ad	A11	3266
Red Lion*	Yk	C7	3377
Seven Valleys	Yk	F4	3478
Shrewsbury Boro	Yk	A8	3584
Shrewsbury Twp	Yk	A2	3584
Spring Garden*	Yk	F11	3271
Spring Grove	Yk	B10	3373
Springettsbury*	Yk	C2	3272
Springfield	Yk	F7	3479
Stewartstown*	Yk	E11	3585
Straban	Ad	D3	3472
Tyrone	Ad	F9	3264
Union	Ad	D11	3578
Warrington	Yk	C11	3058
Washington	Yk	C8	3162
Wellsville	Yk	H3	3162
West Manheim*	Yk	F10	3579
Windsor Boro	Yk	F4	3377
Windsor Twp	Yk	B2	3377
Wrightsville*	Yk	E7	3169
Yoe	Yk	G5	3376
York Haven	Yk	E3	3061
York Springs	Ad	B10	3160
York Boro*	Yk	C8	3271
York Twp*	Yk	A4	3376

PARKS & RECREATION

Albermarle Park	Yk	F6	3271
Allen Field	Yk	E5	3271
American Legion of Hanover Ballfield	Ad	H3	3578
American Legion Park	Ad	B3	3367
Apollo County Park	Yk	D5	3380
Aries Park	Yk	E6	3271
Athletic Association Field	Ad	C3	3578
Attlesburg Park	Yk	D2	3579
August Shaefer Park	Yk	G4	3272
Ball Field (Gifford Pinchot State Park)	Yk	G10	3058
Bantz Park	Yk	A9	3271
Bare Av. Playground	Yk	C2	3579
Bluewater Lee Recreational Area	Ad	B4	3266
Brookside Park	Yk	F11	3164
Caledonia State Park	Ad	C4	3363
Camp Security Trail Park	Yk	F4	3272
Carbaugh Run Natural Area	Ad	G9	3363
Cashtown Community Park	Ad	B7	3365
Catfish Cove Recreational Area	Ad	C3	3266
Cherry Lane Park	Yk	C7	3271
Clayton E. Emig Memorial Park	Yk	C11	3168
Codorus State Park	Yk	H7	3579
Codorus State Park	Yk	B6	3580
Codorus State Park	Yk	G3	3580
Cold Spring Park	Yk	D11	3061
Coover Park	Yk	C2	3056
Cousler Park	Yk	F11	3165
Cousler Park	Yk	F1	3270
Crouse Park	Ad	F1	3681
Deguy Av. Park	Yk	B11	3475
Delon Catholic Ballfield	Ad	G2	3578
Dillsburg Athletic Field	Yk	D3	3056
East Cavalry Historic Site	Ad	C10	3472
Eisenhower National Historic Site	Ad	F4	3574
Elm Av. Playground	Yk	B1	3579
Fairmount Park	Yk	C8	3377
Farquhar Park	Yk	A6	3271
Fayfield Park	Yk	H6	3271
Fitz Park	Yk	F11	3272
Fitz Park	Yk	F1	3376
Fort Richie Raven Rock Site	Ad	B3	3676
Franklin Twp Park	Yk	A9	3056
Freysville Park	Yk	C3	3377
Gettysburg National Military Park	Ad	H6	3470
Gettysburg National Military Park	Ad	A11	3471
Gettysburg National Military Park	Ad	B6	3471
Gettysburg National Military Park	Ad	E5	3471
Gettysburg National Military Park	Ad	C8	3472
Gettysburg National Military Park	Ad	F5	3574
Gettysburg National Military Park	Ad	H5	3574
Gettysburg National Military Park	Ad	H2	3574
Gifford Pinchot State Park	Yk	F1	3163
Gifford Pinchot State Park	Yk	F8	3058
Gifford Pinchot State Park	Yk	A6	3059
Girard Park	Yk	E8	3271
Good Field	Yk	A3	3579
Goose Cove	Ad	H2	3575
Graveyard Park	Yk	C2	3579
Greg A. Crist Memorial Park	Yk	E9	3166
Greiman Park	Yk	G11	3061
Hanover Street Park	Yk	B4	3579
Hellam Recreation Soccer Field	Yk	E9	3168
Heritage Park	Yk	C8	3272
Heritage Rail Trail County Park	Yk	H11	3270
Heritage Rail Trail County Park	Yk	A10	3271
Heritage Rail Trail County Park	Yk	G10	3374
Heritage Rail Trail County Park	Yk	G10	3374
Heritage Rail Trail County Park	Yk	G10	3374
Heritage Rail Trail County Park	Yk	A3	3375
Heritage Rail Trail County Park	Yk	A6	3375
Heritage Rail Trail County Park	Yk	E6	3478
Heritage Rail Trail County Park	Yk	D7	3583
Heritage Rail Trail County Park	Yk	F4	3687
Heron Cove	Ad	A1	3575
Hudson Park	Yk	E5	3271
John Rudy County Park	Yk	F7	3166
Kingston Park	Yk	B6	3272
Klines Run Park	Yk	A3	3275
Lake View	Ad	H3	3575
Lion's Park	Yk	D9	3376
Little Jimmy's Park	Yk	C6	3271
Logan Park	Yk	E2	3056
Longview Recreational Area	Ad	C3	3266
Manchester Community Park	Yk	C1	3166
Martin Luther King Park	Yk	B9	3271
Meadow Lane	Ad	A2	3576
Memorial Field	Ad	G1	3681
Michaux State Forest	Ad	C4	3156
Michaux State Forest	Ad	B1	3261
Michaux State Forest	Ad	A1	3262
Michaux State Forest	Ad	E2	3363
Michaux State Forest	Ad	A1	3364
Michaux State Forest	Ad	B2	3468
Michaux State Forest	Ad	B4	3260
Mouls Field	Yk	D1	3579

Mountain View Park Yk F7 3165
Mud Run Recreational Area Ad B4 3266
Myers Arboretum Yk C4 3579
Myers Memorial Park Yk A2 3579
Noonan Park Yk A6 3271
North Hills Park Yk G3 3271
Oakside Community Park Ad B4 3367
Odeon Park Yk A9 3271
P. Joseph Rabb County Park Yk H6 3477
P. Joseph Rabb County Park Yk A6 3478
Paradise Point Ad A1 3575
Penn Oaks Park Yk D5 3272
Penn Park Yk C8 3271
Penn Twp Community Park Yk C8 3579
Pheasant Cove Recreational Area Ad C5 3266
Pickett Cove Recreational Area Ad C4 3266
Pleasanton Cove Recreational Area Ad A11 3472
Quay Park Yk C4 3056
Radio Controlled Airplane Field Yk B11 3376
Rexroth Park Yk E10 3274
Richard M. Nixon County Park Yk B10 3375
Rockburn Park Yk H4 3271
Rocky Ridge County Park Yk F9 3167
Roof Memorial Park Yk F11 2848
Salems Square Park Yk A8 3271
Samuel S. Lewis State Park Yk B1 3274
Shady Grove Ad H2 3575
Shorewood Recreational Area Ad B4 3266
Shryock Field Yk A5 3376
Small's Park Yk C5 3271
Snyder Park Yk G1 3375
South Cavalry Field Ad G7 3574
Spring Valley County Park Yk E8 3480
Springetts Oaks Park Yk D1 3272
Springettsbury Recreational Area Yk C2 3272
Starview Sportsman Association Yk B6 3167
State Game Lands No 83 Yk E1 3484
State Game Lands No 83 Yk E11 3380
State Game Lands No 181 Yk H7 3484
State Game Lands No 181 Yk B6 3485
State Game Lands No 242 Yk F5 3057
State Game Lands No 243 Yk D1 3161
State Game Lands No 243 Yk C10 3056
State Game Lands Nos 249-70 Ad B11 3264
State Game Lands Nos 249-70 Ad H1 3367
State Game Lands Nos 249-70 Ad G3 3265
State Game Lands Nos 249-70 Ad A8 3265
State Game Lands Nos 249-70 Ad A3 3266
State Game Lands Nos 249-70 Ad B1 3368
Stonewood Park Yk G4 3272
Strawberry Hill Nature Center Ad C2 3572
Sunset Knoll Recreational Area Ad C1 3266
Thackston Park Yk B8 3271
Tri-Twp Park Yk F6 3579
Twp Rec Field (McSherrystown) Ad F2 3578
Veterans Memorial Park Yk F9 3271
Walnut Cove Recreational Area Ad D4 3266
Westminster Park Yk C6 3271
William H. Kain County Park Yk A10 3376
William H. Kain County Park Yk D8 3375
William H. Kain County Park Yk A1 3480
William Park Yk B6 3271
Winebrenner Park Ad A10 3471
Wirt Park Yk B3 3579
York Rifle Range Yk E6 3167
York Township Park Yk B3 3376

PHYSICAL FEATURES

Bakers Knob Ad E1 3572
Barlow Knoll Ad D6 3471
Bear Mountain Ad C6 3262
Beecher Hill Yk D11 3581
Beecher Hill Yk B2 3685
Benner Hill Ad E9 3471
Big Hill Ad B11 3158
Blair Hill Yk B6 3057
Brunner Island Yk F4 3061
Buchanan Valley Ad B11 3261
Buchanan Valley Ad G3 3364
Bushy Hill Ad F3 3365
Buzzards Roost Yk D3 3168
Carr Hill Ad F10 3469
Chamberlains Hill Ad G6 3468
Chestnut Hill Ad H8 3263
Chestnut Hill Ad A8 3264
Chimney Rock Yk C8 3168
Conewago Mountains Yk F8 3163
Conewago Mountains Yk D10 3059
Conewago Mountains Yk D2 3164
Dug Hill Ridge Yk B11 3582
Dug Hill Ridge Yk C6 3685
Dunkard Valley Yk F5 3479
Dunkard Valley Yk A3 3480
East Big Flat Ridge Ad A8 3260
Fairs Valley Yk C3 3686
Fickels Hill Ad F2 3159
Flat Mountain Yk H2 3057
Fox Hill Ad H8 3365
Glen Rock Valley Yk D2 3583
Graefenburg Hill Ad F5 3363
Granite Hill Ad D5 3472
Grave Ridge Ad H3 3260
Grave Ridge Ad B1 3261
Green Ridge Ad H7 3467
Green Ridge Ad A7 3468
Green Ridge Ad E9 3259
Gulp Ridge Ad C5 3572
Harpers Hill Ad G4 3678
Hellam Hills Yk G6 3167
Hellam Hills Yk B5 3168
Herr Ridge Ad E8 3470
High Rock Yk G3 3475
Huntrick Hill Yk D2 3582
Iron Spring Ad F7 3572
Jacks Mountain Ad B10 3572
Johns Knob Yk F4 3058
Kepner Knob Ad H5 3571
Krebs Valley Yk D5 3582
Little Round Top Ad B4 3575
Long Island Yk E3 3580
Lows Island Yk H7 3061
Lows Island Yk A8 3062
Marys Hill Ad H9 3468
McGinley Hill Ad B6 3573
McKee Hill Ad A10 3573
McPherson Ridge Ad H9 3470
Mitten Hill Ad F8 3259
Mt. Newman Ad A9 3364
Neiman Hill Yk A11 2955
Nells Hill Yk F4 3057
Oak Ridge Ad A3 3471
Peavine Island Yk G1 3589
Pigeon Hill Ad G3 3474
Pigeon Hills Yk A11 3372
Pigeon Hills Yk F4 3475
Pine Mountain Ad G10 3571
Pinetown Hill Yk C2 3058
Piney Mountain Ad E10 3260
Piney Mountain Ad B3 3261
Powers Hill Ad E2 3575
Pulpit Rock Yk G3 3475
Quaker Valley Ad G7 3262
Ram Hill Ad D5 3260
Rampike Hill Ad B3 3263
Ramsey Hill Yk G4 3058
Rattlesnake Hill Ad G6 3262
Raven Rock Mountain Ad C3 3676
Rock Top Ad B9 3365
Rocky Knob Ad H8 3259
Rocky Ridge Yk F11 3582
Rocky Ridge Yk D2 3686
Round Hill Ad G9 3265
Round Island Yk F3 3580
Round Top Ad G1 3262
Round Top Ad B5 3575
Round Top Yk B4 3169
Rup Hill Ad F11 3468
Saubel Hill Yk A9 3582
Schulls Rock Yk G2 3167
Sheep Heaven Ad F1 3575
Sier Hill Ad H7 3259
Snaggy Ridge Ad F10 3363
Snyders Hill Ad E7 3159
South Mountain Ad C10 3260
South Mountain Ad A5 3364
South Mountain Ad G10 3467
South Mountain Ad E4 3571
South Mountain Ad C8 3675
South Mountain Ad B1 3261
Stone Head Yk D8 3055
Stone Jug Hill Ad A3 3368
Straight Hill Yk G11 3058
Straight Hill Yk F2 3163
Strasbaugh Hill Ad C6 3260
Sugar Loaf Ad C1 3573
The Narrows Ad F11 3261
Tyson Hill Ad H6 3262
Wickersham Hill Yk G8 2954
Wigwam Hill Ad E11 3259
Wildcat Hill Ad G2 3363
Wildcat Knob Ad H9 3261
Wilson Hill Ad E10 3469
Wolf Hill Ad F9 3259
Wolf Hill Ad G10 3471
Wolfpit Hill Ad E2 3263
Wright Knob Yk D3 3058
Yellow Hill Ad E9 3262
Yellow Ridge Ad E2 3363

PLACES OF WORSHIP

Advent Luth Ch Yk H5 3271
Altersgate Ch Yk G1 3375
Altland Ch Yk C9 3268
Amos Tabernacle Ad D10 3366
Apostolic Ch Ad G11 3571
Asmb of God Ch Yk A7 3377
Barts Ch Ad E2 3682
Benders Luth Ch Ad E2 3367
Bethany UMC Yk H3 3481
Bethel Ch Yk A7 2953
Bethel Ch Yk D7 3380
Bethel Ch of God Yk E10 3055
Bethel Menn Ch Ad A8 3367
Bethlehem Ch Yk G8 3377
Bethlehem Ch Yk G5 3686
Bible Bapt Church Yk F4 3271
Bible Presb Church of York Yk B1 3376
Big Rock Ch Yk D2 3163
Black Rock Ch Yk A5 3685
Blymire Ch Yk F9 3376
Bryansville Ch Yk C1 3693
Calvary Bapt Ch Ad C3 3367
Calvary Bible Ch Yk G6 3274
Calvary UMC Yk E2 3056
Camp Elder Ch Ad F2 3572
Canadochly Ch Yk H5 3273
Canadochly Ch Yk A5 3274
Cassels Ch Yk D5 3061
Cedar Hill Bapt Ch Yk G9 2951
Centre Presb Ch Yk F5 3690
Chanceford Ch Yk D1 3588
Chanceford Tabernacle Yk A5 3380
Chapel Hill Church of God Ad F6 3264
Chestnut Grove Ch Ad A4 3160
Chestnut Grove UMC Yk A2 3057
Chestnut Grove UMC Yk F2 3581
Christ Luth Ch Yk G6 3372
Christ Luth Ch Yk E4 3479
Christian Miss Alliance Ch Yk B10 3168
Church of Christ Yk H6 3271
Church of Christ Yk C1 3686
Church of God Yk E4 3579
Codorus Church of the Breth Yk A4 3480
Codorus Meeting House Yk H7 3373
Community Chapel Yk E6 3061
Conewago Chapel Ad D11 3474
Cross Roads UMC Yk H8 3481
Crossroad Ch Yk C2 2954
Dover Asmb of God Yk B10 3164
Dover Bethany UMC Yk F6 3164
Dover Bible Ch Yk B9 3164
Druck Valley Ch Yk G8 3167
Dubs Ch Yk E5 3580
East End Ch Yk D7 3378
East Side Bible Ch Yk B8 3274
Eastminster Presb Ch Yk B6 3272
Ebenezer UMC Yk B8 3275
Emmanuel Bapt Ch Yk E2 3272
Emmanuel Chr Fellowship Ch Yk A4 3272
Emmanuel Luth Ch Yk D9 3056
Emmanuel Ref Ch Yk C2 3377
Fairmount Ch Yk E6 3168
Fairview Bethel Church of God Yk G10 2848
Faith Alive Yk D2 3272
Fawn AME Zion Ch Yk C9 3587
Fawn UMC Yk G5 3691
Fileys Ch Yk B9 2952
First Church of the Breth Yk B6 3272
First Korean Ch Yk E11 2951
Flohr's Luth Ch Ad D11 3365
Foursquare Gospel Yk C10 3475
Friedensaals Evan Luth Ch Yk B6 3479
Gardners Ch Ad B5 3160
Gettysburg Bible Bapt Ch Ad A7 3368
Grace Bible Chapel Ad D2 3272
Grace Ch Ad F3 3677
Grace Luth Ch Ad C7 3576
Grace Luth Ch Yk B6 3377
Grace UMC Yk B6 3584
Great Conewago Presb Ch Ad C9 3368
Greek Orth Ch Yk F5 3375
Greenmount Ch Yk B1 3582
Guinston Ch Yk A8 3483
Hanover South Congregation Of Jehovah's Witness Yk D6 3579
Harvest Time Temple Yk H6 3579
Hayshire Ch Yk C11 3166
Heritage Ch Ad E5 3470
Hershey Ch Yk H6 3268
Hopewell Ch Yk B1 3586
Huntington Friends Ch Ad F1 3265
Immanuel Evang Free Ch Yk F2 3271
Ind. Fundamental Ch Yk D4 3579
Iron Spring Breth Ch Ad E7 3572
Jehovah's Witness Yk B7 3377
King James Bible Ch Yk E4 3272
Kingdom Hall Ad G7 3470
Kingdom Hall of Jehovah's Witness Yk F8 3475
Kralltown Ch Yk C8 3162
Latimore Ch Ad G6 3160
Lebanon Ch Yk F5 3481
Lighthouse Ch Ad C4 3471
Littlestown Chapel Ad B11 3578
Longstown EUB Ch Yk D7 3272
Lower Bermudian Ch Ad B1 3266
Lower Bermudian Ch Yk G2 3267
Lower Marsh Creek Ch Ad G1 3573
Lutheran Ch Yk D11 3477
Lutheran Theological Seminary Ad A8 3471
Manchester Ch Yk E10 3061
Maple Grove Ch Yk F11 3371
McKendree Ch Yk F10 3484
Memorial Ch Ad B4 3471
Messiah Jerusalem Ch Yk G9 3583
Monaghan Presb Ch Yk C4 3056
Moores Ch Yk D9 2953
Morning Hour Chapel Ad B6 3266
Mountain Grove Chapel Yk G8 3059
Mt. Airy Ch Yk D5 3058
Mt. Carmel Ch Ad F5 3468
Mt. Hope UMC Ad B2 3572
Mt. Joy Ch Ad D1 3679
Mt. Nebo Ch Yk C2 3694
Mt. Olivet Ch Ad B1 3266
Mt. Olivet Ch Yk B7 3163
Mt. Olivet UMC Yk G6 3584
Mt. Olivet UMC Yk D2 3692
Mt. Pisgah Ch Yk A2 3274
Mt. Washington Ch Yk D11 3060
Mt. Zion Ch Yk C10 3057
Mt. Zion Luth Ch Yk A11 3167
Mt. Zion UCC Yk G2 3271
New Bethel Bapt Ch Yk B2 3689
New Cumberland Alliance Ch Yk E8 2848
New Fairview Ch Yk G3 3375
New Freedom Bapt Ch Yk H2 3687
North Hills Bible Ch Yk H2 3271
Oak View Ch Yk H5 3580
Ohev Shalom Cong Yk A6 3272
Open Door Bapt Ch Yk A8 3584
Orrtanna UMC Ad C6 3469
Otterbein UMC Yk A4 3376
Our Savior's Ch Yk F5 3272
Paradise Ch Yk B1 3372
Paradise Church Of God Yk G7 3371
Peace Light Ch Ad G1 3469
Peace United Ch Yk G3 3579
Pinchot Asmb of God Yk E9 3058
Pine Grove UMC Yk F5 3375
Pine Grove United Evangelist Ch Yk F4 3375
Pleasant Hill Ch Yk A2 3481
Pleasant View Breth in Christ Ch Yk D7 3377
Pleasant View Grove UMC Yk A2 3061
Pleasureville EUB Ch Yk F10 3166
Prayer Mission Ch Yk D9 3274
Presb Ch Yk A11 3168
Prospect Ch Yk D8 3587
Red Mountain Ch Yk H11 3161
Red Run Ch Yk F2 3267
Redland Friends Meetinghouse Yk G10 2954
Rohler's Asmb of God Ch Yk C10 3059
Roth Ch Yk G7 3372
Salem Ch Ad F5 3472
Salem Ch Yk G3 2954
Salem Ch Yk H11 3056
Salem Ch Yk F2 3378
Salem Ch Yk E7 3589
Seven Valleys Bapt Ch Yk B1 3479
Seventh Day Adventist Ch Yk F6 3579
Shenbergers Ch Yk B3 3379
Shiloh Luth Ch Yk A4 3270
Shiloh UCC Yk B4 3270
Shrewsbury Asmb of God Yk A7 3584
Shrewsbury Bapt Ch Yk H6 3583
Shrewsbury Church of the Breth Yk B9 3584
Slateville Ch Yk B4 3694
Springville Ch Yk A9 3275
St. Ignatius-Loyola Ch Ad F4 3364
St. Jacobs Stone Ch Yk H8 3581
St. James Ch Ad D3 3680
St. John the Bapt Ch Yk H1 3687
St. Johns Ch Ad E6 3369
St. Johns Ch Ad G2 3469
St. Johns Ch Ad C2 3681
St. Johns Ch Yk C2 3685
St. Johns Luth Ch Yk B8 3272
St. Johns UMC Yk B6 3377
St. Josephs Ch Yk B8 3579
St. Luke Ch Yk D4 3379
St. Lukes Ch Ad A3 3577
St. Marks Ch Ad G4 3575
St. Mary Chapel Yk D8 3169
St. Marys Ch Yk F6 3371
St. Matthews Ch Yk B2 3579
St. Michaels Ch Yk C11 3058
St. Paul Ch Yk C10 2955

St. Paul Ch	Yk	E4	3061
St. Paul Ch	Yk	F8	3377
St. Paul Luth Ch of Hametown	Yk	A2	3584
St. Paul UMC	Yk	C3	3166
St. Paul Zeiglers Luth Ch	Yk	D3	3478
St. Pauls Ch	Ad	B8	3369
St. Pauls Ch	Yk	G3	3376
St. Pauls Lutheran Ch	Yk	D2	3585
St. Pauls Reformed Ch of Shrewsbury	Yk	B9	3584
St. Pauls UCC	Yk	A9	3584
St. Pauls UMC	Yk	G9	3274
St. Pauls Union Ch	Yk	H11	3373
St. Peters Ch	Yk	B7	3479
Sts. Peter and Pauls Ch	Yk	G11	3478
Starview UCC	Yk	G3	3166
Stewartstown Presb Ch	Yk	E11	3585
Stony Brook Menn Ch	Yk	F3	3272
Temple Beth Israel	Yk	H10	3271
Trail Church of the Nazarene	Yk	B2	3688
Trinity Ch	Yk	F1	3274
Trinity UMC	Yk	G2	3687
Union Chapel	Yk	C3	3589
Union EOB Ch	Yk	G8	3055
United Ch	Yk	B3	3056
United Church of Christ	Yk	E11	3477
Upper Bermudian Luth Ch	Ad	B1	3264
Victory Freewill Bapt Ch	Yk	E3	3579
Wildasin Meeting House	Yk	B5	3580
Windsor Ch	Yk	F1	3377
Winterstown UMC	Yk	A6	3481
York Chr Ch	Yk	B2	3272
York Gospel Center	Yk	D7	3375
Yorkana Jehovahs Witness	Yk	D4	3273
Yorkshire UMC	Yk	D5	3272
Zion Ch	Yk	H6	2955
Zion Ch	Yk	F10	3377
Zion Menn Ch	Yk	G3	3271
Zion Shaffers UMC	Yk	B9	3478

POINTS OF INTEREST

Adams County Fair Grounds	Ad	C5	3371
Adams County SPCA	Ad	E7	3367
Agricultural Museum & Workers House	Yk	E7	3271
Amphitheater (Codorus State Park)	Yk	B7	3580
Amphitheater (Gifford Pinchot State Park)	Yk	F1	3163
Amphitheater (GNMP)	Ad	H1	3574
Bailey Spring Convention Center	Yk	D11	3585
Bass Pavilion	Yk	G10	3375
Bear Mountain Orchards	Ad	C8	3262
Black Horse Tavern	Ad	D11	3470
Blue Gill Pavilion	Yk	G10	3375
Boat Ramp (Gifford Pinchot State Park)	Yk	D10	3058
Boat Ramp (Gifford Pinchot State Park)	Yk	H9	3058
Boat Ramp (Susquehanna River)	Yk	C8	3275
Boat Ramp (Susquehanna River)	Yk	H11	3380
Bob Hoffman Softball Stadium	Yk	F8	3271
Bonham House	Yk	D7	3271
Boyer Nurseries & Orchards	Ad	E5	3365
Browns Market	Yk	F5	3479
Cartop Launch (William H. Kain County Park)	Yk	D9	3375
Cartop Launch (William H. Kain County Park)	Yk	H9	3375
Cemetery Hill (GNMP)	Ad	C10	3471
Cemetery Ridge (GNMP)	Ad	C2	3575
Chanceford Community Center	Yk	C2	3483
Charcoal Hearths	Ad	E4	3363
Codorus State Park Marina	Yk	E4	3580
Crestmont Orchards	Ad	F7	3158
Culps Hill (GNMP)	Ad	D10	3471
Cyclorama Center	Ad	B11	3471
Devil's Den (GNMP)	Ad	A4	3575
Dobbin House Tavern Historical Site	Ad	E10	3471
Downtown York Visitors Info Center	Yk	C7	3271
East Berlin Community Center	Ad	C11	3267
East Coast Animal Rescue	Ad	F8	3572
Eichelberg Performing Arts Center	Yk	B1	3579
Eisenhower National Historic Site	Ad	F4	3574
El Vista Orchards	Ad	G11	3468
Environmental Education Center (Richard M. Nixon County Park)	Yk	B10	3375
General Lee's Headquater Museum	Ad	A7	3471
Gettysburg Battle Theater	Ad	A11	3471
Gettysburg Battlefield Tape Tour	Ad	E9	3471
Gettysburg Factory Stores	Ad	G4	3575
Gettysburg Family Fun Center	Ad	F6	3471
Gettysburg National Military Park	Ad	H8	3470
Gettysburg Visitor Center	Ad	E9	3471
Gifford Pinchot State Park Office	Yk	G7	3058
GNMP Visitor's Center (GNMP)	Ad	B11	3471
Golden Plough Tavern/Gates House/Barnett Bobb Log House	Yk	C7	3271
Haar's Drive-In Theatre	Yk	E1	3056
Hanover Community Playhouse	Yk	G4	3579
Hanover Fairgrounds	Yk	D3	3579
Hanover YMCA	Yk	C10	3475
Hanovers Farmers Market	Yk	B2	3579
Harley-Davidson Motorcycle Final Assembly Plant & Museum	Yk	E3	3271
Heritage Rail Trail County Park	Yk	H11	3270
Heritage Rail Trail County Park	Yk	A10	3271
Heritage Rail Trail County Park	Yk	H1	3374
Heritage Rail Trail County Park	Yk	H1	3374
Heritage Rail Trail County Park	Yk	H1	3374
Heritage Rail Trail County Park	Yk	A3	3375
Heritage Rail Trail County Park	Yk	A6	3375
Heritage Rail Trail County Park	Yk	E6	3478
Heritage Rail Trail County Park	Yk	D7	3583
Heritage Rail Trail County Park	Yk	F4	3687
Herr Tavern (Historic Site)	Ad	G6	3470
Historical Society Museum	Yk	D7	3271
Hostetters Metting House	Ad	A6	3578
Howard Tunnel (Historic Site)	Yk	A9	3375
Indian Steps Museum	Yk	H2	3484
Jennie Wade House Museum	Ad	E10	3471
Lake Meade Marine	Ad	C2	3266
Lerews Farm Market	Yk	C5	3057
Lincoln Room Ctr	Ad	E9	3471
Lincoln Speedway	Ad	A1	3475
Lincoln Train Museum	Ad	B10	3471
Maple Lawn Farms	Yk	C10	3587
Maple Lawn Farms	Yk	E7	3587
Marina (Lake Heritage)	Ad	A1	3576
McMillan Woods (GNMP)	Ad	A10	3471
Memorial Ice Skating Rink	Yk	E9	3271
Muskie Pavilion	Yk	G10	3375
National Civil War Wax Museum	Ad	E10	3471
New Oxford Social & Athletic Club	Ad	H2	3473
New Oxford Social & Athletic Club	Ad	A2	3474
North Codorus Community Center	Yk	H9	3373
Oak Ridge Lookout Tower	Ad	A6	3471
Office & Community Center	Ad	C4	3266
Old Wildasin Burial Grounds	Yk	E7	3580
Overlook (Gifford Pinchot State Park)	Yk	A6	3059
Peace Memorial	Ad	A5	3471
Penn Laurel Girl Scouts	Yk	B2	3272
Pennsylvania Welcome Center (I-83N)	Yk	D11	3584
Perch Pavilion	Yk	G10	3375
Plantation Estates Stables	Yk	F6	3587
Police Heritage Museum	Yk	C7	3271
Princess Street Center	Yk	B8	3271
Radio Controlled Airplane Field	Yk	B11	3376
Rotary Kranich Hall	Yk	F6	3271
Rouzerville Gun Club	Ad	F6	3467
Samuel Colt Heritage Museum	Ad	A10	3471
Seminary Ridge (GNMP)	Ad	A9	3471
Shoemaker Field	Yk	B6	2952
Ski Liberty	Ad	A10	3573
Ski Liberty	Ad	H9	3572
Ski Round Top	Yk	B4	3058
Snyder's of Hanover	Yk	F1	3579
Soldier's National Monument	Ad	C10	3471
Soldier's National Museum	Ad	E10	3471
South Cavalry Field	Ad	G7	3574
Spangler Spring	Ad	E11	3471
Stewartstown Community Building	Yk	E11	3585
Strand-Capitol Performing Arts Center	Yk	C7	3271
Susan P. Byrnes Health Education Center	Yk	D8	3271
Susquehanna Orchards	Yk	G2	3694
Susquehanna Speedway	Yk	G3	3059
The Angle (GNMP)	Ad	B11	3471
Trail-Way Sports Club	Ad	H6	3577
Trail-Way Sports Club	Ad	A6	3578
Tri Hill Recreational Center	Yk	F11	3271
TV Tower (WGAL)	Yk	A5	3168
Voni B. Grimes Gym	Yk	D8	3271
Wallace-Cross Mill Historic Site	Yk	D3	3586
Warfield Ridge	Ad	H3	3574
West Shore YMCA Camp	Yk	A9	2849
WNOW Radio/TV Tower	Yk	G1	3271
Wolfgang Candy Company	Yk	C5	3271
WSBA Radio Towers	Yk	A1	3271
WSBA TV Tower	Yk	G11	3271
YMCA	Ad	G1	3681
YMCA	Yk	B5	3167
YMCA East	Ad	A8	3471
York County Chamber of Commerce Convention & Visitors Bureau	Yk	C7	3271
York County Colonial Courthouse	Yk	C7	3271
York County Fairgrounds	Yk	H8	3270
York County Visitors Info Center	Yk	C3	3271
Youth Center & Communtiy Building	Yk	C8	3377
YWCA West	Ad	F10	3470

POLICE STATIONS

*** Includes Municipal Building**

Biglerville	Ad	A2	3367
Carroll*	Yk	B3	3057
Conewago*	Ad	F10	3474
Cumberland*	Ad	G10	3470
East Berlin*	Ad	C11	3267
East Manchester*	Yk	G1	3166
Eastern Adams Regional Police	Ad	D5	3474
Fairfield*	Ad	A5	3573
Fairview*	Yk	F11	2848
Gettysburg*	Ad	C9	3471
Hamilton*	Ad	B5	3371
Hamiltonban*	Ad	B3	3573
Hanover*	Yk	B3	3579
Heidelberg*	Yk	D7	3476
Hellam*	Yk	F9	3168
Jacobus*	Yk	E10	3375
Latimore*	Ad	D9	3160
Liberty*	Ad	B3	3677
Littlestown*	Ad	E1	3681
Lower Windsor*	Yk	F11	3274
Manheim*	Yk	D11	3581
McSherrystown*	Ad	F2	3578
New Freedom*	Yk	G3	3687
New Oxford*	Ad	A2	3474
Newberry	Yk	A10	2955
North Codorus*	Yk	H10	3373
North Hopewell*	Yk	D9	3481
Northern York Co Regional Police	Yk	F10	3164
Oxford*	Ad	C5	3474
Penn*	Yk	D4	3579
Red Lion*	Yk	C7	3377
Spring Garden*	Yk	F11	3271
Springettsbury*	Yk	C2	3272
State Police	Ad	A7	3368
State Police (Loganville)	Yk	G3	3479
Stewartstown*	Yk	E11	3585
West Manheim*	Yk	F10	3579
Wrightsville*	Yk	E7	3169
York Boro*	Yk	C8	3271
York Twp*	Yk	A4	3376

POST OFFICES

*** Denotes Non-Delivery**

Abbottstown	Ad	A10	3371
Airville	Yk	D8	3484
Arendtsville*	Ad	C3	3366
Aspers	Ad	C4	3263
Bendersville*	Ad	A3	3263
Biglerville	Ad	H2	3366
Brogue	Yk	C1	3483
Cashtown*	Ad	C9	3365
Codorus*	Yk	D11	3477
Craley*	Yk	H10	3274
Dallastown	Yk	F7	3376
Delta	Yk	G5	3693
Dillsburg	Yk	D3	3056
Dover	Yk	C11	3163
Dover	Yk	C11	3164
East Berlin	Ad	C11	3267
East Prospect*	Yk	E5	3274
Emigsville*	Yk	C8	3166
Etters	Yk	H7	2955
Fairfield	Ad	B5	3573
Fawn Grove	Yk	G4	3691
Felton	Yk	G4	3481
Franklintown	Yk	E9	3056
Franklintown*	Yk	C3	3056
Gardners*	Ad	F10	3158
Gettysburg	Ad	B8	3471
Glen Rock	Yk	C3	3583
Glenville	Yk	G10	3581
Hanover	Yk	B3	3579
Idaville*	Ad	F9	3158
Jacobus*	Yk	E10	3375
Lewisberry	Yk	B9	2954
Littlestown	Ad	E1	3681
Loganville*	Yk	F3	3479
Manchester	Yk	D1	3166
McKnightstown*	Ad	F1	3469
McSherrystown	Ad	F2	3578
Mount Wolf	Yk	F1	3166
New Freedom	Yk	F3	3687
New Oxford	Ad	A2	3474
New Park	Yk	G4	3690
Orrtanna*	Ad	B5	3469
Porters Sideling*	Yk	F9	3476
Railroad*	Yk	G10	3583
Red Lion	Yk	A6	3377
Rossville*	Yk	B11	3058
Seven Valleys	Yk	F4	3478
Shrewsbury	Yk	B11	3584
Spring Grove	Yk	B11	3373
Stewartstown	Yk	E11	3585
Thomasville	Yk	C2	3373
Wellsville	Yk	H3	3165
Windsor	Yk	E5	3377
Wrightsville	Yk	D7	3169
York	Yk	C8	3271
York	Yk	D2	3272
York	Yk	F7	3270
York Haven	Yk	E3	3061
York New Salem	Yk	D7	3374
York Springs	Ad	B10	3160

SCHOOLS

Adams County Christian Acad	Ad	B11	3367
Alexander D. Goode ES	Yk	D6	3271
Arendtsville ES	Ad	B2	3366
Baresville ES	Yk	E2	3579
Bendersville ES	Ad	A3	3263
Bermudian Springs HS	Ad	F4	3265
Bermudian Springs MS	Ad	F3	3265
Biglerville HS	Ad	A1	3367
Blackberry Sch	Ad	A3	3160
Canadochly ES	Yk	F6	3274
Central York HS	Yk	C4	3271
Central York MS	Yk	G2	3271
Chanceford ES	Yk	C1	3483
Clarence R. Orendorf ES	Yk	E1	3166
Clearview ES	Yk	B11	3475
Clearview ES	Yk	E3	3483
Conewago ES	Yk	D1	3165
Conewago Twp ES	Ad	G1	3578
Crossroads MS	Yk	D1	2954
Dallastown Area HS	Yk	E8	3376
Dallastown Area MS	Yk	E8	3376
Dallastown ES	Yk	G7	3376
Delon Catholic HS	Ad	G2	3578
Delta-Peach Bottom ES	Yk	H3	3693
Devers ES	Yk	A5	3271
Dillsburg ES	Yk	D4	3056
Dover Area ES	Yk	D10	3164
Dover area HS	Yk	C11	3164
Dover Area HS	Yk	C1	3269
Dover Inter Sch	Yk	C11	3164
Dover Inter Sch	Yk	C1	3269
East York ES	Yk	B7	3272
Eastern York HS	Yk	C1	3274
Eastern York MS	Yk	C1	3274
Edgar Moore ES	Yk	B8	3377
Edgar Smith MS	Yk	H7	3270
Eisenhower ES	Ad	D7	3471
Emery Markle Inter Sch	Yk	E5	3579
Fairfield ES	Ad	H6	3572
Fairfield HS	Ad	H6	3572
Fairfield MS	Ad	H6	3572
Fairfield MS & HS	Ad	A6	3573
Fairview ES	Yk	G9	2848
Fawn ES	Yk	E4	3691
Ferguson ES	Yk	B6	3271
Fishing Creek ES	Yk	E2	2954
Franklin Township ES	Ad	C11	3365
Friendship ES	Yk	F10	3582
Gettysburg Area HS	Ad	D5	3471
Gettysburg Area MS	Ad	C9	3471
Hannah Penn Jr HS	Yk	E8	3271
Hanover Christian Acad	Yk	C10	3475
Hanover HS	Yk	D10	3475
Hanover MS	Yk	E10	3475
Hanover Street ES	Yk	C3	3579
Harbolds Sch	Ad	A4	3160
Hayshire ES	Yk	C11	3166
Heidelberg ES	Yk	C8	3476
Immaculate Conception Sch	Ad	A2	3474
Indian Rock ES	Yk	H1	3374
J.F.K. Training Center	Yk	C10	3166
Jackson ES	Yk	D9	3271
James Getty Sch	Ad	B5	3471
Keefauver ES	Ad	C9	3471
Kennard-Dale HS	Yk	E3	3691
Kralltown ES	Yk	C1	3267
Kreutz Creek ES	Yk	B10	3168
Leaders Heights ES	Yk	E5	3375
Leib ES	Yk	F5	3269
Lincoln ES	Ad	C9	3471
Lincoln ES	Yk	A8	3271
Lincolnway ES	Yk	D9	3270
Littlestown SHS	Ad	F11	3577
Littlestown Sr HS	Ad	G1	3681
Locust Grove ES	Yk	A7	3272
Loganville-Springfield ES	Yk	G3	3479
Loucks ES	Yk	G9	3270
Manheim ES	Yk	C9	3581
Maple Ave MS	Ad	E1	3681
Mazie Gable ES	Yk	B6	3377
McKinley ES	Yk	C9	3271
Mt. Wolf ES	Yk	F1	3166
Mt. Zion Sch	Yk	G3	2953
New Oxford MS	Ad	B2	3474
New Oxford Sr HS	Ad	B1	3474
New Salem ES	Yk	B7	3374
Newberry ES	Yk	B11	2955
North Hills ES	Yk	G3	3271
North Hopewell/Winterstown ES	Yk	A7	3481
North Salem ES	Yk	B1	3269
Northeastern HS	Yk	E10	3061

SHOPPING CENTERS & MALLS

TRAILS

NOTES

NOTES

NOTES